WILFRID

ABBOT, BISHOP, SAINT

This volume is dedicated to the memory of Richard Andrew Hall

WILFRID

ABBOT, BISHOP, SAINT

Papers from the 1300th
Anniversary Conferences

Edited by

N. J. Higham

SHAUN TYAS
DONINGTON
2013
.

© The Contributors
Published in 2013 by
SHAUN TYAS
(an imprint of 'Paul Watkins')
1 High Street
Donington
Lincolnshire
PE11 4TA

ISBN
978–1–907730–27–6 (paperback)
978–1–907730–29–0 (hardback)

Typeset and designed from the texts of the authors and editor
by Shaun Tyas

Printed and bound in Great Britain by
Butler, Tanner and Dennis, Frome, Somerset

CONTENTS

LIST OF CONTRIBUTORS

Richard N. Bailey	University of Newcastle
Paul Bidwell	Tyne and Wear Archives and Museums
Jesse D. Billett	University of Toronto
Eric Cambridge	Chester-le-Street
Morn Capper	British Museum
T. M. Charles-Edwards	Jesus College, University of Oxford
Catherine Cubitt	University of York
Sandra Duncan	Chester
W. Trent Foley	Davidson College
Sarah Foot	Christ Church, Oxford
Paul Fouracre	University of Manchester
Christopher Grocock	Bedales School
Jane Hawkes	University of York
N. J. Higham	University of Manchester
Mark Laynesmith	University of Reading
Francisco José Álvarez Lopez	Institute of Historical Research, University of London
Éamonn Ó Carragáin	University of Cork
James T. Palmer	University of St Andrews
Clare Stancliffe	University of Durham
Alan Thacker	Institute of Historical Research, University of London
Alaric A. Trousdale	Western Oregon University
Damian J. Tyler	Manchester Metropolitan University
I. N. Wood	University of Leeds

LIST OF ILLUSTRATIONS

Tables

LIST OF ABBREVIATIONS

Archaeol. J	*Archaeological Journal*
ASC, E	Irvine, S., & Dumville, D. (eds), 2004, *The Anglo-Saxon Chronicle: a Collaborative Edition, vol. 7, MS E*, Cambridge: D. S. Brewer
BAR	British Archaeological Reports
BKS	Godman, P. (ed. and trans.), 1982, *Alcuin: The Bishops, Kings, and Saints of York*, Oxford Medieval Texts. Oxford: Clarendon Press
CASSS	*Corpus of Anglo-Saxon Stone Sculpture*
CBA	Council for British Archaeology
CBCR	Krautheimer, R., et al. (eds), *Corpus basilicarum christianarum Romae: the Early Christian Basilicas of Rome (IV–IX Cent)*, 5 vols, Rome: Pontificio Istituto di Archeologia Cristiana, 1937–1977
CCSL	*Corpus Christianorum series Latina*
CSEL	*Corpus Scriptorium Ecclesiasticorum Latinorum*
CTR	Valentini, R., e Zucchetti, G., 1942, *Codice topografico della città di Roma* II, Rome: Fonti per la Storia d'Italia, 88
DTR	Bede, *De Temporum Ratione,* ed. C. W. Jones, Corpus Christianorum Series Latina 123B (Turnhout: Brepols, 1997)
EEE	*Epistola Beda ad Ecgbertum Episcopum*, ed. Plummer, 1896, I, 405–23
Enarr in Ps	Augustine, *Enarrationes in Psalmos*, ed. E. Dekkers & J. Fraipoint, *Aurelii Augustina opera*, 10, Turnholt: Brepols, 1956
HA	Bede, *Historia Abbatum*, ed. Plummer, C., 1896, *Baedae Opera Historica* I, 364–87
HE	Bede, *Historia Ecclesiastica Gentis Anglorum*, ed. B. Colgrave and R. A. B. Mynors, 2nd edn, Oxford: Oxford University Press, 1991
ILCV	*Inscriptiones Latinae Christianae Veteres* I–III, ed. E. Diehl, Berlin: Weidmann, 1925–31
Itin.	*Itineraria et Alia Geographica*, ed. P. Geyer *et al.*, Corpus Christianorum, Series Latina, 175-6, Turnhout: Brepols, 1965
LP	*Liber Pontificalis*, ed. L. Duchesne, *Le Liber Pontificalis*, 2 vols (Paris, 1886–92). Reprinted with a third volume, *Additions et Corrections de Mgr L. Duchesne*, ed. C. Vogel, Paris: De Boccard, 1981
MGH	*Monumenta Germaniae Historica*
MT	Lawlor, H. J., & Best, R. I. (eds), 1931, *Martyrology of Tallaght*, London: Henry Bradshaw Society 68.

NCH	Hinds, A. B. (ed.), 1896, *Northumberland County History, vol. 3: Hexhamshire, Pt 1*. Newcastle upon Tyne: Andrew Reid & Co.
n.d.	not dated
PL	*Patrologia Latina*, ed. Migne
Ps	Psalm
RSB	Farmer, D. H. (ed.), 1968, *The Rule of St Benedict: Oxford, Bodleian Library, Hatton 48*. Copenhagen: Rosenkilde & Bagger
S	Sawyer, P. H., 1968 *Anglo-Saxon Charters: An Annotated List and Bibliography*, London: Royal Historical Society Guides and Handbooks, 8, with additions and revisions by Susan Kelly and Rebecca Rushforth, www.esawyer.org.uk
TWM	Tyne and Wear Archives and Museums
VC	Anon., *Vita Ceolfridi*, ed. Plummer, C., 1896, *Baedae Opera Historica*, I, 388–404
VCM	Bede, *Vita Sancti Cuthberti Metrica*, Jaager, W. (ed.), 1935, *Bedas metrische Vita Sancti Cuthberti*, Palaestra **198**, Leipzig: Mayer & Müller
VCP	Bede, *Vita Sancti Cuthberti*, ed. Colgrave, B., 1940, *Two Lives of St Cuthbert*, Cambridge: Cambridge University Press
VG	*Vita Guthlaci* – Colgrave, B., (ed. & trans.) 1956, *Felix's Life of St Guthlac*, Cambridge: Cambridge University Press
VW	Stephanus, *Vita Sancti Wilfridi I, Episcopi Eboracensis*, ed. W. Levison, Monumenta Germaniae Historica, Scriptores Rerum Merovingicarum VI (Hannover and Leipzig, 1913), 163–263; see also/alternatively Colgrave, B. (ed. & trans.), 1927, *The Life of Bishop Stephen by Eddius Stephanus*, Cambridge: Cambridge University Press.

Preface

N. J. HIGHAM

The academic focus of this volume is fixed firmly on the career and achievements of just one individual, that charismatic but divisive figure of the early English Church, Bishop Wilfrid of York, then of Hexham. Indeed, it has throughout been the collective intention of all the participants herein to mark the 1300th centenary of Wilfrid's death (traditionally 709, more probably 710, see Stancliffe below). The essays gathered together here originated in papers which were delivered at two conferences designed to re-examine Wilfrid's life, both of which occurred in 2009; the first was arranged by myself under the auspices of the Manchester Centre for Anglo-Saxon Studies, at Manchester in April, the second was organised by Richard Hall at St William's College, York in September, in collaboration with York Minster. During the planning processes, neither of us were aware of the other initiative but when we did become conscious of the fact that we were attempting two very similar events we decided to proceed with both, to each attend the other's and then collaborate with the publication of both sets of papers in a single volume, edited jointly. However, unbeknown to all but his closest family and friends, Richard was already suffering from cancer by the time the conferences occurred. Tragically, as papers were coming in across 2010 and 2011 and the business of putting the volume together moved forward, Richard's health deteriorated ever further and he eventually died on 13 September 2011. While this volume is therefore a testament to the life of Wilfrid, whose activities serve as the dominant theme running throughout these essays, it is also our wish that it should serve as a memorial to Richard, without whose enthusiasm, energy and commitment the ambitious program of the York conference would never have got off the ground and this volume would have been infinitely the poorer.

First a few words of introduction regarding Bishop Wilfrid: Wilfrid is one of the best-known figures of his age in Anglo-Saxon England owing primarily to a 68-chapter-length work of history, hagiography and polemic written shortly after his death but in his support by one of the close associates of his later life, Stephen a monk of Ripon. This is today widely accessible, published in several translations, the most widely read probably being that in the Penguin Classic, *The Age of Bede* (Farmer & Webb 1998), first published in 1965. Very few such works of the period were written, let alone have come down to us, particularly of this length, so its survival directs particular attention to Wilfrid's career. Bede then commented extensively on Wilfrid in his *Ecclesiastical History* in 731: he had both read Stephen's work and himself knew Wilfrid in the last few years of the latter's life (706–10), when he was the bishop responsible for the region in which Monkwearmouth/Jarrow lay. Bede's *Ecclesiastical History* makes it very clear that they had met and conversed at least once, probably they met several times. Bede was also well-acquainted with several of the priests of Wilfrid's household, with at least one of whom he had corresponded. Bede's thoughts on Wilfrid are, therefore, not entirely independent of Stephen's but there again they are far from entirely derivative either; he had his own agenda, very separate from Stephen's, so his focus is very different, but he does bring new knowledge to the table in addition. Although it is probably fair to say that all later comments regarding Wilfrid were in some sense or other derivative of these two primary sources, by the standards of the seventh and early eighth centuries, when we know so little about so many, these provide a comparatively lavish account. To this we are able to add a surprisingly rich material record: we know where Wilfrid was based in Northumbria at particular periods of his life and so can connect him with particular architectural and sculptural remains. Wilfrid was clearly an important patron of the arts and a significant force for innovation in Anglo-Saxon Northumbria and northern Britain more generally, in the later seventh and early eighth centuries.

The bare outlines of Wilfrid's life are fairly well known (for an excellent summary see Thacker 1999; 2004a). To date, our understanding of the chronology has rested heavily on contributions by Charles Plummer (1896, vol. 2), whose central interest was the work of Bede, and Bertram Colgrave (1927), whose focus was on Stephen's Life. The results have, however, not always proved satisfactory and this volume benefits from a thorough review of the evidence by Catherine Cubitt (appendix 2), which makes use of a greater variety of external sources than previous scholars considered, including charters, the comparatively well documented succession of the papacy and a variety of Frankish materials. Cubitt concludes that Stephen's chronology is robust, allowing us to provide a comparatively tight framework for Wilfrid's life and career. He was born, then, to noble parents in Northumbria, probably somewhere north of the Tees so in Bernicia rather than Deira (Charles-Edwards, below), around the time that a group of Irish or Scottish monks from Iona were invited by King Oswald to establish themselves at Lindisfarne (*c.*635, Wilfrid was probably born in 634). When aged about 14 he was presented at court to Queen Eanflæd and was deputed by her to attend on an elderly and infirm royal retainer who was just then retiring to the Lindisfarne community. There Wilfrid was introduced to monastic life as practiced by the Ionan monks and there too he developed the desire to visit Rome. He left in the early 650s, again with Eanflæd's assistance, stayed for some time at Lyons in Gaul on the way before visiting St Peter's. It was as a student that he tarried in Rome, then completed his education at Lyons where he was also tonsured during a lengthy stay (see Fouracre, Cubitt and Wood, below). Among Northumbrians, this lengthy exposure to continental ideas about Christian practice marked Wilfrid out as different; of his peers only the somewhat older Benedict Biscop had similar experiences at this date and relations between these two figures were at times perhaps somewhat frosty following disagreement between them in Gaul during Wilfrid's first visit abroad, when they parted company at Lyons, then Benedict's close association with King Ecgfrith when Wilfrid was in exile (see Grocock and Wood, below).

Returning to England in the early 660s Wilfrid was brought to the attention of Alhfrith, Oswiu's son and with his father jointly king of the Northumbrians, by his ally King Coenwalh of the West Saxons. From the young king he received an estate to found a religious community at Stamford, then the monastery at Ripon for which Alhfrith had recently granted 30 hides to monks of the Ionan Church led by Eata from Melrose. He rapidly therefore became an abbot. At the same time, the king's re-granting of the Ripon estate opened a life-long struggle for power and influence between Wilfrid and those Northumbrian monks and clergy who had been trained within the Ionan Church. Wilfrid was ordained a priest at Ripon by the Franco-Gaulish Agilbert, erstwhile bishop of the West Saxons, for whom he then served as the mouthpiece of the Romanist party at the synod of Whitby in 664, where King Oswiu finally threw his weight behind the Roman formula for calculating Easter and the Roman tonsure.

Wilfrid was perhaps at this juncture almost the only Northumbrian whose ordination and training were consistent with the Romanist tradition; the Ionan Bishop Colmán and those of his followers who did not wish to accept the decision of the synod departed from Northumbria, but others who had been trained in the Scottish Church accepted the decisions of the synod and remained in post (as Bishop Cedd) or were promoted (as Eata and Cuthbert), despite the shortcomings of any previous ordination, at least in the eyes of the Roman Church. King Oswiu initially appointed to the bishopric one Tuda, who had, so Bede tells us, been trained in southern Ireland in the Roman tradition, but he died in the great plague which struck in 664 (EH III, 27). Alhfrith then despatched Wilfrid to Gaul to be ordained but the young king was eclipsed in his absence and disappears from history, so Bede informs us as a consequence of rebellion against his father. Wilfrid diplomatically remained abroad for several years, then returning only to take up his abbacy at Ripon. In his absence Oswiu had promoted a Scottish-educated candidate, Cedd's brother Chad, to the diocese. On Theodore's arrival in 669 as archbishop of Canterbury, however, Chad was degraded, then re-ordained and appointed to Mercia, and Wilfrid was finally accepted as bishop of York, with the whole of Northumbria and Lindsey as his see.

There followed the re-building of Paulinus's stone church at York and the construction of an ambitious new church at Ripon (see Bailey and Cambridge, below). The early to mid-670s were the period when Wilfrid was at his most powerful and most secure, making common cause with Oswiu's heir and successor, King Ecgfrith, and patronised particularly by his first wife, the East Anglian virgin queen, Æthelthryth, who gave him the estate at Hexham where he built his second great monastic church (see Bailey, Cambridge and Bidwell, below). Once Æthelthryth had retired to become a nun, however, and then departed south (Capper, below), Wilfrid's position became progressively less secure: Ecgfrith's second wife seems to have been particularly opposed to him, perhaps wanting the return of the Hexham estate; Ecgfrith himself may have resented his first wife's unwillingness to bear him children and held Wilfrid in part responsible; he may well also have had considerable doubts about a bishop who had been so favoured by his elder half-brother and one-time rival for the succession, and who was clearly by this date extremely powerful. Ecgfrith was close to several major figures who had been trained within the Scottish Church, such as Cuthbert, and to Benedict Biscop, on whom he lavished estates for the foundation of Monkwearmouth. Wilfrid and his followers, along with the papacy, viewed all those baptised and/or ordained outside the Church of Rome as heretics. Such views poisoned relations between different sections of the Northumbrian Church and between Christians in different traditions across northern parts of the British Isles at this date (see Laynesmith and Charles-Edwards, below). Stephen's *Life* presents Wilfrid in terms of a variety of figures drawn from the Testaments (Duncan, below), so his various adversaries via negative stereotypes drawn from the same sources (Laynesmith, below). Finally, Wilfrid fell foul of Archbishop Theodore's ambition to remodel the larger sees of Anglo-Saxon England, sub-dividing them and instituting more numerous bishoprics, so lost the support of the one figure who might have shored up his position in Northumbria.

Wilfrid was ousted, therefore, in the late 670s by Ecgfrith and Theodore working in tandem and he departed from England to present his case at Rome before Pope Agatho (678–81), pausing on the way to undertake Christian mission in Frisia (see Palmer below). In synod at Rome, Stephen tells us that it was agreed that Wilfrid should be restored, that the three bishops appointed in the meantime to Northumbrian sees should be expelled and that Wilfrid should nominate his own candidates to be appointed by the archbishop. Additionally, his monasteries were exempted from diocesan oversight, by papal privilege. Back in Northumbria this proved unacceptable to Ecgfrith and his advisors and Wilfrid was imprisoned, then driven into exile, eventually ending up in Sussex, where he set about converting the South Saxons to Christianity, under the patronage of their king. Then allying himself with the West Saxon Cædwalla, even against his erstwhile hosts, Wilfrid involved himself with Cædwalla's successful conquest of the Isle of Wight, where he gained vast new estates. Given the king's influence across the south it seems likely that Wilfrid's subsequent reconciliation with Archbishop Theodore was largely brought about through Cædwalla's good offices.

Ecgfrith's death in battle in 685 and Theodore's support for his reinstatement clearly facilitated his return to Northumbria c.686, in the second year of King Aldfrith's reign, as bishop of York and with Ripon too restored to him. He still had powerful enemies within the Northumbrian church, however, particularly centred on Lindisfarne and Whitby. After five years Wilfrid was once again exiled, this time retiring to Mercia and the patronage there of King Æthelræd (see Tyler and Capper, below). Stephen lists the causes (VW 45) as disagreements over the lands of St Peter's (Ripon), its status as an episcopal see, and Wilfrid's opposition to Theodore's decrees, which had of course brought about his expulsion in the first place. There followed perhaps eleven years of exile which is scarcely recorded by either Stephen or Bede, when Wilfrid seems to have exercised diocesan responsibilities as and when required by his royal protector. Wilfrid was then summoned to a synod at *Ouestraefelda* presided over by Archbishop Berhtwald, Theodore's successor, but reconciliation proved impossible and Wilfrid was suspended from diocesan duties. He once again journeyed to Rome to lay his case before the papacy, in the person of John VI (701–5), leading to his excommunication in England. John's decision was that Berhtwald should hold another synod, which was to be attended by the incumbent bishops of York and Hexham, where matters should be resolved.

En route back, Wilfrid suffered a seizure, probably a stroke, at Meaux, from which he seems never to have fully recovered. He was reconciled with Berhtwald, and Aldfrith's death a few months later enabled Wilfrid to involve himself once more in Northumbrian politics. He recovered partial control of his see in 706, being reinstated to Hexham but not York. Wilfrid survived only another four years, suffering a further stroke which apparently led him to make a final disposal of his wealth between the abbots he had appointed over Ripon and Hexham, his wider following, two churches at Rome and the poor. Called to Mercia to consult with the king, he died at his monastery at Oundle, probably on 24 April 710 (Stancliffe, below).

Wilfrid's achievements were many: Stephen considered that he was responsible for the introduction of the Rule of St Benedict to England (Álvarez Lopez, below) and Bede saw him as the first Anglo-Saxon who really merited inclusion alongside the great continental figures credited with spreading the true faith among the English; he established monasteries the length and breadth of England (Foot, below), from Wessex and Sussex in the south to Northumbria in the north, and he had a major influence on Northumbria's developing Roman Church, not least in terms of new investment in architecture, sculpture and music (Bailey, Hawkes and Billett, below). Certainly, Wilfrid much increased continental influence in English Christianity and was foundational to the long tradition of English pilgrims of all sorts journeying to experience for themselves the concentration of Christian shrines, relics and practices to be found at Rome (Cubitt and Ó Carragáin and Thacker, below). Although his reputation was far from even thereafter, it has to be remembered that his sanctity has attracted numerous church dedications to the present day and that successive efforts have been made, first by his followers but subsequently by other interested parties, to commemorate him and keep his memory alive (see Thacker, Trousdale), though he has often been a victim of very negative attitudes within English historiography of the last few centuries (Foley, below).

That said, it is probably equally fair to argue that Wilfrid failed in many of his ambitions: the great northern metropolitan church over which he seems to have seen himself presiding, with power or at least influence reaching out across all of northern Britain and even northern Ireland, was virtually still born, although a rather more modest northern English archdiocese was (re-)established in 735; the extensive family of monasteries which he had founded (Foot below) seems to have unravelled within a short time, as local pressures and political ties outweighed any urge to retain unity with Wilfrid's successors at Ripon. More particularly, Wilfrid was unable for long to regain the power and authority which he had been able to exercise before his expulsion in the late 670s; within Northumbria particularly he remained a figure who attracted controversy almost to the end of his days.

Across the twentieth century, both Wilfrid and his biographer were very much overshadowed by Bede, whose *Ecclesiastical History* provided the dominant text from which seventh- and early-eighth-century history was written. Bede was generally complimentary about Wilfrid but his great historical work centred on the desirability of close collaboration between kings and bishops, and in that context Wilfrid's career was problematic, to say the least. Where Bede and Stephen differed in their accounts, it has generally been customary to prefer the later writer to the earlier, as the less polemical. In these circumstances, both Wilfrid and his life have received less academic attention than they arguably deserved. There are notable exceptions of course: in 1974 David Kirby edited a slim, multi-authored study, *St Wilfrid at Hexham*, with six essays and a further four appendices which collectively have proved seminal, but this is the sole academic book-length study of the bishop himself in his immediate cultural context written within the last half century. Alongside, only W. Trent Foley's *Images of Sanctity in Eddius Stephanus' 'Life of Saint Wilfrid', An Early English Saint's Life*, published in the US in 1992, has offered a modern scholarly analysis at comparable length of Stephen's *Life*. In their different ways both these major works underlie much that is offered here: it is a particular pleasure to acknowledge these debts, even more so since Richard Bailey, who contributed to the 1974 volume, and Trent Foley both made important contributions to the two conferences in 2009 and have both provided papers for this new study.

Even while acknowledging these many debts, the 1300th centenary of Wilfrid's death offers a valuable opportunity to return to both Wilfrid and his *Life*. This volume is made up of twenty-three separate essays, and two appendices, each of which focuses on a particular aspect of Wilfrid's life, his career, reputation and/or legacy, each from a unique standpoint. With this format overlaps are inevitable, with scholars often necessarily using the same pieces of evidence in different ways. There are certainly divergences of opinion and/or emphasis on many issues. In the process of editing and publication, no attempt has been made to avoid a degree of repetition nor to reconcile differences of opinion, which are rather all included here in the belief that dialogues between different authors, such as occurred at the conferences, have the potential to enrich the reading experience, enhance understandings and offer valuable new insights. Some cross-referencing is offered, in order to help the reader navigate between and compare the approaches of different authors and a loose gathering together of papers according to theme has been attempted, although many could easily have appeared under a different heading.

The Wilfrid story which emerges is not, therefore, in any sense a single, final and considered judgement capable of summing up his place in history. Rather it is a portfolio of different scholarly insights, reflections and suggestions: between some there remain tensions but all benefited from the processes of discussion and debate within the two conferences. The hope is that these will not just illuminate Wilfrid and his world in the present, but also drive forward further work on the subject, offering a platform for the next generation to strive towards ever better understandings of this pivotal figure in Anglo-Saxon history.

* * *

Wilfrid, then is the principal focus of the papers gathered together in this book. It is, however, also our wish as authors to commemorate Richard Andrew Hall, who died on 13 September 2011, before this volume could be brought to completion. In that cause I will offer here a brief summary of Richard's life.[1] Richard was born in Ilford (Essex) but moved as a child with his family to Northern Ireland where he attended the Royal Belfast Academical Institution and then Queen's University Belfast, studying archaeology. Already as an undergraduate his interests were clearly focused on the Viking Age and he followed up his BA with a PhD at Southampton University under the supervision

---

[1] My thanks to Ailsa Mainman, who kindly read and proposed several corrections to the Preface in draft, all of which I have gratefully accepted. I would also like here to acknowledge the contribution of Brian Ayers, on whose obituary in the *Guardian* (Friday 14 October 2011) I have based some details of what follows regarding Richard's career.

of Peter Addyman, researching the Anglo-Scandinavian towns of the Danelaw. Soon after Addyman became Director of the newly established York Archaeological Trust, Richard joined him there, having in the meantime involved himself in excavations on both sides of the Irish Sea. Beginning as excavations director, he was successively appointed Deputy Director and finally Director of Archaeology at the Trust, serving there throughout his extraordinary and distinguished career.

At York, Richard's greatest triumph was undoubtedly his magnificently successful direction of the excavation of 16–22 Coppergate from 1975 to 1981, and the subsequent management of the processes of post-excavation research and publication of the vast quantity of material recovered from the deep, waterlogged deposits which he found there, from which resulted a whole string of authoritative specialist reports as well as his own overview, *The Viking Dig* (1984). He was working on the final volume of these specialist reports, on the structures themselves, when he died and this will be completed by colleagues at the Trust. These outputs for the first time placed Viking-Age towns in England at the forefront of public attention, and established the emergence of towns in eastern England in the tenth and eleventh centuries as an academic area of interest in its own right. At the core was a new engagement with trade contacts reaching out across much of Europe, trade which is, of course, virtually un-documented and for which we are almost entirely reliant on the archaeological record. Even while the excavations were on-going, it was Richard's concern to inform and involve as many of his fellow citizens as possible that led to maximal circulation of the general public through specially constructed viewing platforms erected around the excavations. In the same vein he then went on to provide the academic underpinning for the Jorvik Viking Centre, which opened in the Coppergate development in 1984 and rapidly established itself as a favourite among Britain's visitor attractions. Through such means the rich legacy of the Coppergate 'Viking Dig' has reached a far wider audience than would otherwise have been possible, influencing the ways in which an entire generation sees and values the past.

His success at Coppergate naturally propelled Richard into the elite of Viking-Age archaeologists not just in Britain but across the Viking World: his work had important implications in America, Greenland and Iceland in the west through to Scandinavia and the British Isles. He became involved in an advisory capacity with sites elsewhere, including the Kaupang Excavation Project in Norway and excavations by the Swedish state archaeological service at the Viking-Age town of Birka. His attention on York's archaeology never wavered, though: there followed both further up-dates regarding the on-going work on the Viking period, as *Viking Age York* (1994) and *York* (1996), but this was drawn together with his wider interests by a magisterial oversight of the entire Viking

Age in *Exploring the World of the Vikings* (2007), published in seven languages.

But his role at York was by definition not a single period, and Richard was responsible for numerous further excavations across the city, including major Roman sites at Blake Street and Coney Street, overseeing it is estimated more than 1,000 in total across his career. Even so, he took great pleasure in knowing that the most recent open-area excavation, at Hungate, had uncovered new areas of early medieval York which offered the opportunity to explore another part of Viking-Age York, an opportunity that Richard relished, last visiting the site only three weeks before he died. Here activity has been demonstrated from the early tenth century, with timber-lined cellars indicative of two-storey houses and warehouses some 3m below modern street level dating to the mid- to late-tenth century, comparable to the structures found at Coppergate.

Outside the City, Richard recorded the seventh-century crypt at Ripon in 1974, where building work was then taking place without any archaeological oversight. Such was his impact in this theatre that he eventually became chairman of the Fabric Advisory Committee and then consultant cathedral archaeologist, directing substantial excavations which enabled him to recover much of the topography of the seventh-century monastery. This work led directly to his engagement with the Cathedral's Fabric Commission and also facilitated the invitation to take up the role of consultant archaeologist to York Minster. Richard's growing stature in his chosen field led to numerous invitations to lend his weight to learned bodies. He was elected a fellow of the Society of Antiquaries in 1981 and served on its Council in the late '80s and early '90s; he was chairman of the Institute of Field Archaeologists (the IFA, now the Institute for Archaeologists) from 1987 to '89; he served as president of the Society for Medieval Archaeology, and the Yorkshire Archaeological Society, and as a trustee and secretary of the Council for British Archaeology. From 2002 to 2004, he was Honorary Visiting Professor in the Department of Archaeology at the University of York.

Richard's commitment to help others was not limited to such causes, however, for he was at the same time a warm friend to many both within and without archaeology, a loving partner to his second wife, Ailsa Mainman, and a deeply committed and devoted father to their sons, Alasdair and Guy. All his many colleagues and associates will bear witness to his deep reservoirs of humanity, his sociability, and his keenness always to help those around him, to engage, to teach and to edify as well as to learn. It is as a great advocate and enthusiast for his subject that he will be remembered chiefly, and as a man whose warmth of personality, whose generosity and whose dry wit touched so many. At the last, his funeral in York Minster on Monday 26 September reflected the ways that Richard was appreciated by so many, with the Choir filled by mourners, many of whom had come from far and wide, including some from overseas, with distinguished academics attending in considerable numbers alongside relatives, friends and neighbours.

While the subject of this volume is, therefore, Bishop Wilfrid, his life, times and career, it is dedicated to the memory of Richard Andrew Hall, who did so much to bring about the volume and the conferences that it represents. His own lecture on the archaeology of Wilfrid's first great monastery, at Ripon, given with his customary wit and sharp intelligence at the York conference, was not available to be included, but will be remembered for its acute insights by those who attended (see the final plate, below).

Bibliography of the Writings of Richard Andrew Hall, FSA, MIFA

AILSA MAINMAN

1. ARTICLES

'An Excavation at Full Street, Derby, 1972', *Derbyshire Archaeological Journal* 92 (1972), 29–77 [with G. Coppack].

'A Hoard of Viking-Age Silver Bracelets from Cushalogurt, Co. Mayo', *Journal of the Royal Society of Antiquaries of Ireland* 103 (1973), 78–85.

'The Pre-Conquest *Burh* of Derby', *Derbyshire Archaeological Journal* 94 (1974), 16–23.

'A Viking Grave in the Phoenix Park, Co Dublin', *Journal of the Royal Society of Antiquaries of Ireland* 104 (1974), 39–43.

'An Excavation at Hunter Street, Buckingham, 1974', *Records of Buckinghamshire* 20 (1975), 100–33.

'Biological Evidence for the usage of Roman Riverside Warehouses', *Britannia* 7 (1976), 274-6. [with H. K. Kenward].

'Rescue Excavation in the Crypt of Ripon Cathedral', *Yorkshire Archaeological Journal* 49 (1977), 59–63.

'The Topography of Anglo-Scandinavian York', in *Viking Age York and the North*, 31–6.

'A Viking Grave at Donnybrook, Co Dublin', *Medieval Archaeology* 22 (1978), 64–83.

'A Copper-Alloy Statuette found near Chalfont St Peter', *Records of Buckinghamshire* 20 (1978), 69–70.

'An Anglo-Scandinavian Cross-Shaft from Haxby, North Yorkshire', *Yorkshire Archaeological Journal* 53 (1981), 123–5.

'10th Century Woodworking in Coppergate, York', *Woodworking Techniques before AD 1500,* ed. S. McGrail, British Archaeological Reports,

International Series 129 (1982), 231–44.

'Miniature Amphorae from Norton, North Yorkshire', *Britannia* 14 (1983), 262.

'St Mary's Church, Levisham, North Yorkshire', *Yorkshire Archaeological Journal* 58 (1986), 57–84 [with J. T. Lang].

'Viking-Age York – an Introductory Survey', in H. Galinie (ed.), *Les Mondes Normandes (VIII–XIIs)*, Actes du lie Congres International d' Archeologie Medievale (Caen, 1989), 85–93.

'York 700–1050', in R. Hodges and B. Hobley (eds), *The Rebirth of Towns in the West. Council for British Archaeology, Research Report* 68 (1988), 125–32.

'The Making of Domesday York', in *Anglo-Saxon Settlements,* ed. D. Hooke (Oxford 1988), 233–47.

'Sources for Pre-Conquest York', in *People and Places in Northern Europe 500–1500,* ed. I. Wood (Woodbridge 1990), 83–94.

'The Waterfronts of York', in G . L. Good, R. H. Jones and M. W. Ponsford (eds), *Waterfront Archaeology. Proceedings of the Third International Conference, Bristol, 1988.* CBA Research Report 74 (London, 1991), 177–84.

'York', in E. Roesdahl and D. Wilson (eds) *From Viking to Crusader* (no place of publication), 1992, 101.

'Numismatic Discoveries and Research in York: an Update', *Yorkshire Numismatist* 2 (1992), 97–9.

'Observations in Ripon Cathedral Crypt 1989', *Yorkshire Archaeological Journal* 65 (1993), 39–53.

'Vikings Gone West? A Summary Review', in B. Ambrosiani and H. Clarke (eds) *The Twelfth Viking Congress* (Stockholm 1994), 32–49.

'Antiquaries and Archaeology in and Around Ripon Minster', in L. R. Hoey (ed.), *Yorkshire Monasticism. Archaeology, Art and Architecture from the 11th to 16th Centuries,* British Archaeological Association Conference Transactions XVI (1995), 12–30.

'Ports of the East and South Coasts in the Anglo-Saxon Era', in P. Carrington (ed.), *Where Deva Spreads her Wizard Stream. Trade and the Port of Chester: Papers from a Seminar held at Chester November* 1995. Chester Archaeology Occasional Papers 3 (1996), 40–48.

The Oxford Companion to Archaeology, ed. B. M. Fagan (Oxford, 1996); contributions as follows:

'Viking Raids and Settlement in the British Isles', pp. 104–6.

'Oseberg', pp. 541–2.

'Scandinavia in the Viking Age', pp. 626–7.

'Uppsala', p. 730.

'Settlement and Monasticism at Ripon, North Yorkshire, from the 7th to 11th

Centuries AD', *Medieval Archaeology* 40 (1996), 62–150 [with M. Whyman].

'Archaeology in York', *Lubecker Kolloquium zur Stadtarchaologie im Hanseraum I: Stand, Aufgaben und Perspectiven*, ed. M. Glaser (1997), 51–65.

'A Silver Applique from St Mary Bishophill Senior, York', *Yorkshire Archaeological Journal* 70 (1998), 61–6.

'The Ripon Jewel', in J. Hawkes and S. Mills (eds), *The Golden Age of Northumbria* (1999), 268–80.

'York', in M Lapidge *et al.* (eds), *The Blackwell Encyclopaedia of Anglo-Saxon England* (Oxford, 1999), 497–9.

'York 700–1050', in C. E. Karkov (ed.), *The Archaeology of Anglo-Saxon England Basic Readings* (New York, 1999), 119–36 [reprint of 1988 article].

'The Archaeology of Medieval Trade – Observations from York', in M. Glaser (ed.), *Der Handel. Lubecker Kolloquium zur Stadtarchaologie im Hanseraum II* (Lubeck, 1999), 111–21.

'The Decline of the Wic?', in T. Slater (ed.), *Towns in Decline AD 100–1600*, (Ashgate, Aldershot, 2000), 120–36.

'Archaeology at York Minster', *The Friends of York Minster 71st Annual Report 2000* (2000), 69–74.

'Scandinavian Settlement in England – the Archaeological Evidence', in S. Stummann Hansen & K. Randsborg (eds), *Vikings in the West. Acta Archaeologica* 71 (2000), 147–57.

'Secular Domestic Buildings in Medieval York', in M. Glaser (ed.), *Lubecker Kolloquium zur Stadtarchaologie im Hanseraum* III (Lubeck, 2001), 77–99.

'Anglo-Scandinavian Attitudes. Archaeological Ambiguities in Late 9th–Mid 11th Century York', in D. Hadley and J. D. Richards (eds), *Cultures in Contact* (Turnhout, 2001), 311–24.

'Anglo-Scandinavian Urbanism in the East Midlands', in J. Graham-Campbell, R. A. Hall, J. Jesch and D. Parsons (eds), *Vikings and the Danelaw*. Proceedings of the 13th Viking Congress (Oxford, 2001), 143–55.

'A Kingdom Too Far –York in the Early 10th Century', in N. J. Higham and D. H. Hill (eds), *Edward The Elder 899–924* (London, 2001), 188–99.

'Anglo-Saxon and Viking-Age York', in P. Nuttgens (ed.), *History of York* (Pickering, 2001), 39–67.

' "The YPS is Very Flourishing" ', *Annual Report of the Yorkshire Philosophical Society 2001*, 77–81.

'Archaeology at York Minster and in the Dean and Chapter Estate, 2001', *The Friends of York Minster 73rd Annual Report 2002*, 21–9.

'Yorkshire 700–1066', in T. G. Manby, S. Moorhouse and P. J. Ottaway (eds), *The Archaeology of Yorkshire. An Assessment at the Beginning of the 21st*

Century. Yorkshire Archaeological Society Occasional Paper 3 (2003), 171–80.

'York', in R. A. Butlin (ed.), *Historical Atlas of North Yorkshire* (2003), 72–4.

'A High Status Burial from Ripon Cathedral, North Yorkshire, England: Differential Diagnosis of a Chest Deformity', *International Journal of Osteology* 13 (2003), 358–68 [with S. Groves, C. Roberts, C. Johnstone and K. Dobney].

'Jorvik – A Viking-Age City', in J. Hines, A. Lane and M. Rednap (eds), *Land, Sea And Home* (Society for Medieval Archaeology Monograph Series) (2004), 283–6.

'York's Medieval Infrastructure', in M. Gläser (ed.), *Lubecker Kolloquium zur Stadtarchaologie im Hanseraum IV Die Infrastructur* (Lubeck, 2004), 75–86.

'Drengs, Vikings, Countrymen: Raiding, Conquering and Settling in Ninth- and Tenth-Century England', in S. Lewis-Simpson (ed.), *Vinland Revisited. The Norse World at the Turn of the First Millenium. Selected Papers from the Viking Millennium International Symposium* (2004), 37–44.

'Archaeology at York Minster', *The Friends of York Minster 76th Annual Report 2005*, 80–85.

'Local Antiquarians, Thornborough Henges and Other Prehistoric Monuments near Ripon', *Yorkshire Archaeological Journal* 77 (2005), 1–16.

'Medieval Craft and Industry', in M. Gläser (ed.), *Lubecker Kolloquium zur Stadtarchaologie im Hanseraum V Das Handwerk* (Lubeck, 2006), 93–103.

'Archaeology at York Minster', *Friends of York Minster 77th Annual Report 2006*, 50–59.

'York', in *Reallexikon der Germanischen Altertumskunde* 34 (Berlin/New York 2007), 387–90.

'Archaeology at York Minster 2006', *Friends of York Minster 78th Annual Report 2007*, 41–3.

'A Striking Discovery: the Seal of a Horologiarius', *Antiquarian Horology* 30/2 (2007), 223–4 [with N. Rogers].

'Archaeology at York Minster 2007', *Friends of York Minster 69th Annual Report 2008*, 53–63.

'The Earliest Record of a Clock at York Minster?', *Friends of York Minster 69th Annual Report 2008*, 69–73.

'The Medieval Cemetery at Riccall Landing: A Reappraisal' *Yorkshire Archaeological Journal* 80 (2008), 55–92 [with J. Buckberry, R. Storm, W. D. Hamilton, P. Budd *et al.*]

'Luxury in Medieval York', in M. Gläser (ed.), *Lubecker Kolloquium zur Stadtarchaologie im Hanseraum VI Luxus und Lifestyle* (Lubeck, 2008), 95–104.

'York', in S. Brink (ed.), *The Viking World* (London, 2008), 379–84.

'York im Zeitalter der Wikinger', in *Die Wikinger* (Historisches Museum der Pfalz Speyer/Munich, 2008), 224–5.

'St Helen's Church, Skipwith, North Yorkshire', *Church Archaeology* 11 (2007), 35–40.

'St Helen's Church, Skipwith, Yorkshire', *Archaeological Journal* 165 (2008), 393–464 [with T. Kendal and C. Briden]

'Archaeology at York Minster 2008', in *Friends of York Minster 80th Annual Report 2009*, 37–41 [with K. Giles *et al.*]

'Archaeology at York Minster 2009', in *Friends of York Minster 81st Annual Report 2010*, 41–45 [with K. Giles *et al.*]

'*Eoforwic* (York) du VII au milieu du IX siècle: Questions de définition', in S. Lebecq, B. Béthouart and L. Verslype (eds), *Quentovic. Environnement, Archéologie, Histoire*, Collection Travaux et Recherches de l'Université de Lille 3, 2010, 367–80.

'The Defences of York', in M. Gläser (ed.), *Lubecker Kolloquium zur Stadtarchaologie im Hanseraum VII Die Befestigungen* (Lubeck, 2010), 71–86.

'Archaeology at York Minster 2010', in *Friends of York Minster 82nd Annual Report 2011* [with Kate Giles].

'Erik Bloodaxe Rules OK': 'The Viking Dig' at Coppergate, York', in J. Schofield (ed.), *Great Excavations. Shaping the Archaeological Profession* (Oxford, 2011), 181–93.

2. CONTRIBUTIONS TO *THE ARCHAEOLOGY OF YORK* SERIES

Medieval Tenements in Aldwark, and Other Sites by R. A. Hall, H. MacGregor and M. Stockwell, *The Archaeology of York* 10/2, 1988. Includes:

'Structures Adjacent to 1–5 Aldwark. Interpretation', pp. 80–88 [with H. MacGregor].

'Medieval Aldwark –The Werkdyke, King's Ditch and Queen's Dyke', pp. 129–32.

'Excavations at 21–33 Aldwark. Trenches IV, VI and X', pp. 133–4 [with R. F. Smith, E. King and T. Tolhurst].

'Observations at 34 Shambles', pp. 133–4.

'Observations at 11–13 Parliament Street', pp. 135–7 [with T. Tolhurst].

Urban Structures and Defences by P. V. Addyman and R. A. Hall, *The Archaeology of York* 8/3 (1991). Includes:

'Structures at 5–7 Coppergate, with a Reassessment of Benson's Observations of 1902', pp. 238–50.

'A Watching Brief at 11–13 Parliament Street', pp. 256–7 [with J. Hinchliffe].

'Anglo-Scandinavian Defences North-East of the Ouse', pp. 264–77.

'Observations in Pavement, 1990', pp. 278–81.

Excavations and Observations on the Defences and Adjacent Sites, 1971–90, by P. J. Ottaway, *The Archaeology of York* 3/3 (1996), includes:
'An Observation of the Fortress Wall in Parliament Street', pp. 227–34.
'B. K. Davison's Investigations of York's Defences between the Multangular and Anglian Towers, 1970', pp. 256–72 [with P. Ottaway and B. K. Davison].

Excavations in the Praetentura: 9 Blake Street. The Archaeology of York 3/4 (1997).

Later Medieval Occupation at 16–22 Coppergate. The Archaeology of York 10/6. (2002) [with K. Hunter-Mann].

Aspects of Anglo-Scandinavian York. The Archaeology of York 8/4 (2004). Includes:
'A Historiographical Introduction to Anglo-Scandinavian York', pp. 293–304.
'The Topography of Anglo-Scandinavian York', pp. 488–97.
'Afterword', pp. 498–502.

3. BOOKS
The Viking Dig (London, 1984).
Viking Age York (London, 1994).
York (London, 1996).
Exploring the World of the Vikings (London, 2007) [Also published in Norwegian, Swedish, Finnish, Spanish, Danish and Estonian translations].

4. EDITED WORKS
Viking Age York and the North, London, 1978.
Vikings and the Danelaw. Proceedings of the 13th Viking Congress, Oxford, 2001 [with J. Graham-Campbell, J. Jesch and D. Parsons].
Aspects of Anglo-Scandinavian York, The Archaeology of York 8/4, 2004.
Vicars Choral in English Cathedrals, Cantate Domino. *History, Architecture, Archaeology*, Oxford, 2005 [with D. Stocker].

1: *Wilfrid, his Cult and his Biographer*

ALAN THACKER

The Establishment of the Cult

There can be no doubt that the cult of Wilfrid was established among his followers immediately after his death. That is made clear by his biographer, Stephen of Ripon, upon whom our knowledge of the cult, as of the man himself, primarily depends. Stephen, as Clare Stancliffe shows so convincingly, wrote his Life very soon after Wilfrid's death, probably in 712 or 713, and certainly before the death of Ælfflæd, abbess of Whitby, in 714 (see below pp. 23–5). At Oundle, in ceremonies which resemble those honouring other early English saints, most notably Æthelthryth of Ely and Cuthbert of Lindisfarne in the 690s, the body was brought into a tent or marquee and laid out, washed, and clothed in appropriate ecclesiastical vestments. Water used in the washing was ritually poured away at a site thereby rendered sacred and marked with a wooden cross, soon to become the scene of miracles. The robe on which Wilfrid's body had been laid out was also preserved and esteemed a holy and wonder-working relic. The house where the saint had died had miraculous properties and when the monastery was attacked and destroyed by fire, it alone survived (VW 66–7; Thacker 2002, 45–6).

After the ceremonious and public laying out at Oundle, Wilfrid's body was taken to Ripon where the whole community came out bearing relics to greet the funeral cortège in a ritual modelled on those for the *adventus* or reception of a saint. Tatberht, as abbot of Ripon and Wilfrid's designated heir, established the formal apparatus of a cult, celebrating a daily private mass in Wilfrid's honour and keeping Thursday, the day on which he died, as a feast day equivalent to Sunday (VW 66). The anniversary of the saint's death became an even more solemn occasion, attended by a great gathering of Wilfrid's abbots and followers. There were vigils at the tomb and on one occasion (evidently at night) the event was marked by a wonderful sign in the sky, a white arc surrounding the whole monastery, like, says Stephen, 'a rainbow by day but without its various colours' (VW 68). This has been most ingeniously interpreted by Clare Stancliffe (p. 23) as a 'moonbow', a rare astronomical event which could plausibly have occurred in April 711. Stephen was probably writing very soon after this event.

Stephen tells us that he wrote at the behest of Wilfrid's heirs, whom he names as Bishop Acca of Hexham and Abbot Tatberht of Ripon. Curiously, the work nevertheless contains references to Acca as *beatae memoriae*, 'of blessed memory', and it has been argued that the original text was revised, either after

1

Acca had been expelled from his see in 731 or after his death in 740 (VW 22, 56; Kirby 1983, 101–14). These references, however, need not imply a wholesale redrafting; they may simply have been inserted by a later copyist.

In pre-Conquest England, Wilfrid was commemorated by two feasts, 24 April and 12 October. In 709 neither was a Thursday. But 24 April was indeed a Thursday in 710, which must undoubtedly therefore be the year of Wilfrid's death (Levison 1946, 278–9; Thacker 2004b). The emphasis on the October feast developed later, perhaps because that in April was likely to conflict with Lent and Easter. We have good independent evidence that April 24 was Wilfrid's original *dies natalis*. The martyrology of Tallaght, a ninth-century compilation but one with much earlier Northumbrian antecedents, commemorates Wilfrid (*Uldbrith*), together with Ecgberht the Saxon, on that day (MT 36). The latter was the English bishop who was responsible for the conversion of Iona to the Catholic Easter and whose death in 729 is recorded in elegiac terms in the penultimate book of Bede's *Ecclesiastical History*. Bede regarded the fact that Ecgberht died on Easter day as a marvellous sign, and placed especial emphasis on the fact that in that year it fell on April 24, an exceptionally late date only permitted under the new Catholic dispensation (HE V, 22)

The earliest strand in the martyrology of Tallaght was probably a breviate of the Hieronymian martyrology which commemorated a number of seventh-century Northumbrian kings, bishops, hermits and martyrs, the latest being the two Hewalds, who were killed in Saxony *c.* 695, and the hermit Oethilwald, who died on Farne 699 (MT 35, 77; Ó Riain 1993, 6–16; 2006, 43–55, 72n). One notable absentee is Abbot Ceolfrith of Wearmouth-Jarrow, who died 716 and who had a particular interest in ritual commemoration. That perhaps indicates that the breviate was compiled before that date (Ó Riain 2002, 327, 340). If so, and if Wilfrid was part of this original phase, the breviate must date from 710–16 and would suggest that Wilfrid's feast was well-established very soon after his death, even in non-Wilfridian churches. One problem with this, however, is the fact that the breviate exhibits especially strong ties with Lindisfarne, perhaps the least likely of Northumbrian monasteries to commemorate Wilfrid in the years immediately after his death (Ó Riain 2006, 22, 48–9, 55). A second and slightly later strand of the martyrology was added at Iona, sometime probably shortly after 729 and certainly before *c.* 740 (Ó Riain 2006, 61–3). It is quite possible that Wilfrid, the leading Northumbrian champion of the Roman Easter, was included at this stage, along with Ecgberht, the man who had brought the monastery to catholic ways.

Also relevant here is the calender evidence from York. The mid-eighth century York metrical calendar commemorates Wilfrid on 24 April (Wilmart 1934, 57, 66; Bullough 1984, 79–80; 2004, 215), and he also appears on the same date in another early calendar, preserved in a manuscript (Berlin, Phillips

1869) transcribed at Prüm in the mid ninth century, but perhaps originating at Wearmouth-Jarrow in the earlier eighth, and remodelled at York in the late 760s or 770s (Bullough 2003, 334, 350–1; Borst 1998, 268). By the mid eighth century, then, if not immediately after his death, Wilfrid was commemorated not only in his own monastic churches in Northumbria, Mercia and elsewhere but perhaps also in other important centres. In Alcuin's York, his position as one of the city's major saints was not in doubt. Alcuin's poem presents Wilfrid as 'a straightforward figure of uncontested sanctity,' a renowned missionary among the South Saxons and the Frisians whose bitter conflicts with the Northumbrian kings are not mentioned (BKS li–lii, 48–54). Significantly, Wilfrid's fifth successor in the see, Archbishop Ælberht (767–779/80), was consecrated on 24 April, Wilfrid's *dies natalis*. The choice of the day (Friday) and season (after Easter) was unusual, and can only suggest that Wilfrid's feast and hence his cult mattered then at York (BKS 116–17; Bullough 2004, 247). It is also worth noting that, unusually, on 12 January the calendar in the Berlin manuscript records the *dies depositionis* of Pope John VI, who heard Wilfrid's second appeal to Rome in 704 and who wrote to the kings Aldfrith of Northumbria and Æthelræd of Mercia on Wilfrid's behalf (VW 50–5; Bullough 2003, 335). It was presumably the pope's relationship with Wilfrid which recommended him. Undoubtedly, there was life in Wilfrid's cult throughout the eighth century, even if he never achieved the same importance as, say, St Cuthbert. In late-eighth-century York indeed, he had become 'an example to his successors' (Bullough 1984, 79).

Stephen and Bede

A key figure in the development of this cult is clearly Stephen himself. Probably a companion of Wilfrid's in his latter years, he was especially interested in Wilfrid's primary foundation, the monastery of Ripon, of which he was evidently an inmate, and in Wilfrid's Mercian affairs. Indeed, it has been suggested that he may himself have been Mercian. Stephen's *Life* is a remarkable work, vivid and revealing, at once deeply partisan and replete with historical detail. In general, early medieval hagiographers tended not to be interested in the particularities of their hero's earthly life, but Stephen in this respect was wholly exceptional. Although he mentions Wilfrid's asceticism and wonder-working power, he was primarily concerned with his earthly career, and inserted documents relating to this into his text, according to the conventions of the day a feature of history rather than hagiography. Stephen, in fact, was writing an apologia. His work was primarily defensive: to show that Wilfrid was always right and always holy. Stephen's agenda is more blatant than Bede's, and his moral and cultural outlook is very different indeed; but nevertheless it is one of the few works of its kind about a major figure of the late seventh and early eighth century which can be set against Bede and which measures up to the latter in quality (Thacker 2004a).

And so to Bede. The monk of Jarrow's attitude to Wilfrid is famously controversial. To my mind, whatever Bede's personal views (and almost certainly they were less than unconditionally admiring) his account of the bishop in the *Ecclesiastical History* is not in itself intended to be read as hostile, rather indeed to be edifying (*HE* V.19). Even if he is not explicitly presented as a saint, he is among the great and good whose epitaphs are included – indeed it has been suggested that Bede wrote the poem himself (Bullough, 2004, 219, 220). Wilfrid's activities were crucial to Bede's narrative. He could not be ignored, but the picture presented in Stephen's *Life* – which Bede had certainly read – had to be customized to serve Bede's purposes. Undoubtedly, the *Ecclesiastical History* was intended to evoke and illustrate values often in conflict with those of Wilfrid and his biographer. Bede's account could not then be other than ambivalent. And as such it tells us a lot about the pressures which shaped Stephen's work.

Stephen's Presentation of Wilfrid

A principal aim of this paper is to show how Stephen shaped Wilfrid as a patron and protector and a figure of cult. It will examine Stephen's aims in writing his *Life* and then draw out some implications about the wider political and ecclesiastical context. The main themes to be emphasized are as follows: first, the insistent presentation of Wilfrid as Old Testament prophet and New Testament apostle; second, his distinctive approach to Wilfrid's ecclesiastical and political career – one which would have been highly distasteful to Northumbria's ruling elite; and third, how the development of the cult of Cuthbert of Lindisfarne throws light on the circumstances in which Stephen was writing.

Prophet and Apostle

One way to answer critics such as Bede was to place Wilfrid in the company of the patriarchs, prophets and apostles. At one point indeed Stephen expressly says that Wilfrid was 'a prophet of God'(VW 8). The Old Testament typology was applied with particular thoroughness. It permeates the entire text. Through it, Stephen was able to present Wilfrid as one of God's holy men and his followers as a chosen people. Abraham and Jacob provided examples of God's elect living as homeless wanderers, setting out for distant lands accompanied only by their household (VW 2, 3, 4, 65). Joseph was a dignified and edifying prototype for the imprisoned Wilfrid – both were brought forth to perform wonders after an unjust confinement (VW 38, 42). Exodus provided even more satisfactory models: Moses and the children of Israel persecuted by Pharaoh (VW 13); Moses building an earthly tabernacle to stir up the faith of the children of God (VW 17). The kings and prophets of Israel were equally compelling: like Elijah, Wilfrid was persecuted by a wicked queen, a second Jezebel (VW 34); like King David, he was chosen from infancy and judged worthy of the gift of prophecy (VW 9); like Solomon, he dedicated a temple to the Lord (VW 17); like the great high priest Jehoida, he brought his king victory over his enemies (VW 19). His and his followers' enemies were like the Philistines, who seized the ark of God: when they laid hands of Wilfrid's holy relics it did them no good (VW 34).

Wilfrid then was a patriarch and prophet of the new dispensation. He and his followers constituted a people of God, a latter-day Israel fighting and overcoming their enemies against all odds. The long periods of exile, the humiliating expulsions and imprisonment, could be infused with new meaning in the light of these models. Stephen himself became a servant of that earthly tabernacle of the New Israel which was Ripon (VW 17).

When it came to using the New Testament, Stephen generally stopped short of direct comparisons with Christ, although he did compare the scattering of Wilfrid's *familia* with the dispersal of Christ's disciples (VW 36). Most characteristically, Wilfrid was *apostolus*. He had a special relationship with St Andrew, formed on his first visit in Rome (VW 5). He is compared repeatedly to Peter, Paul and John the Evangelist. Thus, when he is imprisoned by Ecgfrith, like St Peter he is consoled by an angel and released from his chains (VW 36), while at Lyons he was revealed as a confessor who, like John the Evangelist, confronted martyrdom but was spared, unharmed (VW 6). After his death Wilfrid's apostolic status was divinely confirmed by the miraculous sign, given to his followers, which declared him the equal of Peter and Andrew (VW 68). This New Testament typology again provided Stephen with a means of vindicating Wilfrid's temporal vicissitudes. It carried especial conviction when Wilfrid's missionary activities were being described: like Peter and Andrew, he was a fisher of men (VW 26, 41).

Politician and High Ecclesiastic

Central to Stephen's presentation of Wilfrid's political and ecclesiastical career were his hero's relations with the powers that be in Northumbria and Mercia. That stands in marked contrast to Bede's account in the *Ecclesiastical History*, the main concern of which was to record Wilfrid as missionary amongst the pagans rather than his entanglements in Christian Northumbria or his divided, Mercian-orientated, loyalties. In general, Stephen does little to link his subject in a positive way with the Bernician ruling house (until the surprising alliance with King Aldfrith's son Osred in 706). Rather he places great emphasis upon his hero's supra-national connections and upon his links with Deira, Kent and, above all, Mercia. This contrasts strongly with Bede's treatment. Certain episodes illustrate the differences very clearly.

I. Stephen's preoccupations are especially evident in his presentation of Wilfrid's consecration to and entry into the Northumbrian see, which the

Northumbrian king Oswiu's son, Alhfrith, had secured for him in 664 (VW 11–12, 14–15). Here, interestingly, he is tendentious. He does not mention the removal of the see-seat from discredited Bernician Lindisfarne, but misleadingly presents Wilfrid as succeeding Bishop Colmán (the brief pontificate of Tuda is ignored) as metropolitan bishop of York (VW 10), thus evoking the ecclesiastical plan devised by Pope Gregory the Great (HE I, 29; Thacker 2007, 44–5, 55). Wilfrid appears as the restorer of the ruined cathedral church of York, built in stone, *iuxta Romanorum … morem*, by Paulinus, the first metropolitan (VW 16; HA 5). This emphasis on metropolitan status is highly significant, and accords with Wilfrid's own ensuing consecration in Gaul, the grandeur of which indicates he evaluated his own position in precisely those terms. Stephen describes a splendid ceremony, conducted by twelve bishops at the Merovingian royal palace of Compiègne (Bede is less effusive). Certainly expressive of Wilfrid's high view of the episcopal office in general, it suggests that he regarded himself as a cut above the surviving English bishops, perhaps indeed endowed with metropolitan status (VW 12; HE III, 28).

At this climactic moment, however, Wilfrid's patron Alhfrith disappeared from the scene. Stephen is silent on the subject, but Bede expressly says that he rebelled against his father, Oswiu (HE III, 14). Oswiu reacted by intruding his own candidate in place of his son's absent protégé, an act condemned by Stephen as instigated by diabolic envy and ignorance (whereas Bede implies that it was Wilfrid's fault for lingering abroad). When the new bishop finally returned in 666, he withdrew to his monastery of Ripon, his base for the next three years, from which, resourceful as ever, he exercised his episcopal authority in Mercia and Kent by permission of their friendly kings. In Mercia in particular, he seems to have been favoured by King Wulfhere, who granted him considerable estates on which he established religious communities. Although reported favourably by Stephen, such activities probably did him little good in Oswiu's eyes. Wilfrid's activities in Kent are noted by Bede but the links with Wulfhere are ignored (VW 14; HE III, 18, V, 19).

It was almost certainly to resolve this situation that in 668 (as Bede, but not Stephen, records) the kings Oswiu of Northumbria and Ecgberht of Kent jointly sent a candidate to Rome to receive the pallium and take over the leadership of the English church as a whole (HE IV, 1). It seems highly likely that Oswiu was prepared to accept Wilfrid as bishop but sought an agreed ecclesiastical superior to keep him under control. One of the first acts of Theodore, the papal nominee, on arriving in England in 669 was to regularize the situation at York. Wilfrid was restored and another see found for the intruder Chad, who was sent to Mercia to be based at the large estate of Lichfield that Wulfhere had originally given to Wilfrid. Already then, Stephen is showing how crucial Wilfrid's Mercian links were to his position in Northumbria (VW 15; HE IV, 2).

Stephen's account of these events differs significantly from Bede's. Unlike Bede, he presents Chad's translation to Lichfield as primarily Wilfrid's initiative; moreover, he implicitly associates Wilfrid with the whole process. Chad is said to have accepted the judgement of 'the bishops', to have obeyed 'the bishops' in all things, and to have received a second consecration from them. By 'the bishops', Stephen presumably means Theodore and Wilfrid. So by implication Wilfrid is being accorded higher episcopal authority, although it is clear that there was no formal recognition of York's metropolitan status. Bede, significantly, makes Theodore alone responsible for Chad's reconsecration and again does not mention Wilfrid's links with Wulfhere (HE IV, 2–3).

II. Another telling episode is Stephen's presentation of the years 669–78, the period when Wilfrid, unchallenged at York, was most successful (VW 16–23). Stephen depicts the bishop restoring the church at York and investing in new building at Ripon and Hexham, making much of the structures themselves and their splendid furnishings, vestments and books. In an attempt, perhaps, to call attention to the bishop's special relationship with Ripon, he notes that at Hexham it was Acca, rather than Wilfrid, who provided the ornaments (VW 17, 22). While Wilfrid thus enriched and enlarged his *regnum ecclesiarum*, the Northumbrian kings, with whom he then lived in amity, expanded their dominion among the Saxons, British, Picts and Scots (VW 19–21). There is no hint at this time of subordination to Theodore, although the precise basis of Wilfrid's authority is not discussed. Wilfrid's pretensions are revealed by two episodes. The first, recorded by Bede, but not by Stephen, is his response to the council convened by Theodore, at Hertford in 672: he did not attend in person, but simply sent legates, surely an indication that he regarded York as lying outside the province of Canterbury, in effect as a separate metropolitan see (HE IV, 5; Thacker 2008, 57). Secondly, when he was at Rome in 679–80, seeking restoration after his fall, Stephen relates that Wilfrid subscribed to the synod convened to condemn Monothelitism on behalf of northern Britain and the islands of Hibernia, inhabited by English, British, Scots and Picts, a story confirmed by the acts of the synod and repeated by Bede. It seems, then, that despite his quarrel with King Ecgfrith of Northumbria, Wilfrid was still looking to establish a northern British province which rivalled, perhaps indeed undermined, that set up for Theodore. (VW 53; Thacker 2008, 60; Charles-Edwards 2000, 432–5).

III. Stephen's treatment of Wilfrid's second spell as bishop in Northumbria, 686–690/1, is equally revealing (VW 43–5). He relates that the ailing archbishop, Theodore, wished to make peace with him and sent letters to Aldfrith, Ecgfrith's successor as king of Northumbria, and to Abbess Ælfflæd, then perhaps the leading figure in the Northumbrian church, urging them to do likewise. Stephen also adds a letter commending Wilfrid to the Mercian king Æthelræd and even claims that Theodore wanted Wilfrid to be his successor. Again Bede's account is significantly different; he says nothing of Theodore's intervention or of any restoration in Mercia but simply notes that Wilfrid regained his bishopric at the invitation of King Aldfrith. Neither Stephen nor Bede directly disclose the fact that the restoration was only partial, and that, while Wilfrid regained his privileged monasteries of Ripon and Hexham, he only received the see of York in a reduced form (VW 43; HE V, 19). In the end, when Aldfrith sought to establish a see at Ripon, perhaps Wilfrid's most favoured community, the quarrel flared up again and by 692 Wilfrid had left for Mercia, where King Æthelræd had restored his monasteries and estates, and where he remained under royal protection for some eleven years. Strangely, Stephen either knew or chose to say little about this long sojourn in Mercia, simply recording that Wilfrid 'lived in the profound respect of that bishopric which Bishop Seaxwulf had formerly ruled before his death' (VW 45). The episode is only mentioned in passing by Bede, with reference to two episcopal consecrations performed by Wilfrid at the beginning of his exile. One, that of Oftfor as bishop of the Hwicce, was, he says, made while Wilfrid had charge of the bishopric of the Middle Angles (*qui tunc temporis Mediterraneorum Anglorum episcopatum gerebat*), after the death of Theodore and before the appointment of his successor, that is between 19 September 690 and 30 June 692 (HE IV, 23). The other, that of Swithberht as bishop of the Frisians, he places during Wilfrid's exile in Mercia (*qui ... in Merciorum exulebat*), while the archbishop-elect, Berhtwald was abroad himself, seeking consecration in Gaul, between 1 July 692 and August 693 (HE V, 8, 11). Stephen, although he does not mention the consecrations, appears to have been more accurate in his treatment of these events. His careful wording makes it plain that Wilfrid was not formally assigned a bishopric but that he simply operated within the boundaries of Seaxwulf's former see, which almost certainly comprised the entire Mercian heartlands, Lichfield as well as Leicester. There is no good evidence for a see at Leicester before 737,[1] and it is not clear why Bede suggests that Wilfrid's activity was confined to the Middle Angles in the early 690s.

IV. In 702 came the final crisis of Wilfrid's life. Prompted by Aldfrith, Theodore's successor, Archbishop Berhtwald, presided over a Northumbrian church council, which sought to resolve the bishop's anomalous position by depriving him of all his possessions except the monastery of Ripon, where he was to remain without exercising his episcopal office. This council, the synod of Austerfield, is not mentioned by Bede, so perhaps it was afterwards regarded as ill-judged. In Stephen's account it is notable for Wilfrid's justification of his career, in which he lays stress on his extension of universal Roman observance, his introduction of catholic liturgical chant and of the rule of St Benedict. At this

[1]   I am most grateful for Dr Paul Bowman for discussion on this point.

point, Stephen tells of Wilfrid consulting with King Æthelræd, who continued to guarantee his Mercian holdings (information again omitted by Bede), before determining on a further appeal to Rome. Stephen (but not Bede) tells us that Berhtwald responded by excommunicating the bishop and all his supporters (VW 46–9).

By 704 both Wilfrid and his party were once again in Rome. Basing himself upon earlier papal judgements, Wilfrid appealed to the pope for a confirmation of his predecessor's privilege for his two great communities and for the retention, in accordance with King Æthelræd's wishes, of his monasteries and estates in Mercia. Pope John confirmed the judgments of his predecessors, but anxious to avoid dissension in Britain, ordered that the matter be resolved at a synod convoked by Berhtwald, 'with Bishop Wilfrid' (wording which provides perhaps another indication that Wilfrid was not regarded as one of the archbishop's suffragans). All these events were carefully documented and recorded by Stephen, who was clearly in attendance on Wilfrid at this time and who often applies the first person plural to the bishop and his followers. Again Bede, by contrast, downplayed Wilfrid's strong dependence on King Æthelræd and his retention of his Mercian possessions, although he did note that the pope wrote to Æthelræd as well as Aldfrith urging Wilfrid's restoration (VW 50–4; HE V,19).

After this ruling, Wilfrid eventually, and according to Stephen reluctantly, set out for England only returning in 705, after being struck down by a seizure at Meaux. He met first with Berhtwald, whom Stephen presents as anxious now to make peace, and afterwards with Æthelræd, by then abbot of Bardney. Stephen emphasizes Æthelræd's and his successor's friendship for Wilfrid, and contrasts this with the continuing hostility of the dying Aldfrith, who was soon to be succeeded by Eadwulf, an intruder of unknown lineage, not mentioned by Bede. Interestingly, Stephen says that Wilfrid responded to this usurpation by returning from exile in the company of Eadwulf's son, whom he had presumably met in Mercia. The Mercians may, then, have been involved in this coup. Surprisingly, however, Eadwulf rejected Wilfrid, and shortly afterwards, in 706, was overthrown by a conspiracy, in which, Stephen implies, Wilfrid was involved. Remarkably, Stephen describes the new king, Aldfrith's young son, Osred (still ruling as he was writing), as the bishop's *filius adoptivus*: Wilfrid, perhaps by then a sick man, had at last come to terms with the house of Oswiu (VW 55–9).

The outcome of these intrigues was a settlement, enacted at a synod in 706, in the presence of Wilfrid and Berhtwald, the young king and his chief minister, and three Northumbrian bishops (presumably Bosa of York, John of Hexham and the bishop of Lindisfarne). According to Stephen, the archbishop acknowledged that Rome required a reconciliation and spelt out the options: the Northumbrian bishops could either be reconciled to Wilfrid and yield up to him such parts of the churches he had formerly ruled that Berhtwald and the royal counsellors should determine, or they would have to take the matter in person to the Holy See. The bishops demurred, but their hands were forced by Abbess Ælfflæd. Described by Stephen in the warmest terms as 'always the best councillor of the whole kingdom', she related that Aldfrith had attributed his mortal illness to his failure to observe the pope's request for reconciliation and had expressed his desire to see Wilfrid restored. Her intervention was supported by the chief minister and seems to have been decisive: Wilfrid was to regain the monasteries of Ripon and Hexham. Stephen is rather vague about the settlement, perhaps because he regarded it as a defeat. Bishop Bosa conveniently died about this time but was replaced not by Wilfrid but by John of Beverley, translated from Hexham, leaving Wilfrid with episcopal authority over his own monastery. Stephen ignores this episode and Bede is more informative here, for he says correctly, if rather evasively, that, after some argument, Wilfrid was 'received back into the bishopric of his own church' (*in praesulatum sit suae receptus ecclesiae*). All this must still have been fresh in men's minds when Stephen was writing, some six years after these events (VW 60–1; HE V, 19).

V. Finally, let us look at Stephen's account of Wilfrid's provisions for his followers. Made at Ripon, probably early in 710, they were in two stages, often regarded as inconsistent, though arguably they can be reconciled. The first stage was enacted before a select band of ten witnesses, which apparently included two abbots sent by the Mercian king, and two priests and a *magister*, one of them Wilfrid's intended heir, all probably kinsmen. Wilfrid laid out his treasure, brought from the monastery's strong room, commanding it to be divided into four parts, the best going to two great Roman basilicas, and the remainder to the poor, to the heads of the monasteries of Ripon and Hexham 'to purchase the friendship of kings and bishops', and to his faithful followers in exile. He then confirmed to this inner group that his kinsman Tatberht was to be his successor at Ripon and his coadjutor while he lived (VW 63).

This done, Wilfrid caused the whole community to be summoned. He announced the (perhaps compulsory) retirement of Caelin, evidently an earlier coadjutor, and his departure for Mercia, promising if he returned alive to bring his successor as abbot with him and if not to send five named witnesses to relate his decision (VW 64). Wilfrid then left to confer with King Ceolred about the provision for his Mercian monasteries. Although he failed to reach the king, he did meet his Mercian abbots, to some of whom he revealed the provisions of his will, and distributed gifts of money and land. He died at Oundle in April 710, only there on his deathbed making formal provision for Hexham – allotted to Acca, who was apparently not present at any of these events, perhaps because he was already in charge of the monastery (VW 65).

All this is a world away from the ideal Benedictine practice as

10

recommended by the Rule, which laid especial emphasis on the community's role in electing a superior chosen purely on personal merit (RSB 64). And, needless to say, not a word is said about this by Bede. Wilfrid's arrangements seem highly autocratic and entirely kept from the great majority of his monks, perhaps to forestall intervention from his opponents. That the Wilfridians were indeed alarmed and defensive is suggested by the bequest to buy the friendship of the powerful and the tone of the final chapters of Stephen's Life, which tell of the burial at Ripon, the accession of Tatberht, and the provision made for Wilfrid's cult (VW 66–8; below).

Wilfrid and Cuthbert

A context for Stephen's presentation of Wilfrid is provided by contemporary depictions of St Cuthbert, bishop of Lindisfarne (685–7). Cuthbert, who in life seems to have been closely associated with the royal house of Oswiu, was in death to become the Northumbrian establishment's favourite saint, the ascetic and miracle-working patron of the royal house and its plans for ecclesiastical reform (Thacker 1983, 136–49). Cuthbert's cult was probably associated with a rejection of Wilfridian values and at Lindisfarne, if not elsewhere, with a repudiation of Wilfrid himself. Developing very soon after his death on 20 March 687, it flourished in the years after Wilfrid's second expulsion in 692, culminating in a carefully orchestrated translation in 698 (Thacker 1989; Kirby 1995, 383–97). Shortly afterwards, Cuthbert became the subject of an ambitious and monumental *Vita* written by a monk of Lindisfarne (Colgrave 1940). Very curiously, however, that Life came to be supplemented and ultimately superseded within a few years of its composition. Almost certainly, this process was closely related to the activities of Wilfrid towards the end of his life and his emergence as a figure of cult in the hands of his biographer.

The first phase of the revision of the anonymous *Life* dates from *c.* 706, when Bede composed a metrical Life of Cuthbert (Jaager 1935). This included new material on Cuthbert's last days and death, more fully revealed in Bede's new prose *Life*, composed sometime after 713 and certainly not later than 721 (Colgrave 1940; Lapidge 1989). In the prose *Life*, this new material is presented in the form of a *relatio* delivered by Herefrith, abbot of Lindisfarne in Cuthbert's time and still alive when Bede was writing (VCP 37–40). The *relatio* is composed in the first person and is presented as Herefrith's *ipsissima verba*, although in the later sections the Latin seems to have been improved by Bede (Berschin 1989, 102). It was clearly a written text since it was evidently already in existence *c.* 706 when it informed the metrical *Life* (VCM 33–7).

The *relatio* opens with a description of the bishop's final illness and his commands about his burial, in which he displayed foreknowledge of his future status as a saint (VCM 33; VCP 37) and which is clearly designed to reinforce

Cuthbert's saintly reputation. The most interesting section, however, is that which describes the dramatic announcement of his death to the community, initially made by Herefrith to his companions on Farne and immediately transmitted by a signal to the rest of the community on the main island of Lindisfarne (VCM 37; VCP 40). On both occasions the brethren were singing the psalm which begins 'O God thou hast cast us off and hast broken us down; thou hast been angry and hast had compassion on us' (Ps. 59.3). The psalm is presented as a prophetic text referring to the great blast of trial (*temptationis aura, perosa ... flabra*) which attacked the brethren for a year after Cuthbert's death until the tensions were assuaged and healed by the appointment of Eadberht as bishop of Lindisfarne (VCM 37; VCP 40;). These testing experiences were almost certainly inflicted on the brethren during Wilfrid's tenure of the see of Lindisfarne (687–8), soon after his return to Northumbria (an event which perhaps precipitated Cuthbert's retirement). The episode is discreetly mentioned by Bede in the *Ecclesiastical History* as extending from Cuthbert's burial until the consecration of his successor, although he makes no explicit mention of the crisis (HE IV, 29).

It is highly significant that this material first makes its appearance in the Cuthbertine corpus *c.* 706, just after Wilfrid had made his settlement with the new regime established by the young Osred's guardians and as a result had regained Hexham. Lindisfarne, it seems, feared and resented the returning bishop. A further indicator of the community's sentiments is the deathbed speech attributed to Cuthbert. The saint exhorts the brethren to keep peace with one another, with other communities and with those who visit them. He urges that they have no communion with those who do not keep the proper Easter and that they should leave Lindisfarne, taking his bones with them, rather than fall under the power of schismatics (VCP 39). Although included only in Bede's prose *Life*, it forms part of Herefrith's *relatio* and so may have been composed *c.* 706. If so, it seems possible that it represents a coded condemnation of the Wilfridians, who had only recently (702–3) been excommunicated, an episode expressly mentioned by Stephen in the bitterest and most explicit terms (VW 49).

It is clear then that work was going on to amend the Cuthbertine corpus in an anti-Wilfridian manner, shortly before Stephen took up his pen. Although Bede's *Vita metrica* was perhaps primarily for private meditative use, Herefrith's *relatio* may already have been in circulation. Stephen's own contribution to the debate was to appropriate and upstage the Lindisfarne *Life*'s presentation of its hero's sanctity (Goffart 1988, 283–5). In particular, he countered Herefrith's allusions to schism by treating the pre-Whitby Northumbrian Irish as schismatics along with the obdurate British, thereby establishing Wilfrid's superior credentials as a patron of orthodoxy. The skill and effectiveness of Stephen's achievement is discussed elsewhere in this volume and so will not be dwelt on here (Stancliffe, below). In this paper, it is sufficient to note that his implied contrast between Wilfrid's unimpeachable credentials as the champion of Roman customs, the customs adopted by the Northumbrian elite at Whitby, with Cuthbert's dubiously Irish background, mattered enough to elicit a highly significant response at Lindisfarne: the commissioning of Bede to replace the anonymous portrait. That suggests that Stephen's intervention was important and that the audience he was addressing remained highly influential.

Stephen and His Audience

The *Life* is clearly addressed to the Wilfridian communities, especially Ripon and those in Mercia. Wilfrid is constantly associated with those whom Stephen variously called his comrades or companions (*sodales*, *socii*), brethren (*fratres*), and subjects (*subiecti*, *subditi*), and who might be abbots, monks, priests, deacons (VW 53), clerics, or even anchorites (VW 62).[2] Stephen, as his frequent use of the first person shows, identified with them very closely, regarding them as a special brotherhood linked by unique bonds. They were an elect band in a hostile world and he wrote to sustain their morale. It is this need which explains the rhetoric of his work. He had to justify Wilfrid's problematic career, his failures and misfortunes and the opposition which he had encountered from holy and respected men and women such as Theodore and Æfflæd. To accomplish this, he examined Wilfrid's life in quite exceptional detail, fleshing out his account with biblical typology and documentary evidence, to explain how Wilfrid was always supported by God, if not always, in worldly terms, successful.[3]

Above all, Stephen had to provide something to sustain the bonds of Wilfrid's connection after the saint's death had removed the principal focus of loyalty. This emerges most clearly in the closing chapters. Stephen stresses the eventual triumph of the Wilfridian fellowship over its enemies; his provision for his followers and for the succession; and divine signs vindicating that settlement after Wilfrid's death. The work concludes with Wilfrid's bishops and abbots gathered in Ripon to celebrate his anniversary, strengthened by the comforting

---

[2] *socii*: VW 7, 28, 35, 39, 55; *sodales*: VW 13, 24, 40, 59; *fratres*: VW 41, 50, 53, 56, 58, 63; *subiecti*: VW 24, 34, 41, 44, 50, 68; *subditi*: VW 56, 68; *abbates*: VW 49, 53, 57, 62, 63, 64; *monachi*: VW 40, 44; *presbyteri*: VW 49, 50, 53; *diaconi*: VW 53; *cleri*, *clerici*: VW 13, 30, 50; *anachoritae*: VW 62.

[3] The most compelling parallels, hagiographical works packed with rich historical detail, and deeply concerned with worldly politics, are, as we might expect, from Merovingian Gaul, in particular the Lives and Passions of controversial seventh-century political bishops, men such as Leodegarius of Autun (d. 679), significantly like Wilfrid an enemy of Ebroin, and Prajectus of Clermont (d. 676). See Fouracre, pp. 186–99, below; Thacker, 1977.

sign of the moonbow surrounding the whole monastery. Revealingly, they noted that while, during his life, they endured many trials from kings and princes which on the whole ended well, now after his death they had to believe that Wilfrid had become the equal of the apostles and hence would be able to defend his followers without ceasing. It is a highly defensive image, witness to the insecurity already evinced in Wilfrid's will, that the brotherhood would be under attack (VW 68).

Stephen's account makes clear the degree to which, throughout his life, Wilfrid was dependent upon the good will of kings. His death undoubtedly left his followers highly vulnerable. It was, of course, Wilfrid – magnificent, pugnacious and ambitious – who was really the outsider, not the unworldly and ascetic Cuthbert. That his strong ties with Mercia did not appeal to the political world focused upon Bamburgh is apparent from the way in which they are played down by Bede. That indeed Wilfrid's connnexion was under attack in physical as well as ideological terms is suggested by Stephen's story of the burning of Oundle, the Mercian monastery in which the bishop died, and which was evidently an important centre of his cult, perhaps indeed its major Mercian focus (VW 67). We do not know who the band of noble exiles responsible for the attack might have been; but we may wonder whether they were perhaps Northumbrian and whether their intervention was in some way connected with Wilfrid's involvement in the coups and countercoups in Northumbria in the confused period after Aldfrith's death. Could they have been followers of the deposed Eadwulf, of whom Wilfrid had evidently once had expectations but whom he had deserted in 706 after he himself had been rejected (VW 59)?

The Impact of Stephen's Work

This paper has suggested that the origins of Wilfrid's cult and the nature of Stephen's portrait were largely determined by the fragility of Wilfrid's supranational connexion and the hostility it had generated in Northumbria. That, it might seem, was further borne out by the apparently low-key reception of Stephen's work. The fact that only two medieval (eleventh or early twelfth-century) manuscripts of the *Life* survive has been taken as evidence that it had a very limited circulation (Levison 1913, 183–9; Colgrave 1927, pp. xiii–xvii). There must, however, originally have been more; the two survivors derive from a text which was not itself the archetype, and a copy must also have been known to Frithegod in the tenth century. It seems likely, however, that, after its initial dissemination, the unconventionality of Stephen's *Life* meant that, once the very specific political and cultural circumstances which it addressed no longer had resonance, it came to seem strange and fell into neglect.

In 713, however, it had urgent purpose. One particularly important and unresolved issue was the status of York. It is clear that the main reason why the Northumbrian kings collaborated with Theodore and Berhtwald as sole archbishop is that they needed them to deal with Wilfrid, whom they did not trust but of whom they had to take account (Thacker 2004a). Yet with Wilfrid still around, the legitimacy of the incumbent bishops of York remained questionable; certainly it would have been difficult for them to have obtained the papal pallium. Wilfrid's death opened up the possibility of once again restoring York's metropolitan authority. That is the great unmentioned issue in Bede's treatment of his career. Bede made no allusion to Wilfrid's rights under the Gregorian plan, although by the time he was writing the *Ecclesiastical History* the revival of that plan through the creation of a northern archbishopric was clearly in the air. By contrast Stephen himself ascribed metropolitan status to Wilfridian York (VW 10, 16), and presents a Wilfrid who seems to have regarded himself as a metropolitan, even if, he eventually concluded that it was not worth making this a major issue.

That is not necessarily to say that Wilfrid, or indeed Stephen, was aware of the Gregorian decrees. It is quite possible that after Paulinus's flight in 633 they had been forgotten and only rediscovered after Nothelm's work in the papal archives on Bede's behalf in the 720s. Even so, both Wilfrid and Stephen would almost certainly have been aware of York's status as the metropolis of a Roman province, and their continental travels would have made them conscious of the association of such status with metropolitan authority in bishops.[4] There can be little doubt that, at least until 678, Wilfrid regarded himself as having some kind of higher episcopacy. But when he was thrown out he did not resort to this as a remedy. That may be partly because he was aware of the comparatively weak standing of Gallic metropolitans; partly because Theodore, armed with archiepiscopal authority and the pallium, was unquestionably his superior; and partly because his resistance to the division of his see meant that he had no suffragans, an essential prerequisite of authentic metropolitan status (Thacker 2008, 56–9).

Stephen, as we have seen, was writing just before Ælfflæd's death, which probably occurred in February 714 (Plummer 1896, II, 185; Colgrave 1968, 48). If the Wilfridians were aware of her sickness, it may have increased their sense of insecurity, since by then they seem to have regarded her as a protector. Her death, moreover, seems to have been closely followed by change at the see of York. We do not know exactly when John, who succeeded Bosa in 706, resigned. In the *Historia Ecclesiastica* Bede says that it was because of advancing years, implying that it was soon before his death (HE V, 6). But an early Northumbrian annal indicates that it was around 714, since it records that Wilfrid II died in retirement in 29 April 744, having been a bishop for thirty years (Plummer 1896, I, 362). A change at this time could have been made with new opportunities in

---

[4]   I am grateful to Ian Wood for this suggestion.

mind. If so, it did not succeed. Bede later records that John himself consecrated Wilfrid II, whom he described as John's priest and whom Alcuin says had been his deputy and abbot of York (HE V, 6; BKS, 94). Such a proceeding was uncanonical and may only have been adopted to pre-empt other arrangements (Goffart 1988, 290–1). We do not know what part the Wilfridians played in this but their presence may still have been perceived as a threat.

So Stephen was writing just before a period of significant change in the higher echelons of the Northumbrian church and one which focused upon the controversial see of York. When he was shaping his portrait of Wilfrid, York remained without any clear primacy over the Northumbrian episcopate. Whitby seems to have kept control – since Wilfrid II, like John and Bosa before him, was trained at that house (HE IV, 23). Whitby, however, had had close links with Theodore and seems long to have favoured the single archbishopric of Britain (Thacker 1998, 76–7; 2008, 62). Indeed, the issue was only finally resolved in 732, with the retirement of Wilfrid II and his replacement by Ecgberht, brother of Eadberht, probably by then King Ceolwulf's designated successor – a move which significantly coincided with the expulsion of Acca, Wilfrid's episcopal heir and which was a prelude to the establishment of an archbishopric at York (Plummer 1896, I, 361–2).

It was perhaps around 714, when the Wilfridians seemed at once threatening and vulnerable that, in collaboration with the Lindisfarne community, Bede presented his finished portrait of Cuthbert, remodelled in response to Stephen's newly-minted depiction of Wilfrid (Goffart 1988, 290–3; Stancliffe, below). The new Cuthbert is at once an ascetic, a pastor and an active monk in the spirit of Benedict as interpreted by Gregrory the Great (Thacker 1983, 137–42). His concern with church order and his rejection of all association with schismatics is perhaps a coded but pointed reminder to the Wilfridians of their own tumultuous and excommunicated past. All this suggests that Wilfrid still mattered as a vehicle for propaganda in the factional world of Northumbrian politics. We may set alongside this the evidence of ritual commemoration of Wilfrid's feast. It clearly got off to an early start, probably not only among the Wilfridians. It was certainly well-established at York by the mid eighth century. And if Stephen's Life was still being modified (in however restricted a manner) in the 730s, it still mattered enough to be copied down. The factional world of Northumbrian high politics was a febrile one, and it was probably only after 737, when a firm alliance was established between the new archbishop and the new king, that the outsider Wilfrid was finally given a new and less threatening identity and adopted as a patron by the revivified see of York.

2: *Dating Wilfrid's Death and Stephen's* Life

CLARE STANCLIFFE

Chronology is usually regarded as the humble handmaid of history, yet it is an essential one. Unless a historian can get the sequence of events right, he or she cannot interpret how they relate to each other, and what the probable causes were. For a churchman who died thirteen hundred years ago, yet is regarded by some as a saint, by others as a villain, and by scholars as significant enough to merit two conferences in his honour, it is obviously appropriate to establish the year in which the centenary falls, that is, the year of Wilfrid's death. In a volume focused on Wilfrid, it will also be helpful to establish more certainty as regards the chief source for Wilfrid's life, the *Life of St Wilfrid* written by Stephen, a priest of Wilfrid's monastery of Ripon (VW, pref; Colgrave 1927, x, though there is inadequate evidence to accept his identification of Stephen with Aedde or Eddius: Kirby 1983). We shall here be concerned with dating that *Life* more accurately than has been possible hitherto, and with the question of whether its author undertook a substantial revision of this *Life* in the early 730s, as David Kirby has argued (1983). In this instance the dating of Stephen's *Life* is of particular interest as it has been regarded by some historians as a vehicle whereby Wilfrid's followers engaged in polemic with the Lindisfarne community. It has even been suggested that its remarkable reuse of passages of the anonymous Lindisfarne *Life of St Cuthbert* and application of them to Wilfrid was a major factor in leading the Lindisfarne community to seek a new prose *Life of St Cuthbert* from Bede (Goffart 1988, 281–5; Thacker 1989, 117–22; Kirby 1995; Stancliffe forthcoming). If we are to penetrate this murky world of factionalism within the Northumbrian church, precision on the dating of the relevant Lives is a prerequisite. It is also, of course, of crucial importance for estimating the value which we may attach to Stephen's account of events.

We begin with the dating of Wilfrid's death. There should today be no quibbling with the calendar date of 24 April for this: this is the date attested in all the earliest calendars, as Levison long since established (1913, 178–9; 1946, 278–9). These calendars include a metrical one from York (or possibly Ripon) that can be dated to shortly after the death of Boniface in 755, the most recent saint commemorated.[1] Its evidence is therefore very significant. But the point

---

[1] Wilmart 1934. Included are Paulinus, Wilfrid I, Bosa, John of Beverley, and Wilfrid II, but also Tatberht of Ripon. Wilmart regarded the calendar as dating from the end of the eighth century, because it includes the feast of All Saints on 1 November, which he thought was only introduced then. However, it is now recognised that this feast

needs making because Colgrave, in his edition, gave the date of 12 October, dismissing the 24 April feast as that of Wilfrid's translation (1927, 186). Unfortunately he got this the wrong way round: the 24 April feast is that of Wilfrid's death, while the 12 October feast is found only from *c.*970, and represents his translation (Levison 1946, 279). Colgrave was, however, responsible for misleading David Farmer in the *Saint Wilfrid at Hexham* volume (1974, 57).

A far harder task is that of establishing the year in which Wilfrid died, with historians hesitating between 709 and 710. The problem arises because contemporary sources point in different directions. The verse epitaph on Wilfrid's tomb, quoted by Bede, gives no dates, but says '*Quindecies ternos postquam egit episcopus annos*': 'Thrice fifteen years he bore a bishop's charge'. (HE V, 19.) Since Bede tells us that he was made a bishop in 664 in the same year as Tuda, following Colmán's departure after the synod of Whitby (HE V, 24; III, 26), this would yield the date 709; and this, indeed, appears to be Bede's view of when Wilfrid died. (He dates the death of Hadrian to the year after Wilfrid died, and equates it with the fifth year of Osred's reign, which according to his reckoning would be 710, thus yielding a date of 709 for Wilfrid's death: HE V, 20 and 24; Yorke 2009, 20–3.) At the same time, however, we should recognise that Bede's chronology of events round then is unsure, with some indications pointing to 709 for Hadrian's death, and so presumably 708 for Wilfrid's (Plummer 1896, vol II, 329; Harrison 1976, 89–92; Yorke 2009, 20–3).

Our other major source is Stephen's *Life of St Wilfrid*. This, as we shall see below, can be accurately dated to between July 712 and March 714, thus within at most five years of Wilfrid's death. In addition, it was written by someone excellently placed to know, since Wilfrid was buried at Ripon, the monastery to which Stephen belonged. The Life was thus approximately contemporary with the verse epitaph, whereas Bede was writing around 731, some twenty years after the event. Further, Stephen gives us considerably more detail, and numbers of years that look accurate in their specificity, rather than round numbers that might represent literary approximations. He does not attempt to equate the events of Wilfrid's life with AD (or *anno mundi*) years or with the regnal dates of kings; but he does provide us with an internally consistent chronological narrative that can, at various points, be checked against events that are datable

---

goes back to the pontificate of Gregory III, who died in 741 (Cross and Livingstone 1997, 42). In addition to the English and continental calendars cited by Levison that give 24 April, note also the evidence of the Irish early-ninth-century *Martyrology of Tallaght*: Ó Riain (1993), 10 and n. 56. Kirby's discussion (1983, 113) is confusing: while he cites Levison as his authority, he mistakenly gives 23 (not 24) April as the date of Wilfrid's commemoration in ecclesiastical calendars, and as the date that was a Thursday in 709!

from other sources. First, we should note that he says that Wilfrid was in his seventy-sixth year when he died, and had been a bishop for forty-six years (VW 66). Counting from Bede's date of 664 for Wilfrid's consecration, that would give 710 as the year of his death. Secondly, it says that the abbot whom Wilfrid had appointed to succeed him (at Ripon, where he was buried) 'decided to celebrate a private Mass for him every day, and every week to celebrate Thursday, the day on which he died, as a feast as though it were Sunday' (VW 65). We have already examined the evidence for Wilfrid having died on 24 April; and in 710, 24 April fell on a Thursday, whereas in 709 it fell on a Wednesday. Thirdly, Stephen gives a full narrative of the last eight years of Wilfrid's career, from the synod of Austerfield, where he was excommunicated, to his death. The tumultuous events of these years will still have been fresh in the minds of Wilfrid's supporters, and Stephen was probably present at many of them himself (Levison 1913, 180–1), as well as being able to talk to his abbot, Tatberht, a relative of Wilfrid, to whom Wilfrid had narrated the whole course of his life (VW 65), and to Acca, a priest who had been particularly close to Wilfrid (VW 66): Tatberht and Acca had been appointed to succeed Wilfrid at Ripon and Hexham respectively, and they had jointly commissioned Stephen's work (VW, preface). The numerous details which Stephen gives tally with each other and thus create a convincing narrative. This will require detailed treatment.

We shall begin with the synod of Austerfield. There, Wilfrid had castigated the assembled company for resisting for twenty-two years the papacy's written judgment exonerating him after his initial expulsion from Northumbria (VW 46, and cf. 24–34). Twenty-two years on from the date when Wilfrid had arrived back in Northumbria after his first appeal to the papacy brings us to 702 or 703 for the synod of Austerfield (Plummer 1896, vol II, 318–20). On his excommunication at the latter synod, Wilfrid went first to Mercia, and then again made his way to Rome, say in 703, where his case might then have been heard in the spring to summer of 704. The hearing in Rome under Pope John was a protracted event, requiring over seventy sittings and lasting for four months (VW 53). He was finally exonerated after the decrees of the 679–80 synod were read out along with Wilfrid's attestation of them. At that, Boniface and others who remembered Wilfrid from his earlier visits to Rome denounced Wilfrid's accusers, claiming that 'for forty years and more he had held the office of bishop' (VW 53). This might be an exaggeration – and note the suspiciously round number! However, it is not impossible that it is true: that Alhfrith had promoted Wilfrid to be bishop of York for his subkingdom of Deira (cf HE, III, 28) at the same time as Oswiu had promoted Tuda to the bishopric of Lindisfarne, i.e. straight after the synod of Whitby (cf VW 11; John 1970, 42–50; Wallace-Hadrill 1988, 129). That synod had probably been held in late April, immediately after Easter ('Celtic', 14 April; 'Roman', 21 April), as Bede's placing of it in his *Ecclesiastical History* immediately before the eclipse of 3 May (*recte* 1 May) implies (HE III, 25–27). Wilfrid might then have been consecrated in May 664, and would indeed have been bishop for more than forty years by (say) June 704. Be that as it may, the hearing before Pope John must have been completed before the latter's death in January 705 (Levison 1913, 248–9, note 8), and we can envisage Wilfrid setting off back home later in the summer of 704 (Levison 1946, 279, note 7). On the way, however, he suffered a serious illness near Meaux. While lying unconscious, he had a vision of the Archangel Michael, who assured him that in response to intercession 'years of life have been added to you'; but that 'after the space of four years I shall visit you again' (VW 56). Wilfrid then recovered sufficiently to return home, where he found that King Æthelræd, who had been ruling Mercia when he left, had retired into a monastery after appointing Coenred as his successor. This occurred in 704 and, according to charter evidence, Coenred was on the throne by 13 June 704 (VW 57; HE V, 24; Harrison 1976, 91). Although welcomed in Mercia, Aldfrith of Northumbria refused to receive Wilfrid, and the king's subsequent illness and death were interpreted by Stephen as divine vengeance for this (VW 58–9). We can deduce from other sources that Aldfrith died in December either of 704 or 705 (Yorke 2009, 20–3, favours 705, but note Levison's support for 704: 1946, 273–4 and 279 note 7). After Eadwulf's two-month reign, Osred became king, and Wilfrid regained his monasteries of Hexham and Ripon, and was restored to the bishopric of Hexham (VW 59–60). However, Stephen passes rapidly over the years during which the Wilfridians once more enjoyed good fortune: 'But the joy of this world will be mixed with grief … When the time drew near that the Archangel Michael had foretold', Wilfrid suffered a recurrence of the illness that had afflicted him near Meaux: probably a second stroke (VW 62). His communities prayed earnestly for his recovery, and Wilfrid 'received back his intellect and memory and his power of speech', and lived for another year and a half, during which he settled his affairs (VW 62–3). If the initial stroke near Meaux had occurred around September 704 (cf Levison 1946, 279 note 7), and the second four years later, this would tally neatly with Wilfrid actually dying on 24 April 710. Thus Stephen's chronology is both internally consistent, and consistent with other sources where it can be checked against these.

How should we decide between the verse epitaph and Bede, on the one hand, and Stephen on the other? To me, the answer is clear. The 'thrice fifteen years' of the epitaph is flowery language, and, as such, may well represent an approximation (Harrison 1976, 91). Stephen's forty-six years for Wilfrid's episcopate, on the other hand, convinces by the very fact that it is not a round number. What, however, is decisive for me is the evidence that the abbot of Ripon had been celebrating every Thursday as though it were a Sunday in memory of Wilfrid's death. Stephen, as a priest of Ripon, knew what he was writing about at first hand; and this continuous custom of celebration must mean that the year in which 24 April fell on a Thursday was the year in which Wilfrid died, that is, 710. Finally, I am impressed by the coherence and the detail of Stephen's account of Wilfrid's final years, and the sequence that (following Levison's lead) I have spelt out is as coherent as – and not very different from – that suggested by Plummer (1896, II, 318–20), while fitting with both Stephen's narrative and with other external facts like the date of Pope John's death. As regards Bede giving an erroneous date, I would suggest that he calculated it from the flowery 'quindecies ternos ... annos' of the verse epitaph that he cited, where a round number is understandable (HE V, 19).[2] In any case, when writing about an event that occurred twenty years previously, it is very difficult to be absolutely accurate, and, as we have seen, there are indications that Bede was not on secure ground for the dating of the deaths of Aldfrith, Wilfrid, and Hadrian.

One last question remains to be answered: why, if the evidence for 710 is so much more compelling than that for 709, have so many historians been so loth to adopt it? I suggest that the answer is partly that we are always reluctant to go against Bede ; and that, in this instance, it is also because Plummer gave such a valuable overview of Wilfridian chronology, and favoured Bede's date of 709 (1896, II, 316–20); and, finally, because Colgrave, Stephen's editor, himself largely adopted Plummer's chronology in the dates that he added in square brackets at the head of many chapters, while making no attempt to see whether Stephen's chronology was internally consistent, and potentially more reliable. This is remarkable, because it meant that he totally ignored the detailed discussion which Wilhelm Levison had published fourteen years previously in his Monumenta edition of Stephen's *Vita Wilfridi* (1913, 178–9). Where Levison differed from Plummer (1896, II, 320) was in realising that when the Archangel Michael had told Wilfrid in a vision at Meaux that he would return in four years, this could most plausibly be taken as referring to the onset of Wilfrid's second stroke, not to his death. This same insight renders unnecessary David Kirby's complicated theory (1983, 112–13) about separate Hexham and Ripon traditions as to the length of time Wilfrid lived since his illness at Meaux. Levison, of course, had the advantage not only of his towering intellect, but also of coming to the question as an editor of saints' Lives. He was therefore alert to

---

2   Jaager (1935, 50–1) suggested that Bede himself wrote the epitaph for Wilfrid, on the grounds that its text is transmitted only by Bede, and not Stephen, and that it has many parallels to Bede's metrical *Life of St Cuthbert*. Further, Wallace-Hadrill (1988, 194) comments: 'It insists on achievements with which Bede could have no quarrel.' However, although accepted without comment by Lapidge (1996a, 17), the fact that the epitaph contains four references to gold, despite Bede's normal reticence on gold (Campbell 2010, 123), makes this unlikely. All that the parallels actually show is that whoever composed it had access to Bede's metrical *Vita Sancti Cuthberti*. Might Ceolfrith be a possible candidate?

the significance of the Thursday celebration, and at the same time able to avoid looking at Stephen's *Life* through the prism of Bede's *Ecclesiastical History*. When we turn from Levison's well-argued case to Colgrave's confused note (1926, 186), claiming that 'October 12th is the day always kept in his honour', and that although the early verse martyrology dates Wilfrid's obit to 24 April, 'this however does not fit with the events', we can scarcely temper our disbelief. Levison's clear restatement of the evidence in 1946 (278–9) should have settled the matter; but it lies buried in an appendix, out of sight of historians who have tended to rely on Plummer and on Colgrave's edition.

Now that we have established the date of Wilfrid's death, let us turn to consider the date of Stephen's *Life of St Wilfrid*. Obviously this must postdate Wilfrid's death, but closer examination enables us further to refine its *terminus a quo*. Wilfrid had died at Oundle, and his body had been brought back to Ripon for burial. Three posthumous miracles are then given: the healing of a nun who washed the shroud that had come into contact with Wilfrid's body; the punishment of a warband who had burnt Wilfrid's monastery at Oundle; and, finally, a white arc that had appeared in the sky on the anniversary of Wilfrid's death, when Wilfridian bishops and abbots had gathered at Ripon to celebrate the solemn day. This was first observed by some of the less devout of Wilfrid's followers, who had been standing outside the church while the bishops and abbots had been keeping vigil inside the church on the eve of the anniversary. The following evening, that of the actual day, 'the abbots went out with the whole community to compline in the evening twilight. Suddenly they saw a wonderful sign in the sky, namely a white arc, surrounding the whole monastery, like a rainbow by day, but without its various colours' (VW 68). Thanks to Stephen's precise description, this white arc can be identified as a moonbow. This is the nocturnal equivalent of a rainbow, and is seen when looking in the opposite direction from the moon at a time when it is both raining and the moon is shining brightly, and when the moon is fairly low in the sky. The moonbow (or 'lunar rainbow') appears white because the moonlight is so much weaker than sunlight; and it can only be seen at all when the moon is bright enough, which occurs just around the time of the full moon. Dr Daniel P. Mc Carthy has kindly computed the lunar data for sunset (7.25 pm) on 23–4 April for the years 710–714 in the right area for us (table 2.1).[3] In the following table, the column headed 'illumination' gives the percentage of the lunar disc that is illuminated, while 'elevation' gives the elevation of the moon above the horizon – and here, a negative value indicates that the moon is below the horizon.

[3]   Dr Mc Carthy (Dept of Computer Science, Trinity College, Dublin) computed these results based on Stockton-on-Tees, (1° 13' West, 54° 34' North), which lies some 30 miles north-east of Ripon, using Voyager Interactive Desktop Planetarium version 1.2, on 5 February 2007. I am extremely grateful to him for his help.

Table 2.1: Table illustrating the moon's brightness
on the anniversary of Wilfrid's death, 710–714.

Date	Lunar Age days	Illumination %	Elevation Degrees
23 Apr. 710	21	66	−44 °
24 Apr. 710	22	56	−47 °
23 Apr. 711	1	1	+7 °
24 Apr. 711	2	4	+15 °
23 Apr. 712	12	94	+22 °
24 Apr. 712	13	98	+12 °
23 Apr. 713	24	34	−47 °
24 Apr. 713	25	23	−42 °
23 Apr. 714	5	26	+39 °
24 Apr. 714	6	35	+45 °

From this it is obvious that this incident occurred not, as usually thought, on the first anniversary of Wilfrid's death, but no earlier than April 712. The age of the moon would also have enabled a moonbow to be seen (provided other conditions were right) on 23–4 April 715, a year in which the full moon fell on 23 April. However, Stephen's narrative implies that the Life was written shortly after Wilfrid's death, at a time when, with their patron dead, they still felt threatened and insecure: the Oundle miracle enabled Wilfrid's followers, fearful of 'the snares of their old enemies', to begin to postulate that Wilfrid was now on the same level as the apostles Peter and Andrew, and able to guard his followers. The moonbow was then taken as a confirmatory sign 'that the wall of divine help was around the elect vineyard of the Lord's family.' (VW 68; cf. also Hayward 1999, 135–7.) By 715, however, Acca was well ensconced at Hexham, and the immediate crisis that Wilfrid's death caused for his followers was a thing of the past. In any case, Stephen wrote while Ælfflæd, abbess of Whitby, was still alive, as his reference to her in the present tense makes clear: 'one [witness of King Aldfrith's last words] is the abbess and most prudent virgin Aelffled, who is indeed the daughter of a king' (VW 59; Kirby 1983, 106). Careful reading of Bede shows that he dated her death to late 713, or possibly early 714 (but not 715, as Kirby claims, loc cit).[4] 713 is the date given independently by the Irish annals, in this case probably derived from the (no longer extant) 'Chronicle of Ireland', at this time being kept contemporaneously on Iona (Charles-Edwards 2006, I, 187, and cf. 1–59). This means that we can now date Stephen's *Life of*

---

[4]   After his victory at the Winwæd on 15 November 655 (see Plummer 1896, II, 185 for the date), Oswiu dedicated his daughter, Ælfflæd, then 'scarcely a year old' to the monastic life; and she died 'conpleto unde LX annorum numero', 'after 59 years had been completed.' (HE III, 24.) Ælfflæd will therefore have been born around the autumn of 654, and died around the end of 713: cf. Plummer, loc cit.

St Wilfrid with some precision: it will have been completed between July 712 and March 714.[5]

Was this text, however, the same as the one that we now know as Stephen's *Life of St Wilfrid*, or did Stephen revise his work in the early 730s, as David Kirby has suggested (1983, 107–12)? Kirby adduced three main arguments in support of his hypothesis. First, there are some inconsistencies within the *Life*, which on his reading would stem from a rather ham-fisted revision. Secondly, in three places Stephen refers to Acca with the words, 'of blessed memory', although on two of these occasions he makes it clear that Acca was still alive. Kirby suggests that this strange wording might make sense in the early 730s, as Acca was expelled from his bishopric of Hexham in 731, but did not die till *c*.740.[6] Thirdly, Kirby notes various differences between the accounts of Wilfrid in the text of Stephen's Life that has come down to us, and in Bede's *Ecclesiastical History*, and suggests that Bede might have been using an earlier version of Stephen's Life. In addition to these arguments based on a close examination of the text, Kirby argues that the tensions which led to the expulsion of Acca might well have led Stephen to revise his account, and to associate the appointments of Acca (to Hexham) and Tatberht (to Ripon) more closely with Wilfrid, to try and bolster their positions. In assessing the plausiblity of these arguments, let us grant that the tensions in Northumbria in the early 730s (Kirby 1991, 148–9) could well have led to the rewriting of parts of the *Life of St Wilfrid*. On the other hand, if that was the primary motivation for the revision, one would expect it to show more clearly. In particular, if Stephen had decided to replace an original account of how Wilfrid's successor at Ripon would be found with a revised version where Wilfrid nominates Tatberht, surely Stephen would have had the sense to delete his earlier version? It is therefore more plausible to see the two accounts as arising from different oral traditions, which Stephen failed to reconcile; and the same reason probably explains the existence

[5] Goffart's suggestion of composition near the beginning of Osric's reign (718–29) probably owes much to his conviction that Bede's prose *Life of St Cuthbert*, datable to 721 or shortly before, was commissioned as a riposte (1988, 281–90). His point about Stephen's anti-Irish slant can be stood on its head: it would be more relevant prior to Iona conforming to the Roman Easter in 716. More importantly, he does not adequately address the fact that Stephen uses the present tense when writing of Ælfflæd (cf. ibid 281, n 210), nor the palpable sense of urgency and insecurity for his followers following on from Wilfrid's death that is evident in VW, 68. Again, neither of these points are addressed by Wood (1995, 8); and the Barnabas analogy of VW, 3 fits into a pattern of biblical analogies drawn by Stephen (cf Laynesmith below), and so can more plausibly be seen as inspiring that in the *Vita Ceolfridi*, rather than vice versa.

[6] Acca's expulsion is given in the contemporary annals appended to the Moore manuscript of Bede (Colgrave and Mynors 1969, 572–3). For the later sources on his death, see Plummer (II, 1896, 330).

of the two versions of King Aldfrith's dying wishes. As regards the fact that Bede does not tell us that Wilfrid nominated Acca to Hexham, there was no need for him to do so – particularly as he would probably have regarded it as more correct for an election to have taken place. Bede's discretion would also explain his omission of any reference to the synod of Austerfield, and his playing down of the involvement of bishops in Wilfrid's expulsion (Campbell 1986, 19–22). As regards Bede's account of Wilfrid and the South Saxons, he clearly had access to other sources than the existing version of Stephen's Life; but, as Kirby himself argues (1983, 110–12), this is probably because Stephen was affiliated to Ripon, whereas Bede's primary Wilfridian contact will have been with Hexham. There is, moreover, no need to limit Bede's sources to Acca and Hexham; he may well have drawn on material supplied by Bishop Daniel, and Ceolfrith may also have provided a conduit for information about Wilfrid (cf. Wallace-Hadrill 1988, 151–6, 191). Thus our conclusion must be that the differences between Bede's and Stephen's accounts of Wilfrid arise from other causes than Bede's use of a different version of Stephen's *Life* than that which has come down to us.

The only significant piece of evidence in favour of Kirby's hypothesis of a revised edition is the reference to ' Bishop Acca of blessed memory, who by the grace of God is still alive' (VW 22, and similarly 56 and 65). This is indeed a very odd way of referring to someone who was still alive; and Kirby's suggestion that it would fit the circumstances of Acca's life in the 730s, after he had been expelled from his bishopric but before his death, is possible. This on its own, however, is too slender grounds on which to posit a substantial revision of the *Life*. Instead I would suggest that the phrase 'of blessed memory' was inserted in all three places by a scribe copying the *Life*: possibly, but not necessarily, in the 730s. One might compare the way in which Bothelm, the subject of one of Wilfrid's healing miracles, was treated in the two manuscripts in which the *Life* has been preserved. Oxford, Bodleian Library, MS Fell 3 reads, '*adhuc vivit, nomenque eius est Bothelm, gratias agens Deo*', whereas London, British Library, MS Cotton Vespasian D VI, reads, '*et multo tempore vixit, nomenque est Boðhelm, gratias agens Deo*' (VW 23). Here, the insertion of Bothelm's name is awkward and may have been the first alteration to the original text, probably arising from the incorporation of a marginal gloss. More significantly for us, the original wording has clearly been altered in a copy that lies behind the Cotton Vespasian manuscript to reflect the fact that Bothelm had died since the *Life* was first written. When all copies had to be made by hand, such minor updating or adjustment was very easily made; and neither in the instance of Bothelm, nor that of Acca, do they give us grounds for positing substantial revision of the *Life* such as Kirby suggested. In my view, then, the text of the *Life of St Wilfrid* that has come down to us is essentially that which Stephen completed between July 712 and March 714.

This paper has argued that Stephen's date for Wilfrid's death should be preferred to that of Bede's *Ecclesiastical History*; that Stephen wrote *c.*713, very shortly after Wilfrid had died; and that the Life that he wrote then is essentially the one that has come down to us today. What all three findings have in common is that they point us towards a very positive evaluation of Stephen's *Life of St Wilfrid* as a historical source. Of course, such a judgment must be regarded as provisional when, as in this case, it is based on only a small section of Stephen's work; and it may be that the last part of Stephen's *Life*, which has concerned us here, is more accurate than the earlier parts, both because it was nearer to the date of composition, and because Stephen was personally involved in at least some of the events that he describes there. Nonetheless Stephen has emerged as an accurate recorder, with a fine eye for detail. The most obvious instance is his precise description of a moonbow, which has enabled that sight to be interpreted thirteen hundred years after the event. Other examples are his descriptions of Wilfrid's illnesses, which make it highly likely that what Wilfrid suffered both near Meaux and en route to Hexham were strokes; and his account of the examination of Wilfrid's case by the papacy, with the detail of the papal court talking in Greek amongst themselves (VW 53). It is now over forty years since James Campbell's ground-breaking study of Bede, when he first argued that, as regards Wilfrid, Stephen 'gives a better, though partisan, account of what really happened while Bede steers a careful course', and may sometimes have '"through necessity concealed the truth by the use of very cautious words"' (1966, reprinted in Campbell 1986, 22, with a comment by Bede on King David enclosed within double quotation marks). We have still fully to work out the implications; and, as we do so, scrutinising Stephen's account and setting it alongside Bede and our other sources, let us also remember to avail ourselves of the excellent introduction and notes which another great scholar, Wilhelm Levison, supplied to his edition of Stephen's *Vita Wilfridi* a century ago.

3: *Wilfrid's Monastic Empire*

SARAH FOOT

During Wilfrid's exile overseas (either in 677/8 or in the early 690s) Aldhelm of Malmesbury wrote to the abbots of Wilfrid's monasteries urging them to share their bishop's exile with him:

> ... the necessity of event requires that you along with your own bishop, who has been deprived of the honour of his office, be expelled from your native land and go to any transmarine country in the wide world that is suitable. What harsh or cruel burden in existence, I ask, would separate you and hold you apart from that bishop, who like a wet-nurse caressed you, his beloved, foster-children, warming you in the folds of his arms and nourishing you in the bosom of charity, and who brought you forward in his paternal love by rearing, teaching, and castigating you from your very first exposure to the rudiments of education and from your early childhood and tender years up to the flower of your maturity. (Lapidge and Herren 1979, 169)

Evidently, Aldhelm considered the abbots of Wilfrid's own circle, heads of the various monasteries which had connections with the bishop, to constitute a distinct and self-defined group. It is as members of that collectivity that Aldhelm appealed to the abbots' sense of shame, pointing to the social opprobrium that would fall on those who chose to abandon their lord in his time of greatest misfortune:

> Now then, if worldly men, exiles from divine teaching, were to desert a devoted lord (*devotum dominum*), whom they embraced in prosperity, but once the opulence of good times began to diminish and the adversity of bad fortune began its onslaught, they preferred the secure peace of their dear country to the burdens of a banished lord, are they not deemed worthy of the scorn of scathing laughter and the noise of mockery from all? What, then will be said of you, if you cast into solitary exile the bishop who nourished and raised you? (Lapidge and Herren 1979, 169–70)

More than one social code underpins Aldhelm's rhetoric here: the conventions of Germanic secular society, reflected in the mutual obligations common to the military *comitatus* or the mead-hall; the debts owed by grateful

27

pupils to a master who had taught them the rudiments of faith; and further, the responsibilities of children to the loving father who reared them from spiritual infancy into mature independence. Yet whichever the context colouring Aldhelm's message its import remained constant: these abbots owed it to Wilfrid not to leave him alone in exile.

Aldhelm's letter provides a useful way into a discussion of the widely-dispersed collection of monasteries associated with Bishop Wilfrid. From his acquisition of a monastic house at Ripon and subsequent foundation of a community at Hexham (VW 23), Wilfrid established several monasteries spread across the separate English kingdoms and into northern Britain. Further, he persuaded the abbots and abbesses of other, independent houses to affiliate themselves to him, so creating a monastic confederation that transcended conventional geographical, political, and ecclesiastical boundaries. How should we describe these monasteries collectively? The familial model suggested by some of the language of Aldhelm's letter to Wilfrid's abbots points towards an extended Wilfridian family, spatially-apart but emotionally – and spiritually – united. Or might the worldly resonances we also heard in Aldhelm's letter seem more appropriate, considering the extent to which Wilfrid's contemporaries frequently saw him in secular terms? The size and economic power of his monastic empire certainly made the bishop's contemporaries nervous as well as jealous. Stephen attributed the enmity of Ecgfrith's queen, Iurminburh, towards Wilfrid to her envy of his temporal glories (VW 24). Alternatively, we might pursue the metaphor of the schoolroom and see Wilfrid's abbots as fledged pupils, launched from his tender nurture into the uncertainties of the world without ever wholly severing their ties with their teacher and spiritual mentor.

One modern term also suggests itself: a network. Wilfrid fits the contemporary image of the archetypal networker, for he made high-status contacts everywhere he went; especially when exiled he proved adept at engaging with the sources of power and using those contacts proficiently to further his own ends. Outwardly, his monastic confederation might conform to the modern sociological category of the social network, a structure of individuals or organisations ('actors' or 'nodes') bound by one or more types of interdependency ('ties'): friendship, kinship, money, belief (in this case expressed in a particular, monastic form), knowledge or status (Scott 2000; Erickson 1997). Social Network Analysis examines the social relationships tying separate actors together but it generally involves the application of mathematical models to large data-sets, for which purpose the Wilfridian network is both too small and too uncertainly defined. Appealing as this concept appears, its methodology does not readily adapt to the small-scale nature of the surviving evidence for this period. The specifically modern, indeed largely twentieth-century coining of the noun 'network' also renders the term less than ideal to describe late-seventh-century social groupings.

Clearly Wilfrid's various religious houses appeared to his contemporaries to form a collective unit. Our questions relate to the kind of wider community that Wilfrid created, or at least permitted to grow up around him. What factors – if any – beyond the individual abbots' (and their monks') personal loyalty to Wilfrid bound them together? How different was this dispersed community from other confederations, groups or clusters of monastic houses found in different parts of England in the same period? Did Wilfrid's monastic empire parallel similar arrangements made elsewhere or did his collective stand apart, representing a different sort of connected organisation? Exploring the language that might best describe Wilfrid's monasteries as a group helps to answer these questions as well as having intrinsic merits in shedding light on contemporaries' perceptions of his monastic 'empire'.

Various other monastic houses of the same period lay in close proximity one to another, sustaining intimate associations: Wearmouth with Jarrow, Whitby with Hackness, Chertsey with Barking, Malmesbury with Frome and Bradford, and so on (Foot 2006, 251–82). In some parts of Northumbria, such as the Vale of Pickering and the Tyne valley, there are clusters of closely-connected monasteries which lie within a relatively-defined geographical area (Wood, 2008). Other identifiable groups stand out for their production of distinctive styles of sculpture (Cambridge 1983). But Wilfrid's two best monasteries at Ripon and Hexham, lay slightly tangential to those other identifiable Northumbrian clusters and distant also from most of his other houses, which were dispersed across England (Wood 2008, 25). One possible parallel might be *Medeshamstede* – later Peterborough – which sustained connections with a group of other institutions or colonies which were almost as scattered as Wilfrid's houses (Stenton 1970; Foot 2006, 268–76). Similarly, despite their physical separation, a close tie bound the monasteries at Icanho in Suffolk and Wenlock in Shropshire. Yet Wilfrid's network differed from all these instances. His connection rather resembles an imagined community, an overarching entity extending beyond the immediate, familial and local and constructed into a conceptual whole which existed within the minds of its constituent members (Anderson 1991). We shall need to explore whether Wilfrid's monastic empire did indeed exist in the imaginations of its separate members, depending on shared ideas and a common ethos sustained over time and space which enabled it to function beyond the realms of the immediately visible and tangible, without continuous direct interpersonal reinforcement.

Wilfrid's Monastic Empire

Before exploring different possible models that might help to understand or explain it, we should summarise what we know about the size and shape of

Wilfrid's monastic connection. At its core lay Wilfrid's two favourite monasteries, Ripon and Hexham; founded early in the bishop's career, these remained the institutions closest to his heart. Attempting to prevent the outside interference of kings, nobles and other holders of the episcopal office he thought rightly his own, Wilfrid obtained a privilege from Pope Agatho for Ripon and Hexham which placed them under direct papal control, seemingly modelling this on the privilege for the Columbanan house at Bobbio (VW 51; Wormald 1976, 147–8; Wood 1990, 10–11). Even when absent, Wilfrid continued to think of himself as Ripon's abbot. He appointed his kinsman Tatberht to rule with him over Ripon during his own lifetime, only to possess the house 'without any question' after Wilfrid's death (VW 63). Hexham should have presented Wilfrid with greater problems, having become an independent bishopric held by Tunberht from *c.* 680 when Wilfrid was expelled and his see divided into five distinct dioceses (HE IV, 12). Yet Wilfrid obviously thought Hexham also remained under his own control and thus was his to bequeath, nominating Acca as his successor there soon before his death (VW 65). Although each of these two houses had its own separate landed endowment, both may have enjoyed a share of the bishop's substantial wealth during his lifetime. When he was dying, Wilfrid made specific provision for Ripon and Hexham, allocating to them together one quarter of his total material resources; this he divided between the two *praepositi* in order that they might be able to purchase the friendship of kings and bishops (VW 63).

The Wilfridian empire extended far beyond these two Northumbrian houses and it is in the geographical extent of his sphere of influence that Wilfrid's career diverges most sharply from that of his contemporaries. He may have had other estates devoted to monastic use in Northumbria, but no other monasteries connected with him can be identified with confidence in that region. In fact Stephen, Wilfrid's biographer, named few other houses within this *regnum ecclesiarum* (VW 21). He did devote some attention to Oundle in Northamptonshire, a house dedicated to St Andrew which lay deep in the kingdom of Mercia, far from Wilfrid's heartland in North Yorkshire. The saint spent his last hours and died at Oundle; the monks there prepared his body to be taken for burial at his church in Ripon (VW 66–7). Oundle's abbot – Bede called him Cuthbald – showed his devotion to Wilfrid's memory by keeping Thursday (the day on which he had died) always as a feast day and making generous gifts to the poor on the anniversary of the saint's death each year (VW 65; HE V, 19).

Wilfrid's associations with the Mercian kingdom went back to the late 660s, the period after he had been consecrated (in Gaul) to the Northumbrian see but on his return found Chad appointed to his diocese. Before Theodore's arrival as archbishop of Canterbury, Wilfrid exercised some episcopal authority in Mercia with the support of his *fidelissimus amicus*, Wulfhere of Mercia. In that time he received various pieces of land on which to found monasteries for the servants of God, including Lichfield as a site suitable for an episcopal see either for him or for any other to whom he might wish to give it. Thus when in 669 Theodore expelled Chad from Wilfrid's see at York to restore Wilfrid, Lichfield was conveniently available for Chad to assume episcopal care of the Mercians (VW 15). There may have been another Wilfridian monastery at Ripple in Worcestershire, possibly to be equated with the *Rippel* included in the list of royal estates owned by Wilfrid and read out in the dedication of the church at Ripon (VW 17). The church at Worcester, dedicated to St Peter and St Benedict, could also have had a Wilfridian connection (Sims-Williams 1990, 118). During Chad's tenure of the bishopric of York, Wilfrid had found favour also in Kent where Ecgberht (brother-in-law to Wulfhere of Mercia) sought his episcopal authority and encouraged him to ordain more priests, presumably giving him additional lands and monasteries in that kingdom, although Stephen named none of these (VW 14; Farmer 1974, 52; Higham 1999, 211–12).

Wilfrid renewed his links in Mercia after his exile from Northumbria on the division of his diocese around 680. Stephen reported that he went first to Berhtwald, nephew of the Mercian king, Æthelred, who seems to have had charge of a Mercian dependency in northern Wessex. Berhtwald gave Wilfrid an estate from his own lands, on which Wilfrid founded a little minster (*monasteriolum*) which – Stephen reported – his monks possess 'to this day' (VW 40). Although Wilfrid himself could not stay there long, being driven out to Wessex and on into Sussex, his brothers remained behind in the unnamed minster, not following their abbot. Perhaps this event spurred Aldhelm into writing to Wilfrid's brethren urging them to follow their abbot into exile (Sims-Williams 1990, 104–5). Beyond these examples, it is impossible either to identify or even count Wilfrid's other houses, although there were seemingly a large number in Mercia by the end of his life, perhaps including Evesham where later generations of monks believed Wilfrid had consecrated their church (Keynes 1994, 34; Hillaby 1998, 79 and 106). On the last occasion before his death when Wilfrid met his *familia* at Ripon, two of his Mercian abbots were also present, sent to Wilfrid's side by Ceolred of Mercia. These men, Tibba and Eabba, persuaded the bishop to agree to travel to meet with the Mercian king 'for the sake of the position of our minsters' in Ceolred's kingdom (VW 64). Wilfrid thus travelled with them from Northumbria 'to the southern lands where he found all his abbots rejoicing at his coming' (VW 65), although that joy would soon turn to grief when it became apparent that this would be Wilfrid's final journey.

If identifying Wilfrid's Mercian houses is difficult, locating the sites of his monasteries in Wessex and Sussex – kingdoms where he also apparently exercised some episcopal authority – is harder still. Given what we know of his personality and methods elsewhere, it seems unlikely that his closeness to the royal courts of both kingdoms failed to find material reward in the shape of lands for the creation of new monastic houses. In increasing the possible numbers of houses linked with the bishop we should also give some credence to Stephen's statements both about the size of the Wilfridian empire – *coenobiorum multitudo* – and the number of abbots it encompassed. Driven into Wessex, the exiled bishop sought refuge briefly with the West Saxon king, Centwine, *c.* 681 but again encountered the enmity of the queen (another sister of Iurminburh, wife of Ecgfrith of Northumbria) and had to move on (VW 40). Glastonbury's archives preserve a record of transactions between Centwine and Wilfrid possibly relating to a grant of land for monasteries in Centwine's territory. One estate of seventy hides at Wedmore in Somerset the bishop later gave to Beorhweald abbot of Glastonbury, perhaps as part of the general reordering of his affairs in the last year of his life (Scott 1981, 94–5; Abrams 1996, 90–2). When Cædwalla came to the West Saxon throne in 686 after a period in exile, he summoned Wilfrid to him and gave him 'innumerable pieces of land and other gifts out of the love of his heart and for God's sake, and honoured his father [Wilfrid] exceedingly (VW 43). Where those places were, however, remains uncertain. We are on firmer ground in Sussex, where Wilfrid acquired a religious house at Selsey to found an episcopal see, supposedly with eighty-seven hides of land for its support. Stephen reported that he also established a retreat house at Selsey for him and his followers to withdraw for private prayer (VW 41). Beyond these named places, Wilfrid cannot be identified with any other specific locations. As Nick Higham has suggested, the underlying political agendas at work in the different southern kingdoms played as significant a part in Wilfrid's relationships in this region as did contemporary ecclesiastical politics, notably Wilfrid's far from cordial relations with Theodore in Canterbury (Higham 1999).

Considering the complications of Wilfrid's itinerary, few of the monastic institutions he founded, or that sought to associate under his banner, can have had frequent contact with the bishop in person. Belonging to his affinity must, therefore, have required some imagination among the members of the separate congregations to sustain their sense of participation in so wide and geographically-dispersed an entity. If they each contributed in some manner to the material support of the bishop and his entourage, or to other houses connected with him (as suggested below), that would of course have made their belonging more tangible. Wilfrid's monasteries may have shared other characteristics that marked them out from unrelated houses. All, or at least all those founded by Wilfrid himself, probably followed similar rules of life. By his own account (reported by Stephen, but not mentioned by Bede) Wilfrid had introduced the Rule of St Benedict to his foundation at Ripon (VW 47; Goffart 1988, 314–5). Knowledge of the Rule (and perhaps also that of Columbanus, with which it was associated in the Frankish monasteries that Wilfrid had visited) could have spread from Yorkshire to his southern houses. The earliest extant English manuscript copy of the Rule has a Worcester provenance and may have been copied for one of Wilfrid's Mercian houses, possibly that at Worcester (Oxford, Bodleian Library, MS Hatton 48; Sims-Williams 1990, 118). Wilfrid claimed to have introduced double-choir singing at Hexham and we might again look for the performance of a similar liturgy in many of the houses associated with the bishop (see Billett, this volume). Such shared practices would have enhanced a common ethos underlying the monastic life of each of the separate institutions that sought connection with the bishop, helping to reinforce their sense of a distinctive collective identity. Returning to the question of how best to describe this confederation, the different analogies suggested by Aldhelm's letter to Wilfrid's abbots warrant further exploration.

Regnum

Stephen described how, when King Ecgfrith was at the height of his power and his earthly realm was extending both north and south, at the same time Wilfrid's 'ecclesiastical kingdom' (*regnum ecclesiarum*) increased both to the south among the Saxons (viz. the people of Mercia) and to the north among the British, the Picts and the Scots (VW 21; Goffart 1988, 286–8). Wilfrid advanced the Church's interests so successfully, while presenting an impressive example of pious devotion, that 'almost all the abbots and abbesses of the monasteries dedicated their substance to him by vow, either keeping it themselves in his name, or intending him to be their heir after their death' (VW 21). This may point towards an economic dimension to this federation; perhaps as already suggested, constituent houses paid a financial contribution (a tithe of their own resources) to the wider collective body, a sum that could in part have funded the bishop's retinue and his mobile lifestyle. To Stephen, the distinctiveness of this affinity lay less in its treatment of shared material resources than in its size and geographical extent. Yet outsiders responded markedly less positively to Wilfrid's accumulated wealth. We have already mentioned the jealousy of Queen Iurminburh, and the fact that Stephen attributed the queen's enmity to Wilfrid's temporal glories: 'his wealth, the number of his monasteries, the greatness of his buildings, and his countless army of followers arrayed in royal vestments and arms' (VW 24).

More monks than those with direct personal ties to the bishop recognised the potential advantages of alliance with Wilfrid: his affinity grew because of the reputation, wealth and power it accumulated through its association with the saint, which brought visible material benefits. Stephen's choice of the noun *regnum* to describe this wide-spread confederation is interesting, for it does not convey its geographical extent across contemporary political borders in the way that the use, for example, of the word *imperium* might have done. It does, however, convey the sense that the members of these congregations were all Wilfrid's subjects. This was no cross-ethnic, multi-national group, a confederation binding together other people's abbots in a loose federation: all were Wilfrid's own men. In one chapter Stephen described them specifically as his warband: *exercitum sodalium* (VW 63). Those soldiers fought for God under Wilfrid's banner, arrayed in their royal vestments (*regalibus vestimentis*) and bearing arms. Sometimes their fight took place in the mission field; more often they strove against the forces of darkness represented by those secular kings unable to recognise Wilfrid's worth. To Stephen this was a realm, a kingdom with a single ruler. To those who shared that sense of identity within this *regnum*, Aldhelm's call to follow their master loyally into exile would indeed have resonated in secular terms. One other collective term used by Stephen of the Wilfridian connection has, however, ecclesiastical rather than secular overtones.

Parochia

When he spoke of Wilfrid's *regnum ecclesiarum*, Stephen seemingly referred to the entire realm of the bishop's influence, not merely to 'his' monastic houses. On one occasion he used instead the term *parochia* to serve as a collective noun for these houses. Recording the names for the new bishops among whom Wilfrid's former dominion was divided — Bosa from Whitby, Eata from Lindisfarne and Eadhæd who had been Oswiu's priest — Stephen observed that all three of them came from outside Wilfrid's *parochia* (VW 24). As Alan Thacker argues elsewhere in this volume, Wilfrid had no objection in principle to the appointment of suffragan bishops under his overall (metropolitan) authority, but he wanted all such appointments to come from his own monastic network, not from houses subject to different authority and traditions. He objected to Bosa, Eata and Eadhæd as outsiders. Colgrave, commenting on his edition of Stephen's Life, took *parochia* here to mean diocese; these were men from beyond Wilfrid's episcopal territory, beyond the spatial unit or realm that he governed as a Northumbrian bishop (Colgrave 1927, 168). Eric John suggested, however, that we should understand *parochia* in the Irish sense of a monastic connection, an idea for which Catherine Cubitt has recently offered some support (John 1970, 50 and 60; Cubitt 1989, 23).

The classic understanding of the Irish confederation or *paruchia* is the grouping of monastic churches into non territorial units of jurisdiction under the headship of their founder or their heirs, on the model of the *paruchia Patricii*, dependent on Armagh, or the confederation of houses associated with St Columba. Recent work has challenged this notion, distinguishing between two sorts of confederation, the monastic one of houses such as that based on, and subject to Iona (dependent houses all ultimately under the control of Iona's abbot), and the rather different economic sort of federations concerned with the control of temporal possessions, sometimes spreading across wide territorial areas (Charles-Edwards 2000, 245 and 250–59). Certainly Wilfrid's monasteries do not fit the Ionan model closely; this was not a single monastic family governed by *praepositi* all answerable to a sole abbot at a parent house. Yet we should recall in this context that Wilfrid showed some enthusiasm for extending his authority among the Picts between 670 and 678, and may even have hoped to replace Iona's authority in Pictland with his own; in that case his creation of a rival network of houses might have encompassed some element of imitation. More convincingly, we might categorise Wilfrid's monastic empire as a non-territorial connection of houses bound under the nominal authority of one bishop in an economically-dependent federation, not dissimilar to the Irish model but not entirely equivalent to that organisational form, either.

More important as a model influencing Wilfrid's ideas about monastic organisation than the Irish was the extended period of time he spent in Gaul, first with Bishop Aunemundus of Lyons (655–8) and then with Agilbert. He had connections with monasteries associated with the Irish monk Columbanus, who had founded a number of houses in Gaul and in Italy. Frankish models were patently useful to Wilfrid here. The close bond felt between these houses and particularly their first founder, Columbanus, finds some parallels in the manner in which Wilfrid's minsters were connected. Wilfrid may also have known that Frankish bishops often held possessions far distant from their own cathedral seats; the bishopric of Lyons, for example, had lands in Provence (Roper 1974, 65). There are also important differences, however. In many ways, as Ian Wood has stressed, it was the second generation of Columbanus's followers who were the most significant in spreading the Columbanian tradition; the influence of the saint's rule often proved more important in spreading his spiritual ideas than did direct contact with his main foundation at Luxeuil (Wood 1994, 189). Wilfrid may have modelled his monastic connection on patterns he had observed in Francia, but his monastic affinity differed from the Columbanian connection through the closeness of the personal bond between the bishop and his followers. His connection consisted of independent establishments, none dependent on any other institution but all linked by their devotion to the person of the bishop and, after his death, to his cult. Writing to Wilfrid's followers on their bishop's exile, Aldhelm placed considerable emphasis on the abbots' personal links to their lord (*dominus*). But Aldhelm also played on the obligations of this group to the one who had taught and nourished them in the rudiments of learning.

Schola

Since Aldhelm used the metaphor of the schoolroom in his exhortation to Wilfrid's abbots to stand by their teacher in his exile, might we think of this as a 'school' of Wilfrid's? Monks at Ripon and Hexham were taught by Wilfrid;

they benefited from his oral exposition of the scriptures, his biblical exegesis, and his theological instruction, drawing on the teachings of the fathers. He will have advised those in clerical orders about the performance of their priestly ministry, the most effective modes of teaching and probably gave instruction also on matters relating to the economic exploitation of his monasteries' earthly resources. Both of Wilfrid's houses had libraries. We could comment more readily on the curriculum followed in his 'school' if we knew more about the books they contained beyond the fact that Wilfrid's endowment of Ripon included gifts of manuscripts (VW 17). Among the books to which Stephen had access while he was writing the bishop's life were the anonymous *Life of Cuthbert* written at Lindisfarne, Isidore's *De ortu et obitu patrum*, and Rufinus' translation of Eusebius' *Historia ecclesiastica*. But, as Michael Lapidge has observed, no book from Ripon has ever been identified among surviving manuscripts of this period (Lapidge 2006, 42–3). At Hexham, too, there was once a substantial collection of books dependent not only on Wilfrid's generosity but also the efforts of Bishop Acca, who had travelled to Rome to collect books and built up a substantial library (HE V, 20). If Acca was, as Lapidge has argued, the author of the now-lost Latin martyrology which served as the base text for the ninth-century *Old English Martyrology*, then Acca had access to about eighty passions of martyrs as well as a number of patristic texts when he wrote. Yet, no manuscripts from Acca's library have ever been identified, either (Lapidge 2006, 42).

One might envisage a Wilfridian school in a slightly different, aesthetic sense of a shared artistic style between his houses, evident most obviously in their common architectural mode of church building, but also perhaps in the production of manuscripts and liturgical and other artefacts within the monasteries' workshops. The surviving crypts at Ripon and Hexham both date from Wilfrid's day and share certain exclusive features and similar dimensions (Bailey 1991, 4–9). Yet beyond Ripon and Hexham there are no other sculptural remains from places linked with Wilfrid from which to identify stylistic clusters in the same way that Cambridge and more recently Wood have done in different parts of Northumbria (Cambridge 1984; Wood 2008). In his account of the dedication of the church of Ripon, Stephen reported that Wilfrid had had four gospels written out in letters of purest gold on purpled parchment and illuminated, for which bejewelled covers were made. Yet without any known manuscripts from Wilfrid's houses we cannot associate a particular, distinctive style of book-production or decoration with his circle. Of extant physical artefacts the most promising in this context is the Franks Casket, a magnificent piece of craftsmanship fusing the cultures of the Germanic and Christian world, which might have been produced at Ripon. Certainly Wilfrid's circle with its Frankish connections might indeed, as Ian Wood has argued, offer the sort of intellectual context in which a work of this nature could be created, and where its riddles could have been enjoyed and understood (Wood 1990). Given the paucity of the evidence, it is thus difficult to talk in more than the most general terms of an intellectual, educational or artistic school connected with Bishop Wilfrid. Aldhelm's letter suggested one final analogy: that of the family.

Familia

In his account of the young St Wilfrid's rejection of the Bishop of Lyons' offer to adopt him, give him his daughter in marriage and provide him with a substantial earthly patronage, Stephen placed in the saint's mouth a conventional assertion of the merits of the religious over the secular life, quoting Jesus' words from Matthew's gospel (Matt 19: 29):

> My vows have been rendered to the Lord and I will fulfil them, leaving my kin and my father's house as Abraham did, to visit the Apostolic See, and to learn the rules of ecclesiastical discipline, so that our nation may grow in the service of God. My desire is to receive from God the reward He has promised to those who love Him, saying, 'Everyone that hath forsaken father or mother and so forth shall receive a hundredfold and shall inherit everlasting life'. (VW, 4)

Although Wilfrid initially chose pilgrimage to Rome over temporal preferment, he did return from Rome to his patron, the bishop of Lyons Aunemundus (called Dalfinus by both Stephen and Bede). Receiving from him the Roman form of tonsure he thus committed himself to the monastic way of life for which his previous study and travel had equipped him. Stephen presented Wilfrid's entry to religion as made in complete conformity with the conventional tropes of early medieval hagiography. Having left his father's fields to seek the kingdom of heaven at the age of fourteen, Wilfrid took a slightly circuitous route into the cloister, but that he did so in isolation from family and indeed most personal ties represents a central theme of Stephen's narrative of the process.

Just as entry to the cloister for Wilfrid meant the renunciation of his blood kin, so all those who entered houses in his federation cut themselves off from the emotional bonds of home and severed their links with and obligations to their relatives: professed religious cleaved to Christ, or perhaps to Wilfrid personally, not to father or mother. Monastic life did not, however, deny its adherents the emotional comfort and support of family life, for monastic society was organised analogously to secular kinship. The families of Wilfrid's monastic houses were social brotherhoods, shaped by their collective commitment to a life of communal prayer and shared devotion to the saints dear to Wilfrid's own heart, and to their founding father. When Wilfrid received the monastery at Ripon from King Alhfrith and was ordained abbot, he collected around him a community bound by fraternal attachments, a spiritual brotherhood formed on the model of secular kinship (VW 8). It reflected the same elements of separation from and integration with the world as any secular kin group (Foot 1998, 40). That model apparently extended across Wilfrid's wider *parochia* or *regnum*, extending both north and south from its Northumbrian base.

The familial relationship felt between Wilfrid and his own monks is striking. When in old age the bishop fell ill while travelling to Hexham, his *familia* was dismayed; they prayed urgently that the Lord 'would grant him an extension of life, at any rate so that he could speak to them, and dispose of his monasteries and divide his possessions and not leave us as it were orphans, without any abbots'. As reports of his illness spread, all his abbots from their minsters and his anchorites came hastening by day and night to reach him while he was still alive, and so it happened that 'he arranged the lives of all of us in various places according to his desire, under the superiors chosen by himself, and shared his substance ... between God and men according to his judgement' (VW 62). Stephen devoted most attention to the arrangements Wilfrid made before his death for his two favourite monasteries, but the bishop did not forget the others. On his final visit to Mercia Wilfrid reiterated his testamentary arrangements in detail to certain of his abbots 'and for each of them in due proportion he either increased the livelihood of their brethren by gifts of land, or rejoiced their hearts with money, as though, endowed with the spirit of prophecy, he were sharing his inheritance among his heirs before his death' (VW 65).

If adoption of the religious life necessitated separation from family and kin, familial terminology might seem inappropriate to describe Wilfrid's monastic connections. Yet it is striking how far the language of the family and imagery of its personal relationships dominate Stephen's account of Wilfrid's active life and ministry. Trent Foley has emphasised the place Wilfrid's paternal role takes within Stephen's narrative. Stephen depicted the bishop as spiritual father in different guises: as teacher, but also as provider and protector, especially from the hostile forces of the outside world not just in life but also in his post-mortem miracles. Having protected and succoured them in life as a father supports, cherishes and protects his children, so Wilfrid continued to provide for his monks materially and care for them physically and spiritually, even in death (Foley 1992, 53–70).

Now that we have explored the various possibilities, we need to decide how best to refer to this collection of monastic houses. Clearly all the congregations of Wilfrid's minsters saw themselves as connected by their association with their bishop; they found themselves scattered widely both north and south of the Humber and each had their own abbot, but they continued to look to Wilfrid for authority, approval and support, economic as well as spiritual. Previously I described the Wilfridian confederation as an affinity, a word that has resonances of close connection or relationship created by something other than ties of blood, bonds of lordship or marriage or the spiritual kinship created in baptism (Foot 2006, 258–68). An affinity could function as an overarching community, a network existing in the imagination of its members, who did not necessarily depend for their sense of belonging on direct and repeated contact with Wilfrid's person (although that was the experience of some of its members). In this context, we see readily why Stephen chose to call Wilfrid's own followers across this extended realm *his* men: 'So our bishop lived to the joy of his own – *in gaudio suorum* – and in perfect peace' (VW 63). On a more pragmatic level, Wilfrid's own contemporaries observed the secular, and indeed military, parallels between his lifestyle and the band of warriors for Christ he gathered around him. Much is often made of this, notably the contrast between Wilfrid's outward displays of wealth and the more ascetic and understated modes adopted by Irish missionaries such as Aidan, or monks raised in that environment like Cuthbert. Bede's apparent caution and seeming lack of enthusiasm for Wilfrid in contrast to his admiration for the Irish is also sometimes attributed to this cause (Goffart 1988, 326–7). The political dimensions of Wilfrid's career, and the wider implications of his creation of a monastic federation that transcended contemporary political and ecclesiastical boundaries, cannot be denied. Stephen's description of it as a *regnum ecclesiarum* is thus particularly apt.

Yet in the end I find myself rejecting the language of the *comitatus* for that of the family, which serves as the most powerful metaphor in Aldhelm's letter to Wilfrid's monks. Stephen used the father/son relationship to particular effect to underpin his message about the importance of the bonds that linked Wilfrid to the abbots and monks in his various churches and monasteries (Foley 1992, 53). Stephen's Wilfrid was a father-figure to his monks; he nourished, taught, reproved and raised them in fatherly love, as Aldhelm reminded them. Affinity may seem too neutral a term and empire too loaded, too redolent of the secular spheres in which many of Wilfrid's most difficult battles played out. On reflection, I return again to the family and to the appropriateness of familial language: Wilfrid's collection of monastic communities might best be termed the 'Wilfridian family'.

4: *The* Rule of St. Benedict *in England at the Time of Wilfrid*

FRANCISCO JOSÉ ÁLVAREZ LÓPEZ

Uncertainty about the exact date of arrival in England of the *Rule of St. Benedict* (henceforth RSB) should not be cause for dismissing the fact that most key figures of the early Anglo-Saxon ecclesiastical elite were familiar with most (if not all) of its principles. Evidence suggests that figures such as Benedict Biscop, Ceolfrith, Bede, Aldhelm and Boniface had first-hand knowledge of the RSB from which, in some cases, they drew for the benefit of their own communities (Wormald 2006a, 7). But among these, a particular individual stands out. Wilfrid has been described (Mayr-Harting 1972, 157) as the founder and spiritual leader of a true monastic empire which held to the RSB as a safeguard of unity and uniform observance rather in the manner of ninth- and tenth-century monastic reformers. His federation, led from Ripon and Hexham, had establishments across different kingdoms, a symptom of the unwillingness of his new monasticism to accept submission to royal and episcopal authority. Again, this brings to mind later monastic networks which transcended the borders of individual kingdoms. However, it remains to be shown whether or not it was Wilfrid's decision which was the foundation for the later establishment of the RSB and its pragmatic and practical approach as the most important monastic customary in English ecclesiastical history.

Early Days of Monasticism and RSB

The earliest traditions of individuals leaving their mundane lives for an existence of ascetic prayer and solitude appeared around the Eastern Mediterranean shores and deserts in the fourth century (Dunn 2000, 1–24). Among them, two main practices developed. The first, believed to have been established by Anthony (*c*.251–*c*.356), proposed a solitary withdrawal from the world into the desert (*eremos* being the Greek word for desert), which would prove popular in Egypt and Palestine as shown by the large colonies of hermits found in those areas (Lawrence 1989, 4; Gregg 1989; Dunn 2000, 2–6). On the other hand, in about 320 a divergent perspective emerged which firmly advocated the benefits of communal asceticism. Its founder is agreed (Goehring 1986; Kardong 1990; Rosseau 1999; Brakke 2006, ch. 4) to have been Pachomius (*c*.292–346) and in his 'monasteries (*cenobia*), monks lived in a highly regulated fashion, eating and sleeping in common refectories and dormitories and meeting in church at more regular intervals than their eremitic counterparts' (Lawrence 1989, 25). Shortly after their deaths, Anthonian and Pachomian teachings reached and developed in the West (Brakke 1995, 111–29; Rosseau 2002, 256–7), where coenobitic communities quickly spread under the further examples set out by individuals such as Martin of Tours (*c*.315–397) and Honoratus of Arles (*c*.350–429) throughout Gaul, Italy and even Ireland (Walsh & Beadley 1991, chs. 5–6).

In the last few decades opinion as to which *regulae* these communities followed has seen a dramatic change. Whereas the conventional view had long been that the RSB had been the cornerstone of western monasticism since its composition in the early sixth century, the early work of scholars such as Hallinger (1957) and Ferrari (1957) brought to light a much more complex situation where monastic communities followed an amalgamation of regulations collected from different sources. Indeed, early coenobitic foundations do not in general seem to have lived under the observance of a single, unique rule of communal existence aimed at the highest degree of religious perfection. Rather, they followed a range of prescriptive regulations for the common life which, in most cases, would be drafted by their founder or superior with reference to a range of different regulations composed by early Christian authors deeply influenced by the aforementioned Desert Fathers. St Augustine of Hippo (354–430) and John Cassian (*c*.360–435) stand out among those who contributed most decisively to these early monastic developments. The case of the latter is of paramount importance as his precepts would be maintained and followed well into the eighth century, especially in southern Gaul, where he founded twin monasteries at Marseilles. The writings of Cassian (Petschenig 1886; 1888) were among those drawn upon by Benedict of Nursia (*c*.480–550) in his endeavour to establish a set of observances for his foundation at Monte Cassino (Dunn 1990; de Vogué 1992; Dunn 1992; Dunn 2000, 114–17). Although his initial aim was, like most contemporary monastic legislators, to compose a guide for the internal organisation of coenobitic life in his own community, overall 'the *Rule* represents a solution to the problems of monastic instability and disobedience, reinforcing the bonds of community life by a strengthening of the powers of the abbot, an insistence on absolute obedience and the severing, as far as possible, of contacts with the secular world' (Dunn 2000, 127–8).

By the seventh century, the RSB was being used alongside those texts of Cassian or Cassiodorus, among others, as yet another source in the compilation of individual legislations across Western Europe. This has been described (Foot 2006, 52; Wormald 2006a, 4) as the 'age of *regula mixta*'.

RSB: Arrival in Anglo-Saxon England

The popularity that Benedict's text enjoyed in Italy and Gaul from a very early stage after the saint's decease was assumed by most early scholars to explain its transfer to England, which was frequently set as early as Gregory's mission.

Thus, for example, in his edition and translation of Stephen's *Life of Bishop Wilfrid*, Colgrave (1927, 160) states that 'The rule of St Benedict was of course introduced to England by St Augustine and his fellow-monks in 597'. Such an assertion derived from the prevailing 'tendency to exaggerate both [the Rule's] influence and the rapidity with which it spread' (Hunter Blair 1970, 125) and the belief that both Augustine and Pope Gregory, who had composed the life and miracles of Benedict almost half a century after the saint's death, had been Benedictines themselves. However, although it is known that both men were monks and were familiar with the RSB, no evidence has been found to support their exclusively Benedictine character (Foot 2006, 150–2). Indeed, 'no sixth- or seventh-century monastery could be called "Benedictine" in the sense in which a modern audience would understand the term' (Foot 2006, 52).

As on the continent, early monastic foundations in England followed regulations devised by their abbot/abbess (or founder) drawing on the most popular customaries of the period (including those by Basil, Columbanus and Augustine of Hippo) as well as on those particularly favoured within their own geographical context and/or previous experiences (Mayr-Harting 1976, 6–7; Sims-Williams 1990, 121–8; Plummer 1896, I, 415–6). A well-known example of this is found at Wearmouth and Jarrow. As the founder and abbot Benedict Biscop was approaching his last hour, Bede tells us that one of his main concerns was that his brothers would continue observing the regulations (*decreta*) that he had selected from 17 monasteries he had visited during his journeys: *ex decem quipped et septem monasteriis quae inter longos meae crebae peregrinationis discursus optima comperi* (HA 11). One is left to assume that some Benedictine principles must have been part of this amalgamation (Blair 2005, 80; Foot 2006, 3). This is perhaps confirmed by Biscop's insistence on an elective abbatial selection procedure. He urged his brethren that his successor should be selected from among the members of the community rather than passing his office through inheritance to his own brother, as was common in contemporary dynastic foundations (HA 11; VC, 16; Hanslik 1960, 148–52; Wormald 1978, 62).

If the case for the introduction of the RSB to the English shores with the Augustinian mission must be abandoned, therefore, one faces a vacuum in terms of sources containing any reference to the use of the RSB in early Anglo-Saxon communities, let alone to its initial introduction. Nonetheless, a few scattered references may allow a sketchy insight into the early presence of the RSB in Anglo-Saxon England. The earliest instance is found in the anonymous *Life of St Cuthbert*. Book three narrates how Cuthbert, after having served as prior at Melrose, was invited by Bishop Eata to join the Lindisfarne community where, we are told, 'both present and absent, he healed those possessed of devils and cured various other infirmities' (Colgrave 1940, 94–5). The author highlights the fact that Cuthbert's function also involved rearranging the community's regulations as he claims that 'he arranged our rule of life which we composed then for the first time and which we observe even to this day along with the rule of St Benedict (*quam usque hodie cum regula Benedicti obseruamus*)' (Colgrave 1940, 94–7). The quotation provides evidence that the RSB was known (and consciously used) in England by the last quarter of the seventh century, when the author was composing this *Vita*. Furthermore, it shows that, alongside the aforementioned case of Benedict Biscop's Wearmouth and Jarrow, a *regula mixta* with potential Irish connections to which the RSB had been added or overlain was being used in other Northumbrian monasteries.

Two decades after the anonymous Lindisfarne monk had put in writing Cuthbert's life story, Bede decided to take the work a step further and produced his own prose *Life of St Cuthbert*. Indeed, there is no doubt that he used the previous version as his main source (Higham 2006, 66), but he did not limit himself to changing the words and rhetorical devices. As an appropriate example, Bede describes Cuthbert's move to Lindisfarne in the following terms:

> So when the venerable servant of God had passed many years in the monastery at Melrose and had distinguished himself by the many signs of his spiritual powers, his most reverend abbot Eata transferred him to the monastery which is situated in the island of Lindisfarne, in order that there also he might both teach the rule of monastic perfection (*regulam monachicae perfectionis*) by his authority as prior and illustrate it by the example of his virtue (Colgrave 1940, 206–7).

It is noticeable that Bede, following the anonymous biographer, describes Lindisfarne's regulation in the singular, but contrastingly omits any direct reference to the RSB. Indeed, the former must respond to the common idea that, although composed from different sources, any *regula mixta* was still regarded as a single work. Another interesting reference provided by Bede (though not found in the anonymous account) relates to 'certain brethren in the monastery who preferred to conform to their older usage rather than to the monastic rule' (*in monasterio fratres, qui priscae suae consuetudini quam regulari mallent obtemperare custodiae*: Colgrave 1940, 210–11). This episode of unrest and lack of proper monastic observance among the members of a community is not uncommon when new stricter customs are introduced. Other such incidents, sometimes leading to violent conclusions, are recorded in later narratives such as Simeon of Durham's *Historia Dunelmensis*, where he reports the murder of Bishop Walcher (1071–1080) by his own community (Rollason 2000, 4.8). The absence of this incident from the anonymous *Vita* can be justified on the grounds of shame felt by a member of the same community. However, Bede would have surely known about that unrest and may have decided to include a reference in order to highlight the progress of Cuthbert as 'he overcame these by his modest patience and virtue' (*ille modesta patientiae suae uirtute superabat*: VCP, 208–9). Still, when considered in conjunction with his omission of an explicit reference to the RSB one wonders why Bede shows a degree of reluctance regarding the benefits of the Benedictine text (Wormald 2006, 7).

References to the RSB can also be found in earlier works by Bede. It has been mentioned above that the account found in his HA regarding Benedict Biscop's *decreta* had been collected from seventeen different houses. Some time after Biscop's death, Ceolfrith, who had been appointed abbot of both Jarrow and Wearmouth, decided to leave for Rome and before departing he admonished his brethren on the necessity of selecting a new abbot following the directions of the RSB (*ut iuxta sui statuta priuilegii iuxtaque regulam sancti abbatis Benedicti, de suis sibi ipsi patrem, qui aptior esset, elegerent*: HA 16). The same event is recorded in the anonymous *Vita Ceolfridi* in almost the same words (*iuxta regulam sancti patris Benedicti et sua statute priuilegii ... abbatem sibi constituissent*: VC 25), alongside Ceolfrith's appointment as abbot of both houses immediately before Biscop's passing (McClure 1984, 71–84; Goffart 1988, 277). Both occasions are reminiscent of chapter 64 in the RSB (Hanslik 1960, 148), where the selection of a new abbot/abbess is stipulated according to the community's preference (*omnis concors congregatio*) rather than family inheritance.

RSB in Early Anglo-Saxon England: Wilfrid's Role

The only other explicit references to the RSB in Anglo-Saxon texts from the period are found in another hagiographic work narrating the life of one of the central figures of the Anglo-Saxon Church. Wilfrid (*c*.634–710), abbot of Ripon and Hexham and the bishop of York, enjoyed a position of power like no other English ecclesiastic of his time. It should come as no surprise that this eventually brought him almost as many enemies as devoted followers (Goffart 1988, 258). His progress can be followed both in his *vita*, as written by his disciple Stephen, and in Bede's HE, although the differences between these two portraits of the same individual have already been discussed (Higham 2006, 58–63). However, some of the dissimilarities between these two works may be relevant to this discussion. Thus, whereas Bede omits any reference to the RSB in relation to the Bishop of York (HE V, 19), Stephen suggestively presents his hero claiming that he had arranged 'the life of the monks in accordance with the rule of the holy father Benedict which none had previously introduced' to Northumbria (VW 47). The absence of such a claim from the HE should not be cause for surprise as Bede's attitude towards Wilfrid's merits has been found (Kirby 1983, 101–14; Goffart 1988, 235–328; Goffart 1990; Goffart 2005) to be rather ungenerous by many, though not by all (Higham 2006, 58–69). In Bede's defence, it could be argued that he had already covered Stephen's claim when he affirmed that Wilfrid 'was the first bishop of the English race to introduce the Catholic way of life to the English churches' (HE IV, 2), even though his *catholicum uiuendi morem* may simply refer to Wilfrid's role in the eradication of the Celtic tradition from the Anglo-Saxon ecclesiastical landscape. This seems to be supported in the VW when Stephen explains that Wilfrid was consecrated bishop *ad Galliarum regionem, ubi catholici episcopi multi habentur* (V 12). Surely, the term 'catholic' is here related to the fact that these prelates were followers of the Roman tradition rather than Celtic schismatics.

Even though Stephen's rendering should not necessarily be taken at face value, Wilfrid's role in the transmission of the RSB must not be undermined by his biographer's potential bias. Wilfrid's claim may respond to a comprehensive effort to set the RSB as the regulatory code of practice throughout the network of foundations he established and controlled, though not throughout his diocese (Blair 2005, 97). As did Biscop, Wilfrid may have seen the benefits of a single customary, to be adhered to by all 'his' communities. The founder of Wearmouth and Jarrow devised his own regulations after visiting many a monastic community throughout the continent and made sure that his two monasteries, even when under the direction of two different individuals, were ruled by those principles. Similarly, Wilfrid, who did not see the need for his own regulatory composition, must have realised the benefits of such a thorough text as the RSB to provide his abbots with the path to perfect monastic observance during his absences.

The lack of evidence by which to contradict Stephen makes it feasible that Wilfrid was in fact the first to introduce the RSB in the lands north of the Humber. However, the question remains as to the customary's introduction in the South. There is evidence of the presence of the RSB in Wessex in the mid-seventh century, with Gaulish figures taking important ecclesiastical roles. Among them, the figure of Agilbert stands out. He was appointed bishop of Wessex some time after having been Wilfrid's host for two years at Jouarre (Wormald 2006, 6). It has been argued that Wilfrid may have experienced the RSB in this Gaulish community, where it may have been used in combination with other regulations, as was common among the monasteries of the Columbanian connection (Wormald 2006, 7). Needless to say, this would require him to identify the RSB as a component of that compilation.

Wilfrid visited Rome after spending three months in Lyons, where he decided to stay for three years halfway through his return journey. It was during this second stay that he received the tonsure 'in the shape of the crown of thorns' (VW 6) from Archbishop Aunemundus. This event, considered within the context of a lengthy stay in Gaul, might hold the key to Wilfrid's attachment to the monastic ideal and his presumably first-hand contact with monastic customaries, amongst them the RSB. Although Stephen provides us with no explicit evidence as to the life experienced by his hero in Lyons, this seems to be the most likely period for Wilfrid's exposure to the Benedictine principles. Earlier, while in Rome, Stephen recounts how the archdeacon Boniface taught Wilfrid 'the four Gospels of Christ ... and the Easter rule ..., and many other rules of ecclesiastical discipline' (VW 3). During the 'many months' he stayed in the Apostolic see, he is also said to have visited the shrines of the saints and martyrs on a daily basis, when he would have become familiar with the lavishly decorated churches built by Pope Honorius (625–638). It has been argued that Honorius' example had a deep influence on Wilfrid's building and refurbishing programmes after his first pilgrimage to Rome (Foley 1992, 95). Besides, Foley goes on to conclude (103) that Wilfrid had also learnt from Gregory's disciple how to be a 'Benedictine-styled monk'. Whereas the former statement seems plausible given the archaeological evidence, the Benedictine nature of Honorius' rule is much more questionable, in the light of the arguments presented above. Still, returning to Boniface's teaching, it is possible that amongst those 'rules of ecclesiastical discipline' he taught Wilfrid, some Benedictine principles might have been included.

The impact that continental practices, traditions and powerful prelates had on Wilfrid's character and ecclesiastical practices seems unquestionable. However, perhaps one should consider two early Christian cities rather than one: Rome and Lyons. The appeal of Gaul may be one of the reasons behind Wilfrid's request to be consecrated there, a country he was familiar with. This may also go some length to explaining his delay in returning to his newly appointed see and the appointment of Chad in his absence. Likewise, as has also been pointed out, the figure of Archbishop Aunemundus seems to have played a key role in his development of a strong and powerful character as bishop. However, the role-models offered by some seventh-century popes may have had an equally important impact on Wilfrid. As argued by Foley (1992, 95), the figures of Pope Honorius, with his 'ascetic-monastic streak' and 'his taste for newly built and lavishly decorated churches', and Pope Theodore (642–649), with 'his concern for observing strictly Rome's sacred canons in all things' (98), can be mirrored in the abbot of Ripon's personality throughout his ecclesiastical career. Overall, 'the popes of the mid-seventh century showed themselves every bit as capable as their Gallic counterparts of wielding immense authority, standing up to secular power, building magnificent churches, and patronizing the flock' (Foley 1992, 102–3). All of these characteristics pervade Stephen's portrayal of Wilfrid, for instance, when (VW 27) he adopted the 'dignity and grandeur of the Roman buildings he had seen in Gaul and Italy' into his own (re)building programme at Ripon, Hexham and Paulinus' church in York by lavishly developing stone buildings and endowing them with lands, golden vestments, new vessels, glazed windows and even, in the case of his new church at Ripon, with a copy of 'the four gospels to be written in letters of gold on purpled parchment' (*quattuor evangelia de auro purissimo in membranis de purpuratis*) and a binding 'all made of purest gold and set with most precious gems' (*omnem de auro purissimo et gemmis pretiotissimis*). The question remains as to how his inclination for lavish architectural projects presumably inherited from the Latin Mediterranean churches in Rome and Gaul was to be balanced against the Benedictine principles of poverty and simplicity.

We cannot be sure of the exact moment when Wilfrid decided to implement the RSB in any of his communities, but it might be reasonable to think that this happened when he became abbot of Ripon. As it has been shown, by this time he had just returned from his first visit to Rome and a lengthy stay at Lyons, where besides having possibly been in contact with the RSB, he had been tonsured. However, upon retuning from his consecration as bishop and finding Chad in his see, we are told that Wilfrid went back to Ripon as abbot, from where he was asked to perform various episcopal duties in Mercia and Kent at the request of their kings. After this, Stephen reports that Wilfrid 'returned to his own land with the singers Æddi and Aeona, and with masons and artisans of almost every kind, and there, by introducing the rule of St Benedict, he greatly improved the ordinances of the churches of God' (VW 14).

Early Manuscripts of RSB in Anglo-Saxon England

In addition to the importation of monastic ideals, episcopal policies and architectural inspiration, occasional Anglo-Saxon ecclesiastical travellers brought back from their frequent journeys to the continent books for their (increasingly) well-stocked libraries. We are reminded that Benedict Biscop 'brought copies of innumerable books of all genres' (*innumerabilem librorum omnis generis copiam apportavit*) from one of his visits to Rome, in imitation of the gifts sent by Gregory to Augustine's community at Canterbury in 601 (HA 6; HE I, 29; Brown 2003, 355–8). Although the reference to *librorum omnis generis* is rather generic, one is inclined to assume that it included items on patristic literature, liturgical books and perhaps even monastic regulations (Ogilvy 1967, 3).

The case of Wearmouth and Jarrow is usually taken as a paramount example of the development of an early monastic library in Anglo-Saxon England and, along the same lines, a monastic scriptorium (Peers and Ralegh Radford 1943, 64–5; Campbell 1986, 63; Parkes 1991, 93–120; Cramp 2005, i, 346–7; Lapidge 2006, 34–7). On a similar scale must have been the libraries of other important monastic communities, such as those at Canterbury (Lapidge 2006, 31–3; Barker-Benfield 2008, pp. xlix–li), Whitby (Lapidge 2006, 43) or Hexham (Lapidge 2006, 42), all of which must have contained a sufficient range of items to cater for the needs of a rapidly evolving monastic culture of the book. Due to the absence of manuscript evidence, our most reliable source here is yet again Bede. In his only explicit reference to a library in the HE, Bede describes how Bishop Acca had built up '*amplissimam ... ac nobilissimam bibliothecam*' at Hexham containing hagiographical texts and other ecclesiastical volumes (HE V, 20). Similarly, he provides a list of topics taught at Canterbury by Theodore and Hadrian, which therefore presumes a supply of manuscripts on those areas (HE IV, 2). As for his own community, the *Historia Abbatum* highlights how his various journeys to Rome had allowed Benedict Biscop to establish a '*nobilissimam copiosissimamque*' collection, as well as the fact that his successor Ceolfrith was able to even double the monastery's holdings (HA 11 and 15). Besides their duties concerning the Divine Office and their contemplative and pastoral nature, seventh- and eighth-century monasteries became centres of learning, powerhouses of the knowledge needed to cater for the relentless spread of new monastic foundations. The example to be followed had been laid out a century earlier in southern Italy by Cassiodorus (Dunn 2000, 113–14; Lapidge 2006, 16–20).

The different subjects included in monastic education at the time in each community were obviously dependent on the contents of its library. Yet again, the example of Bede's community must have been beyond the limitations experienced by most Anglo-Saxon houses. The evidence gathered from Bede's own works reflects an impressive collection of Patristic authors which allowed the venerable monk to produce an equally impressive set of historical and exegetic works without needing to leave his own monastery, though occasionally borrowing items from neighbouring houses (Laistner 1943, 1; Lapidge 2006, 191–228).

It may not be far-fetched to suppose that many of these monastic libraries would have contained the works of Gregory the Great, Cassian, Cassiodorus and, of special importance to us here, Benedict of Nursia. There is no physical evidence to allow us to locate in time and place the arrival of the first copies of the RSB in Anglo-Saxon England. However, as has been discussed above, knowledge of the text (even if partial) must have reached England by the second half of the seventh century. Therefore, written copies must have circulated from that time, in all probability in combination with other regulatory works. Thus if one assumes, as has been argued above, the impact of the monastic ideal on Wilfrid along with Stephen's claim to his introduction of the RSB in (at least) Northumbria, it logically follows that copies of the RSB (full or partial) must have been used within his network of monasteries. In addition, if we entertain the view that Wilfrid's pseudo-Benedictinism arose during his journey to Rome and Lyons, it is perfectly possible that he may have brought at least one exemplar of the RSB with him. Interestingly enough, the earliest surviving copy of the RSB is an Anglo-Saxon manuscript (below) probably produced towards the end of Wilfrid's lifetime.

The Case of Hatton 48

Oxford, Bodleian Library, Hatton 48 is a manuscript from the late seventh century or the early decades of the eighth and it contains, in a remarkably good condition, the earliest surviving copy of Benedict's *Regula* (Lowe 1934, ii, no. 240; Ker 1941; Farmer 1968; Gneuss 2001, no. 631). Although its place of origin remains unknown, the possibilities have been narrowed down to a monastic scriptorium south of the Humber (Sims-Williams 1990, 204–5; Foot 2006, 50). Furthermore, the manuscript's provenance is linked to Worcester from at least the eleventh century.

The codex has been described (Farmer 1968, 7) as an impressive witness 'to the remarkable combination of spiritual, intellectual and artistic forces in English civilization at that time'. Hatton 48 contains the 'chief representative [copy] of the revised and interpolated text, that is, of the *textus interpolatus*, which was current in the West up to the ninth century' (Lowe 1929, 7). After Benedict composed his *Regula*, the text underwent a complex process of transmission which would eventually give way to the circulation of three main recensions (Meyvaert 1963; Gretsch 1999, 241–51). The *textus purus* originates from an Aachen manuscript copied for Charlemagne from an exemplar at Monte Cassino thought to have been Benedict's own autograph (Gretsch 1999, 243). This recension does not seem to have ever enjoyed much popularity beyond northern Gaul and probably as a result, it never reached England at all. Instead, the *textus interpolatus* was arguably the most widely used recension across Europe before 850 (Gretsch 1999, 243–5). Originating from Rome at the beginning of the seventh century, this thoroughly revised text (in linguistic terms rather than content-wise) seems to have been popular in England, not only because its earliest surviving copy was produced here but also because other copies of the same recension are known to have existed in this area before the tenth-century monastic reform. The main Hatton scribe left enough traces to show that he/she had corrected this copy against a second exemplar which also belonged to the *interpolatus* tradition (Gretsch 1999, 243), providing some further evidence of the circulation of this recension in early Anglo-Saxon England. In addition, Gretsch (1999, 244) has shown that 'an interpolatus text of the Regula was carefully studied in the school of Archbishop Theodore and Abbot Hadrian at Canterbury at the end of the seventh century', despite not having been implemented as the monastery's sole rule.

A final recension, *textus receptus*, originated from the mid-ninth-century reforms carried out in the Carolingian empire under the spiritual guidance of Benedict of Aniane (c.750–821) and the sponsorship of Charlemagne's successor,

Louis the Pious (814–40). This reforming process established 'the universal and exclusive observance of the *Regula S. Benedicti* in its *textus purus*, made available in the Carolingian empire by Charlemagne himself' (Gretsch 1999, 245). 'Contamination' of the *purus* version with the most popular *interpolatus* one resulted in a new recension 'originating not from a single centre but from individual monasteries all over the Carolingian empire and beyond and embracing in various degrees *purus*, *interpolatus* as well as idiosyncratic readings' (Gretsch 1999, 246). Although the moment when this recension reached England remains unknown, it seems that by the mid-tenth century, when the Benedictine Reform movement was leaving its imprint on the Anglo-Saxon monastic landscape, it had already planted itself among English coenobitic communities (Parsons 1975; Scragg 2008; Barrow 2010). Apart from Hatton 48, all other English copies of the RSB produced before 1100 contain the *textus receptus*, and they all date from the mid-tenth century onwards (Gretsch 1974, 126). In view of this, it logically follows that the introduction of this Carolingian recension into England is likely to have been intimately connected with the tenth-century Anglo-Saxon Benedictine movement.

As already mentioned, Hatton 48 contains the RSB as a single item. This is a fact which in itself raises a good deal of interest as it is common (in most copies) to find a selection of secondary texts in the manner of appendices to the main item, which highlight and develop the Benedictine nature of the codex. That is the case of C, CCC, 57, an Abingdon copy of the RSB from around 1000, which contains some Carolingian texts produced at the time of the ecclesiastical and monastic reform led by Benedict of Aniane – including the *Memoriale Qualiter* and the *Aachen Capitulary* (Gretsch 1999, 274). In other copies, one can also find items referring to the daily life of a particular community (e.g. Durham, B.iv 24 and O, CCC, 197). The relevance of these secondary items is therefore given by the information they provide about the use made of a particular manuscript in the community for which it was made or where it was kept after its production. Moreover, the absence of any references or extracts from other monastic regulations in Hatton 48 should be highlighted as unexpected in a product of the 'age of *regula mixta*'.

Hatton 48 is made of 76 original parchment leaves containing the full Benedictine text except for part of the last chapter and the colophon. It is followed by a medieval binding leaf which had been removed from a later manuscript containing a section of St Augustine's *Enchiridion* in a Worcester hand from the second half of the eleventh century. The text of the RSB is laid out in double columns of 22 lines copied in the so-called *scriptura continua*, whereby no spaces are left between words in the same line. Although the manuscript was originally made of 8 quires of 8 leaves each, plus an additional ninth with 6 leaves, the last two folios of this last quire were lost and with them the aforementioned ending of chapter 72 and the *Rule*'s colophon. Each quire is marked out on the bottom margin of the last verso with quire-signatures in the form of a letter 'q' underneath the first column and a Roman numeral underneath the second. Both figures are inserted between two rows of three lively horizontal strokes.

The manuscript is preserved in an unusually good condition. When describing its palaeographical and codicological features, Farmer went as far as to state that 'some leaves in the middle of the book (27v–31r and 55r–18r) are almost as fresh as when they left the scriptorium' (Farmer 1968, 12). This implies lack of use of the codex, at least on a daily basis, for example in the community's daily chapter meetings, where the abbot/abbess would read out and explain a pertinent chapter to the congregation. This is further emphasized by the absence of a thorough process of correction, annotation or glossing. In this sense, only a limited effort was made by the main scribe probably not long after finishing the original copy (Lowe 1929, 10–11). Although up to four other hands (ninth century?; tenth century; late-tenth/early eleventh; and thirteenth century) can be identified as having done some work on the pages of Hatton 48, none of them attempted a systematic revision of the main text and as a consequence many of the original mistakes were left untouched. Most notable were those involving the use of *s* for *ss*: for example, *misas* (fo. 30r) and *egresurus* (fo. 42v); indeed, the scribe might just have copied these Insular spellings from the exemplar; other mistakes include *praeceta* (fo. 9r), *tun* (fo. 61v) and *recauendum* (fo. 74v).

The script is also of great importance when considering this manuscript against its historical background. This is 'the only manuscript of the Rule written in uncial characters' and the fact that those Roman letterforms were used in an English scriptorium 'renders' this manuscript 'of particular interest both to the historian and to the palaeographer' (Lowe 1960, 7). Indeed, Hatton 48 provides an impressive, albeit late, example of the way in which this originally Italian script was acquired, adapted and developed in an insular context under the pressure of the Irish scripts which would subsequently give way to Anglo-Saxon minuscule. Its large and regular letterforms are the work of a highly disciplined scribe who must have been familiar with a script which had reached England directly from one of its foremost centres of production, such as Cassiodorus's own monastery at Vivarium in southern Italy. Among the literary treasures brought to England by Augustine, Theodore and Benedict Biscop there were some codices produced at this scriptorium. The best evidence for this is found in the use that Bede made of the so-called *Codex Grandior*, an illustrated copy of the Bible which had been produced at the very monastery of Cassiodorus at Vivarium (Lapidge 2006, 28–9).

The acquisition of Uncial script represents not only a palaeographical feat, but perhaps more importantly, a symbolic achievement of the Roman tradition in England. Because of this, it is perhaps odd that the most impressive surviving examples of Uncial in England would come from a Northumbrian scriptorium. The *Codex Amiatinus*, now kept in Florence, and for centuries believed to have been produced in Italy, unquestionably represents the peak of Uncial production in Britain (Bischoff 1990, 71; Roberts 2005, 13). This product of the nine scribes reported to have worked on the manuscript instigated by Abbot Ceolfrith is not a piece of imitative skill but an outstanding example of expertise. As with the scribe of Hatton 48, these scribes were experts in the writing of Uncial who had presumably been trained at insular schools (perhaps at Wearmouth-Jarrow itself).

Nevertheless, any attempt to link Hatton 48 to Bede's community has been discredited on palaeographical grounds (Farmer 1968, 13). The Irish features found in the products from the Northumbrian house are not present here. Rather, the pure Uncial nature of the letterforms and a particular set of decorative patterns resemble those found in Southumbrian codices (Farmer 1968, 22–3; Sims-Williams 1990, 201–2). In addition, the lavishness of its production, the size of its letters and an apparent disregard of production costs all point to a wealthy patron who, in view of the manuscript's content, must have held the RSB in high regard. One such individual who would suitably fit this description at this particular period was Wilfrid, whose lavish building endeavours at Ripon, Hexham and York immediately spring to mind.

Although Wilfrid based his power and dominions mostly in Northumbria, it should not be forgotten, as already pointed out, that one of the unique features of his monastic federation was the fact that its foundations spread far beyond that realm. It has already been argued that it is not unlikely that Benedict's text presented itself as a useful tool for the bishop/abbot and as a practical customary which would allow him to keep control of his communities in his physical absences. With this in mind, one needs to consider the evidence for Wilfrid's involvement in the development of Southumbrian monasticism in the late seventh century.

The RSB is likely to have arrived from Gaul, particularly given that Hatton 48 shows decorative features closely linked to continental manuscripts. Besides, the route from Francia to Southumbrian England seems to have been a fertile one at this time, as shown by Wormald (2006b, 148–53) in relation to early Anglo-Saxon charters. Therefore, a community south of the Humber with foundational connections across the Channel would perfectly suit here. Sims-Williams (1990: 204–5) has put forward the case of Bath, pointing out that both Bath's first abbess and the bishop of Wessex at the time of its foundation were of Frankish origin. Moreover, the house's establishment took place in 675 and the foundation charter was attested by Wilfrid, which would support the Bath hypothesis even further. Finally, the manuscript's transmission to Worcester, where it was in the eleventh century, might have taken place during the period in which Bath became part of Worcester's estate in the eighth century. Incidentally, this might also help explain the lack of use evidenced in the manuscript's pages.

Conclusions

Whatever its origin, the reverence shown by the scribal and artistic quality of Hatton 48 towards a text which, by most accounts, was not fully established as a single monastic regulation at this stage, betrays a particular veneration on the part of the individual who commissioned its production. Its palaeographical features show the work of an exquisite (and expert) hand, almost certainly trained in England and therefore an example of the scriptorial standards already existing in England from, at least, the times of Wilfrid south of the Humber.

The remarkable size of the codex, along with the splendour and beauty of its decorations and script, make Hatton 48 a rather impractical item for regular, daily reading (for example, in chapter meetings). This is probably another reason why it was never much corrected or used. Although one is greatly intrigued by the possibility that other such examples of the proficiency of early Anglo-Saxon scriptoria may have been commissioned and produced at the time, the survival of Hatton 48 should still be regarded as the best evidence of a period of increasing monastic expansion where the RSB was gaining ground as the main monastic customary. The survival of such an early copy of the RSB on its own (along with the evidence it provides for the existence of at least two earlier copies in England) is evidence that this text was not only identified as an individual customary in the age of the *regula mixta*, but it was also being commissioned with a higher degree of veneration than any other monastic customary of the time. This was part of a process which must be considered within a prolific culture of the book which by Wilfrid's later years was already reaching its prime, not only in the South, but also in the powerful Northumbrian monasteries.

5: *Wilfrid and Bede's* Historia

N. J. HIGHAM

There has been a very long-held suspicion that Bede was less than enthusiastic regarding Wilfrid (Plummer 1896, II, 315–16; Levison 1935, 146; Kirby 1983, 101). This finally crystallised in 1988, with Walter Goffart proposing that Bede should be read as a mouthpiece for an 'anti-Wilfridian' lobby competing with the 'Wilfridians' for control of the archdiocese of York, which was eventually [re]created in 735. His arguments were subsequently reinforced by new articles, published in 1990 and 2005, and have gained a degree of acceptance. However, Goffart's position requires very particular interpretations of highly ambiguous passages in several texts, and quite specific dates of composition, none of which are certain (see Higham 2006, 58–69). Such is the complexity of the argument that even significant doubt regarding any part of it necessarily brings down the whole edifice. Goffart's interpretation of Bede as a factional mouthpiece should be viewed as at best uncertain, therefore, and it is now time to put aside this grandiose interpretation of the several texts involved and seek a new understanding of the interaction of Bede with Wilfrid. This paper explores where such a quest might take us.

That Wilfrid only appears in a single work of Bede's, the *Ecclesiastical History*, requires some explanation. Cuthbert's time at Ripon, before it was re-granted to Wilfrid, might have occasioned at least passing mention of Wilfrid in Bede's prose *Life of Cuthbert*. Additionally, Bede's remark in the EH (IV, 29) that Wilfrid took control of Lindisfarne following Cuthbert's death might have warranted his inclusion (whether or not the 'storm of trouble' noted in the *vita* (40) was consequent upon Wilfrid's custody of the see, as Goffart maintained). Given that Benedict Biscop and Wilfrid travelled to Gaul together (VW 3), one might similarly have expected some reference to Wilfrid in the *History of the Abbots* (Plummer 1896, I, 364–87), although Bede would arguably have not welcomed Stephen's depiction of Biscop as Wilfrid's guide since he was the elder figure. Wilfrid might equally have featured in the *Greater Chronicle*, which has brief accounts of the deeds of King Edwin, Queen Æthelthryth, Bishop Cuthbert, Bishop Willibrord, St. Ecgberht and Abbot Ceolfrith (see Higham 2006, 118–20). As explanation it is probably sufficient to state the obvious, that Wilfrid's absence better suited Bede's purposes as author in each of these works. Such was Wilfrid's stature that his presence in Cuthbert's *Life* or the *History of the Abbots* might have threatened the centrality of their key figures, and introduced at the least the appearance of dissension that would have detracted from Bede's agenda in each text. His omission from the *Greater Chronicle* is more complex, but Wilfrid may simply have seemed too contentious for a work of this kind, which was written for a monastic community established by one of Wilfrid's competitors for royal patronage and influence and which owed little to Wilfrid (although he was helpful to Abbot Ceofrith after the latter's retirement to Ripon: VC 8). The English figures included by Bede in this work were few and arguably intended to serve as empathetic exemplars from different sectors of society. Wilfrid's lengthy periods as an exile, his captivity by and quarrels with successive kings and the tensions between him and Benedict Biscop following their apparent fall-out in Francia in the 650s arguably each rendered him a poor fit to Bede's purposes here. Bede was nothing if not politic, in almost all his works.

It is solely in the *Ecclesiastical History*, therefore, that Bede chose to include Wilfrid. Here Bede was addressing an elite secular audience and interpreting English history in terms of the growth of Christianity among the English via exemplary stories capable of steering his listeners towards God. In comparison with earlier works, he was deploying a very large cast of characters, so it would have been quite extraordinary if he had excluded from his *History* a man who had been bishop of the Northumbrians from the late 660s, intermittently at least, until his death, and who presided latterly over Bede's home diocese of Hexham. Wilfrid was, of course, frequently out of favour with the Northumbrian court and/or the English archdiocese at Canterbury, but he was a pivotal figure in the Northumbria into which Bede was born, and only very recently exiled when Bede entered Wearmouth as a novice.

Bede certainly knew Wilfrid personally in the period 706–10. The bishop probably visited Wearmouth/Jarrow, given it's presence a mere day's journey from his own church. Bede in turn very probably visited Hexham and certainly knew several brethren there well enough to write to one asking him to engage another to intercede for him with Wilfrid himself. It seems likely that Bede's close friendship with Acca, Wilfrid's priest, companion and eventual successor, began before Wilfrid's death. They were about the same age, they had similar interests and their relationship extended across the early eighth century, right up to 731, when Bede praised him handsomely (HE V, 20). However, the most convincing evidence for a face-to-face relationship lies in Bede's remarks concerning Æthelthryth, King Ecgfrith's first wife, where he noted that he had asked Wilfrid for confirmation of her virginity. Wilfrid responded, '*dicens* ['saying'] that he had the most perfect proof of it' (HE IV, 19(17)). Assuming that Bede meant this literally, then he was in 731 recalling a conversation which he had himself had with Wilfrid. The delicacy of the matter implies that other conversations had occurred already and that they knew each other comparatively well, as one might expect of the most experienced bishop of his age and the best theologian in Western Europe when living so close.

More importantly, we can be entirely confident that Bede knew the *Life* written by Stephen shortly after Wilfrid's death, since he followed it to a degree which cannot have been fortuitous when offering his own synopsis of Wilfrid's life (EH V, 19). It is the opportunity to compare this work with Bede's *Ecclesiastical History* that allows us to consider Bede's attitude towards Wilfrid at some length. First of all, let us explore the language each author used, beginning with Stephen. His *vita* is a defensive work, stressing Wilfrid's rightful tenure of a see of which he had been unlawfully deprived: *episcopus* ('bishop') is attached to him in all some fifty-six times across the work, while being used of other churchmen on a mere thirteen occasions, almost all of them individuals positively associated with his life (namely Acca (twice); 'Dalfinus' (i.e. Aunemundus, bishop of Lyons, three times); Agilbert; Agatho (twice); Andrew and John – others were Deusdedit, Chad and Paulinus). Stephen bombarded his audience with Wilfrid's name and status, combined together in a welter of phrases asserting divine approval. Take, for example, the formuli used to distinguish him in chapter 29. We have: *Deo amabilis Wilfrithus episcopus* ('Bishop Wilfrid beloved of God'); *Wilfrithus Deo amabilis episcopo sanctae Eboracae ecclesiae* ('Wilfrid the beloved of God, bishop of the holy church of York'); *memoratus Deo amabilis Wilfrithus episcopus* ('the celebrated Bishop Wilfrid, beloved of God'); *Wilfrithus Deo amabilis episcopus sanctae Eboraicae ecclesiae* ('Wilfrid the beloved of God, bishop of the holy church of York') and finally, *Wilfrithus Deo amabilis episcopus* ('Bishop Wilfrid, the beloved of God': two occurrences). Repetition coincides with a variety of voices. In this passage, he used his own authorial voice twice, but also had recourse to direct speech, twice using the voice of Pope Agatho and twice the bishops Andrew of Ostia and John of Porto. The next chapter then opens with Wilfrid's own petition, in his own voice: *Wilfrithus humilis et indignus episcopus Saxoniae ...* ('I, Wilfrid, a humble and unworthy bishop of England ...'). Stephen clearly intended that such repetition should reinforce his core message regarding Wiflrid's exceptional qualities and unquestionable right to high ecclesiastical office.

Stephen also used several other terms for a bishop: *antistes* occurs just once (VW 42) and *praesul* once of Wilfrid (38) and only occasionally of others. However, *pontifex* is used of Wilfrid fifty-nine times but never of any other named individual and only once of unnamed bishops (46). Otherwise, Stephen used the term *episcopus metropolitanus* once each of Colmán and Wilfrid as bishops of York (10; 16), apparently to convey their exceptional authority and the extent of their dioceses (Thacker 2008, 48–52, and this volume). Stephen used the term *archiepiscopus* sixteen times but, apart from three references to 'Dalphinus' in Gaul, this was exclusive to archbishops of Canterbury, using it of Honorius once, of Theodore eight times and Berhtwald four times. He never used it of Wilfrid.

Bede deployed a comparable range of terminology in relation to Wilfrid. *Episcopus* was his preferred term for a bishop, and this occurs (HE IV, 2; V, 11, 24); *antistes* is a somewhat less common alternative, though he actually applied it to Wilfrid more frequently (HE III, 13; IV, 12, 13, 19(17), 29(27)); *pontifex* is in this work most often used of popes but it is applied to Wilfrid in V, 19, where Bede was particularly indebted to Stephen, as well as in Theodore's epitaph, from which Bede quoted approvingly (HE V, 8). Like Stephen, Bede failed to use the term *archiepiscopus* of Wilfrid, but he did refer to him as *pater* ('father': HE V, 20), and offered several highly complimentary phrases. He followed Stephen in terming him *Deo amabilis* ('the beloved of God': HE V, 19), and depicted him variously as *magister* (in the sense of 'teacher'), *uir doctissimus* ('most learned man': HE III, 25), *vir reverentissimus* ('most reverend man'), *reverentissimus antistes* and *reverentissimus episcopus* ('most reverend bishop': HE III, 25), and referred to him three times as *beatae memoriae* ('of blessed memory': HE IV, 19 (17), 23 (21); V, 18). Overall Bede used such complimentary language with great care; its generous application to Wilfrid was no accident.

Name (No. occurrences)	Augustine (64)	Gregory (54)	Wilfrid (51)	Theodore (50)	Paulinus (40)
Doctissimus	–	–	1	–	–
Beatae memoriae, beatae recordationis,	–	–	3	8	1
beatus	2	21	–	–	–
venerabilis	–	1	1	–	2
sanctus	4	4	–	–	–
reverentissimus	2	–	4	1	1
Vir Domini, servus Dei, servus Domini	5	–	1	–	–
Deo dilectus, Deo amabilis	1	–	1	1	1

Table 5.1: Frequently-named individuals in *HE*
and examples of the language which Bede associated with them.

It is also worth emphasising the frequency with which Bede referred to Wilfrid. With sixty-four occurrences, Augustine of Canterbury was easily the individual named most often in the EH but this is largely due to Bede's inclusion of Gregory's letters – Augustine is named ten times in I, 27 alone. Behind Augustine comes a small group of individuals with thirty or more mentions, led by Gregory the Great with fifty-four. Theodore has fifty, Paulinus forty, and kings Edwin and Oswiu have forty-seven and forty-four respectively. Wilfrid lies well within this leading pack, with a total of fifty-one making him the third most commonly named individual. Others of Bede's acknowledged heroes appear less frequently: so, for example, Oswald, king and saint, is named twenty-nine times and St. Ecgberht twenty-three times, St Cuthbert twenty, Ceolfrith eight and John of Beverley a mere five. When considering Bede's treatment of Wilfrid, therefore, we need to take account not just of what Bede wrote but also the frequency with which he appears.

Given his prominence, it seems best to compare the language used with that applied to other major characters. Wilfrid is associated with as broad a range of complimentary language as any other of this group, is less the subject of repeated usage than some but appears in the listings if anything more consistently than others (Table 5.1). Bede clearly felt that particular adjectives were peculiarly apt for specific individuals. So Gregory is strongly associated with the simplex adjective *beatus* ('blessed'), which was used most often otherwise of the apostles, then the saints (it is used of Alban three times, then singly of Cuthbert, Fursey, Lupus, Germanus, Laurence and Pope Martin) but never of Wilfrid. In contrast, the phrase *beatae memoriae* ('of blessed memory') occurs sixteen times in all, eight times of Theodore, with or without Hadrian, three each of Wilfrid and Pope Agatho and once each of Paulinus and Cuthbert. *Doctissimus* ('most learned') is used in the Preface and fourteen chapters relative to only twelve named individuals. Wilfrid was distinguished by this superlative alongside such figures as Abbot Albinus at Canterbury and Bishop Tobias of Rochester, both of whom were graduates of Theodore's school, but Theodore himself is absent from this list. *Eruditio* ('learning') is also associated with Wilfrid (HE III, 25): again this is used sparingly, in only twelve passages.

In terms of the language with which he was associated, therefore, Wilfrid was clearly one of a highly select company in the *Ecclesiastical History*. On this basis it is impossible to distinguish Bede's treatment of him from that of numerous others who received similarly honourable mention. Additionally it is noticeable that Wilfrid's close associates often attract praise. So, for example, Archdeacon Boniface, who befriended and tutored him at Rome, is *vir sanctissimus ac doctissimus* and Acca, his close companion and Bede's source for some stories, is the subject of arguably the densest praise passage applied to a living figure in the entire work (HE V, 20), introduced by reference to Wilfrid's death. Praise of his friends and followers and approving reference to their connection with the cult of St. Oswald (HE III, 13; IV, 14) also necessarily rebound to Wilfrid's credit.

We can be confident, therefore, that Bede was offering a positive view of Wilfrid, who he placed centrally within his collection of stories. What, then, was the role which he was developed to perform in the *Ecclesiastical History*? He was not introduced until early in the second half of the work, appearing first in III, 25 in relation to the synod of Whitby. This chapter was the fourth longest overall and recounts the pivotal moment when the decision was made in Northumbria to conform to Roman practices. Bede's account is an elaboration of Stephen's, giving considerable prominence to Wilfrid and underlining the probity of his advice. The young Wilfrid, fresh from his journey from Rome, is portrayed as the *discipulus* of Bishop Agilbert, the continental leader of the Romanist party, contesting on his behalf, as the more fluent speaker of English, with learned figures in the Scottish Church. Wilfrid was, we are told, a 'most learned man' who had trained in Rome, and had received in Gaul the 'ecclesiastical tonsure in the form of a crown'. Having acted as the mouthpiece of Catholicism at Whitby, he was then sent back to Gaul to be consecrated by Agilbert with other Frankish bishops assisting, *magno cum honore* ('with great honour': HE III, 28). On his return, Bede wrote:

> Now Wilfrid was made bishop, he brought to the churches of the English many Catholic doctrines and observances. With this occurring, with Catholic institutions growing day by day, all the Scots who had remained among the English either gave themselves into his hands or returned to their fatherland.

Bede was hereby representing Wilfrid as the prime mover in the Catholicisation of those parts of England hitherto influenced by Ionan Christianity just before his own birth, performing a role which had hitherto been exclusive to foreign missionaries. This account is reminiscent of Augustine's activities around 600: like Wilfrid, Augustine was the disciple of a continental figure, who had journeyed to Britain from Rome; he had been consecrated in Gaul and he confronted the insular church as a champion of Catholicism. Implicitly at least, Bede was therefore presenting Wilfrid as an English type of Augustine.

Bede was careful to stress that Wilfrid's role predated the glorious achievements of Theodore and Hadrian, to which he turned in book IV, but even when praising their contribution he made sure to recall Wilfrid's successes. Church music spread across England under their patronage but he mentioned both James the Deacon's excellence in this area (HE IV, 2, harping back to II, 20) and the first singing master in Northumbria's churches, Ædddi, who had been invited from Kent by the *reverentissimus vir* Wilfrid, 'who was the first among the bishops who were from the people of the English to introduce the Catholic way of life to the churches of the English.' This is not strictly true, of course, since several Romanist English bishops had preceded him but Wilfrid was the first English-born bishop of the Northumbrians to have been to Rome and/or to be Catholic.

This is fulsome praise which is entirely impossible to associate with any significant antagonism towards the bishop's memory on Bede's part. In contrast, Bede's account of Wilfrid's subsequent expulsion (HE IV, 12) was economical in the extreme, despite far more extended treatment by Stephen (VW 24). Following mention of a comet – perhaps included as a portent, 'a dissension occurred between king Ecgfrith and the *reverentissimus* bishop Wilfrid, the same bishop was driven from his episcopal see, and two bishops were substituted in his place'. Despite including no more regarding the dispute than the absolute minimum, his use of the superlative surely registers where Bede's sympathies lay. His reference to a portent implies that Bede saw this as of considerable significance. Ecgfrith was, of course, the figure who had donated the estates for the foundation of Wearmouth/Jarrow, so we might have expected Bede's sympathies to have lain with him. He instead gave admittedly tangential support to Wilfrid, so establishing this as the starting point for Ecgfrith's slide towards an unworthy death, adrift from the advice of those close to God (HE IV, 26 (24)).

In the next chapter Bede offered further support to Wilfrid, with a lengthy account of his mission among the South Saxons which emphasised his success as an evangelist. Such clearly validates the bishop's continuing activities and demonstrates divine support for him while in exile. This account builds on Stephen's (VW 41) but elaborates to present Wilfrid as a hero of Catholic mission. Wilfrid's triumph is underscored by the ineffectual efforts preceding his: the Mercian king Wulfhere had already had the South Saxon king baptised but made no further progress; the queen was Christian but had attempted nothing in Sussex and an Irish monastery at Bosham had made no converts. Wilfrid's coming, by contrast, initiated a veritable orgy of baptism and the establishment of a new bishopric and monastery, at Selsey. Bede wrapped Wilfrid's achievements in New Testament imagery, with his teaching this coastal people to fish, and his coming bringing to an end a three-year drought which had led to mass suicides on account of famine. The whole is peppered with biblical numbering and built on analogies already offered by Stephen to present Wilfrid as a type of Christ.

Bede then reinforced his message via a string of associated stories. First is a miracle at Selsey (HE IV, 14), recounted by the *reverentissimus antistes* Acca, which demonstrates divine approval of Wilfrid's followers without mentioning him by name. Then he refers to dire events among the South Saxons and the loss of the diocese once Wilfrid was called home (HE IV, 15), so stressing his personal significance within the wider process. There follows a brief account of the deeds of Cædwalla (HE IV, 16 (14)), who killed the South Saxon king but then emerged as the agent through whom Wilfrid was able to convert yet another people, on the Isle of Wight. Bede then moved on to describe the synod of Hatfield (HE IV, 17 (15)) but focused on the life of Æthelthryth in IV, 19 (17), in which Wilfrid appears both as witness to her virginity and as the agent through whom she became a nun. Wilfrid thereby benefits from association with one of the most highly revered female characters in the work, who had likewise separated from King Ecgfrith, exiling herself for love of Christ. Wilfrid appears again in IV, 23 (21), which is centrally devoted to the memory of St Hild: the career of her acolyte, Oftfor, takes him from Whitby to Canterbury under Theodore, then Rome, before preaching among the Hwicce and then being consecrated as their bishop by Bishop Wilfrid *beatae memoriae*, giving him some responsibility and further credit here too.

King Ecgfrith's final defeat and death were set out in HE, IV, 26 (24), then Bede included a series of stories relating to Cuthbert to terminate the book (HE, 27 (25) – 32 (30)), but even here Wilfrid was accorded honourable mention: in a passage recounting the death of the *pater reverentissimus* Cuthbert, Bede added that the *venerabilis antistes* Wilfrid held the bishopric of Lindisfarne for a year until a successor was consecrated, thereby associating Wilfrid positively with the saintly Cuthbert: Goffart's reading of this passage (1988, 291) as hostile towards Wilfrid must be rejected in the face of the language used. That does not mean that Wilfrid was necessarily innocent of any hostility towards Lindisfarne, merely that Bede was not here inclined to offer any sort of criticism.

Memories of Cuthbert still overshadow V, 1, centring on the *venerabilis* Oethilwald as his successor as hermit on Farne Island, but Oethilwald was a long-time monk at Wilfrid's Ripon, which was later Stephen's own house and ruled by one of his patrons and informants. Use of the same adjective of Oethilwald and Wilfrid serves to reinforce the inclusiveness here of Bede's vision of the Northumbrian religious community under divine protection and oversight. There then follows a sequence of miracle stories centring on John of Beverley, but Bede broke off to contextualise the second of these by reference to the return of the *reverentissimus vir* Wilfrid from exile (V, 3), so once again engaging Wilfrid in stories designed principally to underline the sanctity of another. Then, in V, 11, Bede discussed the English mission to the continental Germans, centring on the deeds of Willibrord, with whom he had already linked Wilfrid, but here remarking approvingly the *reverentissimus episcopus* Wilfrid's consecration of the eminently suitable Swithberht as bishop to the Frisians.

However, it is in HE V, 19 that Bede really focuses on Wilfrid. While there are parallels elsewhere in this work between Wilfrid and Augustine, there are implicit comparisons here between Wilfrid and Gregory, the apostle to the English. Bede quoted only five epitaphs in this work. The first and earliest was Gregory's in II, 1, followed rapidly by his servant Augustine's in II, 2, then three occur close together in book V: that of Cædwalla, the West Saxon king (V, 7); then Theodore's, from which Bede only quotes the first and last verses (V, 8), then Wilfrid's (V, 19). Inclusion of just five *in toto* marks out these individuals as exceptional within the context of this work, with Theodore somewhat peripheral as only warranting partial quotation. The common link is surely Rome: Pope Gregory spent his life there, Augustine left Rome to convert the Anglo-Saxons, Cædwalla was the first English king to die there, following baptism by Pope Sergius, Theodore travelled to England from Rome at Pope Vitalian's instigation, and Wilfrid travelled repeatedly to Rome for his education, guidance and support. These are, therefore, five Rome-centric individuals whose epitaphs were used by Bede to embed their roles within his *Historia*.

Bede likewise included only a small number of exceptionally long chapters. The longest was not of his authorship (HE I, 27) and the second longest (HE V, 21) purports not to be but the next three in length were his review of Wilfrid's life (V, 19), his description of the synod of Whitby (III, 25), in which Wilfrid played such a leading role, and his commemoration of Gregory (II, 1). Several other individuals were the subjects of shorter passages of the same kind (HE IV, 23 (21); V, 12) but only Wilfrid and Gregory were accorded extended chapter-length appreciations, and the similarity of treatment necessarily once again invites comparison of Wilfrid with Gregory.

HE V, 19 is prefaced by an account of two English kings laying down their crowns to go to Rome. This is reminiscent of Bede's assertion in IV, 5, that Oswiu had so intended and that Wilfrid was to have been his guide, so making connections back to the inception of the practice four decades earlier, to Wilfrid's benefit. Wilfrid had, of course, also been Cædwalla's counsellor, so his retirement to Rome might also be recalled here. Thereafter, this chapter is very largely a précis of Stephen's *Life*. However, even one of the longest passages in the *Ecclesiastical History* cannot encompass a *vita* of sixty-eight chapters without massive compression and Bede's selections offers lessons in what he considered important.

Apart from the pre-natal miracle in chapter I, treatment of Wilfrid's early life is comparatively inclusive, summarising Stephen's chapters 2 to 9, which cover boyhood through to ordination, on occasion using the same language (as, for example, his use of *modestus* and *bona indoles* from 2). He added, however, the detail that Ripon had previously been granted by Alhfrith to Scottish monks, so introducing Wilfrid's role as an agent of Catholicisation. He then referred back to his earlier treatment of the synod of Whitby (HE III, 25), Stephen's 10, and summarised 11, dealing with Wilfrid's consecration. He omitted the near shipwreck (12) but went on to deal with Chad's consecration to York, the excellence of his governance of the Church (on which Stephen had likewise commented), and Wilfrid's appointment on Chad's retirement (VW 14–15). To this point, Bede had included all the major events in Stephen's narrative, other than the synod which he had already described elsewhere at exceptional length and to which he here directed attention.

The next few chapters of the *vita Wilfridi* are, however, ignored. These cover restoration of the church at York (16), the building of Ripon and then

Hexham (17, 22), miracles validating those accounts (18, 23), Ecgfrith's victories (19, 20) and a general summation of Wilfrid's goodness (21). Instead, Bede jumped from Wilfrid's enthronement to his expulsion, perhaps ten years later. He addressed that in the baldest of terms, referring back to his earlier treatment, in HE IV, 13, but that too had been terse compared to Stephen's in VW 24. He then focused directly on Wilfrid's achievements as a missionary, connecting his activities in Frisia once again with those of Willibrord in the present.

Bede now moved forward to Pope Agatho in Rome, again extending Stephen's account by quoting material which Stephen only included in retrospect (VW 53). He then ignored Stephen's chapters 33 to 40, so Wilfrid's journey back and his reception in England, passing directly to notice of his conversion of the South Saxons (41) and mission to the Isle of Wight, both of which he had already described at length (HE IV, 13; 16 (14)). Stephen had neglected the latter episode, marking this as new material which redounded to Wilfrid's credit. Bede then passed over Stephen's chapters 43 and much of 44, to refer very briefly to his restoration and then exclusion once more after five years (Stephen's 44 to 47). There is nothing on his journey south via Mercia (48), or his excommunication (49), but Bede focused on his reappearance in Rome, including a letter written to the English kings (50–54). Stephen had Wilfrid wishing to remain in Rome and having to be sent back (55), which Bede omitted, but he offered extended treatment of Wilfrid's illness on the return journey at Meaux (56), a skeletal account of his recovery and return to England, including his support from southern England (57), rejection by King Aldfrith (58–59), then reconciliation with the Northumbrians following Aldfrith's death (60, 61). Bede then left out passages regarding Wilfrid's poor health, his disposition of his wealth and concerns for his monasteries (62–64), claiming merely that he lived peacefully for four years until he died at Oundle (65: this was, of course, the period when Bede knew Wilfrid best) and was then carried back to Ripon for burial (66), adding in at this point the lengthy epitaph over his tomb which Stephen had omitted (it may of course not yet have been written). The epitaph closes the chapter, omitting the post mortem miracle stories which Stephen had appended (67, 68).

Across this entire chapter, then, Bede had different objectives to those of Stephen. He was keen to depict Wilfrid as an exemplary cleric, introducing him as *antistes eximius* – 'the famous bishop', who was buried with *honoris tanto pontifici* – 'the honour befitting so great a pontiff', his character as a child was praised, his ambitions were 'celestial' and he exhibited all the virtues which contemporaries might look for in a priest, scholar and bishop. The entirety is spiced with affirmative commentary original to Bede until his consecration; thereafter, affirmation is left to successive popes, with their complimentary addresses being quoted extensively without further comment. This combination assures the reader that Wilfrid's character had been entirely worthy of the dignity of a bishop and that his consecration was beyond criticism. Thereafter affirmation centres exclusively on Wilfrid's close relationship with Rome and his work as a missionary, focusing on a minority of the chapters provided by Stephen. Bede here included his ministry to the Frisians in some detail, having not referred to it previously, and mentioned both his mission to the South Saxons and his responsibility for that also to the Isle of Wight, both of which he had dealt with already. He was thereby foregrounding Wilfrid's achievements as a missionary, both among the English and on the Continent, and stressing his responsibility for initiating work later brought to fruition by Willibrord and others. He also highlighted papal approval and the judgements made in his support, so stressing his Roman credentials. His disagreements with both English and Frankish authorities are by contrast marginalised, noted very briefly or not at all.

What comes out of this chapter is, therefore, a picture of the exemplary bishop, stressing his excellence of character, the validity of his ministry, his closeness to the Lord, his role as a champion of Roman Christianity and the centrality of his work as a missionary. Beyond a skeletal narrative, anything contentious is absent, thus rendering Wilfrid far less controversial than as described by Stephen. We are left in no doubt that Wilfrid's career was a key part of the divine plan for the English, for, as Bede reminds his audience: *Uilfrid ad suae potius, hoc est Anglorum, gentis episcopatum reseruatus*; 'Wilfrid was reserved for the episcopacy of his own people, that is of the English'.

Conclusion

Although in other, earlier works Wilfrid goes unmentioned by Bede, he was important to the *Ecclesiastical History* and depicted therein in very honourable terms. The language used shows that Bede's Wilfrid parallels other clerical heroes as a figure whose qualities should in the present be emulated. He was one of the most frequently mentioned individuals in the *Historia*, but the only one of the leading group who was English. This is fundamental to his value to Bede, for he set out in his Preface that he intended to use 'illustrious men of our race' as exemplars. In the *History of the Abbots* (3) Bede put into the mouth of King Egberht of Kent the desire to have as archbishop a learned man of his own race and language. 'English bishops for the English people' was clearly an issue with which Bede empathised and in the *Historia* he made Wilfrid its focus. Wilfrid had gone to Rome to be trained, and had then become a distinguished English mouthpiece for the promotion of Catholic practices, confounding the heretic champions of Scottish Christianity and persuading pagans in both England and on the Continent to accept baptism into the Roman Church. He was presented as the home-grown father of Roman-Englishness, therefore, via whom the English could dispense with foreign missions, becoming instead full members of the Christian world and committed to mission at home and abroad. One might suspect that Bede reinforced this characterisation via implicit parallels with both Augustine and Gregory. Wilfrid does not stand alone in this role in the *Ecclesiastical History*, for Willibrord and Ecgberht were likewise depicted implicitly as English types of Augustine and Gregory, but Wilfrid is the earliest and the most prominent, although not the first mentioned for Ecgberht has that honour, in III, 4.

Bede's intentions are most transparent in V, 19, where he had Stephen's work very much in mind; he was almost certainly leafing through it as he wrote this chapter. Instead of the sometime exile, excommunicant and hate-figure that Stephen defended, Bede portrayed Wilfrid as especially chosen by God to become the first great English advocate of Rome in England. Of course, from Bede's perspective Wilfrid was undoubtedly problematic; it is important to note that he was also supportive of several of Wilfrid's clerical opponents, including Archbishop Theodore, Bosa of York and John of Hexham. Bede accommodated them all by glossing over the divisions between them, while at the same time encouraging his audience to believe that the difficulties lay primarily between Wilfrid and successive kings, rather than Wilfrid and other churchmen.

Wilfrid's inclusion in the *Ecclesiastical History* and his prominence therein therefore required fundamental manipulation of the received story, leading Bede to under-report the controversies in which he was mired and foreground particular aspects of his career which were capable of a positive portrayal. The result is a very different version to that offered by Stephen. This is not because Bede wrote against Stephen and his patrons; on the contrary the so-called 'Wilfridians' actually emerge from the pages of the *Historia* at least as well as their opponents. One could better argue that Bede developed his Wilfrid here to please Acca than that he was writing for Acca's opponents, but in fact neither is obviously the case. Rather, his approach reflects the different ways in which Bede was seeking to utilise Wilfrid. Stephen was writing to a commission from Wilfrid's close friends and followers, to invest in his memory, to highlight his extended martyrdom at the hands of political opponents and to further the cult at Ripon and Hexham. Bede had no particular concern with these issues but was writing for a more secular audience and for essentially pastoral purposes, to raise the moral and spiritual aspirations of the secular elite and to encourage close co-operation between the secular and religious leadership. His Wilfrid was therefore an exemplary English bishop, learned, a committed missionary and the first great English champion of Rome. He kept to a minimum those aspects which did not serve his purpose, retaining sufficient of the controversy only to make his story intelligible. Bede was not attempting to inform later audiences just what was going on in ecclesiastical politics in the later seventh and early eighth centuries and he did so only to the extent that that accorded with his primary purposes. The two accounts offered by Stephen and Bede therefore provide an opportunity to explore different authorial agendas. Both authors portrayed the Wilfrid that suited their own needs, as opposed to setting out the historical figure critically as a fully formed character.

6: *Anti-Jewish Rhetoric in the* Life of Wilfrid

MARK LAYNESMITH

Stephen described his text as a *humili excusatione* ('humble apology': VW, preface) for a bishop worthy of remembrance, but the *Life of Wilfrid* reads more like an embattled defence written under fire. From the very start Stephen refers to *antiqui hostis millenos invidiae stimulos* ('the thousand envious pricks of the ancient foe': VW, preface) and the penultimate image in the *Life* is of those who *arcus tendentium et sagittas mittentium* ('drew their bow and shot their arrows': 68) against the author's fellow monks. The story Stephen narrates between these images indicates that he was clearly trying to fight back. Alongside other weapons that he used, including the quotation of papal rulings in Wilfrid's favour, one of the less obvious is the deployment of anti-Jewish rhetoric. Though encoded in a manner that renders it not necessarily immediately recognisable to the modern reader, this rhetoric features throughout the *Life* in ways that surreptitiously cast Wilfrid's opponents as types of unbelieving and sometimes persecuting Jews. However, by setting the *Life* within the context of other polemical Christian texts and Biblical commentaries of the period it is possible to make Stephen's rhetorical strategy visible and to clarify the ways in which he sought to defend his subject and to rally his audience.

Before engaging with Stephen's text though, comment should first be made concerning real (rather than imagined) Jews. There are a number of first person plural passages in the *Life* (50, 52, 53). It may be that these are merely a stylistic device designed to echo the Acts of the Apostles (Farmer 1974, 38) or they may possibly indicate Stephen's incorporation of a first-hand source (Thacker 2004c, 424), but if taken at face value these would seem to indicate that Stephen himself accompanied Wilfrid abroad. If he did so it is not inconceivable that he might have encountered Judaism as a living religion. Sadly the *Life* itself shows no interest in such realities. 'The Jews' are only mentioned explicitly twice (24, 35) and neither of these references refer to Jews living in the British Isles or elsewhere in Europe. Stephen's engagement with Judaism is then, as with many other Christian writers, entirely imaginative.

It is tempting to speculate whether Stephen's deployment of anti-Jewish rhetoric drew on the record of his martyred Biblical namesake who as a gentile reportedly castigated a council of Jewish leaders for being Christ's *proditores et homicidae* ('betrayers and murderers': Douay-Rheims translation, Acts VII, 52). Indeed elsewhere I have speculated that 'Stephen' might have been a pen name (Laynesmith 2000, 178). Nevertheless, Stephen was not the only Anglo-Saxon author to use anti-Jewish rhetoric and indeed it can be evidenced in most periods of Church history often regrettably with detrimental effects to Jews (Schweitzer, 1994; Scheil 2004). Stephen's use, however, was particularly related to the vexed issue of paschal orthodoxy. In this he was not alone, for the idea of Judaism appears to have loomed large in the imaginations of a number of seventh- and eighth-century insular writers as they sought both to understand themselves and to respond to the diverse forms Christianity had taken in the British Isles. Stephen's text is not the first to use anti-Jewish rhetoric in this particular manner though it is, prior to Bede's related usage in the *Ecclesiastical History*, perhaps the most extensive example of its kind (Smith 1998; Foley and Higham 2009).

'Quartodecimans' as Types of Jews

One point of entry to Stephen's use of anti-Jewish rhetoric is by way of an examination of the term 'quartodeciman'. In his post-Whitby account of Wilfrid's purge of allegedly schismatic bishops, Stephen has his hero allege: *sunt enim hic in Britannia multi episcopi quorum nullum meum est accusare, quamvis veraciter sciam quod <u>quattuordecimanni</u> sunt ut Brittones et Scotti* ('now there are in Britain many bishops whom it is not for me to criticize, but I know for a fact that they are *Quartodecimans* like the Britons and the Irish': VW 12). Wilfrid's certitude however is misplaced. In so far as the term is technically understood none of the participants of the conference at Whitby would have qualified for the term. So what is its significance and why use it? In origin the term referred to Christians who continued the Johannine tradition of celebrating Easter on the same day as the Jewish Passover (XIV Nisan), which meant that Easter could be celebrated on any day of the week (for background see Wallis 1999, xxxiv–lxiii). These Christians came to be labelled 'quartodecimans'. It is significant to note though that there appears to have been some slippage of meaning regarding the word. By the fourth century the term seems not merely to designate those who always held Easter on the same day as the Passover, but it was also being applied more loosely to those who, though agreeing that Easter should only be celebrated on a Sunday, nevertheless were prepared to allow that Easter Sunday might sometimes coincide with the Passover. Thus the term came to designate those Christians whose Easter Sunday fell within XIV–XX Nisan parameters.

The Council of Nicaea seems to have been concerned that these Christians were in danger of undermining the novelty of the Christian revelation and that their choice of dating suggested that Christ's death and resurrection added nothing more to what the Passover had already revealed and achieved. Eusebius' *Life of Constantine* records the emperor warning the churches that Nicaea had decided 'it was decreed unworthy to observe that most sacred festival in accordance with the practice of the Jews; having sullied their own hands with a heinous crime, such bloodstained men are as one might expect mentally blind ... let there be nothing in common between you and the detestable mob of Jews! We have received from the Saviour another way' (Cameron and Hall 1999, 128). Thus according to Nicaea, Easter Sunday could never be held on XIV Nisan and those who did allow it to happen, even occasionally, were guilty of quartodecimanism.

Quartodecimanism in its original Johannine sense was never an issue for insular Christians. Indeed it is unlikely that at the time there were Christians anywhere in Europe who deliberately chose to celebrate Easter on the same day as Passover. However in the looser secondary sense used at Nicaea, as referring to Christians whose Easter might occasionally coincide with Passover if Passover fell on a Sunday, then the term could have some application for Bishop Colmán and his followers who relied upon the ancient XIV–XX Nisan dates for calculating the Easter limits (so HE III, 25, although perhaps due to scribal error Stephen ascribes to Colmán the rather odd limits of XIV–XXII Nisan: VW 10). Stephen puts into Colmán's mouth the defence that *patres nostri et antecessores eorum, manifeste spiritu sancto inspirati, ut erat Collumcillae, <u>XIIII luna</u> die dominica pascha celebrandum sanxerunt, exemplum tenentes Iohannis apostoli et evangelistae* ('our fathers and their predecessors, plainly inspired by the Holy Spirit as was Columba, ordained the celebration of Easter on *the fourteenth day of the moon*, if it was a Sunday, following the example of the Apostle and Evangelist John'). By contrast Wilfrid appears to have argued for XV–XXI Nisan limits so as to avoid Easter Sunday ever coinciding with the Passover (so HE III, 25 although interestingly Stephen in fact omits to tell us which dates Wilfrid endorsed). Thus Colmán and his supporters were open to the charge of quartodecimanism, albeit only in its Nicaean usage. To the unsympathetic eyes of a critic, it could serve to mark them out as quasi-Jews or Judaizing Christians who undervalued the novelty of the Christian revelation.

Bede himself was careful not to use the term in his *History*, and neither does Stephen actually employ the word in his account of Whitby's discussions. The label only appears *after* Whitby where it is chiefly used to describe those who opposed Wilfrid's elevation to the episcopacy (VW 14, 15). Stephen's use of 'quartodeciman' suggests that though he knew of its strict irrelevance to the paschal dispute, its wider rhetorical associations were useful to his purposes. It functioned, I suggest, as code for those supporters of an old regime, those types of Jews or Judaizers, who were denying the fullness of a new revelation.

Stephen was not the only person after the Council of Nicaea to use the term in this way. In the late-sixth century an anonymous Frankish author writing against the Celtic-84 cycle used by Columbanus (which relied upon XIV–XX Nisan limits) darkly referred to *eos, qui cum in superficie Christiani videantur, <u>per Iudaici</u> sensus impietatem corpus Christi, id est ecclesiam, suis schismatibus* *scindare non metuunt* ('those persons who, though they appear superficially as Christians, yet in the ungodliness of their leanings *towards Judaism* do not fear to rend the body of Christ, that is the Church, by their schisms': Walker 1957, 206–07). Thirty years later, in a letter to the abbot of Iona, the rhetorical link resurfaces. The author, Cummian, referred to a defender of the Celtic-84 cycle as *paries dealbatus, traditionem seniorum seruare se simulans ... quem Dominus, ut spero, percutiet quoquo modo uouerit* ('a certain *whited wall ... pretending to preserve the traditions of our elders ...* I hope *the Lord shall strike him down in whatever way he wills'*: Walsh and Ó Crónín 1988, 92–93). Cummian here combined two quotations. One is from the Gospel of Mark in which those who pretend *traditionem seniorum servare* are identified with the Pharisees and the scribes (Mark VII, 1–9). The other reference comes from the Acts of the Apostles which recounts an acrimonious exchange between Paul and the Jewish High Priest during which the Apostle declares: *percutiet te Deus paries dealbate* ('God shall *strike* thee, thou *whited wall'*: Douay-Rheims translation, Acts XXIII, 3). Cummian's Biblical quotations were thus both drawn from Christian-Jewish confrontations and his use of them seems to have been to associate his own opponents with the Jewish authorities who opposed Paul and Christ.

The imaginative association between paschal heterodoxy and Judaizing is repeated in a papal letter of 640 to the Irish: *repperimus quosdam prouinciae uestrae contra orthodoxam fidam nouam ex ueteri heresim renouare conantes pascha nostrum, in quo immolatus est Christus, nebulosa caligine refutantes et XIIII luna cum Hebreis celebrare nitentes* ('we [have] discovered that certain men of your kingdom were attempting to revive a new heresy out of an old one and, befogged with mental blindness, to reject our Easter in which Christ was sacrificed for us, contending *with the Hebrews* that it should be celebrated on the fourteenth day of the moon': HE II, 19). Bede himself appears to have been somewhat embarrassed by the suggestion that the Irish were authentic Johannine quartodecimans for he excised the word in his transcription. He did however retain the Pope's allegation that a XIV Nisan celebration would indicate a theological undervaluation of Easter and of grace, and be indicative of (to his mind) the quasi-Jewish legalistic Christian heresy Pelagianism (Ó Crónín, 1985).

The anti-Jewish rhetoric surfaces again in 672 in Aldhelm's letter to Gerontius. Aldhelm alleges that the British bishops *cum Judeis paschale sacramentum celebrant* (Ehwald, 1919, 483; 'observe the paschal solemnity ... *along with the Jews'*: Lapidge and Herren, 1979, 157). Like Cummian, Aldhelm developed this link by likening the refusal of the British bishops to share food with their Anglo-Saxon neighbours as being akin to those Jews who, unlike Christ, refused to eat with sinners: *totum hoc contra evangelii praecepta secundum Phariseorum inanes traditiones agere noscuntur* (Ehwald, 1919, 484; 'they are known to do all this contrary to the teachings of the Gospel according to *the hollow traditions of the Pharisees*': Lapidge and Herren, 1979, 158). Even closer in time to the *Life* penitential material probably originating with Theodore of Canterbury ordered complete excommunication *si quis contempserit Nicenum concilium et pecerit Pascha cum Iudaeis* (Van Rhijn, 2009, 74; if anyone 'flouts the Council of Nicaea and keeps Easter *with the Jews*': McNeill and Gamer, 1938, 188).

In strict terms each of these quartodeciman allegations was simply untrue. As Charles Plummer (1896, II, 114) noted, the slur 'was always a handy stick with which to beat the Celtic dog'. What Plummer perhaps overlooked was the precise *nature* of the slur for by the time Stephen came to use the term it had for nearly four hundred years served to associate those who bore the label with Judaism or Judaizing. Still, one might argue that on their own too much ought not to be made of Stephen's quartodeciman references. After all Stephen did only use the term three times. However there are in the *Life* a number of other indications that he was resorting more widely to anti-Jewish rhetoric for, like Cummian, in addition to drawing upon the anti-Jewish rhetorical baggage associated with the quartodeciman libel, Stephen also appears to have utilised specific Biblical quotations and allusions in order to frame Wilfrid's opponents typologically as kinds of Jews.

Stephen's Old Testament Supercessionist Typology

Stephen's is a text replete with biblical typology (Foley 1992, 21–70, 137–139). Naturally any hagiographer would wish to align a saint with biblical archetypes. However among Stephen's numerous typological matches his use of three Old Testament figures stands out in that his reference to them is more than passing. These are Samuel, David and Jacob. What they have in common is that all of them are younger characters who supplant their apparently divinely-appointed elders.

Wilfrid and Samuel

At the start of the *Life* Stephen relates how the young Wilfrid was recommended by Queen Eanflæd to Cudda *ut sibi ministraret et Deo serviret* ('to minister to him and to serve God': VW 2). After Wilfrid is shown taking his place as an adopted son at Lindisfarne Stephen concludes the story with a biblical allusion. Wilfrid *partem cum Samuele Heli sacerdoti ministrante benedictionis accipere meruit* ('therefore deserved to receive a share of the blessing which *Samuel* received when he ministered to Eli the priest': VW 2). The underlying biblical reference is to the story of the boy Samuel's dedication by his mother to the Temple of Shiloh. Stephen's allusion sets up a number of interesting parallels not least between Wilfrid and Samuel, but also between Cudda and Eli, Lindisfarne and the Temple, and even between Samuel's mother Hannah and

Wilfrid's patron Queen Eanfled. Stephen's reason for mentioning Samuel is not mere flattery for, if followed through, the reference functions to explain Wilfrid's wider significance. This can be seen by a closer inspection of the story. Having told of Samuel's arrival the biblical passage goes on to record God's dissatisfaction with Eli's corrupt sons and the divine decision to remove Eli's heirs from the hereditary priesthood. In their place God intends to raise up a more faithful priest and to establish his heirs as a dynasty (I Samuel II, 35). Two chapters later God's judgement comes to pass, Eli and his sons die, and Samuel rises to succeed them.

In Stephen's account Wilfrid's similar receipt of God's blessing and consequent rise to power comes after his eventual installation as bishop at York. In a climactic and deeply symbolic chapter, Stephen invites the reader to pause and reflect on Wilfrid's dizzying rise: *tunc sententia Dei de Samuhele et omnibus sanctis in eo implebatur: Qui, inquit, me honorificat, honorificabo eum* ('then the word of the Lord *concerning Samuel* and all the saints was fulfilled in him: *"Them that honour me, I will honour"'*: VW 16). Stephen's reference here to Samuel seems designed to remind us of the earlier promise and the link is reinforced by the careful choice of biblical allusion. The phrase that Stephen applies to Wilfrid, 'them that honour me, I will honour' echoes God's speech to Eli foretelling Samuel's rise, *quicumque glorificaverit me glorificabo eum* (I Samuel II, 30). Stephen's use of Samuel as a biblical antetype not only neatly frames Wilfrid's own rise to power, it also serves to provide an explanatory paradigm to demonstrate how someone from within an earlier religious system could nevertheless challenge and eventually supplant it. It is a remarkably diplomatic strategy for it ascribes a certain degree of reverence to the Eli figure (Cudda) but it is also simultaneously a damning one, for it writes off Cudda's 'heirs' (the Irish church in Northumbria) as corrupt and warranting replacement.

Both Samuel and Eli are of course Jewish figures. On the face of it one would appear hard put to read anti-Jewish rhetoric into Stephen's use of them. Nevertheless, Christian biblical commentators had long been adept at prising Jewish figures out of their original contexts and making them stand for quite different values. This is the case with Samuel and Eli for by Stephen's time the story of Eli's replacement had come to symbolise the replacement of Judaism by gentile Christianity. Commenting on the significance of the two men in his commentary on Samuel, Bede stated:

> *sub figura Samuhelis de domino sulatore summo uidelicet ac uero*
> *pontifice debet intellegi quia nimirum sicut Samuhel defuncto Heli*
> *successit in sacerdotium non de stirpe Aaron sed de alia Leui*
> *familia electus ... ita mediator Dei et hominum ut esset nobis*
> *pontifex non de Leui sed de alia itique tribu, id est Iuda, carnis*

originem sumpsit aliam quam legalem hostiam, id est ipsam suam carnem, obtulit patri pro nobis alios quam de genere Aaron pontificatus sui reliquit <u>heredes filios uidelicet gratiae noui testamenti de uniuersa gentium natione collectos</u> (Hurst, 1962, 296).

'Samuel must be understood as a figure of the Lord, Saviour and true High Priest for this clear reason: just as Samuel succeeded the dead Eli to the priesthood, having been chosen not from Aaron's lineage, but from another household, namely Levi's ... so also did the mediator of God and humans [ie Christ] take his fleshly origin not from Levi, but from another tribe, namely Judah, so that he might be our priest. He offered the Father a sacrifice other than what the Law required, namely his own flesh; he left for us heirs of his priesthood other than those of Aaron's line, *namely the sons of grace of the New Covenant, gathered from every Gentile nation*': Foley & Holder 1999, 91–92).

For Bede Samuel not only personally represented Christ, but the contrast between his Levitical lineage and Eli's Aaronic origins signified the transference of the spiritual inheritance from the Jews to the gentiles. In likening Wilfrid to Samuel, Stephen may have been drawing not merely on a particular biblical story, but also upon the deeper theological resonances this story had come to possess to colour his interpretation of Wilfrid's rise to power and to augment the use of the quartodeciman slur in characterising Wilfrid's enemies as types of Jews.

Wilfrid and David

A similar supercessionary typology seems to obtain in Stephen's use of the story of David and his predecessor Saul. An early allusion notes the similarity between David and Wilfrid: *<u>sicut autem David puer electus a Domino est</u> et, per Samuelem unctus, dona prophetiae accipere post multas temptationes meruit; ita sanctus Wilfrithus presbitur post multas benedictiones sanctorum Dei tam multiplices donationes coram Deo et hominibus, quam enumerare nullus potest* ('*thus as David was chosen of God while a boy* and anointed by Samuel and, after many tribulations, was judged worthy to receive the gift of prophecy, so Wilfrid the priest, after many blessings from the saints of God, received so many gifts in the presence of God and men that no one can enumerate them': VW 9). Like David, Wilfrid's actual rise to power takes place when he is older. The Davidic parallel thus lies waiting to be picked up just at the moment of his elevation to York. Prior to this, having written of Wilfrid's refusal to accept consecration by *quattuordecimanni* (12), Stephen tells of his journey to the continent for valid consecration. On his return Stephen relates that Wilfrid discovered that an envious King Oswiu, inspired by *quartamdecimanam partem* ('the Quartodeciman party': 14), had had Chad consecrated in his place. According to Stephen Wilfrid only claimed his rightful See three years later when (and here they are mentioned for a third time) the *quattuordecimanni* were rebutted by Archbishop Theodore (15). Stephen's account is probably rather imaginative. It glosses over the fact that, according to Bede at least, Chad was neither archbishop of York nor metropolitan. Further the short-lived episcopacy of Tuda is omitted. Nevertheless Stephen's version economically reshapes history as a simple story of the replacement of a false authority (Chad) by a rightful one (Wilfrid) and the story ultimately condenses in an allusion to David and Saul. Having been enthroned Wilfrid has Chad sent to Mercia, apparently with no hard feelings on either part, with Stephen commenting *tunc sanctus pontifex noster secundum praeceptum Domini non malum pro malo, sed bonum, ut David Saulo, pro malo reddens, qui dixit, non mittam manum meam in christum Domini* ('then our holy bishop, in accordance with the command of the Lord, returned good for evil, not evil for evil, just as *David* did to Saul when he said *"I will not stretch forth my hand against the Lord's anointed"*': 15).

Like the Eli-Samuel analogy, the Saul-David reference is fascinatingly diplomatic. As a type of Saul, Chad is at least granted a degree of divine approval. But importantly it does create a parallel between Saul, whose appointment in the biblical account is said to have been at the behest of the sinful and ignorant Israelites, and Chad, whose appointment Stephen ascribes to the sinful and ignorant demands of those quasi-Jewish characters 'the quartodecimans' (cf I Samuel VIII). Wilfrid emerges as a type of David, divinely approved and appropriately replacing an earlier discredited regime, but apparently by divine action rather than human political machination. Stephen's choice of quotation, *non mittam manum meam in christum Domini*, recalls the account of Saul's violent pursuit of David and the latter's refusal to respond in kind (...*ut mittam manum meam in* eum quoniam *christum Domini* est: I Samuel XXIV, 7). In particular the text refers to David's refusal to strike Saul whilst the king drops his trousers to defecate in a cave in which David is hiding. Typologically Stephen's use of the passage thus masterfully invokes the idea of the divine inevitability of Wilfrid's elevation, depicts his hero as patient and pious, and moreover carefully discredits Chad with scatological humour.

Though Saul and David are of course both Jewish figures, nevertheless like Eli and Samuel their relationship could be interpreted as one emblematic of the relationship between Judaism and Christianity. Bede remarked in a homily that *Dauid pro Saule regnum Israheliticae gentis sortitur humilis innocens et mitis exul porro ille cuius iniusta diu persecutione cruciabatur ... in Saule Iudaeos persequentes in David Christum et ecclesiam significari* (Hurst 1955, 100; 'David was allotted the kingdom of the Israelites in place of Saul. He was a humble, innocent and gentle exile, yet he was for a long time tormented by [Saul's] unjust persecution ... *Saul signifies the persecuting Jews, and David signifies Christ and the Church*': Martin and Hurst 1991, I, 141). Once more, if one listens to Stephen's use of scripture with an ear for the wider resonances, it appears he may be drawing on anti-Jewish rhetoric.

Wilfrid and Jacob

More briefly, the links that Stephen forged between Wilfrid and Jacob seem to continue the theme. Jacob is a curious choice, a rather unsavoury and wily biblical character but whose most obvious merit is his alternative name: Israel. In linking Wilfrid with Jacob, Stephen thus casts his subject in the form of patriarch and founder of a holy people. Wilfrid's monastic communities thereby take on the guise of tribes within a new Israel, or as Stephen describes his colleagues with an allusion to Jeremiah's description of Israel *vineam familiae Domini electam* ('the elect vineyard of the Lord's family': 68; *vineam electam*: Jeremiah II, 21). Jacob however is another example of a younger figure replacing a presumed natural heir. There are three allusions to him in the *Life*. Twice at the start Wilfrid is referred to as receiving blessings from parents and kinsmen *sicut Iacob* (2, 3). The corresponding biblical episode, Isaac's blessing of Jacob, significantly refers to Jacob's supplanting of Esau ('be thou lord of thy brethren, and let thy mother's children bow down before thee': Douay-Rheims translation, Genesis XXVII, 29). The link between Wilfrid and Jacob is reiterated a third time when Stephen describes Wilfrid on his death bed: *postquam pauca locutus est, benedixit eos, sicut Iacob benedixit filios suos* ('after speaking a few words he blessed them, just *as Jacob* blessed his sons': 65).

Aside from the generally edifying nature of the Jacob/Wilfrid association, Stephen may also have seen in Jacob something of a template for Wilfrid: a restless and powerful patriarch whose surprise divine election steered the line of blessing away from its earlier course towards a new holy family among whose number Stephen counted himself. However the Esau-Jacob relationship was also susceptible to an anti-Jewish supercessionist reading. Indeed this particular patriarchal fraternal conflict was iconic in Paul's reflection on the relationship between the older Jewish and younger gentile peoples. Indeed his discussion on the subject took as its departure the verse *Iacob dilexi Esau autem odio habui* ('Jacob I have loved but Esau I have hated': Douay-Rheims translation, Romans IX, 13). In turn, Paul's meditation became a springboard for later writers. Bede, for example, (quoting Augustine) explained Paul's reflections on Esau and Jacob thus: 'As to the words, "The elder shall serve the younger," scarcely anyone among us has taken this to mean anything else than that the elder people of the Jews was going to serve the younger Christian people' (Hurst 1999, 85). Such an understanding of the typological interpretation of Jacob ought then to be considered in reading Stephen's text. In linking Wilfrid with Jacob the shadow of anti-Jewish rhetoric lurks once more in the background with Wilfrid again playing the role of the younger Christian heir upstaging his quasi-Jewish elders.

Stephen and New Testament Christian-Jewish Conflict

Thus far in addition to the polemical use of the title 'quartodeciman' several typological examples of anti-Jewish rhetoric have been advanced. These have all been drawn from Christian interpretations of Old Testament figures. The image of Wilfrid as a zealous young man in conflict with a corrupt older religion makes its most obvious presence felt in a set of quotations that figure in both Old and New Testaments. In the description of the restoration of the church in York Stephen describes Wilfrid's reaction on seeing the dilapidated building thus: *videns itaque haec omnia sanctus pontifex noster, secundum Danielem horruit spiritus eius in eo, quod domus Dei orationes quasi speluncam latronem factam agnovit* ('when our holy Bishop saw all this his spirit was vexed within him, as *Daniel's* was, because he saw that the house of God and the *house of prayer* had become like *a den of thieves*': XVI). Alongside the passing Daniel reference, Stephen's allusion to Jesus' so-called cleansing of the Temple is arguably unmistakable: the phrases *domus … orationes* and *speluncam latronem* repeat Jesus' own words (Matthew XXI, 13; Mark XI, 17; Luke XIX, 46). Stephen it would appear was once more intimating that Wilfrid, as a purging Christ-type, was sweeping away a corrupt quasi-Jewish system, a system that by this point Stephen has identified explicitly three times with the term 'quartodeciman'.

Stephen's supercessionist rhetoric is however only one half of his anti-Jewish repertoire. While serving to interpret Wilfrid's reforming agenda and his successes, this rhetorical ploy of associating Wilfrid's enemies with Judaism also functions to make sense of Wilfrid's set backs. To illustrate this we may focus further on Stephen's use of Christ and also of Paul.

Wilfrid and Christ

Naturally any hagiographer would wish to forge parallels between his subject and Christ. Stephen's deployment of Christ-typology though is particularly focused on interpreting Wilfrid's political failures. This can be seen most explicitly just prior to Wilfrid's imprisonment when the saint comforts his followers with examples of adversity borne with patience, citing several Old Testament figures by name, but climaxing with the supreme example: *legimus quoque in novi Testamento pastorem magnum ovium et totius ecclesiae caput Iesum Christum a Iudaeis crucifixum et discipulus suos dispersos* ('we read also in the New Testament that the great *Shepherd* of the *sheep* and Head of the whole Church, *Jesus Christ, was crucified by the Jews* and his disciples *scattered*':

35). Here in addition to the explicit reference to the crucifixion Stephen alludes to the final words of the Last Supper where Christ predicts his betrayal and quotes to his disciples a verse from Zechariah: *percutiam <u>pastorem</u> et <u>dispergentur</u> <u>oves</u> gregis* ('I will strike the *shepherd*, and the *sheep* of the flock will be *scattered*': Douay-Rheims translation, Matthew XXVI, 31; Mark XIV, 27). In the following chapter, as Wilfrid is escorted to prison, Stephen reinforces the Christ-typology by describing him being led *quasi <u>ovem ad occasionem</u> qui <u>non aperuit os suum</u>* ('as a lamb to the slaughter, which opened not his mouth': 36). Though this image was originally used of the suffering servant in Isaiah, it was quickly taken up by Christians to describe Christ himself (*<u>ovis ad occisionem</u> ductus est ... sine voce sic <u>non aperuit os suum</u>*: Acts VIII, 32; Isaiah LIII, 7). Stephen's successive references to Christ in these two chapters thus serve to interpret Wilfrid's arrest in the light of Christ's own imprisonment.

Those who hold Christ under arrest in the Gospel accounts are of course the Roman authorities who are working in conjunction with the Jewish ones. In his account of Wilfrid's arrest Stephen explicitly likens Iurminburh, the wife of Ecgfrith the king who imprisons the saint, to Pontius Pilate's wife. Both women suffer nightmares during their sleep: *regina illa nocte arrepta a daemone, <u>sicut uxor Pilati</u>* ('the queen became possessed with a devil that same night ... *like Pilate's wife*': VW 39; cf Matthew XXVII, 19). Stephen's setting up of these Wilfrid/Christ, Ecgfrith/Pilate links also encourage a further imaginative development, for they invite the reader to reflect who in the story might function as a parallel to the Jewish authorities who work with the Romans. Who precisely Stephen wants the reader to consider the quasi-Jewish authorities to be is not clear. He refers to Ecgfrith summoning *omnibus principibus* ('all the chief men') as well as *servis Dei* ('the servants of God') to a synod to listen to Wilfrid, and says that the decision to imprison Wilfrid came at *iusiones regis et eius consiliatorum cum consensu episcoporum, qui eius episcopatum tenebant* ('the command of the king and his counsellors with the consent of the bishops who held his bishopric': 34). This miscellaneous group of clerics and elders, among whom were Theodore's three appointed bishops Bosa, Eata and Eadhæd, would seem if pressed to play for Stephen the role of Jewish Sanhedrin alongside the Pilate-like Ecgfrith. Whilst Wilfrid is thus cast in the role of Christ, Theodore's bishops occupy the role of corrupt Jewish rulers.

Wilfrid and Paul

Stephen's strategy of aligning Wilfrid's enemies with Jewish authorities is even more clearly seen in his use of allusions to the Apostle Paul. For a text whose ideology hinges on Petrine orthodoxy, it is surprising to note that the Biblical character with whom Wilfrid is associated at least as much as with Peter (if not more) is the Apostle Paul. Stephen explicitly links Wilfrid by name, or title, to

Paul at least six times (3, 5, 14, 21, 24, 26, 41). Key life events are said to link the two, for example with Stephen noting that just as Paul after his conversion went to the fount of his faith, Jerusalem, to learn more, so Wilfrid too went to the fount of his faith, Rome, for further study (5). As a bishop, Stephen says that Wilfrid conforms to ideals expressed in Pauline texts: he is a *benignum, sobrium, modestum ... prudentem, non vinolentum* ('kind, sober, discrete ... prudent, not given to wine': 9; cf Titus I, 7–8, I Timothy III, 3). Twice the result of Wilfrid's successful tours of evangelism is that *magnum ostium fidei ... apertum est* ('a great door of faith was opened': 14, 41), a description used of Paul's own missionary successes (Acts XIV, 26; I Corinthians XVI, 9). The list of minor resemblances is much longer (Foley 1992, 138–9; Laynesmith 2000, 175–6). Indeed it may even be that a Pauline formula of 'foreknowing, predestination, calling, justification and glorification' may pattern the overall structure of Stephen's description of Wilfrid's *Life* (Foley 1992, 21–52).

The association between Wilfrid and the Apostle Paul has though a significance beyond the norms of hagiographical name-dropping. One of the most explicit episodes in which Wilfrid is linked with Paul takes place after the Council of Hertford. There Stephen describes Wilfrid's decision to appeal to Rome as being precisely analogous to Paul's own appeal to Rome following his dispute with the Jewish authorities in Jerusalem. After the decision to split his See three ways, Wilfrid is shown attempting to defend himself before Ecgfrith and Theodore. Stephen relates that their response is freely to admit the bishop's innocence whilst continuing to deny him justice: *illi responderunt famosum verbum ... 'Nullam criminis culpam in aliquo nocendi tibi ascribimus'* ('They made ... a scandalous reply ... "we do not ... ascribe to you any criminal offence"': 24). Stephen then says of Wilfrid, that *iudicium apostolicae sedis magis elegit, <u>sicut Paulus apostolus, sine causa dampnatus a Iudaeis, Caesarem apellavit</u>* ('he sought the judgement of the Apostolic See, *as the Apostle Paul, when he had been condemned by the Jews without cause, appealed to Caesar'*: 24; cf Acts XXIV–XXV). As in the earlier link between Christ's arrest at the hands of the Jewish authorities, so here too Stephen can be shown by making his hero a type of Paul to be casting Wilfrid's opponents as types of Jewish adversaries with Theodore perhaps playing the Jewish High Priest Ananias opposite Ecgfrith as Roman governor. The use of this Jewish imagery enables Stephen to interpret Wilfrid's difficulties as essentially a continuation of his earlier struggles with his quasi-Jewish opponents. After this key episode, Stephen's frequent allusions to Wilfrid as a type of Paul throughout his several journeys to and from Rome, and importantly during his period of imprisonment where there are a number of parallels between Wilfrid and Paul (Laynesmith 2000, 176), function to maintain this imaginary interpretation of Wilfrid's troubles. They serve to cement his various political clashes within an ideology of

Jewish-Christian conflict and to cast his opponents as types of Jews.

Conclusion

Doubtless to modern readers Stephen's use of anti-Jewish rhetoric appears simply distasteful. However this should not obscure the fact that alongside his other apologetic techniques it does serve two important functions. One is that it acts as a biblical hermeneutical key to make sense of Wilfrid's career. Stephen interprets Wilfrid's life by showing how his story works in parallel with the stories of the turbulent confrontations Christ and Paul had with the Jewish authorities of their day. The stories of Samuel, David and Jacob, and the charge of quartodecimanism work in a similar way, albeit with a further intervening layer of typological interpretation. Wilfrid is thus shown to be the true replacement of a corrupt system, a system staffed by individuals who may be likened to those perennially stubborn and unbelieving biblical Jewish figures, who mysteriously and maliciously acted against the rightful representatives of the New Covenant, Christ and Paul.

The second important function of such rhetoric is one of encouragement. If Wilfrid suffered at the hands of his enemies, Stephen is able to assure his readers that for the faithful it was ever thus. But in likening Wilfrid to various biblical figures, Stephen can further demonstrate that right ultimately prevailed. David *did* triumph over Saul; Christ *did* rise from the dead despite the machinations of the Jewish leaders. Wilfrid, too, ultimately triumphed, and one particularly notes the significance Stephen may have seen in the apparent timing of Wilfrid's final exoneration at Rome as falling *in sancto pascha, tertia die* ('at Holy Eastertide, on the third day': VW 53). Thus if Wilfrid, like his biblical predecessors, can be shown ultimately to have been victorious over his enemies, indeed even to have been resurrected, so too might Wilfrid's surviving communities have hope in their own struggles. Centuries of supercessionist anti-Jewish rhetoric provide the force that invigorates Stephen's ultimate message to his community that despite hardship it is inevitable that they too will triumph, a point underlined by Stephen's choice of final words borrowed from a Psalm of vindication: *nos autem in nomine Domini magnificabimur* ('But "we shall be magnified in the name of the Lord"': 68; Psalm XIX, 6 (XX, 5)).

7: *Prophets Shining in Dark Places: Biblical Themes and Theological Motifs in the* Vita Sancti Wilfridi

SANDRA DUNCAN

When Stephen of Ripon described the building of Bishop Wilfrid's great monastery at Hexham he emphasised that its foundations were laid deep in the earth. In more ways than one this emphasis sums up Stephen's view of Wilfrid's Church which, of all those portrayed in the Northumbrian lives of this period, is probably grounded most deeply in the real world. The Church of Wilfrid as viewed by Stephen is one in which leaders interfere, churchmen play at politics and are seduced by corruption and church congregations are made up of a mixture of people with very few saints and very many sinners.

For Augustine of Hippo the Church was the city of God. According to his idea, two cities, one of God and the second of the devil, existed side by side. Within the city of God, as well as without, however, there are those destined both for damnation and salvation. According to Stephen, it was this church, containing both saints and sinners, on which, from his birth, Wilfrid was destined to shed light and it was his role as bishop which was obviously the dominant theme of the whole *Life*. The work, therefore, had to deal with the central problem of the doctrine of the Church, namely the tension which existed between an idealised communion of saints and the harsh reality that the *ecclesia mundi* was made up of fallen humankind.

Wilfrid may not be the most popular of saints but as a conduit for viewing the realities of the Church his story is arguably more realistic, instructive and useful than the more idealised Cuthbert and as such it has been mined for information about the interplay between leaders of different ecclesiastical factions and between the state and the Church. Traditionally this has meant concentrating on the parts of the work that have seemed the most accessible to the modern mind – i.e. the straightforward narrative parts – and rather passing by the passages that contain the obscure and the miraculous.

This approach, however, misses the all too salient fact that Stephen, whoever else he may have been, was a churchman. He was not interested in recording history for posterity; he wanted to place the founder and patron of his monastic community within the wider communion of the saints and that necessarily straddled the interface between the politics and events of the kingdoms of this world and the truths and realities of the Kingdom of God. This means that those events that also straddled the two realities and allowed the divine to break into this world, namely the miraculous, were actually of the most significance to him. Whilst it is obviously true that Stephen wished to justify Wilfrid, it is also true that, in order to achieve this, he needed to do more than merely defend the bishop's stance within a temporary and shifting set of events; he needed to show his place within the eternal will and purpose of God. To this end it may be claimed that the pre-eminent theme of the *Life of Wilfrid* is the Church and Stephen's purpose in writing is to delineate how the saint's activities brought the true Church to Northumbria.

The Concept of Signa *and Biblical Exegesis*

In order to appreciate how a hagiographer such as Stephen conveyed to his audience the interplay between this world and the next it is necessary to look beyond the words used and to enter into the Augustinian world of signs. Augustine's first discussion of signs was in *De magistro* which was written in about 389 but his developed teaching is found in *De doctrina christiana* which was written over a period of twenty years between 396 and 426. The western world of this time was one which was acutely aware of, and constantly on the lookout for, 'signs' of the presence of the spiritual in the material world. Generally speaking the 'sign' was held to be that which signified something other than itself. Augustine was interested in the signs themselves as well as what they signified but as the years passed, interest in the West became almost exclusively concerned with the figurative meaning of things (Evans 1984, 53). Typical in this respect was Gregory the Great for whom what mattered most was not word or the thing signified by the word but what the thing itself signified – in other words the deepest, the spiritual, level of meaning (Markus 1996, 67).

Augustine's discussion about signs in *De doctrina christiana* was a precursor to a discussion about the way to read and understand the Scriptures. The medieval church in the Latin West was undoubtedly most influenced by the allegorizing Alexandrian School of biblical exegesis. The allegorical method, in which the word as a sign was merely a pointer to deeper meanings, was the tradition normally espoused by Bede. As a result of the Fall, God was seen as no longer able to communicate directly with mankind and so was forced to use analogies based on physical and concrete ideas. At the root of this is the shared assumption, to quote David Dawson, 'that everywhere matter and spirit interpenetrate' (Dawson 1998, 356).

What all of this means is that when reading the hagiographical works of this period the reader should be at least aware that the writers were viewing their world through semiological lenses. Robert Markus observed that, for both Augustine and Gregory the Great, their 'habits of reading the biblical text had profound repercussions' for the way they read their worlds (Markus 1996, 29) and, beyond this, the shared word and imagery associations of Stephen and much of his audience, derived from lives immersed in daily study of the Bible and informed by interpretative texts from the Church Fathers, meant that this must have impacted on them until they became an almost instinctive way of expression. Frances Young (1997, 217–47) has suggested that hagiography was among the various genres of Christian writing which had an on-going exegetical function as a way of interpreting the Bible for the Church, using biblical types and metaphors to create Christian heroes and thus bolster the Christian identity.

For the purposes of this paper I am proposing to look in detail at a few chapters of the *Life of Wilfrid* to draw from them an overview of the doctrine of the Church as it was understood by Stephen, using as a tool the exegetical tradition that would have been known by a monk in the Latin West at this time, including principally Augustine, Jerome, Ambrose, Cassian and Gregory the Great and also adding Bede as a representative of contemporary and relatively local thought. It needs always to be borne in mind, however, that medieval writers avoided conscious innovation and that, for a text to be authoritative, it needed to be grounded on what had gone before, so biblical exegesis was a cumulative process with each new generation accepting the readings of those who had gone before as it suited their purpose and largely without criticism.

Wilfrid as builder of the church

The most obvious and indisputable point that can be made regarding Stephen's view of the church established by Wilfrid is that it was grounded firmly in that of Rome, the See of Peter. Given the crucial biblical text supportive of the supremacy of Rome, the *tu es Petrus* from *Matthew* 16: 18–19, which includes the promise that 'on this rock' (i.e. Peter) Christ would build His Church, it is perhaps not surprising that Stephen places some emphasis upon his saint's activities as a builder. Stephen's descriptions of Wilfrid as church builder and restorer are found primarily in chapters 16, 17 and 22. Ann Meyer (2003) has recently demonstrated how the allegorical interpretation of key biblical passages, in particular the building of the tabernacle and the temple in the Old Testament and the descent of the Heavenly Jerusalem in the New, influenced writing and architecture in the Middle Ages. In relation to the eighth-century Northumbrian lives, it has been suggested that key texts concerning the building activities in particular of Cuthbert and Wilfrid make statements about the role of each prelate that transcend their various architectural achievements. (Duncan 1998, 166–9; Duncan 2000, 401–5; Laynesmith 2000, 172–4).

Whereas Wilfrid was responsible for laying the foundations of Hexham and Ripon, this work had already been done at York by Paulinus, a member of the Gregorian mission and the first archbishop of York, but since his time the church had fallen into a semi-ruined state – an obvious side-swipe at the Irish bishops who had held sway in recent years. Wilfrid, like the prophet Daniel, was horrified because the house of God had become like a den of thieves, which echoes the words of Jesus during his cleansing of the temple (Mark XI: 15–17). Both biblical allusions, therefore, would suggest that more was at stake here than mere physical buildings.

So what caused such extreme feelings in Wilfrid? In short the aged roof let in water, the unglazed windows allowed birds into the building and the walls were in a filthy condition due to the aforementioned rain and birds. A brief look at the development of the interpretation of these symbols in the biblical exegesis of the early church allows us to see how these few sentences would have been meaningful for Stephen's readers in ways that far outweighed the actual significance of the buildings themselves.

As Mark Laynesmith has observed (2000, 173–4), for Bede in *De templo* the walls indicated Christian believers, the windows those who teach the laity, and the roof the celibate, and it is likely that a similar concept of the totality of the Church is to be implied in Stephen's picture. Looking in more detail at the elements in a wider range of writers supports this view.

The image of Christian believers forming a wall rising up from Christ as the corner stone was known from a series of commentators on the Bible, including Augustine (*Enarr in Ps.* 47: 3: Dekkers and Fraipont 1956a, 540), or, in a variation on the same theme, walls were the Church as a whole enclosing her "tender offspring" as in Ambrose of Milan (*De Virginibus*, I: 8.49: Migne 1863a, 202). In particular verses from the Song of Songs (Song of Songs VIII: 9–10) were a popular support for this image. Bede in commenting on these verses speaks of Christ as the wall fortifying His Church and goes on to say, 'Truly he who by becoming manifest in flesh deigned to make the Church his sister, also himself conferred upon her participation in his name, with the result that she was called both 'wall' and 'gate' – 'wall' in those, supplied with greater learning and with the power of the Spirit, were able to fortify the minds of believers against the attacks of those in error and defend them boldly with arms by resisting wickedness.'(*Verum qui apparendo in carne Ecclesiam sibi sororem facere dignatus est, ipse ei etiam sui partipationem nominis donavit, ut et murus videlicet diceretur et ostium: murus quidem in eis qui maiori eruditione ac virtute Spiritus praediti mentes fidelium ab incursionibus errantium munire ac defensare fortiter armis nequitiae resistendo sufficerent* (*in cant.* VI, 37: Migne 1862, 216; Norris 2003, 290).

Again, windows were meaningful in the allegorical interpretation of the Church. Gregory the Great (*Hom. in Ez.* II, 5, 20: Adriaen 1971, 142) had spoken of the 'front windows' as being the *rectores* through whom the light of heaven might enter the building and the 'side windows' as those who, although more lowly, desired heavenly wisdom. Bede likewise likened the windows of the

Temple to the teachers and spiritual people of the Church who revealed to the wider ecclesiastical community the fruit of their contemplation and thus illumined the Church (*De templo* I, 7, 1: Hurst 1969, 162).

The image of the roof could be associated with spiritual heights. Bede in his commentary on Nehemiah 8: 16 (*In Ezr.* III: 1250–75: Hurst 1969, 370–1) and Augustine commenting on II Samuel XI: 2–27 (*Contra Faust.* 22: 87: Zycha 1891/92) both likened it to spiritual contemplation. Similarly, Cassian, in an interesting passage in his *Conferences* in the light of Stephen's words, commenting on *Ecclesiastes* X: 18, likens a mind that has neglected spiritual disciplines to an ignored roof through which drippings of temptation begin to seep and that will, on a stormy day (time of temptation and the attack of the devil) be destroyed (*Collat.* VI: 17.1: Petschenig 1886).

If we accept, therefore, that in the walls, windows and roof we have a symbolic representation of the Church in its entirety, then Stephen was clearly establishing a negative view of the state of the Northumbrian Church when Wilfrid came on the scene. This can be extended to include his treatment of birds. The symbol of the bird was used in a multitude of ways. In this context, however, it is obvious that the birds are unwelcome visitors. Several writers such as Augustine (*In Ioh. evang. tract.* X: 9, 5–12: Willems 1954) liken the devil or the powers of evil to birds, the foundation of this image probably being found in birds described in the Parable of the Sower (Mark IV: 1–20) which Jesus Himself identifies with Satan. In the biblical story the sower sowed the seed of the Gospel in the hearts of men, not all of which actually produced a harvest. Some of the grain was stolen by birds. The unglazed windows, therefore, imply that, prior to Wilfrid, insufficient precautions were taken to ensure that those within the protection of the Church were kept safe from inappropriate teaching and influences.

Bede in his description of the Tabernacle, saw rain as one of the things to be protected against (*De tab.* II, 3: Hurst 1969, 56–7). The storm in the biblical parable of the house built on the rock (Matthew VII: 24–27) was interpreted as temptation by both Bede (*Hom. evang.* II, 25: Hurst and Fraipont 1955, 368–78) and Augustine (*In Ioh. evang. tract.* VII: 14, 14–45: Willems 1954). This was obviously replete with symbolic teaching about building on the rock that was Christ or Peter in order to withstand the onslaught of rains that stood for corrupted teaching and the temptations of the devil. As we have seen this was a theme also used by Cassian. It is worth noting that *distillantia*, which is used to describe the water dripping through the aged roof, is found only three times in the Vulgate, twice in the Song of Songs in connection with myrrh and honey dripping from lips. In later exegesis the image was invariably understood to indicate teaching. In the present context, therefore, it may not be a coincidental use of the word, indicating a rather less desirable type of teaching that had permeated even to the loftier parts of the Church structures.

The result of the birds and the rain was filth on the walls. The word used is *spurcitia* which is rarely found in the Vulgate but is employed in Matthew XXIII: 27 in one of the pronouncements made against the hypocrisy of the Scribes and Pharisees, "Woe to you, teachers of the law and Pharisees, you hypocrites! You are like whitewashed tombs, which look beautiful on the outside but on the inside are full of dead men's bones and everything unclean." Augustine speaks of this passage as a warning against hypocrisy and iniquity (*Enarr in Psa.* LXXXVIII: *10*: Dekkers and Fraipont 1956b) and Jerome warns that this is a trap that can beset those who have been in the Church for a long time (*Ep.* LVIII: 1: Migne 1845, 579–80).

The Church inherited by Wilfrid, therefore, had been badly neglected by those who had previously had custody and was sullied with hypocrisy and iniquity from the walls that represented the wider Christian community right up to the loftier heights of the contemplative rafters. Wilfrid repaired the roof with "pure" lead and put glass in the windows, thus preventing the entry of evil influences but, significantly, not blocking the rays of light. By properly equipping it with priests of the Roman tradition, therefore, he kept the Northumbrian Church free of the influences of evil whilst allowing in the light of the true faith. Wilfrid also cleansed the walls of the Church making them "whiter than snow". As a final act of building Stephen noted how Wilfrid richly adorned the interior of the church and endowed it with lands and riches. In one chapter Stephen thus provided a picture which illustrated his belief in the real significance of Wilfrid the builder, who saved, cleansed, enriched and empowered the Church. Wilfrid brought the adornment of the disciplines and customs of the Roman Church.

If Wilfrid was responsible for the cleansing of the Church, he was also responsible for building it and Stephen shows this in his accounts of the building of both Ripon and Hexham. Stephen placed great emphasis on the laying of foundations and the building of columns. Although this was obviously literally true, it also meant more in the history of the Church. Among the standard texts quoted about the Church is the following from *I Timothy*, 'If I am delayed, you will know how people ought to conduct themselves in God's household, which is the church of the living God, the **pillar** and **foundation** of the truth' (I Timothy III: 15).

This idea of the Church as the pillar and the foundation of the truth was developed by several Christian writers including Augustine (*Serm.* 214; XI: Migne 1865, 1071) and Ambrose (*De Jacob et beata libri* II: 5–20: Migne 1882, 652). Furthermore at Hexham there were winding stairs connecting the various passages. Bede in his writings made much of the image of winding stairs in the temple (I Kings VI: 8), seeing in it a reference to the Body of Christ and the ascent of the Christian through baptism in the Church to the heavenly realms after death (see for example *Hom. evang.* II: 1: Hurst and Fraipont 1955, 190–1; *De temp.* I: 8, 1: Hurst 1969, 166; *In Ezram et Neemiam* II, 500–25: Hurst 1969, 300–1). Wilfrid had worked according to the divine will ('being taught by the Holy Spirit' – VW 22) and properly ('completed in a canonical manner' – VW 17).

As Mark Laynesmith (2000, 179–82) has suggested, it could well be of significance that the two sections on building are followed immediately by passages in which Wilfrid performed resuscitation miracles. The first is the healing of a dead baby brought to Wilfrid by its mother in the hope that baptism might heal the child. The passage is introduced by direct reference to similar healings by Elijah and Elisha, Elijah in the raising of the son of the widow of Zarephath (I Kings 17: 17–24) and Elisha in the raising of the Shunammite woman's son (II Kings 4: 17–29). In both cases biblical commentators had seen the mothers as types of Mother Church bringing her children to the prophets, as types of Christ, for restoration to life (see for instance Caesarius of Arles *Serm.* 40: 2: Migne 1863b, 1824; *Serm.* 42: 8: Migne 1863b, 1830) . The woman confronting Wilfrid is likened by Stephen to the Syro-Phoenican woman who successfully confronted Jesus (Matthew XV: 21–28) and succeeded in bringing about the healing of her daughter who had been possessed by a demon. Once again biblical commentators were fairly consistent in seeing this woman as symbolic of the Gentile Church interceding on behalf of a child led astray by idolatry and sin (for instance Bede, *Hom. evang.* I: 22: Hurst and Fraipont 1955, 158). We have here, therefore, a typological representation of Bishop Wilfrid bringing to life a dead Church.

Similarly, Wilfrid is likened to Elijah and Elisha in the second healing miracle that takes place following the account of the building of Hexham. In this incident a young man named Bothelm falls from a high pinnacle to the ground and is at the point of death. The inspiration for this story obviously is derived from the healing of Eutychus, the unfortunate young man who fell asleep during a sermon by Saint Paul and tumbled three storeys out of a window (Acts XX: 7–12). For biblical commentators Eutychus came to represent negligence and fall from spiritual heights. Cassian observed, 'But we must not imagine that anyone slips and comes to grief by a sudden fall, but that he falls by a hopeless collapse either from being deceived by beginning his training badly, or from the good qualities of his soul failing through a long course of carelessness of mind, and so his faults gain ground upon him little by little' (*Lapsus vero quispiam nequaquam subitanea ruina conruisse credendus est, sed aut pravae institutionis deceptus exordio aut per longam mentis incuriam paulatim virtute animi decedente et per hoc sensim vitiis increscentibus casu miserabili concidisse*: Coll. VI: 17: Migne 1874, 667–8; Roberts *et al.* 1994, ser.2, vol. 11, 571).

It was Wilfrid again who, in his role as bishop commissioned and equipped by the See of Rome and, therefore, as Christ's representative, bestowed new life even within the upper floors of the Northumbrian Church (that is the monastic and ascetic circles) corrupted by the drips of bad teaching.

The Powers of Evil

All Christian writers recognised that the Church existed within a world that was basically evil. Stephen likewise saw Wilfrid's enemy as the devil (VW preface, 14, 21, 24) but this saint confronted the ancient adversary not so much in the desert or in the face of hostile pagans but in the actions of people. In the *Vita Wilfridi* evil was personified in the actions of the people opposing the saint and, by association, the Church. Stephen's is a legalistic view of the life of the Christian in which salvation is equated simply with membership of a church which adhered to the canon law of Rome. Sin was that which led to the breaking of such laws, following on from which there was a necessity for repentance and penance.

There is obviously more than one example of individuals falling into sin (as interpreted by Stephen) in the *Life* but I would like in this paper to concentrate on two incidents that I believe provide allegorised representations of Stephen's worldview concerning sin, salvation and the role of Wilfrid. This role was, according to Stephen, predestined for Wilfrid from before his birth. In the first chapter of the *Life* we have the account of a phantasmal fire which beset the house in which Wilfrid's mother was in labour. Stephen himself explained the portent by identifying the fire with the Holy Spirit and the whole incident as showing Wilfrid to be sanctified by God, as was the prophet Jeremiah. The biblical imagery in this incident is very rich and it sets metaphorical themes that echo throughout the rest of the book. Although Stephen does not attempt to expand upon the image of a woman in labour, given that the Church was a main motif of his work and given also the strong associations this motif would have had in the minds of his hearers, it seems safe to assume that few of them would have missed the biblical echoes.

Staying with this passage, the image of a mother bearing a child was replete with associations of the Virgin Mary and the Mother Church. For example the apocalyptic image beloved of biblical commentators is that of the woman in labour, frequently associated both with the Virgin Mary and also with the Church, in *Revelation* 12. Despite attacks by Satan (resisted by the Archangel Michael), amidst lightning, thunder, a hailstorm and an earthquake, as a '*signum magnum ... in caelo*', she bears her child. The commentators frequently interpreted the child as a type of the people of the body of Christ. Although this image is not made explicit by Stephen, it would probably have been natural for his original audience to have called to mind associations connected with such an important and emotive motif when hearing or reading this account of the birth of Wilfrid, an archetypal son of the true Church. The rest of the scene presents a prophetic illustration of what would happen in Wilfrid's life, for the flames were raised up (*elevatam*) to heaven from the house (Acts 1: 9). The imagery of this miracle, as Stephen himself explains, is twofold. Firstly there is the image of the fire of God consuming sinners and the picture of people attempting, in a flurry of confusion and panic, to rescue the victims in the fire. Those waiting outside were concerned and desired to extinguish the flames and to rescue or tear away (*eripere*) the people from the fire – for 'people' the male *homines* is used despite the fact that there were explicitly only women in the house.

Additionally, the image is of the illuminations of that same fire of God shining through the righteous, in this case the child who was just come into the world, who would give light to all the churches. Stephen himself linked the miraculous fact that the house was not destroyed by the fire to Moses and the burning bush, frequently identified with the Holy Spirit. Another comparison may be found in the use of the words *magnalia Dei* which are also used in Acts 2: 11 to express the reactions of the crowd to the impact of the coming of the Holy Spirit as a tongue of flame and a rushing wind on the disciples at Pentecost.

Specifically here is the message that, before Wilfrid, the soteriological activity of the Church in Britain was lacking in the divine power which was bestowed through the saint, presumably because so much of the Church (from Stephen's perspective at least) was tainted by Scottish Christianity. More fundamentally, however, there is the very blunt view that pervades Stephen's work, that the same power of God that illuminates those within the Church is a fire of destruction for those outside.

If the theme of light was a favourite one in Stephen's *Life* (see VW 5, 36, 53) another was that of the sea. According to chapter 21, Wilfrid as bishop steered the vessel that was the Church through the "tossing billows" of the world. The only occasion on which a storm at sea posed a real problem for Wilfrid occurred in chapter 13 when he was returning to England after his consecration as bishop in Gaul. Having been tossed by the seas onto a shore of the pagan South Saxons, Wilfrid and his companions found themselves forced to fight for their freedom. Whatever may be said about the historicity of this tale, for the original hearers it must have seemed to convey a profound truth. The bishop first of all tried to use money to save the lives of his companions in the time-honoured fashion of the Church dealing with barbarian hordes, although the words *animas redimere* ('to redeem souls') doubtless had a double meaning for Stephen's readers, for the powers of evil in this strange land were threatening to snatch away the people of God. The peaceful overtures of the bishop were initially of no use in the face of the ferocity of the pagan army, led by their chief priest, a *magus*. The magician's curses (*maledicere*) were, however, no match against the blessings (*benedictum*) Wilfrid's group bestowed upon a rock with which the priest was killed. In the face of the ensuing attacks of the enemy the company worked together, with the bishop and his clergy praying for help and thus supporting those Christian companions who repulsed the might of the pagan army. The fact that the enemy forces were repulsed three times is probably on its own a signal that this story was intended to be understood at more than just its surface meaning.

Looking in a little bit more depth at the elements within this story, one begins to appreciate its symbolic background. The first part of the chapter pictures Wilfrid and his companions in a boat at sea. This was a standard image for the Church within the world, the boat representing the safety of the Church as the only means for safe passage for the Christian through the difficulties of life. The image of Wilfrid and his companions through the singing of psalms and hymns giving time to the oarsmen, and therefore, ensuring a correct progress through the waves, is quite fitting in this context. One of the standard 'proof texts' of this image is actually given by Stephen when he refers to the storm faced by the disciples of Jesus on Galilee (Matthew VIII: 23–27; XIV: 32–33). In the case of Wilfrid and his company they were cast by the sea onto an unknown land, an 'alien shore' so to speak, whilst the sea itself retreats to the womb of the abyss.

The confrontation with the pagan army is littered with references to similar biblical victories of the people of God against overwhelming odds – David against Goliath, Gideon against the Midianites, Moses and Joshua against the Amalekites. Mayr-Harting (1991, 140) noted connections between Stephen's work and Bede's Old Testament commentaries, which were being written at about the same time and for the same patron, Acca. It is notable from this point of view that from the outset Bede saw Goliath as a type of the devil (*In I Sam.* 421–25: Hurst 1962, 147), which was a common interpretation in other writers, and David as a type of Christ. This struggle could also be seen as a representation of the fight of the Church against the powers of evil (for instance Caesarius of Arles, *Serm.* XXXVII: 7, Migne 1863b, 1820). Not surprisingly, the stone that killed Goliath was likened by most commentators with the biblical spiritual rock of Christ.

The battle of the Children of Israel against the Amalekites, complete with the evocative account of Moses holding up his hands, supported physically by Hur and Aaron, to ensure victory, was a standard image of the power of good battling against and overcoming evil (Exodus XVII: 8–16). So, for example, to Augustine, the name 'Amalek' signified 'sinful people': 'By his opposition he denies the passage to the land of promise. He then must be overcome by the cross of Christ, which was prefigured by the extended hands of Moses' (*et ad terram promissionis repugnando transitum negans, per crucem Domini quae Moysi manibus extensis est praefigurata, superetur*) (*De trinitate* IV: 15.20:

Mountain and Glorie 1968; Deferrari 1963, 156).

It is probably worth mentioning here as well the fact that the high priest of the pagans is referred to as a *magus* and took his stand on a "high mound" which may well have reminded its audience of the apocryphal battles between Peter and Simon Magus, including that set in Rome where Peter and Paul overcame the 'father of heretics' through prayer in a set piece struggle probably inspired by the defeat of the Amalekites in Acts of Peter, 32 (James 1983, 331–2). In the later stories the imagery allows a microcosmic depiction of the supernatural battle between good and evil and Simon Magus himself was frequently depicted as the coming Antichrist or one who would precede Antichrist (Emmerson 1981, 27–8).

Through its evocative imagery and typology this chapter displays more than just a miraculous victory by Wilfrid over a group of pagans. It illustrates the struggle of the Church in the ongoing cosmic battle against evil. The work of defeating the devil was ultimately achieved through the power of Christ but the daily struggle against the powers of evil continues when the Church works in union to achieve victory. As the clergy in the boat had kept the oarsmen in time, so it was through their prayers that the rest of the contingent was able to defeat the enemy. The supremacy of the bishop in this arrangement is underlined by the fact that it was Wilfrid alone who obtained an early return of the tide, and thus the means of escape, through his prayers. The overarching theme of the story is that when the canonical structure of the Church is observed then victory against the powers of evil is ensured.

Binding and Loosing

The *magus* in the previous story tried in vain to bind (*alligare*) the hands of the Christians. This failure is unsurprising according to Stephen's worldview because the power of binding and loosing is held firmly by the Church. The theme is obviously derived from the words of Jesus in *Matthew* XVI: 19, 'I will give you the keys of the kingdom of heaven: whatever you bind on earth will be bound in heaven and whatever you loose on earth will be loosed in heaven.' Leaving aside the question of the association with the primacy of Rome, the passage was important in the development of the practices of confession and penitence.

Chapters 37–39 of Wilfrid's *Life* contain a series of miracles connected by the theme of binding and loosing. The king and his servants were unable to bind Wilfrid, much as earlier authorities had been unable to bind St Peter, for the power of true binding (in heaven) was given to the apostle and his successor, Wilfrid (VW 38). In order to emphasise this further, the wife of the reeve holding the bishop captive is 'bound' or 'fettered' (*alligata*) by a palsy. She is healed only when her husband appeals to Wilfrid for his intercession on her behalf. Following her healing she ministers to the bishop and later becomes a nun. In this the situation is likened to the healing of Peter's mother-in-law by Jesus, a story that was understood by some biblical commentators, including Jerome (*Tracti in Marci evangelium 333–41*: Morin, Capelle, and Fraipont 1958), as indicating a healing from sin as well as from disease.

In this case as in the earlier act of healing of the infant in chapter 18, the act of restoring to health led to those healed finding salvation for their souls too. This was not merely spiritual regeneration, however. In keeping with the whole tenor of the work the result had an institutional flavour, for the recipients of healing became members of monastic communities. Salvation is only within the institution of the Church which is thus extended and strengthened.

Similarly, Ecgfrith's Queen, Iurminburh was seized or even 'arrested' (*arrepta*) by a demon following the arrest and imprisonment of the saint (VW 37, 39) and in this case the power of binding and loosing is explicitly mentioned. Ecgfrith had acted against the canons of the Church, ignoring the decrees of Rome, and Iurminburh had stolen for herself the relics brought by Wilfrid from Rome for the Church as a whole. Similarly later in the work King Aldfrith died because he refused to accept the decrees of the Apostolic See regarding Wilfrid (VW 58–59). Stephen states that he was struck by the apostolic power (*ab apostolica potestate*). It was the Church itself, utilising the Petrine power, which was the power house dispensing divine justice.

The evil in the world that necessitated the use of such justice was not moral failure but opposition to the Church and its laws. Just as the *magus* in chapter 13 stands in opposition to the Christian body, so evil comports itself daily in the world. In a work where the main theme was the institution of the Church it is not surprising that evil was that which split the body of Christ asunder, whether that be schism or the breakdown of proper hierarchical relationships and the laws which held the structure together. In the end, however, none of the evil powers could overcome the might of God, particularly that which rested in the Apostolic See (VW 32, 34, 59).

Conclusion

The main thrust of Stephen's argument, therefore, tended towards seeing Wilfrid the bishop as a pillar of an institutional church (VW 47). The contrast between the bishop of the *Vita Wilfridi* and the figure of Cuthbert as depicted by the author of the Lindisfarne *Life* could not be starker. Where Cuthbert derived his authority from his experience as an ascetic, which gave him the power to guide and guard his flock, Stephen's Wilfrid derived his authority from canon law and his associations with the See of Peter, which gave him the judicial power of binding and loosing.

For Stephen, the Church as both restored and built by Wilfrid was one that drew within its walls and then protected all who would be saved. The Church is an institution with set norms and laws. What was important was that it had its foundations firmly in the apostolic succession and was informed by the traditions of the Fathers, notably canon law. Stephen's world view was one that saw a constant cosmic battle between good and evil but evil was not really manifested in external forces such as demons and natural disasters; it was incarnate in the actions of men and women. What was of most importance was membership of a church which adhered to the canon law of Rome. Sin was that which led to the breaking of such laws. This was a legalistic view of the Christian life; in the end obedience to the true Church was all that was needful.

8: *Wilfrid, Benedict Biscop, and Bede – the Monk who Knew Too Much?*

CHRISTOPHER GROCOCK

Bede provides us with fascinating and sympathetic portrayals of many of the leading figures of his day, a habit he shares with many another intelligent and politically astute writer, and much of what he gives us is interesting as much (if not more) because of what he leaves out as because of what he puts in. The material in this paper takes as its starting-point work done with Ian Wood on a new edition of Bede's minor historical works under the title *Abbots of Wearmouth and Jarrow* for the *Oxford Medieval Texts* series.[1] In particular, the germ of the paper lay in a cryptic e-mail from Wood which bore the ominous title 'a radical thought', and which led us to conclude that a large number of the oddities we encountered in Bede's *Historia Abbatum* (HA) – in particular the amount of material he appears to omit which is found in the *Vita Ceolfridi* (VC) – could be resolved at a stroke by reversing their putative order of composition. The possibility that this might be the case was also raised, independently and contemporaneously, by Nick Higham, who notes that (as with the question of authorship of the two works) 'there is just insufficient evidence to make either case that strongly' (Higham 2006, 67–8). Looking at the two texts, there was no reason to suppose that Bede's version had to come second. Bede's HA could have been completed immediately following the arrival back from Langres of Ceolfrith's companions as winter 716 drew on, whereas the inclusion of a papal letter (otherwise inexplicably omitted by Bede) in the VC would permit the supposition that *this* text was composed after the return of those who had got as far as Rome and then come back to Jarrow with the papal communication – over-wintering in Rome during 716×717 and only then being able to cross the Alps. Some argument can be adduced that the texts were either composed – or at least rewritten? – in the 730s (Higham 2006, 67) – though the *incipit* (not a 'preface' – and only found in one of the two manuscripts) is almost certainly not by the author of the rest of the text. 716×717 is a definite *terminus post quem* and early composition cannot be ruled out.

If Bede omitted much of which he must clearly have been aware in *this* work, then what of other characters he depicts elsewhere? How full a picture

[1]   Grocock and Wood, Oxford, forthcoming; translations from the *Historia Abbatum* in this paper are taken from this edition). Thanks are also due to the kind guidance and generosity of Nick Higham in preparing this paper.

93

628–650	c.627 birth of Benedict Biscop
	c.635 birth of Cuthbert
	c.636 birth of Wilfrid

| 651–660 | 653 Benedict Biscop and Wilfrid depart for Rome |

661–670	664 Benedict Biscop's 2nd visit to Rome; Synod of Whitby
	665 Wilfrid consecrated in Gaul
	666 Benedict Biscop in Lérins; Wilfrid 'bishop of York and all Northumbria'
	668 Benedict Biscop's 3rd visit to Rome (so John of Worcester); Theodore consecrated
	669 Benedict Biscop returns with Theodore
	670 Benedict Biscop abbot of SS Peter and Paul; arrival of Hadrian

671–680	672×3 birth of Bede
	673 Wearmouth founded; Council of Hertford
	674 Wearmouth building
	678 Wilfrid's diocese divided; ? Benedict Biscop's 4th journey to Rome
	679 Wilfrid appeals to Rome; ?Bede enters Wearmouth (or 680)

681–690	681 Wilfrid in Sussex (to 687); Jarrow founded
	682 Jarrow building
	685 dedication of Jarrow; death of Ecgfrith
	687 Wilfrid reconciled; death of Cuthbert
	688 Wilfrid has Ripon and Hexham restored to him
	689 death of Benedict Biscop

691–700	691 (or 692) Bede becomes a deacon
	692 Wilfrid's second exile to Mercia – Bishop of Leicester 692–702
	695 Wilfrid founds monasteries in Mercia; Bede composes *De Arte Metrica* and (?696) *De Orthographia*

701–710	703 Wilfrid's further petition to Rome; Council at *Austerfeld*; Bede is made priest; composes *De Temporibus*
	705 Wilfrid returns to Hexham; Council at R. Nidd
	708 *Commentary ad Pleguinum* composed
	709 (?or 710) death of Wilfrid; Bede, *Commentaries* ?709–716
	710?*Vita Wilfridi* composed

| 711–720 | 716 death of Ceolfrith; *Historia Abbatum*? |
| | 717 *Vita Ceolfridi* composed? |

Table 8.1: Bede, Benedict Biscop and Wilfrid, AD 628–717.

might we have of them? And in particular, what can we make of his portrayals of two towering figures in the early medieval Northumbrian Church, Benedict Biscop and Wilfrid? We may begin with a brief overview of Bede's relations with Benedict Biscop, using the well-known passage of Book V of the *Historia Ecclesiastica* (HE) and some of the *Historia Abbatum*, then spend a little while looking at Bede's relationship with Wilfrid before looking in depth at the passage about the two great leaders from HE, V, 19 which describes their departure from Kent in 653. Finally, an examination of some other passages, in particular HE, IV, 19, will provide some context for Bede's portrayals, treatment of, and relationships with, Biscop and Wilfrid.

Table 8.1 illustrates how much Bede's lifetime overlapped with that of Benedict Biscop, Wilfrid, and other key events. Some obvious points arise from this: for example, Bede was sixteen when Benedict Biscop died, old enough for him to have made a formative impression on Bede, as illustrated by the student's reminiscences in HE, V, 24: 'When I was seven years of age I was, by the care of my kinsmen, put into the charge of the reverend abbot Benedict and then of Ceolfrith, to be educated.'

As any teacher knows, the connections made and the impact they can have (for good or ill) on students in these formative years is often more striking than either party realise at the time. Bede's comments suggest warm reminiscence on his part, and also imply his relatively lowly status as a child, perhaps even as an orphan (though the name 'Bede' meaning 'prayer' or 'supplication' may suggest that Bede was marked out for dedication to God in the monastery from the outset: see Higham 2006, 9). Such would have set him apart from the noblemen who came to dominate the Northumbrian church and about whom he was to write so copiously, and point to a different conclusion to that of Campbell (2004), who suggested a more elevated view of his social origins. That said, in his mature years Bede clearly saw himself as 'moral guide to both court and country' and 'far from subservient towards his royal patron' in the *Preface* to the HE (Higham 2006, 12).

In the *Historia Abbatum*, which is in many respects a résumé of Bede's *Homily* I, 13 on Benedict Biscop (text, translation and commentary in Grocock and Wood, forthcoming), we have a more distant but still respectful assessment of Benedict Biscop:

> The pious servant of Christ Biscop, also called Benedict, was inspired by the grace from above and built a monastery in honour of Peter, the most blessed prince of the apostles, next to the mouth of the river Wear on the northern bank. Ecgfrith, the venerable and most dutiful king of that people, assisted him and gave him land. Benedict himself zealously ruled over the monastery for sixteen years with the same devotion with which he had built it, suffering numerous hardships on account of his pilgrimages and physical weaknesses. If I may use the words of the blessed pope Gregory with which he praises the life of the abbot of that name, 'He was a man of admirable character, 'called Blessed' by name and by grace. He had a mature outlook even from the time of his childhood,

transcending his age in his behaviour, and gave his soul over to no lustful passion.' He was in fact born of a noble family of the race of the Angles, and yet with no less nobility of mind he was determined on constantly meriting the company of angels. In short, at the age of about twenty-five, he was in King Oswiu's service, and received as a gift from him property in the form of possession of land befitting his rank. He spurned the ownership of transient things so that he could acquire eternal ones, and shunned earthly military service with its perishable reward so that he might be worthy to fight for the true king and to have an everlasting kingdom in the city that is above. He left his home, his family, and his fatherland for the sake of Christ and for the sake of the gospel, so that he might receive a hundredfold and possess eternal life; he refused to subject himself to marriage in the flesh so that he might be worthy of the lamb shining with the glory of virginity in the heavenly realms; he declined to father mortal children according to the flesh, predestined as he was by Christ to bring up for him with spiritual teaching sons who live forever in the heavenly life.

In amongst the expected hagiographic qualities are some salient details which highlight Benedict Biscop's status and background, which are used to counterpoint his sacrifices and holiness; noble birth no doubt provided access to the highest ranks of Northumbrian society and the royal court. Bede goes on to stress that he was marked out for service to the king, a role which he continued to play even after his founding of Wearmouth, and was appropriately honoured by the customary granting of land. The passage concludes with a comment whose relevance in other circumstances will be discussed later: '[he] refused to subject himself to marriage in the flesh so that he might be worthy of the lamb shining with the glory of virginity in the heavenly realms; he declined to father mortal children according to the flesh'. The stress here is not merely on the rejection of a secular career, but on chastity and a refusal to engage in sexual activity, which Bede saw as a hallmark of saintliness, however strange an attitude it may seem to the modern mind. It comes as no surprise to find that later, in HA 4, Benedict Biscop was in extremely good standing with Oswiu's son, Ecgfrith, and received more land, this time to build a monastery:'[on his return to Northumbria] he received such a great and gracious welcome from the king that the latter immediately endowed him with seventy hides of his own land and instructed him to build a monastery there [dedicated] to the first pastor of the church.'

Wood (Grocock and Wood, forthcoming) notes that Bede presents Ecgfrith as the prime mover – perhaps trying to tie Benedict Biscop down. However, it is for religious purposes, not on account of his noble status, that the gift is made, and there is no mention of the previous grant of land (or even whether or not they were one and the same). This down-playing of noble rank is also seen in HA 8, regarding Eosterwine – and the family tie to Benedict Biscop is stated, but is then immediately qualified and carefully circumscribed so that it cannot be seen as having any bearing on his elevation:

> He was a noble man in the eyes of the world, but remarkably was devoted not to boasting about the topic of his noble birth, as some do, and looking down on others, but to the greater nobility of the soul, as befits a servant of God. He was actually the paternal cousin of his abbot Benedict, but both were so noble in heart, and thought so little of worldly status, counting it as nothing, that when Eosterwine entered the monastery he did not look for any favour over the rest on account of respect for his being related by blood or the deference due to his noble birth, and Benedict did not think it should be shown him. Rather, this young man of good resolution was delighted to keep the teaching of the rule on an equal footing with the brothers in every way. And in fact, although he had been in king Ecgfrith's service, once he had left worldly business behind him, he laid down his arms and enlisted in spiritual service; he remained so lowly, and so very like the other brothers, that he rejoiced to work cheerfully and obediently at winnowing and threshing with them, at milking the ewes and the cows, in the bakehouse, in the garden, in the kitchen and in all the work of the monastery. Even when he took the name and rank of abbot, he maintained the same attitude towards all, following the advice of that wise man who said 'when they have made you their overseer, do not be exalted, but be like one of them among them,' gentle, kind and warm-hearted to all.

Bede's comment that Eosterwine was 'devoted not to boasting about the topic of his noble birth, as some do', implies that there were monks who *did* insist on their noble origins, and hold to their former ranks, as does his insistence that Eosterwine 'did not look for any favour over the rest.' Had Bede's own lowly origins given him experience of other monks 'lording it over him', one wonders? At any rate, this seems to reflect Bede's own ideal for a spiritual leader, summed up in the citation from *Ecclesiasticus* 32: 1 which rounds off the passage, and his views on class and status are closely associated with those found in the Rule of Benedict (*Regula* 89; Mayr Harting 1976). Since Wilfrid's apparent insistence on retaining the trappings which befitted his noble origins – such as an extensive retinue – and his refusal to make the most of the wealth which came his way provided raw material for much of the criticism aimed at him (even Stephanus in the *Vita Wilfridi* does not downplay these aspects of his conduct), one might expect that when Bede came to write about Wilfrid, this characteristic might at least get some mention in the latter's portrayal of him; so to this we should now turn.

From the timeline in Table 8.1 it is clear that Bede might just have had some contact with Wilfrid during his brief stay in the North East in 689×691, before being exiled to Mercia, but this seems unlikely, as Bede was not even a deacon until 691×692, and their paths are unlikely to have crossed at this time. In the light of an illuminating, not to say surprising, description of a meeting Bede had with Wilfrid on one occasion, we are given the distinct impression that at some stage Bede was on familiar terms with Wilfrid, and apparently unafraid to ask quite pertinent questions connected with his research. The passage in question is HE IV, 19, cited below in the translation by Colgrave and Mynors (1969, 519–21). It is remarkable not only because of the ease with which Bede interacts with Wilfrid (at variance with the deferential view seen above in the *Historia Abbatum*), but also because of Bede's portrayal in it of kingly behaviour much more redolent of *realpolitik* than anything we find in the HA – and shows in addition that Ecgfrith certainly seems to have hoped that the opportunity to acquire wealth might motivate Wilfrid to fall in with his wishes (which, on this occasion, it clearly did not):

> King Ecgfrith married a wife named Æthelthryth, the daughter of Anna, king of the East Angles, who has often been referred to, a very religious man and noble both in mind and deed. She had previously been married to an ealdorman of the South Gyrwe, named Tondberht. But he died shortly after the marriage and on his death she was given to King Ecgfrith. Though she lived with him for twelve years she still preserved the glory of perfect virginity.

The narrative here is straightforward, and matter-of-fact (though 'twelve' may reflect a symbolic perfection, following the numbers found in biblical texts); the final sentence above mirrors the stress on chastity noted above about Benedict Biscop in HA 1, though even in Bede's day it probably seemed unlikely to some:

> When I asked Bishop Wilfrid of blessed memory whether this was true, because certain people doubted it, he told me that he had the most perfect proof of her virginity; in fact Ecgfrith had promised to give him estates and money if he could persuade the queen to consummate their marriage, because he knew that there was none whom she loved more than Wilfrid himself.

Clearly a marriage to a queen devoted to chastity could do nothing to help Ecgfrith in his desire for an heir. What seems even more remarkable is the way in which this section of HE IV, 19 shows Bede to have been assured and confident enough in the company of Wilfrid to be able to discuss sensitive matters of some 25 years earlier; and any details which might be regarded as putting Ecgfrith in a bad light have *not* been edited out. We will search in vain for such a depiction of the king in the *Historia Abbatum*, no doubt because any negative depiction there would water down the idealistic portrayal of the monastic founders. Given Wilfrid's later reputation perhaps it may show how canny Ecgfrith was, exploiting his weak spot; but it may also be regarded as a reflection on Wilfrid's career before relations between the king and the bishop became soured. Given its incorporation in the HE it indicates a marked difference in the ways in which Bede portrays this monarch when it is put alongside the outline sketch found in the *Historia Abbatum*. Goffart (1988, 323) notes that 'Wilfrid's reply, as reported by Bede, reflects on the bishop as well as the queen. It gives the curious impression that Wilfrid had taken the king's side: even the prospect of a large bribe did not arouse Wilfrid to enough eloquence to talk Æthelthryth into the royal marriage bed.'

When could this encounter have taken place? The continuation of the timeline of events in the lives of Bede and Wilfrid in Table 8.1 indicates a date following Wilfrid's return to Hexham, in 706. Goffart (1988, 322) says 'it must have taken place between 706 and 709, when Wilfrid held the see of Hexham and was the ordinary of Jarrow; perhaps he visited Bede's monastery.' Plummer (1896, I, xlix) noted that 'most of Bede's theological works are dedicated to Acca, bishop of Hexham, for whom he evidently cherished a warm affection', and it is not impossible that the meeting took place at Hexham, not at Wearmouth/Jarrow. Whitelock (1976) and Higham (2006) give a good summary of the widespread contacts Bede had made as a student and as a writer. By 706×709 Wilfrid was more than likely old and infirm, while Bede was priested in 703 and already an established scholar aged about thirty. He portrays himself as an assiduous and confident researcher, unafraid to discuss delicate issues: 'their talk was detached from the incident often thought to have alienated Bede from Wilfrid, in which his chronological writings were impugned before the old bishop as being heretical' (Goffart 1988, 322). That said, the events were some time past, and at this point Bede did not seem to feel the need to distance himself from them in the deferential way in which he had treated the noble founders of his own monastic institution, though the conversation did not raise all the questions we might want answered (or if it did, Bede does not report them): Goffart (1988, 323) notes that 'two subsidiary facts worth ascertaining would have been how the queen's retirement to monastic life was arranged and how Ecgfrith obtained permission to remarry. Unasked, both questions remain unanswered.' By the time of the completion and dedication of the HE, those events were even further in the past, and in the latter work he was evidently prepared to include material which cast Ecgfrith in a rather less saintly light than was the case in the HA.

A further passage from HE V, 19 sheds more light on Bede's attitudes toward Wilfrid:

> He was a boy of good disposition and virtuous beyond his years. He behaved himself with such modesty and discretion that in all things he was deservedly loved, honoured, and cherished by his elders as though he were one of themselves. After he had reached the age of fourteen, he chose the monastic rather than the secular life. When he told his father this, for his mother was dead, he readily consented to the boy's godly desires and aspirations and bade him persevere in his profitable undertaking. So he came to the island of Lindisfarne and there devoted himself to the service of the monks, diligently striving to learn how to live a life of monastic purity and devotion. Since he was quick-witted he speedily learned the psalms and a number of other books; although he had not yet been tonsured, he was in no small measure distinguished for the virtues of humility and obedience, which are more important than the tonsure; and for this reason he was rightly loved by the older monks as well as by his contemporaries.

Wilfrid's patron was Eanflæd, Oswiu's Queen, and the episode must be dated before the year 653. Colgrave and Mynors (1969, 517 n. 5) note that Bede relied very greatly on Stephanus VW 2 (Colgrave 1927, 5–7) in this chapter, a point made earlier by Plummer (1896, II, 315ff.). This is very obvious when we read the two accounts, but detailed consideration shows that Bede has provided only a short summary, with the result that much material found elsewhere is left out (as Higham 2006, 58 comments on this issue in all Bede's works, 'Bede certainly said less than he might have about Wilfrid'). For example, in VW 2, Wilfrid did not get on with his step-mother (*molesta et inmitis erat* – she was 'harsh and cruel'), a relationship Bede leaves out of his story; it does not fit in with his depiction of the youth's 'modesty and discretion.' Stephanus says that Wilfrid 'organized his own retinue to be presented in the palace.' Was he intending to become a monk yet? Bede leaves this detail out, and says instead that Wilfrid 'chose the monastic rather than the secular life' as early as fourteen. Stephanus stresses that Wilfrid went to Eanflæd (this *is* mentioned by Bede, but as an afterthought – playing down royal connections as he does in the HA), and says he is 'comely of appearance' (mentioned by Bede at a later point). Bede completely omits the information provided by Stephanus that Wilfrid was sent to Lindisfarne as a *minister* to Cudda, one the king's 'truest friends' but struck by 'a paralytic infirmity.'

This final point merits more detailed consideration. The other omissions smooth out the brief picture of Wilfrid, but if Bede had wanted to stress Wilfrid's humility even more positively, along the lines of his portrayal of Eosterwine at Wearmouth-Jarrow, this point would surely have been something to highlight. The fact that he leaves it out of his account might support the arguments put forward by Goffart (1988, 307–28) that Bede was writing a refutation of Stephen's *Vita Wilfridi*, reflecting the view at Wearmouth/Jarrow that Wilfrid was really a character who had always lacked humility (an understandable attitude, given the conflict which had arisen in the region during Wilfrid's career, especially between Wilfrid and King Ecgfrith). However, Bede's writing is not polemical; indeed, there is nothing in Bede's accounts which come anywhere near the vitriolic depiction of Ecgfrith by Stephanus (Colgrave 1927, 71). Higham (2006, 69) concludes that 'there is far more evidence of his friendship with Stephen's dedicatees than of hostility towards them and he treated both Wilfrid and Acca with due honour.' If Bede *had* wanted to stress Wilfrid's arrogance or insistence on his noble status, he could have included it and contrasted this role with the ones which Wilfrid quickly sought for himself. Bede does no such thing; as is his practice in writing the *Historia Abbatum*, he simply lets it go by, and in so doing pours oil on long-past troubled waters (even Goffart (1988, 317) comments 'Wilfrid enters the *H.E.* very early and quietly'). If Bede had felt any animosity in his own mature years towards a long-dead Wilfrid, he would surely have had no hesitation in expressing it; after all he was not reticent about his own achievements (HE V, 24), and the tone of the preface to the *Retractio in Acts Apostolorum* (Laistner 1939) is evidence of his confidence as a scholar in these years; above all his *Letter to Bishop Ecgberht* shows how strongly he could feel on matters close to his heart and express them to a bishop, too. As we have seen, Bede was at ease in his conversation and research with Wilfrid in the latter's final years. Did he recognize in the Wilfrid he had come to know a more sympathetic individual than the one who may have been depicted in the hostile attitudes to the great prelate which emanated from the Northumbrian court?

Neither does the vocabulary used by Bede support the view that 'as a monk of Jarrow under the rule of an abbot, he was better suited to contribute . . . to an opposition to Wilfrid's successors' (Goffart 1988, 295). Stephanus uses fairly standard, anodyne terms to describe his saintly hero in VW 2: he is 'obedient to his parents, dear to all, handsome in appearance, of good disposition, gentle, modest, and stable', the last of these qualities being a key monastic virtue which he was not to exemplify for all kinds of reasons: *parentibus oboediens, omnibus carus, pulcher aspectu, bonae indolis, mitis, modestus, stabilis* (Colgrave 1927, 4–7). The vocabulary Bede uses expands on this description, while omitting *stabilis*, which after all hardly fits Wilfrid's character or career: he is 'of good disposition, virtuous beyond his years', has 'modesty and discretion', was 'deservedly loved, honoured, and cherished by his elders as though he were one of themselves' (a considerable expansion on 'dear to all'); he had 'godly desires and aspirations', was 'quick-witted' and 'although he had not yet been tonsured, he was in no small measure distinguished for the virtues of humility and obedience' (*bonae indolis, se modeste et circumspecte gerens, uotis ac desideriis caelestibus, acris ingenii, necdum quidem adtonsus, humilitatis et oboedientiae non mediocriter insignitus*). Bede sums up Wilfrid's character with the phrase *adulescens animi sagacis*, 'a youth with a wise soul' (picked up from VW 3, which also later calls Wilfrid *mente sagax*). This is fulsome praise for the now long-dead adversary of Northumbria's king.

Bede's narrative continues with more expansion of the account in the *Vita Wilfridi*, as follows:

> After he had served God in that monastery for some years, being a youth of shrewd understanding, he gradually came to realize that the traditional way of virtuous life followed by the Irish was by no means perfect; so he resolved to go to Rome to see what ecclesiastical and monastic practices were observed in the apostolic see. When he told the brothers they commended his plan and persuaded (?or 'urged') him to carry out his purpose. He went at once to Queen Eanflæd because she knew him and because it was through her counsel and at her request that he had been admitted to the monastery. He told her of his desire to visit the shrines of the blessed apostles. She was delighted with the youth's excellent plan and sent him to King Eorcenberht of Kent, who was her cousin, asking him to send Wilfrid honourably to Rome. At that time Honorius, one of the disciples of the blessed Pope Gregory, was archbishop there, a man deeply versed in ecclesiastical matters. The youth, who was very active-minded, spent some time in Kent, diligently setting himself to learn all that he saw, until another young man came, named Biscop, known also as Benedict, an Anglian of noble family, who also wished to go to Rome, and who has already been mentioned.

There is a different stress in VW 3, which is considerably shorter:

> It came into the heart of this same young man, by the promptings of the Holy Spirit, to pay a visit to the see of the Apostle Peter, the chief of the Apostles, and to attempt a road hitherto un-trodden by any of our race. By so doing he believed that he would cleanse himself from every blot and stain and receive the joy of the divine blessing.

Bede's account is more fulsome and works in Wilfrid's royal connections and patronage as though *this* were the means of divine grace and purpose, while Stephanus separates these out, and Wilfrid's motivation is due to a charismatic 'hot line to God', the 'promptings of the holy spirit'.

Further deliberate changes of detail and emphasis are introduced by Bede in his account of what then happened in Kent. Earlier discussions of the divergences in the accounts are made by Goffart (1988, 307–24) and Fletcher (1981, 3–4). According to Stephanus, VW 3, 'After a year of weary waiting from day to day, the king, in accordance with the queen's request, found him a guide, a man of high rank and of remarkable understanding named Biscop Baducing, who was bound for the Apostolic See, and prevailed upon him to take the youth in his company ...' Wilfrid's frustration and the urgency of his intentions is neatly conveyed by 'a year of weary waiting from day to day'; Benedict Biscop (here, Benedict Baducing) is described as 'a guide, a man of high rank and of remarkable understanding', a *ducem nobilem et admirabilis ingenii*, which is flattering given Benedict Biscop's close connections to the much-maligned Ecgfrith; whereas in Bede HE V, 19, the relative positions of Wilfrid and Benedict Biscop are reversed: 'The king gave Wilfrid to Biscop as a companion and ordered Biscop to take him to Rome with him.' This is compatible with the bald statement about Benedict Biscop in HA 2, 'and so he left his homeland and went to Rome.' The contrast is more evident in the Latin phrasing, with key phrases set out in bold: Stephanus writes **ducem ... inueniens** *ad sedem apostilicam properantem ut in suo comitatu esset* **adquisiuit**, which rather indicates his view of Benedict Biscop at this point as an impersonal object to be acquired. By contrast, Bede made it clear that Benedict was leader of the party, though both he and Wilfrid are subject to royal command: *huius ergo* **comitatui sociauit** *Vilfridum, utque illum secum Romam perduceret* **iussit**. In both accounts, Wilfrid has extended royal patronage at the outset – and given the divergence in the accounts about their relative positions, one wonders whether this revision of detail in the narrative – namely, who was in charge and who was the junior party – was due to Bede's own rewriting, or a recollection of the way his own teacher Benedict had told the story to an eager young pupil.

Bede's account in HE V, 19 continues with events in Lyons: 'When they reached Lyons, Wilfrid was held back by Dalfinus, the bishop of the city, while Benedict eagerly continued with his journey to Rome.' Note that Dalfinus is given sole responsibility by Bede for their separation (given that Benedict Biscop had earlier been given the charge to get him to Rome). Stephanus gave a quite different reason, which Bede once again simply airbrushes out: 'There [Wilfrid] remained with his companions a certain time, *his stern guide having left him*, just as Barnabas separated from Paul on account of John, whose surname was Mark.' Here it is understandable that Bede would have found the description of

Benedict Biscop as 'a stern guide' unacceptable; and given his earlier account of the royal order issued to Benedict Biscop to escort Wilfrid to Rome, it is clear that from the Wearmouth-Jarrow standpoint, the breach did not so much involve Benedict moving on as Wilfrid refusing to budge, though Stephanus stresses the opposite, as his Latin makes clear: *ibique cum suis sociis aliquod spatium mansit, discedente ab eo austerae mentis duce, sicut a Paulo Barnabas propter Iohannem recessit.* What caused this breach is impossible to say – perhaps it was an early indication of Wilfrid's headstrong nature. It must have been Wilfrid's doing, since his earlier express wish had been to go to Rome, and Benedict Biscop did just that. For Stephanus, the parallel with Paul and Barnabas may have seemed apposite; in the Acts narrative, Barnabas is seen as the lesser party who moved (and Benedict Biscop is equated to him), while the senior, more important one (Paul/Wilfrid) stayed put. Incidentally, *ducem* here is definitely a 'guide' (so Colgrave), but we should remember that Benedict Biscop was also a *dux* in a military sense, and went on to play a major role as a 'leader' in the Northumbrian court.

By contrast, in the *Homily* I, 13 on Benedict Biscop, Bede gives a quite different account of Benedict Biscop's first journey to Rome:

> Spurning his achievements in the service of the king and the prospects he might have expected, since he was a nobleman by birth, he hastened to set out on his journey to Rome, to the abodes of the blessed apostles, in order to take up a more perfect manner of living there where the glorious head of the whole church shines forth through the most exalted apostles of Christ, because the faith and teaching of the churches among the peoples of the English was as yet undeveloped. As a result he was educated in Christ there, took the tonsure in that part of the world, became thoroughly acquainted with monastic teaching there, and was to have passed the whole span of his life there too had not the apostolic authority of the lord pope prevented him and instructed him to return to his homeland, in order to escort to Britain Archbishop Theodore of holy recollection.

Unsurprisingly, here the focus is totally on Wearmouth-Jarrow's patron and founder, and there is no mention of Wilfrid. In addition, this account seems to have conflated Benedict Biscop's first three visits to Rome, since he is represented only as returning with Theodore, in 669, but actually first went around 653/4 and had also gone once more in between (Higham, pers. comm.).

Let us return to HE V, 19 and Bede's description of Wilfrid's activity in Lyons:

The bishop was delighted with the youth's prudent talk, his grace and his beauty, his eager activity, and his consistent and mature way of thinking. So as long as he remained, he supplied him and his companions plentifully with all they needed; and furthermore he offered Wilfrid, if he would accept them, a considerable part of Gaul to rule over, his unmarried niece as his wife, and to adopt him as his son. Wilfrid thanked him for the kindness he had deigned to show him, a stranger, but answered that he had resolved upon another course of life and for that reason had left his native land and set out for Rome.

When the bishop heard this, he sent him to Rome, providing him with a guide for his journey, supplying him with an abundance of all things necessary for the road and earnestly begging that, on his return to his own country, he would come that way. When Wilfrid arrived in Rome he perseveringly devoted himself day by day, as he had intended, to constant prayer and the study of ecclesiastical matters ... after he had spent some months in these happy studies, he returned to Dalfinus in Gaul, where he spent three years, being tonsured by him and so greatly beloved that he proposed to make Wilfrid his successor. But the bishop was cut off by a cruel death and so this was prevented; indeed, Wilfrid was reserved for the task of being a bishop over his own people, the Angles.

In the final sentence cited about it is surely Bede's own comment that 'Wilfrid was *reserved* for the task of being a bishop over his own people' – reserved as part of the overall divine plan for the Angles, one assumes. We should also note how flattering Bede's vocabulary about Wilfrid is here, stressing that 'the bishop was delighted with the youth's prudent talk, his grace and his beauty, his eager activity, and his consistent and mature way of thinking', *adulescens animi uiuacis delectabatur enim antistes pudentia uerborum iuuenis, uenusti uultus, alacritate actionis, et constantia ac maturitate cogitationis*. As Wallace-Hadrill (1988, 192) reflects, 'it is hard to see why [Wilfrid's] Merovingian career and contacts should figure at all prominently in Bede's account.' In addition he adds detail about Honorius and Wilfrid's devotion to the parallel account in VW 4, while cutting out much of the detail included in Stephanus' narrative. Bede felt at liberty to paint a positive picture of Wilfrid – who after all, by this time was no threat to the established ecclesiastical hegemony in Northumbria (it faced quite different problems).

Let us now consider a second passage which describes the appeal by Wilfrid against his deposition, which seems to have coincided with Benedict Biscop's fourth visit to the holy city, a visit whose timing may therefore not have been accidental, though there is no record of Benedict Biscop's involvement in the debates about it, and Bede does not make any mention of a specific visit (see Table 8.1; Grocock and Wood, forthcoming; Plummer 1896, II, 359–60). This is the account found later on in HE V, 19:

> Later on, *during the reign of Ecgfrith*, Wilfrid was driven from the see and other bishops were consecrated in his place, as has already been related [i.e. in HE IV, 12–13] ... after his case had been considered in the presence of Pope Agatho and many bishops, it was decided by their unanimous judgement that he had been wrongly accused, and so he was declared worthy to hold his bishopric.
>
> At that time Pope Agatho had called a synod of 125 bishops to Rome to testify against those who declared that there was only one will and operation in our Lord and Saviour. He ordered Wilfrid to sit among the bishops, to declare his own faith and that of the kingdom and the island from which he had come. When it was found that he and his people were catholic in their faith, they decided to insert the following words among the rest of the acts of the synod:
>
> Wilfrid, beloved of God, bishop of the city of York, appealing to the apostolic see concerning his own case and having been freed by its authority from all other charges, specified and unspecified, and being appointed to sit in the synod with 125 other bishops, has confessed the true and catholic faith on behalf of the whole northern part of Britain and Ireland, as well as the Irish and Picts, and has confirmed it with his signature.

Now what is going on here? Wilfrid is fully justified by the pope and Bede does not gloss over it one whit. Wilfrid is even credited with speaking on behalf of 'the whole northern part of Britain and Ireland, as well as the Irish and Picts' (and one wonders what the Irish and Picts would have thought of such a statement, if they ever did). Now Stephanus uses *exactly* these terms in VW 21 (Colgrave 1927, 42–3); Bede is copying what he found in Stephanus' account without question; this may well be the actual wording of the post Wilfrid was thought to have held. Wallace-Hadrill (1988, 194) comments that 'Bede ... was unwilling to record Wilfrid's differences with Archbishop Theodore as well as his subsequent treatment by King Ecgfrith and his allies', but he seems happy to have repeated the extent of Wilfrid's possessions without qualification. Compare the treatment of Benedict Biscop's role in the same event in HA 6:

> Moreover, so that this tireless provider might bring back from the area around Rome attractive and useful items for his church which

could not be found even in Gaul, once the monastery was established according to the rule he completed a fourth journey, and returned profitably laden with many more spiritual acquisitions than before ... Fourthly, Benedict brought a gift of no little worth, a letter of privilege from the venerable pope Agatho. It was freely received with the agreement, express wishes and encouragement of king Ecgfrith.

Wood (Grocock and Wood forthcoming) has commented that 'the presence of Wilfrid in Rome, and the purpose of his visit, must have been known to Bede'; but here he stresses the benefits gained for Wearmouth by a fourth visit to Rome by Benedict Biscop and makes no mention of Wilfrid at all. Is this because Benedict Biscop's mission failed (at least as far as Wilfrid was concerned)? Or simply because mention of Wilfrid in the HA was irrelevant to his hagiographical purpose? The importance of the papal privileges is shown by the stress placed on Agatho's privilege for Wearmouth in Bede's *Homily* I, 13, 12 and those for Ripon and/or Hexham in Stephanus, VW 45, 47, 51.

The true nature of the visit to Rome may be illuminated by this comment on Benedict Biscop's role in VC 12:

> Benedict himself used often to be summoned to the king because of his innate wisdom and the maturity of his advice, and he did not always have the time to be caught up in the cares of guiding and regulating the monastery, so he sought for himself a colleague with whose assistance he might more easily and confidently bear his onerous duty as ruler. Over and above this he used to make *hasty* journeys to Rome, so that he could bring back the good things which were required for the monasteries which he had found from abroad to his homeland.

Wood (Grocock and Wood) notes on this passage that 'this places Biscop at the heart of the Northumbrian court.' One might ask why the VC qualified Benedict Biscop's journeys as 'hasty'; was this one because of Wilfrid's appeal? It is worth noting that Bede treats not only his own superiors but also Wilfrid (and Wilfrid's memory too) with deference and respect. The same cannot be said of Stephanus' treatment of Ecgfrith, and there are marked differences between Bede's treatment of the breach between Ecgfrith (and/or Theodore) and Wilfrid and that of Wilfrid's disciple and biographer (Higham 2006, 68–9). As we have seen, HE IV, 19 portrays the relationship of Ecgfrith and Wilfrid in a businesslike manner; the concluding part of Bede's narrative here also reveals that he was on good terms with Wilfrid, and was prepared to repeat the latter's version of events quite freely.

Bede follows this with the accounts of Æthelthryth and her sister Seaxburh, widow of Eorconberht king of Kent, as abbesses of Ely (the daughter-house of Coldingham) and his *hymnus uirginitatis*. Now this is no doubt very laudable as a then-orthodox, religious/pious view of virginity, but the principal reason for a royal wedding is to *breed*. The dynastic implications for Ecgfrith and those close to him must have been extraordinary, and the support this virgin queen apparently received from Wilfrid can have done little to foster good relations between a bishop and his king:'(Wilfrid) had been her spiritual counsellor, perhaps to his detriment' (Goffart 1988: 261). Wallace-Hadrill (1988, xxviii) regards Bede's treatment of Æthelthryth as an example of his regard for the 'Church at a higher level ... principally revealed for him in the lives of its saints.' At the same time, he comments on this passage of the HE, that Æthelthryth 'is Bede's ideal of the virgin queen; an ideal, if widely practised, that could not have been congenial to kings in search of heirs'(Wallace-Hadrill 1988, 159). Higham (2006, 119) comments that 'Æthelthryth was here being developed as a unique exemplar of English, Christian womanhood.' Stephanus attributed the breach between Ecgfrith and Wilfrid to Iurminburh in VW 24:

> For Ecgfrith's queen, named Iurminburh, was at that time tortured with envy owing to the persuasions of the devil, although, after the death of the king, from being a she-wolf she was changed into a lamb of God, a perfect abbess and an excellent mother of the community ... She eloquently described to [Ecgfrith] all the temporal glories of St Wilfrid, his riches, the number of his monasteries, the greatness of his buildings, his countless army of followers arrayed in royal vestments and arms.

The latter phrase, even more in the original Latin *magnitudinem innumerumque exercitum sodalium regalibus uestimentis et armis ornatum*, suggests that Wilfrid may also have been seen as a rival in the temporal sphere. Colgrave (1927, 159) comments that Ecgfrith must have married again before the death of Æthelthryth in 679x680; Bede omits this episode entirely (perhaps he did not think the remarriage appropriate), and there is no reference to Iurminburh at all in the HE; in IV, 12 Bede simply says that in 678 'there arose a dissension between King Ecgfrith and the most reverend bishop Wilfrid with the result that the bishop was driven from his see', *orta inter ipsum regem Ecgfridum et reuerentissimum antistem Vilfridum dissensione pulsus est idem antistes a sede sui episcopatus* (Colgrave and Mynors 1969, 370–1). The basis of the rift has been discussed at length; was it because of the amount of power garnered by Wilfrid? Wallace-Hadrill (1988, 150) suggests that the lack of explanation in the HE about why the breach occurred was because 'Bede seems to be in some uncertainty about what happened when Wilfrid was deposed by Ecgfrith', whereas Stephanus makes it clear in VW 24, cited above, that it was jealousy aroused by Iurminburg. The later tradition in the *Vita Sancti Wilfridi* of Eadmer has Wilfrid exorcizing 'Ermenburg' (40), and Wilfrid seeing in a vision the soul of Ecgfrith after the death of the king being borne to hell by devils (47), while Theodore has a death-bed change of heart and is reconciled to Wilfrid (48: Muir and Turner, 1998). There may have been theological differences between Theodore and Wilfrid. In addition, it seems that, after 664, Wilfrid's ambition and drive simply could not help attempting to fill the vacuum left after the departure of the Irish from Lindisfarne (his title, cited above, was after all 'bishop of the whole northern part of Britain and Ireland, as well as the Irish and Picts')– whereas Theodore had a clear remit which had originally been committed to Augustine, namely to complete the establishment of bishoprics (Goffart 1988, 255 n.101; Bede, *Epistola ad Egbertum Episcopum*, 7 and 13) Questions of authority might easily have been raised from what must have appeared as a quasi-secular rule over swathes of Ecgfrith's kingdom – especially from the perspective of Wearmouth-Jarrow, whose independence was guaranteed by papal privilege. But it is noteworthy that Bede omits all reference to Wilfrid's *regalibus uestimentis et armis*, openly depicted in the *Via Wilfridi*; Bede was not afraid to record Benedict Biscop's secular service, so this in itself did not detract from service to God, but the reference to regal military power was not helpful in his depiction of Wilfrid, and he makes no use of it whatsoever.

The terms used about Wilfrid by Bede in HE IV, 19 seem respectful, if sometimes slightly stylised and platitudinous; when Wallace-Hadrill (1998, 191–2) states that 'Bede does seem to admire Wilfrid though not to like him', I find myself in agreement with the first part of his judgement but not able to see how one could tell regarding the second. Bede was capable of expressing downright anger (for example EEE 4, 'it is common gossip about some bishops that they serve Christ in such a way that they have no men with them of any kind of religion or restraint, but rather those who are steeped in mockery and pranks, made-up stories feasting together and drunkenness and other wanton pursuits of a rather lax way of life, and who feed their stomachs with daily banquets more than their minds with heavenly sacrifices'; 11 'it is a foul thing to say that those men who have absolutely no experience of monastic life have received so many places to rule over with the title of monasteries, as you yourself know perfectly well ... being therefore idle and unable to marry when they have left the time of their youth, they may not contain themselves with any suggestion of self-control, and because of this situation ... since their minds are not set on chaste living, they become slaves to riotous living and whoring, a greater and more shameless crime, and they do not refrain even from virgins sacred to God!'). By contrast, there seems to be no expression of distaste in the passages discussed here. If the breach was between Wilfrid and Theodore, the former would have found himself in a tricky situation – he could hardly appeal direct to the pope against Theodore when Theodore was carrying out the pope's wishes – hence perhaps the emphasis on his mistreatment by Ecgfrith and his queen in the recollections of Stephanus.

To conclude: in his portrayals of Benedict Biscop and Wilfrid, Bede may be seen to be a consummate selector of material, including points about Benedict Biscop's secular background and close involvement with Ecgfrith as well as stressing his pious character as befitting the founder of Wearmouth; in the case of Wilfrid, much more is omitted than might have been included if he had followed Stephanus slavishly or uncreatively. It seems impossible that he was unaware of all the details in the *Vita Wilfridi*, given his familiarity with both the persons and the material in it; it therefore appears that where Stephanus provides us with detail about Wilfrid not repeated by Bede, either Bede thought it should *not* be said, or he did not consider that he was the person to say it. Taking the second point first, Bede's lowly status meant that he was not in a position to be indiscreet about the weaknesses of those who were, or who had recently been, in positions of authority, and his spiritual superiors. He might equally have thought that some things ought *not* to be said because of good pastoral reasons (repeating unseemly material could hardly be seen as building up the faith of his readers – edifying them – and this was clearly part of Bede's overall agenda in his scholarly activities). The passage of time undoubtedly had some effect, too: 'while it is fair to argue that Wilfrid had had some committed opponents and had been a factional figure, his reconciliation with the Northumbrian establishment c. 705 and death a few years later does seem to have been the end of the matter' (Higham 2006, 96). Bede probably had political reasons too, though he may himself not have been so aware of them as we might imagine – the ultimate patron and founder of his beloved Wearmouth and Jarrow being a king whose reputation, character, motivations and general disposition is utterly at odds in the HA with the (literally) damning account provided by Wilfrid's biographer (though Bede's account of Ecgfrith is less flattering in the HE). Thus when we come to consider depictions of Wilfrid, and in particular the first breach between Wilfrid and his opponents and its (albeit temporary) resolution, we might note that the *breach* certainly for Stephanus is with *Ecgfrith* because of Iurminburh, an 'Anglian Jezebel', for which he suffered his second exile to Mercia, and was Bishop of Leicester 692–702, but the *reconciliation* is with Theodore. Stephanus' language is vitriolic and polemical; Bede counters it by focusing on the positive – his images of Wilfrid are replete with natural characteristics of which none could disapprove, entirely appropriate for a bishop-to-be; as for the Wilfrid of the later crisis, his descriptions (if they can be called that) are sparse, and he goes so far as to apply his principle of *omission* to the limit (Iurminburh is air-brushed out of the *HE* in a manner upon which Stalin would surely have smiled).

This is in line with Bede's aim in all his historical writings, to write *ecclesiastical* history: its focus is the *gesta erga fidem Christi* and it regards events as divine as much as human in origin, if not more. Davidse (1996, 9–10) draws attention to the approach taken to history by Augustine in the *De Doctrina Christiana*: '*historia* ... depends on research into what is effectuated by time or is instituted by God ... the "biblicization" of time, fact and meaning.' We might also note Nora Chadwick's view that what Bede was writing is 'cautionary ecclesiastical saga' (Chadwick 1958, 23). Bede's omissions of what seem to us salient or significant events may have been due to political expediency, but there is also for a monk and scholar the desire to make sure that what he includes in his narrative is *edifying*, despite the fact that in large part this is an idea of history 'from which we have become totally estranged' (Davidse 1996, 5). Higham (2006, 97) suggests that 'his purpose should be framed in terms of his wish to set before his audience a series of exemplary relationships between God and his peoples in an insular context ... in terms designed to inculcate appropriate behaviour among his fellow countrymen in the present.' For Bede, as he composed his histories, the injunction of St Paul from Philippians IV. 8 seems to have been colouring his processes of selecting material: 'whatsoever things are true, whatsoever things are honest, whatsoever things are just, whatsoever things are pure, whatsoever things are lovely, whatsoever things are of good report; if there be any virtue, and if there be any praise, think on *these* things.'

Bede appears above all to have left a positive picture of Wilfrid, who despite his shortcomings (however exaggerated they may have been in some quarters) *was* a duly consecrated bishop, and whose time at Hexham overlapped with some of Bede's most productive time – and may also have been a time when he was gathering together what was to prove to be the raw material of the HE. Higham (above, this volume) suggests that in HE V, 19, Bede 'is in fact holding up [Wilfrid] as an exemplary figure', in the tradition of summary obituaries comparable to that which he offered in II, 1 for Gregory the Great. By contrast, although in the HA he showed no disrespect to the memory of Ecgfrith, who was royal patron of his own monastic house and the donor of all the land on which it was founded, in the HE 'Ecgfrith provides a case study as to how a king should not behave' (Higham forthcoming). Bede's accounts of Wilfrid also reflect the current *realpolitik* in Northumbria – and in his view of ecclesiastical history, the will of God *had* been done, and saintliness *must* have triumphed.

9: *St Wilfrid – a European Anglo-Saxon*

RICHARD N. BAILEY

I

Rudyard Kipling doesn't appear on most reading lists for St Wilfrid. Which is a pity, because his collection of essays entitled *Rewards and Fairies*, has an entertaining short story about Una, Jimmy and Puck (Kipling 1910; see Pl. 9.8). They meet up with a very loquacious St. Wilfrid, whom the children perceptively observe is 'awfully princely'. Inevitably, he is a somewhat Edwardian figure. Thus his analysis of seventh-century Anglo-Saxon society in Sussex closely resembles a later view of colonial peoples in Africa and India: 'there is little one can do with that class of native except make them stop killing each other'. He is also surprisingly sceptical about the miraculous power of prayer, and about the effectiveness of (what we would now call) top-down conversion – and he is amazingly liberal in his understanding of the hold of traditional religious and social practices. The section which most historians will savour, however, occurs when he looks back on his life and sums it all up: 'On sea and land my life seems to have been one long shipwreck'. Here Kipling comes close to the words on Wilfrid's epitaph in Ripon, as recorded by Bede:

> *... multisque domique forisque*
> *Iactatus nimium per tempora longa periclis*
> ('At home, abroad, long time on tempests tossed'. HE V, 19)

The other essays in this volume will examine some of these shipwrecks and tempests. Here I am concerned to look at the fragmentary physical evidence for the impact on Northumbria of Wilfrid's voyages – both actual and intellectual.

II

Most of what Wilfrid created and patronised has disappeared. The gold and purple silks with which he draped the walls and altars of Ripon's church, together with the vestments of purple and silk he purchased in Rome, can now only be re-created in the mind's eye from the fragments of Byzantine and Mediterranean textiles which survive from St Cuthbert's tomb in Durham and in the great treasuries at Aachen, Lyons and Sens (HE V, 19; VW 17, 55; Bonner *et al.* 1989, 303–66; Chartraire 1911; Martiniani-Reber 1986). Similarly we must turn to the ninth-century Royal Bible, B.L. MS 1 E VI, to sense something of the exotic visual impact of the gospel books, written in 'letters of purest gold on purpled parchment', which the saint's biographer Stephen describes as part of Wilfrid's legacy to Ripon (VW 17; Alexander 1978, no. 32; Webster and

Backhouse 1991, no. 171; see also Henderson 1999, 122–35 on the Late Antique and imperial associations of the colour purple).

We are marginally more fortunate in possessing two fragments of rich metalwork to set against the literary record of a golden cross and gem-encrusted shrine which Bede and Stephen list among Wilfrid's offerings to his church (HE V, 19; VW 17). The gold, amber and garnet cloisonné mount discovered at the Ripon Old Deanery in 1977 is clearly work of the later seventh century – and thus roughly contemporary with Wilfrid's *floruit*; it may have come from a small shrine (Hall and Paterson 1999).

More interesting however, and more relevant to the material to be discussed in the rest of this paper, is the silver sheet now in the British Museum, which emerged from Hexham in the nineteenth century (Pl. 9.1; Kirby 1974, 156–8; Webster and Backhouse 1991, no. 104). About five inches high it carries an incised figure, haloed and holding a book or reliquary, who is set within a diagonally hatched border. His linear features recall those of the figures on the late seventh-century reliquary coffin of St Cuthbert and, like them, his links lie in contemporary continental work. A good parallel is offered by the so-called shrine of St Mumma from S. Benoit sur Loire, whose decorative plates are attached to the wooden core of a reliquary and carry similar crude incised figures placed within hachured borders (Périn and Feffer 1985, cat. 31, pl. 91). We cannot, obviously, prove this is actually a Wilfridian survival but, like the exotic silks and the purpled manuscript pages, it hints at the continental and Mediterranean tastes to which the saint was, through his travels and his training, understandably addicted.

III

It is, however, in stone carving that we can now better trace the way in which Wilfrid transplanted the world of Lyons, Rome and Compiègne to his native Northumbria. I begin with speculation about one group of sculptures whose origins have been somewhat neglected. They were discovered by Derek Phillips in his heroic excavations of the 1970s below York Minster (Phillips and Heywood 1995). Most of the carvings he found belonged to a Viking-age cemetery, but alongside them there were fragments from a much earlier stratum of monumental sculpture – a type which had not been clearly evidenced before in Northumbria. Frustratingly, none of these carvings survived complete but they can be convincingly restored as a form of stèle, shaped like an Ordnance Survey trig point, tapering, four-sided, flat topped and about a metre high (Pl. 9.2; Lang 1991, 18, 60–7; Bailey 1996a, 36, fig 17). Carved in a smooth, finely-finished limestone they obviously originally stood indoors; some carried inscriptions whilst others were decorated with a series of incised motifs: outline crosses, zig-zags, diamonds and – in one case – a half marigold.

When Jim Lang published these carvings in the early 1980s he recognised that, in features like the half marigold, they had Merovingian connections. But at the time he was unaware of the discovery of a range of similar, if cruder, sixth- and seventh-century carvings in the Vexin area to the north of Paris whose shape and ornamental repertoire offer close parallels to the York stèles (Sirat 1983, fig. on 74; Bailey 1996, 36, fig. 17). I suggest that these carvings may have Wilfridian connections and originate in the period of his York pontificate. This phase of Wilfrid's career began with his decision to seek consecration in Gaul, his return being delayed to the point where St Chad was intruded in his place. Whatever the reasons for his prolonged stay in France – the decline in the fortunes of his Northumbrian royal patron may not be unconnected – we know that for at least some of that period he was at Compiègne in the valley of the river Oise to the north-east of Paris (HE III, 28). Thirty miles downstream from there is Pontoise in Vexin where these very distinctive forms of monument are concentrated. Did he see them there? When he eventually succeeded to York he restored St Peter's church, putting in glass – and from what we know from the documentary evidence at Monkwearmouth that must have involved bringing in Merovingian technological expertise from Gaul (VW 16; Plummer 1896, 368). Did he then add further Merovingian features by placing these memorial stèles around the church at St Peter's?

Such notions of a Wilfridian transplantation of continental tastes to Northumbria are supported by evidence from both Hexham and Ripon. The saint's biographer, Stephen, was rhetorically agog as he described the main monastic church at Hexham, built at some date after the 671/673 donation (VW 22; Roper 1974a, 169). His feeble tongue prevented him from fully describing the depth of its foundations, its crypts of wonderfully dressed stone, its columns and porticus, its winding passages with spiral stairs, its great height and length. The description is shot through with biblical imagery (O'Reilly 1995, xlix; Laynesmith 2000), but essentially Stephen is describing an ambitious structure which clearly worked at several levels. We can deduce that it stood on what is now the site of the early twentieth-century nave – an area which, through most of the post-medieval period, had been a wasteland of ruins and graves known as Campy Hill. Gradually, through the later nineteenth century and during the first decade of the twentieth century, the site was cleared and the local architect C. C. Hodges plotted the foundations and walling which were then revealed (Taylor and Taylor 1965–78, 297–311; Bailey 1976; Cambridge 1979; Cambridge and Williams 1995). Not all of these foundations belong to Wilfrid's period but there is general agreement that what he recorded included the remains of two Anglo-Saxon buildings: a large one to the west with the surviving crypt under its east end, and a smaller apsed structure to the east (Cambridge 1995, 76–80). During this site clearance various fragments of sculpture also emerged which were once part of the architectural and furniture decoration of the larger multi-storied building. To these I now turn.

Best known among these carvings is the 'frithstol', which would once have stood behind the altar as the seat or throne of the abbot or bishop, flanked by the bench of the lesser clergy (Pl. 9.3; Cramp 1984, I, 192–3; II, ills 1028–32). Even in its present incomplete state it is an impressive piece: monolithic, low-backed and bucket-shaped. What is significant here is that its form cannot be matched among surviving thrones in England; the oft-quoted parallel in Beverley is quite distinct being, like the fragmentary throne in Norwich, composite in construction (Lang 1991, 224, ills 885–887; Radford 1961). We need to look abroad for its origins. And we find the best parallel at the church of S. Vigor le Grand near Bayeux, where precisely this kind of throne exists associated with a sixth-century saint (Bailey 1996a, pl. 15). The ancestory of Hexham's frithstol is Frankish; it is furniture design of *European* Christianity.

Something of the same story is told by several of the architectural carvings now scattered around the niches in the nave at Hexham. These sculptures are quite distinct from the general run of Anglo-Saxon ecclesiastical ornament; they represent survivals of a short-lived phase of Northumbrian stone carving in the late seventh century. The most obvious is an impost decorated on one face with a cut circle (Pl. 9.4; Cramp 1984, I, 190; ills 1012–1015). This is a very rare pattern in English sculpture – another occurs at Jarrow where it is probably a legacy of Benedict Biscop who had trodden the same continental paths as Wilfrid in the late seventh century (Cramp 1984, fig. 17; Bailey 1992, 31–3; 1996a, 31–2) – but it is a Late Antique motif which is found scattered across sixth and seventh-century churches on the continent. There is, for instance, a fine sculptured example, dated by inscription to within a decade of the foundation of Hexham, forming a frieze around the chancel of King Reccaswinth's foundation at S. Juan de Baños in central Spain (Schlunk and Hauschild 1978, taf. 104, 106). Others are spread through Portugal and the rest of the Iberian peninsular (Cordoba, Guadalajara), in France at Periguex and Narbonne, in Italy at Spoleto, Ravenna and Brescia, and even across in Christian North Africa (Bailey 1992, 32; Schlunk and Hauschild 1978, abb. 30, 32; taf. 60, 65, 67, 93). That small fragment in its Hexham niche draws on the seventh-century ornamental vocabulary of the Christian Mediterranean world.

Other carvings make the same point. On the adjoining face of the cut circle impost is a beast, with the original white gesso still adhering to its body (Pl. 9.5). The pacing animal is naturalistically modelled and can be grouped with another beast, with bovine head and small ears, on a second impost from the site as well as the elegant rear end of yet another animal which is now set in the west wall of the nave (Pl. 9.6; Cramp 1984, I, 189–91; ills 1010, 1011). None of these are normal Anglo-Saxon carvings – though the frieze above the west door at Monkwearmouth shows the same influences at work (Bailey 1996a, fig. 14) – but similar smooth-skinned beasts can be found on the continent at sites like Nantes, Ravenna and Grenoble in the sixth and seventh centuries (Bailey 1996a, pl. 11).

There is one carving from Ripon which is part of the same narrative. This is a large gritstone drum, seemingly originally functioning as a capital, which was found during excavations over the crypt in 1930 (Pl. 9.7; Coatsworth 2008, 240–1, no. 10; Hall 1995, 25, pls IA, IIA–B). When discovered it was loosely incorporated into an east-west foundation which flanked the north side of the crypt; its wider face lay uppermost. The stone is encircled by three plain *fasciae* which, if the fragment is properly interpreted as a capital, were stepped out from bottom to top; that this is the original orientation is supported by the presence of a shallow circular seating on the narrower face which could have been intended for the associated column. More firmly embedded in a similar position in a foundation on the south side was a similar drum, though in this case lacking *fasciae* and carved in limestone; this was left *in situ* and encountered again in the 1997 excavations (Clarke and Hall n.d., 9). The east-west foundations seemingly ran under the existing Norman piers but are otherwise not closely dated: they could belong to Wilfrid's period or to some later pre-Conquest reconstruction (Taylor and Taylor 1965–78, 2, 517–18). Like the decorated Roman stone found acting as a step in the crypt, this capital was clearly being re-used in a secondary position (Jones 1932, 74–5; Hall 1997, 32–3, 34; Bailey forthcoming). In the *Corpus of Anglo-Saxon Stone Sculpture* Coatsworth (2008, 240–1) identified close – though not exact – analogues among capitals at Reculver in Kent which are convincingly dated to the seventh century, and Blagg's analysis of the Kentish examples suggested that the origins of this type lay in the impost block placed above the capital in Mediterranean churches from the fifth century (Tweddle *et al.* 1995, 162–3, ills 123–38; Blagg 1981, 52–3). The implications of this early dating for the Ripon carving are two-fold. Firstly, the foundations must either belong to a post-Wilfridian period or have been much restored after Wilfrid's date. Secondly, and more significantly in this context, they imply that Wilfrid's church, which according to his biographer was supported by *variis columnis*, contained capitals whose form had been transmitted through the ecclesiastical architecture of the late Roman and Byzantine Mediterranean.

These York, Hexham and Ripon carvings are visual statements of allegiance. Like the silks and the silver plaque they are an assertion of what was implicit in Wilfrid's early training in Lyons and Rome, in his consecration in Gaul, in his speech at the Conference of Whitby and in his appeals to Rome: his English communities were part of a much wider church which stretched far beyond Britain. Northumbria's Christians may have lived, in Bede's words, 'almost under the North Pole' (HE I, 1) but for Wilfrid they were always part of a Mediterranean-centred European faith.

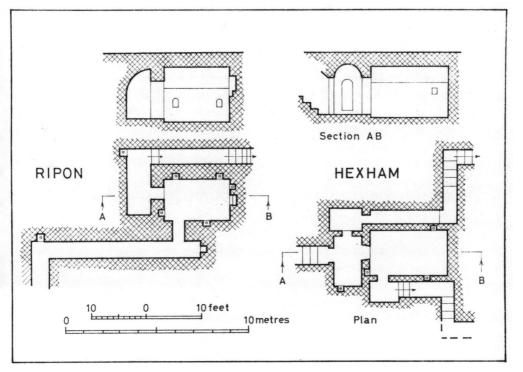

9.1 The crypts at Ripon and Hexham(courtesy: the late H. M. Taylor and Cambridge University Press).

IV

So far we have been looking at scraps but we have, of course, got two much larger survivals from Wilfrid's period, which indisputably reflect his direct involvement: the crypts at Ripon and Hexham (Fig. 9.1). That these two structures should be dated to his period depends upon the identification of Hexham's crypt as being the *domibus mire politis lapidibus* described by Wilfrid's contemporary biographer Stephen as forming part of the main monastic church built by the saint after he had received a land-grant here in 671×673 (VW 22; Roper 1974). I see no reason to doubt this identity. It is true that Stephen writes of *domibus*, in the plural, but this is readily explained as referring to the chambers into which the crypt is divided. Nor is there any trace of another crypt on the site which might be claimed as the structure described by Stephen; the extensive trenching of the monastic area in its post-medieval phase would certainly have encountered any such had it ever existed. And finally, in this catalogue of reasoning for a Wilfridian survival, the excavations of 1978 demonstrated that the crypt is of the same build as a substantial east-west wall which pre-dates the foundations of the twelfth-century south wall utilised in the present nave (Bailey and O'Sullivan 1979).

That Hexham's crypt goes with Ripon's is clear, as Walbran was the first to recognise (Walbran 1848, 4). Admittedly Stephen makes no mention of this part of Ripon's church in his description of the dedication of that building (VW 17). But this is not fatal to the case for a Wilfridian origin: Stephen's concern was to record the impressive dedication ceremonies and the land grants which accompanied Wilfrid's foundation. In purely negative terms, Ripon and Hexham belong together in the sense that their plans – though not identical – are totally unlike any others known in Britain or Europe (in general see: Thümmler 1958, 97–104; Taylor 1968; Taylor and Taylor 1965–78, 3, 1014–17; Grabar 1972, 436–52; Heitz 1977; Magni 1979; Crook 2000). More positively, they share distinctive elements of their layout, constructional techniques and metrology (Bailey 1991, 6–9; Hall 1993, 39–40, 42; 1997; Bidwell 2010 and this volume). Both were built of recycled Roman stone in large holes which were then backfilled against the rising walls. Both have walls underpinned by plinths and were heavily buttressed by rubble against the east wall of the main chamber. Both have western ante-chambers, with air vents to the surface, which preface vaulted main chambers of identical width. The two entrances to the main chamber stand in the same relationship to each other at both sites and are of the same height. Both have northern passages of near-identical width flanking the main chamber. Both, as Jones, Hall and Bidwell have shown, use the same unusual system of rib vaulting (Jones 1932, 75–6; Hall 1997, 31–2; Bidwell 2010 and this volume). And both use similar kinds of mortar (Hall 1993, 42).

Against these identities must be placed obvious differences: in the direction of the southern passages; in the presence of a western entrance at Hexham; in the half or full-vaulted nature of the antechambers; in the precise positioning and form of the lamp niches; in the presence of a shallow relic niche in the east wall at Ripon. But all are explicable in terms of the assimilation of lessons learned at one site (Ripon c.669×678) in building at a second (Hexham post-671×673). In summary, a Wilfridian attribution of these two crypts is incontestable. Thus not only are these rare (and well-dated) survivals from the earliest centuries of English Christianity; they also bring us into direct contact with the mind of one of our major saints who, guided by the Holy Spirit, *opera facere excogitavit* ('thought out how to construct these buildings' – VW 22).

Before we engage with the sources for Wilfrid's crypts it would be helpful briefly to summarise their function. Sited below the main altar at the east end of the main monastic church, one of their purposes was probably that of holding relics – among them no doubt the carefully catalogued material which Wilfrid had brought back from his frequent journeys to Rome and to continental shrines (e.g. VW 33). Some years ago I argued that access to the reliquary chamber was *via* the north passage at both sites; this approach would best explain the function of the smaller western ante-chamber. Importantly, the implication of the 1978 excavations at Hexham was that this passage was probably entered from a side porticus or from outside the main body of the building (Bailey and O'Sullivan 1979; Bailey 1996b, 11). An entrance from the north side – particularly at Hexham where the evidence survives best – would work theatrically by bringing the pilgrim down a dark narrow passage, with confusing changes of direction and levels, into a gloomy ante-chamber which in turn opened out into a well-lit chamber in which the jewelled reliquaries would stand, reflecting the light from the niches set around the chamber. It was precisely this type of architectural drama, involving disorientation and sudden revelation, which intrigued William the Cantor in describing the tenth-century crypt at Winchester – and it would also well exemplify what Peter Brown identified as a characteristic of shrine architecture in providing 'a microcosm of pilgrimage' by 'playing out the long delays of pilgrimage in miniature' (Campbell, A. 1950, 69; Brown 1981, 87).

What was the inspiration behind these two idiosyncratic crypts? They are often said to be derived from the so-called 'annular' crypts of Rome, of which the most famous is that traditionally attributed to Gregory Great in St Peter's and dated to 590×604, a form which was revived on the continent in the Carolingian period (Taylor 1968; Crook 2000, 80–2). In this type a subterranean corridor, accessed by steps to the north and south of the sanctuary, curves to the east beneath the altar; at the apex of the curve a straight corridor runs westward to the small relic chamber (Crook 2000, 80–3). It is, in fact, not entirely certain that the St Peter's arrangement was of Gregory's date, but the type was certainly established in Rome by the time Wilfrid was touring its sites: S Pancrazio of c.625 provides one such well-dated survival (Crook 2000, 82–3). However, though some examples of this plan do have angular forms (see Heitz 1977, pl. 1; Taylor 1968, figs 1, 6; Crook 2000, fig 33), the relatively large size of the Wilfridian main chambers and the presence of ante-chambers in combination with eastern entrances suggest that they are not closely related to these annular plans and that, indeed, they were designed to function in a very different manner from the types spawned by these early Roman examples. In particular, the space available for liturgical activity in the English structures is noticeable; Ripon certainly had an altar here in the sixteenth century (Hall 1995, 19, 24).

It is possible, of course, that Wilfrid was drawing upon some continental prototypes which have failed to survive. Such hypothetical ancestors might be reflected in other crypts: the complex eighth-century phase of the crypt at Saint-Laurent in Grenoble, for example, has a chamber flanked by passages which approach from the east whilst a church at Disentis in Switzerland preserves a crypt, inserted in the eighth century, which offers a parallel to Ripon in its combination of eastern and western passages (Girard 1961, figs 20–3; Sennhauser 1979, fig 14; see also: Fernie 1983, 62–3; Crook 2000, 60, fig 13).

Unwilling to accept the notion of lost prototypes, and in the absence of any clear parallels among other crypts, some scholars have argued for the influence of other types of structure on the Ripon and Hexham forms. Prominent among these are the catacombs of Rome (Gem 1983, 3; Crook 2000, 92–3). Wilfrid himself must have visited them, for they were part of the tourist attractions of the seventh-century city – and they must have been the source of many of the carefully catalogued relics with which he returned laden to England (for such labelled material at Senlis see Laporte 1988, 133–50). True, the catacombs are like Hexham and Ripon in that they are made up of narrow corridors which open into vaulted *cubicula*, where the funeral feasts could be held. Miniaturised and, by contrast with the Roman catacombs, more formally integrated into the above-ground structures at Ripon and Hexham, these Roman passages might have provided some inspiration. But it is all pretty tenuous.

Some twenty years ago I suggested another approach to this problem, which fits well with what we have seen of Wilfrid's awareness of the place of Northumbria in a wider Christian church centred on the Mediterranean (Bailey 1991, 20–2; 1996, 16–17). The crypts, I suggested, embody architectural allusions to one of the seminal buildings of Christian architecture: the tomb of Christ in Jerusalem (Conant 1956; Krautheimer 1971b; 1971c; Biddle 1994; 1999; Wilkinson 2002, 365–8).

At first brush, admittedly, this seems highly unlikely. There is, first, the problem of general shape: incorporated into Constantine's great ecclesiastical complex, Christ's grave was surmounted by a great rotunda. The Church of the Holy Sepulchre was essentially round. This is the feature which draws comments from all early medieval travellers and writers: thus Adamnan, the late seventh-century abbot of Iona, claimed that the Gaulish traveller Arculf had described it to him as *mira rotunditate ex omni parte conlocata* ('shaped to wondrous roundness on every side'), whilst Bede, drawing on Adamnan, identifies it as 'the round church of the Anastasis' in his influential *De Locis Sanctis* (Meehan 1958; Fraipont 1965, 254–6, translation in Foley and Holder, 1999, 7–8; see also HE, V, 16). The various plans which accompany ninth-century copies of Adamnan and Bede's works, all drawing ultimately on the wax tablet sketch which Adamnan claimed had been made for him by Arculf, further reinforce this description by showing a complex circular structure (Wilkinson 2002, 379–84). Whether Adamnan's account and its drawings are an elaborate literary fiction or not, it nevertheless provides information on what an insular scholar *might have* believed about Jerusalem in the later seventh century (O'Loughlin 2007). And it is similarly as a rotunda that it is reproduced on pilgrim mementoes and on countless medieval ivory and manuscript illustrations, as well as becoming a defining feature of Holy Sepulchre churches spread across Europe (Krautheimer 1971c, 117–30; Biddle 1999, 22–8). So, on the face of it, the Anastasis church seems fairly unlikely as a model for Hexham and Ripon's crypts.

But some of the early medieval depictions in ivory, metalwork and pottery show the actual tomb chamber at the base of the monument as rectangular (Elbern 1962, 386; Biddle 1999, 71, fig. 21; Morris 2005, figs 3.5, 3.6). What is more, the Anglo-Saxon traveller Willibald in the 720s was quite explicit on this issue: *est quadrans in imo et in summo subtilis* ('at the bottom it is square, and it is pointed/slender on top'; Wilkinson 2002, 241; Biddle 1999, 71). The absence of a circular plan is thus no absolute bar to identification with the Holy Sepulchre.

Even more telling at this point is an argument based upon medieval concepts of copying. Here we are best guided by an elegant, and much quoted, paper by Richard Krautheimer, first appearing in 1942, which examined buildings claimed by contemporaries to be imitations of the Holy Sepulchre, but which were 'also astonishingly different from the prototype which they mean to follow' (Krautheimer 1971c, 117). His analysis concluded that medieval 'copying' involved a very different concept to that denoted by modern usage of that word. There is an indifference to precise imitation of given architectural shapes. Rather, copying involved 'the disintegration of the prototype into its single elements, the selective transfer of these parts, and their re-shuffling in the copy' (Krautheimer 1971c, 126). Not everything in the original model need thus be adopted in the copy, nor need those parts which have been selected be set in the same relationship to each other as they are in the original.

In the light of all this, what information about 'single elements' in the Holy Sepulchre would be available to Wilfrid for copying? There is no certain answer, but the early travellers' descriptions and the pilgrim souvenirs in various media mentioned above provide some indication (Biddle 1999, 21–8, 65–73; Wilkinson 2002, 367–8). Thus all sources agree that the entry to the tomb is from the east, and the descriptions and the Adamnan/Bede plans show the central area as surrounded by passages (Wilkinson 2002, 371–3, pl. 2). The main chamber, according to Adamnan, was vaulted overhead (Meehan 1958, 44; see the discussion of the term *camera* in Biddle 1999, 112), and Adamnan describes its height as 'a foot and a half' higher than a fairly tall man and big enough for nine people; Bede expresses the same dimensions by saying that a man can reach its roof (Meehan 1958, 45; Hurst 1960, 638; 1955, 251; Martin and Hurst 1991, 95). All of these 'constituent parts' of Christ's tomb are present at Ripon and, more systematically, at Hexham. What is more, the combination of main and smaller prefacing chambers echoes the two-part structure of the Holy Sepulchre (Biddle 1999, 69, 109, 116–17, figs 64B and C; see also Conant 1956, 4 and Wilkinson 2002, fig. 7).

Parenthetically, in view of the current discussion about the degree to which the two Northumbrian crypts were plastered so as to obscure the Roman tooling and decorative stonework, it may be relevant to note that Adamnan, followed by Bede, comments that masons' chisel marks were visible over the whole interior surface of Christ's tomb (Meehan 1958, 48; Fraipont 1965, 255; HE V, 16).

There are two other supporting arguments which might be deployed in favour of this Holy Sepulchre interpretation. The first is that, in both crypts, the emphasis is on the north side. At Hexham there are two lights in this area, one of them filled by a later image bracket. And Paul Bidwell has noted that the western entrance is so placed that the first glimpse anyone entering from that direction – perhaps in some liturgical procession – would have of the crypt chamber is of that north-east corner (Bidwell, 2010). At Ripon there are equally two lights in virtually the same position, one of which was later expanded into the 'Needle' through which Camden, in the later sixteenth century, recorded that women were passed to prove their virginity (Camden 1637, 700). Under those lights is a stone 'step'; in the nineteenth century Micklethwaite recorded that it was customary to lay flowers and other offerings on this stone (Micklethwaite 1882, 350). The significance, in the present context, of this emphasis by lighting, sightline and tributes is that Christ's tomb was traditionally known to lie on the northern side of his vault, a location which is echoed in the positioning of Easter sepulchres and chapels in many Holy Sepulchre churches (for the north side position see: Wilkinson 2002, 173, 241; Fraipont 1965, 255; Hurst 1960, 638; 1965, 251).

A final argument depends upon metrology. This is a field which is fraught with methodological controversy, and more work is needed on Hexham and Ripon now that we are beginning to get more accurate plans of both crypts (for some of the issues see: Huggins *et al.* 1982; Fernie 1985; 1991; Kjølbye-Biddle, B, 1986). Some 20 years ago I argued that the main lines of the two structures were laid out in terms of rod lengths of 5.03 m (16½ modern English feet; Bailey 1991, 7–9, fig. 2); this conclusion now needs re-examination, though certain key dimensions do seem to reflect that unit of length. Of more immediate relevance here is the smaller unit of the 'foot' – a unit which varies in length across the differing systems seemingly in use in the early medieval period. We have already noticed that the main chambers at Ripon and Hexham share an identical width; this varies between seven feet six inches and seven feet nine inches at both sites when measured (in Imperial terms) from wall face to wall face. When I first wrote on this topic I argued that such a measurement equated neatly to seven 'Drusian' feet, thus invoking a unit which we know to have been used in seventh-century Winchester (Kjolbye-Biddle 1986). What I had ignored at that point was the fact that construction trenches for the chamber would be laid out to accommodate the width of the plinths underpinning the walls, rather than the widths of the walls themselves. The distance between the *inner* faces of the plinths emerges as seven modern English feet – and Fernie's work has conclusively demonstrated that the English foot of 0.3048 m was in widespread use in the Anglo-Saxon period (Fernie 1991). Whichever measurement system was in use, it does appear therefore that seven feet is a significant dimension, shared between the two sites. The importance of this conclusion here is that seven feet is the well-attested length of Christ's tomb; Adamnan and Bede both assert this and Arculf, indeed, had measured it *mensus est manu* 'with his own hand' (Meehan 1958, 44; Fraipont 1965, 255; Hurst 1965, 251). Such transfer of significant measurements was a vital element of medieval copies (Krautheimer; 1971b, 93–6; 1971c, 124–5).

Inevitably this architectural invocation of Jerusalem remains speculative. But, in its defence, one could argue that Wilfrid was not a lone figure in seeking such Anastasius inspiration in the period. For Victor Elbern has convincingly demonstrated that the seventh-century tomb of Mellibaud near Poitiers, with its rectangular chamber entered from the east, arched tomb on the north side and accompanying inscriptions, were all designed to evoke the same Holy Sepulchre source (Elbern 1962, 383–92).

V

Kipling's Wilfrid recognised the shipwrecks in his life. We now have to use what flotsam has survived to us in order to reach the man and to tease out his complex personality. But what I would argue is that, among what can be recovered, his sculpture and his crypts suggest a mind which looked far beyond Britain. Surrounding the daily liturgy of York, Ripon and Hexham were constant visual reminders of – and architectural allusions to – the Mediterranean heartland of the faith which he so vigorously embraced.

Acknowledgements

This paper draws on parts of my general lecture, delivered in York Minster, at the opening of the York Ripon conference in 2009. I am deeply grateful to the Dean and the conference organisers for their kind invitation to play a part in an enormously successful conference. I must also thank Paul Bidwell, Eric Cambridge and the late Richard Hall for their help and advice, though necessarily absolving them from responsibility for the use I made of it.

10: *A Sculptural Legacy: Stones of the North from the 'Age of Wilfrid'*

JANE HAWKES

Introduction

When Wilfrid died *c.*710 the carved stone monuments of Anglo-Saxon North-umbria, which have come to define the public arts of the region, were perhaps not as numerous or significant a part of the landscape as they were to be by the end of the eighth century. Yet, the means by which the ecclesiastical culture of Northumbria would come to be 'cast in stone' had been established: churches had been constructed in stone, as had their architectural and liturgical furnishings, while public displays of death and commemoration were also being articulated in this more permanent medium, and the free-standing stone crosses, which have come to be identified with the public arts of Anglo-Saxon England, were starting to be erected.

At Ripon and Hexham, Wilfrid's churches had been standing for some 40 years (VW 17, 22), their crypts being still extant (Bailey 1993), along with the frith stool and some of the elaborate carved stonework that decorated the building(s) at Hexham (Cramp 1984, 174–93, pls 167–88); and from the church at York which Wilfrid had restored (VW 16) are the distinctive funerary *stèles* from the seventh-century cemetery (Lang 1991, 60–7, pls 44–102). And, of course there were other centres marked by stone buildings: the stone church at Corbridge, for instance, five miles down-river from Hexham, which stands in the *vicus* area of the Stanegate fort of *Corstopitum*, preserves stone features from the fort in the form of the large and imposing arch at the west end of the nave, marking the point of entry from the western porch into the body of the church (Taylor and Taylor 1965, 172–6). Although no monumental stone crosses survive from this site, at Hexham itself is the lower part of a cross-shaft, dated to the mid-eighth century, decorated on one face with the image of the crucifixion, the other three faces being filled with stylised plant scrolls (Hexham 2: Cramp 1984, 176–7, pl 173); at York are the remains of another such monument which can be dated to the eighth century (York Minster 1: Lang 1991, 53–4, pls 1–2). While the plant-scrolls filling the shaft from Hexham are uninhabited, those at York are filled with various creatures receiving sustenance from the fruit of the plants, as do the similar scrolls on the cross fragments from Croft-on-Tees (Co. Durham) and Easby, in North Yorkshire (Croft 1; Easby 1: Lang 2001, 89–92, pls 147–52; 98–102, pls 198–200, 207–9).

So, although at the time of Wilfrid's death the stone buildings and monuments which have come to define the material culture of Northumbria were perhaps not as familiar as they were to be a century later, the earliest articulations of these public art forms were clearly present. Moreover, they manifested some of the extraordinary inventiveness that characterises the early Christian art of the region which, more importantly, Wilfrid and his contemporaries were instrumental in establishing (Hawkes 2007b).

The New Art of Stone

And here, it is perhaps worth pointing out that when the stone monuments and buildings first began to appear over the course of the 7th century, they represented an entirely new and innovative art form; the art of working in stone is generally understood to have been one not practised by the early Germanic settlers in the region in the immediate post-Roman period (Bailey 1996, 23–4; Lang 1999, 271; Hawkes 2003b). But, as a result of contacts with peoples in the west and northwest, the establishment of the papal mission at the turn of the seventh century and other encounters with the late Roman/early Christian world, stone came to be a medium embraced by the Anglo-Saxons for purposes of visual public expression.

Those living in the west and northwest, for instance, had continued to use stone as a medium for erecting churches and funerary monuments throughout the post-Roman period – albeit infrequently. At Whithorn, as even Bede was forced to admit, there was 'a church of stone, which was not usual among the Britons' (HE III, 4), but which has nevertheless been confirmed by excavation (Hill 1997). And, at this site, and elsewhere in the region, funerary monuments still survive that further demonstrate a continuum of working in stone for this purpose (Hill 1997, 437–41; Thomas 1992; Craig 1992).

Nevertheless, it was with the arrival and establishment of the papal mission that stone as a medium for art and architecture was re-introduced into the Anglo-Saxon territories on a large scale, by travellers such as Wilfrid passing through Canterbury on their way to and from continental Europe. The churches of the monastery at Canterbury itself were erected with re-used Roman material, as was the Church of Christ Saviour, set up within the walls of the old Roman cantonal capital, to serve as the head-quarters of the mission (HE I, 33; Cambridge 1999; Hawkes 2003b; 2006). And, most significantly, there was the church – built of stone from the foundations – which was dedicated to *Coronati Quattuor*, the Four Crowned Martyrs. This is an unusual dedication which existed elsewhere only in Rome – and Pannonia, where the saints in question were martyred under Diocletian in 305. In Rome, a fourth-century *titulus* on the Coelian Hill was rededicated to *Coronati Quattuor* in the early decades of the seventh century to mark the translation there of the martyrs' relics (HE II, 7; Cambridge 1999, 211-12). It has been suggested that the Canterbury dedication may mark the further translation of some of these relics to Anglo-Saxon England. What is important here is that the martyrs in question were understood to be stonemasons (Colgrave and Mynors 1969, 158, n 1); a new 'stone' church dedicated to them, set up *within* the confines of the Romano-British cantonal capital of Canterbury, whose landscape had been systematically redefined by its new stone churches, clearly reflects the importance that was being placed on that medium in the first papal ecclesiastical centre in Anglo-Saxon England (Hawkes 2003b).

Precepts and Perceptions of the New Art of Stone
The use of stone also reflects the importance invested in the medium by early Anglo-Saxon churchmen such as Wilfrid due to its perceived potential to express things Roman (Cramp 1974; Hawkes 2003b; 2006; 2007). Wilfrid's staunch defence of the Roman (papal) Church (e.g. VW 10), and his much publicised replacement of the wooden church of the Iona mission at Ripon with a stone church dedicated to Peter provides strong evidence of this (VW 8, 17). But Bede makes the equation clear in his explicit association of stone with Rome in his account of the stone churches (of Peter and Paul) set up at Wearmouth and Jarrow (HA 5). Here the Roman associations were further expressed through the use of *opus signinum*, used for the flooring of Romano-British remains still visible in the landscape of the northeast, as for example, at *Vinovium*/Binchester, Co. Durham (Ferris and Jones 1991; 1995; 2000). It was from this fort that Roman *spolia* was reclaimed in the building of the church at Escomb, often associated with the Wearmouth-Jarrow centre (e.g. Taylor and Taylor 1965, 234–8; c.f. Ó Carragáin 1999; Hawkes 2003b; 2006).

Association with the world of late imperial Rome and the papal Church is also reflected in the design of the stone monuments that began to be erected in Northumbria at this time (Bailey 1996, 46–52; Mitchell 2001; Hawkes 2002b; 2009). For, among the monument forms that would have been encountered by those, such as Wilfrid, who visited Rome were the obelisks. With their squared tapering monolithic form they had become ubiquitous signifiers of imperial victory, and they included in their number the obelisk that stood to the southwest of St Peter's (Mitchell 2001, 90–5). With these connections and the association of Constantine with the 'victory sign' of the cross in Anglo-Saxon England – evident both in the liturgical sculpture at Jarrow (Jarrow 16a–b: Cramp 1984, 112–13, pl. 96), and in the symbolic act of erecting a cross attributed to Oswald by Bede prior to his victory at the Battle of Heavenfield in 634/5 (HE III, 2; Mac Lean 1997) – it is not inconceivable that the triumphal form of the obelisk may have played a part in the development of the squared and slightly tapered monumental stone crosses that were set up in Northumbria during the course of the eighth century. Indeed, such connections may well have influenced contemporary references to, and perceptions of these crosses. The runic inscription on the early eighth-century monument at Bewcastle (Cumbria), for instance, refers to the cross unequivocally as *þis sigbecn*, 'victory sign' (Bewcastle 1: Bailey and Cramp 1988, 61, pl 116; Hawkes 2006).

Similar sources of influence may also lie behind the distinctive monumental columns that were set up in Northumbria in the late eighth and early ninth centuries: at Masham and Dewsbury, in Yorkshire (Masham 1: Lang 2001, 168–71, pls 597–681; Dewsbury 1–3: Coatsworth 2008, 129–33, pls 190–7; Hawkes 2002b; 2006; 2009). While these recall the imperial triumphal columns of late antiquity with their arrangement of figural ornament in horizontal registers encircling the length of the columns, their smaller dimensions may equally reflect the influence of the Jupiter columns (Bauchhenss and Noelke 1981) that stood throughout the early middle ages in the landscape of north-western Europe which was traversed by those travelling to and from Rome (e.g. VW 3–4, 6, 12, 27–28, 56).

Such encounters with the triumphal stone monuments of the earlier Roman imperial world would have been further enhanced by the sight of the stone furnishings in the Christian churches that came to inhabit it. As has often been noted, the unusual monolithic nature of the so-called 'frithstol' preserved at Hexham has its best parallels in episcopal thrones from the Merovingian world (Hexham 41: Cramp 1984, 192–3, pls 186–7; Bailey 1996, 36–7 and this volume), but it is also highly reminiscent of the thrones that were set at the centre of the clerical bench that encircled the interior of the eastern apses of churches throughout Italy and Western Europe and which have been postulated for the seventh-century church at Reculver (e.g. Fernie 1985, 35–6, figs 13–14).

Certainly, the decorative motifs and iconographic schemes carved on the crosses reveal the strong influence of this Roman world – imperial and Christian. As Kitzinger (1936) noted, any consideration of the inhabited plant-scrolls – which are so ubiquitous to the cross-shafts, and serve to transform them at one level into the Tree of Life (Hawkes 2002a, 90–3; 2003a) – should include the pilasters that stood in the Oratory of John VII (705–7) in St Peter's. These comprised five first-century spoliated pilasters, and a sixth, commissioned by John, to complete the set. Square in section and standing upright along the wall, these made prominent the motif of a plant-scroll growing from the ground upwards, filled with all variety of animals, birds and even human figures; above them were mosaics depicting the iconic figure of the Virgin and events from the life of Christ and Peter (Nordhagen 1965; 1968; 1969). While the inspiration for the individual foliate designs presented on the Northumbrian sculptures may lie in a complex genealogy of sources (Mitchell forthcoming), it is not unlikely that the association of the motif with one of the most important spaces in St Peter's will have played a part in decisions to adopt and display the plant-scroll in the Anglo-Saxon north.

As far as the figural images are concerned, the influence of the Roman world can be seen in the production of iconographic schemes as well as individual images. At Rothbury, for instance, the iconography of imperial rule, from an object such as an imperial diptych, was adapted to present the divine rule of Christ in the late-eighth century (Hawkes 1996, 84–5), while at Easby, North Yorkshire, at the turn of the ninth century, carvings of Christ and the busts of the apostles are clearly based on similar portrait busts found in numerous contexts in late antique and early Christian contexts (Longhurst 1931; Lang 1993; 1999, 273).

The Art of Relief and the Stone Icon

Against this background of potential inspiration, appropriation, adaptation and innovation in the material, form and decoration of the (relatively new) art of stone sculpture in the seventh and eighth centuries in Anglo-Saxon Northumbria, the art of relief carving itself perhaps deserves further consideration. For, not only was this fairly innovative, it was also highly polychromed and incorporated multiple media in its appearance. In their original state the stone monuments would have stood out, brightly coloured and inset with paste glass and/or pieces of metal. Numerous pieces of sculpture attest to its coloured appearance: as Bailey has noted, the shaft of the cross from Ruthwell (Dumfries), which was preserved in the church after its demolition in the seventeenth century, is recorded in the eighteenth entury as still retaining green paint on its surface (Bailey 2009, 26, n 48), while the base of the slightly later eighth-century cross-shaft at Rothbury still retains traces of red paint (Rothbury 1: Cramp 1984, 217–21, pls 211–15). Later sculptures, such as the tenth-century pieces from Burnsall, also preserve traces of gesso and polychromy (Burnsall 1–2: Coatsworth 2008, 107–12, pls 79–92); as do the earlier, ninth-century fragments from Reculver (Tweddle *et al.* 1995, 46–61, 138, 151–61; Bailey 1996; Hawkes 2006, 109–10). And of course, the more recent find from Lichfield provides perhaps the best-known instance of the phenomenon, as well as giving clear insight into the quality of painterly techniques that could be brought to bear in this medium. The subtlety of shading, gradations of colour, and fine-line highlighting are all abundantly clear (Rodwell *et al.* 2008). Furthermore, the deeply drilled eyes of many of the figures, such as those at Easby, attest to the use of insets, most probably in the form of paste glass, rendering them analogous to the studded eyes of contemporary ivories such as the eighth-century Northumbrian Genoels-Eldern Diptych (Webster and Backhouse 1991, cat. 141, 180–3). And the presence of additional recesses and drilled holes (as on the cross-head from Lastingham), bear witness to the appliqués that were attached to the stone carvings – a metalwork boss set at the centre of the cross-head (Lastingham 4: Lang 1991, 169, pls 582–3; Hawkes 1999b, 413–15). The fragmentary and monochrome remains that today provide evidence of the existence of Anglo-Saxon stone sculpture are clearly far removed in appearance from what was once set up in the churches and across the landscape. The bright colours and (occasionally) glittering nature of the free-standing crosses would have made them instantly visible to those encountering them, whether on landed estates, as possibly suggested in the *Hodoeporican of Willibald* (Talbot 1954, 154–55), or within ecclesiastical enclosures, while the effect of glittering candlelight on the carvings within a church would have been considerable (Cramp 1984, pls 214–15; Hawkes 1999a, 214–15).

With this in mind, it is necessary to consider the carvings themselves in more detail. To a certain extent, this subject has a bearing on the way in which the carvings have been deemed to conform, or not, to certain classical norms. In the early scholarship the 'barbarity' of the carved figures was, at best, noted, but was more often castigated for its inability (or, more accurately, the inability of the carvers), to produce figures carved in relief that replicated the perceived, although resolutely undefined, refinement of classical carving; these deficiencies – lack of proportion, stylisation and flattening – were cited as proof of the influence of the barbaric arts of the Germanic peoples who were incapable of achieving the heights of civilised cultures expressed in the public art of relief carving (Clapham 1930; Kendrick 1939; Saxl 1943; Schapiro 1944; Saxl and Wittkower 1948). These attitudes can, of course, be recognised as the products of the time in which they were published: in the years leading up to the outbreak of World War II, during the War itself, and in its immediate aftermath; thus much of the rhetoric used to frame the premise can perhaps be discounted. Nevertheless, it remains the case that discussion of Anglo-Saxon art, generally, has regarded the tendency to render figures and animals as less than realistic or naturalistic entities, as a result of the Germanic Anglo-Saxon tendency to abstraction and stylisation evident in the traditional arts of the metalworker (Spearman and Higgitt 1993, 1–2; Kendrick 1939, 111–12; Wilson 1984, 53–6; Henderson 1999, 56–8.).

While this may indeed be the case, it was certainly not a characteristic unique to the arts of the Anglo-Saxons (Bailey 1996). A brief consideration of the carvings circulating in the late Roman, early Christian world of the fifth and sixth centuries demonstrates many features analogous to those identified in the Northumbrian carvings. The consular diptychs for instance, reused on the altars of Anglo-Saxon churches in the seventh and eighth centuries, are characterized by considerable stylization, abstract flattening, and odd proportions, in the context of representing the apparently 'real' event of the inaugural games officiated by the consul (Pl. 10.1). By elevating and enlarging the consul with the symbols of his office and magisterial authority, and isolating him from the circus depicted below, man and games are presented 'non-realistically'; the circus itself is reduced to a series of diminutive figures placed, apparently randomly, on an 'empty' ground framed by the semi-circle demarcating the arena. This organisation negates any notion of perspective, of the games taking place 'within' an arena 'before' the consul enthroned in his 'box'. Events taking place in 3-dimensional space have been effectively reduced to a two-dimensional planar surface. The result is the articulation of the visual rhetoric of *aulic* art that distorts representations of space and form to emphasise, in this case, the consul's majesty and authority within the imperial hierarchy (Hawkes 2011).

Reconsidering Anglo-Saxon carvings in the light of such late antique visual articulations, it is clear that there are many instances of such phenomena, one of the most notable perhaps being the manner in which the Old Testament figure of David dictating the Psalms is rendered on the column at Masham (Pl. 10.2; Lang 2001, 71, pl 614; Hawkes 2002b; 2009). In most insular carvings it is the reduced scheme of David the Psalmist which is depicted, David himself being shown in profile facing one or more musicians who confront him, also in profile (Henderson 1986; Hawkes 2005, 267; 2009, 35). This is also the case at Masham, but here, unlike the other insular versions, it is the full scheme of David in the act of dictating that is illustrated, and he is depicted as enlarged in relation to the three figures accompanying him. In fact, he is articulated in keeping with the principles of *aulic* art which, when employed to illustrate the Psalmist with his musicians, depict David as the largest figure at the 'back' of the scene, surrounded by his courtiers and musicians who are reduced in scale relative to the space they occupy to the 'front' of the scene; it is an articulation of space that prioritises degrees of individual human/social importance at the expense of perspectival logic (Wright 1967, 72). The result, as at Masham, elevates and 'foregrounds' David as the principal figure in the scene, while those recording his divinely inspired words and song are appropriately reduced in relation to him, being presented as diminishing in size the further they are from him in conceptual space. The whole is a complex expression of three-dimensional space organised on the two-dimensional surface of the stone column that successfully combines the 'traditional' profile presentation of the figures with the late antique visual rhetoric of *aulic* art.

With this in mind, it is worth reconsidering the 'style' of the Northumbrian carved figures, for if they can be removed from the categories of 'inadequate' classicism, or cultural hybridity, it is possible that they may usefully be regarded as reflecting quite deliberate visual manipulation. Rather than presenting a stylised, ill-proportioned and 'flattened' version of classical art under the presumed influence of more traditional artistic vocabularies, the act of visual re-location involved in the presentation of David dictating the Psalms at Masham – of removing the subject from the visual illusion of 'real' time and space – serves to render the figure of David all important, foregrounding the authority inherent in his role as divinely inspired Psalmist, prophet and forefather of Christ.

Elsewhere, such 'dis-proportion' is used for similar purposes, but in different ways – especially in the panels depicting individual figures in non-narrative settings, such as the busts of the apostles that cluster in the panels on one face of the cross from Easby (Pl. 10.3a; Lang 1999, 273, pl 1; 2001, pls 195–6, 201–3). Here, presented in groups of three and six in the three panels set below that containing the figure of an enthroned Christ, each apostle is portrayed as a bust emerging from the frame containing the group, or from 'behind' the halo of the apostle 'in front'. At the base (Pl. 10.3b), the haloes of the lowermost row of figures cross over one another and on each side stand proud of the spiral columns supporting the arch containing the panel, while being cut off by the inner roll moulding running the length of the shaft; above them two further figures emerge from behind the lower row of haloes, and, although theirs too cross over one another, both are contained by the spiral columns. This has the effect of apparently crowding the apostles into a confined space, while placing two of them coherently behind the other three. Such coherence is broken, however, with the figure surmounting the group who logically could be considered as placed far 'behind' the others. Yet this expectation is denied by the fact that his halo, unlike those of the apostles 'before' him, obtrudes over the upper arch enclosing the group, and by the fact that twisted strands of plant scroll emerge from 'behind' his shoulders and pass behind the arch. Illogically he is thus placed on the same plane as the three figures at the 'front' of the group.

Here, the art of relief carving has been exploited to contradict the expected means of expressing depth and varied planes of existence which were well-established in late antique and early Christian carving. Yet even here, such expectations could be exploited to achieve the required effect, as with the ivory relief panels from the sixth-century throne of Maximianus in Ravenna. The five panels set below the seat of the throne each contain a single standing figure; at first glance these figures each appear to be standing in a row alongside one another (Bovini 1990, pl. on 22). However, the panels are arranged so that the outer and middle panels stand proud of the other two; the illusion of a shared plane is created by the fact that the figures in the outer panels stand with their feet on the lower horizontal frame while those in the inner panels stand with their feet obtruding over the frame or over the columns flanking them. While this creates the illusion of setting the two pairs of outermost figures on the same level, the overall effect sets the central figure of John the Baptist on a plane slightly further forward than those flanking him. It is a subtle but effective means, made possible by the art of relief carving, of presenting figures which occupy varied surfaces as if they exist on only two planes, with a single figure standing forward of the others. An analogous artifice has been used at Easby to present figures that exist both in a receding plane and on the same planar level.

Rather than indicating an incomplete understanding of the sophisticated effects that can be achieved in expressing varied planes of diminishing space in relief carving, it seems that the apparently contradictory presentation at Easby may well have been intended. One result of the visual conceit is to foreground the books and scrolls held out in front of the apostles who cluster in the foreground of each panel, and so highlight the New Law.

Another perhaps more important consequence is the resulting prominence placed on the figure of Christ in the panel above the apostles (Pl. 10.3c). As each 'uppermost' figure in the apostle panels is emphasised by the distortions of varied surfaces within each panel, so the figure of Christ is fore-grounded in relation to those 'below' him. Furthermore, like the figures of Christ in Majesty at Bewcastle, Cumbria, and Ruthwell, Dumfriesshire (Bailey and Cramp 1988, pls 94, 683) the Christ at Easby is enlarged within the frame, his arms held tightly at his side, effectively reduced to the absolute essence of majesty and authority – in a manner analogous to, but perhaps articulated with more emphasis than that expressed by the official portraits of the consular diptychs. At Easby, where the panel has been identified as presenting the *Traditio Legis* (Lang 1999, 273), the enthroned Christ is given additional emphasis by being carved in a plane apparently forward of the two saints flanking him whose bodies stand half hidden by him and the surrounding frame. The effect is further exaggerated by the way in which the deeply dished halo of Christ, like those of the uppermost figures in the panels below, extends forward of the upper arched frame. Rather than contradicting the logic of receding space, however, the overall effect here serves to dissolve the frame, allowing the figure to move from one plane into another – in this case, situating the Divine within the space that lies between sculptural surface and viewer. The result is a three-dimensional icon, which achieves a complex re-presentation of the Divine.

And here, the term 'icon' is worth considering further. Evidence from the sixth century onwards provides many examples of the painted panels which are understood to be 'icons': wooden boards painted with depictions of a holy being or object. The most common subjects were Christ, the Virgin, saints, angels and the cross, but 'events' such as the Crucifixion were also included. Yet, while it is the painted wooden board that is commonly considered to constitute the material icon, it is clear that they could be constructed in other media and still serve the same function, so as portals through which the human viewer could gain understanding of the divine. Or, put another way, they might serve as the means by which the viewer could contemplate the nature of the divine. Thus, in Rome during the seventh and eighth centuries, painted panel icons, generally of the Virgin and Child but also of Christ, became prominent features in sacred spaces. At the same time, icons in other media were also venerated: the almost life-size panel contained within its painted frame in the Catacomb of Comodilla provides one such example; graffiti nearby testifies to the presence of Anglo-Saxon visitors to and viewers of the image (Nicolai *et al.* 1999, pl. 121). Elsewhere, at S. Maria Antiqua, the church serving a papal *diaconium* and so frequented by early pilgrims to Rome, are the icons of the Three Holy Mothers and the Virgin and Child, as well as a single framed figure on one of the columns (Nordhagen 1968; Izzi 2010). In each case there is a strong sense of frontality, with the gaze of the figure engaging with that of the viewer, while the figure itself fills but is contained firmly within the space of the painted panel, be that wood, stone or brick. All serve the purpose of facilitating access by the viewer to the divine – to understanding the idea that in the incarnation of Christ, the Second Person of the Trinity was united to human nature, thus making salvation possible by breaking down the wall separating God and humanity (Bell 2010).

Thus, images defined by multi-media, polychromy and the clearly defined limits of a framed space, are all aspects of the icons familiar in the context of Christian spaces in the seventh and eighth centuries. These are also the features which characterise the carved figures of Northumbrian sculpture, such as those at Easby. But here, the art of relief carving has been exploited to enable the figures to break through the frames confining them, to inhabit, physically, the space between the divine and the human – something that can only be intimated in the two-dimensional medium of the painted surface.

Furthermore, the documentary sources indicate that panel paintings of divine figures and salvationary episodes were known in Anglo-Saxon England; the earliest account of Christian art in the region is, after all, Bede's description of the Augustine mission's progress to their headquarters within Canterbury bearing a panel painting of Christ (HE, I, 25); the most famous such painting, was of course, the sixth- or seventh-century icon now displayed in the Lateran *Sancta Sanctorum* (Nees 2002, 138–9). There is also the often-cited account of painted boards publicly displayed in the chapel of St Mary at Wearmouth and the church of St Paul at Jarrow, which included not just figures of Christ, the Virgin and Saints, but events such as the Crucifixion (HA 9). Furthermore, in one of his more extensive defences of the role of figural art in sacred spaces, as part of the contemporary debate concerning icons within the Church, Bede invoked these images, in a manner that is not irrelevant to consideration of the figural sculptures:

> If it was permissible [he says] to lift up a brazen serpent on a piece of wood ... why should it not be allowable to recall to the memory of the faithful, by a painting, that exaltation of our Lord Saviour on the cross through which he conquered death, and also his other miracles and healings through which he wonderfully triumphed over the same author of death, and especially since their sight is

wont also to produce a feeling of great compunction in the beholder
... And again, if it was not contrary to that same law to make
historiated sculptures ... why should it be considered contrary to
the law to sculpture or to paint as panels the stories of the saints
and martyrs of Christ, who by their observance of the divine law,
have earned the glory of an eternal reward? (*De Temp.* II, Connolly
1995, 91–2).[1]

Here, there are two points to emphasise: one is the fact that for Bede,
images could be justified because they produced 'great compunction'
(*compunctionis*). This was understood to be the specific feeling inspired by the
act of contemplation; and this, as Gregory the Great put it, was the means by
which 'we rise to the love of God' (*Moralia* VI. xxxvii. 56: Bliss 1844, 339–40;
Adriaen 1979, 326; see also *Moralia*, XXXI. xxv. 49; *H.Ez.* I. iii. 9; Markus
1997, 23; Hawkes 2007a). In other words, contemplating images was considered
the means by which understanding of the divine could be accessed through
compunction – the process of 'seeing' that was expected in the viewing of icons,
and which provided their *raison d'être* in sacred spaces. Second, and perhaps
more remarkable, is the fact that – in the only surviving reference we have to
carved sculpture *per se* in the pre-Viking world – we find it being invoked as
painted panels (Hawkes 2007b, 23–7). The implication is that in the
ecclesiastical culture of Northumbria at the turn of the eighth century the figures
sculpted in relief in stone panels and highlighted with paint and other media
were considered synonymous with figures painted on wooden panels. It follows
that the two may well have been considered to function in relation to the viewer
in the manner of icons – eliciting contemplation, 'great compunction' and thus
the understanding necessary to achieve salvation.

---

[1] *Si enim licebat serpentem exaltari aeneum in ligno quem aspicientes filii Israhel
viverent, cur non licet exaltationem domini saluatoris in cruce qua mortem uicit ad
memoriam fidelibus depingendo reduci vel etiam alia eius miracula et sanationes
quibus de eodem mortis auctore mirabiliter triumphauit cum horum aspectus multum
saepe compunctionis soleat praestare contuentibus et eis quoque qui litteras ignorant
quasi uiuam dominicae historiae pandere lectionem? ... Si licuit duodecim boves
aeneos facere qui mare superpositum ferentes quattuor mundi plagas terni
respicerent, quid prohibet duodecim apostolos pingere quomodo euntes docerent
omnes gentes baptizantes eos in nomine patris et filii et spiritus sancti uiua ut ita
dixerim prae oculis omnium designare scriptura? Si eidem legi contrarium non fuit
in eodem mari scalpturas histriatas ... quomodo legi contrarium putabatur si historias
sanctorum ac martyrum Christi sculpamus siue pingamus in tabulis qui per
custodiam diuinae legis ad gloriam meruerunt aeternae retributionis attingere* (Hurst
1969, 212–13).

Summary

From this review of the Northumbrian Anglo-Saxon sculptural legacy of the 'Age of Wilfrid', it has become clear that, under the initial influence of churchmen like Wilfrid, the Church in Northumbria adopted rich and varied means in its initial displays of public art in sculptural form during the later seventh and early eighth centuries. The ways in which the medium represented, at the time, a new and innovative art form has allowed some insight into what its materiality might have signified, as a result of its means of transmission, to those responsible for its production, and its anticipated viewers. Further insight has been gained from an exploration of the motives informing the selection of the various monument forms, and the motifs and images used to decorate them. In the light of these observations, it is also clear that the results of such experimentation may well have included the deliberate manipulation of the art of carved relief and the presentation of the human form. The fact that the material and the image were originally highly coloured and inset with other materials may well indicate that the carved figures should be understood to represent attempts to re-create the painted icon; such panels were widely familiar in ecclesiastical contexts and played a specific role in sacred settings as the image made 'real' (Maguire 1996). In the medium of carved stone the art of relief was exploited to present these images as performative – as mimicking, in the way they were carved, to appear as if they inhabited more than one plane of existence. This was the process by which the viewer, engaging in the act of contemplation, was expected to move beyond the material surface to achieve understanding of that which lies beyond. Whether the 'sacred vessels, lamps and other objects', such as 'all kinds of decoration and works of art' (HE V, 20),[2] that Wilfrid, and Acca after him, brought back from Rome, included painted panels/icons like those imported by Ceolfrith, cannot be ascertained, but clearly the cultural legacy of Rome and the papal Church to which Wilfrid contributed involved complex approaches to the visual arts of that culture, and in the sculpture of the North following the 'Age of Wilfrid' it seems that those approaches may have resulted in the sophisticated articulation of stone icons.

[2] *... qui et ipsius ecclesiae suae, ... aedificium multifario decore ac mirificis ampliauit operibus. Dedit namque operam, quod et hodie facit, ut adquisitis undecumque reliquiis beatorum apostolorum et martyrum Christi in uenerationem illorum poneret altaria, distinctis porticibus. ... Sed et historias passionis eorum, una cum ceteris ecclesiasticis uoluminibus, summa industria congregans, amplissimam ibi ac nobilissimam bibliothecam fecit, necnon et uasa sancta et luminaria aliaque huiusmodi, quae ad ornatum domus Dei pertinent, studiosissime parauit (HE V, 20).*

11: *The Sources and Function of Wilfrid's Architecture at Ripon and Hexham*

ERIC CAMBRIDGE

The sources of the architecture of Wilfrid's churches at Ripon and Hexham have been the subject of lively debate as old as the scholarly study of the remains themselves. Many commentators have interpreted Hexham in particular as reproducing specifically Roman architectural forms. Their arguments rely in part upon inferences from the historical information about Wilfrid's continental journeys in which visits to Rome figure prominently. We should certainly not disregard this evidence in seeking to understand the scope and variety of the cultural influences to which Wilfrid was exposed; drawing the inference that specific features of the churches that he erected in Northumbria were derived from particular buildings that he had encountered in Rome is, however, another matter entirely. If we are to avoid the risk of a historically deterministic answer to the question of identifying the architectural sources of Wilfrid's Northumbrian churches we must begin by asking a logically prior archaeological one: what is the distribution of the comparanda to the material evidence from both sites? In contrast to the debate about their architectural sources the question of the function of those churches and, more specifically, of their crypts, is an issue that arguably has not been considered nearly enough. The general tendency has been to interpret them as, in some sense, pilgrimage churches, the objects of veneration being the relic collections assembled by Wilfrid, particularly in Rome, and the location of that veneration being the two crypts. That account may, of course, be correct; yet there are difficulties with it which should at least warn us against uncritical acceptance. Further, the two issues are interrelated: the more weight that is given to Rome as a source of architectural ideas the more readily the traditional view of the function of the churches and their crypts tends to be accepted.

We know nothing about Ripon above ground, so it is only possible to attempt a substantive evaluation of the archaeological context of Hexham; and even there, the only material evidence for its elevation derives from ex situ fragments of architectural sculpture likely to be of Wilfridian date. The most recent analysis of this material (Bailey 1996a) has strongly emphasised its Gallic context. Thus, the closest analogy outside Northumbria to the motif of profile animals on a number of architectural friezes from Hexham is to be found in north-western Gaul, at Nantes (Barral i Altet 1989, 220, fig. 11). They are also paralleled at Monkwearmouth, where Gallic influence is also likely (Bailey

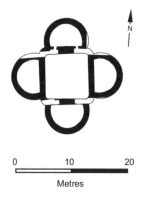

11.1 Rosny-sur-Seine, Saint-Lubin, excavated ground-plan (after Dufaÿ & Bourgeois 1998, fig. on p. 228).

If the rounded corners of the foundation platform of the central vessel continued into the superstructure, it might have been a similar arrangement at Hexham that prompted Prior Richard to describe the church of St Mary there as *fere rotunda* ('almost (or 'approximately') round').

KEY TO FIGURES:

Fabric extant/observed

Fabric inferred

1996a, 33–4). Again, the closest continental parallel to the so-called 'frithstool' is at Bayeux in Normandy (Bailey 1996, 36–7, pls 10–11). Other aspects of the buildings at Hexham also plausibly reflect Gallic connections. For example, though the relationship between the church of St Andrew and the small axial chapel to the east of it (Fig 11.2A) has been compared to that between Old St Peter's in Rome and the Basilica Probi attached to its apse (McClendon 2005, 70), the Hexham chapel was probably freestanding (Taylor and Taylor 1965–78, I, 306–8), and both the layout and likely comparative proportions of the chapel and the church to which it was adjacent are more closely paralleled in Gaul, for example, in the mortuary chapel added to the east of Cologne Cathedral probably in the sixth century (Doppelfeld and Weyres 1980, 574–5, Abb. 3). The layout of Saint-Martin at Autun, an important monastery founded probably in the 590s under Burgundian royal patronage, probably fossilises a similar arrangement beneath a later medieval reconstruction of its eastern chapel (Fig 11.4A: Sapin 1986, 145–6); while a very close (though non-axial) parallel to the plan of the Hexham chapel can be found in the oratory of Saint-Georges within the complex at Saint-Pierre, Vienne (Jannet-Vallat 1995, 258, 262–4; Cambridge 1995, 80).

The evidence relating to one further building at Hexham is pertinent in this context though no archaeological evidence of it has yet been identified. Prior Richard, writing in the twelfth century, refers to a church there that is probably to be identified with the one that Wilfrid erected to the Virgin late in his life following a vision while he lay seriously ill at Meaux (VW 57; Cambridge 1995, 73, note 25). If Richard's description (turriform, almost (or approximately) round, with *porticus* opening from each of its four sides: Raine 1864, 14–15) is a reliable guide to its original early eighth-century form, the closest analogy (and

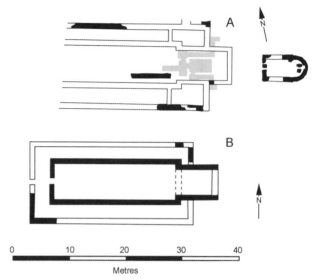

11.2 A, Hexham, St Andrew, ground-plan, possible partial reconstruction by the author and Alan Williams (grey tone indicates crypt). B, Monkwearmouth, St Peter, ground-plan, possible partial reconstruction (after Cramp 2005, I, fig. 6.17).

the one most likely comparable in scale) is to be found not among the more elaborate centrally planned structures of Rome or Perugia (McClendon 2005, 71–2) but in northern Gaul, at Rosny-sur-Seine, a church probably erected in the late seventh or early eighth century, the ground-plan of which is known from late nineteenth-century excavations (Fig 11.1). Unfor-tunately nothing certain is known about its original dedication or context (Dufaÿ and Bourgeois 1998); a centrally planned (though not, alas, closely dated) church dedicated to the Virgin is, however, attested archaeologically at the Auvergnat monastery of Manglieu (Fournier 1996), the location of which relative to the principal church of the complex also closely resembles the likely arrangement at Hexham (Cambridge 1995, 74–6, fig. 14). Cumulatively this evidence suggests a Gallic context for Wilfrid's Hexham, just as the remains from Wearmouth and Jarrow do for their respective churches (Cramp 2005, II, 162–8). In the case of Wearmouth the implication of the material evidence is corroborated in near-contemporaneous sources, for its founder, Benedict Biscop, is recorded as having obtained his masons from Gaul (Plummer 1896, I, 368, 390).

Unfortunately the evidence for the ground-plan of the principal building of the Hexham complex, Wilfrid's church of St Andrew, is too fragmentary to permit more than partial and highly tentative reconstructions, my own and Bidwell's (Figs 11.2A, 11.3A) highlighting some of the options (Cambridge 1995, 76–9; Bidwell 2010, 121–5). The most that can be said is that neither is incompatible with a Gallic origin: if, as I have suggested (Fig 11.2A), the ground-plan resembled Biscop's contemporary church at Wearmouth (Fig 11.2B: Cramp 2005, I, fig. 6.17), that would also imply a Gallic origin for Hexham; if, on the other hand, the more elaborate layout reconstructed by Bidwell is correct (Fig

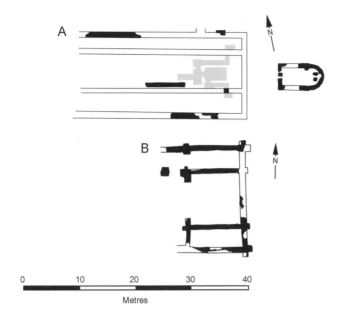

11.3 A: Hexham, St Andrew, ground-plan, possible partial reconstruction by Paul Bidwell (grey tone indicates crypt).

B: Notre-Dame-de-Bondeville, excavated ground-plan (after Zadora-Rio 2005, fig. 1).

0   10   20   30   40
Metres

11.3A) that also finds its closest parallel in Gaul, in the ground-plan of a church recently excavated at Notre-Dame-de-Bondeville, near Rouen (Fig 11.3B). Though its historical context and function remain uncertain (Anon 2001), it is dated to the early seventh century and consists of a squarish sanctuary bay completely flanked by narrow eastern chambers which continued westwards as aisles divided from the nave by columnar arcades (Zadora-Rio 2005, 16–17). The early sixth-century basilica recently excavated at Rezé near Nantes allows us to glimpse something of the earlier history of this aisled rectangular plan type in late Antique Gaul (Pirault 2009, 187, fig. 5).

It may be significant that many of the comparanda of the remains at Hexham are located in the kingdom of Neustria and immediately adjacent regions (Fig 11.5). This territory does not figure prominently in Wilfrid's documented contacts, though it was where his episcopal consecration took place (at Compiègne) and in which the see of his erstwhile patron, Agilbert, was situated (at Paris). If, however, one broadens the discussion to consider material-cultural contacts as a whole, the closeness of the relationship between the Northumbrian material and sites in this region is striking (Bailey 1996a, Chapter 2). They include the closest known analogues of a number of funerary *stèles* from York Minster which very likely date from Wilfrid's lifetime (Bailey 1996, 36–7, fig. 17) and which may even be associated with his episcopate (perhaps commemorating members of his *familia*). These connections may not have been entirely a consequence of geographical proximity: significant numbers of new religious foundations were established in Neustria well into the seventh century, which probably made it increasingly the main theatre of cultural activity and, more specifically, of architectural patronage, in Gaul (James 1988, 151); so, by the late seventh century, this was probably the area of Gaul from which masons were most easily recruited.

So far we have seen that the material evidence for Wilfrid's churches contains a number of features which point to a Gallic origin and others which are at least not incompatible with that hypothesis. Those who support a Roman origin for Wilfrid's architecture interpret this evidence restrictively, as indicating no more than the place of origin of the masons who executed Hexham, while contending that the major features of its design were deliberate copies of architecture that he had encountered at Rome, perhaps transmitted via sketch-plans made during his first visit there (McClendon 2005, 70). The argument depends primarily on the interpretation of documentary evidence, but before turning to a critical evaluation of the relevant texts, the crypt systems at Hexham and Ripon need to be considered first, for these are the material remains that are widely accepted as reflecting a Roman origin. Yet the closest formal parallels to their barrel-vaulted ashlar crypt chambers are arguably to be found not in Rome, but in the funerary structures of Gaul, of which the best known and most complete is the Hypogée des Dunes at Poitiers (Barral i Altet 1996). The completely sub-floor position of the Northumbrian examples can also be paralleled in the chambers underlying the funerary basilica of Saint-Just at Lyons following its mid-sixth-century reconstruction (Reynaud 1995, 275–7). Burial chambers are, of course, commonplace in the catacombs of Rome, though none ever seems to have been preserved as the focus of a cult beneath the sanctuary of a later basilica. The city does, however, provide examples of churches the principal altars of which are located directly above venerated tombs. This is at least broadly analogous to the arrangement at Ripon and Hexham, where the crypt chambers are likely to have underlain the sanctuaries (though not certainly the principal altars) of the churches above them. Further, in contrast to the surviving Gallic crypt chambers, which have only a single entrance stair at one narrow end, some of the Roman tombs are accessed by means of multiple subterranean passages, whether reusing a catacomb gallery, as at Sant' Agnese, or a purpose-built replication of one, as in the corridor crypt of San Valentino (Crook 2000, 90–1). Despite uncertainty as to its precise early medieval arrangement the crypt of San Paolo fuori le Mura, with its entirely sub-floor layout and passages with right-angled turns, provides the closest surviving formal analogy to Wilfrid's crypt passages (McClendon 2005, 30–1), though, as elsewhere in Rome, the focus is again a venerated tomb and not a chamber.

The surviving evidence thus appears to suggest that the design of the Ripon and Hexham crypts should be seen as eclectic hybrids, combining Gallic sources for the central chambers with Roman ones for the access system and their relationship to the upper churches. There is, however, an important caveat: uneven survival may have produced a distorted impression, causing features that might formerly have been present in Gaul to appear distinctively Roman now purely because they happen to have survived there. For example, some Gallic single-entrance mortuary chambers may well have acquired additional entrances the better to accommodate pilgrim traffic once their occupants had become the focus of a cult; others are likely to have assumed a liturgically significant relationship by becoming incorporated into pilgrimage churches erected over them after their occupants had become venerated (Crook 2000, 50–2) and, in that context, the principal altar is likely to have been sited directly above the chamber. Given the exceptionally poor survival of Gallic architecture of this period, the possibility that precedents for all the components of Wilfrid's crypt systems (though not necessarily their precise configurations) might once have existed in Gaul should therefore not be discounted; and if the influence of Roman buildings did play any part in their genesis, that may have been more at the level of generalised recollection than as specific architectural precedents.

One might have expected that, as the documentary source closest in date to the construction of Wilfrid's buildings, Stephen's *Life* would also be the most informative as to their architectural appearance, and hence as to the sources of their design, but his accounts (VW 17, 22) are so permeated by Biblical allusion (Laynesmith 2000, 172–3) that it is tantalisingly difficult to distil specific architectural information from them. Crypts apart, the only attributes that Stephen ascribes to both churches are that they were supported by *variis* (differently-coloured?) columns and *porticus* (aisles or chambers). This is often taken to imply fully basilican plans, but that is not necessarily so, for the reference to columns might equally well describe a structure like the nave of Saint-Pierre at Vienne (Gilbert 1974, 103–4; Bailey 1991, 17), the sole example of a major early Gallic church to have survived in elevation, which has a solid walled nave idiosyncratically articulated by superimposed zones of blind arcading carried on engaged columns (Jannet-Vallat 1995). The point that actually emerges most strongly from Stephen's account is not so much information about the appearance of either building as a concern to distinguish the two. He describes Hexham alone as *multiplex* (manifold?), supported by 'many' *porticus*, and equipped with winding passages on more than one level connected by turning or spiral stairs. His evident admiration for multi-level spatial complexity may itself reflect a distinctively Gallic aesthetic preference (Wood 1986, 75). The contrast with Ripon was presumably deliberate since, as an inmate of the latter, Stephen would surely have exercised any personal bias in favour of the church of his own community. We should therefore be cautious about assuming that the superstructures of the two churches resembled one another as closely as the common features of their crypt systems might otherwise appear to suggest; in turn, that leaves open the possibility that their architectural sources were not necessarily identical either.

The argument that key architectural concepts of the design of Wilfrid's church of St Andrew at Hexham originated in Rome in fact relies upon the evidence of much later sources and in particular on the most extensive account, written towards the middle of the twelfth century by Prior Richard (Raine 1864). But Richard appears uncritically to have identified the structure as it was in his own day with Wilfrid's original church, an unsafe assumption given Bede's evidence that it apparently underwent significant modification as early as the episcopate of his successor, Acca (HE, V, 20) quite apart from the possibility of later undocumented alterations. What is more, the greater part of Richard's text is an elaboration of the description in Stephen's *Life,* so has little independent evidential value as to the architectural form of the church (Brown 1925, 151–5), though it does contain unique information about its decoration. In particular, Richard's account has been interpreted as supplying a specific piece of otherwise unattested architectural information: that the nave elevation incorporated a gallery extending over side aisles. If correct that would indeed be significant, not least because galleries were a prominent feature of recent architectural developments at Rome (Brown 1925, 176–81; Fernie 1983, 61–2; McClendon 2005, 69–70). But the interpretation entails, firstly, taking Richard's description of the main elevations of the church as divided into three stories or zones (*tribus tabulatis distinctos*) to mean that the middle stage was occupied by a gallery, and, secondly, interpreting his remark that it was possible for a multitude of men to surround the nave 'without being able to be seen by anyone below' (*a nemine tamen infra in eum* (sc. '*corpus ecclesiae*') *existentium videri queat*: Raine 1864, 12) as envisaging them concealed from view on a gallery. But the latter requires *infra* to be translated in its classical sense of 'below' (Brown 1925, 152), whereas in medieval Latin the word had come to mean 'inside' or 'within' and therefore need not imply that those concealed were on a different level to that of their hypothetical observer; and there are other ways of envisaging how large numbers of men might have been concealed in self-contained subsidiary chambers on one or more levels. Likewise, a tripartite vertical division of the nave elevation is perfectly conceivable without supposing that the middle stage consisted of a gallery (though it probably does imply that the uppermost stage should be envisaged as a clerestory: Fernie 1983, 61). Since there is no good reason to suppose that any architectural feature of St Andrew's was derived from specifically Roman forms, it follows that neither are there any grounds for hypothesising a disjunction between the sources of the design of Wilfrid's architecture and the Gallic context implied by its material remains.

To postulate a Gallic origin for the architecture of St Andrew's church at Hexham is not, of course, to deny that it may also have embodied more widespread late Antique architectural trends: Gallic architecture no doubt had its regional idiosyncrasies but it was far from being an isolated phenomenon.

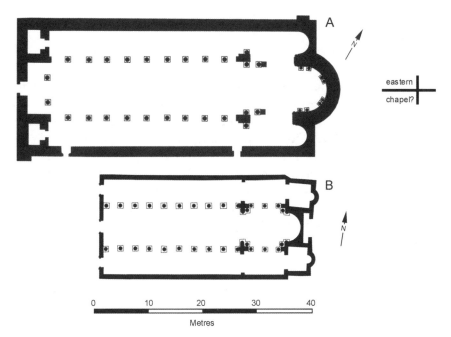

11.4 A: Autun, Saint-Martin, ground-plan, after a plan of 1658 (Sapin 1986, fig. 88);
B: Spoleto, San Salvatore, ground-plan (after Jäggi 1998, fig. 64).

For example, the plans of Wearmouth and Jarrow have been compared to the architecture of provincial northern Italy as well as to buildings much further east (Cramp 2005, I, 353). Though we have already noted the evidence for its Gallic antecedents (above, p. 139) there are hints that the church at Bondeville (Fig 11.3B) also belongs in a wider context. Thus the plan of the late-sixth-century church of Saint-Martin at Autun, though a larger and more elaborately articulated structure than Bondeville, has a comparable basic plan, an aisled rectangle (with the addition of eastern apses) with a squarish chancel, here slightly narrower than the nave, flanked by narrow chambers (Fig 11.4A). In turn, the plan of Autun may be compared to that of San Salvatore at Spoleto (Fig 11.4B), the recent re-dating of which to the long seventh century (Jäggi 1998, 61–78) places it within the same broad chronological horizon. Allowing for regional variations the generic similarity of its plan to that of Autun is striking, and resemblances between some of the decorative elements of the elevation of San Salvatore and those of the later phases of the Poitiers baptistery suggest that the architectural vocabulary of the latter should be seen as a provincial version of contemporary developments south of the Alps (McClendon 2005, 54). Through the relationships hinted at in these fragmentary survivals we may catch a fleeting glimpse of Gallic architecture in its wider Late Antique context, sometimes participating in the mainstream (as at Autun), while at others producing provincial reflexes in more peripheral areas (as arguably at Poitiers and Bondeville).

If Wilfrid's architecture was indeed derived from Gaul in conception as well as execution, one implication is that the supposed contrast between his architectural patronage and that of Benedict Biscop is illusory, a reification of the limitations of our evidence rather than of any substantive difference; to abandon that contrast is not, of course, to rule out the possibility that Hexham was a more ambitious and elaborate structure than either Wearmouth or Jarrow. What is more, an identity in the cultural outlook of the two men, in which Rome was seen as a source of relics and cultural artefacts, but not apparently as a repository of architectural models, is arguably itself thoroughly Gallic, as the closely comparable attitude attributed in near-contemporary sources to monastic patrons in Gaul suggests (Krusch 1888, 456–7 (cap. 2); Palmer 2009, 215–22). The wider architectural-historical implications are no less important, for they suggest that deliberately replicating specific architectural forms as an iconographical statement was essentially a product of the Carolingian renaissance and any attempt to interpret earlier buildings in those terms is anachronistic. The obvious exception would be the possible allusions to Jerusalem and specifically to the Holy Sepulchre explored below (pp. 146–9); but Jerusalem, familiar from the Bible, central to the liturgy, and the birthplace of the apostolic church, is clearly a special case. The issue is ultimately one of *mentalités*: in Wilfrid's day the fact of building a church of dressed stone (or perhaps more specifically of reused Roman stonework) was arguably sufficient to establish its iconographic conformity *iuxta Romanorum morem* (Gem 1983, 2–5).

* * *

It is generally accepted that a significant proportion of the extensive collection of relics assembled by Wilfrid would have been housed at his two principal monasteries (*optima coenobia*: VW 60) of Hexham and Ripon. Precisely where and how they would have been located and displayed at each site is, however, uncertain. It is often further assumed that the primary (if not the sole) purpose of the crypts at Ripon and Hexham was to house those relics and provide access to them for pilgrims; yet no contemporary source corroborates that, Stephen's *Life* being silent on the point. The association of crypt chambers with relics probably came about in Gaul when a number of them acquired a supervening function as settings for a cult and the architectural form underwent a parallel transformation of meaning (see above, pp. 140–1). But these structures would by definition have housed primary relics – whole and undisturbed bodies venerated *in situ* – whereas Wilfrid's collection (and particularly that part of it acquired in Rome) probably consisted mostly of secondary contact relics. This contrast highlights a peculiarity of the sacral landscape of Northumbria, at least as seen from Wilfrid's standpoint, that was surely unique in contemporary Christendom: it lacked a network of primary relic cults. This was almost certainly not due to an absence of candidates but was rather a direct consequence of Wilfrid's aggressively intolerant attitude towards British Christianity, which would surely have entailed a rejection of indigenous cults (Charles-Edwards, this volume, pp. 243–59). Indeed Archbishop Theodore's prescription that all such relics were to be burned (Haddan and Stubbs 1869–78, III, 182 (V, 13)) tellingly reveals their power to perpetuate heresy unless eradicated (Stancliffe 2003, 25). Conversely, the use of orthodox relics to counter heresy or paganism was a papal strategy promoted at least from the time of Gregory the Great (de Vogüé and Antin 1979, 380–1 (III, 30); Norberg 1982, 165 (III, 19)), which must have assumed a particular topicality in the theologically charged atmosphere of Wilfrid's Northumbria.

Contemporary evidence for the way in which secondary relics were housed and displayed is much more elusive than that relating to the primary relics from which they were derived. By the early sixth century at least they seem to have been housed in small, portable reliquaries, often placed in readily accessible cavities in altars (Arndt and Krusch 1884, 505–7 (cap. 30); Van Dam 1988, 48–50) with which they were commonly associated (Norberg 1982, 961 (XI, 56)) and frequently containing relics of more than one saint (Michaud 1999, 201–3). The tendency toward multiplication of altars within a single church is also documented by the time of Gregory the Great, who refers in a letter of 596 to a church containing thirteen altars recently erected by Bishop Palladius of Saintes (Norberg 1982, 423 (VI, 50). If correctly identified as a rebuilding of his cathedral (Vieillard-Troïekouroff 1976, 280–1) this may be the earliest record of a church of a kind which traditionally would not have been expected to contain relics at all being provided with an extensive collection of (surely secondary) apostolic and martyrial relics. The implication is that the association between relics and churches generally (or, more specifically, between relics and altars) was by then coming to be regarded as the norm, and may itself have stimulated the demand for secondary relics. While the latter doubtless played a significant role in the liturgy of the churches into which they were imported, there is no indication that they were regarded as a substitute for primary relics to the extent of becoming objects of pilgrimage in their own right, nor that they were accommodated specifically in crypts.

These Late Antique developments had presumably become established convention by the time that Wilfrid and Benedict Biscop were planning and equipping their Northumbrian churches and what little evidence we have appears to be consistent with that. Biscop's relic collection appears to have been comparable in size and scope to Wilfrid's yet, however he accommodated it within his own churches, he appears to have achieved that without recourse to crypts. Likewise Bishop Acca, whom Bede describes as having assembled a significant relic collection of his own, did not choose to house it in the crypt at Hexham; instead, he is said to have 'placed altars in veneration (*sc.* of the saints and martyrs whose relics he had acquired) in separate chambers within the walls of the church' (HE V, 20). The implication is presumably that Acca placed his relics in (or on) altars, each in a separate chapel. This evidence does not, of course, imply that Wilfrid's crypts were devoid of relics, but it does suggest that, if they did contain them, they would most likely have been associated with one or more altars, and probably formed part of a more dispersed distribution pattern throughout the two churches. It also raises more fundamental problems of interpretation, for even if the crypts had some association with relics, that no longer seems to provide a full explanation of the choice of that particular architectural form but suggests that some additional factor was involved.

If, notwithstanding the reservations outlined above, we consider that the traditional account of the crypts as primarily conceived to house secondary relics is correct, the implication would then presumably be that an architectural form associated with the cult of primary relics was being deliberately chosen in an attempt to compensate for the presence of a less popular substitute. Indeed, contact relics might have needed all the promotional assistance that they could get, for they seem to have met with a significant degree of scepticism in early medieval Northumbria. That presumably explains why the Whitby *Life* of Gregory the Great recycles what was in origin itself a piece of Gregorian propaganda, the miracle story of the *brandea* or strips of cloth which, when cut, demonstrated their credentials by bleeding with the blood of the martyrs with whose remains they had once been in contact (Colgrave 1968, 109–11).

Alternatively, the iconography of the crypts may provide a clue as to why Wilfrid selected this particular architectural form. Bailey has tentatively proposed that elements of the layout of the crypt systems and of the metrology of the main crypt chambers at Ripon and Hexham were intended to allude to the tomb of Christ in Jerusalem (Bailey 1991, 20–2; idem 1993, 12). This hypothesis builds upon Elbern's fundamental reinterpretation of the Hypogée des Dunes outside Poitiers as embodying that same allusion (Elbern 1962, 384–92). The Hypogée is a mortuary structure and the remains interred there do not themselves appear to have become venerated (though relics were deposited with them). We have already noted that the type is well attested in Gaul, the Poitiers example being distinguished by the preservation of features which enable its iconographical programme to be reconstructed. That iconography seems particularly apposite for a mortuary structure and we might therefore speculate that it originated in such a context and would already have been deployed in others elsewhere in Gaul where Wilfrid might have encountered it.

An allusion to the Holy Sepulchre may also be implied – if they do not simply exemplify a common topos in praise of ecclesiastical architectural patronage – by the references to Solomon's Temple in Stephen's descriptions of Hexham and Ripon (Laynesmith 2000, 172–3), for the Sepulchre complex was conceived as a re-creation of the Temple and by Wilfrid's time had come to acquire some of the specific features traditionally ascribed to its Old Testament antecedent (Barker 2007, 65–7; O'Reilly 1995, xlix–l). Other evidence may suggest a more general intention to evoke Jerusalem. The very presence at Ripon and Hexham of an ensemble of apostolic contact relics may have signified that, for it seems to have been specifically the importation of apostolic relics by Bishop Victricius of Rouen into his cathedral city which prompted Paulinus of Nola to describe him as having turned it into the image of Jerusalem (Hartel and Kamptner 1999, 132 (Ep. XVIII.5); Walsh 1966, I, 171). Likewise Wilfrid's church of St Mary appears to have been in some sense centrally planned (above, p. 137), and while he would certainly have been familiar with other examples in the West, most obviously the rededicated Pantheon in Rome (McClendon 2005, 71–2), he may well also have been aware that the ultimate origin of that tradition was probably the church outside Jerusalem which housed the Virgin's cenotaph (Krautheimer 1971a, 111–14) and have intended a specific allusion to that structure.

The key feature of the crypt systems that is not explained by reference to an iconographic evocation of Christ's tomb is the presence of multiple entrances and exits, including specifically two means of accessing the main crypt chambers, one preceded by a vestibule. This is usually interpreted as intended to regulate the flow of pilgrims coming to venerate relics located in the main chamber. But we have already suggested that, while the concept may have originated in devising improved access for the veneration of primary relics (above, pp. 140–1), there are reasons to doubt both that secondary relics were objects of veneration by pilgrims in the same way (above, p. 145) and that they were particularly associated with crypts. Any alternative explanation would, however, still need to account for the evidence of control of circulation that appears to be implied by the common features of the layout of both systems. Two, not mutually exclusive, possibilities may very tentatively be proposed.

If we accept that the main crypt chambers at Ripon and Hexham contained an iconographic allusion to the Holy Sepulchre, they may have provided an appropriate setting for parts of the Passion and Easter liturgy. This was undergoing rapid change in the later seventh century, both at Rome itself (Ó Carragáin 2005, especially chapters 3 and 4) and probably also elsewhere, though evidence of liturgical practice outside Rome, including in Gaul, is as fragmentary as that of the buildings in which it was performed. Wilfrid must have been aware of, and keenly interested in, such developments, which may therefore have influenced his liturgical prescription for the principal churches at Ripon and Hexham, just as his erection of St Mary's at Hexham a generation later may have reflected more recent liturgical developments at Rome (Ó Carragáin 2005, 245). What remains unclear, however, is what recent liturgical innovations might specifically have suggested crypts as an appropriate setting. If the hypothesis that the Hypogée des Dunes at Poitiers also contained a prominent representation of the Crucifixion is accepted (Elbern 1962, 377–83) and, further, if we are prepared to entertain the hypothesis that this was also the case with Wilfrid's crypts, they might conceivably have been associated with recent developments in the veneration of the cross (Ó Carragáin 2005, 189–93). Liturgical associations of this kind might have been reinforced by the presence of appropriate secondary relics, such as oil which had been in contact with Christ's tomb, or even a cross-relic.

An alternative explanation arises from the implications of the possibility that Ripon and Hexham were conceived by Wilfrid as playing pivotal roles in his policy of eliminating heresy among the British population of Northumbria (Charles-Edwards, this volume, pp. 153–4). Preventing the clergy who perpetuated that heresy from exercising their ministry must have been a key priority, and we may speculate that both monasteries might have accommodated numbers of intransigent British clergy, as the practice of exploiting monasteries for the detention of clerical offenders was well established in the western church (Vogel 1952, 194; Bruns 1839, 60 (printing Council of Narbonne, AD 589, canons 5 and 6)) and the security that they offered is not likely to have been a feature of Wilfrid's cathedral complex at York. Ripon and Hexham were probably also close to major royal centres (and therefore, perhaps, to places of assembly) at or near Aldborough and at Corbridge respectively, which may also have made them convenient locations for the reconciliation of large numbers of lay heretics, reminiscent of the settings for the mass baptisms of a generation earlier. Structures embodying the Holy Sepulchre iconography might have been perceived as a particularly appropriate setting for the abjuration of a heresy in which observance of the correct date of Easter was the central issue, and the disorientating spatial complexities of the crypt systems (Bailey 1993, 2) might have been deliberately intended to reinforce that liturgical experience. That the Hexham crypt at least could be circumambulated via its eastern passages independently of the main liturgical space of the church (or, perhaps, without needing to enter it at all: Fig 11.2A) may be significant here, for some rites (including Archbishop Theodore's) excluded penitents from the church altogether during the initial stage of their penance (Charles-Edwards 1995, 163–6). In turn, that might help to explain why Wilfrid's churches were provided with crypts while Benedict Biscop's apparently were not, for the reconciliation of heretics in Theodore's teaching was still an exclusively episcopal prerogative (Charles-Edwards 1995, 166–7).

It may be objected that Wilfrid's hard line approach to dealing with heresy was a comparatively brief episode in the history of the Northumbrian church and is therefore unlikely to have entailed specific architectural consequences. As

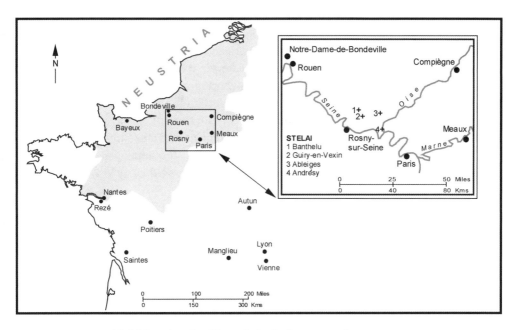

11.5 Map showing Neustria in the later seventh century
(after Rouche 1989, Carte 1, p. 11) and sites in Gaul mentioned in text.

things turned out the policy was indeed short-lived and in its extreme form presumably did not outlast his fall in 678. But that should not lead us to underestimate either the fervour with which Wilfrid, at the zenith of his personal power in the preceding years, and with the backing of Archbishop Theodore and King Ecgfrith, pursued this policy, or the numbers potentially affected by it, for it was very much the ecclesiastical counterpart of Ecgfrith's expansionist policies northwards and westwards into territory where encounter with significant numbers of so-called 'Quartodeciman' heretics might reasonably have been anticipated (Charles-Edwards 2000, 432–8). Ripon, likewise, might have been associated with the tightening of Northumbrian control over the British population in, and west of, the Pennines, areas in which it was granted former British church property (VW 17). The design of a building necessarily fossilises the priorities of its patron at the time of its conception, and though the relative chronology of Ripon and Hexham continues to be disputed there is widespread consensus that both designs date from the decade or so preceding 678. The possibility that they reflect the particular ideological agenda and political circumstances of those years therefore deserves serious consideration.

Whether we interpret the crypts as designed to bolster the cult of secondary relics in the face of local scepticism, or as a setting for contemporary liturgical developments, or as devices for dealing with endemic heresy, or a combination of these, we are still confronted by the same paradox: an architectural form originally intended for one purpose was apparently being adapted for a quite different one. Exactly the same may have been true of the iconography, as an allusion originally conceived as appropriate for funerary structures – evoking the place of Christ's resurrection while awaiting one's own – was adapted to other contexts. There may therefore have been a number of respects in which Wilfrid's crypts were genuinely innovative. If so, that might have been directly attributable to his own personal input, for Stephen portrays him as a proactive patron: at Hexham, taught by the Holy Spirit, he 'thought out (*sc.* 'how') to carry out the (*sc.* 'building') works' *(opera facere excogitavit*: VW 22).

* * *

If a Gallic context for both Wilfrid's architectural and iconographical ideas is accepted, we are left with one final question: how then did the tradition of associating Wilfrid's architecture (particularly at Hexham) with Rome arise at all? By the twelfth century William of Malmesbury believed that Wilfrid's Hexham reflected the glories of Rome and that he had actually lured masons from Rome to build it (Winterbottom 2007, 388–9); but that is not attested in any earlier source and is more likely to reflect contemporary perceptions (Brown 1925, 150), and specifically Malmesbury's own preoccupation with episcopal architectural patronage, than to convey information about seventh-century reality. As Malmesbury's text suggests, the kernel of the tradition of a Roman origin is probably Stephen's well-known remark about Hexham, that he had never heard of any other building on this side of the Alps built in such a manner (VW 22). This may already have been interpreted in the twelfth century (as it sometimes still is (McClendon 2005, 69; cf. Gem 1983, 3)) as implying a specific comparison with Rome, though that goes significantly beyond the text. *Two* comparisons are arguably implied here: between Gallic and Italian architecture in general; and between Gallic buildings in particular, the latter surely being the primary focus of the remark (Wood 1990, 10). But how far did Stephen intend to assert specific factual information about architecture at all? Rhetorical convention is surely also a major contributory factor; the *Life* is, after all, not only avowedly apologetic but also encomiastic, a form in which deliberate exaggeration is only to be expected (Laynesmith 2000, 166–7). That accords with the material evidence which suggests that, though Hexham would not have been out of place in contemporary Gaul, nor would it have stood out as exceptional there. Might Stephen's remark echo the sort of conventional praise that Gallic bishops bestowed upon one another's building projects? If so, his prime concern was to portray Wilfrid as demonstrating the standard of architectural patronage expected of a good Gallic bishop (Wood 1986, 77) and, by implication, to assert his membership of an exclusive continental episcopal confraternity. Thus, even the terms in which Stephen celebrates Wilfrid's architectural achievement are as much a product of Gallic ecclesiastical culture as we have argued is the case with both the stylistic and the iconographical sources of his architecture. Wilfrid's life-long preoccupation with Rome is not in doubt; but that need not imply that he chose to express that by imitating Roman architecture and nor should it be allowed to obscure how profoundly his outlook was shaped by the distinctive ecclesiastical culture of Merovingian Gaul. It was that Gallic nexus which proved to be decisive in determining the sources of his architectural patronage.

Acknowledgements

Profound thanks are due above all to Richard Bailey, to whose friendship and learning my indebtedness over many years is even greater than is apparent from the citations of his published works. I have also received helpful discussion and comment on particular points from Paul Bidwell, Rosemary Cramp, the late Richard Hall, Joyce Hill, Éamonn Ó Carragáin, Clare Stancliffe, and Ian Wood. I am particularly grateful to Alan Williams for his wise advice and infinite patience in producing the line drawings. The University Library in Durham generously permits free consultation of its collections by *bona fide* external researchers; without access to that incomparable resource the production of this paper would not have been possible.

12: *Wilfrid at Hexham: The Anglo-Saxon Crypt*

PAUL BIDWELL

Introduction

A survey of the Anglo-Saxon crypt at Hexham was part of a wider programme of work by TWM Archaeology, which began at Corbridge in 1995 with an investigation on the north side of the river of what had been recognised shortly before as the basement of an Anglo-Saxon water-mill (Snape 2003). At the same time, part of the Roman bridge on the south side of the river was exposed. It was at serious risk of destruction because of long-term changes in the course of the river, and from 2004–8 was excavated, dismantled and finally re-erected on a site nearby where the impressive remains were safe from further damage. The crypt at Hexham, and presumably the church above it, had been built entirely of reused Roman stonework, some of which was thought to have come from the Roman bridge at Corbridge. The fabric of the crypt was analysed partly to see whether this identification could be confirmed and to establish the origins of the other reused stonework, particularly the fine architectural ornament. Much, it was hoped, would also be learnt about the construction and function of the crypt. The survey results and a discussion of their significance have now been published, and this article is a summary of that report (Bidwell 2010).

Wilfrid built the church of St. Andrew at Hexham shortly after 671–3. Stephen, his contemporary and biographer, wrote in praise of the church, built: '... *cum domibus mire politis lapidibus* ...' ('... with crypts [or chambers: *domus*] of wonderfully dressed stone ...': Eddius Stephanus, VW, 22). There are no further references to the crypt until the mid-twelfth century, when Prior Richard of Hexham described it as follows: '*Igitur profunditatem ipsius ecclesiae criptis et oratoriis subterraneis, et viarum anfractibus, inferius cum magna industria fundavit*' ('[Wilfrid] laid crypts and underground oratories beneath the foundations of his church, with branching [or twisting] passages, at a great depth and with great labour': Raine 1864, *Prior Richard*, Bk I, ch. iii; translation as in Hinds 1896, 177). The crypt was probably still open and in use during Richard's time: Eric Cambridge considers that an image bracket in the E wall of the main chamber is unlikely to be earlier than *c.*1200 (pers. comm.). The building of the existing crossing-piers in the early thirteenth century probably obstructed access to the two E stair-wells, but the W stair-well could still have been used. After the suppression of the Priory, the nave of the church was largely dismantled and its site was used as a cemetery which became known as Campy Hill. The crypt was forgotten, only to be re-discovered in 1725 when a large buttress, built to shore up the north-west pier of the crossing, cut through the north entrance (Bailey 1976, 63–5). Its earliest published notices are in the works of antiquaries who recorded the Roman inscriptions reused in its fabric (Gordon 1726, 174–7; Horsley 1732, 248; Stukeley 1776, 62–3). In 1737 the Lecturer of the church was granted a licence to use the main chamber in the crypt as a burying-place for his family, and at some later stage the remains of the west stair-well were converted into an entrance shaft (Hinds 1896, 175; Bailey 1976, 63, n. 68).

In 1845 and 1846 T. Hudson Turner and J. R. Walbran linked the crypts at Hexham and Ripon with Wilfrid's churches (Turner 1845, 240–1; cf. Walbran 1848, 4, where it is explained that the association of the crypts with Wilfrid was made by Turner and Walbran independently, and Hall 1995, 20–1). Raine included a long essay, mostly written by Walbran, on the architecture of the church and crypt in his Surtees Society publication on Hexham (Raine 1865, i–c). Measured plans and elevations together with perspective sketches were prepared by Hodges for his comprehensive account of the crypt in *Ecclesia Hagustaldensis, etc.*, which was published in 1888. The present state of the crypt dates largely from 1908, when during the rebuilding of the nave 'the extremities of the two eastern passages were built up … as it was necessary to underpin the tower piers. The western passage was completed, the floor of the main chamber cemented, the head stones laid down in the floor, and electric lights provided' (Hodges and Gibson 1919, 81–2). In recent years, an altar has been inserted at the east end of the main chamber and the lighting has been replaced, but no other significant alterations have been made since 1908.

Hodges' work was the foundation of all subsequent research, and the publication in 1961 of his plan of discoveries made during the rebuilding in 1907–10 led to a revival of interest in the Anglo-Saxon church and its crypt (Taylor and Taylor 1961, appearing again in Taylor and Taylor 1965, 297–312, with few alterations; Gilbert 1974). New information about the plan of the church emerged in 1978 when excavations above the east part of the crypt established that the floor of the Anglo-Saxon church had been roughly at the same level as the present building: the crypt was therefore wholly subterranean (Bailey and O'Sullivan 1979). Another important discovery was of a short length of wall built at the same time as the crypt and which formed the south wall of the sanctuary – the first, and still the only structural element above ground which can definitely be shown to have been part of Wilfrid's church (cf. Cambridge 1979). Further important studies of the crypt and the Anglo-Saxon church followed (Bailey 1991 and 1996b: studies of the church and crypt; Cambridge 1995, 72–80: on the significance of excavations outside the church).

The Survey of the Crypt

The main survey was carried out in May and June 2005. A total of 490 blocks

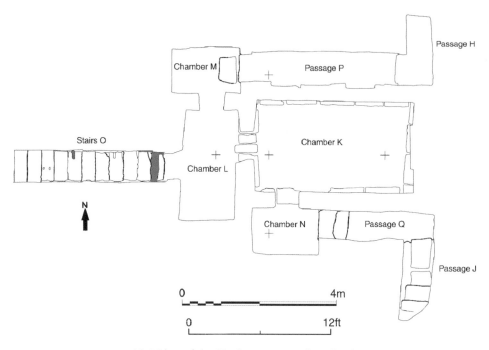

Chamber M

Passage P

Passage H

Stairs O

Chamber K

Chamber L

N

Chamber N

Passage Q

Passage J

0   4m

0   12ft

12.1 Plan of the Hexham crypt at floor level,
with letters used by Hodges to identify its various elements.

and 61 smaller stones were catalogued, but many of the walls are still partly covered by plaster, which prevented the recording of every block used to form the crypt walls (although in some cases the edges of the blocks could be discerned beneath the plaster). The crypt consists of a main chamber with an ante-chamber to its west, which is flanked to north and south by two side-chambers (Fig. 12.1). Passages run eastwards from the side-chambers and then turn north and south to connect with stair-wells which led up into the church. A third stair-well leads up into the nave of the church from the ante-chamber.

This summary account concentrates on new discoveries which improve our understanding of the construction and use of the crypt. Perhaps the most important was the recognition that the vaulted roofs of the ante-chamber and side-chambers incorporated stone ribs, as in the crypt at Ripon (Peers 1931). In the barrel-vault of the ante-chamber at Hexham, there were five ribs each about 0.23m in width and about 0.28–0.30m apart, the spaces between the ribs being filled with small slabs (Fig. 12.2). In the northern side-chamber, which had a vault of triangular section, there were two pairs of ribs, those to the east having been cut from a large Roman altar (Pl. 12.1). The stonework in the vault of the southern side-chamber is still largely concealed by plaster. There were no ribs in the vault of the main chamber, which was built of roughly-worked voussoirs. The use of ribbing in the construction of small stone vaults was a Roman technique, and it is a curious coincidence that the only surviving examples are in

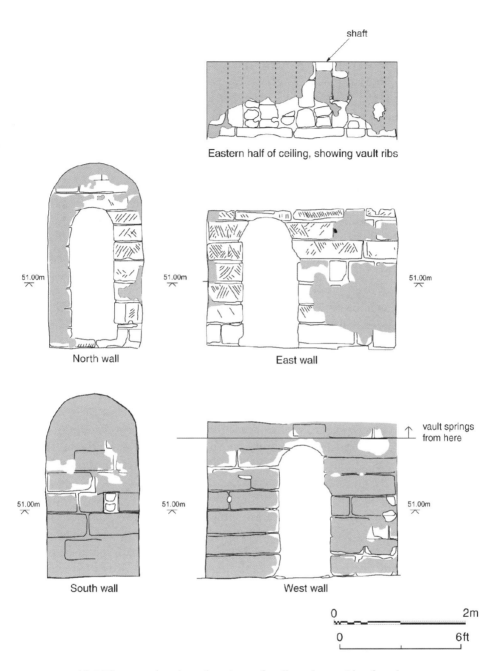

shaft

Eastern half of ceiling, showing vault ribs

North wall

East wall

South wall

West wall

vault springs from here

51.00m

51.00m

51.00m

51.00m

51.00m

51.00m

0   2m

0   6ft

12.2 The ante-chamber: elevations of walls and east side of vault.

the strongrooms of the Roman *principia* at the forts of Chesters and Great Chesters on Hadrian's Wall. Chesters was one of the sources of the stone used at Hexham, but it is most unlikely that the strongroom was still visible in the later seventh century. The use of ribs was probably part of the tradition of small-scale Roman architecture which Wilfrid's masons had inherited.

Much of the interior of the crypt, both walls and vaults, is covered with plaster, and it is likely that all the floors were originally plastered. As far as can be determined by the naked eye or by low magnification, mortar of the same mix was used to plaster the surfaces and to bond together the stone blocks in the walls, and the plaster was probably applied as the walls were built. Modern cement, readily distinguishable from the ancient mortar, has been used in various repairs. When the crypt was opened in 1725, some of the plaster was missing, and two reused Roman inscriptions and some of the other reused stonework were visible. More plaster was removed in the nineteenth century to expose decorated Roman blocks. A new feature recognised in the main chamber is the remains of a rectangular recess forming a sort of hood over the door into the south side-chamber; the same feature has been recorded over the door in the equivalent position in the crypt at Ripon.

All the doors in the crypt are round-headed, and two of their lintels are monolithic. None preserves any traces of door-hangings, but the door connecting the north side-chamber and north passage has a rebate perhaps for a wooden door-leaf or hinged iron grille which was never inserted. The only door or grille in the crypt, its hinges represented by iron shanks set in lead, is at the east end of the south passage; its date is uncertain, but there is no reason to associate it with the post-medieval use of the crypt as a burial vault.

As at Ripon, the crypt was lit from lamp-niches in the walls: three remain in the main chamber, and there was probably a fourth in the east wall, its recess now occupied by a projecting stone bracket; there is a single lamp-niche in the ante-chamber. In the vault of the ante-chamber, there is a small, square-sectioned shaft which still opens into the floor of the nave above. Immediately to the north, an iron shank is set in the vault. It is probably part of a hook to suspend a hanging lamp or candelabrum, and the shaft was perhaps provided to evacuate the smoke. There is another iron shank in the vault further to the north. The plaster in the crypt is heavily smoke-blackened, not only from the various lamps but perhaps also from hand-held torches: the latter would seem to have been the only means of illumination in the side-chambers and passages.

Apart from the inscriptions, the most striking reused Roman fragments are lengths from a series of four separate architectural friezes: they are of the same size and in the same style, consisting of combinations of leaf-and-berry ornament, dentils and bead-and-reel motifs, and came from the same building, which can be identified with some confidence as the enormous mausoleum at

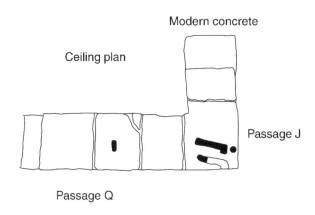

Modern concrete

Ceiling plan

Passage J

Passage Q

Passage J

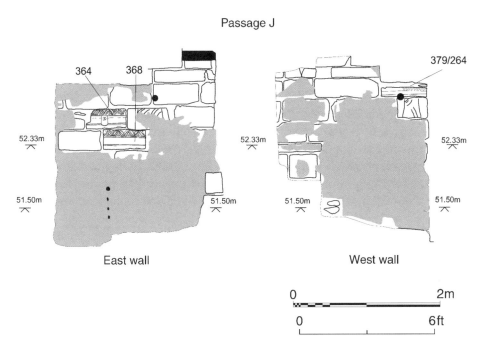

East wall

West wall

0 _____ 2m

0 _____ 6ft

12.3 Ceiling of south passage and elevations of east and west walls
of north-south turn of passage.

Shorden Brae, about 1 km west of Corbridge. The position of these blocks in the
crypt does not appear to be random; they are placed as follows:

South passage, south turn, east wall: two sections of leaf-and-berry
ornament placed one above the other in overlapping positions with the band of
ornament uppermost, probably in the fourth and fifth courses up (the lower
courses are entirely covered with plaster: Fig. 12.3).

South side-chamber, south wall, east end: two sections of leaf-and-berry ornament in the fourth and fifth courses up and in the same relative positions as the first group, although the upper section is longer and completely overlaps the lower section.

North passage, north wall: three sections, one in the sixth course up having leaf-and-berry ornament, with the decorated zone at the bottom, and two sections in the course above, one having a cable moulding below a row of dentils, and the other a coarser cable moulding and a bead-and-reel motif.

These are the only complete frieze-sections visible in the crypt and are the only architectural fragments which are grouped together. They are all placed at about eye-level. The surfaces of all three groups are now bare stone, the frieze-sections in the north passage have been cleaned with a claw chisel in the later nineteenth century. The other two groups have specks of mortar or lime adhering to their surfaces; if they were originally covered with plaster, gentler methods than those employed in the north passage must have been used for its removal. The faces of the frieze-sections were roughly flush with those of the surrounding blocks, and the plaster covering the latter preserves no evidence, such as finished edges, that the decorated blocks were left exposed. However, in Roman and early medieval buildings, stone mouldings and ornamentation were often covered with a thin layer of plaster as a ground for painted decoration, and on some of the Anglo-Saxon sculpture from Hexham and Wearmouth traces of such plaster survive (Cramp 1984, 13). The grouping of the frieze-sections and the positions of two of the groups on significant lines of sight make it likely that they were displayed, perhaps with their details picked out in paint applied to a thin wash of lime or plaster covering. The group in the north passage is not on any particular line of sight but is nevertheless at eye-level. Although, it seems, invisible beneath plaster when found by Robson, this group of frieze sections might originally have been meant to be seen. They might have been plastered over at a later date, or even during the original building work because of a change of mind.

The possible display of these Roman architectural fragments is one of a number of possible visual factors which suggest how the crypt was used. The route from the north to south entries offers five striking lines of sight:

1. Turning into the east-west length of the north passage, the visitor would see the door leading down into the north side-chamber, which would have been dimly lit by lighting in the ante-chamber, not only from the lamp-niche but probably also from hanging-lamps.

2. Looking from the north side-chamber into the ante-chamber, the eye would be drawn to the south wall with its lamp-niche and a possible display of relics.

3. From the east door of the ante-chamber, the visual emphasis would be

very much on the east wall of the main chamber, illuminated by lamps in the flanking niches. It was surely the main focal point of the crypt. Victorian plans marked traces of an altar in this position (Wilson 1862, 11; Raine 1864, 11, note n). The later stone bracket and the object it supported were placed to the north of this possible altar, on the line of sight from the west stair-well door.

4. Someone taking a step through the west door into the main chamber and looking through the south door would see the two blocks with leaf-and-berry ornament in the south-east corner of the south side-chamber, if, as argued above, they were marked out in some way.

5. Moving through the side-chamber into the south passage, the visitor would perhaps be able to see two further blocks with this ornament in the wall at the turn of the passage at its east end.

A route from south to north would certainly include a view from the west turn of the south passage to the door to the south side-chamber, which was comparable to no. 1 above, though less impressive because of the shorter east-west length of the south passage (2.95 m rather than the 5.0 m length of the north passage). There would have been nothing to substitute for the other views. The design of the crypt seems therefore to have been conceived for progress from north to south. This is certainly supported by the greater length of the approach to the main chamber from the north, 10.9 m from the north stair-well to the west door as opposed to 5.9 m from the south door to the south stair-well. The east-west length of the north passage is also 0.10 m wider than the equivalent length of the south passage.

This route through the crypt would have made no use of the western stair-well. The door at the foot of the stairs and the door beyond are aligned on the north side of the main chamber, where some object of devotion was perhaps positioned. On certain occasions this aspect of the crypt might have assumed special importance and required use of the western stairs, which opened into the nave of the church. There are indications that usually this entry was closed. The need for ventilation and additional lighting in the ante-chamber, represented by the shaft in the vault and possible hooks for hanging lamps or candelabra, does not fit with an open or partly covered stair-well to the west. Perhaps the opening of the stair-well when not in use was covered with a trap door or planks at the floor-level of the church.

As already noted, in 1978 Bailey and O'Sullivan (1979) recorded a length of masonry which they identified as the south wall of the sanctuary and which was associated with the construction of the crypt. The wall was built over the southern end of the north-south length of the southern passage; the adjacent stair-well was built outside the sanctuary, against its southern wall. The northern stair-well and its adjacent length of passage were described by Walbran (in Raine 1865, xl–xlii); they were illustrated by Hodges (1888, pl. 39A), although it is uncertain how much of the fabric was still visible and to what extent he depended on Walbran's description. Where the passage opened onto the stair-well, there appears to have been a sloping tunnel-vault, as if to support a wall above the north end of the passage. This suggests the same arrangement as to the south, with the northern stair-well sited outside the sanctuary and built against its northern wall. If so, the width of the sanctuary would have been 6.42m internally, assuming both of its side walls were 0.9m in width. For the plan of the remainder of the church, we have to rely on Hodges' observations. Several of the walls and foundations which he thought were part of Wilfrid's church have been shown to be of later medieval date. From what remains, Bailey and Cambridge reconstructed a church with a narrower sanctuary than is proposed here and a wider nave (Fig. 12.4). Although Hodges' plan was a sketch, a church with a nave and sanctuary of the same width fits rather better with what he showed. Its internal width of 6.42m is larger than the widths of the naves at Wearmouth (5.64m) and in the west church at Jarrow (5.49m) (Cramp 2005, 56, 160).

A final observation is that the position of the north and south stair-wells ought to have lain within the church. Crook's (2000) extensive series of plans, ranging from the late Roman to later medieval periods, includes no examples of crypts with entrances outside churches. At Hexham the stair-wells would have been situated in aisles or *porticus* flanking the sanctuary and which presumably extended westwards along the sides of the nave.

The Reused Roman Stonework

The main sources of Roman building materials for the church at Hexham were the Roman bridge at Corbridge, as has long been recognised, and also the bridge at Chesters. At both of these structures, most of the stone was taken from the abutments and the massive stone ramps which carried the roads up to the level of the carriageways of the bridges (Pls. 12.2 and 12.3).

These parts were easily accessible. Removing the stone from the piers and arches would have been far more difficult, and their fabric seems to have been pitched into the river in order to obtain the many tonnes of lead bars which tied each course together. Another important source of stonework was the enormous mausoleum at Shorden Brae which probably survived intact until it was demolished by Wilfrid's builders. The four different friezes, which were probably from the central tower-tomb, have already been referred to. There are also fragments from several very large fluted pilasters which would have been c 5.5m in height; they were probably part of the wall enclosing the tower-tomb. Also from the mausoleum are a series of blocks with smooth (rubbed) faces.

Other identifiable stones are altars which came from a temple dedicated to Jupiter Dolichenus, almost certainly at Chesters, and a temple of Apollo

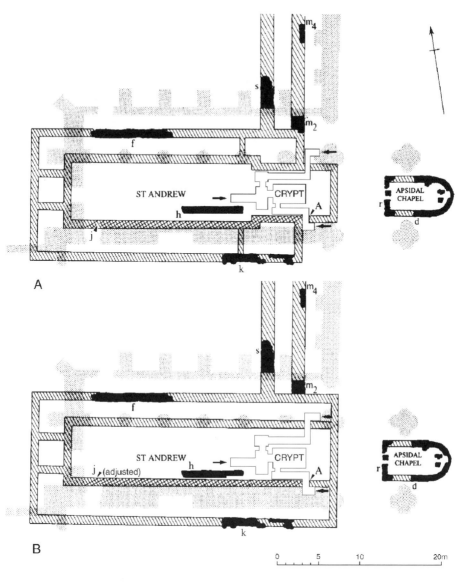

12.4 A: Reconstructed plan of Wilfrid's church (existing church shown in grey scale), after Cambridge 1995, fig 16.

B: Adaptation of Plan A, showing new position for north wall of sanctuary, position of wall 'j', as indicated by Hodges, adjusted to align with south wall of sanctuary seen in 1978, and aisles or *porticus* extended eastwards to include north and south stair-wells of crypt.

Maponus, probably at Corbridge. Other stones include a Severan inscription from a granary, and various reliefs and sculptures of uncertain origin. There are only two tombstones; one is the famous Flavinus stone, commemorating a late first-century cavalryman of the *ala Petriana*; the other is a fragment which might have come from the mausoleum.

Most of the Roman stonework was obtained not by the random robbing of ruins but by the systematic demolition of standing buildings, which supplied large amounts of lead and probably some iron, as well as building stone. The ready availability of these materials, which could have been transported along Roman roads, must have made the building-work at Hexham much speedier than that of the churches at Jarrow and Wearmouth, where much of the stone seems to have been freshly-quarried, though at both sites there is some reused material. At most Roman military sites in Britain – indeed, at most settlements, whether towns or villas – there were few structures which incorporated the large stone blocks of the type reused at Hexham, and they were usually employed for specific features such as the framing of gates or large entries or as stylobates. The landscape around Hexham, with its bridges and mausoleum, and the ruins of Hadrian's Wall and its forts and milecastles, was quite different from that of most of Britain in the later seventh century. One inspiration for Wilfrid's building program was what he had seen in the Mediterranean areas, but another was surely its setting amongst monuments to Roman power and its architectural achievements.

Acknowledgements
The main funder of this survey was the Heritage Lottery Fund, with other contributions from English Heritage, Tyne and Wear Archives and Museums and the Arbeia Society.

13: *Wilfrid and Music*

JESSE D. BILLETT

The title of this chapter, which was suggested by Nick Higham in advance of the Manchester 'Wilfrid' conference in 2009, reflects a widely and justly held view that Wilfrid materially influenced the history of music in the Anglo-Saxon Church (our sources never mention Wilfrid in connection with secular music – see Lawson and Rankin 1999; Lawson 1999). Taken comprehensively, the title may be treated under three headings. First, Wilfrid's experience of music: what music will he have heard (and sung) in England and abroad at different times in his career, and what were the major traditions to which he will have been exposed? Secondly, Wilfrid's influence on music: did he make a distinctive contribution to the musical life of the English Church, and if so, how is this to be interpreted in the light of his wider career? And finally, music about Wilfrid: did music play a part in Wilfrid's cult after his death?

Wilfrid's Experience of Music
We hear of Wilfrid himself singing only once, during his nine months' imprisonment under King Ecgfrith, when in the darkness of his cell his psalmody produced a supernatural light that terrified his jailers (VW 36). We are probably correct in understanding *psalmodia* here in its usual sense of 'singing of psalms'. However, Wilfrid's biographer was not far removed in time from a monk of St Gall who could apply the words *canire* and *melodia* to the barely audible murmuring of the priest during the Canon of the Mass, so we cannot entirely exclude the possibility that Wilfrid was merely reciting the psalms in his natural speaking voice (*Ordo Romanus* XV, 39; ed. Andrieu 1931–61, 3, 103). Assuming that Wilfrid was indeed singing, what did his singing sound like? The question is ultimately unanswerable but it may serve as a convenient conceit around which to organise the available data on Wilfrid's experience of music, revealing two basic 'hermeneutical contrasts': Canterbury vs Iona (played up by Bede and Stephen of Ripon), and Rome vs Gaul (a contrast more pertinent to the interests of modern musicology).

It is not surprising that Wilfrid should be able to sing. In an age when almost every word of the liturgy was sung, whether to simple recitation formulae or to florid melodies, a measure of competence in singing was expected of prelates. Music is a familiar topos in the careers of the Merovingian bishops whom Wilfrid tried to imitate. Gregory of Tours (573–94) possessed so powerful a singing voice that it was a surprise to him that his chanting of Nocturns did not rouse a scoundrel passed out drunk in the church (*Decem Libri Historiarum*, IX, 6; trans. Thorpe 1974, 486). Nicetius of Lyons (552–73) was constantly preoccupied with the chanting of psalms, whether outwardly during the canonical hours or inwardly in his ceaseless contemplation (Mayr-Harting 1991, 133). But no English music manuscripts survive from the seventh or early eighth centuries, and there is precious little of that date from anywhere else either. We are well into the ninth century before musical notation makes its first appearance, and then in forms useful only to singers who already knew the melodies by heart. The oldest English music books date from the tenth century (*contra* Haines 2008), though narrative and canonical texts refer to them much earlier (Rankin 2011). An attempt to reconstruct Wilfrid's experience of music must therefore use much later musical sources to interpret the maddeningly vague references to music in the main narrative accounts of his career. Such references are surprisingly abundant.

The main early sources of information about Wilfrid's life, Bede's *Historia ecclesiastica* and Stephen of Ripon's *Vita Wilfridi*, show a special interest in music. Bede himself testifies to his dedication to 'the daily task of singing in the church' (HE V, 24). If Ian Wood is right in arguing that the anonymous *Vita Ceolfrithi* is an adaptation of Bede's *Historia abbatum*, rather than the other way round (Grocock and Wood forthcoming), there will be even more reason to believe that Bede was the *puerulus* who, together with Ceolfrith, maintained the tradition of chanting antiphons and responsories in the daily offices after the plague at Jarrow and who 'until the present day holds the rank of priest in the same monastery and commends the abbot's laudable actions in words and writings to all who wish to know them' (*Vita Ceolfrithi*, 14; ed. Plummer 1896, 1, 393; trans Farmer and Webb 1998, 218). The many references to singers in Bede's *Historia ecclesiastica* therefore reflect the interests of an accomplished church musician (Willis 1968, 201–2; McKinnon 2000, 89–93).

As for Stephen of Ripon, doubt has been cast on the traditional identific-ation of him with the singing master Ædde (Eddius Stephanus) mentioned by Bede (HE, IV, 2; see Kirby 1983; *contra* Plummer 1896, 2, 206; Colgrave 1927, x). But it is nevertheless clear that the author of the *Vita Wilfridi* was interested in music. His narrative includes musical details that others might overlook, as when he describes how Wilfrid's clergy sang psalms to set the pace for the oarsmen (*pro celeumate*) on Wilfrid's stormy journey back to England following his episcopal consecration (VW 13). Stephen is also capable of abstract musical imagery. As Wilfrid's body is being prepared for burial, the monks hear the sound of birds, 'their wings making sweet melody' (*cum suavi modulamine pennarum*; VW 66). And when the young Wilfrid returns to England c.658 after extended sojourns in Rome and Lyons, King Alhfrith begs him to stay and preach to the whole nation 'with the music of the Spirit singing through him' (*organo spiritale de se canente*; VW 7). Stephen puts into the king's mouth an ambiguous musical term, *organum*. In some contexts it can simply mean 'music' or 'singing' – in the ninth century it came especially to denote singing in harmony. It can also refer to the vibrations of vessels at different frequencies. But in texts of the sixth and seventh centuries, *organum* most commonly means a musical instrument, the organ, and this was the meaning understood in Frithegod's verse *Breviloquium Vitae Wilfridi*, which renders Stephen's *organum* as *ydraulia*, the storied 'water organs' of antiquity (Campbell 1950, 13; line 217 in MSS C, P). It is highly unlikely that Alhfrith, Wilfrid or Stephen had ever seen a real organ. The instrument was known mainly from commentaries on the psalms, as seems to be the case in Aldhelm's reference to an organ in his *Carmen de virginitate* (lines 66–73): 'If anyone [...] eagerly desires to feed his mind with great euphony [...] let him listen to the greatest instrument with a thousand breaths, let it delight his hearing with bellows full of wind' (Ehwald 1919, 355–6; trans Williams 2001, 107). Aldhelm probably has in mind an image of the Body of Christ, with its many members (the 'thousand breaths') all sounding in perfect consonance (Williams 2001, 107). Taken in this sense, Stephen's *organum spiritale*, a 'spiritual organ' with many voices sounding in harmony, becomes a wonderful image of the Catholic (i.e. universal) Christianity that Wilfrid championed.

All this means that when Bede and Stephen mention technical details about music, they are probably to be trusted as authorities well versed in the subject. But for neither of them is music merely a technical matter for clerics and monks. Bede and Stephen both depict the spread of Roman Christianity in England as essentially coterminous with the spread of Roman music, and it is in his role as champion of Roman orthodoxy that Wilfrid's contributions to English music are made.

Contrast 1: Canterbury vs Iona

Bede and Stephen portray the history of music in England in terms of a polarised contest between Canterbury and Iona, between St Gregory and St Columba. Augustine and his fellow missionaries came to Canterbury singing in procession (HE I, 25), and Bede recounts how this Roman music also attained supremacy in the North, after some initial disasters. The defeat of King Edwin in 633 crippled the Roman mission in York. A Roman singing master, James the Deacon, bravely remained in York when Bishop Paulinus retreated to Kent. But his isolated efforts to teach singing 'after the manner of Rome and the Kentish people' (HE II, 20) were insufficient to establish a self-sustaining musical tradition. All music at this date was transmitted orally from teacher to pupil, a process requiring institutional resources that will not have been available. We have little evidence for the kind of music that Bishop Aidan and his Irish monks brought with them when, at King Oswald's invitation, they established a new mission and episcopal see at Lindisfarne *c*.635 (HE III, 3). The famous 'Antiphonary of Bangor' (Milan, Biblioteca Ambrosiana, MS C 5 inf), usually thought to have been copied at the monastery of Bend-Chor in Ireland during the period 680–91, contains a number of chant texts (Warren 1893–5; Curran 1984; Jeffery 1985). But the obliteration of the Irish liturgical tradition in subsequent centuries has made it impossible to interpret these texts against later, fuller witnesses, and it has been suggested that the manuscript may have been made somewhat later, on the Continent, by Irish missionaries (Jeffery 2000, 112–13). Whatever music was sung by Aidan's monks, Bede apparently considered it no music at all, for he says without qualification that 'the knowledge of sacred music' reached the North only when Archbishop Theodore installed Wilfrid as bishop of York in place of Chad in 669 (HE IV, 2). Inviting the Kentish singing expert Æddi to York, Wilfrid finally completed the triumph of Canterbury over Iona, becoming the first, as he would later claim at *Ouestraefelda*, to uproot the 'poisonous weeds' of the Irish and to set the Kentish-Roman chant tradition on a firm footing in the North (VW 47).

There are obvious problems with this simplistic narrative framework, but it accurately reflects a choice that Wilfrid had to make early in his career. Wilfrid memorised the whole Latin psalter as a teenager at Lindisfarne, where, following Irish tradition, the version later known as the *Gallicanum* or 'Vulgate' was used. When he spent a year in Canterbury before his first trip to Rome, Wilfrid memorized the *Vetus Latina* version of the psalter that was used *more Romanorum* (VW 2–3; see Gretsch 2005, 15–18). Differences between the *Gallicanum* and the *Romanum* are small but pervasive, as may be seen from the first few lines of Psalm 26, which in the Roman liturgy was sung weekly at Monday Nocturns. The *Romanum* text is given on the left; variant readings are marked in bold type, with *Gallicanum* readings given on the right (from Weber 1953):

Dominus inluminatio mea et salus mea : quem timebo?
Dominus **defensor** uitae meae : a quo trepidabo?　　　　　*Ga.* protector
Dum adpropiant super me nocentes : ut edant carnes meas,
Qui tribulant **me** inimici mei : ipsi infirmati sunt et ceciderunt. *Ga.* me et
Si consistant **aduersum** me castra : non timebit cor meum. 　*Ga.* aduersus
Si exsurgat **in** me proelium : in hoc ego sperabo. 　　　　　*Ga.* aduersus
Unam petii a domino hanc requiram : ut inhabitem in domo
　　domini **omnibus** diebus uitae meae. 　　　　　　　　*Ga.* omnes

Both of Wilfrid's feats of memorisation were to serve a musical end: a monk or cleric could not participate in the singing of the liturgy without first knowing the psalter by heart. Learning the *Romanum* version of the psalter was Wilfrid's first concrete act of conversion away from Irish to Roman liturgical music (Ó Carragáin 1994, 6). Stephen's report of Wilfrid's death includes a quotation from the *Romanum* text of the psalter (VW 65; Ps 103:30, with the variant *emitte* in place of the Gallican *emittes*), so it would seem that Wilfrid's monks and clergy persisted in the use of the *Romanum* psalter. Confusion between the two versions would seriously impair any attempt at choral recitation of the psalms, which, as we shall see, was Wilfrid's favoured practice, so it would certainly be difficult for any religious community to sustain more than one 'change of course' in each generation. In our imaginative exercise of reconstructing Wilfrid's prison psalmody, it is almost certain that Wilfrid sang words from the *Romanum* psalter, and presumably in a style of recitation derived from the Kentish-Roman musical tradition.

What was this 'Kentish-Roman' musical tradition? A superficial reading of Bede would equate it with the musical tradition of the churches and monasteries of the city of Rome, but Bede never actually says as much. We read instead of 'the manner of Rome and the Kentish people' (HE II, 20), of chant learned from 'the disciples of the blessed Pope Gregory' (HE IV, 2) or from 'the successors of the disciples of St Gregory in Kent' (HE V, 20). Wilfrid did not claim to have introduced a 'Roman' practice of singing, but that of the 'primitive Church' (VW 47); the singing masters Aedde and Aeona are mentioned among assets acquired by Wilfrid in the course of his episcopal activities in Mercia (VW 14). Only John, the abbot of St Martin's in Rome, whom Benedict Biscop brought to Wearmouth in 679 to teach his monks to sing, is said specifically to have taught the musical and liturgical practices of St Peter's basilica, where he was 'archcantor' (*archicantator*, a title that Bede seems to have invented for him; HE IV, 18; cf HA 6, and VC, 10.

The little evidence available to us indicates that the 'Kentish-Roman' musical tradition was eclectic, making use of chants from both Rome and, chiefly, Gaul. The florilegium *De laude Dei* by Alcuin, apparently written before 786, includes a section entitled *De antiphonario* containing ninety-three chant texts that are the only surviving witness to the ancient chant repertory of York (or of any other English Church). The *De antiphonario*'s first editor made a beguiling case that the compiler of the antiphoner from which Alcuin drew these texts was none other than John the 'archcantor' (Constantinescu 1974, 52–4). An emphasis in some of the *De antiphonario*'s chants on Christ's two natures could suggest that they originate in the context of doctrinal controversy – one of them even resorts to Greek, calling Christ *homoousion Patris*, 'consubstantial with the Father' (Billett 2011, 97–100). John's mission to England was primarily doctrinal, not musical: he had been charged by Pope Agatho to obtain the English Church's assent to the anti-monothelite decree promulgated at the Lateran Council of 649 (HE, IV, 18). But even if a few of the chants in *De laude*

Dei arrived in England with John, he cannot be credited with the whole of the York antiphoner. As Susan Rankin has recently demonstrated, about half of the chants in the *De laude Dei* must be considered as non-Roman in origin – though to prove this is a tricky matter since we actually have no Roman chant books older than the eleventh century; we must rely instead on comparisons with Frankish books that claim to transmit a Roman repertory (Rankin forthcoming). The non-Roman chants in the *De laude Dei* have striking parallels with Gallican sources, and sometimes also with later books of Milan and Spain.

Contrast 2: Rome vs Gaul

An attempt to reconstruct the musical world of Wilfrid's times must therefore grapple with a second hermeneutical contrast, namely Rome vs Gaul. It is a contrast largely elided by Bede and Stephen. Bede was certainly aware of it: he records Augustine's surprised question to Pope Gregory about the dramatic differences between the Roman and Gallican forms of the Mass (HE I, 27). Stephen will have experienced the differences at first hand when he accompanied Wilfrid on his travels to Frisia and to Rome. But, for both, the Gallican Church was first and foremost a body in full communion with Rome, in contrast with the Ionan Church – a view that the Irish would no doubt contest (Jeffery 2000, 100). Wilfrid sought episcopal consecration from bishops in Gaul, not because they would use a Roman liturgical form (which they manifestly did not), but because they were in unquestioned communion with the Holy See (VW 12). Pope Gregory himself seems to have envisioned from the beginning that the English Church would benefit from a measure of co-operation with the Gallican Church, foreseeing that Gallican bishops would work in England and *vice versa* (Wallace-Hadrill 1960b, 534–5). Frankish priests joined the Roman missionaries who landed at Thanet in 597 (HE I, 25; cf Gregory *Registrum epistolarum*, VI, 49, 57; Gregory I, *Registrum*, ed. Ewald and Hartmann 1899–91, 1, 424, 431).

The Gallican liturgy, with its distinctive musical repertory, was largely wiped away by Romanising reforms in the eighth and ninth centuries (see McKitterick 1977, 115–54; Hen 2001, 65–94; Claussen 2004, 263–76; McKitterick 2008, 340–43). Even the earliest surviving Gallican liturgical books and fragments are already more or less Romanised, probably through the influence of Anglo-Saxon missionaries (though a contrary view holds that the Anglo-Saxon missionaries used the Gallican liturgy largely as they found it: Hen 2002; 2007). Beginning late in the eighth century, a Romano-Frankish musical hybrid later called 'Gregorian' chant gradually supplanted all but two or three local chant traditions in Western Europe. Nevertheless, a few chants from the Gallican repertory, identifiable on textual, liturgical and musical grounds, seem to have survived within the 'Gregorian' corpus. Several of these chants are of interest in relation to Wilfrid's career.

Musical Example 13.1: A Gallican antiphon for the consecration of a bishop.

Source: Paris, Bibliothèque nationale de France, ms. lat. 12044 (Antiphoner of the abbey of Saint-Maur-des-Fossés, s. xii), fol. 209r. The manuscript lacks barlines. Hollow note-heads signify liquescence. Abbreviations have been silently expanded.

Pax e- ter- na ab e- ter- no pa-tre hu- ic do-mu- i

pax per- hen-nis uer-bum pa- tris sit pax hu- ic do- mu- i

pa-cem pi- us con-so- la- tor hu- ic pre-stet

do- mu- i

Eternal peace from the eternal Father be unto this house.
Perennial peace, O Word of the Father! Peace be unto this house.
May the benevolent Comforter grant peace to this house.

When he received episcopal consecration at Compiègne, Wilfrid was carried into the church, seated on a golden chair, by a dozen Gallican bishops singing 'hymns and canticles' (VW 12). Carrying a new bishop into his church seems to have been a common element in Gallican rituals for episcopal consecration (Heinzelmann 2001, 62). It is found in a complete *Ordo ad suscipiendum novum pontificem*, from a twelfth-century *rituale* of the diocese of Soissons, printed in Edmond Martène's *De antiquis ecclesiae ritibus* (1736–8, 2, 80–81 = Lib I, cap 8, art 10, 19). It prescribes the singing of various chants, notably the *Te Deum*. When the new bishop has reached the middle of the church, a cantor begins the antiphon *Pax aeterna*, after which the procession enters the quire. The antiphon thus functions as a kind of blessing on the bishop's 'new house', just as Wilfrid blessed the house of King Alhfrith saying *Pax huic domui* (VW, 7). *Pax aeterna* is assigned to the liturgy for the dedication of a church in books of Gregorian chant; but its melody and grandiloquent text, given in Example 13.1, mark it out as a survival of the old Gallican repertory (Huglo 2001, 463). It is possible that this very chant was sung at Wilfrid's consecration.

Similar speculation is possible for the music that would have been sung at the dedication of Wilfrid's new church at Ripon, which, as Henry Mayr-Harting

(1991, 180–81) perceptively noticed, must have been performed according to a Gallican form, since Stephen notes that the bases of the altar were dedicated (VW 17). A complete Gallican rite for the consecration of a church may be reconstructed from the 'Sacramentary of Angoulême' (BnF lat 816; s. viii/ix) and the *Missale Francorum* (BAV Reg lat 257; s. viii). The musical provisions are minimal: at three points in the ceremony – the entry into the church, the consecration of the altar, and a procession with relics – a litany (*laetania*) is chanted (Chavasse 1958, 41–2).

Bede says that Augustine and his monks chanted a *laetania* as they went to Canterbury, and he quotes the antiphon *Deprecamur te*, which is sung as part of the 'lesser litanies' (or 'Ember Days') four times a year (HE, I, 25). The lesser litanies originated in Gaul and were not adopted in Rome until the second half of the eighth century (Bullough 1991, 6, 209 n. 15; Cubitt 1995, 129–30). They were observed at Jarrow in Bede's lifetime, and texts for the antiphons sung in procession as part of the lesser litanies, including *Deprecamur te*, are included in Alcuin's *De laude Dei* (Constantinescu 1974, no. 70). Kenneth Levy (1998, 19–30) has identified three melodies for *Deprecamur te*, suggesting that all may derive from a Beneventan source. Another of the antiphons included for the lesser litanies in Alcuin's *De laude Dei*, *Invocantes Dominum exclamemus* (Constantinescu 1974, no 73), specifically pleads for protection of the *templum* from wicked persons, which would be appropriate for the consecration of a church.

In the Gallican liturgy, *laetania* tends to refer to longer sets of *preces* that were sung responsively by deacon and choir as a general intercession during the Mass. They are the most numerous Gallican chants to have survived in later Gregorian books (Huglo 2001, 469). One of these, the *Deprecatio Gelasii*, seems to have originated in Rome, very likely with Pope Gelasius I (492–6), and draws on Eastern models. It spread widely in the West and was still in use in Gaul, in several different textual traditions, after it had been abandoned in Rome itself (Capelle 1934; De Clerck 1977, 166–205). The *Deprecatio Gelasii* is included in a collection of private devotions commonly attributed to Alcuin and printed among his works as *Officia per ferias* in the *PL* (101, 509–612, at 560–62). The collection is not in fact Alcuin's work, but it certainly dates to the ninth century and was very probably compiled by his disciples (Bullough 2004, 7). Example 13.2 gives the melodies of the refrain and opening two petitions of a later Frankish adaptation of the *Deprecatio Gelasii*, preserved in an eleventh-century Aquitainian gradual (it is printed from another manuscript in Stäblein 1955, 1313). A chant of this kind may have served for at least one of the *laetaniae* in the Gallican rite used at Ripon's dedication.

These imaginative musical reconstructions of two events in Wilfrid's career may serve to illustrate the 'mixed economy' that probably characterised the

Musical Example 13.2: Refrain and first two verses of a litany from the Gallican chant repertory.

Source: Paris, Bibliothèque nationale de France, ms. lat. 776 (noted gradual, Gaillac, s. xi), fols 83v–84r. The manuscript lacks punctuation, barlines and clefs. Hollow note-heads signify liquescence. A saw-toothed symbol denotes a quilisma (a neume of uncertain interpretation, but in this case probably indicating that the note following it should be flattened).

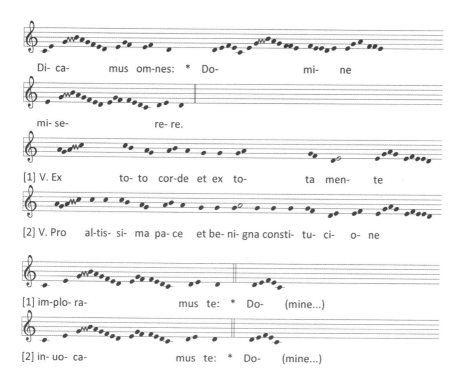

Di- ca- mus om-nes: * Do- mi- ne

mi- se- re- re.

[1] V. Ex to- to cor-de et ex to- ta men- te

[2] V. Pro al-tis- si- ma pa- ce et be- ni- gna consti- tu- ci- o- ne

[1] im-plo- ra- mus te: * Do- (mine...)

[2] in- uo- ca- mus te: * Do- (mine...)

*Deacon: Let us all say, 'Lord, have mercy.' Choir: Lord, have mercy. Deacon: With all our heart and all our mind, we implore you. Choir: Lord, have mercy. Deacon: For heavenly peace and a favourable ordering [of the world], we call upon you. Choir: Lord, have mercy. (*There follow petitions for the universal church, for the king and his army, for the abbot of the house and his congregation, and for the dead and the penitent, all set to the same melody.)

'Kentish-Roman' chant tradition in England in the seventh and early eighth centuries. As I have argued elsewhere, this seems to have operated within a basically Roman liturgical framework, at least in regard to the Divine Office (Billett 2011, 92–7). When it came to 'one-off' liturgical events, like ordinations and church dedications, it would be possible to use a pure Gallican liturgy, without the admixture of Roman elements. Indeed, the only books available for such rites may have been Gallican: 'Rome for all her riches was not near' (Wallace-Hadrill 1960b, 534).

A Special Problem: Roman vs Gallican Monastic Psalmody

Some Roman and Gallican musical practices, however, were not interchangeable. As will be argued here, the two traditions seem to have had fundamentally different approaches to the singing of the psalms in the monastic Office.

Research on the chanting of liturgical psalmody has dealt primarily with two central themes. The first of these is the transition, in different contexts, from 'lector chant' to 'schola chant', a dichotomy first proposed by Dom Jean Claire (1962) and further developed by James McKinnon (1995; 2000, 62–5). 'Lector chant' refers to liturgical music that is chosen *ad hoc* for the liturgy of the day (the term usually refers to the Mass) and is sung by a soloist, with or without a congregational or choral refrain. The singing is regarded as a heightened form of reading a biblical text, and the text may be the topic of the homily. This was the universal practice of the fourth-century Church. 'Schola chant' refers to a much larger repertory of chants ordered according to a fixed annual cycle, an achievement requiring a stable group of professional singers. These chants would consequently cease to function as readings and would become distinct liturgical elements in their own right. McKinnon (2000, 65–76) has argued that the Gallican chant remained fundamentally of the 'lector' type, while the work of the *schola cantorum* in Rome in the seventh century produced a repertory and practice of the 'schola' type, the Roman 'Proper of the Mass' – though most musicologists would hold that the process was underway earlier and for longer, and that it was not as straightforward or deliberate as McKinnon suggests (see Jeffery 2003a; Rankin 2002). The dilemma for the question of psalmody is that it is not at all clear how the melodically austere psalmody of the Divine Office, as attested in the Gregorian repertory, can be related to a pro-gression from a quasi-improvisatory, more or less elaborate 'lector chant' to an even more elaborate 'schola chant'.

The second theme, related to the first, is the transition from solo psalmody to choral psalmody, particularly in the Divine Office. The earliest monastic practice was for psalms to be chanted by a soloist while others listened silently, sometimes adding a refrain (Dyer 1989a). By the later Middle Ages, however, monks and canons chanted the psalms chorally. Joseph Dyer (1989b) has argued that this must have been a relatively late and gradual development: the earliest witness to the musical tones for reciting the psalms, the late-ninth-century Frankish treatise *Commemoratio brevis de tonis et psalmis modulandis* (ed and trans T. Bailey 1979), together with later witnesses, describes a practice too diverse and too complex to be imagined as a primarily choral practice. The psalms were intoned by soloists, while others contributed short refrains. By contrast, Edward Nowacki (1990; 1995) urges exactly the opposite interpretation: while all monks would know the psalter by heart, the large repertory of antiphons sung with the psalms could only be managed by a few expert singers in any one community. It is telling that each scholar can adduce the same passage from the ninth-century liturgist Amalarius of Metz to support his conclusions (Dyer 1989a, 68–9; Nowacki 1995, 312–13; commenting on *Liber officialis* IV, 7; ed. Hanssens 1948–50, **2**, 433).

These two problems of musical history – lector chant vs schola chant, solo psalmody vs choral psalmody – have usually been lumped together because of a basic assumption that the relatively simple recitation tones used for singing the psalms in the Divine Office share a common origin with the much more elaborate melodies of the Roman Mass Proper. It is often proposed that the solo psalmody described in the writings of Athanasius and Augustine could have been as simple as the familiar Gregorian psalm tones (eg Dyer 1989a, 52–3). As Peter Jeffery (2003b) has recently argued, however, this is probably not the case.

The fifth and sixth centuries saw a shift in theologians' (and musicians') treatment of the psalms. Where at first they had been read as part of God's word to humanity (as in Augustine of Hippo), they came to be internalised as human prayers to God (as in Cassiodorus). In this newer approach, a monk studied the psalter so as to be able to make its words his own personal prayer. The almost inevitable corollary was that the monk could no longer merely listen to the psalms being recited; 'the monk at worship now sang them with his own lips' (Jeffery 2003b, 77). This new 'psalmodic ethos', which found prominent expression in the writings of Gregory the Great – combined with a collapse of general literacy that left monks and clerics in sole possession of the psalter – was the impetus for the emergence of a 'schola type' repertory of Mass chants (Jeffery 2003b, 83). Jeffery's findings corroborate the argument of Terence Bailey (1980, 97) that the extremely simple psalm tones of Milanese ('Ambrosian') chant were devised independently of the chants of the Mass to serve a newly introduced choral psalmody in the monastic Office. While Bailey (1980, 97) thought that choral monastic psalmody could not be dated earlier than the seventh century, Jeffery (2003b, 72–80) finds it attested in texts written in a sixth-century Roman milieu.

The extremely contingent character of this theory hardly needs to be pointed out: it involves extrapolating backwards from the musical practice of the ninth century and later, guided by theological and other texts open to varied interpretation. Nevertheless, it is striking that choral psalmody makes its first clear appearance in the neighbourhood of Rome in the sixth century – in the 'Rule of Paul and Stephen', which shows awareness of the Roman chant repertory (Dyer 1989a, 66–7; Jeffery 2003b, 80) – whereas it appears in Frankish texts only at the end of the eighth century, and then clearly within the context of the Romanising reforms of the Carolingian kings (Dyer 1989a, 67–8). Earlier Gallican practice, which probably varied greatly from place to place, may best be represented by the sixth-century monastic rules of Caesarius and Aurelian of Arles, which envisage only solo psalmody in the monastic Office (Dyer 1989a, 56–7; Jeffery 2003b, 70).

Returning to the question of Wilfrid's prison psalmody, it seems very probable that, just as he had to choose which version of the psalter to recite (*Romanum* vs *Gallicanum*), he will also have had to choose between a 'Roman' choral psalmody and a 'Gallican' solo psalmody. Wilfrid may well have learned a solo psalmodic practice as a boy on Lindisfarne or as a cleric in Lyons. But as we shall see when we come to look at Wilfrid's influence on Anglo-Saxon music, there is fairly strong evidence that as a bishop Wilfrid favoured the Roman option.

In terms of the musical characteristics of the two practices, we have no extant examples of the musical style of the earlier solo psalmody, though something like it may be preserved in later Gregorian chants of the Mass (the graduals and tracts) and Office (the verses of the great responsories sung at Nocturns), and especially in certain chants of the Mozarabic (Spanish) repertory, which survives only in an adiastematic neumatic notation (see Cullin 1991; Claire 2006–7). The 'choral' style will have been, by contrast, something very like the Milanese tones, which may preserve an extremely early Roman approach (Bailey 1980, 84–5; and see Bailey 1978). Though they are only found in comparatively late manuscripts, they probably represent 'the primordial forms of what was to become a ubiquitous and elaborate practice' (Bailey 1980, 98). Our earliest sources for the Gregorian psalm tones, especially the *Commemoratio brevis*, already show considerable elaboration (perhaps under the influence of the native Gallican solo style) and have already been made to conform, with some exceptions, to the system of eight musical modes (Bailey 1979, 16). The system of eight modes was devised during the Carolingian centuries, in imitation of the Byzantine *oktoechos*, as a means of controlling the oral tradition of the emerging Romano-Frankish chant repertory (Cohen 2002, 309–10). It is foreign to the monastic psalmody of the Milanese and urban Roman traditions (Bailey 1980, 94–5).

Example 13.3 gives sample psalm tones from three different repertories – Milanese, Gregorian, and 'Gallican' – to illustrate what can be surmised about the early choral style. The bulk of the psalmody of the Divine Office in the early Middle Ages was sung 'direct' (*in directum*), without any sort of refrain. The music for this direct choral psalmody seems almost never to have been written down. In its modern chant books the Roman Catholic Church provides three tones for direct psalmody, but their age and origin seem never to have been published (Ferretti 1938, 155–7). The only tone *in directum* with a certain

Musical Example 13.3: Gregorian, Milanese ('Ambrosian'), and 'Gallican' psalm tones.

Sources:
Gre: Munich, Bayerische Stadtbibliothek, Clm 19558 (tonary and cantor's manual, prov. Tegernsee Abbey, s. xiv/xv); this tone ed. Wagner 1921, 86.
Amb: Vimercate, Basilica S Stefano, MS D (s. xiii); this tone ed. Bailey 1993, 186.
Gal: *Commemoratio brevis* (s. ix); this tone ed. Bailey 1979, 55.

Each example shows how the words '*Sicut erat in principio et nunc et semper: et in saecula saeculorum. Amen.*' would be adapted to the recitation tone (this is the conclusion of the 'little doxology' sung at the end of most psalms in the Divine Office).

    Gre and *Gal* are 'accentual' tones, that is, pitches under the accent sign (>) always coincide with a stressed syllable (in *Gre* the final *g* is used only when the verse ends on a monosyllable or a Hebrew word with the stress on the last syllable, like *Amen*); extra pitches, represented by hollow note-heads, are added depending on the number of unaccented syllables. *Amb* is a 'cursive' tone in which the pitches of the final cadence are applied mechanically without regard to the accentuation of the text.

medieval pedigree is that given as *Gre* in Example 13.3. An even earlier tone *in directum*, however, may be represented in the second tone (*Amb*). In many early Office liturgies – eg in the *Regula Magistri*, the *Regula S Benedicti* and the Roman Office as described by Amalarius of Metz – psalms are often prescribed to be sung *cum Alleluia*, that is, with the word *Alleluia* added somehow to each verse (Oury 1965). *Amb* is a reconstruction of the early Milanese version of this practice, and simple psalmody *in directum* at Milan may have used an identical tone (Bailey 1993). The third tone (*Gal*) is from the *Commemoratio brevis*, where it is one of several recitation tones that found no permanent place in the Romano-Frankish repertory. It is in this limited sense 'Gallican' (Huglo 2001,

466–7). The *Commemoratio brevis* is not concerned with direct psalmody. This tone was apparently used only with the antiphon *Anima mea exultabit* (Bailey 1979, 55).

Alb is the simplest of the tones: the first half of the psalm verse is sung on a single reciting tone ('tenor'), and a final cadence ('termination') is applied mechanically to the last six syllables of the second half. *Gre* likewise has a simple reciting tone for the first and second halves of the verse, but it has a cadence at the midpoint of the verse as well ('mediant'). Both cadences respect the accentuation of the text. *Gal* is the most complex. Each half verse begins with an opening gesture ('intonation') and concludes with its own cadence ('mediant', 'termination'). Unlike most tones in the *Commemoratio brevis*, this tone seems also to pay attention to the accentuation of the text, which Bailey (1976) judges to be a late development. The choral psalmodic practice of sixth-century Rome, and therefore perhaps also of seventh-century Canterbury, was probably closest to the Milanese style.

We have so far examined the 'mixed economy' of liturgical and musical practices that will have shaped Wilfrid's experience of music at home and abroad: Irish, Roman-Kentish, Gallican and Roman. Although his experience will have been eclectic, Wilfrid's personal allegiance was to the Kentish-Roman tradition, at least when it came to the chanting of the psalms. We may now consider the question of how Wilfrid may in turn have influenced the music of the English Church.

Wilfrid's Influence on Music
Bede and Stephen present Wilfrid as pivotal for the history of ecclesiastical music in the North. This seems to have been as a facilitator, not as a teacher or practitioner: there is no suggestion that Wilfrid himself possessed any special musical talents. But he does seem to have had a personal connection to most of the singing experts mentioned by Bede. We have already noted Wilfrid's Kentish singing master Aedde and Aeona (Bede does not mention the latter). Ceolfrith, whose musical skills are documented in the famous story of the plague at Jarrow, was received as a monk at Ripon and ordained to the priesthood by Wilfrid (VC 3). Wilfrid also ordained Putta, later bishop of Rochester (VW 14), who, says Bede, was 'especially skilled in liturgical chanting after the Roman manner, which he had learned from the disciples of the blessed Pope Gregory' (HE IV, 2). Wilfrid's priest Acca, who succeeded him as bishop, was a highly skilled musician, and Acca imitated Wilfrid's example in bringing a Kentish singing master to teach in Hexham (HE V, 20). This was Maban, who taught there for twelve years. This was, incidentally, the approximate time it took to train one cantor in the whole of the Roman chant repertory before the advent of diastematic musical notation (Rankin 1985, 323).

Wilfrid, however, could claim no responsibility for having trained these singers. Æddi, Aeona and Putta were trained in Kent. Ceolfrith may have had his first musical training at Gilling before coming to Ripon. Most important, Acca was trained at York by Bishop Bosa (HE V, 20). This was during the years 678–86, when Wilfrid, having been expelled from his diocese, was performing episcopal duties in the South of England, travelling on the Continent, or singing psalms in King Ecgfrith's dungeon. Alcuin, in his *Versus de patribus*, describes Bosa's attention to liturgy and music in the church of York (lines 857–70; ed Godman 1982, 70–73), and these activities may have been inspired by the teaching of John the 'archcantor' at Wearmouth around the same time.

Therefore, when Wilfrid is put forward as a decisive musical figure, this must mean that he both determined a musical policy for his diocese (and for his network of monasteries) and acquired expert teachers to implement it. His use of Kentish teachers further shows that he was not introducing a new practice from abroad (eg Rome), but promoting a tradition that was already well established in the south of England.

We may now turn to the specific claims that Stephen puts in Wilfrid's mouth in the account of his defence before the hostile council at *Ouestraefelda*:

> And did I not instruct them, in accordance with the rite of the primitive Church, to stand in double choirs with resounding melody of the voice, singing joyfully with responsories and alternating antiphons?
>
> *Aut quomodo iuxta ritum primitivae ecclesiae assono vocis modulamine, binis adstantibus choris, persultare responsoriis antiphonisque reciprocis instruerem?* (VW, 47)

There are four key concepts in this statement that need careful attention: antiphons, responsories, 'double choirs' and the 'primitive Church'.

Antiphons and responsories are refrains inserted between the verses of psalms. What distinguishes an antiphon from a responsory is a question that has occupied students of music since Isidore of Seville (*Etymologiae* VI, 19, 7–8; ed. Lindsay 1911; more recently, Hourlier 1973). The sources are ambiguous, the bibliography is vast, and nothing like a definitive solution can be proposed here.

Responsorial psalmody is the older form, attested in the second century. A soloist chants a psalm, and the congregation periodically interrupts him with a refrain: either *Alleluia* or, more commonly, a verse from the same psalm (Taft 2003, 17–19).

Antiphonal psalmody is a later development, attested in the fourth century. In Greek music theory, and in the Hellenistic-Jewish writings of Philo of Alexandria, 'antiphonal' had referred to the sound that results when men and women attempted to sing in unison: a perfect consonance at the octave. Early

Christians read Philo, but when they first use the word 'antiphon' they meant it in the more general etymological sense of 'alternation' (Jeffery 2003c, 170–74). A soloist continued to sing the psalm verses; but the congregation was divided into two groups (at first probably the already segregated groups of men and women), and the refrain was passed from one side to the other. Sometimes each side of the congregation would have its own refrain text (Taft 2003, 19–22). The refrain was usually a non-biblical 'piece of ecclesiastical poetry' (Taft 1993, 54).

The same terminology is found in the medieval West, but with different shades of meaning. In the Western repertories available for us to study, 'responsorial' is best understood to describe a *literary form*: a psalm that is not sung straight through, but is rather punctuated with a repeated refrain. 'Antiphonal' denotes a *performance practice*, namely alternation between two soloists or two choirs (which could be done with or without a refrain). Thus the term *responsorium* was applied to refrains that were sung by everyone together, and the term *antiphona* was applied to refrains that were sung in alternation between two choirs (Cullin 1991, 23–4). While Latin antiphons are overwhelmingly biblical in their texts, they often exhibit a textual and musical 'caesura' where the singing could pass from one soloist or choir to the other. Edward Nowacki (1990) has shown that such a practice was known in twelfth-century Rome. This practical distinction may not have applied throughout the West. The Antiphonary of Bangor, for instance, includes texts that are labelled as *antiphonae*, and certain Irish hymns seem to refer to alternation between two choirs, but the two concepts were not necessarily connected (Stevenson, J. B. 1996, 113). The distinction had become meaningless by the later Middle Ages, when both types of refrain were performed identically.

Stephen seems to be aware of the different performance practices implied by these terms *responsorium* and *antiphona* – at least if we understand *reciprocae* to modify only *antiphonae*, as suggested in the translation above. For Wilfrid and his English contemporaries, however, 'antiphons and responsories' meant, above all, a repertory of chants that had to be learned and retained in the memory through constant use. When the monastery of Jarrow was founded, Abbot Ceolfrith worked hard to establish there the repertory of antiphons and responsories that had been learned at Wearmouth a couple of years previously with the help of John the 'archcantor'. When a plague subsequently carried off everyone in Jarrow who could sing these chants except Ceolfrith himself and the 'little boy' traditionally believed to be Bede, the repertory was preserved and passed on only through intense labour (*non paruo cum labore*) (VC 14). Alcuin's *De laude Dei* preserves the texts of many antiphons and responsories, but their melodies could only be transmitted orally and retained through constant practice. Acca's singing master Maban both taught new musical pieces and restored familiar ones that 'had begun to deteriorate by long use or by neglect' (HE V, 20).

Two-choir psalmody is another bugbear of medieval musicology. It has long been equated with 'antiphonal' psalmody, which, as will now be clear, originally entailed the recitation of the psalms by a soloist. Under the influence of the new theological 'ethos' of psalmody that emerged in the fifth and sixth centuries, however, it would seem that choral psalmody, shared between the two choirs that had previously sung only the refrains, came to predominate (*contra* Dyer 1989b). The simple psalmody of Milan is inseparable from a practice of alternation between two choirs, and the same practice is explicit in the earliest Gregorian tones in the *Commemoratio brevis* (Bailey 1980, 97; Bernard 2004, 320–21).

Two-choir psalmody seems to have been an important part of the monastic Office as it was celebrated in the major basilicas of Rome. These churches were served by adjacent monasteries – John the 'archcantor' was abbot of St Martin's next to St Peter's basilica – who were responsible for Nocturns and the daytime offices, while the secular clergy led Mass, Lauds and Vespers. Each monastery was responsible for one of the two choirs needed for the daily Office (Ferrari 1957, 365–6). The practice is recorded several times in the *Liber pontificalis*, as in this description of the reforms carried out by Hadrian I (772–95) at the Lateran basilica (XCVII, 68; trans Davis 1992, 157):

> He laid down that they should celebrate the office – matins, prime, terce, sext, none and vespers – in the Saviour's basilica also called Constantinian close to the Lateran patriarchate, in two choirs: one (*ab uno choro*), the monks of St Pancras' monastery located there, who formerly used to chant on their own antiphonally (*qui dudum singulariter in utrosque psallebant* – 'who formerly used to sing on both sides'); the other, the monks of the just-mentioned monastery of SS Andrew and Bartholomew called that of Pope Honorius.

This implies that two-choir singing had been the norm at the Lateran for some time before Hadrian's intervention. References to two-choir psalmody in Gaul begin to appear only in the second half of the eighth century, when Roman musical practices were being deliberately imitated (Bernard 2004, 316–21; and see Bernard 2005).

The church in Canterbury, as founded by Augustine, had much in common with the Lateran basilica: its church was dedicated to the Holy Saviour, and it had a neighbouring monastery. Its liturgical arrangements, too, may have paralleled those of the Lateran basilica (Brooks 1984, 91–2).

Two-choir singing is mentioned in several independent Anglo-Saxon literary sources. Aldhelm refers to it in three separate works: his third *Carmen ecclesiasticum* (lines 46–58; ed. Ehwald 1919, 14–18), his *Carmen rhythmicum* (lines 123–30; p 527), and the prose *De virginitate* (cap 30; pp 268–9). Aediluulf's *De abbatibus*, an early ninth-century verse history of an unknown Northern monastery, describes the monks in two choirs (*classes geminae*) singing psalms and antiphons (lines 495–8; ed. Campbell 1967, 39). Benedict Biscop continued to recite the psalms of the Divine Office during his final illness, with the assistance of a few brethren standing in two choirs on either side of his bed (HA 12; ed. Plummer 1896, 1, 376). In each case the language seems more readily to admit an interpretation of choral psalmody, not solo psalmody with choral refrains.

Anglo-Saxon writers evidently thought that the practice was worth mentioning explicitly. If we are right in thinking that two-choir psalmody at this date was a Roman rather than a Gallican practice, then it will have been a distinctive feature of the nascent English Church's liturgical identity. And if, as seems almost certain, this ceremonial arrangement was accompanied by a new style of singing – many voices joined in the simple recitation tones of the Milanese type – the fragility of this recently learned oral tradition will have made it all the more special in the daily life of the Church.

What did Wilfrid mean by the 'primitive Church'? Was he referring to the widespread belief that antiphonal singing was introduced by Ambrose of Milan in the fourth century, in imitation of an Eastern practice? Was it based on his time in Rome, where the palpable presence of the early martyrs – and of Peter's authority (cf HE III, 25) – lent to this relatively young musical practice a sense of deep antiquity? Both suggestions are entirely plausible. A third may be added. Nicetius, bishop of Lyons (552–73), was noted for a devotion to chant unusual in a bishop: he participated personally in the offices of the day and night, and was known to meditate on the psalms so intently that if he were asked a question he would answer with the words of the psalm that he had just been pondering (Krusch 1896, 522). An inscription on his tomb recorded this musical interest (ed Krusch 1896, 519):

> *Psallere praecepit normamque tenere canendi*
> *Primus et alterutrum tendere voce chorum*
>
> (He was the first to teach singing and the rule of chant, and to strive
> for either choir with the voice.)

The passage does not admit of an easy translation, and it has often been taken to mean that Nicetius introduced two-choir psalmody at Lyons. Philippe Bernard (2004, 295–6) has demonstrated why such an interpretation is implausible. But might Wilfrid have read this inscription during his time in Lyons? If he did, he may have surmised that a great bishop of Lyons – a Church hallowed by the blood of the martyrs of AD 177 – had introduced a form of singing that Wilfrid already associated with Rome and the ancient East. Wilfrid seems to have understood himself as a bishop in the Merovingian mould, and Nicetius may have provided a model for how such a bishop ought to superintend the quality of ecclesiastical music in his diocese.

Ultimately, Wilfrid's role in spreading the Kentish-Roman chant tradition in the North can be demonstrated only from two or three references to his musical importance in Bede and Stephen. Wilfrid was not the only Anglo-Saxon cleric interested in Roman chant; Benedict Biscop and Ceolfrith were probably just as important for the process. Nevertheless, our examination of Wilfrid's 'experience' of the mixed musical economy of early Anglo-Saxon England and of the language used to describe his own contribution has at least allowed us to formulate a theory of what he specifically wanted to promote, namely, the choral recitation of the psalms by monks in two choirs, with a carefully preserved treasury of antiphons and responsories, according to the tradition of Rome as practised in Canterbury. This conclusion, if it is accepted, will overturn some frequently repeated assumptions about the supposedly solo character of early Anglo-Saxon psalmody (eg Ó Carragáin 1994, 6; Billett 2011, 101 n. 68). It may also offer some insight into what Wilfrid was doing as he sang the psalms alone in his darkest hour.

Music about Wilfrid

A reflection on music for Wilfrid's thirteenth centenary would not be complete without a brief notice of music for Wilfrid's cult. So far as we know, Wilfrid's early cult had no special music in his honour, nor would this be expected. The earliest English example of a specially composed saint's Office with chants is that for St Cuthbert, dating from the first half of the tenth century (Hohler 1956, 156–7). Music for Wilfrid is first mentioned in Eadmer's early-twelfth-century *Breviloquium*, a sermon on Wilfrid's life written for the community of Christ Church, Canterbury, to be read on Wilfrid's death day. In Canterbury this may have been observed on 12 October, which marked both the (disputed) translation of Wilfrid's remains to Canterbury by Archbishop Oda (941–58) and their re-interment on that date in 1070 or 1071 under Archbishop Lanfranc (Muir and Turner 1998, xxiii). Eadmer recounts a miracle in which the Christ Church sacristan Godwin was awakened just before the time for Nocturns by angelic singers in the church singing an invitatory antiphon in Wilfrid's honour in the first Gregorian mode (149; ed. and trans. Muir and Turner 1998, 178–9):

Unum Deum in Trinitate fideliter adoremus, cuius fide Deo vivit sanctus presul Wilfridus.

(Let us faithfully worship the One God in Trinity, by faith in whom the holy prelate Wilfrid lives unto God.)

Musical Example 13.4: An Invitatory antiphon from the
Common of Confessor Bishops.

Source: Cambridge, University Library, Mm. 2. 9 (antiphoner following Salisbury Use, St Giles Abbey [Augustinian], Barnwell, England, s. xiii$^{2/4}$) ; facsimile in Frere 1901–24, plate 650. The manuscript lacks barlines. Hollow note-heads signify liquescence.

U-num de-   um in tri-ni-ta-   te   fi-de-li-ter   a-do-re-mus.

Cu-ius fi-de de-o ui- uit sanctus pre-sul Wil-fri-dus.

deo uiuit] deum uiuit MS
Wilfridus] 'N' MS (name of the appropriate saint to be inserted)

Let us faithfully worship the One God in Trinity, by faith in whom the holy prelate Wilfrid lives unto God. (Cf Rom 6:10–13)

This antiphon is not unique to Wilfrid. Its text is from the Common of a Confessor Bishop, which was sung to a first-mode melody in the medieval use of Salisbury (see Example 13.4). It would seem that no special music was composed for Wilfrid at Canterbury.

Wilfrid was also honoured in the liturgy of York. Here too his feasts were observed with chants from the Common of a Confessor Bishop, with one important exception: a sequence, i.e. a poetic chant sung before the reading of the Gospel at Mass. This is the only piece of music written specifically about Wilfrid that has come down to us with a melody (Example 13.5, pp. 184–5). The first part of the text refers to Luke's version of the Parable of the Talents (Luke 19: 13–2), which is the Gospel reading assigned to the Common of Confessor Bishops (so the York breviary: Hughes 2000, 905; the Matthaean version is prescribed in the missal: Henderson 1874, 2, 31). The remainder draws predictably on two prominent miracles in Wilfrid's career as recounted in the *Vita Sancti Wilfridi*. The text and melody are unique to York (Hiley 1995, ix).

An early-fifteenth-century liturgical psalter from Ripon collegiate church, now Ripon Cathedral MS 8 (currently held at the Brotherton Library, Leeds), contains, on fols 162–88, texts, without musical notation, of through-composed Offices for three feasts of St Wilfrid (Fowler 1875, 382–3; Ker 1969–2002, 4, 211–13). In most of England, Wilfrid had two feasts: his Deposition on 24 April, and his Translation (to Canterbury) on 12 October. In medieval Ripon and in York, these dates were reversed, reflecting Ripon's claim that Wilfrid's body had never been removed. To these two feasts Ripon added a third, Wilfrid's birthday, which was observed on the Sunday after the feast of St Peter's Chains (1 August).

WILFRID AND MUSIC

Musical Example 13.5: Sequence for the Translation of St Wilfrid (24 April) from the York Gradual (continued on next page).

Source: Oxford, Bodleian Library, Lat liturg b 5 (use of York, prov East Drayton, Nottinghamshire, s. xv). Facsimile: Hiley 1995, fols 96r–97v. Hollow note heads represent liquescent neumes. Abbreviations in the text have been silently expanded.

(1) Sal- ua-to- ris cle-menci-e dul-cem pan-gat ar- mo-ni- e modu- lum ecc-le- si- a.
(2) Qui in sanctis mi-ra- bi-lis est et mundo pla-ca bi- lis ho-rum per suf-fra-gi- a.

(3) Hic est pa- ter-fami- li- as qui mnas ser-uis dans singu-las pro-fec- tu- rus pe- re-gre.
(4) Pro ta- len-tis gemi-na-tis pre-ci- um fi- de- li- ta- tis sto-lam red-dit glo-ri- e.

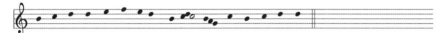

(5) Glo-ri- a- tur hac in-dutus Wil-fri- dus in ce- le-sti-bus.
(6) La- pis domo col- lo-catus ce- le- sti de-cen-tis-si-mus.

(7) Hic est la- pis am-plex- an- dus ue-la-men non ha-ben- ti- bus.
(8) Pre-ce tol-lens cul-pe pon-dus et in- du- ens uir-tu ti- bus.

Textual corrections (following W. G. Henderson 1872, **2**, 30–31): 1 clemencie] clemencia MS.

Translation:

[1] *Let the Church sing the sweet, harmonious song of the Saviour's mercy,* [2] *who is wonderful in his saints* (VW 18; quoting Ps. LXVIII: 36) *and who is placated towards the world through their intercessions.* [3] *This is the householder about to set off abroad who, giving one coin to each of his slaves* (Luke XIX, 13–26), [4] *for doubled talents* (Matt. XXV, 14–28) *gives in return the reward for faithfulness, the garment of glory.* [5] *Clothed with this, Wilfrid glories in the heavens,* [6] *placed as a most seemly stone in the heavenly house* (1 Pet. 11, 5). [7] *This is the stone worthy of embrace, a shelter to those having none,* [8] *taking away by prayer the burden of guilt, and clothing with virtues.*

The feast had both religious and civic significance in the parish; in the nineteenth century it was still known as 'Wilfrid Sunday' (Fowler 1875, 17 n. 2).

What little attention this manuscript has attracted has been focused almost entirely on the lengthy readings provided for the office of Nocturns on the three feasts and during their octaves (Fowler 1882, 26–30, 49; Muir and Turner 1998,

183

(9) Quod in ter- ris me-ru- it in-nu- me-ris cla-ru- it per or- bem mi- ra- cu- lis.
(10) Que chri- stus ex- hi- bu- it cu-i es- se stu-du-it pla-cens si- ne ma-cu- lis.

(11) Confir-ma-ri dum de-fer-tur o- bit infans et of- fer-tur su-sci- tandus pre-su- li.
(12) Su- sci-ta- tus con- fir-ma-tur et post annos manci- pa-tur ob-se- qui-o do- mi- ni.

(13) Vir ex al- to la- bi-tur et de-fun-ctus cre-di-tur ar- tu-bus at-tri-tis.
(14) Sed mors statim pel-li- tur et uir sa- nus red-di-tur tactu pon-ti- fi- cis.

(15) Est et mor-bis a- li- is sa-lus da-ta plu-ri- mis e- ius-dem pre- ca-mi- ne.
(16) Cu-ius chri-stus preci- bus ue-ro in ce-le- sti-bus nos il- lu- stret lu-mi- ne.

Textual corrections: 10 maculis] macula MS; 11 defertur] differtur MS; 12 obsequio] obsequiis MS; 14 No final punctuation in MS; 15 morbis] morbus MS; 15 data] datur MS

[9] *What he won on earth has shone forth throughout the world in innumerable miracles.* [10] *These Christ produced in proof, to whom he strove to be pleasing without stains.* [11] *While he is being brought to be confirmed, a child dies and is offered to the bishop to be raised up.* [12] *Raised up, he is confirmed, and after some years he is delivered into the Lord's service.* [13] *A man falls from a height and is believed dead, with his limbs broken.* [14] *But death is immediately banished and the man returned to health by the bishop's touch.* [15] *Through his prayer, health is also given to many people with other diseases.* [16] *Through his prayers, may Christ illumine us with the true light in the heavens.*

271–6). These are primarily a conflation of Eadmer's *Vita* and Bede's summary of Wilfrid's career (HE V, 19). The one major alteration is that Eadmer's description of the translation of Wilfrid's relics to Canterbury is replaced with an account of the re-interment of Wilfrid's complete skeleton in a new shrine at Ripon by Archbishop Walter de Gray in 1224.

The Offices and lessons are accessible in a nineteenth-century edition, with modernised Latin spellings and a facing English translation (Whitham 1893). It is not immediately obvious whether the chant texts of the three Offices, as distinct from the new readings, were composed before or after 1224. The chant texts do not refer to a translation of Wilfrid's relics, whether in Ripon or in Canterbury. Stephen's *Vita Wilfridi* seems not to have been used at all, which may mean that it was inaccessible at Ripon in the later Middle Ages. The chant texts are mainly excerpted and adapted from Eadmer's *Vita*. Many of the shorter antiphons are hexameter couplets quoted or modified from Frithegod's tenth-century verse *Breviloquium*. For example, the first antiphon at Lauds on Wilfrid's birthday (fol. 166v) is taken from two consecutive lines in Frithegod, but the opening words have been altered (Campbell 1950, 6):

53 *Presul Wilfridus* [Frithegod: *nil puerile gerens*] *facunde munia lingue*
54 *aspirante deo gestis explebat apertis*

(The prelate Wilfrid, by the assistance of God, supplemented by manifest deeds the gifts of his eloquent tongue. Trans. Whitham 1893, 7)

The second antiphon at Lauds stitches together two disjunct lines (Campbell 1950, 7):

71 *Vir probus ingenio regum meritoque satelles*
69 *acceptus* |acceptis, MS] *cuneis fidei polebat in actis*

(The worthy man, by his ability and merit the attendant on kings, acceptable to all, was mighty in deeds of faith.)

There is a single example of a newly composed rhyming antiphon, which has little literary distinction (fols 166v–167r):

O *Wilfride lux lapsorum / consolator miserorum*
ave decus prelatorum / salus tibi devotorum
intuere nostrum chorum / et post tempus hoc laborum
duc nos ad regna celorum / tua sancta preces [sic]

A properly researched edition of the Offices might yield interesting information about the cult of Wilfrid in late-medieval Ripon.

14: *Wilfrid and the Continent*

PAUL FOURACRE

St Wilfrid's travels on the Continent play a large part in the narrative of his *Life*, not least because the bishop spent over ten years in Francia and in Italy. In the minds of modern historians, his Continental experiences loom just as large, being thought to be the key to Wilfrid's formation as a churchman of princely type. It is, in turn, the perception of Wilfrid's ecclesiastical imperialism that informs our reading of Bede's account of how Archbishop Theodore struggled to bring the fledgling Anglo-Saxon church to good catholic order. And from the viewpoint of relations between England and the Continent, the *Life of Wilfrid* by Stephen the Priest is the most important narrative witness of the seventh century. Yet for nearly all of this we are reliant on the word of Stephen alone. Bede adds only one element to Stephens's account, namely his friend Acca's story of Wilfrid's visit to Frisia in 703 (HE III, 13). No Continental source mentions Wilfrid, nor can be thought to be referring to him even obliquely, so that Wilfrid's probable corroboration of the Roman Council of 680 is, strictly speaking, the only piece of Continental evidence for his ever having left Britain.

Since what Stephen says about Wilfrid on the Continent is clearly invaluable, we must press his account on every point, and this is what will be done in what follows. That is to say, a forensic questioning of the text is needed if we are to estimate its reliability in relation to the Continental episodes. Can we, in short, believe Stephen the Priest? Though every piece of hagiography should be understood as a creative work in its own terms, if we are searching for original detail it is logical to strip out of a work those elements that are copied from elsewhere, or which at least may have origins outside of the strictly biographical detail. But apart from the scriptural references in the work, a search for such borrowings in relation to Wilfrid in Francia draws a blank. Stephen used no identifiable Continental sources, so we cannot say that Wilfrid was, as it were, inserted into someone else's experience, at least outside of the imagined experience of the scriptural. All we can do is to look carefully at what Stephen did say in the light of what we know from other sources about the contexts in which Wilfrid is placed and the people with whom he is associated in the *Life*. We can then ask whether what Stephen tells us has any plausibility and, if it does, how we might interpret it in historical terms. Let us begin with Wilfrid's first journey to Rome, and with the episode said to be formative in his understanding of what a bishop might be like, namely his stay in the southern Gallic or Neustro-Burgundian city of Lyons. It is an episode which is very prominent in Trent Foley's analysis of the structure of the *Vita Wilfridi* (Foley 1992, 31–3; 51–6; 84–5). Foley sees it as the key to the presentation of Wilfrid as the obedient son who is transformed into the 'pious father' figure and was at the same time prepared to undergo martyrdom. To Henry Mayr-Harting (1972, 75), this was simply the time when Wilfrid learned to be the kind of bishop who dealt with the powerful and who expected to exercise worldly as well as spiritual authority.

Wilfrid's first journey to Rome was a long one, lasting at least four years, largely because, according to Stephen, he spent three years in Lyons (VW 4–6). Travelling towards Rome through Francia, on what route we are not told, Wilfrid parted from his companion and guide Benedict Biscop at Lyons. The parting was apparently discordant, for Stephen compared it to the split between Paul and Barnabas (Acts 15, 35–38). No reason is given as to why Wilfrid chose to stay in Lyons apart from the fact that the archbishop of the city, one Dalfinus, took a liking to him and offered lavish hospitality to Wilfrid and his companions. So much did Dalfinus like Wilfrid that he offered him 'a good part of Gaul to rule', his niece to be his wife, and his constant patronage. Wilfrid declined and carried on to Rome with his companions where he spent 'many months' (*per multos menses*) being instructed by the archdeacon Boniface before 'finally' (*postremo*) being blessed by the Pope (VW 5). He then returned to Lyons. His companions are no longer mentioned. He spent three years in Lyons, plenty of time to learn how to be a Frankish-type bishop, and was tonsured in the Roman style. Finally, Dalfinus was persecuted by the wicked Queen Balthild who, like Jezebel (I Kings, 21–22) was attacking the prophets and who had nine bishops killed. Dalfinus was to be one of them. Preparing to die alongside Dalfinus, the dukes in command spared him because he was English, although this near martyrdom made him worthy to be counted amongst the confessors. After Dalfinus's death Wilfrid sailed home. Following Plummer's chronology (in his notes to Bede, HE V, 9), he left England in the year 654 and returned in 658 (Plummer 1896, II, 316–17) This chronology is not, as we shall see, very tight. What should we make of the Lyons story?

Some of the apparent historical detail may be explained by the exigencies of scriptural analogy: as Trent Foley (1992, 30) argues, the offer of a large part of Gaul to rule parallels Satan's tempting of Christ with the offer of a kingdom here on earth. There was certainly a powerful bishop of Lyons, but even Merovingian bishops did not go around offering secular power to young strangers. The bishop known in the *Life* as Dalfinus is otherwise known as Aunemundus, that is, named thus in bishops lists, charters and a set of *Acta*, the *Acta Aunemundi* (Fouracre and Gerberding 1996, 179–192), from which we also learn that he had a brother who was *praefectus*, secular ruler, of Lyons. In later tradition the brother is named as Dalfinus. This tradition was generated in the eleventh century when two Lyons institutions were battling over an Aunemundus cult and producing documents to order (Fouracre and Gerberding 1996, 168). One of these was a spurious will that named the brother, but it seems quite likely that the name came from Bede's précis of Wilfrid's career, possibly influenced by the fact that the name Dalfinus means 'brother' in Greek. Is this somehow how Stephen arrived at the name too?

That Aunemund was killed is certain: he appears in a Lyons martyrology composed before 806 (Dom Quentin 1908, 205). But that Wilfrid was there and prepared to die alongside him has been questioned. Plummer's chronology, which was adopted by Coville, the premier historian of Lyons who published in 1928, had to have Aunemund die in 658, the last moment Wilfrid could have been there (Coville 1928, 389–90). This date is arrived at by counting from 654, allowing for Wilfrid to be several months first in Lyons and then in Rome, before meeting the Pope in 655, that is, when the exiled Pope Martin died and Pope Eugenius, elected in 654, achieved full legitimacy. Then three years in Lyons makes 658, with Wilfrid travelling directly back to England after Aunemund's death. But Aunemund put his name to a privilege for the church of Sens on 26 August 660, in a charter now demonstrated to have been genuine (Fouracre and Gerberding 1996, 174). In fact, Willhelm Levison, editor of the *Life* for the *Monumenta Germaniae Historica*, thought in his 1913 edition that the charter might well be genuine, that is over twenty years before Coville wrote (Levison 1913, 199–200). Coville did not pick this up. So, Aunemund cannot have died before 26 August 660. Wilfrid had thus been back in England for over a year before Aunemund's death. It was Janet Nelson (Nelson 1978), picking up on Levison, who pointed this out in an important paper published in 1978 and drew out the implication that Stephen, or maybe Wilfrid himself as Stephen's informant, was being deliberately misleading. That point in turn weakened our trust in the work as a whole and her reading became generally accepted. However, the traditional chronology, that is to have Wilfrid home and dry in 658, now seems less certain. If he toured the shrines in Rome for *plures menses*, and then was instructed by Boniface, and if the term *postremo* 'fnally' implies a further wait, Wilfrid could have been in Rome a long time, possibly waiting for Eugenius's successor Vitalian to be properly elected in 657 (VW 5). Pope Vitalian is remembered as having showed an especial interest in England, and this could have been prompted by his meeting with Wilfrid. So, if Wilfrid left Rome in 657 he would indeed have been in Lyons in 660. Katy Cubitt (pers. com.) has pointed out that there is no evidence of Wilfrid's presence in England much before the Synod of Whitby in 664. And on reflection it does seem that it would have been extraordinary for Stephen to build his seminal episode around a claim that would have been as risky as it was false, given that Wilfrid was apt to be challenged on his version of the truth. Nevertheless, some of what Janet Nelson in 1978 called

Steigerung, the inflation of Wilfrid's saintly credentials, was certainly built into this narrative.

It is easy enough to see why Stephen would have put his hero alongside Aunemund in his final moment, for he says that by being prepared for death, Wilfrid was worthy to be regarded as a confessor. This for Trent Foley is another important moment in the construction of Wilfrid's apostolic persona (Foley 1992, 32–3). Our Lyons source, the *Acta Aunemundi*, is a tenth-century work, with, as several have argued, a Merovingian narrative at its core (Fouracre and Gerberding 1996, 171). The story it tells is not seriously incompatible with that told by Stephen. In both accounts the bishop and his family were extremely powerful; the decision to kill him originated in the royal court; he was ordered to appear before the court; he had a holy man with him; there were 'dukes' in charge of him, and he was killed. Both versions could embody the same early tradition, with significant *ad hoc* embellishment: Wilfrid was present in Stephen's account, in the *Acta* the holy man was Waldebert, abbot of Luxeuil. In the *Acta* the brother was first called to court and executed. Aunemund was accused of inviting foreign peoples into the realm, a detail that might well fit with either Lombard, or, later, Moorish, intrigues in the Rhône Valley. In the *Acta*, Aunemund was not executed, but assassinated on his way to court. For modern historians of the later Merovingian period, the big difference in the two accounts is Stephen's claim that the queen Balthild, a persecutor of the church and killer of prophets like the Jezebel of old, had Aunemund killed along with eight other bishops (VW 6). If she had had, then this really would be news.

One is surprised to read 'Balthild' here because this queen, who ruled as regent for her son Clothar III (657–664), is otherwise known as a saint. She was the subject of a *Vita* completed by 690 (Fouracre and Gerberding 1996, 118–32). Though this *Life* makes it plain that she used a measure of coercion in reforming the *seniores basilicae* of the Neustro-Burgundian realm, and that she did have enemies at court who eventually forced her from power, nowhere else is there even a hint that she was a serial killer of bishops, and surely this is the kind of thing we would have been told about, not least in the *Acta Aunemundi*. Medieval readers of Stephen and Bede were also puzzled by the name, not because they thought well of Balthild, for there is no evidence that they knew of her, but because the eponymous Jezebel-like Frankish queen was Brunhild, of a fame that lasted from the *Life of Columbanus* composed in the 640s through to modernity via the Niebelungenlied. Jonas, author of the *Vita Columbani*, called her a second Jezebel, for she famously had Bishop Desiderius of Vienne, another Rhône Valley city, stoned to death (Krusch 1902, 86). Of the two eleventh-century manuscripts of the *Vita Wilfridi*, one, the British Library Cotton manuscript, has 'Brunechild' instead of Balthild (Levison 1913, 183–5; 100). If we go back to Frithegod's mid-tenth-century *Brevilogium Vitae Beatae Wilfridi* (line 185) for a reading earlier than that of the two earliest extant *Vita Wilfridi* manuscripts, we find that of the two tenth-century manuscripts of this work, one ('C') has 'Brunhild' and the other ('L') has 'Balthild' (Campbell 1950, 11). This, apparently, is the only substantial difference between 'C' and 'L'. Then if we turn to Bede's précis, we read, in Plummer's critical note, that 'several manuscripts both of Bede and Eddius (ie. Stephen) read 'Brunhild' for 'Baldhild' (Plummer 1896, I, 325; II, 322). Alas he does not say which manuscripts of the *Historia Ecclesiastica* these are, but considering that he otherwise spells out which variants were in the manuscripts he called 'M', 'B', 'C' and 'N', that is the earliest ones which are eighth-century copies, we may deduce that he did not mean any of these, and this suggests that Bede himself had understood Balthild rather than Brunhild, with later copyists assuming that it must have been in error for Brunhild. One could make the same argument for Frithegod's *Brevilogium*. The question here is whether Stephen knew of the *Vita Columbani*, or, at a pinch, the story of Brunhild in *the Fourth Book of the Chronicle of Fredegar*, a work produced *c.*660 which borrows heavily from the *Vita Columbani* (Wallace-Hadrill 1960, 23–9), and whether he had appropriated the story for Wilfrid, in which case this would give us a rather different take on the Lyons episode. If so, there is no other sign of Brunhild-like behaviour apart from the Jezebel epithet, and Stephen could perfectly easily have arrived at the Jezebel analogy on his own: how many other scriptural exemplars of wicked prophet-killing queens are there? Tellingly, he used it again in chapter 24 of the *Life*, in order to criticise Iurminburh, King Ecgfrith of Northumbria's queen, thus in a context entirely removed from that of the *Vita Columbani*. It therefore seems that we cannot show that Stephen was influenced by, or knew of, this Continental source. Nor, apparently, did he know that Balthild was a saint, nor that she was English, for the *Vita Balthildis* tells us that she was *de partibus transmarinis* and *ex genere Saxonum* (Fouracre and Gerberding 1996, 119). That she might actually have been involved in the demise of Aunemund is not implausible, for she was the type of ruler that the Franks termed *strenua*, which carries a hint of force. It is also the case that Aunemund's replacement as bishop was a certain Genesius, whom the *Vita Balthildis* tells us had been her palace chaplain and confidant. Stephen's account of Wilfrid's stay in Lyons thus has a degree of plausibility. Death by violence was something of an occupational hazard for Merovingian bishops: at least sixteen of them were killed over the period as a whole (Fouracre 2003). Balthild was vigorous in reforming the church by inserting her supporters into key bishoprics: Autun and Toulouse are further examples. But important details seem very wrong: the name of the bishop; the offer to Wilfrid of territory to rule and Balthild's murder of eight other bishops, if not Wilfrid's presence at Aunemund's execution. As for Wilfrid learning how to be a bishop in Lyons, I am not sure that that 'the Frankish-type bishop' is not something of an ideal type, a construction of modern historiography that may confuse the episcopal with the simply political. Trent Foley tends to have it both ways. In his view, Stephen constructed an episcopal persona for Wilfrid based on scriptural type, but it was also constructed in the light of recent history that Wilfrid would have known about: the popes versus the Empire, the Gallic bishops versus the centre (Foley 1992, 88–9). This leaves the way open for other lessons, and in Rome and Lyons one would surely be that bishops who got involved in the politics of power needed large towns with thick walls. How, one must ask, might Wilfrid have thought to transport this kind of city-based rule to the very different environment of Northumbria?

Balthild provides a link to our next episode, Wilfrid's consecration as bishop in Francia in 664. A key figure here is Bishop Agilbert. Agilbert appears in Bede (HE, III, 7) as a bishop coming to King Coenwalh of the Gewisse (West Saxons) from Ireland. He was a Gaul or Frank by birth and spent a long time in Ireland studying the scriptures. He left Wessex when Coenwalh, tiring of Agilbert's inability to speak English properly, appointed Wine to the new bishopric of Winchester. Agilbert fetched up in Northumbria (HE III, 25) as a friend of King Ahlfrith and of Wilfrid. According to Stephen he ordained Wilfrid priest in his own monastery, i.e. Ripon. He then appeared at the synod of Whitby as spokesperson for the Roman camp, but asked Wilfrid to speak on his behalf. Afterwards he departed for Gaul/Francia where, according to Bede, he was acting as bishop of Paris (HE V, 19). Eventually (c.670) Coenwalh asked Agilbert to return to Wessex, but as bishop of Paris he was unable to do so, and sent his nephew Leuthere in his place. Leuthere was bishop for six years. Stephen (VW 12) tells us that, after being elected bishop, Wilfrid was sent to Gaul to be consecrated, Bede that Alhfrith sent Wilfrid to the king of Gaul, who in turn sent to him to Agilbert 'who after he left Britain became bishop of Paris'. Agilbert was thus amongst the twelve bishops who met for the consecration and then, according to their custom, bore the newly consecrated Wilfrid into the oratory on a golden throne. This is not a custom seen elsewhere in Gaul/Francia, but as Mayr-Harting pointed out, it is clearly an allusion to Christ in Majesty, a scene that is also depicted on Agilbert's sarcophagus which has survived in the crypt of what had been his family monastery at Jouarre. Bede, in HE III, 28, thus earlier in the work than the précis of Wilfrid's life, adds the detail that the consecration took place in Compiègne, whereas one might have thought that if Agilbert was behind it, it would have taken place in Paris. But, in fact, Agilbert was not made bishop of Paris on his return from Whitby as Bede implied. There may conceivably have been no less than three bishops of Paris in the year 664, none of which was Agilbert. The bishops' list for the diocese shows one Importunus in post until at least 667 when he put his name to an Episcopal Privilege (Ewig 1979, 439). The earliest date post 667 for Agilbert as bishop of

Paris again comes from Bede (HE IV, 1), and is 668, for Theodore was said to have stayed with Agilbert 'bishop of Paris' on his way to England. The details of Agilbert's career were clearly fading from memory, but he was remembered as a touchstone of orthodoxy and probity in the building of the English church. Behind this may lie a mass of Anglo-Frankish contacts that we can now only guess at, but of which we should try to be aware in reading the *Vita Wilfridi*.

Balthild, we have seen, was in all probability English, and it has been reasoned that she came from East Anglia, moving to Francia as a slave possibly taken in the conflict between East Anglia and Mercia (Fouracre and Gerberding 1996, 100). A gold seal-ring matrix found near Norwich in 1998 bears the name 'Baldhild' and may well have been hers. At the same time, three Irish holy men, brothers, moved from East Anglia to Francia the first of them being Fursey, who found a patron in the mayor of the palace, Erchinoald, who was also Balthild's master, and who provided her as a bride for the Merovingian king, Clovis II. Erchinoald, who died in 658, was as mayor the most powerful non-royal ruler in Francia. He is said to have provided his daughter Emma as a bride for the Kentish king Eadbald, following in the footsteps of the provision of Bertha as wife to King Æthelberht. Identification of links by name is a hazardous practice, but the Earcon- element in Southern English names suggests links with Erchinoald, most obviously in Earconwald, the bishop of London (d.692 or 693), bearer of what is basically the same name. The name Agilbert is closely related to that of Æthelberht. Leuthere, the bearer of a name which may be cognate with Hlothhere, was closely associated with Bath Abbey of which the first abbess was another Berta (Sims-Williams 1975). Bede tells us that around the middle of the seventh century, many Anglo-Saxon leaders sent their daughters to convents in Francia, amongst them Chelles, Faremoutiers and Andelys sur Seine (HE III, 8). Hild of Whitby, whose name of course forms the suffix of Balt-hild, had East Anglian connections according to Bede, and had at one time considered joining the monastery/convent at Chelles, of which Balthild was effectively the founder. What is very striking is that several of these ladies became abbesses in their adopted Frankish institutions which indicates that their high status was recognized on the Continent, which is in turn suggestive of family connections. What is even more remarkable is that Bede, having mentioned Chelles and Balthild's royal husband Clovis II, never picked up on the fact that Balthild herself was English.

Turning to Francia itself, we find the great families of north-west Francia (Neustria) frequently at loggerheads with each other. It is again hazardous to work out who was on which side, for they changed sides, intermarried and attacked each other with what seems equal enthusiasm, but it seems almost clear that in the 650s Balthild and Erchinoald were one side and Agilbert was on another. His trip to Ireland may thus have been some kind of exile. While he was away, Balthild demanded nuns from his sister Teodechilde, abbess of Jouarre the family monastery, in order to stock her own foundation of Chelles. Teodechilde, we are told, 'hesitated for a long time' before coming up with up her lead nun, Bertila (note, another of the Berta name group), and many others (Levison 1913, 104). The phrasing might indicate that Teodechilde was being coerced. Finally, it seems more than a coincidence that Agilbert returned to Francia in 664, the year Balthild was driven from power. This was an eventful year. Both Balthild and Chrodbert, long-standing bishop of Paris, are attested in a charter of September 664. In August 665 we have a charter in which Balthild's son, Clothar III appeared alone; the mother had gone. By then both Chrodbert and his successor as bishop of Paris, one Sigobrand, were dead. Sigobrand's successor was Importunus. The *Vita Balthildis* tells us that the occasion of the queen's downfall was the murder of bishop Sigobrand. The latter can only have been in post for a very short time before he was killed, apparently on account of his *superbia*. Fearing Balthild's revenge, the court ousted her and confined her to Chelles. All this has to have happened between September 664 and August 665. We do not know when in 664 the Synod of Whitby took place, although in Bede's narrative sequence it comes before the solar eclipse of 1 May 664 (HE, III, 27). We cannot say when Agilbert got back to Francia, nor when Wilfrid arrived there, but we can infer that both of them were in the thick of things. That this was indeed in the year 664 is confirmed by Stephen himself when he says that when Wilfrid died (709/10) he had been a bishop for 46 years (VW 65). Either just before, or maybe just after, or, even, during the Sigobrand affair, the convocation of twelve Frankish bishops must have been, to say the least, a politically charged moment. And even if Wilfrid was consecrated before Balthild's demise, he certainly lived through the events of her downfall, for he remained in Francia until 666. Agilbert went on to become a fixture in the new regime. Re-reading the *Vita Wilfridi* in the light of these observations, one perhaps better understands the emphasis on Balthild's villainy in the Lyons episode, if that is, we are right in thinking that Agilbert had been her opponent. By the same token, we must ask whether in reality Wilfrid was more likely to have been influenced by his stay in Lyons than by the events in Francia in 664/5. The episode also reminds us of the selective nature of Stephen's account. Lyons figures prominently because, as Trent Foley explains, it provided the arena in which the various paradigms of the saintly bishop could be set out. Wilfrid's stay in Francia 664–6, apparently, was not memorable in these terms, though because of Stephen's silence, we can never know what Wilfrid did do after consecration at Compiègne and before arriving in Sussex. Importunus, bishop of Paris at this time, cuts a very different figure to that of Aunemund. We have a scurrilous correspondence between Importunus and a Frodebert or Chrodobert of Tours which shows the bishop to have been highly educated and the master of exquisite literary genres of insult and innuendo (Shanzer 2010). This is a type of Merovingian bishop rarely mentioned and never considered as a figure who might have influenced Wilfrid. Finally, if we accept Stephen's word that Wilfrid's consecration as bishop was a splendid occasion and one of great honour, we should ask what might have been given in return by the English, for we must remember that we are dealing with societies bound by strong principles of reciprocity. One suspects, however, either that Wilfrid did not reciprocate satisfactorily, or that he changed sides, for when he came back to Francia thirteen years later, the Neustrian elite were out for his blood.

We might guess that Wilfrid was involved in Frankish politics in the years 664–6, but in relation to his second journey to Rome in 678–680 we can be more certain that he was. This sequence, chapters 25–33 in the *Vita Wilfridi*, begins with the story of Winfrith of Lichfield's ill-fated journey to Quentovic where, mistaken for Wilfrid, he was beaten up by agents of King Theuderic and the *impius dux* Ebroin who had been bribed by Wilfrid's enemies. Wilfrid meanwhile sailed to Frisia, a pagan land, where he converted many thousands of people and all but a few of the leaders. For Wilfrid's missionary work in Frisia there is no corroboration, but it could be that it was because of this first contact, that Willibrord, a missionary monk from Wilfrid's foundation of Ripon, later made Frisia his destination.

Stephen tells us that Ebroin offered a barrel full of gold to the Frisian king to get him to deliver up Wilfrid, dead or alive. The king, Aldgisl, (otherwise unknown) though a pagan, shows his moral superiority to Ebroin by reading out the letter in which the bribe was offered, tearing it up and burning it, then making a speech in which he condemned Ebroin for blasphemy. Ebroin makes a final appearance in the narrative at the end of the sequence where Wilfrid is threatened with being arrested and sent to 'Ebroin's judgement'. Ebroin was Erchinoald's successor as 'mayor of the palace' in Neustria-Burgundy. Much vilified in later tradition, he ruled from 658–672 and from 675–680. Stephen's account is traditionally used to demonstrate that he was still alive into 680, at which point he was assassinated (Poole 1934, 61). We can track the vilification of the Ebroin figure through one particular hagiographical work, the *Passio Leudegarii* (Fouracre and Gerberding 1996, 215–53) which was composed in the early 690s, for Ebroin was the opponent of the hero of this text. Did Stephen, or Wilfrid, know of it? Again, as in the case of the *Vita Columbani*, we cannot pin Stephen down to any demonstrable borrowing. Bede, in his one reference to Ebroin, that it is in the story of Theodore's journey to England in 668, refers to the mayor in neutral terms, which suggests that he was unaware of the views put forward in the *Passio Leudegarii* (HE IV, 1). From this we might infer that in English church circles little attention was paid to what we might term Frankish internal affairs, by which I mean Francia outside the missionary context. If so, this casts further light on the uniqueness of Wilfrid as one who *was* in touch with events there.

After leaving Frisia, Wilfrid moved south into the Frankish kingdom of Austrasia. There he met with its king, Dagobert, whom we know as Dagobert II. He welcomed Wilfrid warmly because Wilfrid had helped him regain the throne of Austrasia. As a youth he had been exiled to Ireland. Much later his friends, hearing he was alive, asked Wilfrid to find him and get him back to Francia. This Wilfrid did, in style fit for a king. Dagobert now offered Wilfrid the bishopric of Strasbourg, and when the offer was refused, gave him 'his' bishop Deodatus as guide to Rome. Wilfrid then proceeded to 'Campania', by which presumably Lombardy was meant, for there he was welcomed by King Perctarit, who told him that he had been bribed to prevent Wilfrid reaching Rome, but he refused because of his own experiences, which were rather similar to those Wilfrid had just had in Frisia. As a youth Pectarit had been an exile amongst the Huns. The king of the Huns had been offered a barrel full of gold to hand him over to be slain, but refused because he feared his gods would harm him as he had sworn to protect the exile. If a pagan could be so noble, as a Christian ruler Perctarit could not even begin to countenance betraying Wilfrid. The barrels full of gold doublet make, in fact, the same point about the ability of some pagan rulers to act honourably, and the contrasting wickedness of some, but not all, Christian rulers. The stories thus point up the wickedness of Ebroin, and arguably this prepares the audience to think the worst of Wilfrid's Nothumbrian persecutor, King Ecgfrith.

After a lengthy stay in Rome, in 680 Wilfrid returned, laden with relics. Upon reaching Francia he found that Dagobert had recently been assassinated, for he had been an oppressive king, spurning the advice of elders, wasting the cities, imposing humiliating tributes on the people and showing contempt for the church. Thus even the bishops condoned his murder. One of them, at the head of a huge army, blamed Wilfrid for sending them this awful ruler, and threatened him, as we have seen, with the judgement of Ebroin. His answer, that in sending Dagobert to Francia he had only been doing his duty as a man of faith and honour, shamed his accuser who promptly asked for forgiveness. To historians of Merovingian Francia these passages are crucial, for they provide two missing pieces of a jigsaw otherwise impossible to make sense of. This we can easily demonstrate, and I shall do so, albeit as briefly as possible as this discussion is recently in print (Fouracre, 2008), but such a demonstration is necessary in order to evaluate the story.

According to the Frankish chronicle, the *Liber Historiae Francorum*, which was completed by the year 727 (Gerberding 1987; Fouracre and Gerberding 1996, 79–96), after the death of King Sigibert III of Austrasia in, probably, 656, the mayor of the palace Grimoald took the dead king's young son Dagobert, had him tonsured and then conducted to Ireland. We can work out that he then placed his own son on the throne, but, the *Liber Historiae* tells us, Grimoald was put to death for acting against his rightful lord (Gerberding 1987). Incidentally, one of the accusations Importunus made against Frodebert was that the latter had had sex with Grimoald's widow (Shanzer 2010, 379). After Grimoald's demise, Balthild's son Childeric was made king in Austrasia. The source says no more about this Dagobert who had gone into exile in Ireland. Now, Dagobert is a relatively common Merovingian name: counting Wilfrid's Dagobert there were at least four of them, and one of them died violently, for there was a cult of a Dagobert king and martyr. The *Life* eventually generated by this cult clearly had no idea who the subject of the royal cult had actually been. Only two other texts mention any ruler who could conceivably have been a king Dagobert ruling in Austrasia at the time of Wilfrid's visit, and these references can scarcely be decoded without the prior knowledge that there was such a king. Thus, since the *Vita Wilfridi* was not known on the Continent before the mid seventeenth century, the Dagobert who had been exiled to Ireland was effectively forgotten, and confusion remained about which Dagobert was which. Bede, who was the source for Continental knowledge of Wilfrid up to this point, had omitted the Frankish episodes in his account of Wilfrid's second journey to Rome, so he was no help. Then in 1655 the Bollandist scholar Godfrey Henschen published a work which attempted to sort out the various Dagoberts, and his breakthrough was that he had read William of Malmesbury's *Gesta Pontificum Anglorum* which drew on Stephen's *Life* and revealed that Wilfrid had encountered Dagobert on his way to Rome (Preest 2002, 148), so it was now clear that Dagobert had returned from Ireland to become king of Austrasia. But William had left out the second part of the story, that is, of Dagobert's murder, which left Henschen speculating about what then happened to Dagobert, and Henschen was still unable positively to identify the king of the martyr cult. Finally, the Maurist Jean Mabillon was made aware of Thomas Gale's work on the *Vita Wilfridi* and published a full edition of the text in 1677 (Mabillon, 1677). Now the whole story of Dagobert's exile, return, murder and construction as martyr made sense. Wilhelm Levison in his 1913 edition gave the *Vita Wilfridi* the solemn approval of the *MGH* as 'reliable' and it has been used ever since as crucial to an understanding of events in Francia in the 670s. We cannot make sense of whatever other information we do have without it, and the engagement with the text in two stages, first through William of Malmesbury's truncated story and then through Stephen's original version is surely one of the best examples one could ever find of how the historical kaleidoscope changes as new information is revealed.

That independent but fragmented information makes sense once the *Vita Wilfridi* narrative of Dagobert's exile, return and murder are in place is a good indicator of that narrative's historical plausibility. Continental historians, however, have been much more interested in Dagobert than in Wilfrid. Rarely asked is whether it is plausible that Wilfrid would have been asked to find and return Dagobert. Well, yes, if we remember that he had been in the thick of Frankish politics a decade earlier at the time of his consecration as bishop, and recall his contacts with Agilbert who was now a magnate in Francia. Agilbert, remember, had also spent time in Ireland and presumably had contacts there, so that he could have been the source of information about Dagobert. It seems anyway likely that Wilfrid would have known about the exile even before he met Agilbert. He was, after all, in Lyons and hobnobbing with the powerful Aunemund when it took place. If Wilfrid *had* been asked to find and return Dagobert, this is further indication that he was well known to the Frankish elite and regarded as an important figure in England. This, in turn, makes it seem more believable that the mayor Ebroin might have been keen to get hold of him. Indeed, Dagobert II's reappearance as king created severe problems for Ebroin. By helping the Autrasians acquire a king of their own, Wilfrid, who had previously been close to the Neustrian elite, had apparently changed sides in Frankish politics. In short, Wilfrid's role in the return is not implausible. One element of the story can be checked more firmly and this is the provision of a bishop Deodatus as guide to Wilfrid. A Deodatus, bishop of Toul appears in the Roman council of 680, named next to Wilfrid. Later tradition had Deodatus as onetime bishop of Nevers, but latterly a holy man in Alsace, from where, Stephen tells us, he was sent off with Wilfrid. That same later tradition has him dying in 679 a date which would make sense if he left Francia with Wilfrid and never came back (Paperbroch 1701, 873). Finally, it is interesting to note that a version of King Perctarit's story about his own exile can be found in Paul the Deacon's *Historia Langobardorum* (Waitz 1878, 180–1). In this late eighth-century work, Pectarit was said to have been a refugee with the Avars (ie. Huns). Perctarit's enemy King Grimoald threated the Khan of the Avars with war if he continued to harbour him. Perctarit was then in effect asked to leave. It seems most likely that Paul the Deacon got this story, as with his other anecdotes about Lombard kings, from local tradition, and that Stephen too had it, presumably via Wilfrid, from a Lombard source. It is thus plausible that Wilfrid did hear a version of the story from Perctarit himself. If we consider too that Wilfrid's name, like that of Deodatus, appears in the record of the Roman council, then taking on board the evidence that Dagobert did return and was murdered, plus the part corroboration of Pectarit's story, we can state that what Stephen says about Wilfrid's second journey to Rome has more support than any of his other Continental forays.

His third journey to Rome from 703–5 (VW 50–56) was much less eventful. The only reference to Francia is to Wilfrid's illness at Meaux. Acca, friend of Bede, bishop of Hexham and one time companion of Wilfrid, and one of the two people to whom Stephen dedicated the *Life* (it being written at his request), was said by Bede to have spoken of how in 703 he and Wilfrid stayed with Willibrord on their way to Rome. This need not have been in Frisia itself, for it could have been in the monastery of Echternach, Willibrord's base, but they apparently heard Willibrord's tales of his preaching in Frisia. It is baffling that this episode is not in Stephen's *Life*. It may be of some significance here that Wilfrid does not appear in Willibrord's *Calendar*, a contemporary document which honours the great and the good of the religious world of Willibrord's time (Wilson 1918). The omission of Wilfrid is all the more surprising given that he had been Willibrord's abbot at Ripon. Had Wilfrid fallen out with Willibrord, as he had done fifty years earlier with Benedict Biscop? The narrative structure of the text may in part explain the near silence about the course of this last journey, for the main thrust of the story is the exhaustive examination and vindication of Wilfrid's case in Rome, and the four extra years of life given to him to fulfil his religious duties. It may also be the case that Francia was a rather quieter place in 703 than it had been at the time of the three previous visits. It was unified and for the time being there was no political in-fighting. Wilfrid had been around so long, for fifty years in fact, that all the people we can associate him with on the earlier visits were dead. Over that period, he had spent at least ten years on the Continent.

We began by asking whether Stephen's account of his time there can be seen to have historical plausibility, and if so, how we might assess the Continental episodes in historical terms. It is the Lyons episode which seems to have been the one most obviously shaped around the *Vita*'s purpose in constructing the religious persona of the saint. But despite obvious infelicities of detail, Stephen's account of the power and fall of the bishop of Lyons is roughly compatible with what we know from the *Acta Aunemundi*. This is not quite the same as saying that it was his experience there that shaped Wilfrid's understanding of what a bishop should be like. One must ask whether his relationship with Agilbert and his sojourn in Francia during the turbulent times of Balthild's downfall might have been at least as formative, not to mention the influence of Importunus and a host of others. Agilbert is a particularly important figure, hitherto somewhat underplayed in Wilfridian scholarship by comparison with Dalfinus/Aunemund. In the *Vita* his unimpeachably orthodox credentials help to guarantee that Wilfrid was perfectly consecrated as an orthodox bishop. But Bede's rather fuller picture of Agilbert's career, the circumstantial evidence of Anglo-Frankish contacts, including the admittedly hazardous evidence of personal names, and what we know of Frankish history in the 660s all point to a plausible historical context in which Wilfrid could have been known to the Neustro-Burgundian elite and to have been regarded as a figure of some importance on the Continent. His role in the return of Dagobert II about a decade after his consecration lends strong supports to this notion. This in turn suggests that he was indeed a churchman of princely stature, and, if he really was able to fit Dagobert II out as a king, one of immense wealth. One can perhaps now see why the Lyons episode is so prominent so early in the *Life*, that is, to establish Wilfrid's saintly credentials as early as possible in the light of what was to follow. Although Stephen did not visibly borrow from Continental sources, he shares with Merovingian authors the difficult task of presenting the worldly and the powerful as saintly and selfless, and this too to an audience likely to have had a direct knowledge of controversial subject matter. In this respect the *Vita Wilfridi* arguably has more in common with Continental works of the same vintage than it does with any other English text. To see this, just compare the use of the term *invidia* across the set (VW 14, 24, 45). Envy was the catalyst for opposition to Wilfrid just as it was in Francia for bishops like Leudegar, Praejectus and Aunemund (Fouracre 1990). But although we can argue that Wilfrid was of a stature to cut an important figure on the Continent, we cannot claim that he left any impression there, in contrast, say, to Columbanus, Fursey, Willibrord, Boniface or Alcuin. The reason is simple: the *Vita Wilfridi* was unknown on the Continent before the time of Mabillon. The fact that once it was recovered it was found to be an important source for Frankish history is perhaps the strongest argument that we should, after all, and with all due caution, take Stephen at his word.

15: *The Continental Journeys of Wilfrid and Biscop*

I. N. WOOD

Wilfrid's continental connections have often been examined: so too, have Benedict Biscop's six visits to Rome (Wormald 1976; Fletcher 1981). Curiously, however, I know of no combined examination of the voyages of the two travellers. Yet there is much overlap: the two set out together on one occasion, and on another they found themselves in Rome at the same time, though this last coincidence has scarcely attracted attention. In combining the evidence for the two great Northumbrians I hope to show that there is a little more to say about Wilfrid's continental journeys than would result from a simple return to the well-known cruces of his career.

Our story begins with the voyage undertaken by both protagonists. In the mid 650s, traditionally in *c*.654, the young aristocrat Wilfrid decided that he wanted to visit the holy places in Rome (VW 2–6). He was, at the time, associated with the household of the Northumbrian queen, Eanflæd, who agreed to support his plans, and sent him to her kinsman, king Eorconberht of Kent, to wait until there was a chance of joining a larger party to make the journey. It may be significant that Eorconberht's mother was Frankish, which would no doubt have meant that his contacts with the Merovingian court were strong (Wood 2011, 459). In Kent Wilfrid teamed up with Benedict Biscop. One wonders why the two did not set out from Northumbria together: was the queen employing Wilfrid on some special errand that required that he contact Eorconberht alone? In the event, the two Northumbrians travelled together as far as the city of Lyons, where they split up. Stephen remarks that they did so just as Paul split with Barnabas over John Mark, which is presumably intended both to imply that Wilfrid was superior to Biscop as Paul was to Barnabas, and also to give some indication of the cause of their disagreement, which would appear to involve a third party, though that remains opaque. Biscop travelled on to Rome without his companion.

Wilfrid, meanwhile, had attracted the attention of the bishop of Lyons, whom Stephen calls Dalfinus. The bishop, says the hagiographer, proposed to adopt the young Northumbrian, offered him his niece for his wife, and promised to put him in charge of a substantial part of Francia – a set of proposals that strain credulity (VW 4). Wilfrid insisted on continuing his journey to Rome – and thus convinced Dalfinus that he was 'a true servant of God'. On his return he stopped at Lyons once again. There, Stephen says, Dalfinus welcomed him as his son and tonsured him (VW 6). Wilfrid stayed on in Lyons for a few years, until, the hagiographer claims, Dalfinus was suddenly martyred on the instigation of the Frankish queen.

It is unfortunate that the surviving evidence for the history of the Rhône valley in the mid seventh century is poor, perhaps as a result of destruction during the wars of the early eighth century – as claimed by Ado of Vienne (Wood 1981, 19). It is a region through which Wilfrid and Biscop passed on a number of occasions, for both of them it was clearly important, indeed it was surely central to their experience of continental Christianity and culture (Foley 1992, 84–6, 100–4, 122), but we lack the detail to trace exactly what they derived from their sojourns in the middle Rhône valley. What little remains in terms of manuscript evidence, and of later historical and hagiographical work, suggests that Lyons was a lively centre, politically, culturally, and ecclesiastically (McKitterick 1981, 177–84) – perhaps still boasting expertise in law, and especially canon law, for the oldest systematic collection of canons known from Francia was apparently made there in the early seventh century (Mordek 1975), a point perhaps of some importance in Wilfrid's intellectual formation. And the Anglo-Saxon would surely have learnt something of the bishop of Lyons' attitude to canon law, for at almost exactly this moment, in 654, Aunemund was among the signatories of Clovis II's confirmation of Landeric of Paris' privilege for St Denis (Kölzer 2001, 216–20: Rosenwein 1999, 75–7).

The story of Wilfrid's relations with Dalfinus as told by Stephen is partly symbolic: the young saint is tempted by, but overcomes the blandishments of the secular world. And there are plenty of elements in it that will not stand historical scrutiny (Nelson 1978, 65–7: Fouracre and Gerberding 1996, 172–6): the bishop of Lyons at this time was called Aunemundus, not Dalfinus – which is what his brother is called in the rather later martyr acts (see Fouracre above). In the earlier of the two manuscripts of the Life of Wilfrid, the queen supposedly responsible for Dalfinus' martyrdom is named as Brunhild, who was long dead, but who had been involved in the harassment of Desiderius of Vienne. Chronologically the queen in question must have been Balthild – a woman apparently of Anglo-Saxon origin. While culted as a saint, she was certainly forceful enough to have ordered the execution of an opponent, though the Frankish sources do not associate her with the death of Aunemundus, which must lessen the likelihood that she was the instigator (Fouracre and Gerberding 1996, 183, n. 54). Nor will the traditional chronology for these events stand. It is usually claimed that Wilfrid returned to England following the bishop's death in c.658, but Aunemundus was still alive to sign a charter in 660 (Fouracre and Gerberding 1996, 166). Not that this rules out Wilfrid's presence at his death, since we have no certain date for his return to England.

Having left Francia Wilfrid seems to have made his way to Wessex (VW 7).

The king, Coenwalh, is a difficult figure to assess: he had come to the throne as a pagan, but had subsequently converted and appointed Agilbert as his bishop, although he would subsequently throw him out. He later sought to reinstate him, but in the end had to settle for installing Agilbert's nephew, Leuthere, in his place (HE III, 7). Although Agilbert was a Frank, he had been living in Ireland before he arrived in Wessex. Leuthere, however, came directly from Francia. The relations between Wessex and Francia were obviously important, perhaps almost as important as those between Francia and Kent, for Hamwic must have been one of the ports with strong connections to Quentovic – hence Wilfrid and later Biscop headed to the court of the West Saxon king on arriving in England. Despite his unpredictability, Coenwalh's dealings with Wilfrid appear to have been cordial, and he recommended the young cleric to the attention of the Northumbrian prince Alhfrith (who Wilfrid must already have known from his early days at the Northumbrian court). Shortly after his return to Northumbria Alhfrith transferred to Wilfrid the monastery of Ripon, which he had previously given to the pro-Irish Eata. The transfer of Ripon to Wilfrid would seem to have taken place in 660 or shortly thereafter (VW 8).

At this point Agilbert turned up in Northumbria and ordained Wilfrid (VW 9). One enters the land of guesswork when trying to reconstruct Agilbert's movements. It is usually thought that he had already been exiled from Wessex by the time he turned up in Northumbria, for that is the implication of the order of events as they appear in Bede, who has already told us that Agilbert left Dorchester for the continent, and became bishop of Paris (HE III, 7, see also III, 28). But in French scholarship (Maillé 1971, 74) it is assumed that it was as bishop of Wessex that he turned up at Whitby, and this does not actually contradict what Bede says (HE III, 25). Although the account of Whitby comes after Bede's reference to Agilbert leaving his see, there is nothing to suggest that the points are in chronological order. If Agilbert did indeed attend Whitby as bishop of Wessex, one would have to consider whether he did so with Coenwalh's approval – not impossible, given the king's links with Alhfrith – or whether this involvement in another kingdom was one of the factors that made him suspect to his king. What is clear is that Agilbert was influential in the run-up to the council, but at that point he let Wilfrid take over as spokesman for the Roman party (VW 10). Whitby would lead to the resignation of Colmán as bishop of Northumbria and the appointment of Wilfrid in his place, at which point the latter decided to head to Francia for consecration on the grounds that not enough canonically appointed bishops could be found to carry out the rite in England (VW 11).

Stephen's description of the consecration ceremony in Compiègne, involving twelve bishops and a golden throne, looks like the stuff of legend. More important is his naming of Agilbert as one of the twelve bishops involved in the ceremony. If he did indeed participate as bishop, it must have been as bishop of Wessex – perhaps another reason for Coenwalh to be aggrieved – for he is not attested as bishop of Paris before 668, and cannot have been appointed before 667 (Lapidge 1999, 21). The neatest reading is certainly to see Agilbert as attending Whitby as bishop of the West Saxons, then accompanying Wilfrid to Francia for consecration, before returning to Wessex and falling foul of Coenwalh: there is nothing in Bede's narrative to contradict this – and in some ways this reading makes Agilbert look more like Wilfrid, a bishop who defied political boundaries and aggravated rulers in so doing.

But if we cannot see Agilbert as bishop of Paris at this point, we can look to his connections with monasticism in the Île-de-France, most notably with Jouarre, in the foundation of which his family was deeply involved: indeed his sister was the first abbess of the house (Maillé 1971, 74–8). Closely associated with Jouarre was Faremoutiers (Prinz 1965, 174–5): both of them were major centres of Columbanian monasticism, which may well have influenced Wilfrid (Wood 1990; 1995). At the end of his life he would visit Meaux (VW 56), the diocese in which Faremoutiers and Jouarre, and indeed the nunnery of Chelles and the male house of Rebais, are to be found. Faremoutiers was also among the houses, alongside Chelles and Les Andelys, that Bede singled out as being nunneries to which a number of Anglo-Saxon princesses went in the mid seventh century (HE III, 8), while Bertila, the first abbess of Chelles, was remembered in her later *vita* for the books she sent to England (Sims-Williams 1990, 110–11). The English connections of these houses must have involved rather more than is stated in Bede's comment, not least because Balthild, the supposed persecutor of Dalfinus/Aunemundus, and foundress of Chelles, would appear to have been Anglo-Saxon. Alongside religious interchange we should probably assume political interest (Wood 2011).

Wilfrid spent an inordinate amount of time in Francia at this point: intriguingly two major political events occurred while he was out of England. The first was the fall of queen Balthild, who was forced into monastic retirement at her foundation of Chelles in 665/6 (Nelson 1978, 70–1). Balthild had not only founded the nunnery, but was also responsible for the transfer of Bertila, from Jouarre (Prinz 1965, 174–5). How Agilbert reacted to Balthild's fall is thus an open question: the bishops of the Île-de-France with whom he was apparently associated seem to have supported what has been called her monastic policy, but that, of course, does not mean that they did not tire of her as a ruler. And Agilbert himself must have been appointed to the bishopric of Paris by the man who emerged as the dominant figure of the kingdom in her place, Ebroin.

Perhaps more significant in explaining Wilfrid's delay is what happened in Northumbria, where his patron, Alhfrith, rebelled unsuccessfully against his father. We know nothing of the rebellion, except its occurrence (HE III, 14), but the prince vanishes from the scene at about this point. This may well have made matters awkward for Wilfrid: as Alhfrith's protégé he would scarcely have been welcomed by Oswiu, who, quite apart from intruding Chad into the Northumbrian diocese (HE III, 28), was also pursuing a very forceful monastic policy at precisely this time (Wood 2008). It is likely, then, that it was Alhfrith's fall that led Wilfrid to stay on in Francia and to the intrusion of Chad into the Northumbrian see.

Before Wilfrid returned to his diocese, which he did only after spending some time in Sussex and Mercia (VW 13–14), another crucial event in the relations between Northumbria and the continent had occurred: the arrival in Canterbury of archbishop Theodore, accompanied by Biscop (HE IV, 1: HA 3–4), who had left Wilfrid way back in c.654. Having continued on to Rome Biscop had returned to Northumbria before Wilfrid, but soon decided to revisit the City of the Apostles (HA 2) together with Alhfrith, the prince who would give Wilfrid Ripon, and would later rebel against his father, Oswiu. In the late 650s or early 660s, then, Biscop was associated with the political group that supported Wilfrid – despite their disagreement at Lyons. Alhfrith, however, was prevented from making the journey by his father, so once again Biscop set out alone. Having reached Rome a second time, Biscop headed back north, only to turn aside to the island monastery of Lérins, where c.665 he became a monk (HA 2): one might ask whether this decision not to travel on to England, like Wilfrid's delaying in Francia, has anything to do with Alhfrith's rebellion, for Biscop too was associated with the prince.

A visit to Lérins at this juncture might have seemed particularly interesting, for the new abbot, Aigulf, who was attempting to reinvigorate the community, had recently been involved in the theft of the relics of Benedict from Monte Cassino (Mews 2011, 131–2). Biscop's stay in Lérins, however, is as problematic as any of the evidence relating to Wilfrid, because the monastery was currently in the midst of a crisis, which would culminate with the murder of Aigulf, at the hands of his recalcitrant monks. Unfortunately we cannot be sure of the chronology, but it may be that it was this murder that prompted Biscop to undertake another journey to Rome in c.665-7 (HA 3; Plummer 1896, vol. 2, 357; Wood 1981, 19; Fletcher 1981, 5). There would then be a nice contrast between Stephen's emphasis of the martyrdom of Dalfinus, and Bede's silence over that of Aigulf. At all costs Biscop was in Rome when Wighard, archbishop-elect of Canterbury arrived to collect his pallium in c.667 (HA 3). However, the latter promptly died of plague, and in 668 Theodore was sent in his place, with Hadrian to advise and with Biscop as guide, much to his disappointment because he had intended to live out his life in Rome.

The journey of Theodore, Hadrian and Biscop sheds further light on connections between Rome, Francia and England (HE IV, 1). The party travelled to Arles, where they had to stay with archbishop John, until given leave to proceed by the mayor of the palace, Ebroin – Bede's account of all this provides us with some of our clearest evidence for governmental control of foreigners travelling in Francia: it reveals an extremely tightly monitored society. Having received permission to continue, Hadrian visited Emmo of Sens, another supporter of monastic reform (Prinz 1965, 162), and Faro of Meaux, a relative of Agilbert (Le Jan 1995, 390–1) and bishop of the diocese in which Jouarre was to be found. This was a world with which Wilfrid had become acquainted at the time of his consecration at Compiègne.

Ecgberht of Kent, hearing that Theodore was on his way north, sent his reeve Rædfrith to make arrangements with Ebroin, for the archbishop's journey via Quentovic. Hadrian, however, was prevented from accompanying him, according to Bede because the Frankish mayor suspected that he was involved in some mission from the emperor to the English (HE IV, 1). One should remember that at precisely this time the Byzantine emperor Constans II was active in southern Italy: he was even suspected of wishing to transfer his capital to Syracuse (Waitz 1878, 186–7). One should also remember that Hadrian came from Naples. Ebroin's suspicions may not have been ridiculous: Hadrian was perhaps held until after news of the murder of Constans in September 668 reached Francia.

Biscop, having accompanied Theodore to Canterbury, took charge of the monastery of SS Peter and Paul for two years. However, at the end of that time, in around 670, he decided to go back to Rome (for a fourth visit), leaving Hadrian as abbot. During his journey to Rome Biscop acquired various objects, above all books, both as gifts and purchases: on his way south he left them with friends in Vienne, collecting them on his return (HA 4). This is the first time we hear of Biscop's acquisitions: on subsequent journeys he would acquire books, paintings, liturgical objects and precious cloth (HA 5–6, 9). Who his friends in Vienne were – and why Bede, who is generally sparing of detail, mentions them – is something of a mystery: we should perhaps assume that Biscop built up a nexus of contacts in the region, much as Wilfrid seems to have done in the Île-de-France. Unfortunately we know as little of Vienne as we know of Lyons in the mid seventh century, though a post-Carolingian text, the *Vita Clari*, reveals it to have been a thriving monastic centre, with, if the figures are correct, 1,525 monks and nuns – and so specific are the numbers given for each monastic house that one needs to think carefully before rejecting the evidence: were they derived from some official register (Wood 1981, 9–10)? From an earlier generation we have evidence of bishop Desiderius, who fell foul not only of Brunhild, but also of Gregory the Great (Norberg 1982, vol. 2, 922), who forbad him from teaching grammar, because it relied on pagan classics. Although Desiderius was long dead by the time that Biscop arrived in Vienne, one might wonder whether his enthusiasm for learning had been passed on to later generations.

Biscop returned to England before the end of 671, and went directly to Wessex, where Coenwalh was still king – thus doing much as Wilfrid had done a decade earlier: again we see the importance of Wessex as a point of entry into England for people travelling from Quentovic (HA 4). But since Coenwalh died soon after, Biscop moved on to Northumbria, where he received from king Ecgfrith land for the foundation of Wearmouth in c.674. When he came to erect a stone building on the site, Biscop turned back to Francia, according to the anonymous author of the *Life of Ceolfrith* to an otherwise unknown abbot Torthelm (who has a suspiciously Anglo-Saxon name: VC 7) – Patrick Wormald was inclined to look to the region around Paris, that is to the circle of Agilbert, to find Torthelm (Wormald 1976, 149) – and given the presence of other Anglo-Saxons in the region this certainly looks a sensible place to start – but he might, of course, have been one of Biscop's friends in Vienne (HA 5; VC 7).

Meanwhile, in England, relations between Theodore and Wilfrid turned sour. Theodore had initially supported Wilfrid's restitution to the see of York (VW 15). Within ten years, however, he had turned against him. Stephen presents this as resulting from the bishop's conflict with queen Iurminburh and her husband Ecgfrith: the two then supposedly bribed the archbishop to act against Wilfrid and to divide his diocese, intruding three bishops from elsewhere into the new sees (VW 24). In fact, Theodore's attempts to reform the English Church were almost bound to cause problems. As a result Wilfrid appealed to Rome.

His opponents attempted to prevent him from reaching the Holy See. Assuming that he would take the normal route via Quentovic and through the Neustrian heartlands of the Frankish kingdom, they asked Ebroin and Theuderic III to arrest him – this would not have been difficult, given Frankish control of foreign travellers, and indeed they did arrest bishop Winfrith of Lichfield by mistake. As it happened Wilfrid had taken a different route, via Frisia, where, according to Stephen (VW 26–7), he was well received by the local ruler, Aldgisl, who refused to betray him: this is the first of three stories about loyalty, which were surely intended to highlight the villainy of Ebroin, and indeed of Wilfrid's Northumbrian persecutors, and which must therefore be seen as having undergone a process of deliberate interpretation on Stephen's part, at the very least.

Moving south from Frisia Wilfrid found support at the court of the Austrasian king Dagobert II (VW 28), who not only welcomed the saint but even offered him the diocese of Strasbourg. This brings us to another problem in Merovingian history. Dagobert was the son of Sigibert III: on his father's death in the mid 650s he had been sent into exile in obscure circumstances, which involved the intrusion of a king known to modern historians as Childebert the

Adopted. Fortunately this part of the story need not concern us here. The young Dagobert was taken into exile in Ireland, apparently to the monastery of Slane (Picard 1991, 43–4). In the crisis that enveloped Francia in the mid 670s, however, a faction in the eastern part of the kingdom decided to invite him back to Francia and to install him as king of Austrasia. According to Stephen, Dagobert's friends had turned to Wilfrid (*c.*675/6) to expedite his return from Ireland (Picard 1991, 48–50). While the story in Stephen has a clear moral, in that Dagobert repays a debt, and in so doing emerges as a far nobler character than Ebroin, the later denouement does not cast the king in such a good light: on his return from Rome, Wilfrid discovered that Dagobert had been murdered because of his tyrannous rule (VW 33).

Jean-Michel Picard has played down Wilfrid's possible role in the return of Dagobert, pointing rather to the Irish monk Ultán as providing a likely connection between the king's Frankish supporters and his place of exile (Picard 1991), though it is unclear that Ultán was still alive at this point. If we wish to identify a possible chain of communication between Wilfrid and the Irish house where Dagobert was in exile, we might rather look to the family of Ceolfrith, abbot of Jarrow. Ceolfrith's monastic career had begun when he entered the community at Gilling, where his brother Cynefrith, was abbot (VC 2-3). Cynefrith, however, decided to pursue the monastic life in Ireland: his position at Gilling was taken over by a relative, Tunbert, but subsequently the whole community, Tunbert and Ceolfrith included, moved to Wilfrid's new foundation of Ripon. After a brief spell at Icanho, Ceolfrith returned to Ripon, only to be transferred to Wearmouth, when Biscop appealed to Wilfrid for help in setting up his monastery. Ceolfrith soon found the monastic standards of Wearmouth rather below what he expected and went back to Ripon, only to be forced to return to Biscop's foundation. Despite what is sometimes said about conflict between Wearmouth-Jarrow and Wilfrid's foundations of Ripon and Hexham, it is clear that Wilfrid, Biscop and Ceolfrith saw no such conflict, at least before the late 670s. An additional connection between Wilfrid and Ireland, and perhaps a more important one in this context, is Agilbert, who had lived in Ireland before becoming bishop in Wessex (HE III, 7). Coming from the Frankish aristocracy, he could well have had an interest in the whereabouts of the deposed Merovingian.

Having left Dagobert, Wilfrid arrived at the kingdom of the Lombards. Here again Stephen presents us with a symbolic tale of loyalty (VW 28). Wilfrid was welcomed by Perctarit, who himself had been exiled when Grimoald usurped the throne in 662. The Lombard prince had fled to the Avar court, where his rival's agents tried in vain to bribe the king to kill him. There is certainly a historical core to this story, but in Paul the Deacon's version (Waitz 1878, 180–2) the denouement is rather different, though it raises a further element of contact between the Lombards and the Anglo-Saxons. According to Paul, who almost certainly did not know Stephen's Life of Wilfrid, when Grimoald's messengers reached the Avar court, the king, knowing he could not protect Perctarit, advised him to leave. The exile decided to risk going back to Italy, but soon found that it was too dangerous to stay there (Waitz 1878, 180–5). Instead, he ended up at the court of Dagobert (which one should admit is chronologically impossible), but still fearing that Grimoald was pursuing him, he decided to cross to England. Just after he had embarked, however, he learnt that Grimoald had died (671), and so he returned to Italy, where he was restored to the throne (Waitz 1878, 197–9.). How much of this story one should believe is an open question (and one might note the parallels between the story of Perctarit at the Avar court, and Bede's account of Edwin at Rædwald's (HE II, 12), which Paul did know), but there is clearly an interesting chain of connections involving Dagobert and Perctarit, of which Stephen was aware. Evidence for Perctarit's English contacts might be bolstered by the fact that his son Cunincpert supposedly married an Anglo-Saxon, Ermelinda (Waitz 1878, 200–1).

From Perctarit's court, Wilfrid moved on to Rome to lodge his appeal before pope Agatho, only to find that a monk called Coenwald had already presented Theodore's side of the case. Stephen (VW 29–32) deals at length with Wilfrid's petition. Although the Roman synod of 679 supported Wilfrid, it did not reverse Theodore's division of the northern see (Cubitt 1989, 18–24). In addition the bishops gathered in Rome instructed John the Archchanter to investigate the views of the English Church in advance of the Council of Constantinople – for Agatho was keen to ensure that he had the general support of the western episcopate in the looming conflict over Monothelitism. As a result the Anglo-Saxon bishops met at Hatfield in September of 679 (Cubitt 1995, 252–8). John travelled to England in the company of Benedict Biscop, who exploited his presence to introduce the proper performance of a Roman style of liturgy to Wearmouth, and from there to other houses (HE IV, 18, V, 24; HA 6; VC 9–10).

Biscop's presence raises an interesting question. What side, if any, did he take in Wilfrid's appeal to the Roman curia? Although the two had fallen out at Lyons, there is nothing to suggest that their disagreement was long-lasting. As we have seen, Biscop had turned to Wilfrid for monks when he founded Wearmouth and it was from Ripon that Ceolfrith joined him. But in the mid 670s both Wilfrid and Biscop were working in harmony with king Ecgfrith. In 679, however, Wilfrid was appealing against the king's rulings, while Biscop was very much the abbot of a royal monastery. Moreover, we are told by the anonymous author of the *Vita Ceolfridi* (VC 12) that when he appointed Eosterwine co-abbot of Wearmouth, Biscop did so because he was often called upon by the king for advice. Since he was in Rome at the time that Wilfrid made his appeal to Agatho, should we conclude that he was there in part on the king's business, in other words to oppose Wilfrid's appeal? Given the statement of the *Vita Ceolfridi*, which is actually a significant modification of Bede, who talks only of Biscop's regular journeying without making any comment on his role as counsellor (HA 7), we should certainly be looking to see where and when he might have been acting as a royal agent. In addition, Biscop had also been an adviser to Theodore: would he therefore side with the archbishop? What then of Ceolfrith, who was with Biscop in Rome at this juncture, and who, if anything, had shown a closer attachment to Wilfrid than he had to Biscop, and had indeed been ordained by him (VC 3)?

The latter must have set out on his fifth visit to Rome at some point in the second half of 678, since he and Ceolfrith only arrived after Agatho had been installed as pope (HA 6: Plummer 1896, vol. 2, 360). It is, therefore, possible that the two left Northumbria before Wilfrid's clash with the king. Even so, with the arrival of Coenwald in Rome they would have been placed in a quandary. To judge from the fact that they did not fall into disfavour with Ecgfrith on their return, it would seem unlikely that they supported Wilfrid openly. On the other hand they may well have deliberately abstained from committing themselves to either party. They were no doubt lucky that they were not official representatives at the synod, and indeed, not having Episcopal status they may well have had no place there at all. For Biscop simply to return to England in the company of John the Archchanter, and to persuade him to teach at Wearmouth, might have been a careful statement of agreement with the synodal decision.

Interestingly both Wilfrid and Biscop lobbied Agatho for papal privileges granting immunity from Episcopal intervention for their respective monasteries at approximately the same time, which suggests that each had an eye on what the other was doing. Since it is likely that the privileges that they obtained were ultimately modelled on that granted by pope Honorius to Bobbio, they may have seen its efficacy in the Columbanian houses of Francia: in particular they may well have been aware of the privilege for Rebais in the diocese of Meaux (Wormald 1976, 148–9). We have already seen that Wilfrid could have learnt in Lyons about Episcopal grants of immunity, such as that given to St Denis by Landeric. The grants obtained by Wilfrid and Biscop, however, would be received very differently back in England, for the immunity for Wearmouth was obtained with the licence, consent, desire and exhortation of the king, according to Bede (HA 6), whilst the documents that Wilfrid produced on his return were denounced as having been purchased (VW 34, 45, 47, 51). Bede's reference to Ecgfrith's support for Biscop implies that this had been given before Biscop set out for Rome, and we might even guess that this, rather than any attempt to sabotage Wilfrid's appeal, was the initial reason for the journey. Indeed, one might wonder whether Ecgfrith's support for a privilege for Wearmouth was actually a contributing factor to the conflict between Wilfrid and the king. It could be read as part of an attempt to limit the bishop's authority – for although scholars have noted that Frankish privileges of immunity should not be understood as an attempt to break Episcopal power (Rosenwein 1999, 75–96), that might not always have been the case: the privilege for Wearmouth would undoubtedly have limited Wilfrid's jurisdiction over the monastery. As for the privileges for Ripon and Hexham, the fact that Wilfrid requested them without having secured royal licence in advance would seem to suggest that he was copying Biscop; and the fact that Agatho granted them, might well reflect a desire to be seen to be even handed.

On his return Wilfrid was met with imprisonment, and subsequently exile, which took him south to Sussex and Wessex for a number of years (VW 41–2). He would only return to Northumbria after the death of Ecgfrith in 685, by which time he had already made his peace with Theodore. By the mid 680s, however, Biscop was in the middle of his sixth and last visit to Rome. This, in its own way raises as many problems as does the previous visit. Biscop, we are told by Bede, set out on his final journey to the Holy See shortly after the foundation of Jarrow (HA 9). Were Biscop to have been the founder of Jarrow, as claimed by Bede, this would seem to be rather odd timing: the evidence, however, suggests that Jarrow was king Ecgfrith's foundation, and that he drew manpower, and in particular the first abbot, Ceolfrith, from Wearmouth (Wood 2006, 68–72). This makes Biscop's journey to Rome rather more explicable, and it certainly helps explain the fact that he made no attempt to return to Northumbria in time for the dedication of the church at Jarrow, which took place in 685: he only returned after the death of Eosterwine and election of Sigfrith, in other words in 686 at the earliest. This final visit would seem to have been intended, at least in part, as another book- and icon-buying venture. The chronology does not suggest any ulterior motive, unless, perhaps, he was indicating disapproval of the foundation of Jarrow.

Biscop returned to Northumbria at approximately the same time as Wilfrid returned to favour following the death of Ecgfrith and the accession of Aldfrith. He was also reconciled to Theodore (VW 43–4). By the time that Aldfrith and Wilfrid fell out, in the early 690s, as they inevitably did, Biscop was dead. Once again it seems that the points of conflict related to Theodore's division of the diocese, and to the infringement of the privileges secured from Agatho for Ripon and Hexham (VW 45) – though, as we have seen, from the Northumbrian point of view these were problematic documents in a way that the privilege for Wearmouth was not. Having been condemned at Austerfield, Wilfrid set out on one last appeal to Rome: and just as had been the case in 679, a rival embassy was sent by the archbishop of Canterbury (VW 50). It was presumably on this journey south that Wilfrid visited Willibrord, who was then working as a missionary in Frisia (HE III, 13): he would thus seem to have taken the same route that he had followed at the time of the earlier appeal. Perhaps, once again, he felt that the more easterly route was the less dangerous. One other document might contain a faint echo of Wilfrid's journey. At some point before 713 the abbess of Whitby, Ælfflæd, wrote to Adula, her counterpart in the abbey of Pfalzel, recommending a nun who was on pilgrimage to Rome (Tangl 1916, 3–4). Since Ælfflæd was one of Wilfrid's chief supporters after his return in 706, and since Pfalzel, on the outskirts of Trier, would be a plausible stopping place on the easterly route to Rome, one wonders whether she was making use of contacts established by the bishop in the course of his journey. According to Stephen, Pope John, after very full consideration of the relevant claims and documents, came down firmly on Wilfrid's side (VW 51–4).

In the course of his journey home Wilfrid fell ill near the town of Meaux. The fact that he was returning through the centre of the Neustrian kingdom may indicate that he felt that the papal ruling had given him some security. Moreover, he had once had a number of allies in the region, for, as we have seen, the diocese of Meaux was the heartland of Agilbert's family. Above all it was where Faro had been bishop. His successor was Ebregisil, brother of Agilberta, second abbess of Jouarre, and perhaps the cousin of Theodechild, the first abbess, and of Agilbert (Maillé 1971, 81: Le Jan 1995, 390–1). Unfortunately we do not know whether Ebregisil was still alive in c.705, but given the importance of family in late Merovingian diocesan history, we might guess that Wilfrid could expect to find a relative of Agilbert in post.

Wilfrid returned to Northumbria, initially to a frosty welcome, though he soon came to some sort of accommodation with the powers that be, and became the guardian of the young King Osred (VW 59). This state of affairs lasted until his death in 710. The journeys of Biscop and Wilfrid shed little light on the realities of Merovingian politics, though they have pointed to recurrent questions of ecclesiastical jurisdiction. Above all they reveal men developing contacts and continuing to exploit them throughout their careers. It was a world of networks that functioned remarkably well despite the political crises – and it was these networks as much as political history that lay behind the development of the Northumbrian Church in the late seventh century.

16: *Wilfrid in Rome*

ÉAMONN Ó CARRAGÁIN AND ALAN THACKER

This paper could perhaps simply have been called 'Wilfrid and Rome'. The word 'Rome', however, has a wide and forbidding metaphorical baggage; that title might well include 'Wilfrid and the papacy', 'Wilfrid and the liturgy' and 'Wilfrid and orthodoxy'. Such matters are beyond the scope of a short paper, and we wish here to focus upon the physical facts of Wilfrid's three visits to Rome. These visits spanned half a century: the mid 650s, 679–680 and 703–4. We shall examine the changing physical topography of the city he encountered; the churches and holy places he probably visited (with the liturgies and cults which they fostered); and, as far as we can now know, the clerics he met, who introduced him to the city and its ecclesiastical and cultural life. We wish to emphasize Wilfrid's relation to the city as a physical and cultural entity. Other, wider, matters will emerge from discussion of Wilfrid's knowledge of, and attitudes to, the city itself.

Rome in the later seventh and very early eighth century was a very different place from the great city of perhaps a million inhabitants of its heyday. By then, after the disasters of the fifth and sixth centuries, it may have numbered no more than 60,000, spread through the vast spaces occupied by the imperial city (Durliat 1980, 117). The walls remained standing and the main thoroughfares were kept clear of debris. Although virtually unused, the great public monuments at the heart of Rome were probably still largely intact. A valuable source of building materials, of *spolia*, and used as such from the days of Constantine, they were the subject of decrees protecting them from private spoliation from at least the mid fifth century. Buildings such as the imperial palace on the Palatine, the Forum Romanum and some of the adjacent imperial fora had been as far as possible maintained, despite the city's vicissitudes in the fifth and sixth century. Officials such as the prefect of the city and the supervisor of the acqueducts survived at least until the late sixth century, and there was still a curator of the imperial palace in 686 (Durliat 1980, 124–8; Ward-Perkins 1986, 47–8; Augenti 1996).

By the seventh century, the *abitato* comprised quite a number of settlements scattered through and just outside the area enclosed by the Aurelian walls (Dey, 2011, 196–8). One important area lay by the Tiber, on either side of the bend in the river where it widens to accommodate the Isola Tiburina. To the south, across the river, lay Trastevere with its little group of early *tituli* (intramural churches with quasi-parochial functions). To the north lay an area stretching eastwards to the Theatre of Marcellus and thence to the Palatine. This included the port, fish market and trading zone, where the Greeks and other easterners established themselves, and where lay the *titulus* of Sant' Anastasia and three early *diaconiae* or welfare centres. There were, however, many other pockets of habitation. Some lay at the foot of the Caelian near the Porta Metronia and around the imperial fora; others were associated with the great papal complexes of the Lateran, in the far south-east by the walls, and of Santa Maria Maggiore on the Esquiline. Just outside the imperial walls, in the far west, lay the growing settlements associated with the apostolic basilicas, in the far west, St Peter's on the Vatican and, to the south on the Via Ostiense, St Paul's, both long linked to gates in the Aurelian wall by colonnaded *porticus* (Reekmans 1970, 206–8; Dey 2011, 222–3). All around the walled city were the *loca sancta* identified and increasingly systematised as places of pilgrimage since the time of Pope Damasus (366–84). Besides the various sanctified *cellae* within the catacombs themselves, there were a number of basilicas commemorating the more significant of Rome's martyrial cults. Of these the most notable were the great imperial funerary basilicas, in particular, Sant'Agnese in the north-east of the city on the Via Nomentana (*CBCR* I, 14–38), and San Lorenzo on the Verano, the latter like the apostolic basilicas also linked to the walls by a *porticus* (*CBCR* II, 1–144; Dey 2011, 222).

Since the end of the Gothic wars, the popes had invested above all in the restoration of the extramural *loca sancta* and, within the walls, in the adaptation of existing buildings to Christian uses or the creation of new (and generally relatively modest) structures to house the increasing number of new, imported, relic cults (Thacker 2007b). Already, in the later fifth century, Pope Simplicius (468–83) had constructed a great rotunda commemorating St Stephen on the Caelian, while on the Esquiline very near Santa Maria Maggiore, he had converted the opulent basilica built by the fourth-century consul Junius Bassus into the first church in Rome to be dedicated to Peter's brother and fellow apostle, St Andrew (*CBCR* I, 62–3; Huelsen 1927, 179–81; Lombardi 1996, 41). The basilica of San Pietro in Vincoli on the Oppidan emerged in the mid fifth century as an important secondary site of the Petrine cult, housing chains which were believed to have fettered the apostle in his imprisonment and which had perhaps been installed in Rome by the Empress Eudoxia, wife of Valentinian III (*CBCR* III, 178–231; Huelsen 1927, 418–19; Thacker 2007b, 48–9).

Around 500, when he was excluded by a rival from the Lateran, Pope Symmachus had enriched the Vatican complex in various ways, building there episcopal accommodation (*episcopia*) and establishing a second cult site to the apostle Andrew, in the more easterly of the two imperial rotundas on the south side of the basilica. At St Paul's the same pope also renewed the apse and made improvements to the *confessio* (*LP* I, 261–2). The Lateran too had been enriched with additional chapels and a growing collection of relics since the time of Pope

Hilary (461–8) (*LP* I, 242; Thacker 2007b, 44–5; idem, 2007a, 39).

From the later sixth century, Rome expanded her role as a centre of pilgrimage. The catacombs, refurbished by John III (561–74), became less places of burial and more places of cult (Osborne 1985). These developments, enhanced in the seventh century by Rome's increasing importance for western pilgrims after the Islamic conquest of Jerusalem, were accompanied by the rise of a new literary genre: itineraries which set out systematic and detailed routes around the extramural cult sites and in so doing provided pilgrims with a memento and aide-memoire of their visit. The earliest surviving examples of these works have long been dated to the second quarter of the seventh century, although more recently arguments have been advanced to place them somewhat later, 650–80 (*CTR*, 29–207; *Itin.* I, 281–343; Geertman 1975, 136, 198–202). If so, they were being compiled at exactly the period Wilfrid was visiting Rome, and we may perhaps imagine him purchasing or commissioning just such a text to commemorate his own visits to Rome's *loca sancta* (below).

The pontificates of Pelagius II (579–90) and Honorius I (625–38) were particularly crucial to this burgeoning pilgrim activity. Despite the siege of Rome by the newly arrived Lombards, at its height when he was elected, Pelagius invested in the cult sites and catacombs. He adorned the shrine of St Peter with silver-gilt panels and perhaps initiated the raising of the level of the sanctuary so that the high altar could be directly located over the apostolic tomb, a work brought to fruition by his successor Gregory the Great (590–604). A similar work was undertaken at St Paul's on theVia Ostiense (*LP* I, 312; *CBCR* V, 99, 174, 195–7; Brandenburg 2005, 128–30; Filippi 2009, 35–7). Most importantly, Pelagius built a new shrine church for St Laurence, on a platform dug from the side of the Verano, so that it might stand right over the martyr's undisturbed tomb (*LP* I, 309; *CBCR* II, 11, 122–27). This building, which made ample use of opulent *spolia* from the decaying public buildings of Rome, was singled out for especial praise in the pilgrim itineraries (*CTR* , 69–70, 102–3, 134–5).

The investment of Rome by the Lombards in the late sixth century does not seem to have prevented its continuing development as a pilgrim city, presumably because visitors could circumvent any difficulties of land access by travelling by sea and disembarking at the port of Ostia (Llewellyn 1971, 173–98). Certainly, Gregory of Tours' deacon was collecting relics in Rome during Pelagius's pontificate. Gregory offers a vivid description of the manufacture of secondary relics at the Petrine tomb (*GM* 27), and expressly tells us that besides relics of the apostles whose feet Christ had washed (presumably Peter and Andrew), his deacon also came back with relics of the apostle Paul, and the Roman martyrs Laurence, Pancras, Chrysanthus and Darius, and John and Paul (*GM* 82; cf. *GM* 28, 37, 38, 41, 45).

Pelagius's and Gregory's successors built on this work. Boniface IV (608–615) converted the greatest temple in Rome, the Pantheon, into the church of Sancta Maria *ad martyres* (*LP* I, 317). Honorius I was especially active: his many enterprises within the city and in the cemeteries included the conversion of the ancient Curia in the Forum Romanum into a church, dedicated to St Hadrian (*CBCR* I, 1; *LP* I, 324), the rebuilding of the cemeterial basilica of St Pancras (*CBCR* III, 153–74), the addition of a new church, dedicated to St Apollinaris, to the eastern atrium of St Peter's (*LP* I, 323) and, most conspicuously of all, the construction of a new basilica *ad sanctam* over the tomb of St Agnes on the Via Nomentana (*CBCR* I, 14–38; Brandenburg 2005, 241–7). This, like Pelagius's San Lorenzo, was presented as an admired sight in the pilgrim itineraries (*CTR*, 79, 115).

Throughout the seventh century, the Lateran remained the seat of the papal administration and treasury and the location of the most important assemblies and councils. The complex received a splendid new addition, the church of St Venantius, installed in the baptistery complex by John IV (640–2) to house relics of some ten saints brought mainly from the abandoned metropolis of Salona in his native Dalmatia, and probably completed only a few years before Wilfrid's first visit to Rome (*LP* I, 330). The presence of the martyrs was recorded in an inscription and in mosaic portraits in the apse and on the eastern wall of the new church (Mackie 2003, 212–30).

After the establishment of what proved to be a lasting peace with the Lombards in 598, the pilgrim traffic to Rome increased. The collecting of relics was, of course, of overriding importance, as Wilfrid's own activities demonstrate. Secondary relics, promoted as having the same wonderworking powers as the corporal remains themselves, were created from strips of cloth or from oil and dust in contact with the holy tomb. At St Peter's in the sixth century, this seems to have been a matter of personal initiative, but later the popes took control; under Gregory the Great, the procedure involved a papal mass celebrated over the relic object (Colgrave 1968, 108–110). The popes also distributed non-corporal *benedictiones* in the form of filings from the apostolic chains, both those of St Peter, displayed in the basilica of San Pietro in vincoli, and of St Paul, perhaps as now on show in the apostle's great *memoria* on the Via Ostiense (Thacker 2007b, 47–9; 2007a, 43–4).[1]

On the whole, Gregory and his successors drew on a relatively restricted group of saints for relic creation (Thacker 2007b, 67–9; Leyser 2000, 300–1). Other relics, as Stephen relates, were distributed at the *loca sancta* by 'chosen men' (*electi viri*), presumably the custodians or *praepositi* of the cemeteries in

---

[1]   The chains were among the relics seen by Palladio in the mid sixteenth century: Hart and Hicks, 2009, 112.

which the saints were interred (VW 33, 55; Thacker 2007b, 59–66). It was clearly the number which impressed: in the early seventh century, the agent of the catholic Lombard queen, Theodelinda (d. 628), brought back with him phials containing secondary relics of some sixty-odd Roman martyrs (*CTR*, 29–47). Wilfrid's repeated visits to the *loca sanctorum* to collect relics suggest that he was of the same mind.

Even so, Rome's leading cults clearly had especial prestige for English pilgrims: in particular, those of the apostles Peter, Paul and Andrew and the city's own particular patron, Laurence. Wilfrid certainly had especial veneration for at least three of these. His relation to the other great cult figure of seventh century Rome, the Virgin Mary, was as we shall see perhaps more complex.

One last point: the cult of Gregory the Great, himself. The Roman pope so vigorously promoted in some English circles in the later seventh century cut less of a dash in his own city (Thacker 1998). Here Wilfrid was probably in tune with the Romans. His relative indifference to Gregory is perhaps reflected in his biography. Stephen only mentions the pope once and that in the context of Wilfrid's claim to have taken up Gregory's work after the failure of the papal mission (VW 47; Dailey 2010, 203).

Wilfrid and His First Visit

Let us look now at the young Wilfrid's attitudes to Rome and the way in which he prepared himself for his first visit, in the mid 650s. By then he was in his late teens or early twenties (for a discussion of the date, see below). He was therefore not yet ordained: he would be tonsured later, in Gaul, and ordained on his return to England. His primary motivation, no doubt, was to become an exile for Christ; but his biographer, Stephen, sees him as also anxious to discover what distinguished Roman from Irish monasticism. Stephen tells us that Wilfrid wished 'to learn the rules of ecclesiastical discipline, so that our nation may grow in the service of God' (VW 4). He sees the young Wilfrid as already wanting to reform the English.

The long journey to Rome, down through Francia and over the Alps, was dangerous. Those making it needed companions, for safety and protection. Wilfrid, having got permission to set off for Rome, waited at Canterbury, until a sufficiently large group of travellers had collected. It included another young Northumbrian nobleman, Benedict Biscop. Benedict was some six years older than Wilfrid, and King Eorcenberht of Kent evidently intended him as a mentor for the younger man (VW 3; HA 2; HE V, 19).

While waiting for the group to gather, Wilfrid by no means wasted his time. How he prepared himself for Rome is of considerable interest. He clearly understood that Canterbury, where Gregory's envoy Augustine had himself preached and sung, was the perfect place in England to prepare for an extended visit to Rome. Stephen tells us that Wilfrid's preparations included committing to memory the psalms which he had first of all read in Jerome's revision in an edition 'after the Roman use' (VW 3). Canterbury followed the city of Rome in singing the Roman Psalter. Wilfrid would have learned the Roman texts of the psalms above all by daily participation in, and listening to, the monastic and cathedral office. He thus prepared himself, in the most practical way, to take his turn singing the office when he got to Rome, taking his place as an aspirant monk and cleric in the Roman tradition. Of course, Wilfrid's relearning of the Psalter was also a declaration of allegiance: from now on, his liturgical life would have Rome as its centre.

However warm the relationship between Wilfrid and Biscop when they set off, on the journey it evidently soured. At Lyons they parted, Biscop going on to Rome, Wilfrid lingering with Bishop Aunemundus. Wilfrid's decision to stay on at Lyons seems either to have caused or to have been caused by tension between the two men. Stephen, who describes the departing Biscop as Wilfrid's 'stern guide' (*austerae mentis dux*), compares the separation to that between Paul and Barnabas, the fruit of bitter dissension (VW 3; Acts 15: 36–40; Plummer 1896, II, 321). This journey marks the beginnings of a difficult relationship that was to have a determining effect on Wilfrid's entire career.

The date of Wilfrid's arrival in Rome is a matter of considerable significance but very difficult to determine. It was probably in 654 but may have been even later. The circumstances, as related by Stephen, present a number of possibilities. Stephen tells us that in the course of several months visiting Rome's holy places, Wilfrid met a man who became his teacher and friend: the Archdeacon Boniface (VW 5). Now the archdeacon of Rome was a very senior figure indeed. In liturgical ceremonies he was literally the pope's right-hand man, the sustainer of his right hand when he advanced in procession (Ó Carragáin 1995, 8). He probably also had a role in effecting papal introductions and indeed, after teaching Wilfrid much about ecclesiastical discipline and, presumably, about the complex and strife-torn politics of contemporary Rome, Boniface went on to present him to the pope (VW 5; see Cubitt, this volume).

Much hinges on the unnamed pope's identity. By the 650s, Rome was a city in crisis, and indeed a city in rebellion against the Emperor. The reason was a theological controversy, Monotheletism, which echoes in a remarkable way throughout Wilfrid's relations with the city, and must certainly have dominated the first two, at least, of his three visits to it. The doctrinal dispute between pope and emperor led to the arrest and deportation of Pope Martin I, who, in a letter written in October or November 653 to the Greek monk Theodore of Sancta Sophia, made it clear that he expected Rome in his absence to be governed by a committee of three, of which Boniface was evidently the most senior (PL 87, 201). Boniface remained in this position of great authority until the election of a new pope, Eugenius I, on 10 August 654, an action in which the exiled Martin reluctantly acquiesced (PL 87, 204; Piazzoni 1992, 207). Plummer long ago conjectured that the reason that Boniface played such a significant role in Wilfrid's introduction to Rome was that there was no resident pope for the newly-arrived Wilfrid to meet (Plummer 1896, II, 321–2). While that is indeed possible, it may also be that a newly arrived young cleric would never have had easy access to the pope himself and that Boniface was merely performing his proper role of introducing Wilfrid at an appropriate time (see Cubitt, this volume). It is worth remembering too that there was another papal interregnum, albeit a much shorter one, in 657, from the death of Eugenius I (2 June) until the election of Vitalian (31 July), when Boniface was presumably again in charge (*LP* I, 338–41).

It is then far from clear whether Wilfrid first arrived in Rome as early as 654 or as late as 657. It is also apparent that, although he had to wait, he did eventually attract the attention of the highest authorities in Rome. There is no evidence that Biscop had any part in this process.

Boniface would doubtless have instructed Wilfrid in the doctrinal and disciplinary issues involved in Martin's dispute with the Byzantine emperor (see Cubitt, this volume). As endorsed by Constans II, Monothelitism asserted that Christ was fully human as well as divine while denying that the man Christ had a will of his own. The orthodox reaction, developed most fully by the Greek theologian Maximus the Confessor, who had come to Rome in 646, affirmed that Christ not only participated in the divine will, which he shared with God the Father and with the Holy Spirit, but could only be fully human if he also had a human will. In 649 the Lateran Synod, presided over by Pope Martin, duly rejected Monotheletism and solemnly proclaimed orthodox doctrine.

Constans knew that doctrinal dissent could easily become a focus for political dissent, that Rome's defiance had quickly to be quashed. His first plan misfired, however, in a way which demonstrates how real the danger then was to the unity of the Empire. The emperor gave the task of asserting his authority to Olympius, his exarch at Ravenna. Arriving at Rome in October 649, when the Lateran council was still in session, Olympius saw how strong the opposition to Monotheletism was, even among the Greek community and the army; in response, he refused to carry out the imperial orders and set himself up as the independent ruler of Italy (Bertolini 1941, 337–50).

This tumultuous period saw the creation of a highly important Christian monument in the heart of Rome: a great cycle of frescoes in Santa Maria Antiqua in the Forum Romanum. That church had clear political as well as ecclesiastical importance within the city. Standing within the shadow of the imperial palace on the Palatine, and near the Greek quarter (*schola Greca*), it provided a centrally-placed basilica for the Greek community of Rome (Nordhagen 1978;

Osborne *et al.*, 2004, 67–82). Beat Brenk has argued that much of this decoration must have been carried out in the pontificates of Theodore and Martin, and especially in the brief period between October 649 and summer 653 when Olympius ruled Rome as an independent city (Osborne *et al.* 2004, 67–82). For the rear wall behind the altar, flanking the apse, Pope Martin commissioned frescoes depicting four fathers of the Church. Each of these held a scroll, inscribed with a text in Greek, taken from his writings, which had been read out at the council of 649 in refutation of Monothelitism. Rome's independence, expressed in this scheme, only came to an end after Olympius's death in 652. To reassert imperial authority, the emperor quickly sent a new exarch, Theodore Calliopas, who entered Rome on 15 June, 653. In vain did Pope Martin, seriously ill, claim refuge by placing his portable bed before the altar in the Lateran basilica (*LP* I, 338). On the morning of 17 June, Theodore arrested him there, and sent him a prisoner to Constantinople, where he was tried and finally, on 16 September 655, martyred, the last pope to suffer that fate (Piazzoni 1992; Bertolini 1941, 349–50).

These events were either being played out or were still very fresh in people's minds when Wilfrid arrived in Rome. Very probably during his extended period of visiting the city's holy places Wilfrid went to the newly frescoed church in the Forum and imbibed the defence, highly popular in Rome, of Christ's human will and human courage. One would like to know whether he was also present in Santa Maria Maggiore in the autumn of 654 when, soon after the election of Pope Eugenius, the Roman clerics and people physically prevented the pope from finishing mass in the basilica until he promised to reject the public profession of faith which the patriarch of Constantinople had sent to him and which was ambivalent on the question of Christ's human will (*LP* I, 341).

Buildings and Cult Sites

One holy site in Rome which Wilfrid certainly did visit at this time was what Stephen terms the 'oratory' of St Andrew (VW 5). By then, there were at least two significant cult sites in Rome devoted to St Peter's brother. The earlier was the church of Sant'Andrea *iuxta praesepe* or cata Barbara, established near Santa Maria Maggiore by Pope Simplicius between 471 and 483 in a richly floored and marbled basilica built by Junius Bassus, consul in 317 (*CBCR* II, 62–3). Simplicius retained the main hall of the basilica unaltered, including the opulent marbles with their pagan figures and motifs, and added an apse to house the altar, adorned with a mosaic of Christ and six apostles, including St Andrew, standing to the left of St Peter (Osborne and Claridge I, 73–7; II, 78–80; Lombardi 1996, 41). Beneath the apse he placed an inscription commemorating Valila, who had left the property to the Christian community, naming himself as Valila's agent, in establishing a church dedicated to the apostolic martyr Andrew, hitherto lacking a dwelling in the city (*LP* I, 250; *ILCV*, 1785).

The other cult site of St Andrew was at the Vatican, established by Pope Symmachus in the early sixth century in the more easterly of the two rotundas on the south side of Old St Peter's. Symmachus richly adorned his foundation both with relics and with opulent furnishings. Besides the silver shrine or *confessio* of the apostle with its silver canopy, he introduced oratories of St Thomas the apostle (whose relics, like Andrew's, were in the Apostoleion in Constantinople), St Apollinaris of Ravenna, and St Sossius, and a *confessio* to house relics of the Roman saints Protus and Hyacinthus and St Cassian of Imola. All the shrines and the arches associated with them were of silver (*LP* I, 261). Andrew's shrine was further enriched by Pope Honorius I, who provided a silver panel to stand in front of the *confessio* (*LP* I, 323), and the basilica was still evidently highly valued in the early eighth century, when Pope John VI (701–5), a pope with whom Wilfrid was to become personally acquainted, provided it with a new ambo (*LP* I, 323).

Stephen does not identify the *oratorium* with its altar furnished with a Gospel book, before which Wilfrid knelt and invoked the apostle's aid in dedicating himself to his mission of converting and reforming the English Church (VW 5). The term *oratorium*, however, suggests that it was the relatively small structure adjoining the large basilica of St Peter's on the Vatican rather than the large free-standing basilica on the Esquiline. Nevertheless, Wilfrid probably visited the latter, since it lay near Santa Maria Maggiore, a church he must have gone to in the course of his months-long visits to the Roman *loca sanctorum* and to which on his deathbed he bequeathed a portion of his treasure (VW 63). In both of Andrew's churches he would have been confronted with an imperial Roman building opulently converted to Christian use. Such experiences are likely to have affected his own aesthetic when establishing churches for his new foundations.

Other sites which Wilfrid almost certainly visited include the Lateran, where he presumably had his delayed meeting with the pope. There he would doubtless have been shown the splendid *novum opus*, the chapel of St Venantius, at the baptistery (Mackie 203, 212–30). Almost certainly, he also visited the other apostolic tomb in the great church of Saint Paul on the Via Ostiense, to which again he bequeathed treasure on his deathbed (VW 63).

The impact of all this became apparent after Wilfrid's return; in particular, his new churches at Ripon and Hexham, dedicated respectively to St Peter and St Andrew and built in the 670s when he was at the height of his power, suggest that he wished to evoke Rome's *loca sancta* in his native land. The crypts, in the proportions of both the curiously angled corridors and the *cellae* to which they led, evoke the holy sites within the catacombs. Their ostentatious reuse of Roman *spolia* in particular recalls Pelagius's beautiful church of San Lorenzo with its splendid set of *pavonazetto* columns and their opulent entablature of reused door-jambs and fragments of friezes, finely carved but of widely different design and dimension (*CBCR* II, 51–2; Brandenburg 2005, 236–40; Andaloro 2006, 77–94). That, of course, is not to say that Wilfrid did not employ Gallic craftsmen or that that those craftsmen did not employ Gallic techniques and lay out the crypts like a Gallic hypogeum (see Cambridge, this volume). Wilfrid would not, of course, have perceived Rome and Gaul as in any way opposed in matters of architecture; like Biscop he would have thought that in Gaul (unlike contemporary Northumbria) buildings were erected *iuxta morem romanorum*. But Stephen's account suggests that it was Roman rather than Gallic *loca sancta* which most impressed him and it seems likely that it was these that he wished primarily to evoke.

Liturgies and Rituals

Wilfrid was clearly interested in liturgy and ritual. He was proud of introducing into Northumbria a double choir singing antiphons and responsories 'in accordance with the rite of the primitive church' (*iuxta ritum primitivae ecclesiae*), by which he probably meant in the Roman manner as transmitted by the Gregorian mission to Kent (VW 47; HE II, 20; IV, 2). But we should note the bewildering variety of liturgies in Rome during this period. Any visitor would have found it necessary to select and organize and simplify, if he or she was to construct his own version of the 'Roman' liturgy. Wilfrid would not have been surprised by this. He would have encountered similar variability in both England and Gaul. But like Benedict Biscop, he clearly accorded especial respect to liturgy and ritual which were in some way thought to be Roman or underwritten by the authority of Rome.

In Gaul, the ancient Gallican rite existed in many forms. In Wilfrid's time these were subjected to increasing influence from Roman liturgical sources or from sources that were regarded as representing Roman practice (Vogel 1960, 185–229). Thus the eclectic *Missale Gothicum*, which seems to have been complied in Burgundy *c*.685–700, contained a version of the Roman canon (Smyth 2003, 71–83). The *Missale Francorum* of the earlier eighth century also contained much that was Roman, again including the core mass text, the canon (Smyth 2003, 104–7). Even if, as has often been suggested, insular agents were involved in the diffusion of this text, its acceptance in late Merovingian Gaul suggests that there, as in England, respect was accorded to Rome. The Old Gelasian, another collection of mass texts in use in Gaul and related to the *Missale Francorum*, has been described as 'fundamentally Roman in nature' and, whatever its origins, would, in the eighth century, have been thought of as representing Roman liturgy, as its title indicates (*Liber Sacramentorum Romanae Aeclesiae Ordinis Anni Circuli*: Smyth 2003, 126–41). Sacramentaries with material close to that of the Old Gelasian were also known in England in Bede's time: such compilations may have included texts, interpreted as exemplifying Roman practice, obtained not only in Rome but also in Gaul by Benedict Biscop and perhaps by Wilfrid himself (Cubitt 1996, 48–52).[2]

With such a lack of textual uniformity, one aspect of the liturgy which was likely to impress as evidence of Romanness or otherwise was the way in which services were performed. Hence Wilfrid's and Biscop's particular interest in singing in the Roman manner. By the early eighth century, if not earlier, the Roman *ordines*, which provided practical guidance in these matters, were beginning to circulate in Francia (Vogel 1960, 217–25). It is highly likely that Wilfrid, like Biscop, took home with him from Rome ideas about how to conduct liturgy as well as liturgical texts.

In the ferment in Rome itself in the 650s, then, Wilfrid would have encountered liturgical innovation and experiment. The Roman opponents of Monothelitism adduced Christ's virgin birth as the reason why there need be no conflict between his human and his divine will and it is surely no coincidence that the first of the four Marian feasts, the *Natale* of 15 August (also styled the *Pausatio*, *Dormitio*, or *Assumptio*) began to be celebrated in Rome from *c.* 650. The opposition to Monothelitism provided an important stimulus for the development of the cult of Christ's mother. We shall see that, by Wilfrid's second visit, and still more by his third, this cult had developed in complex ways.

The Second Visit, 679–80

Wilfrid's second visit, to appeal against his deprivation in 678, brought him again to the Lateran, to meet the bishops gathered in council in the *secretarium* of the basilica (VW 29).[3] Once again, he went around the holy places to obtain relics; Stephen's wording indicates that this included a variety of sites – not just St Peter's (VW 33). He also met a papal *consiliarius* named Boniface, perhaps the archdeacon who befriended him on his earlier visit (VW 53; HE V, 19).

It is important to note that Benedict Biscop was also in Rome in 679. Accompanied by Ceolfrith, then his prior at Wearmouth, he had almost certainly set off after the decision to deprive Wilfrid had been taken. It has been plausibly suggested that he was there as the envoy of King Ecgfrith.[4] He may indeed have

---

[2] The calendars of some of these early English liturgies suggest Neapolitan influence, also apparent in the Vatican Old Gelasian; but material from Naples, which lay within the Rome's suburbicarian province and which was almost certainly promoted in England by papally sponsored clerics, may well have been regarded as underpinned by the authority of Rome.

[3] On the Lateran *secretarium*, see De Blaauw 1994, I, 74–5, 182; Claussen 2008, 61–89.

[4] We are grateful to Eric Goldberg for first making this point in a seminar delivered in

been one of those who, in addition to Coenwald, Archbishop Theodore's official representative, delivered reports to the Roman council against Wilfrid, presenting him as a fugitive making his way to Rome (VW 29). Significantly, one of Biscop's reasons for going to Rome was to obtain a privilege exempting his monastery from the authority of its diocesan – until 678, of course, Wilfrid himself (HA 6; HE IV, 18). Biscop returned to England in 679, with the pope's envoy, the archcantor John, abbot of St Martin's monastery which stood just outside the apse of St Peter's, in time to deliver the acts of the Lateran synod of 649 condemning Monothelitism to the council of Hatfield, held in September of that year.[5]

Wilfrid, meanwhile, after wintering in Frisia and proceeding south through Austrasia and Lombardy, arrived in Rome in time to prepare his case for presentation to pope and synod in October 679 (VW 25–9). Almost certainly, then, the visits of the two men overlapped (Plummer, 1896, II, 360). Significantly, neither Stephen nor Bede mention Biscop in their accounts of Wilfrid's visit, just as Bede says nothing of Wilfrid in his accounts of that of Biscop (VW 29; HE IV, 18; V, 19; HA 6).

Biscop's relations with Wilfrid, perhaps permanently damaged by the events at Lyons in the 650s, may well have worsened in the 670s, not only because of Biscop's close association with King Ecgfrith and Archbishop Theodore (HE IV, 17; HA 9,17; VCP 25), but also perhaps because Wilfrid had interfered in internal dissension in Wearmouth. His coadjutor Ceolfrith had been ordained by Wilfrid when a monk at Ripon and licensed by Wilfrid to work with Biscop in 674, but after a revolt at Wearmouth *c*. 676 had returned to Ripon, whither Biscop had been forced to follow him to persuade him to return (VC 3–4, 8). Having lived and trained under Wilfrid's rule for several years, Ceolfrith's view of his former mentor may have been different from Biscop's, and perhaps more favourable.

Biscop, Wilfrid and the Marian Cult

By 679 there had been major innovations in the Roman cult of the incarnation of divinity in Christ, a dogma of which a central element was Christ's birth from the Virgin Mary. Henceforth, Rome would commemorate Christ's virginal birth, not only in the relatively ancient cult of the Nativity (25 December), celebrated at Rome since the mid-fourth century, but in four other feasts. The feast of Christ's presentation in the Temple (2 February) had been celebrated in the city

---

Kalamazoo in 2008. Cf the comments in Wood and Grocock (forthcoming).

[5] We are following the current consensus on the date of the Hatfield council. It is worth noting, however, that Bede expressly dates it to 680 (HE IV, 24) and that at least one of the regnal years used by the council to date itself (those of Æthelræd of Mercia) also point to that year (HE IV, 17).

since the 630s and that of the Virgin's death and entry into heaven, the Dormition or Assumption (15 August), from the 650s, the period when the Monothelite crisis reached its climax with the martyrdoms of Pope Martin I and Maximus the Confessor. From the 660s, the feast of the Annunciation of the Lord had been celebrated at some Roman basilicas on 25 March (Frénaud 1961, 184), and finally, in the 670s, the feast of the Nativity of the Virgin (8 September) was also introduced. All four feasts, including some at least of the readings assigned to them, were imported from Constantinople. Educated Roman clerics must have appreciated the irony that these Constantinopolitan feasts strengthened devotion to Christ's human birth from the Virgin, and thus reinforced the orthodox Roman theological position that Christ's incorruptible human will stemmed from his birth in Mary's uncorrupted womb, the *thalamus* or bridal chamber in which he forever united the divine and human natures (Ó Carragáin 2005, 61, 82, 322–23). Biscop, then, in the course of his visits in the 660s and 670s (HA 2–4, 6) would have become familiar with at least three of the new feasts: the Purification, the Annunciation, and the greatest of all, the Dormition.

Biscop reacted promptly, and in two remarkable ways, to this Roman atmosphere of increased devotion to Christ's incarnation and to his mother. First, he brought back to Wearmouth, and placed near the altar of the monastic basilica (dedicated to St Peter) an icon of the Virgin Mary accompanied by icons of the twelve apostles (HA 6). Second, in the years immediately following his return to Wearmouth, that is, in the early 680s, he built at Wearmouth a church dedicated to Mary and, on a later trip to Rome (*c*.684–6), acquired icons to decorate this new church. Bede tells us that they represented the life and miracles of Christ: they thus, once more, associated the cult of Mary with the achievements of her son (HA 9).

Further, in his visit of 678 Biscop achieved something still more remarkable: he brought back with him to the ends of the earth – all the way to Wearmouth – the precentor of St Peter's, John the archcantor. After representing the pope at the synod of Hatfield, during the winter of 679–80 the archcantor gave at Wearmouth *viva voce* lessons in the chant and liturgy of St Peter's, not only to the monks of St Peter's, but to monastic cantors from other Northumbrian monasteries who would learn from John's expertise (HE IV, 17–18).

We can be certain that the archcantor was interested in the developing cult of the Virgin, to which his Vatican community had recently made a unique contribution. The feast of the Annunciation (25 March) posed a practical problem. It usually fell during Lent, and quite often during Holy Week, when Christ's passion and death were commemorated. How could the joy of the Annunciation, when Christ took on a human nature, be properly celebrated in Lent, the penitential season that prepared for his passion? Alone among the basilicas of Christendom, St Peter's on the Vatican developed an explicit theology to justify the celebration of the Annunciation during Lent. The Vatican mass for 25 March drew on an ancient Christian tradition that the first Good Friday, the day of Christ's death, fell on 25 March, the anniversary of the Annunciation, when he was conceived in the Virgin's womb. From the 670s, the Vatican basilica celebrated 25 March as *Adnuntiatio Domini et Passio Eiusdem*, the Annunciation of the Lord and his Passion (Ó Carragáin 2005, 85–93). As John was precentor at St Peter's and thus in charge of liturgical performance in that basilica, it seems reasonable to suppose that he may himself have composed this unique mass. It seems equally likely that John the archcantor, Benedict Biscop and also, perhaps, Archbishop Theodore of Canterbury, celebrated as the only person in the Latin West who really understood Monothelitism, were all aware of, and favourable towards, the developing cult of Christ's incarnation and his relationship to his Virgin Mother.

This Roman elaboration of the church's teaching on the Incarnation and the accompanying enhancement of the liturgical cult of the Virgin apparently passed Wilfrid by. Indeed, he was eventually to experience a vision in which the Virgin herself accused him of neglect (below). It may well be that the cause of this indifference lay in the association of these developments in England with Wilfrid's enemies, Theodore and Biscop. It is clearly significant that Bede omits any mention of Wilfrid in the *Historia Abbatum*, despite knowing of his early links with Biscop and despite his early patronage of Ceolfrith. Here, he may well be reflecting Biscop's antipathy as much as his own.

Third Visit 703–4

Wilfrid, aged nearly 70, made his last visit to Rome, once again to defend himself against his enemies, in 703 and 704. The pope at the time was John VI (VW 50–5). In the twenty-five years since Wilfrid's second visit, there had been a major development in the Roman cult of the Virgin: a development which clarified further the relationship between Marian devotion and devotion to the full humanity of her son. As we have seen, the four new feasts celebrating Christ's mother had been introduced at various dates and, possibly, in a variety of different basilicas (though, in the development of this cult, the basilica of Santa Maria *ad Praesepe*, on the Esquiline hill, must always have been important). But Pope Sergius (686–701) had unified and transformed the cult by making all four feasts part of the papal stational liturgy (Baldovin 1987, 122). The official biography of Pope Sergius, in the *Liber Pontificalis*, records that:

> He decreed that on the days of the Lord's Annunciation, of the Falling-asleep and Nativity of St Mary the ever-virgin mother of God, and of St Simeon (which the Greeks call *Ypapante*) a litany

should go out from St Hadrian's and the people should meet up at
St Mary's (trans. Davis 2000, 89).[6]

In the Roman 'stational' liturgy the pope, on particular Sundays or feast
days, went in solemn procession, accompanied by his court, to a particular
basilica, one often with a symbolic relevance to the feast, to celebrate mass
(Baldovin 1987, 105–66). Symbolism clearly played a large part in the stational
processions for the four new feasts. The procession began, not at the Lateran
patriarchate, but at the church of Sant' Adriano in the Forum Romanum: the
building that, until the 630s, had been the Senate House. There, the people
gathered and prayers were recited. From Sant'Adriano, pope and people went in
procession to the basilica of Santa Maria *ad Praesepe* at the top of the Esquiline
Hill. Since it was built in the first half of the fifth century, this basilica had been
the most important centre in Rome, and indeed in Western Europe, of devotion
to the Virgin: it was the symbolic equivalent, at Rome, of Bethlehem, and from
the 640s was believed to possess relics of the crib in which Christ was laid
(Baldovin 1987, 148; *CBCR* III, 6). There the papal mass of the day was
celebrated. By providing matching processions (from the forum to Santa Maria)
for all four feasts, Sergius for the first time made it clear that they formed a 'set',
with a four-fold unity. The two which fell in spring primarily celebrated Christ's
incarnation: the presentation of Christ in the Temple (2 Feb) celebrated the
'meeting' (hence the Greek title 'Ypapante') in the Temple between the new
covenant, embodied in the Christ-child, and the old, symbolized by Simeon the
high priest; the Annunciation (25 March) celebrated the moment of the
Incarnation. Sergius's matching processions now emphasized the close
connection between these two dominical feasts and the two in late summer and
autumn, each of which directly celebrated the death and birth of the Virgin: her
Dormition (15 August) and her Nativity (8 September).

Sergius thus emphasized in a new way that the cult of the Virgin formed a
necessary part of devotion to the incarnation of her son. For the first time, he
made the four feasts official, because episcopal and papal: public events in the
life of the city. The account of the new 'set' in Sergius's official biography is the
earliest surviving official notice of these developments. Henceforth, if a bishop
wanted his city to be truly 'Roman', he needed to imitate this set of Marian
feasts. Bede duly noted Sergius's innovation, and convincingly described the
evolution of the feasts, and their recent unification within the stational liturgy
(*DTR* 323; Ó Carragáin 2005, 238). In their relatively long stay at Rome,

[6] 'Constituit autem ut diebus Adnuntiationis Domini, Dormitionis et Nativitatis
sanctae Dei Genetricis semperque virginis Mariae ac sancti Symeonis, quod Ypapanti
Graeci appellant, letania exeat a sancto Hadriano et ad sanctam Mariam populus
occurrat' (*LP* I, 376).

between 703 and early 705, Wilfrid and his party had ample opportunity to participate in the new papal processions, and so to come to appreciate the new status of the four feasts. As we have seen when discussing Wilfrid's first visit and the beginning of his friendship with the Archdeacon Boniface, stational masses, which usually included refreshments for the curial participants at the stational basilica, provided excellent opportunities for clerical networking.

Wilfrid made his representations about his mistreatment in England at the court of John VI, a pope with a Byzantine background. John VI died on 11 January 705, possibly before Wilfrid and his companions left Rome for Northumbria: they were hardly likely to leave the city in the dead of winter, before the Alpine passes had become negotiable (*LP* I, 383). The new pope, John VII, was elected on 1 March (*LP* I, 384–5). It may be significant that he adopted the same name (chosen on election?) as his predecessor: that may indicate a continuity of policy and a community of interests. If so, Wilfrid may well have become acquainted with him during the reign of his predecessor. John VII, together with Pope Sergius, was one of the most active of the early medieval popes to develop the cult of the Virgin. The monuments he commissioned during his short but fruitful papacy (705–707) were all in her honour, and contained inscriptions, in Greek as well as Latin, calling him *servus Sanctae Mariae*, the slave of St Mary (Ó Carragáin 2005, 240–6).

Wilfrid set off on the long journey to Britain, either towards the end of 704 or in early spring 705 (VW 56). Now old and infirm, he evidently travelled fairly slowly, first on horseback – for he could no longer walk – and then borne on a litter. Even if Wilfrid left Rome in late 704, it is likely that on the journey, he was overtaken by the news of John VI's death and the election of John VII.

Then came a highly significant miracle. At Meaux, near Paris, Wilfrid fell into a coma and seemed to be on his deathbed. But after four days he woke up restored to health. His first words were 'Where is Acca, our chaplain?'. We can be sure that Stephen got these words from Acca himself. Wilfrid personally told Acca that the Archangel Michael had appeared and informed him that the Virgin had interceded for him, so that he, Wilfrid, could carry out an important commission for her. Michael was, with St Peter, one of the gate-keepers of heaven. By the late seventh century, his status was very publicly inscribed in the Roman landscape as ordered by the church. On the Vatican hill, passing along the '*porticus* of St Peter' on their way to worship at the apostle's grave, pilgrims passed the shrine of St Michael atop Hadrian's mausoleum, before finally attaining Rome's *paradisus*, the name given to the atrium or quadriporticus in front of the entrance to the basilica. The *paradisus* was so-called from the fifth-century mosaics which adorned its eastern (entrance) façade and which depicted the *Agnus Dei* in glory, flanked by the Evangelists and the Elders of the Apocalypse – thereby representing the liturgy of heaven, as described in the

Revelation of St John (chs 4–6). Originally executed during the pontificate of Leo I (440–61), they had recently been renovated by Pope Sergius (*LP* I, 375; Andaloro 2006, 24–6).

According to the archangel, the Virgin asked why Wilfrid had failed to honour her with a church and commanded him, in return for adding years to his life, to remedy this neglect (VW 56–7). Responding to this experience, at Hexham, in his final years, 706–10, Wilfrid finally did what Wearmouth had done a whole generation before: he erected a chapel in honour of the Virgin Mary. Presumably from 706, Hexham celebrated the Roman Marian feasts introduced by Pope Sergius: there was no point in building the chapel otherwise. The story is startling evidence of Wilfrid's political awareness. In his experience at Rome in 703–4 of Sergius' 'Marian' feasts, Wilfrid would have grasped that now Marian devotion had become official and papal: the most prestigious new way to imitate episcopal Rome. In his last three years at Hexham, Wilfrid seems to have proclaimed, by his actions, his adherence to the very latest papal devotion, and also to the very latest papal politics, including John VII's masterly description of himself as the servant or slave of Mary: if the pope was a slave of Mary, it is clear that he could not be a slave of anyone else, in particular, not of an interfering emperor in Constantinople. Returning to Northumbria, Wilfrid too was going to be exclusively the servant of the Virgin Mary: not of local bishops, not of local kings. Acca took note, and had the miracle recorded and published (VW 56).

It is remarkable that Bede, who recorded the miracle (HE V, 19), concentrated on the visit of the archangel and left out all mention of the Virgin Mary. That cannot be because the pupil of Benedict Biscop and of John the archcantor had a distaste for the cult of the Virgin. We must look elsewhere for an explanation. Bede's excision of all reference to the Virgin is possibly confirmation of Goffart's theory, that he was determined to cut Wilfrid down to size. Bede knew all about Sergius and John VII. He had read John's official biography, and recorded the chapel John had built for himself at St Peter's, dedicated to St Mary (Ó Carragáin 2005, 245, 274; *DTR* 323, 529–30). We can infer that Bede was very well aware that Wilfrid's account of how Mary had personally interceded for him with Christ in heaven gave Wilfrid a status very like that of John VII. The last thing Bede wanted to stress was that Wilfrid, finally returned to Hexham, was a bit like the newly elected pope or that he presented the Marian policy of his final years as a direct copy of contemporary papal policy. Bede, above all, was aware that Benedict Biscop and his Wearmouth community had anticipated Wilfrid by a generation in developing the cult of Mary along Roman lines.

But it is also perhaps possible to see an element of courtesy in Bede's omission of any reference to Mary's role in Wilfrid's cure. There is a scolding tone in Acca's original story, as told to Stephen the priest: 'Now remember that you have built churches in honour of the Apostles St Peter and St Andrew; but you have built nothing in honour of St Mary, ever Virgin, who is interceding for you. You have to put this right and to dedicate a church in honour of her.' Bede leaves all this out. By doing so he is not merely cutting Wilfrid down to size, eliminating all mention of his papal longings: he is also being courteous to Wilfrid's chaplain and successor Acca, and to the diocese of Hexham, of which Bede was himself a member. Reading the *Historia Ecclesiastica*, no one could infer that Wilfrid and Acca and Hexham had to be scolded by no less a person than the Archangel Michael to do what Benedict Biscop had done at Wearmouth a whole generation before.

The miracle at Meaux provided Wilfrid with a new opportunity to affirm that he accepted the innovations of Sergius, and the policy of the newly-elected John VII. For twenty years and more he had been reluctant to imitate the developed Marian devotion introduced at Wearmouth by Benedict Biscop, but the miracle at Meaux changed all that. It has to be understood in the context of Wilfrid's long visit to Rome in 703–705, which had taught him that the new Marian liturgies had become papal, and therefore a new way of proclaiming 'Romanness'. The importance of such Romanness to Wilfrid received a culminating expression in the final speech recorded by Stephen, which clearly has the character of a last will and testament. In it he expresses his desire to return to Rome for one last time, and 'to carry presents to the church dedicated to St Mary the Mother of the Lord' as well as to other Roman basilicas, in particular to St Paul's outside the Walls (VW 63).

Wilfrid's singling out of these two great Roman basilicas is interesting. They honoured two saints at the very highest universal level who (unlike Peter and Andrew) and least until the miracle at Meaux, had not as far as we know been given churches by Wilfrid in England. It may be that just as Sergius and John VII had promoted the Marian cult in St Peter's and Santa Maria Maggiore, so albeit on a far smaller scale, Sergius and John VI had paid attention to the Pauline cult on the Via Ostiense (*LP* I, 375, 383). Wilfrid was perhaps following in papal footsteps to the very end.

Conclusions

This paper has stressed the importance of the buildings, topography, culture and local politics of Rome for Wilfrid. It was at Rome that some of the most vital turning-points of his career were accomplished. There, he went as an impressionable young man and vowed himself to missionary activity. There, he acquired or refined a taste for church building and for fine ecclesiastical objects. There, he began his collection of apostolic and martyrial relics (there is no evidence that any of these came from Gaul – Stephen's stress is entirely on relic collecting in Rome). It was on the way to Rome and in Rome that Wilfrid's almost certainly difficult and determining relationship with Biscop was played out. Rome was formative in his liturgical and cultic programme, the relics he venerated and the way they were displayed.

Wilfrid's experiences of Gaul were to say the least equivocal; Neustria's good relations with his enemies endangered his life. At Rome he was generally treated with honour and received comfort, even if this had little effect at home in England. Rome, we might argue, played an enormous role in Wilfrid's spiritual imagination, in the way he viewed buildings, liturgy and cult, even if in practice in all those areas Gallic precedents helped to mediate *Romanitas*. In Wilfrid's mind, in these areas, Rome and Gaul were complementary, not opposed.

17: *Wilfrid and the Frisians*

JAMES T. PALMER

Sometimes accidents can take on a significance which far exceed their initial consequences. In 678 Wilfrid was desperately trying to reach Rome in order to appeal against his deposition as bishop of York by King Ecgfrith of Northumbria and Archbishop Theodore of Canterbury. A fortuitous wind took the ship of Wilfrid and his companions more directly east than they had initially intended, thus avoiding capture by King Theuderic III of Neustria and Burgundy (d. 691) and Duke Ebroin (d. *c.*680), who had their own reasons for wishing to inflict injury on the exiled bishop. Wilfrid and his companions overwintered somewhere in Frisia and began to preach Christianity to the people, having first earned the respect and protection of their king, Aldgisl. To Stephanus and Bede, and so to modern scholars, this marked the beginning of the Anglo-Saxon missions to the continent which would be driven forward next by St Willibrord and then by St Boniface, inaugurating, in Levison's words, 'a century of English spiritual influence on the continent' (Levison 1946, 60). But Stephanus's story is not simply a tale about missionary work: it is part of a series of episodes in the *Vita Wilfridi* which serve to make statements about the treatment of exiles by rulers – a theme which is central to understanding the purpose of the work as a whole. A careful examination of the structures of the Frisian episode, and its reception (or lack thereof) by Bede and hagiographers in Frisia, will contribute to a greater understanding of the nature of hagiography and the cult of saints in a period of important interactions between Britain and the continent.

Any consideration of Wilfrid's career must pay due care to the nature of the source material. It is by now well understood that hagiographies and histories are often shaped as much by polemic and external discourses as they are by 'what happened' (Goffart 1988; Wood 2001; Palmer 2009). In the case of the Frisian episode, as it appears in the work of both Stephanus and Bede, we might benefit from paying attention to how the story is structured. Hagiography, as Martínez Pizarro (2008, 181–2) has recently observed, is full of stories which fall between literary topoi and descriptions of ritualised moments, in which there are common expectations about how saints, rulers and other actors should behave in a given situation. By attending to the rules and their subversion, important aspects of authorial strategy can be revealed. Stephanus's *Vita Wilfridi* seems, at least to me, to be largely built up around two kinds of scene: the reception of the hero by kings, and debates at councils, both being played out with different casts and outcomes at critical junctures in the story. Many of these scenes, as Foley (1992) and Laynesmith (2000) have amply demonstrated, owe their logic to biblical models and in particular to the image of the persecuted Old Testament prophet. The language and rules are not simply transposed unaltered from source to product, however, and we must pay attention to how they work in practice. Study of rule-based episodes in the *Vita Wilfridi* is potentially fruitful because, in Bede's reworking of Stephanus's stories, we have a near-contemporary adaptation of those same scenes. By studying the language and the structure of Bede's own Wilfridian episodes we can expose the fluid association between language and the story. Where, for example, Bede chooses different words to describe a particular moment, does he also change the logic of the story? Such questions can also motivate reassessments of our preconceptions about how hagiography works in the context of a cult. We continually make assumptions about how hagiographies are studied and used in relation to the cult of saints, emphasising their potential use as occasional literature (van Egmond, 2000). The language used in ritualised or stock scenes is thus central to constructing an interpretative framework for understanding the message a text might be trying to convey.

Wilfrid in Frisia: Lessons on Honour and Friendship

The world Wilfrid entered provided a natural stage for an episode in the bishop's career. Frisia had long standing connections with Britain before his visit, resulting in many parallels in culture. Frisians were implicated in the *adventus Saxonum*, even if their actual involvement has been doubted (Bremmer 1990). As far as Bede and his friend Ecgberht were concerned, the Frisians were at least spiritual ancestors of the English, and as co-heirs to the regions of *Germania* they were a prime target for mission (HE V, 9). The culture and language of the English and the Frisians was close in many respects, which no doubt reinforced that feeling. Archaeology shows that North Sea trade was lively in the seventh century (Wilson 1986; Mostert 1999, 17–18). Any political structure that existed is now largely lost to us. Although Aldgisl is called *rex* by Stephanus and Bede, these are the only references to Aldgisl, and indeed the only references to any Frisian leader of the seventh century. Radbod, the next leader mentioned half-a-century later, is consistently called *dux* in contemporary Frankish sources, and these treat him largely like any other Frankish aristocrat (van Egmond 2005). Use of the word *rex* in Latin sources is no guarantee that there was an institutional kingship or kingdom outside the imaginations of Stephanus or Bede. Comments by modern historians which assert that Aldgisl was 'succeeded' by Radbod, or that Aldgisl was based in Utrecht like Radbod, rely on guesswork. All we can say for certain about the Frisia Wilfrid might have entered is that it was a vibrant economic area in which the many waterways were overlooked by networks of forts and trading centres, linking to the major trade routes down the Meuse and Rhine. It was a more obvious place for Wilfrid to end up than the 'miracle' of his boat being blown off course might suggest.

Wilfrid's arrival into this world is carefully described in the sources. The crucial first moment, having been blown off course, is Wilfrid's reception by 'King' Aldgisl. There is no scene-setting, negotiations, or people prostrating themselves in deference as there is elsewhere in Stephanus's work. Aldgisl simply receives the bishop 'with honour'. It is an innocuous statement in its own right, but one which brings with it literary baggage from both across the *Vita Wilfridi* and elsewhere. In Stephanus's narrative, the account of Wilfrid's re-election to the see of York follows his 'honourable reception' by King Oswiu (VW 15) and the subsequent restoration of the church culminates with a comparison to Samuel: 'then the words of the Lord concerning Samuel and all saints was fulfilled in him: "Them that honour me", He said, "I will honour"; for he was beloved and honoured both by God and by all the people' (VW 16). In other sources, we find that 'good' exiles such as Wilfrid, expelled from their homes by unjust rulers, are often 'received honourably' by the righteous elsewhere. To cite just two examples, one finds that Jerome emphasised the 'honourable' reception of Athanasius of Alexandria, the lead opponent of the Arian heresy in the early fourth century, by Maximianus of Trier, while Jonas of Bobbio stressed how the Arian Lombard King Agilulf received St Columbanus in identical terms. Stephanus's choice of language, whether directly or indirectly imitating a particular source, immediately conforms to the colouring of similar statements in which a holy man is forced into exile but is received well. The importance of the turn of phrase is exposed in Bede's retelling of the story, because it is nearly the only turn of phrase which was not altered from Stephanus's original. Both Stephanus and Bede wished to maintain the implication that Wilfrid was a good exile who deserved to be honoured.

The honourable treatment of exiles in Stephanus's narrative extended to their protection from their enemies or *inimici*, a term consistently contrasted with Wilfrid's own *amici*. Aldgisl was approached by messengers sent by Duke Ebroin with promises of 'a full measure of gold solidi' in exchange for Wilfrid. Yet the king had already invited Wilfrid to feast (*epulari*) with his followers, reinforcing the bond of friendship through communal eating. The king read the letter out to all the assembled feasters, again indicating the communal responsibility towards the exile. Then, tearing the letter up and burning it before his men, he ordered the messenger to tell King Theuderic that: 'So may the Creator of all things rend and destroy the life and lands of him who perjures himself before God and breaks the pact he has made. Even thus may he be torn to pieces and burn to ashes!' (VW 27). The Christian content of Aldgisl's words, of course, expose the extent to which this is a hagiographical construction. Moreover, the use of direct speech is a dramatic device, here designed to contribute to the impression that the preservation or violation of pacts of friendship were the real issue here. Having received the exile honourably, the pagan king persisted in his good treatment of Wilfrid, and provided a lesson for Christian kings who had not treated the Northumbrian so well.

The themes outlined so far in the Frisian episode are reinforced by the story which immediately follows in the narrative, concerning Wilfrid's reception by King Dagobert II of Austrasia and the previously exiled king Perctarit of the Lombards. Wilfrid was again received 'with honour' by Dagobert, this time because Wilfrid and his friends had helped to restore the king to the throne (VW 28). Friendship needed to be preserved across borders and across circumstance. Wilfrid then continued from the Austrasian court to visit Perctarit, who recalled his own exile in his youth and how he had been treated well by the pagan king of the Huns. The parallel with Wilfrid's reception by Aldgisl is tangible here, as the two pagan kings are revealed to have treated exiles with more honour and respect than had either Ecgfrith or Grimoald in the exiles' homelands. The constructs of Stephanus's story may be highlighted by comparison with the no-less stylised account of Perctarit by Paul the Deacon, which suggests instead that the Lombard and Hunnish kings had not enjoyed friendship for long at all (Bethmann and Waitz 1878, 142). Stephanus's overall theme is nevertheless reinforced through the Perctarit story, as when the king's Hunnish protector was similarly invited to betray his friend for 'a full measure of gold solidi', he declared that 'his gods would cut short his life if he broke his promise to them by this foul deed' (VW 28). Again, promises should not be broken, especially for money. Stephanus returns to this theme later too, writing that when Wilfrid found himself in exile in Sussex, the pagan king Æthelwealh 'promised under a treaty of peace such friendship that none of his enemies should strike terror into him by the threatening of the sword of any warlike foe, or make void the treaty thus inaugurated between them by the offer of rewards and gifts' (VW 41). The elements of a pact, friendship and protection, all being offered to the hero by a pagan king, again offer a lesson for the descendants of kings who had been so hostile to Wilfrid.

The importance of honour runs deeper in Stephanus's narrative overall, and helps us to understand his frames of reference as a writer. In particular, the Frisian episode has its natural antithesis in the story of Wilfrid's imprisonment by Ecgfrith in 680 (indeed one might wonder whether Aldgisl – whose name means 'old hostage' – was little more than a literary creation in that context). Here, Wilfrid was imprisoned explicitly 'without honour' and without access to his friends (VW 34, 35). The temporary denial of honour and friendship had parallels on the continent, where it was a common strategy for giving politically sensitive individuals a 'time out' from which they could be readmitted to political life (de Jong 2001). Stephanus, however, pushes the imagery of the imprisonment further by adding that Wilfrid's light was hidden in dark dungeons and that 'lamps were not lit to honour the night', thus extending a metaphor to conceptualise the treatment of the saint. When the wife of the local reeve fell ill, however, Wilfrid was briefly released to heal her and was thereafter treated with honour by the couple until the threat of the king's wrath forced them to put him back in chains (VW 37–38). In these examples, honour was denied through the imprisonment but could be established anew. The impact was the partial disruption of Wilfrid's different circles: his subjects were dispersed and his friends were not only barred from visiting but kept ignorant of his treatment. Wilfrid's subsequent exile allowed him to regain honour and make new friends. If one wanted to think of Stephanus as a Germanic writer, as many have, one could think of Tacitus's comment that Germanic societies put great stock in always having their homes open to visitors (Hutton and Warmington 1914, 162–7). But for Stephanus as a Latin writer in eighth-century Northumbria, his model is more arguably the Rule of Benedict, which prescribed that all guests should be received with honour (de Vogüé 1972, 610–17). To a monastic writer like Stephanus, who so clearly valued the Rule in his work, this was perhaps more important than the social etiquette of the laity.

Wilfrid's political exile makes the Benedictine model for receiving guests particularly pertinent. There are several instances of the verb *peregrinere* and its cognates in Stephanus's work. Historians have taken the occurrence of these words in insular contexts to refer specifically to Irish ideals of wandering asceticism, forsaking homeland, kin and friends, but these can also reflect hagiographical motifs of asceticism (compare Angenendt 1982, and Palmer 2009). There was, either way, a long history of tension between unregulated wandering and the *stabilitas loci* of monasticism. *Peregrini* appear in the *Regula s. Benedicti* as 'good' wanderers, but in the prevailing mood of the early medieval West 'goodness' needed to be argued for and numerous *vitae* – including the *Vita Bonifatii* – adopted the rhetoric of *peregrinatio* to defend the activities of their saints (Levison 1905, 15). The Wilfridian interest in the *Regula s. Benedicti* no doubt made them aware of such issues. Spending significant amounts of time wandering in exile, therefore, might have grated with some of Wilfrid's followers' sensibilities. When challenged in Francia about the decision to help Dagobert II reclaim the throne, Wilfrid argues that there were parallels with the Israelites for taking in exiles and pilgrims (VW 33). When Wilfrid and his entourage arrive in Canterbury to meet Berhtwald, the nephew of King Æthelræd of Mercia, they are described as 'honourable men' on *peregrinatio* whilst 'in exile' (VW 40). When Wilfrid finally returned to Northumbria in 686/7 from his 'honourable exile', he had his possessions restored to him 'like John returning to Ephesus' (VW 44). The political fact of the exile could readily be folded into the hagiographical and Benedictine world of the *peregrinus* in order to find a language to justify Wilfrid's wanderings. Within this theme, the Frisian episode and the king's reception of Wilfrid again seem to owe a great deal to particular discourses about exile and friendship.

A central claim of Stephanus's Frisian episode is that Wilfrid began the conversion of the Frisians, a task which Willibrord is credited with bringing to fruition. It is naturally repeated by Bede, for whom Willibrord was something of a symbol of the spiritual progress the English had made since the *adventus Saxonum*. Again Stephanus's story does not stand in isolation within the text, and again it needs to be compared to the conversion of the South Saxons. In Stephanus's version, Wilfrid's preaching coincides with a plentiful catch of fish, which affords the holy man the opportunity to preach. The conversion of the South Saxons, on the other hand, proceeded because of the reception given to Wilfrid by the king. Here there is clear evidence for Bede playing with the story, insofar as he reverses their key features: Wilfrid's success among the South Saxons was because of a good harvest, while the work in Frisia was facilitated by the king. Goffart noted the similarity between the stories but argued that it was impossible to know if it was deliberate (Goffart 1988, 318–19). If we were to accept that it was a conscious decision by Bede, then we should avoid the Goffartian conclusion that Bede was attempting to undermine Stephanus's version of events; rather, the transplanting of the story serves to preserve a fuller role for Willibrord as the apostle of the Frisians, while transposing an excellent conversion narrative within the overarching Wilfridian story to a point in which it could still serve a useful purpose. This demonstrates Bede's sensitivity towards balancing the concerns for good storytelling, putting Wilfrid in context, and preserving the essence of Stephanus's construction. Bede does not edit Wilfrid down here, but instead adjusts the structure of his narrated career in order to bring in other characters worthy of greater recognition.

Bede's treatment of Stephanus's story has a further subtle significance. Stephanus had stated that Wilfrid 'baptized many thousands of common people in the name of the Lord'. Bede's rendering of the same sentence is 'he preached Christ to them, teaching the word of truth to many thousands' (HE V, 19). The change is not superficial: the wording now more closely echoed a comment in Bede's own *Commentary on the Acts of the Apostles* (Laistner 1983, 23), which he expanded upon by saying that teachers of the church, 'coming at the end of the world, also preach first to ailing Israel and afterwards to the gentiles'. In Bede's mind, then, Wilfrid was fulfilling the role of the *doctores ecclesiae* by preaching to the gentile Frisians. Again, it does not seem that Bede was systematically 'diluting' Wilfrid, as Goffart argued. If anything, Bede had found a way to keep the story short while escalating the possible significance of the hero through the colouring of the narrative. Indeed, this turn of phrase provided the basis of Alcuin's first poetic celebration of the Frisian mission in the York

Poem, with the refrain 'and soon he converted thousands of the people to Christ' repeated both for Wilfrid and later for Willibrord (Godman 1982, 52, 85). Although Willibrord could be celebrated for building churches and ordaining priests for Frisia, for Wilfrid Alcuin extended a metaphor of sowing seeds to bear fruit in barren lands before exclaiming 'and [his] fame was praised throughout the world'. Notably, for all Wilfrid's professed achievements it was this missionary episode, alongside the evangelisation of the South Saxons, which Alcuin focused upon as the defining dimension of the saint's reputation (*fama*). Wilfrid's work as a missionary was full of apostolic overtones in the Bedan tradition, which accentuated rather than diminished Stephanus's version.

The escalation is further apparent if one looks at another difference between Stephanus and Bede concerning the mission. Curiously, Stephanus is silent regarding a story Bede tells in which the missionary Swithberht was consecrated as bishop for the Frisians by Wilfrid while Willibrord was in Rome obtaining the same office, after which Swithberht relocated to the Pippinid foundation of Kaiserwerth (HE V. 11). While Swithberht's actions could be taken as a provocative act against Willibrord, such an interpretation sits ill at ease with Bede's positive assessment of the bishop, his commemoration in the Echternach calendar associated with Willibrord, and the involvement of Wilfrid in the story. Alternative scenarios were proposed by both Levison (1946, 58) and Schäferdiek (1994, 192–4), the first suggesting that Wilfrid and Swithberht were simply expanding the field of missionary work, and the second arguing that Bede had misdated Swithberht's consecration from the later 680s and that Swithberht had really been established as a pre-Willibrordian Frisian bishop. If one were to read that chapter of Bede's work in the context of the author's 'literary arguments', one could probably make the case that it amplifies the activities of the English abroad by creating a second pro-Pippinid Willibrord in the wake of the gloomier story about the martyrdom of the two Hewalds, murdered for working without support, in the previous chapter (HE V, 10). Stephanus, on the other hand, may have felt that Swithberht added nothing to the outlining of his cause, which reinforces the impression that he only mentioned the Aldgisl incident to develop his plot in relation to a particular theme. Neither Bede nor Stephanus were attempting to relate 'the whole story', only those parts which fitted their immediate purposes. The Swithberht case also invites us to ask how far we can project Wilfrid into the continuation of the Frisian mission. In an authorial note introducing a story about St Oswald's relics, Bede reveals that his story had been told to Wilfrid and Acca when they stayed with Willibrord en route to Rome. But in the context of Wilfrid's career, the bishop was probably hurrying to Rome after his excommunication in *circa* 702 rather than exercising an interest in mission (VW 50). It is not even certain that Willibrord would have been in Frisia, as Stephanus mentions that Wilfrid's route took him through Meaux (VW 56), while charter evidence shows Willibrord active in business between Trier and Thuringia in these years. Stephanus certainly had nothing more to add on Willibrord or mission in this case, as it did not add to the urgency of Wilfrid's final years. It is Stephanus, not Bede, who seems to have cut back the involvement of Wilfrid in the Frisian mission after 679.

We should now be in a position to understand some of the key themes of Stephanus's work as revealed by a contextualisation of the Frisian episode. The inauguration of a long process of conversion had accidental beginnings and, as reported by Stephanus, served primarily to illustrate the apostolic character of Wilfrid and thus to accentuate the poverty of his treatment in Northumbria. That Bede developed this theme further, and added further stories about Wilfrid's involvement in mission, shows that it was Bede rather than Stephanus (and Wilfrid?) for whom Frisia mattered as a theatre for Northumbrian missionary activity. Stephanus's narrative was extended to incorporate a scene in which Aldgisl, having become friends with Wilfrid, refused to hand the exile over to his enemies; and the whole scene, when compared to the treatment of Wilfrid by other kings, and particularly in the language used in those stories, demonstrates that Stephanus was keen to highlight repeatedly the importance of honour and friendship regardless of circumstance. Such a reading of Stephanus's text has striking relevance to the theme of a letter written by Aldhelm to Wilfrid's abbots, probably around the same time as Wilfrid fled to Frisia (Lapidge and Herren 1979, 150–1). It is an exhortation to the abbots not to abandon their exiled lord, who has fled to 'transmarine kingdoms'. But it is also an occasion on which Aldhelm used his famous bees metaphor to emphasise the importance of community, this time apparently casting Wilfrid as a king bee leading his company of friends – *sodalis*, the same word used in Columbanian circles to denote community – out of a winter camp and back again if adversity struck. Stephanus's stories may have been designed to a similar end, this time reinforcing community through the bonds of honour and friendship in the absence of the recently deceased holy man.

Forgetting Wilfrid's Mission in Frisia

A surprising feature of Frisian historical traditions from the eighth and ninth centuries is the absence of Wilfrid. Paul Fouracre's (2008) recent demonstration that Stephanus's work was unknown on the continent until after the seventeenth century may partially explain this, but it is almost certain that Bede's *Ecclesiastical History* was known. This may have been through the agency of St Liudger (d. 809), whose family dominated the early history of Christian Frisia. Liudger was educated by Alcuin in York in his youth and may have become familiar with Bede's works there (Gerschow 2005). When he returned to his family in Utrecht he took books with him, one of which may have been the copy of Bede's work which is now only a fragment in Münster's Staatsbibliothek. Liudger did not, however, take his historical and literary cues from Bede in his one extant composition, *Vita Gregorii abbatis* (*c*.800), about his teacher Gregory of Utrecht. Liudger's debt was to the more recent hagiography of Alcuin and Willibald, and indeed it seems that Alcuin must have sent copies of his *Vita Willibrordi* to Liudger soon after composition (Wood 2001, 111–12). This may have been a crucial factor in the development of hagiographical traditions in Frisia because, unlike in his York Poem, Alcuin omitted the statements of Stephanus and Bede that Willibrord was continuing missionary work begun by Wilfrid. His hand may have been guided in part by the Irish hagiographer whose text Alcuin was rewriting, but since the original is lost it is hard to tell. It may nevertheless be possible to identify the important frames of reference for hagiographers such as Liudger in order to gain an understanding of why Wilfrid's story may not have fitted.

Liudger's omission of Wilfrid's role in the conversion of Frisia is likely a product of his background as a man of Utrecht. Insofar as he provides a narrative of the conversion of the region, it is a narrative which places Utrecht at the heart of significant developments in the North, with few other centres afforded any mention. The mission also began only with Willibrord as the first institutional figure of Frisia, as he was made bishop of the town. Willibrord's direct successors were claimed by Liudger to be St Boniface and Abbot Gregory, not because they were bishops of Utrecht, but because they had continued Willibrord's work, and had done so based in his home town. In this context, only Willibrord could truly be the apostle of the Frisians – Wilfrid's missionary work was not only an accident, but institutionally insignificant, especially if we remember that we do not even know where Wilfrid encountered Aldgisl. Moreover, when Frisian and Westphalian hagiographical traditions were extended in the ninth century through the three lives of Liudger, the *Vita Willehadi* and the *Vita Lebuini antiquior*, the contribution of further English missionaries was readily incorporated into the later parts of the story, but only as continuators of the enterprise begun by Willibrord and Boniface (Wood 2001). These two figures, and these two alone, were the great saints of the early medieval mission. This point must be set alongside evidence for the cult of saints in Liudger's foundations. A litany associated with Werden, now Cologne, Dombibliothek, 106, includes on folio 73v Boniface among a selection of ancient martyr saints, and Willibrord alongside the Frankish and Irish confessors of the Merovingian age, adding only Lebuin and Liudger himself on folio 74r from recent missionary history. More solidly than any extant calendar, it provides the kind of snapshot of the Frankish cult of saints that we might expect on the basis of the saints' lives that we have from the seventh and eighth centuries. In that context, it is not difficult to see that without a continental cult site or saint's life, and no institutional impact upon the Frisian Church, there would have been little to recommend a cult of Wilfrid.

A slightly different perspective on the early Christian history of Utrecht is provided by the anonymous *Vita altera Bonifatii*, which may have been written in the 840s but which is certainly not in its original form now (Levison 1905, lii–liii). The key difference between this text and that of Liudger's is that the author promoted the significance of St Martin's church in Utrecht, while Liudger had promoted his family's favoured church of St Saviour's, where Liudger is even said to have slept at night. The St Martin's priest was, interestingly, more explicit than Liudger in naming Bede's *Ecclesiastical History* as a source of inspiration. Indeed, he mentions the 'sweet smell' which emanated from Britain and which had been carried forward in the saintly works narrated by Bede, identifying Fursey, Willibrord and Boniface as the major protagonists (Levison 1905, 66). Boniface was not, of course, mentioned in Bede's actual text, but he was mentioned in the continuations which accompanied some versions – and indeed it is likely from orthography that the Münster fragment of the *Ecclesiastical History* mentioned above was from such a line of tradition. Fursey, meanwhile, may have been mentioned because he was a saint referred to by Bede who had a functioning cult on the continent, including mention in the Werden litany, even though he had no significance to Frisian history specifically. But here, more so than in the work of Liudger, the omission of Wilfrid speaks volumes, because Wilfrid was overlooked even by someone drawing attention to stories of missionary work in a history which mentioned Wilfrid as missionary.

We can only really speculate about the possible reasons for why the St Martin's monk remained silent about Wilfrid, although we can in the process point to some further features of early Frisian history. We could, for example, note Wilfrid's inauspicious role in Frankish politics. The historical context for the story of Aldgisl refusing to hand over Wilfrid to Theuderic was that Wilfrid had helped to impose Dagobert II, a rival originally exiled to Ireland, on the Austrasian throne. Our only source for what happened is Stephanus, who wrote that Dagobert had subsequently been murdered for behaving like the biblical Roboam: he had preferred the counsel of his own men (from Ireland?) and imposed heavy taxes. Whatever the details of this revolt, the political beneficiaries were the dukes Martin of Laon and Pippin II of Herstal, who took control of Austrasia in the absence of any kings, and who then fought against King Theuderic and Ebroin (Fouracre and Gerberding 1996, 91). The impression from Stephanus is that Theuderic and Ebroin were keen to make a scapegoat of Wilfrid to appease Austrasian factions, although the complete silence of Frankish sources on the matter makes this impression difficult to evaluate. Wilfrid's role in the Dagobert affair had left him tainted by association, with potential enemies from both the Merovingian and Pippinid families as a result. As Dagobert's reign was quickly forgotten in historical records, it is unlikely that this would have had a long-lasting effect, but it could easily account for the apparent reticence about Wilfrid in Willibrord's circle noted by Fouracre (2008, 87, and in this volume).

Wilfrid was, in the end, a saint from another world. He might in many ways be compared to St Boniface, who was well recognised as a great figure in his own day on both sides of the Channel, but whose cult among the English appears to have floundered quickly in the absence of either hagiography or relics on that side of the Channel. Wilfrid, on the other hand, was fundamentally a saint based in England (Mostert 1999, 11). There was space for Wilfrid's name to be inserted into a couple of Carolingian calendars in the ninth century, including one from Hildesheim where there was evident interest in the missionaries to Frisia and Westphalia, but no more (Bischoff 1952). Whether many of the continental scribes knew who this Wilfrid even was is another matter, as is illustrated by the same Hildesheim calendar which includes feast dates for the two Hewalds on consecutive days because two different exemplars used spelt their names differently. What had started to matter in the ninth century anyway was the listing of the names of the saints as an appeal to the holy which operated outside the hagiographical or historiographical (Lifshitz 2006). It is somehow fitting that commemoration of Wilfrid as a saint on the continent could only proceed once his sanctity had become detached from his career on Earth.

Conclusion

Wilfrid's missionary work in Frisia inaugurated the 'Anglo-Saxon missions to the continent'. Nevertheless, it was rarely valued for that significance outside of the work of Bede and, to a lesser extent, Alcuin. Stephanus made capital of the association to portray his hero as an apostolic figure; yet his real concern as a hagiographer was to provide lessons about the importance of honour and friendship within interlocking Christian communities, and he did not elaborate where he could have done on Wilfrid's subsequent interest in Frisia. In Frisia itself Bede's account, with its emphasis on mission, was available to early hagiographers, yet they preferred to concentrate on the role of figures with continental hagiographies and cultic sites. Both sides reveal the centrality of institution to the cult of saints in the eighth and ninth centuries. Wilfrid was a significant figure in Northumbria after his death because he left behind a community who needed to make sense of the experiences of the previous fifty years while re-establishing the bonds of honour and friendship which had been broken in that time. This is the real significance of Stephanus's hagiography. In Frisia, meanwhile, ecclesiastical bonds and Christian communities began only in the days of Willibrord and Boniface, rendering Wilfrid's effectively 'prehistorical' adventure meaningless. Wilfrid's Frisian episode, far from exposing the close ties between England and the continent, in the end demonstrates the extent to which they could be separate.

Acknowledgement
I am grateful to Joanna Thornborough for helping to develop and clarify many aspects of this paper.

18: *Wilfrid and the Celts*

T. M. CHARLES-EDWARDS

My title, 'Wilfrid and the Celts', might suggest a misconception, which I must guard against at the start. Wilfrid knew that he had to do with Britons, Irish, and Picts, but we can be confident that he had no notion of Celts (peoples who spoke a Celtic language). I have, however, a particular reason for addressing the wider question of Wilfrid and the Celts, as opposed to narrower questions, such as Wilfrid and the Irish or the Britons: parts of my topic have been most admirably covered by Clare Stancliffe's Jarrow Lecture (Stancliffe 2004) and her Whithorn Lecture (Stancliffe 2007). I shall concentrate, first, on the relationship between Wilfrid and what Bede called 'the episcopacy of the Irish' under which Wilfrid grew up, the period from 635 to 664 during which the bishops of the Northumbrians were Irishmen sent from Iona. Wilfrid, of course, played a major role in bringing this episcopacy of the Irish to an end. The second aspect of Wilfrid's career I propose to examine is his attitude to the Britons, Picts and Irish and the relationship of that attitude to Northumbrian power.

Wilfrid was of noble background, but his approach as a boy to court, one of the crucial rites of passage for the seventh-century Northumbrian aristocracy, was to Eanflæd, the queen, rather than to Oswiu, the king. Moreover, his service was not within a royal household; instead he was instructed by Eanflæd to serve a nobleman called Cudda, who was afflicted by 'a paralytic infirmity' and wished to enter the monastic community at Lindisfarne (VW 2). Cudda became a monk, but Wilfrid did not; yet, so we are told by Stephen, he strove to live like a monk, learnt the psalms by heart and studied 'several books' (VW 2). He was not to be tonsured for about ten years, until his period in Lyons on his way back from his first visit to Rome (VW 6). The chronology of his life is not entirely certain, but it is clear enough that he began his period of service at Lindisfarne about 648 and thus in the time of Aidan, the first of the three Irish bishops of the Northumbrians, who died on 31 August 651 (Plummer 1896, ii. 316–20). Although Aidan, as bishop, was on the move round his diocese, Wilfrid can hardly have avoided seeing him in the three years 648–51. If we follow Bede's Prose Life of Cuthbert, Aidan will have appointed an abbot to rule the community at Lindisfarne, but we do not know who this person was in 648 (Colgrave 1940, 206–9). He should also have witnessed the burial of Aidan in the monastic cemetery at Lindisfarne.

So far as the Irish were concerned, Wilfrid's first contact with them was, therefore, with Aidan and the other monks of the mission to the Northumbrians that had come from Iona about a year after Wilfrid's birth (634). His first contact with Britons is not known, but the best guess is that there were enough Britons living within Northumbria at that period for it to be likely that he would have come across them from early in his life. Stephen's *Life of Wilfrid* does not reveal where his home was; and in 634 some parts of Northumbria would probably have had a much higher population of Britons than, for example, the heart of Deira in the former East Riding. Wilfrid, however, made his approach as a fourteen-year-old to Eanflæd, Oswiu's queen, in 648, at a date when Deira was ruled by Oswine, of the rival dynasty to which Edwin had belonged: Oswine ruled Deira for seven years, 644–51 (HE III, 14). Although, therefore, Wilfrid subsequently came to prominence in Deira, when he was given land by Oswiu's son, Alhfrith, to establish a monastery at Stamford and then took over the monastery at Ripon, he was probably not a Deiran himself. As soon as Wilfrid became abbot of Ripon, he is likely to have been in contact with Britons, even if he was not familiar with them from an earlier date. As for the Picts, however, any significant contact followed from his consecration as bishop of York.

Not long after Aidan's death, and thus early in the time of Fínán, his successor, Wilfrid made the fateful request that he be allowed to go to Rome.[1] From Rome and from Lyons, he would return to Northumbria with the firm conviction that those who followed the so-called 'Celtic Easter' were heretics and schismatics. From the letter of the pope-elect John, partially reproduced in Bede's *Ecclesiastical History*, we know that in 640 Rome considered the Celtic Easter to amount to heresy and schism (HE II, 19; for some evidence on what Bede left out of this letter, see Ó Cróinín, 1982; Harrison, 1984); and there is no reason to think that this opinion had been modified since. Indeed, since it is implied by the letter of Pope Vitalian to Oswiu *c.*667 (HE III, 29); and since Archbishop Theodore appears to have arrived in Britain in 669 with the same belief, there is every reason to think that this judgement remained in place when Wilfrid was in Rome *c.* 654.

Stephen, in the *Life of Wilfrid*, uses such phrases as 'the schismatics of Britain and Ireland' or 'Quartodecimans like the Britons and the Irish' or just 'Quartodecimans' (VW 5, 12, 14, 15). In origin, 'Quartodeciman', literally 'Fourteenther', was a name given to those Christians who celebrated Easter at the same time as the Jewish passover, on the fourteenth day of the lunar month, the

---

[1] VW 3. An aspect of the text at this point is missed by Colgrave's translation: the text says that 'it entered into the heart of this youth *apellare et uidere sedem apostoli Petri* – not just 'to pay a visit' (Colgrave) but 'to appeal to, and to look upon the see of the apostle Peter'. This sentence also works better syntactically if one omits, with MS C, the *et* after *ascendit*. Wilfrid proposed to *ap[p]ellare sedem apostoli Petri* in the belief that, by his pilgrimage, he would receive from Rome 'a release from every bond of sin'. It was, in other words, a penitential pilgrimage.

day of the full moon, and thus on whatever day of the week that happened to occur. The underlying issue, of fundamental importance to the early Church, was quite how Jewish could a Christian be. However, it was widely believed in the seventh century that the condemnation of the Quartodecimans by the Council of Nicaea in 325 had also embraced those who always celebrated Easter on a Sunday but, by allowing Easter Sunday to be as early as the fourteenth day of the lunar month, would, on occasion, celebrate Easter at the same time as the Jewish passover. They also, and not just the true Quartodecimans, were deemed to have rejected the decree of the Council of Nicaea and were thus schismatics and heretics (HE II, 19; III, 25). It should be noted that Stephen refers to the Britons and the Irish as examples of Quartodecimans. He is suggesting that others also were Quartodecimans, not just the Britons and the Irish. In the context of *The Life of Wilfrid* this is unlikely to be a reference specifically to the Picts, though they would have been included. The Quartodecimans that concerned Wilfrid immediately after he had become a bishop were primarily English: if we believe Stephen, the Quartodecimans left in Northumbria after the third Irish bishop, Colmán, had left were responsible for encouraging King Oswiu to prefer Chad to Wilfrid as the new bishop of the Northumbrians (VW 14). In most of Stephen's *Life*, therefore, Wilfrid's attitude to the Irish, Britons, and Picts was not governed, at least explicitly, by their nationality but by theological considerations allied with ecclesiastical politics.

The status of the Britons, the northern Irish, and the Picts as schismatics and heretics at the time when Wilfrid was consecrated a bishop is fundamental to relations between the peoples in the late-seventh century. We can approach the situation in the early period, between 664, the date of the Synod of Whitby, in which Wilfrid was the spokesman for the Roman party, and 669, when he was installed as bishop of York, by considering briefly the issue of the re-consecration of Chad. The accounts by Stephen and Bede are notoriously difficult because of the issues both political and ecclesiastical that lie, half-hidden, behind them. According to Bede's account in Book III of the *Ecclesiastical History*, Alhfrith son of Oswiu sent Wilfrid to Gaul to be consecrated bishop 'for himself and for his people' (HE III, 28); Alhfrith's people can be identified with the Deirans, since he controlled Ripon, north-west of York, and Stamford to the east (VW 8). When, says Bede, Wilfrid lingered in Gaul, King Oswiu, namely the father of Alhfrith, 'imitated the energy of his son and sent Chad to Kent to be consecrated bishop of York' (HE III, 28). However, Archbishop Deusdedit was already dead, and Chad, accompanied by Oswiu's priest, Eadhæd, moved on to Wessex, where Chad was consecrated by Wine, bishop of the West Saxons and two bishops 'from the British people, who, as has often been noted, celebrate Easter Sunday contrary to canonical custom from the fourteenth to the twentieth day of the lunar month'. What is only just lying beneath the surface of Bede's account is that Alhfrith had rebelled against his father within a year or two of the Synod of Whitby and had been removed from authority (HE III, 14; Mayr-Harting 1972, 108). Wilfrid, however, had been closely linked with Alhfrith and his position in Northumbria was thus uncertain.

Stephen, naturally, does not so much as allude to such matters. He also has a different account of the consecration of Chad. For example, according to Bede (HE III, 23) Chad had been made abbot of Lastingham on the death of his brother, Cedd, in the plague of 664; but, according to Stephen (VW 14), when Chad was made bishop he had just come from Ireland, which might suggest that he was still a Quartodeciman. First, before the idea of consecrating Chad had even been conceived, Wilfrid had made a declaration to Oswiu and Alhfrith proposing that he should go to Gaul for consecration, because there were no acceptable bishops in Britain available (VW 12):

> Now there are here in Britain many bishops whom it is not for me to criticize, but I know for a fact that they are Quartodecimans like the Britons and the Irish. Men have been ordained by them whom the Apostolic See does not receive into communion, neither them nor those who involve themselves with schismatics.

Subsequently, King Oswiu, 'moved by envy', was persuaded by the Quarto-deciman party to allow Chad to be consecrated to York (VW 14). Stephen says nothing explicitly about the mode of Chad's consecration; we are merely left to understand that, since there were no acceptable bishops left in Britain, Chad must have been consecrated by those who were unacceptable.

In Stephen's *Life of Wilfrid*, it is clear that Archbishop Theodore rejected the validity of Chad's consecration. Theodore's action in re-consecrating Chad so that he could become bishop of the Mercians presupposed that his first consecration, which involved the participation of two British bishops (HE III, 28), was rendered null and void because the Britons were heretics and schismatics; indeed, according to Stephen's *Life of Wilfrid*, Chad was re-ordained to all the grades of the Church (VW 15):

> So a friendly arrangement was made with that true servant of God, Chad, who in all things obeyed the bishops: they thereupon consecrated him fully to the said see through all the ecclesiastical degrees. (*per omnes gradus ecclesiasticos ad sedem praedictam plene eum ordinauerunt*)

By implication, no previous ordination in the period that Bede described as 'the episcopacy of the Irish' was accepted as effective (HE IV, 2, and III, 28 for the earlier consecration, by which time Chad was already a priest). Bede's account of the same action is more guarded, but it does not contradict Stephen's statement (HE IV, 2):

> Among these he made it clear to Bishop Chad that his consecration
> had not been regular, whereupon the latter humbly replied ... When
> Theodore heard his humble reply, he said that he ought not to give
> up his office; but he completed his ordination a second time after
> the catholic manner (*sed ipse ordinationem eius denuo catholica
> ratione consummauit*).

The verb *consummauit* 'completed' suggests, indeed, that Chad's orders below
the level of bishop were acknowledged as valid, but not his episcopal
consecration (the one in which British bishops were involved). However, it only
suggests such an interpretation; there is no necessary incompatibility with
Stephen's account. Similarly, the phrase *catholica ratione* might be taken to
suggest that there had been something wrong with the way Chad was
consecrated as opposed to the persons who consecrated him. If *catholica ratio*
merely disallowed the participation of heretical bishops, Bede would be agreeing,
as we shall see, with the early, Greek-influenced Theodore, which is improbable.
It is perhaps more likely that Bede was avoiding being unduly specific.

The *Penitentials* derived from Theodore's teaching also make it clear that
the followers of the Celtic Easter were deemed to be heretics (Finsterwalder
1929, 323–4). Clare Stancliffe has, however, made a persuasive case that two
views are represented in canons preserved in the collections setting out
Theodore's teaching: one set of canons she calls 'the Penance Group', the other
'the Reconciliation Group' (Stancliffe 2004, 12–15). The Penance Group is
explicit in regarding those who did not follow the canonical Easter as heretics;
but the Reconciliation Group only implies that they were schismatics. Similarly,
the Penance Group denounces prayer for, celebrating with, or venerating the
relics of such heretics. The separation between the orthodox and the heretics
was to be absolute. The Penance Group requires re-ordination but the
Reconciliation Group allows someone to be merely confirmed in his orders,
provided he is penitent and of blameless life. Finally, the basis for the
requirement of re-ordination, although contrary to western practice, was to be
found in a canon law collection of the Greek Church, in which Theodore had
been educated, a link which makes it all the more likely that in 669 Theodore did
indeed require re-ordination: Pope Vitalian had been afraid that Theodore might
be too Greek for the good of the English Church (HE IV, 1).

All this is critical for understanding the standpoint of Wilfrid as portrayed
by Stephen. Wilfrid, of course, did not have the Greek background that explained
Theodore's views. One may explain his unwillingness to be consecrated in Britain
by the much more general ban on consorting with heretics and schismatics. In
664 he might simply have believed that one should not be consecrated by those

who held heretical views on Easter, nor by those who, though not themselves Quartodecimans, consorted with them. At this point, he would have thought that Chad's consecration was valid even if it was wrong. Only in 669, when he became acquainted with Theodore and his Greek-inspired hard line on heretical and schismatical orders, would he have realized that Chad had not even been a real bishop. It is easy to read Stephen as suggesting that Wilfrid's reasons for not seeking consecration in Britain were the same as the reasons why Chad was re-ordained in 669; perhaps Stephen intended us to understand him in that way, but it would not be right to do so. In 665, therefore, Chad, who must have accepted the decision made at Whitby, did not think that he was thereby prevented from being consecrated by Wine and two British bishops; Wilfrid did take the view that he should not be involved with Quartodecimans in any such way; but he can hardly have thought that Chad's consecration was invalid until he came into contact with Theodore in 669.

There is reason to think that some harsh views were held in Northumbria even in the first two decades of the eighth century. Evidently, Stephen can tell the story of Chad's re-consecration without a hint that anything had changed since 669. But he was not alone in continuing to condemn the Britons, the Picts, and some, at least, of the Irish as Quartodecimans. One of the things that distinguishes Bede's Prose Life of Cuthbert from the earlier Lindisfarne Life is the detail of his account of Cuthbert's last days, death and burial. In the words he ascribes to Cuthbert before his death, the community of Lindisfarne is ordered not to have communion with those who do not celebrate Easter at the correct time. The latter are explicitly termed *scismatici* (Colgrave 1940, 284–5). Clare Stancliffe has drawn attention to the remarkable nature of the fear said by Bede to have been expressed by Cuthbert in this passage (Stancliffe 2007, 22–3, 28):

> But have no communion with those who depart from the unity of the catholic peace, either in not celebrating Easter at the proper time or in evil living. And you are to know and to remember that if necessity compels you to choose one of two evils, I should much rather that you take my bones from the tomb, carry them with you, and departing from this place dwell wherever God may ordain, than that in any way you should consent to iniquity and put your necks under the yoke of schismatics.

This was not long after the defeat and death of Ecgfrith at Nechtanesmere in 685, and it was plausible to think that 'the schismatics' might impose their yoke even on Lindisfarne, in the very heart of Bernicia. The tone of this passage is quite different from Bede's well-known description of the position during the episcopate of Aidan (HE III, 25):

This disagreement over Easter observance was patiently endured during Aidan's lifetime by all. They had openly accepted that, although he could not celebrate Easter contrary to the custom of those who had sent him, he nevertheless assiduously strived to perform deeds of faith, mercy and charity in the manner observed by all saints. And therefore he was deservedly loved by all, even by those who took an opposed view on Easter – and not only by those of lower rank: he was also held in veneration by the bishops, Honorius of the Kentishmen and Felix of the East Angles.

It is important to note Bede's phrase 'during Aidan's lifetime'. That contrasts with what he had written earlier in the chapter about Aidan's successor as bishop of the Northumbrians, Fínán: that the bishop's Easter observance was denounced in Northumbria by another Irishman, Rónán, and that the dispute made Fínán 'a fiercer and an open opponent of the truth'. This distinction allowed Bede both to maintain full support for the cult of Aidan as a model saintly bishop and to express his opposition to the paschal practices of all three bishops from Iona.

The consequences of the Synod of Whitby were worked out in two phases. In the first, the switch was made from one method of determining the date of Easter to the other. This does not seem to have been taken by those advising Oswiu to imply that the previous bishops of the Northumbrians, the Irishmen Aidan, Fínán, and Colmán had not been true bishops at all: they were just wrong rather than being heretical; and even those, such as Wilfrid, who thought that they were heretics, were not yet aware of Theodore's Greek-inspired under-standing that heretic clergy had to be re-ordained. Chad, as we have seen, saw no insurmountable problem in being consecrated by British bishops, even though Wilfrid preferred to go to Gaul. Two events – the arrival of Theodore and the placing of Wilfrid in his see of York in place of Chad – brought about a fundamental change: the Roman view now prevailed that the followers of the Celtic Easter were not just wrong but were also schismatics and heretical; and, because of Theodore's Greek background that view now necessitated a large-scale re-ordination of clergy previously ordained by those now deemed heretical, not just in Northumbria but also in Mercia, Lindsey, among the Middle Angles and in Essex. Nothing in our sources would lead us to suppose that the treatment of Chad was in any way exceptional. The principle followed by Theodore was clear, and there was no need for Bede or Stephen to list further examples apart from Chad: he was especially important as someone of acknowledged sanctity, with a cult supported by the Mercian kings.

As far as we know, the followers of the Celtic Easter continued to be regarded as heretics by those who agreed with Wilfrid right into the eighth century. There is not a hint in Stephen's *Life of Wilfrid* that any other view was possible. This is why he can quote Wilfrid as saying at the synod of *Ouestrae-felda* in 702 or 703, 'Was I not the first after the first eminent leaders sent by St Gregory to root out the poisonous weeds planted by the Irish?' (VW 47) This appears to be a reference to the parable of the wheat and the tares in which the tares were sown by the enemy (Matth. XIII: 24–30). The enemy in question in the parable was understood to be the Devil, bent on wrecking the labour of the farmer, God. Admittedly, in Matthew's Gospel the farmer tells his servants not to pull up the weeds until the time of the harvest; but, as Jerome explained in his commentary, this applied only to those whose iniquity was not manifest (Hurst and Adriaens 1969, 112): evident tares should be uprooted immediately. This phrase, 'the poisonous weeds planted by the Irish', was by far the harshest reference to them in the whole of Stephen's *Life of Wilfrid*. It was, however, consistent with a significant piece of negative evidence: although Wilfrid spent about four formative years at Lindisfarne, most of them during the episcopate of Aidan, the latter is never mentioned in the *Life*. The contrast with Bede's *Historia Ecclesiastica* is obvious (Thacker 1996) – except for one place. Towards the end of Book III Bede quoted two long passages from a letter of Pope Vitalian to Oswiu. The second passage looks forward to the day when the Pope can send a bishop 'with the instruction ... to root out in accordance with the will of God the tares sown by the enemy from the whole of your island' (HE III, 29). Here the reference to the parable is unambiguous; and here, too, the pope envisaged no waiting until the Day of Judgement.

Attitudes towards the old, pre-Synod of Whitby regime in the Northumbrian Church, namely what Bede called the episcopacy of the Irish, varied from outright hostility on the part of Wilfrid, to an increasingly modified hostility on the part of Theodore and finally to a qualified praise on the part of Bede. Clare Stancliffe has clarified the evidence of the penitential texts deriving from Theodore: what was clearly his original view – that Quartodecimans should be re-ordained – changed to a later view, that, if penitent, they should merely be reconciled. To judge by Stephen's *Life*, no such change was accepted by Wilfrid.

There was, however, a complicating factor, namely the rivalry between what one might call ecclesiastical lordships in late-seventh-century Northumbria. A crucial passage in Stephen's *Life of Wilfrid* has been elucidated for us by Catherine Cubitt, but it is worth considering briefly here (Cubitt 1989, 18–38). Before Wilfrid was expelled from his see of York in 678, his diocese extended throughout the entire territory ruled by Ecgfrith, king of the Northumbrians (VW 21). It therefore included at least some Pictish territory to the north of the Forth and, since 675, Lindsey to the south of the Humber. His responsibilities were, therefore, of colossal extent – roughly, in modern terms, from the Tay to the Wash. When he was expelled, this territory was divided between, from north to south, a diocese for those Picts subject to Ecgfrith, a diocese for the Bernicians, between the Forth and the Tees, a diocese for the Deirans, with its see at York, and a diocese for Lindsey (HE IV, 12). Wilfrid appealed to Rome against the way his diocese had been taken from him. There were several grounds for the appeal, but one of them was that Archbishop Theodore had consecrated to 'his own *loca* belonging to his *episcopatus*' 'three bishops found from elsewhere and not from the subjects of that *parrochia*'; and the effect of their actions was that King Ecgfrith and Archbishop Theodore had, 'like robbers, deprived him of the possessions with which, for God's sake, kings had endowed him' (VW 24). This is clarified, and at the same time further complicated, by the rather different terms of the appeal Wilfrid is said to have made in Rome: if he was to get back his old bishopric (*episcopatus*), 'the intruders' should be driven out *de pristinis parrochiis ecclesiae, cui ego indignus vester famulus praefui* 'from the former *parrochiae* (plural) of the church over which I, your unworthy servant, have been presiding'; even if new bishops were to be consecrated to parts of his old diocese, 'the intruders' should be driven out and the new bishops should be chosen 'from our own clergy' (VW 30). Now, it is abundantly evident that Stephen was using *parrochia* in at least two different senses. One was a normal sense of the word, as found in the acts of the Synod of Hertford: there *parrochia* means diocese, or perhaps rather the territory and people attached to the see (HE IV. 5, caps. 2, where it is roughly equivalent to *plebs* 'people', and 6). The cautionary note is because of the older sense, still preserved in Hiberno-Latin of the period, in which the *urbs* is distinct from the *parochia* (*parrochia*) attached to it. The other use of *parrochia* in the singular, however, was equivalent to Wilfrid's own properties and his supporters, both clergy and monks. This has to be so, since everyone would have known that the bishops consecrated by Theodore in 678, Eata for the Bernicians, Bosa for the Deirans, and Eadhæd for Lindsey, all belonged to Wilfrid's *parrochia* in the first sense. Taking *parrochia* as diocese, these bishops were not 'found from elsewhere' (*aliunde inuentos*) and were not 'intruders' (*inuasores*). The use of the plural *parrochiae* – *parrochiae* said to belong to Wilfrid's former *ecclesia*, namely York – is possibly suggestive of usage in Frankish Gaul, where *parrochia* was used for the rough equivalent of what historians of Anglo-Saxon England have called a minster church; in that case, three senses of the word mingle in Stephen's text. His account only makes sense if we recognize the systematic ambiguity of the word *parrochia*. Because Plummer did not notice the ambiguity, he was able to dismiss this part of Wilfrid's appeal on the grounds that he could assemble a list of bishops promoted from other dioceses (Plummer 1896, II, 324); but that is not what Stephen, and Wilfrid, meant, for one of Wilfrid's abbots from Mercia would have been part of his *parrochia* in the second sense, even though outside his *parrochia* in the first sense.

It is an ambiguity that must make any historian of early-medieval Ireland sit up and pay close attention, since the same word has been at the centre of recent debates over the organization of the early Irish Church. There, too, *parrochia* (*parochia*, *paruchia*) is used in more than one sense: for the territory attached to an episcopal see, but also for the possessions and people attached to such a see or to a monastery (Sharpe 1984, 230–70; Etchingham 1993; 1999, 106–30, 172–5). The *Collectio Canonum Hibernensis* of 716×725 offers some good examples: in I, 22a, *parrochia* is an episcopal diocese attached to a see; in XXXVII, 20b, it seems to refer to the lay people attached to a church; in XLII, 21 (title) it covers everyone and everything attached to a monastery but probably excluding the monastery itself (Wasserschleben 1885, 12, 136, 168). In at least one case of crucial importance to the Northumbrians, namely Iona, this type of link had included other monasteries subject to the abbot of Iona, as well as lesser churches and individual monastic tenants, *manaig*. Early Irish historians have taken, and still take, different views on the relationship of such complexes of institutions and individuals to episcopal dioceses; and, in Northumbria, in the long-running case of Wilfrid, one can see a potential clash between the *parrochia* as diocese and the *parrochia* as ecclesiastical lordship.

In the time of Wilfrid's episcopate his was only one *parrochia*, in the sense of an ecclesiastical lordship, within the great diocese, *parrochia* in the other sense, over which he ruled. Lindisfarne would also have had its *parrochia*. Great rivalry was possible between different *parrochiae*: in addition to Archbishop Theodore, the other ecclesiastical dignitary who wrote to the pope to justify the expulsion of Wilfrid was Hild, abbess of Whitby, who had been close to Aidan (HE IV, 23). Bosa, who was made bishop of York in 678, was from her community (HE IV, 23). Eata, who was made bishop of the Bernicians in 678, was one of the original disciples of Aidan and had been abbot of Lindisfarne (HE III, 27). These new bishops consecrated by Theodore in 678 were, in Stephen's terms, intruders from other *parrochiae*, those of Lindisfarne and Whitby. Ironically, our best example of the trouble that could be caused when someone from one *parrochia*, in the sense of an ecclesiastical lordship, was put in authority over another is Wilfrid himself, when, for a year, 687–8, he was in charge of Lindisfarne, the church founded by Aidan (HE IV, 29 taken together with Colgrave 1940, 286–7).

Rivalry between *parrochiae* expressed itself in many ways but one was a deep difference in the attitude taken to 'the episcopacy of the Irish' between 635 and 664; and a crucial aspect of this division was the issue whether or not the clergy ordained by the Irish bishops could be regarded as having valid orders. This will be a vital issue for the second section of this paper.

My second concern is the role of Wilfrid in the extension of Northumbrian English power, both within Northumbria over the British part of the population and externally over Britons, Picts, and Irish. First, then, we may consider Wilfrid and the internal consolidation of Northumbria as an English kingdom. In his account of the dedication feast of Ripon – a great fund-raising jamboree – Stephen says that Wilfrid read out the names of 'holy places in various *regiones*' which the British clergy had abandoned, fleeing from the hostile swords of our people'. The implication is that these, also, had been given to Ripon.

What is puzzling about this reference to British clergy and their holy *loca* is the chronology. We know from Bede and from the *Historia Brittonum* that a British king of Elmet had been conquered, and presumably deprived of his kingdom, during the reign of Edwin, 616–33 (HE IV, 23 (21); Faral 1929, 43). The known British kingdom lying to the west of York and south of Ripon had therefore been conquered before Wilfrid was born. The dedication of Ripon, however, took place in the 670s, about forty years after Edwin's death in battle against Cadwallon and Penda. What I suspect may have happened is that the flight of the British clergy noted by Stephen did not take place in Edwin's reign but after the Synod of Whitby, and very probably after Wilfrid had been installed as bishop of York. At least during the reigns of Oswald and of Oswiu up to 664, the likelihood is that British clergy continued to minister to the Britons who lived under Northumbrian rule, especially since those kings made conquests after they had been converted to Christianity. That there was a closer link between the Britons and the mission from Iona than Bede acknowledged is suggested by the fact that the Irish knew Lindisfarne by its British not its English name, namely Medcóit (Lawlor and Best 1931, 67, under 31 August; Stokes 1905, 190–1; Faral 1929, 42, 44). However, once Wilfrid was installed as bishop of York, with the firm belief that the Britons were heretics, British clergy who refused to accept the decision of the Synod are likely to have been driven out: Colmán, after all, had to leave, even though, so Bede tells us, Oswiu was deeply attached to him (HE III, 26).

The effects of driving out the British clergy may have been far-reaching. We may compare Cornwall, brought under West Saxon authority in the ninth century, and with its last king, Duniarth, being drowned in 876 (Dumville 2002, *s.a.* 876). A few years earlier, Alfred, not yet king of the West Saxons, had gone hunting in East Cornwall and had prayed at the church of St *Gueriir*, now St Neot's on the south side of Bodmin Moor (Stevenson 1904, 55). This was about three miles west of the memorial stone for Duniarth (Macalister 1949, 184). The comparison, therefore, is between Cornwall, where not long before 868 a West Saxon prince could pray at the church of a British saint, and Deira two hundred years earlier, where the British clergy were forced to flee from their churches and other holy places at the point of the sword. The crucial difference, I suggest, is that the British clergy in the lands around Ripon were caught by that period between 669 and some date in the eighth century when they were regarded as heretics. The British clergy of Cornwall, however, came under direct West-Saxon rule when that controversy was a thing of the past. Bede notes that Aldhelm persuaded those Britons who were under West Saxon rule to adopt the Roman Easter (HE V, 18); he notes no such change for the Britons under Northumbrian rule. The long-term results are obvious: Cornwall has been for more than a millennium part of England, yet the Cornish language only gradually retreated from east to west and finally died out at the beginning of the nineteenth century. Only two areas show a clear predominance of English names: in the far north-east in an area co-extensive with the hundred of Stratton, and in the central east, adjacent to the Tamar, around Callington (Padel 1988, 7–8). In Domesday Book, Stratton was the hundredal centre for what had been and would be again the three hundreds of Stratton, Lesnewth, and Trigg, strung out along the north coast from the boundary with Devon to the mouth of the River Camelford (Thomas 1964, 70–9). The area around Stratton, namely the original eastern-most hundred of the three combined together into one great elongated hundred in Domesday Book, was in terms of place-names a western extension of Devon, and thus an exceptionally anglicized part of Cornwall; and it was also the base of governmental authority over north-east Cornwall. In the secular sphere Cornwall was not always given favourable treatment.

More importantly, however, the religious landscape of Cornwall resembles those of Brittany and Wales (Padel 1985, 91, 142–5). This is because the churches that were the centres of cults of British saints were not subject to a total replacement of personnel and a condemnation of their previous traditions after English rule. In Northumbria, however, the expulsion of British clergy coincided with a period in which churches were given new dedications on a wide scale (Levison 1946, 259–65). I know of no evidence that the Britons or the Irish made any use of the rite of dedication of a church in the form attested in Gaul in the sixth century and in England in the seventh, but the rite was widely used in Northumbria in the time of Wilfrid. Unsurprisingly, it was not used to dedicate a church to a British saint: heretics were not considered worthy of such an honour. Part of the energy behind the process of anglicization was, perhaps, not the mere fact of English rule or of the introduction of an English population, but the condemnation of British Christianity, a condemnation in which Wilfrid took a leading role, and which changed the landscape of Northumbria (Higham 2001, 22). Because Cornwall was conquered after the issue over Easter had been resolved, it was not subject to the kind of wholesale anglicization exemplified by Wilfrid's monastery at Ripon. Devon, however, was, since Exeter was already in English hands at the time of Boniface's childhood, in the 670s (Levison 1905, 6–7). Perhaps the contrast will help to explain the paradox expressed by Margaret Gelling, when she wrote: 'There are parts of western England – Shropshire and Devon in particular – where the scarcity of Celtic names is highly embarrassing.' (Gelling 1993, 51; for further discussion see Padel 2007)

A parallel to the religious topography of Cornwall is the old kingdom of Ergyng, which became, in the late Anglo-Saxon period, a hundred in Herefordshire. Ergyng took its name from the Romano-British town of Ariconium, which lay east of the Wye. Between the sixth and the ninth century Ergyng lost two areas: first, perhaps *c.* 600, the part east of the Wye around Ariconium, and, secondly, the part immediately south of the Wye near Hereford. This second loss of territory probably occurred between 650 and 770 and perhaps at the time, no later than 802, when the see of the Magonsæte was established at Hereford (Sims-Williams 1990, 90–1); the area lost to Ergyng included major churches, headed by abbots (Evans and Rhys 1893, 164–6). The Domesday hundred of Archenfield was the remnant left by successive truncations. After the first loss, of the lands east of the Wye, but before the second, Ergyng still retained its own kings (Davies 1978, 88, 93–4). After the second, the remnant passed under the rule of the kings of Gwent, to the south across the Monnow, and then, probably by the tenth century, under English rule. In the twelfth century Urban, bishop of Llandaff, claimed that Ergyng belonged to his see; but the Ergyng in question was the remnant left after the successive losses of territory (Evans and Rhys 1893, 42–3, 134–5). His claim was buttressed by a list of churches to which Hereward, his predecessor, had ordained priests in the reigns of Edward the Confessor, Harold, and William the Conqueror (Evans and Rhys 1893, 275–8). The settlements to which these churches belonged largely retained their saints' names under English rule, although they acquired anglicized forms (Coplestone-Crow 2009). Thus the *Lann Sanfreyt* of the list came to be known as Bridstow, the *Lann Cein* of the list is Kentchurch, and *Lann Sant Guainerth* was St Weonards. In Domesday Ergyng, namely the remnant left after successive territorial losses, the cults of British saints remained prominent in the landscape. In the parts lost by *c.* 750, however, this was not the case, even though British names in general survived better than they did in Shropshire or Devon.

The contrast between Cornwall and Devon and between the Archenfield of Domesday Book and the rest of Herefordshire is probably the outcome of two processes. First, on the British side, churches were increasingly named after saints, both local ones and those with a wide cult, such as St David, so that *Lann* (Llan) + a personal name became the dominant way of referring to churches. In early seventh-century Ergyng this form of name is already attested, but alongside others, such as *Mochros* (Moccas), 'pig promontory', that make no reference to saints or churches. By the early twelfth century, in the list of Ergyng churches, *lann* + personal name is dominant. This British trend is not, however, the sole explanation, since early names in *lann* + personal name already existed by the seventh century, as with *Lann Deui* in *Liber Landavensis*, 163b, 164, 165 (Evans and Rhys 1893, 164–6), charters dated to *c.*620 and 625 by Wendy Davies; and these were lost under English rule, except in what remained Ergyng. The likelihood, therefore, is that the contrast is to be explained both by the increasing propensity of the Britons to name their churches after saints and by the disfavour into which British saints fell within English-ruled territories in the late-seventh century. As Cornwall and Ergyng illustrate, this disfavour had its chronological limit: its effect was confined to the period between 669 and the second half of the eighth century, to the period when the Britons retained their old Easter reckoning and when influential churchmen in England regarded the Britons as schismatical and even heretical. Admittedly by the ninth and tenth centuries, when Cornwall was coming under direct West Saxon rule, any such fear as that expressed by Cuthbert on his deathbed was no longer pressing; and perhaps West-Saxon rulers from Alfred onwards could afford to be more tolerant of the British identity of Cornwall (Padel 2009, 209–31). Yet what may have made the greatest difference was that kings such as Alfred could now worship in the church of a British saint, and Athelstan could now collect their relics alongside others. It is also likely that there was variation in the degree of ecclesiastical anglicization even in the late-seventh century. Lothian, for example, to judge by the place-names, was less thoroughly assimilated than were Shropshire and Devon; and yet, it too was a frontier territory (Watson 1926, 126–54).

The other way in which Wilfrid may have had an influence on relations between the Northumbrians and the Celtic peoples concerned Northumbrian imperialism in North Britain and the northern half of Ireland. The two were explicitly associated by Stephen in the well-known passage in which he links the growth of Ecgfrith's kingdom both to the north and to the south with the parallel extension of Wilfrid's 'kingdom of churches' to the south over the English and to the north over the Britons, the Irish, and the Picts (VW 21). Stephen, indeed, is much more explicit about Northumbrian ambitions to rule over their northern neighbours than is Bede, for whom some aspects, at least, of this policy were distasteful, and who, in any case, was sparing in introducing secular history not directly relevant to his main task. It is Bede, however, who gives us one critical piece of evidence, the letter of Pope Vitalian to Oswiu (HE III, 29). There are several puzzling aspects of Bede's treatment of this letter, especially how it fits into the sending of Wighard to Rome and the eventual consecration of Theodore (Brooks 1984, 69–71). It is, however, clear that Vitalian's letter was an answer to one from Oswiu, and that the latter's letter, which we do not have, was written after the Synod of Whitby. What concerns me for the purposes of understanding Wilfrid's relations with the Celts is what Vitalian's letter implies about the terms in which Oswiu wrote. This is, naturally, a matter of delicate inference, especially since Bede does not give us the full text of Vitalian's letter.

Vitalian begins by expressing his joy at the news, conveyed in Oswiu's letter, that the king 'has been converted to the true and apostolic faith'. He then gives a string of biblical quotations from Isaiah, messianic prophecies that 'my servant' will 'restore the tribes of Judah and convert the dregs of Israel'. 'My servant', for Christians, was, of course, Christ, but the prophecy could also be applied to others working as the instruments of Christ. That is how Oswiu is presented. It is interesting that Vitalian's quotations embody two distinctions, between Judah and Israel and between both Judah and Israel, on the one hand, and the Gentiles on the other. The supreme mark of the restoration of the whole Jewish people will be when 'the isles', namely 'the peoples from afar' will turn to God. Isaiah's 'isles' had been taken to refer to Britain and Ireland, ever since Patrick laboured in the Irish mission-field in the fifth century. Vitalian also thought in terms of entire islands, as in the sentence already quoted, when he looked forward to sending a bishop 'to root out in accordance with the will of God the tares sown by the enemy from the whole of your island'. I do not think, however, that he was led to do so merely by the text of Isaiah, since he ends with these revealing words:

> May your Highness, we ask, hasten to dedicate to Christ our God, as we wish, his (Oswiu's) entire island. For indeed he has a protector, the redeemer of the human race, our Lord Jesus Christ, who will grant to him that all goes well, so that he may gather together a new people of Christ, establishing there a catholic and apostolic faith. For it is written: 'Seek first the kingdom of God and His justice and all these things will be granted to you.' Indeed, your Highness seeks and will obtain, and all his islands will, as we hope, be made subject to Him.

Vitalian, therefore, takes a hard line on the supposed Quartodecimans: the tares sown throughout the island would logically include the missions of Dimma (Diuma) and others to the Middle Angles and of Cedd to the East Saxons in the time of Fínán (HE III, 21–2). But it would also include the Christianity of the Irish of Dál Riata and of the Picts (for the latter see Kirby 1973, 1976). Oswiu's decision at Whitby is treated as a conversion to 'the true catholic and apostolic faith'.

The notion that there should be an alliance between Northumbrian power and orthodox Christianity goes back before the time when Wilfrid was installed as bishop of York. Wilfrid claimed to be working to spread the faith and customs of Rome; as we can see, his claim was entirely correct. The hope that Oswiu's power could extend the catholic and apostolic faith throughout northern Britain was conceived by Oswiu and his advisers before the king wrote to the pope. The most likely date for that letter must be after Chad had returned from the south bearing the news that Deusdedit had died in 664, very possibly in the plague of that year, and that the see of Canterbury was now vacant. At that time, Wilfrid was still in Francia.

The only extension of this programme that we can link with Wilfrid is the idea that the northern half of Ireland should be treated together with the northern half of Britain. When Wilfrid was in Rome for his second appeal, he was, to judge by Stephen's account, given a hard time in seventy sittings of the papal council. His liberation from what Stephen describes as this 'fiery furnace', to be compared with that fiery furnace into which Nebuchadnezzar had three Jews thrown, Shadrach, Meshach, and Abednego, apparently came when an extract from the acts of the council held by Pope Agatho in 679 was read out. This is quoted by Stephen: 'Wilfrid, bishop of York, beloved of God, appealing to the apostolic see about his case, and absolved by its authority from charges both definite and indefinite, and with 125 other bishops called together in synod in the seat of judgement, confessed the true and catholic faith, and confirmed it with his signature, for all the northern part of Britain and Ireland, and the islands which are tilled by the peoples of the English and the Britons, and also the Irish and the Picts' (VW 53). I have argued elsewhere that the reference to the northern half of Ireland only makes sense if, in 679, Wilfrid made two assumptions: first, that the northern Irish churches were still Quartodeciman; and, secondly, that the authority enjoyed before 664 by Iona in Britain and Ireland should now be held by York, as the northern metropolitan see in Britain, prescribed by Gregory the Great, but also as the champion of the Roman cause in the northern halves of both islands (Charles-Edwards 2000, 434–5). The careful reference to the islands adjacent to Britain and Ireland makes perfect sense if we remember that Iona was one such island and that the power of the Northumbrian king was then sufficient to make Dál Riata, within which Iona was situated, tributary.

When Wilfrid set off for Rome where he made this confession of the faith, Ecgfrith's power was at its peak. In 679, however, he was defeated at the battle of the Trent and lost his power south of the Humber. This did not prevent him from making further military expeditions. One is particularly interesting in the light of Wilfrid's reference to the northern part of Ireland. In May 684 a Northumbrian army led by Berhtred, a member of a powerful family associated with the northern frontier of Northumbria, attacked the Irish province of Brega (HE IV, 26). Brega, however, was the native kingdom of the current king of Tara, Fínsnechtae Fledach, who was thus the leading Uí Néill king. Brega was also part of what is referred to by Stephen and Bede as the northern part of Ireland. Quite what lay behind this attack we do not know; Bede thought it a thoroughly reprehensible action – he describes the Irish as 'a people always most friendly to the English' – and had no interest in explaining its motivation (HE IV, 26; cf. Thacker 1996a). It clearly caused serious and lasting alarm in Ireland, but, again, none of the sources explains why it occurred. My own suspicion is that the Easter issue had become so intertwined with Northumbrian imperialism that the status of the northern half of Ireland as a stronghold of Quartodeciman heretics is likely to have been, at least, a pretext.

In 684, Wilfrid was not in Northumbria at all and cannot have had any influence on the decision to attack Ireland. To judge by Stephen's *Life*, he was, however, entirely sympathetic to the cause of Northumbrian power in northern Britain. Stephen tells the story of Ecgfrith's great victory, early in the 670s, when a Pictish attempt to throw off Northumbrian overlordship was bloodily suppressed. Here Stephen refers to 'the bestial peoples' of the Picts, a classic diminution of the human status of a subject people (VW 19).

The issues I have addressed have been Wilfrid's relationship to 'the episcopacy of the Irish' and Wilfrid's relationship to the Britons within Northumbria and the imperial ambitions of Oswiu and Ecgfrith. For the first, Wilfrid was following in the wake of papal policy and was initially in complete agreement with Archbishop Theodore: Quartodecimans were condemned by General Councils, and the Britons, some at least of the Irish and all the Picts were Quartodecimans. But, whereas Theodore came to soften his stance and thus came close to the heirs of Aidan, Wilfrid did not, partly because of the rivalries which lay behind his expulsions from Northumbria. As for the Britons within Northumbria, their clergy and local cults were highly vulnerable to Wilfrid's hardline position. The comparison with Cornwall and Ergyng suggests that this may have hastened their anglicization. As for Wilfrid and Northumbrian imperialism, seen in the Pictish north and in the invasion of Ireland, he was evidently in sympathy with the first. When, in 684, a Northumbrian army invaded Ireland, he had already been expelled from Northumbria; but the opinions he championed probably had some part in justifying an attack that, on Bede's evidence, many thought unjust.

19: *Prelates and Politics:*
Wilfrid, Oundle and the 'Middle Angles'

MORN CAPPER

Wilfrid is best known for his role as a leading figure in the controversies surrounding the implementation of Christian orthodoxy in the English kingdoms. His early career was founded on his debating prowess at the synod of Whitby in 664 where he upheld the authority of the Roman Church against the Irish traditions of Ionan monasticism (Corning 2006). Early in his episcopate at York, Wilfrid seemingly ruled an episcopal and monastic territory coterminous with the extent of Oswiu's lordship. His career under Ecgfrith also at first seemed promising and support from Queen Æthelthryth earned him the personal gift of Hexham. According to Wilfrid's biographer, Stephen, his Northumbrian monasteries of Ripon and Hexham and his bishopric at York remained Wilfrid's priorities. Yet much of Wilfrid's career was spent in exile, and it was these periods which formed his wider reputation. It is intended here to assess Wilfrid's rarely discussed final exile, during which time he '... went to his faithful friend Æthelræd, King of the Mercians, who received him with great honour ...'; this episode lasted eleven years, which his hagiographer Stephen all but omits from his narrative (VW 45–46).

Athelings frequently spent time in exile. However, bishops were less often cast out, although the experiences of Winfrith of Mercia and Putta of Rochester show that Wilfrid was not alone in his misfortunes. Both these bishops responded to exile by surrendering episcopal status in return for well-endowed Mercian monasteries: Winfrith at Barrow in Lindsey (VW 25; HE IV, 6) and Putta to an unnamed church offered by Bishop Seaxwulf (HE IV, 12). In contrast, Wilfrid's biography suggests that his aristocratic bearing and sizeable military retinue were more like those of other noble exiles, making him an asset to the overlords he served (Mayr-Harting 1972, 134–5; Wormald 1978, 56). However, he remained unusual in seeking to maintain possessions in more than one kingdom. As Wormald observed (1978, 62), Wilfrid was in Bede's eyes a 'flawed model' for episcopal behaviour, but despite exile from his see, he remained influential. It is therefore unsurprising that of his lengthy absences from Northumbria those spent by Wilfrid with Northumbria's traditional enemies were the least reported, despite his biographer Stephen's possibly Mercian origins (Kirby 1983, 104).

Wilfrid's Approach to His Episcopal Duties
Wilfrid's flexible approach to diocesan boundaries was in part a legacy of

Northumbrian overlordship, which had expanded the bounds of his *regnum ecclesiarum* (VW 21). During a five-year vacancy at Canterbury prior to Archbishop Theodore's arrival in 669 (Brooks 1984, 67–71), Wilfrid, though ousted from his see at York by Oswiu's appointment of Chad, was able to exercise episcopal authority in vacant sees, for Ecgberht of Kent and Wulfhere of Mercia (VW 12–13; HE III, 28). Wulfhere '... invited him [Wilfrid] into his realm to fulfil various episcopal duties ...' for which Wulfhere '... granted our bishop many pieces of land in various places, on which he soon founded monasteries' (VW 14). Such gifts included a sizeable estate at Lichfield. Once Wilfrid was reinstated at York, he was obliged to agree to Theodore's consecration of Chad to the Mercian see and to Chad's takeover of this estate 'suitable for an episcopal see' at Lichfield (VW 15). Yet Wilfrid retained other Mercian monasteries since *'multa monasteria'* given by both Wulfhere and Æthelræd are mentioned subsequently (VW 45 and 61). Thacker (2004a) concurred with Farmer (1974) that the years which followed, 669–78, were 'the most obviously successful' for Wilfrid in Northumbria. However, the dismemberment of his Northumbrian possessions orchestrated by Theodore (678 and 681) triggered Wilfrid's exile in 678 (HE IV, 12; Farmer 1974, 47; Brooks 1984, 75). Despite reconciliation with Theodore, Æthelræd of Mercia and Aldfrith of Northumbria in 686, Wilfrid's conflict with the Northumbrian court quickly rekindled and when he was again 'expelled' by King Aldfrith, Wilfrid's network of patrons soon provided alternative opportunities (Colgrave 1940, 287; HE IV, 29).

The Prospect of Canterbury

Wilfrid's Mercian activities of the 690s should also be assessed in view of his prospects of becoming archbishop of Canterbury. It is usually held that the archbishopric was offered first under the aegis of Cædwalla's overlordship, which had triggered Wilfrid's reconciliation with Theodore *c.*686 (Higham 1999, 216–17). Stephen's *Vita* is emphatic that Theodore had intended Wilfrid for the position: '... I adjure you, by God and St Peter, to agree to my appointing you while I am still alive to my archiepiscopal see as my successor and heir' (VW 43). With Gregorian plans for York as a second metropolitan see in abeyance, it would also have been obvious to Wilfrid that Canterbury offered an alternative route to primacy over Northumbria. However, by 688 Cædwalla had retired to Rome, Wilfrid's dispute with Aldfrith had rekindled and Mercian support for a resurgence of East Saxon kingship was enabling King Sæbbi's son Swæfheard to install himself in Kent under Æthelræd's overlordship (c.688/9, see S10; S12; HE, IV, 26; Yorke 1985, Kelly 1995, 143–6). By Theodore's death in 690, Wilfred's preferment to Canterbury most likely relied on Æthelræd's patronage.

That Wilfrid failed to achieve the archbishopric sheds light on important themes also underlying early Mercian overkingship among the middle Angles (Capper 2008). As Mercian overlordship encroached on London it was contested by other overlords, such as Cædwalla at Barking (S1246; S1248), whilst the regional East Saxon lineage used monastic foundations and grants to local bishops in an attempt to preserve territory (S65a; S65b; S1171; S1246; S1783; S1784; S1785; Capper 2008, 116–30). Yet the East Saxon kings also used service to Mercian overlords as a means to rejuvenate their own fortunes. Whether or not Æthelræd invaded Kent in 691, the possibility of Wilfrid's preferment as Archbishop of Canterbury posed notable dangers not only to Kentish autonomy, as Brooks (1984) has argued, but also to regional interest among Mercian clients such as Sæbbi of Essex and even Bishop Eorcenwald of London. This contentious prospect was blocked via the consecration in Gaul and confirmation by the pallium in Rome of the Kentish abbot Berhtwald, of Reculver (Brooks, 1984). Unease over Wilfrid's trustworthiness may also have played its part: Wilfrid had abandoned the South Saxons to their enemy Cædwalla of Wessex (Bede IV, 15–16; Yorke 2004). He may have been viewed, even by close allies, as uncontrollable.

Wilfrid's Years as a Bishop Among the 'Middle Angles'

The eleven years Wilfrid spent as a bishop to the Mercians between 691/2 and 703 represent a notable lacuna in the *Vita Wilfridi*. Bede's main treatment of Wilfrid in the *Historia Ecclesiastica* essentially summarises the *Vita*, also skirting over this part of Wilfrid's life (HE V, 19). Wilfrid's last exile was arguably seen by contemporaries as irrelevant to Northumbrian narratives. It is largely known from retrospective references in his *Vita*, occasional charters and contextual notes in Bede's *Historia Ecclesiastica*. Yet in addition to his extensive network of contacts, one should consider Wilfrid's view of himself as an exile – an attitude he emphasised in his will – in his reliance on his Mercian patrons. When personally dependent on a series of Mercian sponsors and protectors, Bishop Wilfrid remained useful as an agent of their royal authority.

Perhaps in expectation of the archbishopric of Canterbury, Wilfrid used Æthelræd's patronage to intervene in episcopal consecrations after Theodore's death in 690. Canon 8 of the synod of Hertford had established seniority as the determinant in episcopal status (HE IV, 5). Although Wilfrid was never to be archbishop, by the time Berhtwald returned in 693 he had established his influence in an inexperienced Mercian church. Consecrated in c.664/5, Wilfrid was notably senior to Tyrhtel of Hereford, consecrated in 688 and probably consecrated Headda, who became bishop of the principal Mercian see of Lichfield (691–716×727) after Seaxwulf's death in 691. Seniority may also have given Wilfrid a role in the consecration of Eadgar of Lindsey, named in company with Wilfrid and Headda as '*electus*' in a charter of June 693, though Eadgar maybe preferred to await Archbishop Berhtwald's arrival (S1248; Brooks 1984, 76–7). In consecrating the Northumbrian Oftfor as bishop to the Hwicce 'at Æthelræd's command', Wilfrid not only emphasised his own status, but also Mercian power (HE IV, 23). Bede justified Wilfrid's consecration of Oftfor and also Swithberht for the Frisian mission thus: '... for Archbishop Theodore was now dead and no-one had been appointed' (HE IV, 23; V, 11).

Wilfrid's service to Mercia had allowed him to sponsor a clutch of Mercian foundations (VW 51). Even in his most successful years in Northumbria, Wilfrid apparently confirmed his friendship with Æthelræd, Wulfhere's brother and successor, by attesting charters at Bath in 675/6 and so supporting Mercian authority among the Hwicce (S51; Sims-Williams 1990, 104). One of Wilfrid's protégées held his small monastery in southern Mercia, sponsored by Æthelræd's nephew Beorhtwald (VW 40; identified speculatively as Ripple, Worcestershire; S52; Sims-Williams 1990, 104–5). On his return to Æthelræd's court Wilfrid continued to support the development of the Hwiccian church, consecrating Oftfor and being acknowledged with Archbishop Berhtwald in 692×6 among the bishops attesting King Oshere's foundation with Cuthswith of a minster [probably Inkberrow] (S53). Alan Thacker (1982, 200) has speculated that the tradition of Gerald of Wales, though late, suggests that Wilfrid consecrated the church of St John, Chester. By 693, Wilfrid's activities and foundations had embedded his influence widely across the Mercian church.

All of this suggests that entitling Wilfrid 'bishop of the middle Angles' may be misleadingly restrictive. At the consecration of Swithberht, Bede described how Wilfrid '... was at that time acting as bishop for the middle Angles [*Mediterraneorum Anglorum*]', specifically designating Wilfrid to a Mercian diocese. It may be, however, that Bede sought to impose an order on Wilfrid's activities that they lacked. Similar desires for order may underlie the misleadingly simple division of the Mercian see into five at Seaxwulf's death given in early-ninth-century episcopal lists (Page 1965–6; Capper 2008). Berhtwald's return as Archbishop of Canterbury in 693 left Wilfrid in an ambiguous position. Nor is it certain that Wilfrid's seat was at Leicester as is often stated as fact (Farmer 1974, 52; Pelteret 1998, 178; Thacker 2004a). Leicester, located on the River Soar, a tributary of the Trent, suggests a strongly Mercian perspective to Wilfrid's activities. Yet although St Nicholas's Church, Leicester, overlies a major Roman bathhouse, the late-seventh-century archaeological remains are ambiguous (Courtenay 1998, 112). Only the later records of John of Worcester suggest separation of this see from Lichfield prior to Wilfrid's 'tenure' under an otherwise unknown Bishop 'Cuthwine', who should probably be discounted (Page 1965–6, 92; Keynes 1986). The synod of Hertford had ruled that '...no bishop should intrude into the diocese of another...' (HE IV, 5). In contrast, the *Vita Wilfridi*, having skirted Wilfrid's time at Lindisfarne (HE IV, 29), avoided identifying Wilfrid's see and stated only that he lived '...under the protection of God and the king amid the profound respect of that bishopric which the most reverend Seaxwulf had formerly ruled': that of the Mercians, actually held by Headda (VW 45). Wilfrid's role was perhaps focused further east by his holdings at Oundle. Furthermore, Wilfrid does not begin the episcopal lists for the middle Anglian diocese, but is given with Headda as one of two bishops for the Mercians (Page 1966, 5). In 679, dioceses for the Hwicce and *Westerne* [later Hereford] were created and Lindsey became a Mercian bishopric, yet Seaxwulf's diocese for 'Mercia proper' seemingly remained whole and, excepting Wilfrid's questionable tenure, the see of the 'middle Angles' would not reappear until 737, reverting to Headda's governance when Wilfrid left (HR 737; Brooks 1984, 75; Page 1965, 92–3 against which Kirby 1966, 7, n.11). These ambiguities regarding Wilfrid's sphere of authority in Mercia allow interpretations of his usefulness in which regional nuances play a more significant role.

Even if potentially inaccurate, Bede's label 'middle Angles' usefully identifies Wilfrid's primary area of activity, narrowing Stephen's description. It may be that Wilfrid's activities as a bishop, like his possession of Oundle, were 'tangential' to the Mercian community, as Wood (2008) showed for Wilfrid's Northumbrian holdings. Simon Keynes (1994) has highlighted the wealth and group identity of middle Anglian monasteries within the eighth-century Mercian supremacy. In the seventh century, Mercian rule did not yet dominate the region. Dorothy Whitelock (1972, 14) showed that the early conversion of the fens probably stemmed from East Anglia, as shown by the election of Thomas of the Gyrwe as bishop to the East Angles c.648 and Æthelthryth's marriage to Tondberht of the southern Gyrwe in the 650s. Seaxwulf, founder of *Medeshamstede* and bishop of Lichfield, may have been converted and educated by East Angles (HE III, 20). Clear ties with East Anglia are visible in the material culture of the south-east Lincolnshire fens, whilst incomplete Mercian authority may be shown by the later nucleation of villages in the likely territory of the *Spaldingas* and *Bilmigas* mentioned in the Tribal Hidage (Hayes 1988, 325). The 'middle Angles' described a group which did not occur as a kingship or as people in the Tribal Hidage, and whose identity under Mercian rule was seemingly based around a bishopric (Davies 1978b). The later seventh century saw strategic consolidation of Mercian control in the East Midlands (Capper 2008). Oundle was central to the middle Anglian community and it is argued here that Wilfrid arrived at a critical juncture in defining Mercian influence.

Wilfrid's usefulness to Mercian kings is shown in the substantial debt owed by the Mercian church to Oswiu's overlordship and evangelism (Davies 1978b, 19). Even after the murder of Oswiu's son-in-law and puppet, King Peada, in 656, Mercian conversion had continued under four priests sent from Northumbria to his court in the East Midlands, including Diuma the first

Mercian bishop, who died 'among the middle Angles' (HE III, 21). The final transfer of the Mercian see to Lichfield had only occurred around 669. Bishop Chad and his followers from Lastingham, including Winfrith his successor at Lichfield, '...who had been his deacon for some time' represented further Northumbrian influence (HE IV, 3), as did Wilfrid. Æthelræd's wife Osthryth, founder of the cult of Oswald at Bardney, was Northumbrian and Northumbrian intrigue was perhaps still a cause of friction in Lindsey, which had briefly returned to Northumbrian rule with Ecgfrith's victories in the mid-670s and over which Wilfrid himself had exercised authority from c.674 until his expulsion (HE IV, 12). Before assessing Wilfrid's potential in eastern Mercia, it is important to recognise that the Mercian church had absorbed major strands of Northumbrian influence which needed to be reconciled.

If Wilfrid could not rely on strongly defined diocesan powers, a patchwork of authority can be suggested for the East Midlands, reflecting the regional peoples under Mercian rule (Capper 2008). Until recently *Medeshamstede* [Peterborough] was believed to have dominated Mercian monasticism (Stenton 1933). This led Farmer (1974, 52) to surmise that for Wilfrid to rule as bishop of the 'middle Angles' he also held *Medeshamstede*: unfortunately this theory seems reliant on forged papal privileges from Wilfrid. Alternatively, Keynes (1994, 41–3) has suggested that Headda of Lichfield, in addition to his abbacy at Breedon, also inherited control of *Medeshamstede* from Seaxwulf. Such a situation might have hamstrung Wilfrid's episcopal influence. However, since Kelly (2009, 67–75) now argues that the *Medeshamstede* monastic confederation is unlikely to have possessed a strongly hierarchical structure, multiple strands of noble influence and religious authority may be visible in these foundations. The campaigns of Wulfhere and Æthelræd still relied heavily on the followings of key Mercian and regional nobles. A critical balance of overlordship and local interest sponsored the Church in areas of recent Mercian expansion (Fig. 19.1, overleaf).

Medeshamstede (Peterborough) on the Nene seems the earliest significant minster in the East Midlands, alleged to have been founded in the time of Peada, or more likely Wulfhere. Seaxwulf, '*constructor*' of *Medeshamstede* and probably a major local landholder 'in the land of the *regio* of the Gyrwe' was subsequently made bishop of the Mercian diocese by Theodore (HE IV, 6). This was perhaps a vital step in the transfer of regional influence and allegiance to Mercian interests, which may have split the Gyrwas into their Northern and Southern groupings (Capper 2008). Recently Susan Kelly has argued that close ties between *Medeshamstede* and Bishop Headda reflect later attempts to justify forged papal privileges, in which case this house should be viewed as a separate concern in Wilfrid's day (Kelly 2009, 9, 78). However, Candidus also provides an unparalleled and so perhaps accurate assertion that monks were sent from

Figure 19.1: Fenland monasticism, Oundle and its environs.

here to found Brixworth (Mellows 1949, 15; Kelly 2009, 68). Brixworth had been the site of a Roman villa and surviving Church fabric gives clear evidence of its status in the Middle Saxon period, which is lacking in early texts (Audouy 1984; Parsons 2001).

At nearby Castor, which had been a significant Roman temple site, a nunnery or double house was founded under Cyneburh and Cyneswith, two of the better attested daughters of Penda (ASC, E 963; Mellows 1949, 50; Rollason 1978, 63; Ridyard 1988, 60). Associated Middle Saxon female finds are identified by Dallas (1973) as from the 'upper class' of Anglo-Saxon society (Parsons 2001, 60). If Cyneburh can be identified as the widow of Wilfrid's earliest patron, King Alhfrith of Deira, she may have supported Wilfrid's activities (HE III, 21; Stafford 2001, 37). It is unclear whether Castor was paired with *Medeshamstede* [Peterborough], which later absorbed its lands (S68, S72), or was originally an independent foundation, introducing royal oversight and visitation into the area. Like *Medeshamstede*, Castor lay on the Nene, downstream from Wilfrid's foundation at Oundle, but within easy communication.

Re-interpretation of the *Medeshamstede* narrative allows greater independence to Breedon-on-the-Hill (Leicestershire) at the time of Wilfrid's exile. Located within a prehistoric hillfort only one day east of Tamworth, Breedon was probably a significant regional administrative centre associated with the founder, Frithuric *princeps* (S1803; S1805; Dornier 1977; Bullough 1993, 121; Parsons 2001, 56). Abbot Headda of Breedon probably continued to lead the community following his consecration as bishop of Lichfield *c.*691. Through Headda, Kelly argues for ties between Breedon, Bermondsey and Woking, in which Breedon was potentially dominant – the presence of this material at *Medeshamstede* representing a later 'amalgamation of archives' (Kelly 2009, 78). According to Candidus, the early monks were provided by *Medeshamstede*, but Breedon became increasingly powerful; Abbot Tatwine later became Archbishop of Canterbury (Keynes 1994). Blair has suggested that Frithuric was related to Frithuwold of Surrey and that his family sponsored monasteries at Bermondsey, Woking and Chertsey (Blair 1989, 105–7; see also, however, Keynes 1994). If so, Frithuric seemingly represents a noble or collateral royal lineage in the East Midlands, tied by service to Æthelræd and Wulfhere, whose family benefitted from Mercian campaigns in the South East.

At Repton the archaeological evidence indicates a church and a cemetery of three generations in the Mercian heartland, beginning in the earliest period of Christianisation (Biddle and Kjølbe Biddle 2001). These mid-seventh-century features may be identified with the middle Anglian lineage of Frithuric via his grant to Breedon of 31 hides in the territory of the *Hreppingas*, or with Merewalh, an alleged son of Penda, via legends of his burial at Repton. Ties to

Frithuric and Breedon rely on the identification of '... *ad Repingas* ...' with Repton, Derbyshire (S1803–5 and S749; Dornier 1977, 158–9; cf Stenton 1933, 185). More generally, this foundation was linked to the Mercian royal lineage. By *c.*700 Repton was ruled by Ælfthryth, a member of a royal line in dispute with Coenred of Mercia by 704 (Haddan and Stubbs vol. 3, 274–5). Although distant, this royal faction interacted with lineages active in the East Midlands, through Guthlac and potentially with Breedon via Headda's subsequent consecration of Guthlac's church.

Guthlac represents a further influential noble or royal lineage. The complex significance of Guthlac's cult in the region has been considered elsewhere (Higham 2005; Capper 2008). Here it is sufficient to note that his *Vita* claims Guthlac descended from Icel and was a member of the Mercian *stirps regia*, although possibly non-Mercian or local marriage ties may be indicated by the *walh* element, indicating 'foreigner' in his father Penwalh's name. Penwalh's halls 'in the region of the middle Angles' hosted fosterlings, suggestive of regional status and wider influence (Colgrave 1956, 78). Guthlac's birth narrative identifies this affluence with the days of Æthelræd (Colgrave 1956, 72). The hermitage and shrine of Guthlac at Crowland '... on *middan Gyrwan fen*' (Rollason 1978, 89) and of his sister Pega (d.*c.*719) at nearby Peakirk, a less marginal settlement of Roman origin on Carr Dyke, near Peterborough, may offer a general location for Penwalh's territory (Colgrave 1956, 160–2; Blair 2002, 552). Penwalh's family seemingly prospered in Wilfrid's day, although they may have suffered later from Guthlac's involvement with Æthelbald during his exile.

Within this complex framework, Æthelræd sponsored Wilfrid's episcopal influence and an unknown number of foundations including that headed by Cuthbald at Oundle. The latter is described after Wilfrid's death as having thatched buildings bounded by a thorn hedge (VW 67). Although for this early period only small amounts of pottery have been found, there has yet to be significant excavation in the Late Saxon core of Oundle (Foard, n.d.). Wilfrid died at his monastery which lay in what Bede termed the '*provincia*' or sub-kingdom of Oundle, often viewed as a Mercian administrative district (Campbell 1979, 48). Although *Medeshamstede* lay at the bounds of the farmland and fen, as recalled by Candidus (Mellows 1949, 5–6), Wilfrid's Oundle was not part of the fen-edge but lay in more secure Mercian territory upriver, surrounded by good farmland producing 'tithes of herds and flocks' (VW 65). Continuity at Wilfrid's Oundle foundation is suggested by the eighth-century survival of an early cult of St Cett (Rollason 1978, 63; Blair 2002, 520).

In addition to Wilfrid, Æthelræd introduced Wulfhere's daughter, Werburh, into the region, making her the head of Mercian female houses by her death *c.*700; these included Weedon (Northamptonshire), lying on the Nene at its convergence with Watling Street, and Threekingham (Lincolnshire). Her role mirrored a wider strategy introducing Mercian control into strategic regional foundations of the East Midlands (Love 2004, 37; Capper 2008). Æthelræd's sponsorship of Werburh may have placated the lineage of Wulfhere at a critical juncture. Her religious authority was also augmented by her membership of the Ely community and her great-aunt Æthelthryth's sanctity. In this context, legends in the *Liber Eliensis* regarding early foundations by Æthelthryth at *Alftham* (possibly West Halton) and *Ætheldredestowe* (Stowe St Mary, Lincolnshire) merit consideration (Blake 1962, 30). David Roffe suggests that '... the *Liber Eliensis* preserves an authentic seventh- or eighth-century tradition' with '... remarkable awareness of local topography ...' (Roffe 1986; Foot and Roffe 2007, 142, n.112). Yet, taken together, Mercian control of Lindsey at the time of Æthelthryth's journey to Ely (672/3) and the general inventiveness of the *Liber Eliensis* make foundations by Æthelthryth unlikely. Retrospective development of the better attested saint to augment foundations by her great-niece Werburh is more likely, in the early eighth century (Thacker 2004b) or post-Viking when Lincolnshire and Ely lay under the bishops of Dorchester (Kirby 1966, 5).

Overall, in the region broadly identifiable as Wilfrid's preserve in the 690s, local lineages and collateral lines of the Mercian *stirps regia* competed in the sponsorship of monastic foundations. Wilfrid's houses provided him as bishop with resources and with a training ground for his priests, but probably not with overwhelming regional influence. Although his activities among the 'middle Angles' are unrecorded, Wilfrid had demonstrated considerable skills appropriate to Mercian governance of border regions: an experienced politician, he had been authoritarian in handling newly colonised British-Northumbrian (British) subjects (VW 18; Pelteret 1998, 164) and collaborated with Cædwalla's 'merciless slaughter' on the Isle of Wight (HE IV, 16), but also shown himself capable of 'gentle persuasion' in Sussex (VW 41–2). At Oundle, Wilfrid's royal remit, charisma and episcopal status made him a powerful prospective patron for local youths looking to both secular and monastic careers. From his activities in Northumbria, '... secular chief men too, men of noble birth, gave him their sons to be instructed, so that ... they might devote themselves to the service of God, or that, if they preferred, he might give them into the king's charge as warriors when they were grown' (VW 21). Wilfrid had brought the Rule of St Benedict to his monasteries (VW 47; Cubitt 2005, 275). In the web of Wilfrid's own interests, river systems of the Wash connected Oundle and other local communities to East Coast traffic passing between Northumbria, East Anglia, Kent and the continent. Wilfrid supported Æthelræd's consolidation of royal power in the East Midlands and the management of residual Northumbrian strands in the church. However, weaknesses in episcopal authority and resources may be suggested by Headda remaining abbot at Breedon when he became bishop of Lichfield.

The Elevation of Æthelthryth (695)

Wilfrid's support for the cult of St Æthelthryth is one of Stephen of Ripon's more notable omissions, although he mentioned in passing both Æthelthryth's incorrupt body and, in discussing her gift of Hexham, her dedication as '... *Deo ordinata* ...' (VW 19, 22). By contrast, in Bede's *Greater Chronicle* Æthelthryth was the 'unique exemplar of English Christian womanhood' (Higham 2006, 119). Wilfrid was essential to Bede's narrative, consecrating Æthelthryth as a nun, as witness to her virginity and the elevation of her untarnished remains. As abbess she was '... an example of heavenly life and teaching' (HE IV, 19; Ridyard 1988, 177), ideal for the instruction of Wilfrid's own abbesses, such as Cynethrith (VW 47). Stephen's omission of Æthelthryth's cult should be re-evaluated in this context.

Given Mercian expansion, Wilfrid's presence at the elevation of Æthelthryth (695) was taken by Farmer (1974, 52) to imply direct Mercian overlordship of Ely. However, Mercian control of Ely before the mid-eighth century disagrees with Bede's testimony that Ely 'is' in the kingdom of the East Angles (HE IV, 19). Æthelthryth's middle Anglian possessions from her Gyrwan marriage, King Ealdwulf of East Anglia as child of the Northumbrian princess Hereswith, and the Kentish marriage of Æthelthryth's sister Seaxburh all represented traditional anti-Mercian alliances between East Anglia, Northumbria and Kent. Northumbrian power had retreated, but peace following the battle of Trent in 679 probably allowed such ties to be renewed. Wilfrid's place at Æthelthryth's ceremonies affirmed their shared Northumbrian past. Yet it also shows Abbess Seaxburh's influence. As abbess, Seaxburh arranged Æthelthryth's cult to emphasise East Anglia's Frankish links. Her *Vita* follows the formulae of Frankish lives (Rosser 1997, 23), probably those of Seaxburh's sisters Æthelburh and Sæthryth, abbesses of Faremoutiers-en-Brie. At her translation, Æthelthryth, like Æthelburh, was 'untouched by decay', two of only four saints Bede noted as incorrupt (HE III, 8). Wilfrid had a long association with Seaxburh, beginning *c.*653 when he impressed her husband, Eorcenberht of Kent, during a year at his court (VW 3). During the vacancy at Canterbury (666–9) Wilfrid had acted as a bishop for Ecgberht, probably Seaxburh's son, obtaining singers and artisans, and ordaining Kentish priests and deacons (VW 3, 15). Unfortunately, hints from the *Liber Eliensis* that Æthelthryth aided Wilfred's journey to Rome in 678/9 probably reflect later traditions claiming Wilfrid's acquisition of papal privileges for Ely (Blake 1962, 37). In 695 Wilfrid may have hoped that Æthelthryth's sanctification would confirm her gift to him of Hexham, at that time held by the bishopric of Hexham.

The fen edge was a difficult space across which to assert power. Wilfrid's status augmented Mercian royal authority, but also entailed responsibilities. By requesting he witness Æthelthryth's translation, Seaxburh used Wilfrid's

Mercian ties to obtain tacit recognition of Ely's independence, legitimising her house against Mercian strategic interests. In a middle Anglian community rapidly re-defining itself as Mercian, the promotion of Seaxwulf as bishop of Lichfield had drawn *Medeshamstede* and the North Gyrwas toward the Mercian court. The elevation of Æthelthryth supported a matching polarisation of the eastern fen-edge, bringing the South Gyrwas, Bawsey – the second most productive hub of trade in East Anglia after Ipswich (Rogerson 2003, 112–14) – and tribes such as the Wissa more securely into the East Anglian orbit. The events of 695 reaffirmed Ely's status and Seaxburh's role in an influential east-coast network of female religious which included her daughter Eormenhild at Sheppey, Kent in 699 (Kelly 1995, 42), and her grandaughter Werburh at Threekingham. Following a long weakness in East Anglian influence and the intrusion of *'reges dubii vel externii'* into Kent in 688–92 (HE IV, 26), Seaxburh's elevation of Æthelthryth in 695, 16 years after her death (HE IV, 19), took advantage of Kentish resurgence and promoted Ely's status and identity in the face of Mercian consolidation. Werburh is named abbess only by Ely tradition, though her *Vita* suggests she trained there (Love 2004, 34–5; Thacker 1985, 4). It is improbable that if Werburh was recalled to Mercia she also ruled Ely before her death c.700, as implied by the *Liber Eliensis* (Blake 1962, 51). A prestigious monastery headed by East Anglian royal women until at least 700, Ely most likely hosted visitations by East Anglian kings and bishops, just as *Medeshamstede*, Crowland and Oundle hosted their Mercian counterparts. Yet we should not underplay the wider importance of the venerable Wilfrid's endorsement in validating Æthelthryth's sanctity.

Middle Anglia and Austerfeld

The reopening of negotiations for Wilfrid's return to Northumbria indicates the anomalous position he held, both within the Mercian diocese and as an exile at the mercy of Mercian royal sponsors. Wilfrid's experience had aided Æthelræd's expansion and consolidation across the Midlands, yet as questions of succession loomed his usefulness was tempered by a wider anti-Northumbrian reaction, which may have mirrored that which brought Wulfhere to power in 658. The murder of Æthelræd's Northumbrian Queen Osthryth in 697 '... by her own nobles ...' suggests dangerous factionalism at court (HE V, 24). Wilfrid attempted reconciliation at the synod at Austerfeld c.702/3, and the presence of both Northumbrians and Mercian bishops seems likely (Cubitt 1995, 302–3). Stephen blamed the failed negotiations on the Northumbrian King Aldfrith, but an anti-Wilfridian reaction among Mercian bishops may also be implied by threats to deprive Wilfrid of '... all which you were seen to possess in the land of Northumbria, whether bishopric or monasteries ... and whatever you have gained in Mercia under King Æthelræd' (VW 47). Æthelræd gave assurances, but both men probably knew he was unable to assure Wilfrid's future security – shortly before Æthelræd's abdication in 704 Wilfrid returned to Rome to appeal for reinstatement in Northumbria. When Wilfrid returned, Æthelræd orchestrated confirmation of his Mercian holdings by Coenred (VW 57) and Wilfrid returned to the Northumbrian church at the synod of Nidd in 706 (Rollason 2004).

Wilfrid had appointed successors to the communities he founded in exile, often from his Northumbrian following (HE IV, 16). The fate of such communities had caused consternation for Aldhelm (Lapidge and Herren 1979, 169). Designation of the bishop-elect by an incumbent bishop also remained commonplace (Cubitt 1989, 23–9). Once reinstated in Northumbria, Wilfrid's Mercian abbots Tibba and Eabba were '... sent from Ceolred, King of Mercia, asking me [Wilfrid] to go confer with him ... for the sake of the position of our monasteries in his kingdom' (VW 64). When he died with Abbot Cuthbald at Oundle, Wilfrid still held multiple Mercian foundations, some probably in newly consolidated areas. The gathering of abbots to take Wilfrid's remains north was potentially assisted with relief by his Mercian neighbours (VW 66). That Headda re-combined the sees of Lichfield and the middle Angles suggests the ambiguous nature of Wilfrid's tenure, and possibly also Headda's desire to control Wilfrid's legacy.

Wilfrid died at Oundle 23 April 710, on the cusp of a dynastic crisis which shook the 'middle Anglian' region (Capper 2008, 213–38). Soon after Wilfrid's death '... certain exiles of noble birth who were ravaging with an army, because of some wrong done to them, burned the whole of the above-mentioned monastery at Oundle ...'; they in turn were slain soon after (VW 67). Like Æthelbald's visits to Guthlac, the burning of Wilfrid's monastery shows how involved the East Midlands had become in dynastic politics. Antipathy between Guthlac and the entourage of Bishop Headda when he visited Crowland may also hint that distrust remained between the Mercian establishment and regional lineages (Colgrave 1956, 142–6).

Conclusions: Wilfrid's Mercian Exile

Wilfrid's stature in the English church resulted from Northumbrian hegemony. However, it is as an exile that he proves most illuminating to wider questions of Anglo-Saxon history. As is well known, Wilfrid developed his influence using papal authority and ties with the Frankish church. He also took advantage of the overarching unity of the English church, using vacancies at Canterbury in the 660s and 690s to exercise wider authority on behalf of his overlords. Wilfrid might have become Archbishop of Canterbury without losing his Northumbrian possessions, but to become a genuine player in the Mercian polity Wilfrid would have had to become a Mercian bishop and it is unclear whether or not this was offered him. Perhaps from an anachronistic refusal to acknowledge that Northumbrian power had receded, Wilfrid instead maintained a unique position straddling Northumbrian and Mercian interests, unlike other Northumbrian ecclesiastics such as Chad or Oftfor, who were absorbed into the Mercian church. Wilfrid's failure to achieve the archbishopric of Canterbury has perhaps also been over-emphasised. His place 'among the middle Angles' in the 690s allowed Wilfrid episcopal power while maintaining contacts with Northumbria, the Frisian mission and the papacy. At the royal court, at Oundle and potentially also at Leicester, Wilfrid was rewarded for aiding consolidation of the Mercian polity. He led Mercian bishops in seniority – if not, given Headda's links with Breedon, in influence – and was acknowledged in his role by Archbishop Berhtwald, as recorded in charters. However, as Mercian authority strengthened, attitudes towards Osthryth, Wilfrid and other relics of Northumbrian influence hardened in the 690s. The looming potential for a Mercian war of succession and the death of Aldfrith encouraged Wilfrid's re-entry into Northumbrian politics and stimulated Headda's formal assertion of control in the 'middle Anglian' region, re-attaching it to the Mercian see.

In allocating Wilfrid to the bishopric of Leicester there is potential to overlook the challenges of Wilfrid's last exile as bishop to a community in the process of formation. Wilfrid's career in Mercia was a consequence of his own reputation and capabilities, but the Northumbrian foundation of the Mercian Church under Peada also needed to be reconciled. Wilfrid's presence as bishop was part of a wider Mercian strategy introducing royal adherents, often members of the royal lineage, into the region, such as Werburh, Cyneburh and eventually Æthelræd himself. Harnessing the influential middle Anglian regional lineages that had founded fenland monasticism was vital to Mercian royal power in East Midland provinces (Capper 2008, 97–101). Sponsorship of religious foundations and structures of ecclesiastical supervision allowed regional lineages to compete with Mercian royal authority. Wilfrid's prospective holding of Leicester and Oundle may even have continued a policy of integration which managed and utilised prominent East Midlands monastic foundations to resource the weaker diocesan structures: Seaxwulf of *Medeshamstede* and Lichfield; Chad and his long time deacon Winfrith holding Lichfield and Barrow on Humber; Headda at Breedon holding Lichfield. Oundle, tied to a major administrative district, placed Wilfrid at the heart of the middle Anglian community. Access to the Wash allowed him constant news of Northumbrian and church affairs. Potential Northumbrian strands in the East Midland church had been revived by Wilfrid's tenure in Lindsey c.674–8, and remained in the Mercian court through Osthryth and in the community surrounding the Wash through Osthryth's patronage of Oswald at Bardney, Cyneburh at Castor and Æthelthryth's foundation at Ely. Yet although Wilfrid was received at Ely and at Bardney it is unlikely that either represents an episcopal visitation. In focusing on the influence of Wilfrid's unique monastic *familia* we should not forget that as a senior bishop in the 690s he had a spiritual authority which allowed him to authorise sanctity, as for Æthelthryth, beyond the remit of pastoral responsibility. Acknowledging that the 'middle Angles' Wilfrid attempted to lead were a community which remained incompletely assimilated to Mercian rule, to the point that exiles had free reign there, is key to understanding the Mercian political crisis of the early eighth century. Regional families, such as that of Seaxwulf, founder of Peterborough, vied with (potentially imposed) Mercian lineages such as those of Penwalh and Frithuric for influence. The Mercian dynasty on which Wilfrid had relied did not long outlast his return north. His cult was kept alive at Oundle, by his successor Cuthbald, through the giving of alms (VW 65), but Wilfrid's communities were attacked and his legacy diffused. Later Mercian rejection of Wilfrid's time among the middle Angles is indicated in the statement in episcopal lists that he was 'ejected' from the see of Leicester, just as the complex past of Mercian episcopal structures led to the provision of a simplified schema for the division of the Mercian see into five in 679 (Capper 2008, 335). Wilfrid's refusal to commit to a Mercian career inevitably restricted and obscured the legacy of his Mercian achievements.

Acknowledgements

Many thanks are due to the conference organisers, participants and editors, in particular Nick Higham, Sarah Foot, James Palmer, and Katy Cubitt. Additional thanks are offered to Susan Kelly, Philip Shaw, John Blair, Julia Barrow, Jonathan Jarrett and the late Mark Blackburn for their help with surrounding matters discussed in my 2007 thesis. All errors remain those of the author.

20: *Bishop Wilfrid and the Mercians*

DAMIAN J. TYLER

In his long, varied and tempestuous career, Bishop Wilfrid had significant relations with many peoples, both in Britain and in Continental Europe. After his native Northumbria, however, the Mercians were the group with whom he intereacted the most. It is well known that Wilfrid managed to fall foul of three successive Northumbrian kings, Oswiu, Ecgfrith and Aldfrith, and spent long periods in exile or semi exile, much of it in Mercia. He also received extensive patronage from Mercian kings and possessed many monasteries in Mercia. The greater part of Wilfrid's episcopate coincided with the reigns of Kings Wulfhere and Æthelræd, who between them ruled the Mercians from 658 to 704, and the first part of this chapter traces some important developments relating to the Mercian kingdom during this half century. The second part examines Wilfrid's interactions with these two rulers, concentrating on the three periods when he was out of favour with Northumbrian kings.

After his defeat of Penda, king of the Mercians, at the battle of *Winwæd* in 655, the Northumbrian king Oswiu was the most powerful ruler in Britain, and for a while it appeared that the Mercians were to be swallowed up in what we might term a greater Northumbria. Directly annexing the northern part of the Mercian kingdom, he initially gave the kingship of the Southern Mercians to his son-in-law Peada, who was the son of Penda and already the ruler of the Middle Angles. The following spring Peada was assassinated, and thereafter the whole of the Mercian people, and presumably the Middle Angles also, were ruled for Oswiu by Northumbrian ealdormen (or, as Bede calls them, *principes*). In 658, however, the Mercian elites drove out Oswiu's lieutenants and installed Wulfhere, another son of Penda, as king of the Mercians (HE III, 24).

Oswiu's direct power over Mercia was, therefore, short lived, but it seems likely that the new king accepted a tributary status. Penda, famously, was not a Christian, preferring the traditional gods of the English. Wulfhere, in contrast, was Christian from the start of his reign (HE III, 24). This change of cult affiliation was probably partly caused by a consciousness among the Mercian elites of the advantages that the new religion had provided for Oswiu (Stafford 1985, 99). In addition, however, it is likely that, having expelled Oswiu's ealdormen and made Wulfhere their king, the Mercian great and good found it easier to persuade the Northumbrian king to acquiesce to the new *status quo* by their acceptance of both Christianity and a Northumbrian-appointed bishop. The first two Mercian bishops, Diuma and Ceollach, who presided during the period of Northumbrian rule, had been Irishmen, but with the changed political situation Oswiu seems to have decided that a more political appointment was necessary, and Trumhere, the first Mercian bishop of Wulfhere's reign, was a member of the Deiran royal lineage and as such a relative of Oswiu himself (HE III, 24). Appointed by Oswiu and a high-ranking figure in the Northumbrian ecclesiastical and secular hierarchy, Trumhere's presence was a highly visible statement that, despite having regained a measure of autonomy, Mercia was still a Northumbrian dependency (Higham 1997, 246–7). Thus paradoxically the Christianisation of the Mercian kingship was driven by two contradictory but equally strong imperatives, a need to accommodate the still dominant Oswiu, and a desire to gain for themselves some of the advantages which espousal of Christianity had given to the Northumbrian king.

Despite his probably subordinate position Wulfhere seems to have made efforts to regain at least some measure of the dominance over southern Britain that his father had enjoyed. This is shown by his relations with King Æthelwealh of the South Saxons, for whom he acted as godfather and to whom he gave (or more probably gave tributary rights over) the Isle of Wight and the Meonwaras in Hampshire (HE IV, 13), his intervention in Essex during the East Saxons' reversion to traditional religion (HE III, 30), his power over Surrey demonstrated in a charter of the shadowy *subregulus* Frithuwold (Birch 1885, no. 34, S1165), and his ability to sell the diocese of London to Wine (HE III, 7). After Oswiu's death in 670, Wulfhere seems to have renounced any tributary obligations to Ecgfrith, Oswiu's son and successor, and in 673/4 attacked the North-umbrians with the intention of making them tributary, though his defeat led in practice to the opposite result (VW 20). In fact, though probably nominally tributary until Oswiu's death in 670, it is likely that by the mid 660s Wulfhere was able to pursue an independent policy with little regard to the Northumbrian ruler. This brings us to the Synod of Whitby, the occasion where Wilfrid first made a significant impact on the wider political stage. There is not the scope to consider here the context of Whitby, or indeed of Wilfrid's role in it, and these things have been discussed elsewhere (Mayr-Harting 1991, 103–13; Higham 1997, 255–8). We can, however, consider the implications the 'synod' had for Mercia. The early Mercian Church, as we have seen, was to some extent an instrument of Northumbrian control, and derived its spiritual authority from Lindisfarne. After the Synod of Whitby, however, the Northumbrian Church – and therefore its Mercian satellite – looked to Rome for legitimacy (HE III 25, VW 10). To some extent then, Wulfhere in his espousal of Rome was constrained by circumstance, but he may not have found these developments displeasing. A Mercian Church looking for its authority to Rome via Canterbury, rather than to Iona via Holy Island, had a greater potential for independence from Northumbrian oversight. It is true that when, in 669, Archbishop Theodore provided Wulfhere with a bishop to replace the dead Jaruman, Chad, the man chosen by the archbishop, was a Northumbrian, and a member of Oswiu's circle (HE IV, 3), but Oswiu's death the following year may have led to a weakening of Chad's ties to the Northumbrian kingship (Higham 1997, 265–6). By the death of Wulfhere in 675 (HE III, 24; V, 24) then, the Mercian bishopric was a member of the *familia* of Churches subject to the authority of Canterbury, and was *de facto* independent of, and of similar status to, the Northumbrian see.

Wulfhere was succeeded by his brother Æthelræd (HE V, 24). Æthelræd's secular policies are well known, and need only be briefly outlined here. Wulfhere's defeat, followed shortly by his death, probably left his southern hegemony in some disarray, but Æthelræd seems to have lost little time reasserting the dominant position of the Mercians – his attack on Kent in 676 is probably to be interpreted in this light (HE V, 24). By 679 he was in a position to challenge Ecgfrith, defeating him in battle by the River Trent (HE IV, 21). This battle restored Lindsey to the orbit of the Mercians, effectively ended the influence of Northumbrian kings in southern England, and perhaps indirectly precipitated Ecgfrith's disastrous Pictish campaign (HE IV, 26; VW 44). It is also well known that it was during Æthelræd's reign that Mercian kings began to tighten their control over autonomous but tributary peoples on the peripheries of Mercia. This process is most clearly illustrated by a series of charters in which one can trace the changing status of the rulers of the Hwicce (B85, B187, B223; S53, S56, S113).

In all this Æthelræd was continuing the policies of his brother Wulfhere, and it can be suggested that he did likewise in church politics. It was during the episcopate of Archbishop Theodore that the disparate ecclesiastical systems of the various English kingdoms, Mercia among them, were amalgamated and re-organized into what can with some justice be termed an 'English Church' (Brooks 1984, 71–6, Cubitt 1995, 8–11), and, I suggest, Æthelræd supported this process because it was in his own interests. In particular, it facilitated the extension of his power over the kingdoms of the West Midlands. Our knowledge of Church structures in this region before the reforms of Archbishop Theodore is marginal, as neither Bede nor any other extant sources furnish details of them (Bassett 1992, 13). It is sometimes thought that the Hwicce and the Magonsæte – if we can use this term at this early date – were originally subject to the authority of the bishop of the Mercians, but in fact there is cause to suppose the existence of a well-established system of bishoprics in the West Midlands, that formed an integral part of the native British Church of western Britain (Bassett 1992, 2000; Tyler 2007). Exactly when this system was superseded by a Canterbury/Rome oriented one cannot be stated with certainty, though it is likely to have occurred during or after Theodore's diocesan reorganization of 678/9, as none of the bishops attending Theodore's council at Hertford in 673 held sees west of Mercia (HE IV, 5). Certainly the bishop of the Hwicce appears to have been firmly within the Canterbury fold by *c.*690–92. At this time the ailing Bishop Bosel was replaced by Oftfor, who had been educated first at Whitby and later under Theodore at Canterbury. Significantly, Oftfor was installed at the request of King Æthelræd, not a local Hwiccan ruler, and the consecration was performed by Bishop Wilfrid, at that time acting for Æthelræd as bishop of the Middle Angles (HE IV, 23). The personnel of any indigenous Church system in these kingdoms are likely to have been members of the local elites. Consequently, it is probable that ecclesiastical hierarchies in both these kingdoms were intimately involved in the local systems of patronage, power and influence. These clerics would look principally to the local kings for protection and advancement, rather than to the distant and only recently Christian Mercian hegemon. Thus the native Churches would have both expressed and supported the political autonomy of the Hwicce and the Magonsæte. By contrast, incoming Canterbury-focused bishops would lack local ties and influence, and would be much more inclined than their predecessors to look to the Mercian king as their chief patron and protector.

These then were the principal political developments in Mercia during the second half of the seventh century. In the secular sphere, Wulfhere and Æthelræd between them broke the power of Northumbria in southern England, restored on a firmer basis their father's hegemonic position, and started the process of absorbing into their kingdom many of the surrounding polities. If we now turn to matters ecclesiastical, during the same period the Christian Church in Mercia was transformed from a new, small, externally- and politically-imposed missionary endeavour among an essentially non-Christian people, into a regular, well-organized Church dependent on native rulers. It is against this background that we need to see Wilfrid's interactions with these two kings.

Some little time after Whitby, perhaps a year or so, Oswiu and Alhfrith had Wilfrid appointed as bishop. While he was in Francia for his ordination, Oswiu changed his mind and appointed Chad to the see instead (VW: 11–12, 14; HE III, 28, V, 19). The reasons for this are not clear, but Wilfrid at this time was very much the protégé of Alhfrith, Oswiu's son and sub-king of Deira, and it has been noted that it may have had something to do with the strife between Oswiu and his son enigmatically referred to by Bede (HE III, 13; Kirby 1991, 103). On his return to Britain therefore, Wilfrid found himself a bishop without a diocese, and spent the next few years in semi-retirement at his monastery of Ripon. It was during this period that he had his first significant interaction with the Mercian kingdom. Stephen tells us that Wilfrid remained at Ripon throughout this period:

[...] except for the frequent occasions when Wulfhere, King of the

Mercians, out of sincere affection for him, invited him into his realm to fulfil various episcopal duties. The Lord raised up for himself this most kindly monarch, who, amongst his other good deeds, for the benefit of his soul, granted our bishop many pieces of land in various places, on which he forthwith founded monasteries. (VW 14)

In addition to purely spiritual considerations, and any genuine goodwill between the two men, both stood to gain from their relationship, each of them being to some degree opposed to Oswiu. Wilfrid gained property, including Lichfield (VW 15), and an opportunity to fulfill the episcopal functions denied him in Northumbria. At this time he was not, of course, the influential, powerful figure he would become, but nevertheless to Wulfhere he probably seemed a potentially useful tool in relations with Oswiu. Given Wilfrid's role at Whitby, it would have been easy to portray him as the champion of Rome-focused Christianity in England and, as was argued earlier, it was in Wulfhere's political interests to emphasize his adherence to Rome, as such a posture tended to reduce his dependency on Oswiu. Additionally of course, Wulfhere gained the services of a bishop not controlled by the Northumbrian king. It is even possible that he hoped to persuade Wilfrid to abandon his Northumbrian claims and base himself permanently in Mercia. The fact that Wilfrid was given Lichfield may be significant in this regard. Stephen describes Lichfield as a place '[...] suitable as an episcopal see either for himself or for any other to whom he might wish to give it.' (VW 15). What does this mean? It could just be that Stephen knew that Lichfield became the principal church of the Mercian bishop. On the other hand it could be that Wulfhere intended Wilfrid to become the Mercian bishop, with his seat here. Furthermore, there are some faint indications that there was a pre-existing 'British' church at nearby Wall, perhaps even the seat of a bishop (Tyler 2007). If a vestigial 'British' Church structure survived in 'Original Mercia' then Wulfhere may have planned to tie it more firmly to his kingship by imposing Wilfrid, an outsider dependent on his favour, as bishop.

If Wulfhere did hope to 'poach' Wilfrid, however, he did not know his man and was to be disappointed, and this phase in Wilfrid's relations with Mercia ended with the arrival in Britain of Archbishop Theodore in 669, followed by the death of Oswiu in 670 (HE IV, 2, 5, V, 25). Wilfrid was reinstated at York and, still a relatively young man, he entered the most successful, and probably the happiest, period of his life, for nearly a decade enjoying the position of sole Northumbrian bishop. It is unclear to what degree Wilfrid and Wulfhere were in communication with each other during these years, but Wilfrid's probable retention of Mercian properties suggests that there was some contact. Nor do we know what Wilfrid's attitude towards the Mercian ruler was, though Stephen's treatment of him is perhaps illuminating. As noted earlier, when Wulfhere was acting as Wilfrid's patron Stephen describes him as a 'most kindly monarch whom God had raise up for himself' but when, in 673/4, he launched his attack on Northumbria, he is characterized as 'a man of proud mind and insatiable will,' and the defeat of his army is recorded with evident satisfaction (VW 20). It is at least possible therefore that there was a cooling of relations between the two men.

We shall now consider Wilfrid's second fall from grace. While Æthelræd and Ecgfrith were clashing by the River Trent, Wilfrid was in the process of seeking papal support in his quarrel with Ecgfrith and Theodore (VW 24–33). On his return to Northumbria Wilfrid was first imprisoned and then driven into exile, ultimately taking refuge among the South Saxons (VW 34–42). One might have expected Æthelræd to have offered Wilfrid asylum. Not only did he not do so, however, but we are told that when Wilfrid initially sought the protection of the rather shadowy *subregulus* or ealdorman Berhtwald, he was soon forced to leave by the enmity of King Æthelræd. Stephen tells us that Æthelræd did this to oblige Ecgfrith, who was his wife's brother. At first sight this explanation seems exceedingly unlikely, considering the political circumstances. However, Bede informs us that Ecgfrith's brother Ælfwine was killed in the battle, that Æthelræd paid compensation for this death, and that Archbishop Theodore negotiated a peace between the two kings (HE IV, 21). Given these rather delicate negotiations, and given that, as the victor at the Trent, Æthelræd was getting the better of the bargain – regaining control of Lindsey for example – he may have preferred not to irritate his brother-in-law and erstwhile enemy further by offering sanctuary to Wilfrid, whom Ecgfrith clearly detested. Additionally, Æthelræd may just not have wanted to help Wilfrid. Peace had been made, but tensions between Mercia and Northumbria would still have been high, and Wilfrid, despite his current troubles, was a Northumbrian and, after spending almost a decade as sole Northumbrian bishop, he was now a much more powerful and influential figure than he had been when he was the recipient of Wulfhere's patronage in the 660s. If, as was tentatively suggested earlier, relations between Wilfrid and Wulfhere had been strained in the mid 670s, Æthelræd may have looked on the bishop with an unfriendly eye. These factors, together with his possession of extensive property in Mercia, may have made Wilfrid seem an undesirable and destabilizing factor in Mercian political circles.

We should note, however, that Wilfrid's sojourn among the South Saxons probably had Æthelræd's tacit approval. Stephen emphasizes the remoteness of this kingdom, saying that it was the only part of Britain outside the reach of Ecgfrith and that dense forests and rocky coasts had prevented it from being conquered by any other kingdom (VW 51). This is a *topos*, perhaps meant to emphasize the pagan barbarism of the South Saxons, and to highlight Wilfrid's nobility in exile. In fact the South Saxons and their rulers participated fully in southern English politics – they had been tributary to Wulfhere and probably were to Æthelræd also. If Æthelræd wished to prevent Wilfrid's staying there, it seems unlikely that a minor ruler like Æthelwalh king of the South Saxons would have been able, or indeed wished, to resist. So while certainly not amicable to Wilfrid at this time, Æthelræd may not have been as hostile as generally supposed.

Wilfrid's exile among the South Saxons came to an end in the mid 680s. He was reconciled with Archbishop Theodore and King Æthelræd and, after the death of Ecgfrith, with Aldfrith, the new Northumbrian king. Many, if not all, of his Northumbrian and Mercian properties were returned to him, and he was restored to York (VW 43–4). His troubles were not over for long, however, and in 691 he fell from the favour of a third Northumbrian king and went into exile in Mercia. For the next decade and a half – Church councils and trips to Rome aside – Wilfrid acted as bishop for Æthelræd, perhaps based at Leicester (VW 45). This section of Stephen's life of Wilfrid is in many ways the most frustrating, as we are told virtually nothing about the bishop's relations with the Mercian king during this extended period. Unlike in 680, when Wilfrid was *persona non grata* in Mercia, in 691 Æthelræd appears to have welcomed him with open arms, and stood by him throughout his difficulties with King Aldfrith and Archbishop Berhtwald. Why this change of attitude by Æthelræd? Firstly, there may have been a genuine friendship between the two men. The reconciliation between them affected by Theodore in 686 may well have been sincere, and there is nothing in Stephen's cursory account of the period 686–91 to suggest any rift between them during these years. Thus Æthelræd may have been personally inclined to offer asylum to Wilfrid. Also, by 691 it may have been apparent, in a way that it had not been a decade earlier, that active, aggressive competition between the Mercian and Northumbrian kingdoms was a thing of the past. If tensions between the two polities were reduced, Wilfrid's status as a member of the Northumbrian elite may have been less of an issue than it had been previously.

Æthelræd may, therefore, have had less reason to be hostile to Wilfrid in 691 than he had had in the early 680s. He may also have had more positive reasons to welcome the exiled bishop. The see of Canterbury had been vacant since the death of Theodore in 690 and in addition the kingship of Kent was disputed by a variety of native and external claimants. Æthelræd appears to have been actively involved in this process. Stephen tells us that Theodore had expressed a desire for Wilfrid to succeed him at Canterbury (VW 43). This, of course, might not have been the case, Stephen may have wished to give extra lustre to Wilfrid's memory with this statement, but Nicholas Brooks has suggested that Æthelræd himself may have desired to install Wilfrid as

Metropolitan at Canterbury (Brooks 1984, 77). If so, he was of course to be disappointed, as Abbot Berhtwald of Reculver was eventually appointed to the archdiocese (HE V, 8). If, as Brooks argues, Æthelræd found Berhtwald's appointment unsatisfactory, this might partially explain his continuing support of Wilfrid, but it is probable that he also found the bishop a valuable servant in other ways. It's not clear exactly what official status Wilfrid had in the Mercian ecclesiastical hierarchy during these years, but it does seem that in practice he acted as bishop for the southerly and easterly parts of Æthelræd's kingdom. Wilfrid's monastery at Oundle was located in Middle Anglia, and he may have had other properties there also. Despite this he was a relative outsider and dependent on the patronage of the Mercian ruler. Æthelræd may have used him, and his episcopal role, to consolidate his own power over the Middle Angles (Capper, this volume).

Conclusions

In conclusion, we have seen that while it is likely that there was some contact between Wilfrid and the Mercian court throughout his episcopate, the more active phases of this relationship occurred during his quarrels with Northumbria's kings. From the perspective of the Mercian rulers, Wilfrid proved a useful ally in a number of ways. In the 660s patronage of the bishop helped Wulfhere in his attempts to free his kingdom from Northumbrian control. In the early 690s Æthelræd, as we've seen, may have hoped to make Wilfrid Archbishop of Canterbury and, if successful, this would have augmented Æthelræd's authority across Britain. If we look at other aspects of Mercian policy, we see that patronage of Wilfrid may have aided the consolidation of Mercian power over autonomous or semi-autonomous polities on the periphery of Mercia – directly with regard to the Middle Angles, indirectly with the Hwicce.

If we now consider things from Wilfrid's perspective, we can also say a number of things. Looking at his career as a whole, not just his relations with Mercia, it seems clear that Wilfrid saw himself primarily as a Northumbrian bishop, if not 'the' Northumbrian bishop, but he valued his properties in Mercia, and was willing to act as a Mercian bishop when the need arose. It also seems possible that there was a genuine friendship between Wilfrid and Æthelræd during their later years – Stephen's life is generally complimentary to this king, whereas, as we've seen, its treatment of Wulfhere is rather more changeable. Despite all this, however, Wilfrid's determination to pursue his rights in Northumbria, at all stages of his life, even as a septuagenarian, make it clear that any role in Mercia, however honourable, was second best from his viewpoint. It has been noted that in many ways Wilfrid's career and lifestyle look more like those of a secular prince than of an ecclesiastic, and it is possible to interpret his interactions with Mercia in the Anglo-Saxon tradition of secular princely exile. A man might go into exile to take refuge from troubles at home, perhaps even with enemies of his people, but such exile was, ideally, to be a springboard to a triumphant return. So it proved for Wilfrid in 669, in 686 and finally in 706.

21: *Wilfrid, Oda and Eadmer*

ALARIC A. TROUSDALE

When he commissioned the composition of a lyrical poem celebrating Wilfrid's translation from Ripon *c*.948, Archbishop Oda effectively claimed that saint's relics for Canterbury. Half a century later Byrhtferth of Ramsey, in his *Vita S Oswaldi*, made a counter claim that St Oswald of York found and re-housed Wilfrid's relics, still at Ripon, during Oswald's archiepiscopate (971–92). Such claims and counterclaims are nothing new to the student of saints and their relics. The possession of all or some of a potent saint's remains was tremendously important for a church in the Middle Ages. Proper documentation as to how such relics were acquired was of the utmost consequence, whether the translation was a legitimate purchase or a more underhanded matter. The writing of saints' lives was an essential component in the transfer of power involved when one church obtained relics from another.

It has most often been argued that Wilfrid's translation was an essential element of the developing political relationship between Wessex and Northumbria during the middle decades of the tenth century (Brooks 1984, 227–8; Cubitt and Costambeys 2004). This interpretation views the impromptu abduction of Wilfrid from Ripon as a symbol of King Eadred's domination of the Scandinavian kings of York and the supremacy of Canterbury over the Archbishopric of York. This is an entirely justifiable stance, but while such conclusions make for attractive reading, they leave out other possible interpretations.

Through an examination of the relationship between Wilfrid's cult, the purported translators of his relics, Oda of Canterbury and Oswald of York, and the hagiographer of all three saints, Eadmer of Canterbury, two main points will be argued in the present essay. It will initially contend that Oda's involvement with the removal of Wilfrid's relics from Ripon more accurately reflects his concerns with issues of ecclesiastical conduct – the role of bishops in their diocese and church maintenance – than the dispute between Wessex and the men of York. The first point will be addressed through a re-examination of the preface to the *Breviloquium vitae Wilfridi*, where Oda defends Canterbury's acquisition of Wilfrid's bones, in the context of his wider corpus of writings. Secondly, the essay will examine Eadmer's role in interpreting these events. Eadmer wrote lives of SS Wilfrid, Oda and Oswald and was the first writer after Stephen of Ripon to comment on the conflict surrounding Wilfrid's remains. The traditional view of Eadmer's solution to the problem of two divergent traditions surrounding

Wilfrid's translation has been seen solely as part of his resolute defense of Canterbury's relic claims. Here a new interpretation of Eadmer's comments will be proposed as part of a reflection on his particular reverence for Wilfrid and Oda as Anglo-Saxon saints. In Eadmer's writings one observes Oda and Wilfrid reinforcing each other's status through their connected roles as translator and translated. It will be argued that Eadmer effectively wove Oda's and Wilfrid's stories together to strengthen both saints' reputations – not only as part of his respect for Wilfrid's relics and Canterbury's claim on them – but also as part of his efforts to promote Oda's emerging cult in conjunction with Wilfrid's. A fresh examination of Wilfrid's translation and the authors who addressed it will shed valuable light on how Oda's own posthumous reputation and Eadmer's hagiographical energy were affected by their connection with Wilfrid's cult at Canterbury.

In order to better frame the arguments to come, it will prove valuable at the outset to re-examine the circumstances of Wilfrid's translation from Ripon, and how Canterbury's acquisition of Wilfrid's relics can be seen in the context of Archbishop Oda's writings. The 'D' manuscript of the *Anglo-Saxon Chronicle* records that in the year 948: 'King Eadred ravaged all Northumbria, because they had accepted Eric as their king; and in that ravaging the glorious minster at Ripon, which St Wilfrid had built, was burnt down' (Cubbin 1996, 44; Whitelock *et al.* 1961, 72). King Eadred's raid on the north was a direct and violent response to a breach of faith, a reversal of pledges made by the men of York a year before at a meeting at Tanshelf where they chose Eric Bloodaxe as their king (Smyth 1979, 155–7; Woolf 2007, 185–7). While it is not explicitly stated in any source, Eadred's raid was in all likelihood the moment at which Wilfrid's remains were acquired and delivered into the possession of Archbishop Oda of Canterbury.

Oda's career is of considerable interest to historians of the tenth century and his life deserves more study than it has hitherto received. The best full biographical treatment of Archbishop Oda remains that by Nicholas Brooks. The picture of the prelate that emerges is of an energetic, dynamic and conciliatory figure, one who was both traditional and pragmatic (Brooks 1981, 222–37). Before his appointment to the archbishopric in 941, Oda had occupied the see of Ramsbury. During the reigns of King Athelstan (925–39) and his brother Edmund (939–46) Oda was a notable presence at foreign and domestic diplomatic occasions, and appears to have worked closely and productively with both rulers. In 929 he traveled in the company of Bishop Cenwald of Worcester on a tour of German monasteries, and at some point between 941 and 946 he passed through the monastery at Pfäfers, presumably on another diplomatic assignment (Keynes 1985, 198–201). A late source indicates that on one such mission he negotiated with Duke Hugh of the Franks the peaceful return to

France of King Athelstan's nephew, Louis d'Outremer (Latouche 1930, 130).

Oda was instrumental in the legislation of King Edmund, heavily influencing that king's so-called 'first code' (Wormald 1999, 310). To Edmund's reign (939–46) can also be assigned the composition of Oda's ten 'Chapters', a treatise on proper ecclesiastical conduct heavily influenced by the Legatine Decrees of 796 (Schoebe 1962; Whitelock *et al.* 1981, 65–74 and Trousdale, Forthcoming). Archbishop Oda can also be observed, in co-operation with Archbishop Wulfstan of York, negotiating a peace treaty between King Edmund and Óláfr Gothfrithsson after the latter's abortive attack on Mercia in 940 (Stevenson 1858, 68). Oda's own writings and his influence on royal legislation show the archbishop to have been vigorously concerned with the relationship between the church and royal government. This, combined with his international experience and demonstrated energy, leave one with few doubts about Oda's abilities to attract well-educated individuals to his service.

One example of this ability can be found in the figure of Frithegod, a member of Oda's household, an accomplished author of continental origin and, as Michael Lapidge has reminded us on multiple occasions, one of the most learned men in England in the tenth century (Lapidge 1975 & 1988). Frithegod's scholarship and the closeness of his relationship with the archbishop may be demonstrated by the fact that Oda's nephew Oswald, the future saint and archbishop of York, was personally tutored by Frithegod (Lapidge 1988, 47 n.15). That the association between Frithegod and Oda was a robust one is supported by evidence suggesting that upon the archbishop's death in 958, no longer in possession of a patron, Frithegod left Canterbury for the canonry of Brioude in the Auvergne (Lapidge 1988, 62–4).

It was Frithegod also who, upon the arrival of Wilfrid's relics at Canterbury, was assigned by Oda the task of composing a metrical poem in the saint's honour based on the prose life by Stephen of Ripon. Internal evidence from Frithegod's *Breviloquium vitae Wilfridi* has been used to date the poem's composition to a ten-year span, as Ripon Minster was burned in Eadred's invasion of 948, and Archbishop Oda, who enjoys a dedication at the end of the poem, died in 958 (Lapidge 1988, 46).

The *Breviloquium* has a brief, forty-eight line introduction that describes the circumstances of Wilfrid's translation from Ripon, and while the precise language was possibly composed by Frithegod, it is clearly Archbishop Oda's own sentiments that have been recorded in this first-person account. We are told that:

> ... when certain men having the favour of God had translated the most venerable remains of the blessed confessor of Christ, Wilfrid, from there (that is, from the place of his burial), which was rotting

away in the unfitting neglect of a thorny swamp – nay rather what is frightful to say – they were neglected through the revulsion of the prelates, I received them in reverence and gathered them together within the precincts of the metropolitan church over which I preside by the grace of God, compelled especially by the testimony of the evangelist (which is my defense), that wheresoever there will be a body, there the eagles will also be gathered. And so, delighted by the proximity of such a great kinsman and one so worthy of God I have thought it worthwhile both to adorn the remains with a more stately reliquary and to sweeten them with a new poem, using flowers plucked from the book of his life. (Turner and Muir 2006, 272–3).[1]

This passage has been assigned, not without good reason, to the category of *furta sacra* apologia (Brooks 1984; Lapidge 1988; Cubitt and Costambeys, 2004). That Archbishop Oda had ordered St Wilfrid's relics snatched from Ripon and translated to Canterbury, and was single-handedly responsible for reviving Wilfrid's dwindling cult is a very appealing tradition, and one that has remained popular in Anglo-Saxon scholarship. As will now be demonstrated, there is an alternative view of the circumstances surrounding Wilfrid's translation to Canterbury observable through an examination of Archbishop Oda's own corpus of writings. *Furta Sacra* it may have been, but viewed in the context of Oda's opinions on proper ecclesiastical practice it is not the only explanation allowable. A comparison of Oda's legal and clerical output with his justification for Wilfrid's translation will illustrate this point.

Frithegod composed the preface to the *Breviloquium* in the first person, and an authorial voice is noticeably present. While Oda was himself a keen student and practitioner of the hermeneutic Latin style popular in the tenth century, and perfectly capable of composing florid and intricate Latin, Brooks' suggestion that Frithegod enlivened Oda's words with his own linguistic flair seems reasonable (Brooks 1984, 229). The preface provides what at first glance appears to be an extended explanation for Wilfrid's translation (notably omitting the burning of Ripon Minster), but a closer examination reveals the possibility

---

[1] 'Igitur uenerabilissimas beati confessoris Christi Wilfridi reliquias indecenti senticosae uoraginis situ marcidas, immo, quod dictu quoque meticulosum est, praelatorum horripalitione neglectas, cum inde, fauente Deo, scilicet a loco sepulchri eius, quidam transtulissent, reuerenter excepi, atque intra ambitum metropolitanae cui gratia Dei praesideo aecclesiae collocaui, praesertim cogente illo euangelistae testimonio, meo uidelicet apologetico, quia ubicanque fuerit corpus, congregabuntur et aquilae. Itaque tantae tamque Deo dignae affinitatis delectatus uicinitate, et editiore eas entheca decusare, et excerptis de libro uitae eius flosculis, nouo operae praetium duxi carmine uenustare.'

that the choice of language was more deliberate.

The section quoted above highlighting Oda's reasoning for the translation is preceded by a passage emphasizing the discord that had recently struck England, and it sets a pessimistic and exasperated tone for what follows. In this instance Oda places significant emphasis on three aspects of the translation. First, he mentions that 'certain men' performed the act, thus shifting blame from the Canterbury community onto persons unnamed for the theft. He then states that he received the relics gratefully, thus emphasizing that these relics were not acquired at the archbishop's instigation, but given to Canterbury as a gift. Oda appears then to acknowledge that the acquisition of Wilfrid's relics could potentially be considered controversial, and focuses his justification of their safe removal to Canterbury on the contention that the northern prelates were derelict in their duty to maintain Church property adequately. This appears to be the heart of his line of reasoning, and one impression is that this aspect in particular, the 'revulsion of the prelates', has troubled the archbishop.

Following his defense of Wilfrid's translation, Oda proceeds to defend his actions on the basis of good intentions. The final sentences of this justification are especially telling:

> Lest he, who with furrowed brow is snarling that I ought to be criticized, should absurdly strive to thwart the most evident will of God … Moreover I shall sweeten the inadequacies of bitter obstinacy and the throttled cries of robbery with the unworn covering of universality and the ambrosial resin of poeticality … (Brooks 1984, 229–30).

It is not difficult to come away from this with the conclusion that vociferous accusations of theft may indeed have followed Wilfrid's translation to Canterbury, and that they were allegations that Oda felt necessary to appease with honeyed words.

As mentioned above, the accepted view of Oda's translation of Wilfrid places the incident squarely within the context of political expediency in the wake of the mid-century clash between the Archbishop of York and the kings of Wessex. When one examines Oda's words more closely however, additional possibilities to the received interpretation of events emerge. The preface to the *Breviloquium* takes pains to clarify several important issues. Firstly, it states that Wilfrid's translation was the will of God, and God at that moment favored Canterbury over Ripon for Wilfrid's safe keeping. Secondly, derision is cast upon those who neglected the upkeep of the church of Ripon. Ripon, however, is singled out as an example of the neglect that many churches throughout the *'imperium Anglorum'* have lately suffered. Thirdly, stress is placed on the impoverished nature of the northern church and that this fact was intrinsically connected to the difficulties then common throughout England.

All of the above items are of course common topoi of *furta sacra* accounts. However, Oda's abhorrence at the northern prelates' neglect of Wilfrid and Ripon Cathedral, and his gloomy acknowledgement of troubles within the English Church are also well in line with sentiments that are found in other compositions of his that have survived. His 'Ten Chapters' and his 'letter to his suffragan bishops' were composed as instructive and exhortatory expositions. A closer examination of these texts suggests that Oda was concerned less with admonition and rebuke than he was with direction and example. His 'letter to his suffragan bishops', for instance, serves both as an acknowledgement of and apology for the myriad problems afflicting the English church. Oda expresses in heartfelt terms his own inability to solve such dilemmas:

> If it could somehow come about that the riches of the entire world were placed before our eyes, to serve us in their entirety by royal gift, I should willingly give them all away, and sacrifice my own life too for the salvation of your souls; for I desire and hope to be strengthened myself by your Holinesses' zeal, in the sphere in which the Lord God has made us His labourers. (Winterbottom and Thompson 2007, 29).[2]

Oda follows this passage with an exhortation to proper episcopal responsibility, and a collective effort. In addition to this letter, Oda's 'Ten Chapters' show him to have been deeply concerned with proper episcopal conduct as well as with the central role of bishops as the shepherds of their diocese. The third 'Chapter' is directed explicitly at bishops who were inattentive of their duties within their districts (Schoebe 1962, 80–1). It stresses constant vigilance and attention to the everyday acts that take a bishop to the furthest reaches of his diocese, lest a single soul remain open to the 'wolves' mangling jaws' (*lupinus pateat morsibus lacerandus*). The third 'Chapter' outlines a specific warning against precisely the type of neglect that Oda accused the northern prelates of having committed in the preface to the *Breviloquium*: that of the shepherd neglecting his flock.

The law code known as I Edmund, which was heavily influenced by both Archbishops Oda and Wulfstan, presents further evidence of a strong, archiepiscopally driven emphasis on church maintenance. The fifth clause of the code makes this sentiment unequivocal; it stresses the need for the upkeep of

---

[2]   '*Si aliquo modo fieri posse tut totius mundi opes ante nostros ponerentur obtutus, ita ut imperiali munere nobis universaliter deservirent, libenter illa omnia distribuerem, meque ipsum insuper pro vestrarum animarum salute impenderem, quippe quoniam meipsum a vestre sanctitatis studio cupio et spero corroborari super eo in quo Dominus Deus nos operarios constituit.*'

churches and their buildings, and that these essential preservation measures are the responsibility of the bishops: 'Likewise we have ordained that every bishop shall restore the houses of God on his own property, and also exhort the king that all God's churches be well put in order, as we have much need' (Robertson 1925, 6–7).[3] That both archbishops Oda and Wulfstan directly influenced the legislation promulgated by King Edmund reinforces the symbolic importance of Oda's irritated response to the dilapidated state of Ripon church.

Oda's own compositions show him to have been thoroughly concerned with the role of bishops in their own dioceses and the upkeep of proper episcopal discipline, including the physical maintenance of church structures. It is important also to recall that Oda was himself an active church builder and restorer. One of the more significant miracles described in his *vita*, for example, was concerned with the upgrades he made to Canterbury Cathedral. Eadmer's version of these events is the most colourful: 'For the roof of the church was decayed by its very great age, and was sagging, with parts of it half in ruin throughout its length. Oda wished to restore it, and desired also to raise its walls to a much more exalted height …' (Turner and Muir 2006, 24–5).[4] Lacking a building of comparable size to accommodate the large Canterbury crowds, Oda prayed for dry weather and continued to use the cathedral throughout the renovations. *Quid moror*? No rain fell within the walls of the church for three years. This miracle story brings into sharp relief Oda's intimate connection with the buildings of Christ Church. The story also provides further support for the argument that the archbishop was a passionate advocate for the physical upkeep of Church structures. As an intriguing side-note, there are numerous accounts of translations having been used as opportunities for the local display of saints as a means of fundraising for building projects (Geary 1978, 63–5). It is possible, however unprovable, that the display of Wilfrid's relics funded Oda's renovation of Christ Church.

In the preface to the *Breviloquium*, then, Oda can be observed railing against episcopal laziness and inactivity throughout the English Church; neglect of Wilfrid and of Ripon serves as the pertinent example. While there is no need to reject entirely the interpretation of Wilfrid's translation as a retaliatory measure against Archbishop Wulfstan of York for his recalcitrance towards King Eadred, it remains a singularly narrow lens through which to view what was

---

[3] '*Eac we gecwædon, þæt ælc biscop béte Godes hus on his agenum, 7 eac þone cyningc minegige, þæt ealle Godes circan syn wel behworfene, swa us micel þearf is.*'

[4] '*Nam tectum eiusdem aecclesiae nimia uetustate corruptum semirutis per totum partibus pendebat. Quod ille renouare cupiens, murum quoque in porrectiorem caelsitudinem exaltare desiderans, congregatis artificibus praecepit et quod disolutum desuper eminebat penitus tolli, et quod minus in altitudine murus habebat iussit extolli.*'

undoubtedly a very complex situation. There are other ways to consider Wilfrid's translation in light of what is known of Archbishop Oda. Oda was one of the great Anglo-Saxon ambassadors of the tenth-century, sent on various delegations to the Continent by King Athelstan and the chief negotiator between Kings Edmund, Eadred and the Viking kings of York. Oda appears to have been a natural diplomat, and what can be gleaned of his character suggests that he was willing to work together with Archbishop Wulfstan towards productive goals on multiple occasions. If Oda's justification of Wilfrid's translation is considered not as a club with which to berate the archdiocese of York but as a symbol of hope for the rest of the English Church, Oda's protestations of innocence and worthy endeavor in the preface to the *Breviloquium* can be understood in a less cynical light. Such an interpretation aligns well with the evidence offered above.

The significance of Wilfrid's translation to Canterbury, however, differs greatly depending on whose account we read. As noted above, Oda is not the only individual associated with the removal of Wilfrid's relics, and the picture that modern research has established of Wilfrid's translation has not always been so orderly. Historians have long been aware of the competing claim for Wilfrid's remains made on behalf of St Oswald by his first hagiographer, Byrhtferth of Ramsey, and confusion remains to this day regarding the development of the two mutually contradictory traditions (Raine 1879, xliii–xlviii; Thacker 1996, 254–5). Composed sometime between the years 997 and 1002, Byrhtferth's *Vita S. Oswaldi* is a rich source for the history of Benedictine monasticism in the tenth century. However, as Lapidge has made abundantly clear, one uses its pages as a source for the history of tenth-century events and individuals at considerable risk (Lapidge 2009, lxviii). The *Vita S. Oswaldi* contains at its opening several chapters dedicated to Archbishop Oda, Oswald's uncle and benefactor. While these chapters are fully integral to the *Vita*, they also serve as the earliest incarnation of a life dedicated to Oda himself and evidence of a nascent cult at Ramsey. Byrhtferth's commitment to Benedictine monasticism no doubt influenced his appreciation of Oda, who had himself been a monk. But while Byrhtferth recounts several of Oda's miracles and a handful of his virtuous deeds, Wilfrid's translation to Canterbury is not listed amongst Oda's achievements.

In Part V of his *Vita* Byrhtferth relates a story in which Oswald translated Wilfrid's bones to a lovely new reliquary at a location undisclosed:

> Oswald, the tireless soldier of Christ, making a tour of his sheepfolds, arrived happily at the buildings of the monastery which is called Ripon, which had famously been built by the venerable Wilfrid, but was at that point in ruins. While he was setting about his work at that same place, through grace of the All-seeing Saviour he 'discovered a treasure' which had long been hidden from

mortals, which he raised up from the ground with a pure heart and humble intention. For the holy father discovered the blessed remains of Bishop Wilfrid; because of the merit of Oswald's exalted life, the guiding force of his life, the Holy Trinity of God, granted it to him to discover this treasure. (Lapidge 2009, 170–1).[5]

No shortage of scholarly ink has been shed trying to decipher what exactly Byrhtferth meant in this passage, and to this day a significant amount of confusion remains as to how these two mutually exclusive traditions developed. One possibility is that Oswald obtained 'secondary relics' of Wilfrid (Thacker 1996, 254), perhaps by purchase. It has also been suggested that Byrhtferth mistook an anecdote told to him by Oswald late in his life (Lapidge 1988, 45 n.3). Given Lapidge's own more recent arguments demonstrating Byrhtferth's reliance almost exclusively on written sources for the *Vita S. Oswaldi*, as well as his lack of personal contact with Oswald himself, this now seems difficult to accept. Lapidge has since concluded that Byrhtferth was patently unaware of the tradition at Canterbury and of Frithegod's *Breviloquium* (Lapidge 2009, 171 n.97). Unless we are to consider Byrhtferth most disingenuous, this suggestion seems highly likely, whether one accepts Oswald's hypothetical acquisition of derivative relics or not.

There remain, however, a number of reasons for Byrhtferth to have been aware of Canterbury's possession of Wilfrid's relics. An important point requiring consideration, persuasively argued by Alan Thacker, is that when Byrhtferth was writing in the late tenth century it is likely that the cult of St Oda was actually more popular at Ramsey than it was at Canterbury (Thacker 1996, 254). Furthermore, it was Byrhtferth's own personal tutor, Frithegod, who had written the *Breviloquium*, where Oda's claim on Wilfrid's relics was made.

One possible explanation for Byrhtferth's seeming lack of awareness of Canterbury's claim could be that the half-century interim had effectively laid any controversy to rest. But this requires the assumption that Oda succeeded in soothing any fevered Yorkshire brows. If Oda's words are taken to be composed in response to a genuine opposition to Wilfrid's translation, as argued above, then perhaps any vitriol surrounding Wilfrid's translation had, by the closing decade of the tenth century, died down to sufficient levels as to be beyond the hearing of Byrhtferth.

---

[5] 'Osuualdus uero, impiger miles Christi sua ouilia perlustrans, peruenit gaudens ad menia monasterii quod dictum est Ripum, quod tunc dirutum erat, quondam uero a reuerentissimo uiro Wilfrido celebriter constructum. Cumque ibidem insisteret actibus, per gratiam omnia cernentis saluatoris 'inuenit thesaurum' absconditum diu mortalibus, quem puro corde et humili mente e terries leuauit. Inuenit autem presulis beata membra pius pater, cui pro meritis summorum actuum gubernatrix uite sue sancta Dei trinitas talia concessit inuenire munera.'

A stronger possibility is that knowledge of Canterbury's possession of Wilfrid was not widely circulated by the time Byrhtferth was writing. A number of factors behind Lapidge's general suggestion above add weight to this possibility. The *Breviloquium* has been described by Lapidge, mirroring comments by William of Malmesbury, as 'one of the most brilliantly ingenious – but also damnably difficult – Latin products of Anglo-Saxon England' (Lapidge 1988, 56), and contemporary sentiments may have been similar. It is reasonable to imagine that this impenetrability led to the text's marginalization then as now. Only three manuscripts of the *Breviloquium* are extant, and all are likely to have been products of Christ Church's scriptorium. While there is the slim chance that a manuscript made its way to Winchester by the late tenth century, reliable evidence for the *Breviloquium*'s distribution is limited to Canterbury and Glastonbury (Lapidge 1988, 57). One scholar has advised that Canterbury was the sole focus of interest for the work (Brooks 1984, 231). Furthermore, the *Secgan*, an eleventh-century list of saints' resting places, lists Wilfrid as resting not at Canterbury, but at Ripon (Rollason 1978, 64, 89; Liebermann 1889, 10). While it is perhaps hazardous to infer from a single source, it may bear out the suggestion that knowledge of Canterbury's claim was not widespread.

It can be said with slightly more certainty that by the end of the tenth century Byrhtferth was only dimly aware of Oda's life and career. This is made clear when one examines the introductory chapters to Byrhtferth's *Vita S. Oswaldi*. It is true that Byrhtferth is not a reliable source for the sort of biographical information that we might consider valuable, but (despite Lapidge's assertions to the contrary) much of this early material appears to have been garnered from oral, rather than written sources. Byrhtferth says as much when he prefaces Oda's miracles with the admission that his knowledge was based on what he had heard: '*sicuti a fidelibus uiris narrare audiuimus*' (Lapidge 2009, 14–15). Byrhtferth's information on Oda is distinctly vague, and there are hints that he based his statements on rumor (Lapidge 2009, 16–17). It remains difficult to comprehend how Byrhtferth, the student of Frithegod, could have remained wholly uninformed of Oda's translation of Wilfrid. However, to Byrhtferth Oda's deeds seem to have been merely a small part of the much more important story of Oswald's life; his concern was with Oswald and Benedictine monasticism, and even though he felt it necessary to go into detail about Oda's life and influence on Oswald, by the time he was writing Wilfrid's translation to Canterbury had either been wholly divorced from any identification with Oda personally, or the Ramsey monks had never been aware of it to begin with.

One of the first to address the dispute over Wilfrid's relics was Eadmer of Canterbury, writing in the late eleventh century. It is to Eadmer's 'solution' to the problem that we now turn in order to shed light on questions raised in the above discussion of the works of Oda. Eadmer had a profound interest in Oda, and he probably wrote his own *Vita S. Odonis* early in his adult life (Turner and Muir 2006, xxxv–xxxvi). It is the most complete and detailed narrative account that we have for Oda's career; however, it is not in Eadmer's *Vita S. Odonis* but in his own *Life of St Oswald* that he provides clarification as to who possessed Wilfrid's relics.

Composed sometime after the *Vita S. Odonis*, Eadmer's *Vita et Miracula S Oswaldi* relies heavily on Byrhtferth's life while at the same time both omitting and adding much material (Turner and Muir 2006, cvi–cxvi). The work was commissioned by the monks of Worcester (Turner and Muir 2006, cvi, 218–19), and perhaps this explains what its editors identify as 'a change in the focus of Eadmer's work' from that of Byrhtferth (Turner and Muir 2006, cxi). Archbishop Oswald, Eadmer reports, did indeed find the relics of St Wilfrid. However, Oswald discovered the bones of the younger, less famous saint of the same name, who was Bishop of York between 721 and 732, our Wilfrid's nephew. Eadmer puts considerable effort into making matters clear for the reader; his language takes extraordinary care. According to Eadmer, after the relics had been discovered through divine revelation:

> ... when a suitable shrine had been made ready for the body of saint Wilfrid, he [Oswald] enclosed it there with great reverence, because he knew him to be related by blood to the great Wilfrid, that is the founder of that place [Ripon]; he knew that the former had succeeded the latter in governing the church of York, just as venerable Bede relates near the end of his *Historia Gentis Anglorum*, and he considered that just as he had shared the same name, so too was he Wilfrid's heir with respect to his life and morals. For the body of the more renowned Wilfrid, which had had a tomb of its own apart from the others in a prominent location within the church and which was worthily adorned by an epitaph (as this same Bede relates in that history), had been translated to Canterbury by the glorious prelate of the Kentish people, Oda, whom we mentioned briefly at the beginning of this little work, in the manner in which he himself attests in the prologue to the life of this same Wilfrid which he had composed in heroic metre, writing thus: (Turner and Muir 2006, 270–3).[6]

Eadmer then quotes directly from Frithegod's preface the same lengthy extract recounted in full above. Up to this point there are significant similarities

---

[6] '... *ad corpus sancti Wilfridi feretro conuenienter aptato, illud in eo magna cum reuerentia condidit, utpote quem magno Wilfrido fundatori uidelicet loci ipsius consanguinitate iunctum nouerat, quem in regimen aecclesiae Eboracensis, sicut uenerabilis Beda prope finem historiae gentis Anglorum refert, ei successisse sciebat,*

between Eadmer's account and Byrhtferth's. Their divergence here is remarkable. Eadmer effectively splits the difference between the claims of Canterbury and Ripon, allowing both traditions to be recognized by introducing a second Wilfrid and claiming the more famous one for Canterbury. How Eadmer accomplishes this is most important. The direct use of source material, its quotation and identification is extremely uncommon in Eadmer's writing, and this adds to the extraordinary character of this passage (Turner and Muir 2006, cxii). Eadmer was a passionate advocate of Canterbury's saintly possessions, and this reconciliation of disparate traditions has been interpreted as his effort to close the case and lay to rest any further dispute that might injure Christ Church's saints (Muir and Turner 1998, xxiii).

But what if Eadmer had additional motives behind these efforts at reconciliation similar to those identified with Oda above? Let us return, for a moment, to Eadmer's language in the *Vita et Miracula S Oswaldi* and his efforts at making matters as clear as possible for the reader. Let us also consider Eadmer's lengthy emphasis on Oda's role in the translation. To Eadmer the incident was no passing matter; the pains to which he goes to clarify matters underlines the perceived seriousness of the issue by the time he was writing in the late eleventh century. Eadmer's approach to the disparate traditions employs an impressive sense of editorial duty. He cross-references his sources and cites them as diligently as any modern historian. That he engages in such elaborate justification so rarely in his writing underlines the gravity of Eadmer's interest in ensuring recognition not only for Canterbury's claim to Wilfrid, but also for Oda's own role in the saint's translation. Eadmer's lengthy digression and quotation of what he believed, incorrectly but genuinely, to be Oda's own words demonstrates to his reader Oda's dedication to Wilfrid's relics and thus Oda's standing as a protector of Wilfrid and also of Canterbury.

Similar treatment of the dispute, and of Oda, is also found in Eadmer's *Vita S. Wilfridi*. Eadmer takes the bare facts of Oda's self-professed role in Wilfrid's translation found in the preface to Frithegod's *Breviloquium* and with them creates a remarkable scene where awe-inspiring reverence for Oda is expressed by the 'certain men' who initially acquired Wilfrid, and the archbishop is depicted parading Wilfrid's relics triumphantly through the streets of Canterbury (Muir and Turner 1998, 142–6). Eadmer goes on to state that out

---

quemque uti nominis eius consortem, ita et uitae morumque heredem fuisse acceperat. Corpus siquidem illius maioris Wilfridi quod semotum ab aliis per se in eminenti loco in ipsa aecclesia tumbam habuerat, quam et epitaphium, ut idem Beda in eadem historia narrat, digniter decorauerat, a glorioso Cantuariorum antistite Odone, cuius in initio huius opusculi paucis meminimus, translatam Cantuariam fuerat, quemadmodum ipsemet in prologo uitae ipsius Wilfridi quae per eum herioco metro composita est attestatur, ita scribens:'

of respect for Ripon, a small share of the saint was allowed to remain there. While the anecdotes serve the immediate purpose of reinforcing Canterbury's claim, they also allow Eadmer to further establish Oda's prominent and virtuous place in Wilfrid's story, advancing Oda's reputation as a reverent and respectful translator.

Writing in Canterbury, Eadmer had his own prejudices and allegiances. Eadmer's treatment of Anglo-Saxon saints and the context in which he composed his hagiographical works must also be kept in mind. As has recently been argued, Eadmer adored pre-conquest English saints with an uncommon vigor, and sought to protect them both from Archbishop Lanfranc's disparagement and the scepticism of other Christ Church monks (Rubenstein 1999). Rubenstein highlights Eadmer's dedication to Oda specifically, and also points out that Oda's and Wilfrid's cults were effectively revived by Eadmer's strenuous efforts, going so far as to suggest that Oda owes his long-term saintly reputation to Eadmer (Rubenstein 1999, 307). Such arguments are persuasive, and are amplified here. To Eadmer, the acquisition of Wilfrid's relics by Canterbury went beyond the local claim to that saint. Eadmer's own repeated emphasis on Oda's role in the translation seems to be part of Eadmer's drive to maintain Oda's reputation as a father of Christ Church and as a fellow advocate of its saints. In his own *Vita S. Wilfridi*, Eadmer twice mentions Oda in the same sentence as he does Bede, and he describes their reliability as historical sources in similar terms (Muir and Turner 1998, 10–11, 148–9).

The reasons for Eadmer's repeated and detailed emphasis on Wilfrid's translation and Oda's part in it probably stem not only from Eadmer's desire to remove confusion about competing claims for Wilfrid's relics and reinforce Canterbury's case but also from a desire to enhance Oda's own reputation, whom Eadmer greatly admired. His approbation for Oda of course stemmed chiefly from their shared connection with Canterbury, but it is worthwhile to highlight an important point: both Oda and Eadmer composed short *vitae* in honor of Wilfrid on an occasion at which the saint was translated. While the earlier *Breviloquium* has since been attributed to Frithegod, Eadmer believed it to be the work of Oda himself; perhaps Eadmer felt himself conspicuously close to Oda through their shared subject of spiritual veneration and hagiography.

An additional feature of this argument is the suggestion that Eadmer admired Oda not only because they shared a reverence and appreciation for St Wilfrid, but also a devotion to the physical maintenance and upkeep of Christ Church Cathedral, that house of so many English saints. Just as Archbishop Oda sought to revive Wilfrid's cult, admonishing those who neglected the upkeep of churches in his stead, perhaps too Eadmer sought to stimulate interest in Oda's own reputation for similar reasons. Eadmer would have known from his research into Oda of the archbishop's association with the cathedral itself and the miraculously rain-free remodeling. Eadmer seems to have been especially receptive to Canterbury traditions regarding the history of the church buildings themselves, and to have repeated those same stories enthusiastically. In his *De reliquiis S. Audoeni* Eadmer describes how he studied intently the history of the Cathedral building itself, and Rubenstein highlights further Eadmer's 'strong association between that building and its saints' shrines...' (Rubenstein 1999, 299). That Eadmer deeply respected Oda and his sanctity is made clear by the mere existence of the *Vita S Odonis*. But Eadmer's repeated emphasis on Oda's connection to Wilfrid's cult demonstrates the extent to which Eadmer would go to express his dedication to both saints. Wilfrid and Oda's link with each other arguably bound them even tighter to Eadmer's heart than did their affiliation with Canterbury alone.

While it was no doubt a boon to Christ Church's relic collection, the present essay has argued that to Archbishop Oda Wilfrid's translation was probably also seen as an opportunity to inspire the English church into positive action, and the concern with church upkeep and episcopal duty observed in his writings is echoed in the preface to the *Breviloquium* attributed to Frithegod. Whether Eadmer saw things similarly when he read the *Breviloquium* is also worth considering. Eadmer knew that Oda had been a passionate advocate of Wilfrid's cult, and this unquestionably cultivated Eadmer's esteem for Oda. Eadmer also shared Oda's concern for the physical buildings of Christ Church and the preservation of the pre-Conquest Anglo-Saxon saints that were housed within. In the eyes of Eadmer, Oda's reputation benefited significantly from being associated with Wilfrid, and vice versa, as it was Oda who had helped to promote Wilfrid's cult. While it may be entirely coincidental, it is perhaps worth noting that in Eadmer's autograph collection of his combined writings the *Vita S. Odonis* immediately follows the *Vita S. Wilfridi* and the *Breviloquium* (Turner and Muir 2006, xliv–xlv); it is possible that Eadmer associated Wilfrid and Oda together directly. The connection between these figures is of course Canterbury, and it appears that the traditions evident there had not made their way to Ramsey by the late tenth century when Byrhtferth was active.

No new explanation for the disparity between the traditions of Wilfrid's whereabouts can be offered at this time; certainly none better than any that has been voiced before. But the answer may lie with the small number of extant manuscripts of Frithegod's *Breviloquium* and their limited distribution beyond Canterbury. Tied to this notion is the postulation that knowledge of Canterbury's acquisition of Wilfrid was not widely known, and that it was not exclusively meant to symbolize English superiority over York as many have concluded. If such an interpretation were accepted, then it would also seem as though any edificatory motivations on Oda's part were equally confined. Eadmer's commitment to the sanctity of both Wilfrid and Oda arguably helped both of their cults at Canterbury, and it is the contention of this essay that a primary aspect of this was Eadmer's recognition and celebration of Oda's early interest in the revitalization of Wilfrid's cult, which Eadmer perhaps took as an example worthy of imitation.

22: *St Wilfrid in English Historical Writing Since 1688*

W. TRENT FOLEY

In considering how historians since the Glorious Revolution have treated St Wilfrid, I am put in mind of a scene from Arthur Miller's tragedy, *The Death of a Salesman*, in which the play's protagonist, Willy Loman, quizzes his son Biff about Biff's classmate Bernard, who lives just next door. By the play's end Bernard is a successful lawyer, while Biff tragically has squandered his life away, dreaming big but doing little. Ever the salesman wanting his son to cut a prominent figure in the world, Willy asks Biff how friends at school regard Bernard. Biff replies, 'He's liked, but he's not well liked' (1976, 33). And so it is with Wilfrid. One need not read historians' assessments of him for very long to see that if by 'liked' one means that he is conferred a sort of grudging respect, then Wilfrid is 'liked' by a few. But none, I think, would put him among the ranks of the 'well-liked'. When it comes to the early Northumbrian saints, we know who the 'well-liked' are: Aidan, Cuthbert, Chad and of course Bede.

When I first came to the University of Durham to study Wilfrid in the early 1980s, it soon became apparent just how well liked these latter saints were in comparison to Wilfrid. I lived at St Aidan's College; I had friends who lived at the College of Hild and Bede, as well as St Chad's College. Durham, however, boasted of no St Wilfrid's College. And of course, Cuthbert was everywhere. There was a St Cuthbert's society, mostly for postgraduates and, of course, one was quickly made to know that Cuthbert was Durham's whole *raison d'être*, his bones reputedly still resting in its great cathedral. At the 1987 conference commemorating the thirteenth centenary of Cuthbert's death, not only did scholars attend, but so did clergy, laity and armchair historians. Indeed, all paid homage to the great saint at his tomb. Many genuflected and crossed themselves in reverence for him. Who is surprised that at this conference in 2009 no one witnessed a like reverence toward Wilfrid?

Since the Reformation, Wilfrid has received mostly negative press, but sometimes he has just been ignored. In a sermon collection entitled *Leaders in the Northern Church*, Bishop Lightfoot of Durham (1890) offers us one sermon each commemorating SS Columba, Aidan, Cuthbert, Hild and Benedict Biscop, and two commemorating Bede. But the Bishop offers up no sermon in Wilfrid's memory. When he has not been ignored, Wilfrid has often been ill served even by his few friends. In 1844, at the Oxford Movement's peak, before many in it had crossed over to Rome, Frederick William Faber wrote his *Life of St Wilfrid* for Newman's *Lives of the English Saints* series (1844, vol. 9). Before its publication, Newman informed Faber that it contained doctrinal error and that it was generally in bad taste (Wilkinson 2007, 85). Despite Newman's criticisms, the resulting work still gushed with fawning praise of Wilfrid and, more especially, of Rome as the bastion of true Catholic piety. The public hated it. As one biographer of Faber notes, 'There are several passages [in this Life] in which we learn as much, possibly more, about Faber as about St Wilfrid' (Wilkinson 2007, 87). Indeed there are, but the public cared little to discern any difference between the two. It detested them both, especially when Faber converted to Roman Catholicism a year later.

In one sense, one easily sees why Wilfrid has been so despised since the Reformation. As one who continually appealed to the church of Rome for justice during his own lifetime, he has been seen as, in a sense, England's first dogmatically *Roman* Catholic. And in light of the exploits of Bloody Mary, the Spanish Armada, Guy Fawkes and the Old Pretender, what loyal Englishman could love a saint who was so thoroughly Romanized? But to explain Wilfrid's unpopularity merely in terms of his early modern reputation as an inveterate Romanizer misses a broad-ranging complex of resentments that have welled up against him since about 1850. To better appreciate that complex, I should like to focus attention chiefly on three negative images of Wilfrid that emerged in the eighteenth and nineteenth centuries and then to account for why they have continued to enjoy a robust afterlife into the whole of the twentieth century and even into the twenty-first. Specifically, I will argue that the often uncomfortable ground that mid-Victorian Anglo-Catholics had to occupy – squeezed as they were between hostile Evangelicals and Dissenters on the one side and newly energized Roman Catholics on the other – tempted the historians among them to portray Wilfrid in these three uniquely unflattering ways: (1) as Bede's nemesis, (2) as vainglorious and (3) as a Gollum of sorts, that is, as one obsessed with accumulating and hoarding treasure. Let us briefly consider the genesis and development of these images.

Wilfrid as Bede's Nemesis

One need not read modern scholarly literature on Wilfrid very long before encountering the disturbing claim that Bede – scholar, saint and father of English history – pretty much detested Wilfrid. This claim goes at least back to the Augustan era, intensified in the late Victorian period, and has persisted into the twentieth and twenty-first centuries. This claim's chief defect, of course, is Bede's never having directly expressed such a sentiment. Its legitimacy largely depends on the premise that Bede's silence regarding some of Wilfrid's actions reveals Bede's disapproval of them as well as his antipathy for their author. This image of Wilfrid, as well as the two others we will examine shortly, can be traced back to Thomas Carte, who in the first volume of his *A General History of England* utterly skewered Wilfrid. A curious combination of nonjuror, spirited Jacobite and rabid anti-Catholic, Carte alleges that Wilfrid's conduct was condemned by SS Cuthbert, John of Beverley, Hild, 'and even the modest Bede; who says so little of a man, that made the greatest figure of any of that age ... that his very silence may pass for severe censure' (1747, 1: 237). He goes on to say that, unlike Bede, Stephen wrote only for two purposes: to glorify Wilfrid and magnify the court of Rome. But unlike Bede's work, Stephen's 'hath more the air of romance than a history.' According to Carte, Stephen recounts no miracle that Wilfrid performs to convert a nation and leaves us a biography of Wilfrid that is riddled with inaccuracies (1747, 1: 238, n 5). Carte's contempt for Stephen is typical. It is almost an iron law of modern historical scholarship that as Bede's reputation for truthfulness and objectivity rises, Stephen's falls. That law remained in full force during the late Victorian period. Even so warm an admirer of Wilfrid as Oxford ecclesiastical historian William Bright could not resist portraying Stephen vis-à-vis Bede in this way (1888, 291). Neither could Benjamin Wells (1891) nor Reginald Lane Poole (1919), each of whom assailed Stephen's integrity as biographer and historian in the *English Historical Review*.

Not content merely to assert Bede's dislike for Wilfrid, Charles Plummer perhaps better than anyone else drew together the evidence for such a claim and summarized it in notes for his critical edition of Bede's *Ecclesiastical History*. These included Bede's relative silence concerning Wilfrid's working of miracles, Bede's praise of Wilfrid's enemies (including Kings Ecgfrith and Aldfrith) and Bede's lack of criticism for certain actions that Wilfrid opposed (namely, Theodore's division of the Northumbrian diocese and Chad's receiving the see of York from Oswiu). Finally, he asserted that Bede may have disliked Wilfrid's 'Romanising tendencies', a claim for which, uncharacteristically, Plummer offered no supporting evidence (Bede 1896, 2: 316). Plummer also editorialized in a note in his introduction when he asserted, 'Bede's transparent good faith must be plain to everyone who reads his narrative,' but then immediately adds, 'The only point which creates a doubt is suppression of certain incidents in the life of Wilfrid' (Bede 1896, 1: xlv). Plummer suggested that Bede may have been trying here to protect the reputation of either Wilfrid or the kings who opposed him. But his later comments on Bede's dislike of Wilfrid make it clear that he saw Bede's silence as supporting Wilfrid's royal foes more than Wilfrid himself.

Since Plummer, the theory that Bede disliked Wilfrid was revived in 1943 by Charles W. Jones. In his famous edition of Bede's chronological works, Jones suggested that Bede's antipathy toward Wilfrid began when, as a young monk, a confessedly angry Bede learned that Wilfrid's priest, David, had condemned in Wilfrid's presence Bede's views about the six ages of the world. Bede himself narrates this incident in his *Letter to Plegwine* and Jones asserted, certainly more directly than Bede did, that Bede's anger at the priest David boiled over onto the great bishop himself (Bede 1943). More recently, Alan Thacker, in his biography of Wilfrid written for the *Oxford Dictionary of National Biography* repeats Jones' account of the Plegwine letter, but with a bit more nuance. Far from saying that Bede disliked Wilfrid, Thacker (2004a, 949) asserts instead that Bede's account of Wilfrid in the *Ecclesiastical History* 'need not necessarily be read as disapproving.' 'Although,' Thacker adds, 'it is perhaps worth remembering that it was before Wilfrid ... that Bede was accused of heresy.' Apart from the historians just mentioned, Frank Stenton (1943, 145), Benedicta Ward (1990, 127) and Walter Goffart (1988, 307–24) have all asserted, or at least strongly implied, that Bede disliked Wilfrid. Since Nick Higham has offered a detailed counterpoint to this view in his *(Re)-Reading Bede* (2006, 63–9), I will not rehearse his arguments here, but will later try to account for why Bede's reputation as Wilfrid's discreet detractor gained such traction in the Victorian period.

Wilfrid as Vainglorious

Before it became fashionable to conclude that Bede disliked Wilfrid, Protestant historians gave reasons why everyone less saintly than Bede ought to dislike him. The most basic was because Wilfrid grasped after glory and gain in ways they considered un-Christian. In this aspect, Wilfrid compared unfavorably to such monk-bishops as Aidan, Chad and Cuthbert, whose Celtic-style humility led them neither to demand nor even desire anything for themselves as Wilfrid had. Let us examine first the charge that Wilfrid grasped for glory.

As with so many accusations against Wilfrid, this one begins with Thomas Carte, for whom Wilfrid's lack of virtue stems mostly from his Roman connections, but not entirely so. 'It appears plainly from his whole conduct,' Carte wrote of Wilfrid, 'that he was very fond of himself; had a great opinion of his own parts and merits; and was too much elated with the success of his labours on several occasions, and the popularity he had thence acquired. He loved wealth, power, state, pomp, and splendour; perhaps the effect of his natural disposition, and of a certain haughtiness of mind' (1747, 1: 235). As proof, Carte notes that Wilfrid did no miracle, at least in Stephen's telling, that helps convert the nation and thus implies that Wilfrid did miracles only to glorify himself. In another place, Carte railed against 'the haughty, grasping, and assuming temper of Wilfrid' (1747, 254). By himself, the haughty Wilfrid might have done less mischief had he not been egged on by Rome, which, in Carte's words, was 'ready to patronize every restless and seditious spirit, that would sacrifice the liberties of a national church to his selfish ends' (1747, 255).

One might have thought that by the twentieth century, a cooling of anti-Catholic sentiment would have softened such invective against Wilfrid's character. It does not. Surprisingly, one hears it most forcefully not among ecclesiastical historians or religious partisans, but among Anglo-Saxonists. For example, in the first edition of his *A History of the Anglo-Saxons*, Robert Hodgkin – provost and lecturer in Modern History at Queens College, Oxford – attacks Wilfrid with extraordinary virulence. To Hodgkin's mind, Wilfrid had utterly wasted God's good gifts to him: intelligence, unbounded vitality, a good birth, wealth, friends at court, a first-hand knowledge of continental ways, and the early prestige he won at the Synod of Whitby. He had wasted them, Hodgkin concluded, because he had 'failed to assimilate the inner spirit of Christianity, and became more of a curse than a blessing to the Northumbrian Church' (1935, 1: 344). Worse than that, Wilfrid served as the prototype for such English churchmen as Archbishop Thomas Becket and Cardinal Wolsey. But at least Becket and Wolsey could justify themselves by claiming that they had waged principled conflicts against kings. Unlike their cause, said Hodgkin, 'the cause for which [Wilfrid] fought was primarily personal – his own position, his own rights, both of them in the way of the general welfare of his diocese' (1935, 1: 344). In Hodgkin's account, Wilfrid's self-concern was so great that he didn't even really care about Roman Christianity. The true Romanists of that age, says Hodgkin, were Archbishop Theodore and Bede, and the fact that Theodore thwarted Wilfrid's ambitions while Bede refused to record his miracles shows the inauthenticity of Wilfrid's own Romanism (1935, 1: 344).

Though hailed as an improvement over Hodgkin, Frank Stenton's *Anglo-Saxon England*, first published only eight years after Hodgkin's work, treated Wilfrid little better. In one curious paragraph, Stenton first asserted, 'Despite abundant information about Wilfrid's career, it is hard to form an impression of his personality.' But not content to let the matter rest here, Stenton noted that Bede treated Wilfrid 'with a curious detachment' and, more damning, that Wilfrid 'was opposed by many persons whose motives are beyond criticism.' Feeling perhaps that he had been a bit too harsh, and with the grudging respect that so many of Wilfrid's commentators have accorded him, Stenton asserted that Wilfrid was 'one of the greatest men of his generation,' yet could not leave this compliment as his last word. He concluded, 'But [Wilfrid's] abilities were thwarted by his identification of his own interests with the cause of religious order, and for all his insistence on the universal authority of the Roman church, he remained essentially an individualist' (Stenton 1943, 145). It is interesting to note how far the pendulum has swung in the two centuries that separate Carte and Stenton. Whereas for Carte, Wilfrid's vainglory proved his symbiosis with the vainglorious Roman church, for both Hodgkin and Stenton, Wilfrid's vainglory, or 'individualism' as Stenton puts it, showed that Wilfrid didn't really care about the Roman church and its claims at all, but only about himself.

The notion that Wilfrid was something of an insufferable self-seeker still abounds. One still hears echoes of this view, for example, in Alan Thacker's assessment of him as 'undoubtedly ambitious' and 'probably pugnacious' (2004a, 949). At times, one still encounters a Wilfrid who is not merely vainglorious, but downright sinister. In a largely sympathetic portrait of Wilfrid, Catherine Cubitt has argued that Anglo-Saxon ecclesiastical tradition gave Wilfrid good grounds for opposing the manner in which his diocese had been divided and handed to others. But in a jarring conclusion that largely undoes the tone of what came before, she wrote: 'If Wilfrid had had his way, ecclesiastical authority in Northumbria would have been the monopoly of his own foundations: no monk from the royal houses of Lindisfarne or Whitby could have held episcopal office. Wilfrid's *stranglehold* would have been complete' [my emphasis] (1989, 38).

Wilfrid as Gollum

The second aspect of Wilfrid's grasping personality, and the final caricature I will treat here, is his alleged greed for gain, lust for treasure and love of splendour. An apt epithet for this caricature is 'Wilfrid as Gollum'. Like so many of Wilfrid's other unflattering images, this one, as best I can tell, dates back to Carte, who charged Wilfrid with loving wealth and splendour, thus making him the very anti-type of an Aidan and other Celtic-style bishops. Unlike Wilfrid, these latter 'had no notion of providing splendid houses for the reception of great men, or of heaping up riches for their entertainment.' Precisely Wilfrid's antitype, they were, as Carte asserts, 'perfectly free from avarice' (1747, 1: 247).

After Carte, this image of 'Wilfrid the greedy' lies largely dormant for a century and a half. Its resurgence coincides with the Victorian interest in Anglo-Saxon studies and with a tendency to find traces of 'Beowulfish' heroes in the saints of the early Anglo-Saxon church. This tendency is first exemplified in Thomas Hodgkin – Quaker, amateur Anglo-Saxonist, successful Newcastle banker and father of Oxford historian Robert Hodgkin, who was introduced earlier. A wealthy man himself, Hodgkin nevertheless looked askance at Wilfrid's accumulation of wealth for his churches. In *The History of England*, he asserts that a study of relevant sources leaves us in the dark as to why Northumbria's leading men opposed Wilfrid so strenuously. Not content to leave us in the dark, the elder Hodgkin explains:

> When we see the well-filled treasury, blazing with gold and jewels, which after all his reverses gladdens the aged eyes of Wilfrid at the close of his career, we are, perhaps enabled to understand ... the unexpressed grievance in the mind of the Northumbrian kings and bishops against their greatest ecclesiastic ... Whatever view may be taken of the struggle, the very fact of ... the somewhat sordid

interests at stake shows us how far we have already travelled in less than two generations from the days of Oswald and Aidan' (1906, 213).

As with the father, so it was with the son. Robert Hodgkin charged Wilfrid with loving mammon too much. 'Cuthbert,' he tells us, 'had gone to one extreme in the repudiation of worldly goods; Wilfrid went to the other.' He continues, 'It is a memorable picture, that of Wilfrid, the *miles Christi*, the old warrior surveying his hoard as did Beowulf.' Like Beowulf, Hodgkin asserts, Wilfrid gloated over his spoil. As such, he represented the medieval Church's 'possessive spirit,' a spirit that Hodgkin believes eventually sparked the protest of the Reformation (1935, 1: 346–7). Robert Hodgkin did more than anyone else to fuel the image of Wilfrid as Gollum. Like Hodgkin's Wilfrid and Beowulf, Gollum, the famous antagonist in Tolkien's *Lord of the Rings* trilogy, is enraptured by his golden treasure, the Ring, his 'precious'. Himself a scholar of things Anglo-Saxon, including *Beowulf*, Tolkien was Hodgkin's contemporary at Oxford, though I can find no evidence of their acquaintance. For an Anglo-Saxonist to compare someone with Beowulf need not be read as unflattering, but in Hodgkin's case it clearly was. Having already asserted that Wilfrid failed to assimilate the inner spirit of Christianity, that he cursed rather than blessed the Northumbrian church and that he was the archetype for the medieval Church's 'possessive instinct,' Hodgkin clearly sees Wilfrid's lust for treasure as in no sense heroic, his comparison with Beowulf notwithstanding.

This tendency to paint Wilfrid more as a Germanic aristocratic hero than a late antique Christian bishop, as one shaped more by *Beowulf*'s pagan spirit than the Christian spirit of the Latin Fathers, has scarcely let up since Hodgkin. Even Henry Mayr-Harting, who wrote a warmly appreciative chapter on Wilfrid's life and career in *The Coming of Christianity to Anglo-Saxon England*, portrays Wilfrid in this way. He writes, 'At the end of his life Wilfrid is pictured bringing out and disposing of the treasure which he had accumulated, in a certain way as Beowulf, before he died, longed to handle the treasure which he had won from the dragon's hoard' (1991, 228). Just a few years after Mayr-Harting wrote these words, Patrick Wormald repeated the Beowulf comparison, citing not only Wilfrid's meting out of treasure, but also his feasting with kings, his heroic fight with his comrades on the beaches of Sussex and even David – his drunken Bede-libeling priest – as evidence of Wilfrid's Germanic aristocratic manner. Unlike Robert Hodgkin, though, Wormald shows nothing but the greatest respect for Wilfrid, calling him 'the greatest ... of early Anglo-Saxon saints,' even noting that in his personal life, Wilfrid was 'far from worldly' (1978, 54–5).

Such comparisons to Beowulf may obscure rather than clarify Wilfrid's aims and character. After all, Stephen says only that just before dying Wilfrid commanded his treasurer to lay out all the gold, silver and precious stones before those present (VW 63). So, we may count as embellishment Hodgkin's claim that Wilfrid gloated over his treasure, or his father's claim that the sight of this treasure 'gladdened' Wilfrid's aging eyes, or even Mayr-Harting's implication that Wilfrid had, like the aging Beowulf, 'longed to handle his treasure.' These twentieth-century authors all impute to Wilfrid emotions and desires that Stephen does not. And neither does Bede. We do well to remember that the claims and convictions of these modern historians were built on foundations laid by earlier Anglo-Catholic historians who had wanted to posit a stark difference between the authentic ascetic spirituality of Cuthbert and Bede over and against Wilfrid's sham spirituality that gloried in largesse. So while it is tempting to emphasize Wilfrid's Germanic background as an Anglo-Saxon to try to help interpret his style and behaviour, one must be careful not to overdraw the distinction between supposedly Anglo-Saxon styles of episcopal leadership and Gallic or even Roman ones. Stephen clearly viewed Wilfrid more as a Roman Christian than a heroic Anglo-Saxon. His *Life of Wilfrid* abounds in citations from and allusions to the Christian Bible, from Christian apocryphal literature and from the writings of the Latin Fathers. From its first page to its last it portrays a hero who appeals to norms and canons of the Catholic church far more relentlessly than to a Germanic code of heroism (Foley 1992, 21–52).

Wilfrid in Mid-Victorian Anglo-Catholic Historiography

Having considered these three images of Wilfrid, we ought to consider the factors that gave them rise and also to account for their longevity. All three were motivated, at least in their beginnings, by anti-Catholic sentiment. As one who appealed to Rome three times in the late seventh and early eighth century, Wilfrid could not escape his reputation as a Romanist once the Reformation had passed. In so far as eighteenth- and nineteenth-century historians linked him indissolubly to Rome, they reflexively endowed him with those qualities they associated with Rome: pomposity and vainglory, and lust for filthy lucre.

That rare mixture of anti-Romanism and divine-right royalism that Thomas Carte had embodied in the Augustan age had become a commonplace among mid-Victorian Anglo-Catholics, except that the latter could not express their antipathy to Romanism as baldly as Carte had. Nevertheless, now eager to distinguish themselves from such converts to Rome as Newman, Faber and Manning, they were in a quandary. On the one hand, they could not bring themselves to follow Newman to Rome; on the other, they were neither able nor willing to forsake the piety Newman had embodied in the early days of the Oxford Movement. Their anti-Catholicism was thus, at its most extreme, only tepid, especially compared to that of Evangelical Churchmen and Protestant nonconformists. Among these Anglo-Catholics, venomous slurs against Roman

Catholicism went increasingly out of fashion. Their anti-Catholic resentments were expressed only obliquely, if at all. Yet – and this is the cardinal point of my paper – Anglo-Catholics could and did express their usually hidden contempt for Rome through their overt contempt, freely expressed, for Wilfrid and his biographer Stephen. It is as if the mid-Victorian Anglo-Catholic imagination had constructed two catholicisms: an idealized one characterized by ascetic, prayerful humility and a bowdlerized one recognizable through its showy pomp and naked plays for power. Wilfrid represented the latter, while Bede, Cuthbert and Gregory the Great represented the former. Gregory the Great's inclusion in this list of worthies showed why no wholesale indictment of Rome was possible. As pope, Gregory was clearly Roman, but as apostle of the English and Bede's spiritual mentor, his Catholicism was clearly English as well. Because overt expressions of contempt for Rome were unacceptable, the contemptuous expression for Wilfrid's Romanism that we find a century earlier in Carte is largely absent in most English historians of the Victorian era. These latter express their antipathy for Rome in code, as it were, through the accusations they heap upon Wilfrid as one who is greedy, vainglorious and held in low esteem by Bede.

The importance of the Anglo-Catholic party's views in shaping a more generalized view of Wilfrid cannot be underestimated. They wielded immense influence at both Oxford and Cambridge, where they monopolized the fields of modern and ecclesiastical history. Of the major parties in the Church of England, the Evangelicals had little intrinsic interest in early medieval history, thinking that only biblical history and the narratives of more recent Protestant heroes were relevant to faith. By contrast, Anglo-Catholics saw the patristic and early medieval periods as that place in the church's history where its core identity had been formed. They thus enjoyed an outsized influence in Victorian English constructions of both the Age of Bede in general and Wilfrid in particular. When one looks at the enduring legacy of an Anglo-Catholic scholar like Charles Plummer, for example, one can see a few clues as to why Wilfrid was portrayed – even far into the twentieth century – as the bête noire of the early Northumbrian church. As noted earlier, Plummer believed that Bede disliked Wilfrid. Yet Wallace-Hadrill shrewdly noted, 'Bede was not as anti-Wilfrid as Plummer was' (1976, 381). A closer reading of Plummer's Introduction to his first Bede volume may reveal one root of his anti-Wilfridian stance. There, briefly, he let the scholar's mask drop so that we catch a glimpse of the committed High Churchman that he was. Clearly an admirer of Bede, Plummer likens him to Richard W Church and Henry Parry Liddon (Bede 1896, 1: lxxix). Both these luminaries of the late Victorian Church had the strongest of ties to the Oxford movement. Dean Church, once Newman's young disciple, had written a warm and moving history of the movement (1897); while Canon Liddon, perhaps Pusey's most eminent disciple, wrote a massive biography of his old mentor (1894) shortly after Pusey's death. Plummer's comparison provokes the following interesting question: if Dean Church and Canon Liddon resembled Bede, then who in his mind resembled Wilfrid?

Unfortunately, Plummer does not answer that question directly, but we can make some educated guesses. Before doing so, however, we should examine Plummer's statements about Bede's resemblance to Church and Liddon in the context of the Victorian era's more general discussion of the early English church. For much of the later nineteenth century the Church of England found itself in a precarious position, defending itself against a newly confident Catholicism, on the one side, and a dissenting Protestantism increasingly impatient for disestablishment on the other. Of course, Protestant dissent looked with even greater horror at Catholic resurgence than the Church did. To counter Roman claims that the English church owed its founding to Rome, apologists for a dissenting and Low Church viewpoint resorted to an argument that Tudor and Stuart apologists had first put forth (Parker 1853, 111–12; Ussher 1631, 92–117), namely, that the Church of England traces its origins to the ancient church of the Britons. By doing this, they could rightly argue that the Christian faith had been brought to Britain before the 5th-century English invasions and long before Gregory the Great had dispatched St Augustine to Kent. But the High Church party would have none of this. It wanted to draw a clear line between the British Church on the one hand and the English Church on the other. In its estimation, the Church of England began, as its name implies, as a Church of the English, not of the Britons who, as everyone knew, were really the Welsh. The High Church emphasized that the English invaded this island as heathens, having come to Christianity specifically through the efforts of a Roman pontiff, Gregory the Great. Much of this High Church argument was fueled, though not always motivated, by the kind of race theory popularized by historians E A Freeman, J R Green and Bishop Stubbs. To such as these, the English belonged to the Teutonic race. As such, their innate industriousness and capacity for conquest and self-government far surpassed that of Britain's Celtic natives (Curtis 1968, 8–12). Freeman in particular took pains to stress that the Anglican Church had specifically English rather than British origins. Bede, of course, proved a great ally in shoring up High Church and racialist arguments. He showed a deep reverence for Gregory the Great, consistently located the English church's catholicity in Rome (while attributing the faults of the British church to its insularity), emphasized that the English mission originated in Rome and showed how even the Celtic bastions of Lindisfarne and Iona belatedly conformed to Roman custom, most notably in their Easter. In an unsigned editorial for *The [Church] Guardian*, Freeman (1888) took to task both dissenters in the Liberation Society and low churchmen in the Church Defence Institution. Both used the ideal of the 'ancient British church' to further their respective aims: the former to show a church unfriendly to establishment, the latter to show an English Church established, to be sure, but given birth by ancient Christian Britons, not Rome. Freeman had little patience for such claims. Troping St Paul's language in 1 Corinthians 3, he thus summarized the work of converting the English: 'The Roman planted, the Scot watered, the Briton did nothing.' More than that, against those who traced English Christian origins back to the Britons, Freeman's friend and fellow historian at Oxford, the Reverend William Bright, complained that they 'speak and write about the subject without having read their Bede' (Kidd 1903, 207–08).

I relay this debate between Freeman, the Liberation Society and the Church Defence movement to show just how much racialist and High Church positions depended on Bede. To such historians as Freeman and Bright, Bede's account of the English conversion was sacrosanct and justified their disparagement of the Welsh. And while it would be unfair to say that all late Victorian High Churchmen uniformly shared Freeman's racialist views, they did treat Bede's narrative as incontestable and saw in him an early representative of Anglicanism's *via media*. To them, just as Bede steered through the Scylla and Charybdis of a Celtic-church not concerned enough for catholicity and a Roman church perhaps corrupted by arrogance and worldliness, so too did the High Church of the late Victorian period hew to its own *via media* between a Low Church and dissenting evangelicalism on the one hand and an ultramontane Roman Catholicism on the other. I submit to you as a hunch (and I must confess that it is a hunch, for which I can find no direct evidence in my sources) that in this debate, Wilfrid represented the extreme ultramontane Roman pole to which Bede, with his love of the simple ascetic piety of Aidan, had never quite succumbed. It could be conceded that Bede was an apologist for Rome, but Bede's Rome was the Rome of the humble Gregory the Great, whereas Wilfrid's Rome was the Rome of later pompous popes who needlessly meddled in the affairs of the English Church and threatened England's sovereignty. If, to Plummer, Dean Church and Dr. Liddon were latter-day Bedes, then perhaps Cardinals Pole, Richelieu and Archbishop Manning, as later caricatured by Lytton Strachey, were latter-day Wilfrids.

In highlighting these four modern and early modern caricatures of Wilfrid, I do not mean to oppose them to other more accurate portrayals. Indeed, in one sense accuracy has nothing to do with it. Plummer, for example, knew his facts about Wilfrid and was largely true to them. What I have tried to highlight here, however, is how mid-to-late Victorian Anglo-Catholic scholars like Plummer patterned these facts in such a way as to forge congruencies between the ecclesiastical tensions of their own time and those of late seventh-century Northumbria. Nor have I meant to suggest that historians have only vilified Wilfrid. One finds, for example, some very flattering twentieth-century portrayals of him by Henry Mayr-Harting (1991, 129–47) and H. P. R. Finberg (1974, 55), but I hasten to add that these two historians are, or were, Roman Catholic. There are even some Anglican apologists for Wilfrid. The Reverend William Hunt (1900, 242) stands out in this regard, as does the Reverend J. T. Fowler, whose glowing biography of Wilfrid in Baring-Gould's *Lives of the Saints* so annoyed the ardently Anglo-Catholic Baring-Gould that he admitted to editing it heavily, unable to agree with Fowler's good view of Wilfrid's character (1914, 11: 318).

I have focused here on the more negative assessments of Wilfrid, not just because they are more fun to read (and they certainly are), but because they reveal how fully historians have projected the deepest fears and resentments of their own age onto the historical figure of Wilfrid. While we may flatter ourselves by imagining that these quaint old projections belong to a past now dead to us, we do well to remember novelist William Faulkner's oft-cited adage: 'The past is never dead. It is not even past' (1966, 92). If we want to do Wilfrid justice, we must attend to much more than Stephen's and Bede's first narratives about him. We must attend also to the more recent narratives that have mediated the first ones to us. For before we ever get to first ones, our thoughts about them have already been shaped by the concerns and agendas of the more recent ones. About their agendas Wilfrid, of course, could have known nothing and yet they have sometimes done his memory great damage. It is worth considering how a fresh examination of him, one that keeps in mind these historiographical considerations, might yield a different assessment of his life and work.

23: *St Wilfrid: A Man for His Times*

CATHERINE CUBITT

St Wilfrid, whose life and achievements are celebrated in this volume, was a very remarkable figure, a man of exceptional charisma and tenacity, an undoubtedly unique figure. However, there is a tendency to see him as not so much unique but as an anomaly, a towering but lone figure in the early Anglo-Saxon church. This paper aims to place Wilfrid in an Anglo-Saxon and European context which enables his career and his significance to be understood more fully; it will show how the saint's trials and anxieties were shared by many of his contemporaries and place him among a continental collection of saints and bishops with whose careers his own was closely linked. It explores Wilfrid's many conflicts in the light of what is known about church privileges and land tenure in early Anglo-Saxon England, examines how Stephen, his biographer, exploits papal anathemas to protect the position of Wilfrid's foundations and looks more closely at Wilfrid's Roman allegiance, placing him in a network of continental clerics involved in papal affairs.

Wilfrid's isolated position in the historiography of the English church is largely due to the dominance of Bede's *Ecclesiastical History* over our modern perceptions of the church. To put it briefly, Wilfrid seems odd because Bede makes him so: Wilfrid did not fit neatly into Bede's didactic agenda which underpins his *History*. A crucial thread running through Bede's depiction of the growth of the Anglo-Saxon church is the vital importance of harmonious cooperation between kings and bishops to the well-being of a kingdom and to the salvation of its people. This theme is manifest from the very first days of the conversion in the relationships of Augustine of Canterbury and Æthelberht of Kent, Paulinus of York and Edwin of Northumbria, Aidan of Lindisfarne and Oswald of Northumbria, to name only the most prominent episcopal-regal partnerships. It is the bishop's responsibility to preach and teach the king and the king's duty to obey and to apply such teachings; the bishop is an indispensable mediator between the king and God. For example, Bede included in his account of Augustine's mission Pope Gregory's letter to Æthelberht penned on his conversion, describing Augustine of Canterbury as a man filled with scriptural knowledge and good works: 'so whatever counsel he gives you, listen to it gladly, follow it earnestly and keep it carefully in mind. If you listen to him as he speaks on behalf of Almighty God, the same Almighty God will listen to him more readily as he prays for you ...' (HE I, 32). The inverse of this message is given in another episode in the *Ecclesiastical History* where Bede describes how King

Coenwalh of Wessex replaced his bishop, Agilbert (in fact, Wilfrid's patron) with another, Bishop Wine, whom he subsequently expelled. But when Coenwalh's bishopless kingdom then suffered numerous defeats and attacks, the king realized that 'a kingdom which was without a bishop was, at the same time, justly deprived of divine protection' (HE III, 7). Thus bishops were essential for the right running of the kingdom and for the kingdom's wellbeing. The identification between a bishop and his kingdom was close: dioceses and kingdoms were often coterminous and the establishment of a see was often a sign of political independence.

From Bede's *History*, one learns that bishops were intimately involved with the king and were closely identified with the kingdom. It is a clear cut and simple picture, and one which Wilfrid's career fundamentally muddies. The events of Wilfrid's life open up a world not only of royal overlords and great kings but of sub-kings and provincial leaders (Campbell 1986). Wilfrid came to prominence in Northumbria through the patronage of Alhfrith, Oswiu's son, who ruled jointly with his father (HE III, 28; V, 19; VW 7–9). Wilfrid was spiritual adviser not only to Northumbrian kings, but also to Mercian and West Saxon. His closest collaboration was with Æthelræd of Mercia, whom Stephen depicts as an exemplary and pious figure (Thacker 2004; VW 57). Indeed, it is notable that Wilfrid acts almost independently of royal support – out of favour with one royal patron, he finds another. Compare this with the dependence upon royal support enjoyed by Aidan, depicted by Bede as summoned to the missionary field by King Oswald and interceding with God against the attacks of the Mercian enemy, Penda, for example (HE III, 3, 16). Moreover, in Bede's stories, when bishops do oppose kings, as Aidan does Oswine, rebuking the king for his criticism of his almsgiving, the king responds humbly and thankfully (HE III, 14). One suspects that it was not always like this. The assertion of ecclesiastical power was not unproblematic. Take, for example, Bede's description of Theodore's ascendancy over the Anglo-Saxon church – he famously tells us that Theodore was the first archbishop whom the whole Anglo-Saxon church obeyed (HE IV, 2). But many may have put up a fight. Bede tells us that when Bishop Winfrith of Mercia was deposed by Theodore for disobedience, he retired to the monastery of Barrow and there led a very holy life (HE IV, 6). It is only in the pages of Stephen that we find that he journeyed to the continent, perhaps to Rome to appeal against his deposition, like Wilfrid (VW 25).

We are therefore highly fortunate in having Stephen's *Life of Wilfrid* which not only provides us with an alternative to Bede's picture of the seventh-century church but is, in its own right, a remarkable work. The *Life of Wilfrid* is now recognised as an important source whose testimony when it conflicts with that of Bede is of at least equal and perhaps greater weight (Thacker, above). However, it is important to recognise that Stephen's account is also full of puzzling silences and only provides a partial picture, highly influenced as it is by its author's loyalty to Ripon. Stephen's concerns in writing the *Vita* may reflect contemporary vulnerabilities. His careful inclusion of two posthumous miracles, one demonstrating the divine punishment afflicting nobles who attempted to attack Oundle and the second recording the arc of light (Stancliffe's moonbow) which surrounded Ripon on Wilfrid's feastday, are suggestive of the need to safeguard these houses (VW 67–8). Stephen was probably writing shortly after 712 in the reigns of Ceolred of Mercia and Osred of Northumbria who both died in 716 and who, as we will see, were notorious for their treatment of churches (Hahn 1989, no. 73, pp. 152–3; Stancliffe and Thacker, above). Events after the death of Wilfrid as much as those of his lifetime may have had a profound influence on Stephen's narrative.

It is therefore important to set our hero-bishop not against the idealised model of religious life created by Bede's *Ecclesiastical History* but rather against other types of contemporary source which may give us a different perspective on the church. The first part of this article considers issues of ecclesiastical privilege, episcopal authority and church property, matters central to Wilfrid's series of conflicts with secular and religious authority, while the second half places Wilfrid against the background of developments in continental Europe and Rome.

But first it is necessary to review briefly the causes and development of Wilfrid's disputes with the Northumbrian kings and archbishops of Canterbury. Although we have two near contemporary sources for these – Bede and Stephen – neither can be considered neutral voices: Stephen's account is overtly partisan while Bede's habitual discretion may draw a veil over less edifying aspects of Wilfrid's life. Both tell essentially the same tale, with some different emphases and omissions. Indeed, Bede's account of Wilfrid is very largely based upon Stephen's.

Wilfrid's struggles fall into three main episodes. The first occurred in 678 when he was expelled from Northumbria by King Ecgfrith. The king joined forces with Theodore of Canterbury, and the archbishop was able to divide Wilfrid's see and consecrate new bishops in Northumbria. The second occurred in the late 680s or 690s when he lost the royal favour he had regained under King Aldfrith, Ecgfrith's successor, and was again forced out of Northumbria. Aldfrith's continuing hostility culminated in the third assault on Wilfrid's status and powers, when he was summoned to a Council at Austerfield in 702 and threatened with the confiscation of all his religious houses and property, deposition and monastic confinement at his house of Ripon. These attacks provoked Wilfrid to appeal twice to the see of Rome for vindication and restitution. In 678, he immediately made his way to Rome and pleaded his case before a council in October 679, which had been convened by Pope Agatho. Although he received a favourable decision which cleared his name of any accusation, the papal decrees were rejected by Ecgfrith and Theodore, and he was imprisoned and subsequently exiled from Northumbria. Wilfrid again made his way to Rome after the Council of Austerfield, and appeared before a second papal council, this time convened by John VI in 704. This also vindicated his reputation but referred a decision on his complaints back to an English council. While this papal decision may underlie his eventual restitution in 706, it was also initially rejected by King Aldfrith and Wilfrid only returned to Northumbria in the reign of King Osred.

The complaints behind these bitter disputes are far from clear. Stephen asserts emphatically that Wilfrid was cleared of all accusations in 679 and again in 704, but never tells us what these were. Moreover, the conflict between Stephen's assertions of Wilfrid's restoration and what we know of episcopal succession from other sources also highlights the uncertainties of our knowledge. In 678–9, Wilfrid appealed against Theodore's appointment of three new bishops because the latter had acted uncanonically on his own, and without the support of fellow bishops. Wilfrid objected not to the division of his diocese, but to the fact that the new bishops were not chosen from any of his foundations. Stephen represents the Council of Rome in 679 as a triumphant vindication of his hero, and he maintains that Pope Agatho reinstated Wilfrid and allowed him to select his co-bishops. However, the surviving proceedings of this council present the dispute in a rather different light. They deal with complaints from a number of bishops and uphold the need to create more sees, but capped the number at 12 (including that of Canterbury) and made clear that the suffragan bishops were subject to the Archbishop (Levison 1912, 280–1). This suggests that a plea to Rome was made not just by Wilfrid but also by other bishops, perhaps including Bishop Winfrith, challenging Theodore's authority to create new sees. Agatho's ruling may have been a compromise, allowing an increase in the number of bishoprics but restricting it to a lesser number than that desired by Theodore (Brooks, 1984, 71–6).

Bede tell us that Theodore divided Wilfrid's see into two dioceses representing Deira and Bernicia. The former was governed by Bosa from York, and the latter by Eata, initially at Hexham but also temporarily at Lindisfarne (HE IV, 12). Additionally, the newly-conquered province of Lindsey was also provided with a bishop, Eadhæd, who was transferred to Ripon when the region was regained by King Æthelræd of Mercia. In 681, two further bishops were consecrated by Theodore: Trumwine for another newly-conquered region, Pictland, and Tunberht, who replaced Eata at Hexham during the period when he occupied the see at Lindisfarne (c.681–5: HE IV, 12). The fluidity of diocesan organisation in Northumbria at this point is notable: in 684 Cuthbert was elected Bishop of Hexham but transferred to Lindisfarne a year later, causing Eata's return to Hexham (HE IV, 28).

The exact extent and nature of Wilfrid's restoration in 686 and 706 are unclear. Stephen's account of Wilfrid's return from exile in 686 claims that intruded bishops (*alienis episcopis*) were expelled and that Wilfrid then held the houses of Hexham and Ripon and the see of York for five years (VW 44). In the following chapter, Stephen describes how relations between King Aldfrith and Wilfrid alternated between harmony and conflict for many years until eventually the king expelled the saint. The roots of the discord were, according to Stephen, the treatment of the monastery at Ripon which was deprived of its possessions and lands, the fact that it was converted into an episcopal see in contradiction of its privileged status, and that the decrees of Archbishop Theodore's middle period were enforced, not those of his later years when he sought to be reconciled to Wilfrid. The significance of Stephen's account here is a little unclear but can be clarified by close examination of the events during Wilfrid's restoration, from 686 to 691.

Wilfrid's restorations in 686 and 706 have one key element in common (Brooks 1984; Cubitt 1989). On both occasions, the bishop's return to Northumbria seems to have coincided with a vacancy in the see at Hexham. Eata is said to have died at the beginning of Aldfrith's reign, in either 685 or 686. In 706, it was the death of Bosa of York which opened the way for John of Beverley to be translated from Hexham to York. These events suggest that Wilfrid's initial restitution in 686 was to Hexham. In early 687, Cuthbert resigned his see at Lindisfarne, dying a hermit on Farne on 20 March of that year. Wilfrid administered Lindisfarne for one year, a year of exceptional turbulence according to Bede (Colgrave 1940, 284–9). In August 687, John of Beverley was appointed to Hexham and in 688 the community of Lindisfarne were relieved of rule by the outsider, Wilfrid, through the election of Eadfrith, probably one of their own number. Stephen's complaint in VW 45 about the imposition of the decrees of Theodore's middle period probably refers to these two appointments, to the creation of a see at Hexham and the revival of that at Lindisfarne.

At this point, the diplomatic record has important light to shed on Wilfrid's vicissitudes. A charter of King Cædwalla of Wessex granting land in Surrey, S 235, dated to 688, includes the saint in its witness-list, indicating that Wilfrid must have been in Southumbria in this year. The date is given by both indictional and incarnational reckonings, and the appearance of an AD date in this charter have led some to doubt its authenticity. However, Edwards has convincingly defended its reliability and the incarnational date and the indiction agree (Edwards 1988, 132–7; Whitelock 1979, 484). Two other charters – S 1171 and 1246 – also include Wilfrid in their witness lists and may date to 688, but their dating is more problematic (Whitelock 1979, 486). In the light of Wilfrid's difficulties at Lindisfarne, and his replacement there in 688 by Eadfrith, his presence in Surrey in this year may indicate a temporary expulsion or self-imposed exile. Was this one of the alternate episodes of disharmony to which Stephen referred in chapter 45?

Wilfrid's ultimate expulsion by Aldfrith took place in 691. What was Bosa's status during Wilfrid's restoration? Stephen declares that bishops were forced out as a result of his hero's return but does not specify who. Of the three bishops consecrated by Theodore in 678–81, Trumwine had been forced to flee from his see in Pictland after Ecgfrith's defeat at Nechtanesmere in May 685 and retired to Whitby (HE IV, 26). Of Eadhæd, we know nothing after his translation to Ripon from Lindsey c.679. Bede does not indicate any disruption to Bosa's pontificate but this silence may reflect his discretion. Some historians have deduced that his rule at York was interrupted for the five years of Wilfrid's restitution (as Thacker 2004e). Stephen's indignation in VW 45 at the conversion of the monastery at Ripon into an episcopal see suggests that Bosa was moved sideways to Ripon at some point, perhaps after 688, to accommodate Wilfrid at York.

Stephen states explicitly that when Wilfrid was restored in 706 after the Council at Nidd, his two best monasteries at Ripon and Hexham with their possessions were restored to him (VW 55). Bosa's death, as we have seen, allowed John of Beverley to be translated to York, leaving Hexham free for Wilfrid. Ripon, it would appear, was no longer providing an episcopal see. On his final restoration, therefore, Wilfrid did not regain York nor extensive episcopal authority in Northumbria, but was able to take full control of his most prestigious monasteries. It is interesting to note that on his death he was succeeded as bishop at Hexham by one of his own followers, Acca, and not by a man trained in another's foundations.

At the heart of Stephen's narrative lie claims to the privileged status of monasteries and ecclesiastical possessions, exemplified by his outrage at Aldfrith's treatment of Ripon and the violation of its privileges. Control of Wilfrid's foundations and their possessions was also central to the debacle at the Council of Austerfield where, according to Stephen, Wilfrid's properties in Northumbria and Mercia were to be surrendered to the archbishop of Canterbury's control (VW 47; Wood 2006, 198).

The outrage at these actions conveyed by Stephen's *Vita* impresses the reader with a sense of royal and archiepiscopal high-handedness, that his enemies were acting beyond their legitimate authority. In fact, the issues underlying the treatment of Wilfrid's possessions were by no means clear cut and were matters of debate and controversy at this time. Questions about the relationship between episcopal oversight and monastic independence loomed large at this period. What powers did a bishop have over the monasteries in his diocese? Monasteries and their founders sought ways of limiting episcopal interference by grants of immunity (Wood 2006, 186–7, 190–9). The seventh century saw a shift to greater freedoms on the part of monastic houses, evidenced for the first time in an exemption granted by Pope Honorius to Bobbio (Wormald 2006a, 7–9). On his visit to Rome in 679–80, Wilfrid had taken the precaution of obtaining from Pope Agatho a privilege for his monasteries of Hexham and Ripon. He was not the only one at this time to pursue this policy – Agatho also issued privileges for St Augustine's Canterbury, and Benedict Biscop's houses at Monkwearmouth-Jarrow (Levison 1946, 24–6, 187–95; Wormald 2006a, 7) We only know of Wilfrid's and Benedict's privileges from report, while the St Augustine's charter does survive in something like its original form. Wormald's analysis suggests that, at Wearmouth-Jarrow, episcopal interference in abbatial elections was excluded. Stephen emphasises that Ripon's privileges protected the community and its property from conversion into an episcopal see. The St Augustine's privilege also excluded the jurisdiction of any church other than the apostolic see, and we know that the subsequent confirmation which Wilfrid obtained from Pope Sergius did the same (Wormald 2006, 7–9). This clutch of papal privileges for English houses indicates that concerns over relations between bishops and monasteries were widespread. Indeed, English houses continued to seek papal privileges in the eighth century and beyond (Levison, 1946, 24–33; Anton 1975).

Wilfrid's papal privileges failed to achieve their desired aim of protecting his communities. It would appear that the saint obtained these in the face of opposition. Benedict Biscop obtained King Ecgfrith's ratification of his privilege but it seems unlikely that Wilfrid was able to solicit the king's confirmation. Stephen states that Ripon's privilege was confirmed by Pope Agatho and five kings, but this may be a reference to the presence of kings, including Ecgfrith, at Ripon's consecration, rather than an indication that Agatho's privilege had royal confirmation (VW 17 and 45). Royal approval was frequently sought to support papal immunities – the co-operation of the king is explicitly mentioned with regard to Pope Theodore's privilege for Bobbio, and Pope Sergius's for Malmesbury was explicitly endorsed by Kings Æthelræd of Mercia and Ine of Wessex (Anton 1975; Edwards 1988, 100–5; Rauer 2006). It may perhaps be the lack of royal approval for Wilfrid's papal privileges that led Stephen to highlight the spiritual power of papal decrees and the consequences of defying their anathemas.

When Wilfrid returned to Northumbria in 680, armed with Pope Agatho's synodal ruling reinstating him in his see and ordering that he should choose the new Northumbrian bishops, Ecgfrith promptly threw him straight into gaol (VW 34). Stephen's account of this great council in 679 is notable for its lengthy recitation of the anathema which concluded the judgment:

> If anyone therefore attempts with rash daring to withstand the
> decrees of these synodal statutes … we declare by the authority of

the blessed Peter the chief of the Apostles that he shall be punished by this decree; so that if he be a bishop who attempts to flout this pious ordinance, let him be deprived of episcopal rank and be the object of an eternal curse; likewise if he be a priest, deacon ... a cleric, a monk, or a layman of whatever degree, even a king, let him be cut off from the body of our Saviour and the blood of our Lord Jesus Christ ... (VW 32).

This anathema is there for a purpose: it serves as a warning to the Life's audience of the dreadful fate awaiting those who defied the decree and other papal privileges. It informs the rest of the narrative of Stephen's account. Stephen repeatedly emphasizes how Ecgfrith and his successors defied the papal power to bind and loose and demonstrates the fearful ends they meet. Peter's power as chief of the Apostles to bind and loose is explicitly mentioned when Ecgfrith rejects the papal degree and has Wilfrid imprisoned – Ecgfrith 'despised the judgment of Peter the Apostle and chief of the Apostles who has the power from God to loose and to bind [*solvendi ligandique potestatem*]' (VW 34), and reiterated it when his queen and accomplice, Iurminburh, is struck down by demonic possession. Iurminburh is described as close to death with 'her limbs were contracted and tightly bound together [*contractis membris simul in unum stricte alligatam*]'. Abbess Æbbe of Coldingham pleads with the King to release Wilfrid from prison in order to obtain the queen's life, reminding Ecgfrith of how he scorned the papal decrees: 'the writings of the Apostolic See which has, in company with St Peter the Apostle, the power of binding and loosing [*potestatem ligandi et solvendi*]'. Iurminburh's limbs are bound – '*alligatam*' (VW 39). Moreover, Stephen's description of Iurminburh's physical constriction through demonic possession follows immediately upon his chapter concerning Wilfrid's imprisonment at Dunbar when the King ordered that he should be fettered. But Ecgfrith's iron bonds are incapable of binding the saint – the smiths cannot make them fit (VW 38). The counterpoint here is very deliberate: Iurminburh is bound physically by the pope's spiritual power but the king cannot fetter the saint.

When Ecgfrith and the best of his army are slaughtered by the Picts at the Battle of Nechtanesmere, Stephen reports this as an event which ushered in Wilfrid's return from exile (VW 44). He does not need to labour the message that the king's defeat was a result of divine disfavour; it would have been clear to his audience. Ecgfrith's successor, Aldfrith, restores Wilfrid to his see, and eventually fulfills Pope Agatho's decree, expelling the alien bishops and returning Ripon and its possessions to Wilfrid. However, this happy period does not continue and Aldfrith ejects Stephen's hero (VW 44–5). Wilfrid obtains another papal judgment in his favour to which Aldfrith pays no heed. Stephen writes:

Now the divine vengeance did not tarry but, as the prelate of the Apostolic see had prophesied, laid hold upon the king binding him fast by chains of sickness [*vinculis alligatum infirmitatis*]. Being a prudent man he realised that he had been struck by the Apostolic power and, moved by penitence, confessed the sin which he had committed against Bishop Wilfrid in defiance of the judgments of the Apostolic see' (VW 59).

Like Iurminburh, Aldfrith is rendered '*alligatus*' by his disease. Aldfrith vowed that, if he were healed, he would make full amends to Wilfrid and if he was prevented by death from doing so, he would instruct his heir to make peace with the bishop. But his successor, Eadwulf, failed to carry out Aldfrith's command, despatching Wilfrid rudely, but he too soon met an unhappy fate – 'after these rough words, a conspiracy arose against the king and he was driven from the kingdom' after a rule of only two months (VW 59). In the case of Aldfrith, Stephen is explicit about the effect of rejecting the papal decisions. Elsewhere, the threat of the papal anathema is implicit. It may lie behind his depiction of Theodore's reconciliation with Wilfrid, which is explicitly stated to have been prompted by Theodore's premonition of his own imminent death and parallels Aldfrith's own deathbed conversion to the Wilfridian cause (VW 43).

The dreadful consequences of ignoring papal edicts is an important thread running through the *Life of Wilfrid* and must reflect the plight of the communities when Stephen was writing. Ripon and Hexham were safeguarded not only by papal privileges but also by land charters which might also have been reinforced by the inclusion of anathemas. Stephen is careful to include the fact that these were read at the consecration of Ripon in the presence of a great crowd of magnates, spiritual and secular, including Kings Ecgfrith and Ælfwine and other subkings (VW 17). Sadly, these documents, like all other Northumbrian charters, do not survive, a huge loss. However, the charter record for the Southumbrian kingdoms at this time is relatively good, although not numerous, and our saintly bishop does appear, mostly as a witness, in five or six southern charters. These documents are rarely used to shed light on Wilfrid but, as we have already seen, their evidence can help us to comprehend him better, and it is these charters which will now be addressed.[1] With one exception, these all date to periods when Wilfrid was in exile from Northumbria and show Wilfrid in the company of kings, chiefly Cædwalla of Wessex and Æthelræd of

---

[1]   S 45, 692 Nothgyth, King of the South Saxons grants 33 hides to his sister, Nothgyth who transfers it to Wilfrid. S 235, 688 Caedwalla grant of Farnham to three men, S 1171, 685×93 Æthelræd to Æthelburh, abbess of Barking, and S 1248 Cædwalla to Barking and S 1246. S 53 Oshere to Cuthswith abbess grant of Inkberrow and Dyllawida.

Mercia. They are striking corroboration of Stephen's narrative: for example, S 45 is a grant made by the king of the South Saxons to his sister who transfers the land to Wilfrid, a transaction reminiscent of Stephen's comment on how abbots commended their houses to the bishop (VW 21). Another common element is Wilfrid's attestation of charters for women, the beneficiaries of four (including the South Saxon grant just mentioned) are women. Perhaps Wilfrid played a special role in encouraging women's vocations, just as he supported Queen Æthelthryth in her monastic calling, giving her the nun's veil (HE IV, 19 (17)). Two of these are for the double monastery of Barking, affirming Wilfrid's relations with Bishop Eorcenwald of London, its founder, who appears in Stephen's Life on the occasion of Theodore's reconciliation with Wilfrid (VW 43). Edwards suggested that Wilfrid's presence as a witness to S 235, Cædwalla's grant of 688, confirmed Stephen's description of the saint as an influential councillor of the king and she surmised that Wilfrid may have had a role in Cædwalla's retirement to Rome in 688 (Edwards 1988, 137; Pettit 2004).

The late seventh century was a dynamic period in the development of the Anglo-Saxon charter. Although the use of written documents to record the transfer of land to the church may go back rather earlier, authentic charters only survive from the second half of the seventh century. Their formulation suggests that a variety of influences were at work, with some continental influence. Bishop Eorcenwald of London, probably a Merovingian in origin, has been seen as responsible for the use of a number of Frankish features in charters associated with him, including S 235, Cædwalla's grant of 688 and two others attested by Wilfrid (Wormald 2006b, pp. 142–5; Kelly 1990). Loss of the foundation charters for Ripon and Hexham means that we cannot analyse their diplomatic formulation. However, Henry Mayr-Harting's observation that Stephen's account of the consecration of that altar at Ripon indicated that a Gallican, not Roman, rite was used is suggestive of Frankish influence at work in Wilfrid's activities (Mayr-Harting 1972, 180–1). Wilfrid has been credited with the introduction of incarnational dating into charters, a distinct possibility although the use of this form of dating is not consistently linked to him (Harrison 1976, 65–75; Sims-Williams 1995).

The flowering of diplomatic at the end of the seventh century reflects the sudden popularity of monasticism and the establishment of many new monasteries in England, like the foundation of Bishop Eorcenwald for his sister at Barking (Blair 2005, 79–108; Foot 2006). The new craze for the establishment of monasteries posed new questions for the nature of land tenure. One must envisage a situation of innovation and experimentation. The endowment of major churches and monasteries in England not only produced new, written documentation but also transformed land tenure. The introduction of charters, landbooks, allowed for the donation of land in perpetuity with freedom of alienation (Wormald, 2006b, 153–61). In the time of St Wilfrid, the foundation of monasteries gathered pace: new double communities under women abbesses were established and the practice of noble rather than royal foundation began to develop.

Susan Wood's magisterial survey of the medieval proprietary church charts the growth and transformation of ideas governing ecclesiastical property from the Roman Empire onwards (Wood 2006). Although theories of ecclesiastical property had evolved within the late Roman Empire, ideas of property were dynamic and the new popularity of noble foundations initiated in Merovingian Francia by Columbanus and his followers seems to have led to new developments. In England, the rules governing monastic land may not have been static and clearly established. Anglo-Saxon diplomatic shows variety and experimentation in this period, a liveliness which should not be divorced from the evolution of ideas about the nature of religious property (Kelly 1990). The charters attested by Wilfrid highlight a number of issues in the status of ecclesiastical land. They include a number of confirmations by King Æthelræd of Mercia of previous grants by lesser kings, emphasizing that a king's ability to grant land to the church in perpetuity was dependent upon political circumstances: a change of regime or the intrusion of an overlord could place existing tenurial arrangements in jeopardy. One is reminded here of the fact that Wilfrid's first possession, Ripon, was the gift of Alhfrith who appears to have been a subking of Oswiu. It is not surprising that Wilfrid gained confirmation of his charters from the assembled kings at the consecration of Ripon (VW 8).

The fluidity of religious property is evidenced elsewhere in the history of seventh- and eighth-century Northumbria. For example, Alhfrith's decision to make Wilfrid abbot of Ripon presumably displaced the existing abbot and effectively forced the community to leave. So Alhfrith did not regard his original foundation of Ripon as placing it outside his personal control (VW 8; VCP 7). Later, in the eighth century, Bede advocated to Bishop Ecgberht of York that, in cooperation with the king, it was possible to annex monastic foundations to create new sees, just as was attempted with Wilfrid (EEE 10–11). Bede's promotion of this idea indicates that monastic land might be seen as subject both to episcopal control and to royal. John Blair has drawn attention to the tensions between religious aspiration and secular norms and desires in the early endowment of Anglo-Saxon monasteries. He cites an exceptionally interesting sequence of grants concerning a monastery at Bradfield, Berkshire, which had been endowed by King Cissa, probably a West Saxon sub-king. This grant had been annulled by King Ine because of the failure to found a community, and the land redirected to Ine's royal *patricius*, Haeha who seems himself to have taken monastic vows and granted the confiscated land for the foundation of a monastery. Subsequently, however, Haeha sought to leave the monastery and wished to repossess his land, perhaps to become an abbot himself of another foundation, and was allowed to do so by a council of King Ine, Bishop Haeddi, and Abbots Aldhelm and Wintra (Blair 2005, 87–91, S 241; S 1179; Kelly 2000, 11–22). If the land record of these transactions can be trusted, it would appear that monastic land was not immune from the changed priorities of its original donors, nor from royal interference. Wilfrid's clashes with kings over his possession of monasteries reflects not a simple opposition between hostile and greedy kings and a saintly churchman righteously upholding ecclesiastical prerogatives but one aspect of a continuing negotiation between kings and churchmen over the status of church land and its relation to both royal and episcopal authority.

Problems over the status of church land were not restricted to questions of ownership and possession but encompassed the privileged status of monasteries and their lands with regard to royal demands for military and labour service. Royal privileges issued in Kent and Wessex in 699 and 704 respectively – contemporary therefore with Wilfrid's conflicts – show Kings Wihtred and Ine exempting monasteries and churches from certain forms of tribute. These grants required reciprocal action: in Wihtred's case, that the honour and obedience previously shown to Kentish kings should be granted to him and his successors, and in Ine's, the privileges were given in return for prayers for the welfare of the king and kingdom (S 20: Brooks 1971, 75, and 1984, 78, 192; S 245: Edwards 1988, 107–14). These concessions must have been gained by negotiation and argument. They are important reminders that just at the time when Wilfrid was asserting his absolute possession of Ripon and Hexham, kings and churchmen were hammering out agreements about the extent of royal authority over church land. Moreover, both privileges were preceded by royal law-codes enforcing Christian *mores* on the lives of the laity. Wihtred's code in 695 translated a number of the rulings of the Council of Hertford into secular law and protected the status of the Kentish churches, while Ine's code (688×694) enforced ecclesiastical provisions concerning baptism, Sunday work, church dues and the rights of sanctuaries (Liebermann 1903–16, I, 12–14, 89–123; Wormald 1999, 101–2; Cubitt 2007, 154–6). It would appear that Kings Wihtred and Ine came to important agreements with the Church over the obligations of Christian conduct and the protected status of churches and monasteries. Similar evidence is lacking for the kingdoms of Mercia and Northumbria at this time and, while it is dangerous to argue from silence, it may be that churches in these kingdoms did not obtain similar privileges in this period. In the mid-eighth century, St Boniface castigated King Æthelbald of Mercia for his contravention of church and monastic privileges, for his confiscation of their properties and the abusive exploitation of monks within his kingdom. Boniface claimed that the violation of church privileges had been initiated by the early eighth-century kings, Ceolred of Mercia and Osred of Northumbria (Tangl 1916, no. 73, pp. 152–3). His admonitions to Æthelbald seem to have been heeded in 749, when the king issued a privilege at a synod at Gumley for the Mercian church (S 92; Brooks 1971, 76–8). The boundaries between royal right and ecclesiastical privilege were, therefore, disputed territory in the late seventh and early eighth centuries and Wilfrid's rancorous disputes over the rights and status of his communities took place within this context. It is significant that the royal privileges promulgated by Wihtred and Ine are drafted as resulting in reciprocal obligations of prayer or honour on the part of the privileged communities. Churches had to earn their privileged status by their close alliance with royal power, a collaboration which Wilfrid signally failed to achieve. The vulnerability of his foundations to attack is evidenced in Stephen's *Vita*, a text which was written in the reigns of Ceolred and Osred (both died in 716) and must reflect the insecurities and anxieties of this time.

Wilfrid's links with the continent form an important background to his ambitions and achievements. His eagerness to protect his foundations with papal privileges and to restrict episcopal power can be mirrored in continental developments, particularly in the communities founded by Columbanus and individuals associated with them. It was his foundation at Bobbio which received Pope Honorius's privilege of exemption (Wormald 1976, 5–7). Wilfrid's advocacy of the Benedictine Rule associates him with Columbanus and his foundations, which adopted the *Regula Benedicti* as part of mixed rules, just as Wilfrid may have done. Further, Ian Wood has pointed out that the practice of nobles receiving a grant of royal land from the king in order to found their own monastery is evidenced in Columbanian circles on the continent, in the grants of Dagobert to Bishop Eligius of Noyon, to St Amandus and to the family of Bishop Audoin of Rouen, and he noted the parallel with Anglo-Saxon customs. In a number of cases, royal intervention also secured privileges limiting episcopal control (Wood 1982, 77). It looks very strongly as though Wilfrid and his English contemporaries were directly influenced by continental practices not only in the types of community which they founded but also in the process of endowment.

The significance of Frankish and particularly Columbanian influence for our understanding of Wilfrid was signalled long ago by Henry Mayr-Harting and Ian Wood. (Mayr-Harting 1972, 157, 180–1; Wood 1990) Seeking for comparable figures in the early medieval world to Wilfrid, an immediate candidate is Columbanus himself, an Irish monk who left his native land as a perpetual pilgrim and settled initially in Francia, where his violent clashes with royal authority led to his departure to Italy and establishment of a monastery at Bobbio. He died in 615. Like Wilfrid, Columbanus's own foundations crossed national boundaries and his great charisma provoked a rash of monastic foundations and vocations among the nobility, rather like Stephen's account of abbots and nobles seeking Wilfrid's protection and patronage (Wallace-Hadrill 1983, 55–74; Bullough 1997). But Wilfrid's aims and activities are better paralleled not by those of Columbanus himself but rather by the next generation of bishops working under his influence, St Amandus (dying *c*.675) , St Eligius, bishop of Noyon and St Audoin, Bishop of Rouen, both consecrated bishop in 641 (Wood 1994, 184–9; Fouracre 1996, 133–52; Wood 2001, 39–42).

Here not only are the parallels quite precise but one can trace personal links. Wilfrid owed his early promotion to Bishop Agilbert of Wessex who later became bishop of Paris (VW 9). He was buried at Jouarre, the double house founded by Ado, brother of Audoin of Rouen. Audoin's family was active in monastic foundations in the region of Meaux, the place where Wilfrid recuperated from illness in 704 and received his vision of St Michael (Fouracre, above). Wilfrid's association with the network of churchmen linked with Columbanus and his foundations may date back to his days at Lyons under Bishop Aunemundus. If the *acta Aunemundi* are to be trusted, Aunemundus was educated at the court of King Dagobert, where earlier Audoin and Eligius had been trained. He seems to have acted as godfather to Clothar III, or to have baptised him – another link to Eligius who was the king's godfather. Finally, when summoned by the king for trial, Aunemundus sought the support of Abbot Waldebert of Luxeuil, the premier Columbanian foundation (Fouracre 1996, 166–80). So it is possible that Wilfrid's links to the circle of Columbanus and even to Agilbert were initiated in Lyons.

There are further key parallels between Wilfrid and these men in matters of Christian mission and papal affiliation. On Wilfrid's first visit to Rome, Stephen tells us that Wilfrid prayed in an oratory dedicated to St Andrew (probably the basilica close to St Peter's), before an altar on which was placed the Gospels, and asked that he might be granted 'a ready mind both to read and to teach the words of the Gospels among the nations'(VW 5). By this episode Stephen signals Wilfrid's commitment to missionary activities, as is later evidenced by his actions in Frisia and Sussex. Wilfrid's missionary commission can be paralleled by that of St Amandus who received his own on the steps of St Peter's in a vision from the prince of the Apostles himself (Wood 2001, 39–42; *Vita sancti Amandi*, ed. Krusch, c. 7, p. 434). Wolfgang Fritze has expounded the significance of this and other episodes in the *Life of St Amandus* to the idea of universal Christian mission, founded on Christ's commission to his disciples at the end of the Gospel of St Matthew to 'go therefore and make disciples of all nations', an idea propagated by the early seventh-century papacy (Fritze 1969; Wood 2001, 39). Stephen's careful comment that the Gospels was placed on the altar before which he prayed may be an oblique reference to this Gospel passage and Wilfrid's choice of the basilica of Andrew linked to the latter's status as a missionary saint. Fritze (1969, 84–106) argued that the idea of universal Christian mission can been seen as a distinctive feature of a circle of Frankish bishops and abbots linked to St Columbanus, whose number included Eligius and Audoin, or to monasteries associated with him. Wilfrid can be further linked to this circle by the proximity of his own missionary activities and those of his disciple Willibrord in Frisia to their mission fields (VW 26; HE III, 13; V, 11, 19; Fritze 1969, 81–84).

The idea of universal Christian mission was promoted by the seventh-century papacy (Fritze 1969, 106–113). Wilfrid shares with Amandus, Audoin and Eligius direct involvement in papal politics, with links to the opposition of the seventh-century papacy to the doctrines of monoenergism and monotheletism, the teachings advocated by the Byzantine Emperor and the Patriarch of Constantinople that Christ possessed only one operation or will. The conflict within the Byzantine Empire between opponents of this doctrine and the imperial church over-spilled into the west through the involvement of the papacy, prompted by eastern refugees. Pope Martin convened a council in Rome in 649 which anathematised the new doctrine and declared a series of Patriarchs of Constantinople heretics. Martin and other opponents of monotheletism were severely punished: Martin was tried in Constantinople and brutally treated. He was exiled to Cherson where he died. The *acta* of the Lateran synod were drafted in Greek and translated into Latin and circulated in both east and west (Herrin 1987, 250–9; *Book of the Pontiffs*, tr. Davis 1989, 68–71; Haldon 1997, 297–317). The Lateran synod and Martin's opposition to Byzantine religious policy should be seen as a crucial episode in papal history when Martin and subsequent popes, particularly Pope Agatho, sought to inform the western churches of their opposition and to seek their support in the preparations for the 680/1 Council of Constantinople. In the west, Amandus, Eligius and Audoin all had significant involvement in this papal initiative.

Pope Martin sent the Lateran *acta* to the western churches; we know that he wrote to St Amandus, sending the Lateran *acta* and asking him to condemn the monothelete doctrine. He asked that other Frankish bishops join in this condemnation and that the Frankish king send a delegation to Constantinople. It is likely that the Council of Chalon-sur-Saone, which took place in between 647–53 (probably, in my view, in 650) was convened in response to this papal initiative. This affirmed its adherence to the ecumenical councils thus implicitly condemning any doctrine which contravened them (Pontal 1989, 216–20; Cubitt and Price forthcoming). Eligius was deputed to travel to Rome to affirm Frankish orthodoxy. Thus all three, Amandus, Eligius and Audoin were involved in supporting papal opposition to the new doctrine.

Wilfrid's participation in this seventh-century doctrinal controversy is a little more oblique. In 680, he was present at the Roman Easter Council of Pope

Agatho, convened to affirm western orthodoxy in preparation for the 680–1 Council of Constantinople, the ecumenical council by which the papacy and emperor were reconciled in doctrinal matters. By 680, Byzantine support for monotheletism had waned and the emperor was ready to condemn the doctrine (Herrin 1987, 250–9; Haldon 1997, 297–317) Wilfrid attests the conciliar *acta* and his presence at this council appears to be a by-product of his presence in Rome in 679 appealing against the division of his see, but this may not represent the whole picture. In fact, Wilfrid's awareness and engagement with papal opposition to monoenergism and monotheletism may have long predated this council and can be traced to his very first visit to Rome, made at a time when the effects of papal resistance to imperial policy were strongly felt.

However, the timing and details of Wilfrid's first visit to Rome are not easy to unravel and there are two key issues which must be addressed. The first is the question of exactly when Wilfrid was in Rome, and secondly the identity of his friend and mentor, the papal Archdeacon Boniface. Stephen's chronology for his subject's early years is vague and date limits for the bishop's first continental journey are broad. The date of his departure for Rome is unclear – Wilfrid left Lindisfarne after a number of years [*post circulum annorum*] after he joined in 648 (VW 3). He then spent a year in Kent before proceeding to the continent with Benedict Biscop. He stayed in Lyons on his way to Rome but, again, we do not know for how long (VW 3). This account suggests that Wilfrid was unlikely to have arrived in Rome before 654 at the earliest. We know that he returned to England at some point before the Synod of Whitby in 664 after three years in Lyons; the latest that he could have been in Rome must therefore have been 660–1.

These were years of turmoil in Rome: Pope Martin was arrested and taken to Constantinople on 15 June 653 (Winkelmann 2001, 286), where he was tried and sentenced to exile, dying on 16 September 655. The violent abstraction of the pope left a vacancy in papal administration which the Pope instructed should be filled by the archdeacon, together with the *primicerius* and the *archipresbyter* (Bresslau 1912–31; Cubitt and Price forthcoming). His successor, Eugenius, was consecrated on 10 August 654, somewhat irregularly since Martin was still alive. It is possible that the Archdeacon Boniface, whom Stephen says instructed Wilfrid in religious teaching, was Pope Martin's delegated deputy and Wilfrid's encounter with him took place while he was responsible for the see (VW 5). On the other hand, it may be that the archdeacon was acting as a mediator for papal visitors, since Stephen also tells us that he eventually presented the young Englishman to the pope, whom, lamentably, Stephen fails to name. The broad date range of Wilfrid's first visit to Rome does not enable us to exclude the possibility that this was Eugenius's successor, Vitalian, consecrated on 30 July 657, after a vacancy of nearly two months. The monothelete controversy must have been a live issue in Rome at this time. Pope Eugenius was coerced into rejecting the synodica of the new Patriarch, Peter of Constantinople by the Roman people and clergy (Davis (trans.) 1989, 71). Pope Vitalian, on the other hand, did not oppose imperial policy and sent his synodica to the Emperor. Wilfrid's religious instruction in Rome and his missionary calling took place in the context of this controversy.

The identity of Wilfrid's friend, the Archdeacon Boniface, is problematic. Stephen describes him as 'one of the wisest of the counsellors [*unum ex consiliariis sapientissimum*]' (VW 5). Bede, perhaps paraphrasing Stephen, says that Wilfrid gained the friendship of 'Archdeacon Boniface, a most holy and learned man, who was also a counsellor to the pope [*amicitiam uiri sanctissimi ac doctissimi, Bonifatii uidelicet archidiaconi, qui etiam erat consiliarius papae*]' (HE V, 19). A lead bull found at Whitby in the name of an archdeacon Boniface (illustrated by Levison 1946, 17–18) may be associated with him. Berschin has identified this man with the later seventh-century papal councillor of the same name who was involved in Wilfrid's Roman pleas in 679 and 704, a figure of some note (Berschin 1989, 25–40, esp. p. 26, n. 8). However, this identification is very uncertain for two weighty reasons. Firstly, the archdeacon was one of the most important officials in the papal administration, head of the college of deacons and prominent in papal affairs (Richards 1979, 250, 290). This would suggest that he was already a senior figure when he mentored Wilfrid in the 650s, and was unlikely to have been a young man. It is improbable therefore that he would still be prominent in papal affairs over forty years later. Secondly, the Bonifatius *consiliarius* who took Wilfrid's part in 704 is not designated archdeacon, a more prestigius office than the role of *consiliarius*, and it seems unlikely that the lesser position would be mentioned rather than the greater (Richards 1979, 299–300).

The later Bonifatius *consiliarius* who was present when Wilfrid's case was presented at both the 679 and 704 Roman synods was also a very considerable figure. Stephen tells us that a man named Boniface spoke up for the Bishop at the Council of 704, recalling Wilfrid's vindication at the Council of 679 (VW 53). The list of those attending the 679 Council precedes the decrees and includes at the head of the priests present, one Bonifatius (Levison 1912, 278). It is Bede who, in his resumé of Stephen's account, designates this Bonifatius as a papal councillor [*Bonifatius consiliarius apostolici papae*] (HE V, 19). He played a significant part in the aftermath of the Council of Constantinople and was entrusted with the responsibility of de-hereticising a leading monothelete, Macarius of Antioch, who was sent to Rome for this purpose. He appears to have been strongly linked to the dyothelete party since he translated from Greek a hagiographical text of the Patriarch Sophronius of Jerusalem, a leading anti-monothelete. In the pontificate of Pope Sergius, he was arrested and taken to

Constantinople as a reprisal for the pope's opposition to the Byzantine Council in Trullo, an episode which looks like a further indicator of his opposition to imperial ecclesiastical policy (Davis (trans.) 1989, p. 84; Berschin 1989; Oekonomou 2007, p. 223). Another of the Roman emissaries was also arrested in Constantinople, Bishop John of Porto, who may also be identified with the bishop of the same name whose names appears in the attendance list of the 679 Council, where Stephen records that he also spoke up in Wilfrid's defence (VW 29; Levison 1912, 278 and note 8). This bishop was subsequently part of the papal delegation to the Council of Constantinople and celebrated Latin mass in the church of the St Sophia in April 681 in the presence of the emperor (VW 29; Herren 1987, 279). Bonifatius *consiliarius* and John of Porto play a prominent role in the adjudication of Wilfrid's pleas; both were significantly involved in the condemnation of monotheletism in 680/1.

Wilfrid's involvement in the great politico-ecclesiastical issue of the day is further evidenced by his journey to Rome in 678–9. Stephen tells that he broke his journey to Rome with visits to Kings Dagobert and Perctarit and that he was accompanied from Francia by Bishop Deodatus. Deodatus of Toul was in fact travelling to Rome to attend Pope Agatho's Easter Council, the *acta* of which he also witnessed. He was also present at Agatho's Council of 679 which ruled on the question of English dioceses (Levison 1912, 278). The sojourn of these two men with the Lombard king, Perctarit, probably also has an anti-monothelete dimension since in his reign, the metropolitan, Mansuetus of Milan, convened a synod at Milan to condemn the heresy, probably at exactly this time. Mansuetus also attested the acta of the Easter Council of 680 (Riedinger 1990, 149; Picard 1988, 84–5).

The fact that Wilfrid's own personal crisis coincided with the renewed papal initiatives over the condemnation of monotheletism may not be pure coincidence. His struggles with Theodore of Canterbury over the division of his see were occasioned by the latter's claims to authority over the whole of Britain and to his archiepiscopal status. As Thomas Charles-Edwards has pointed out (2000, 429–38), Theodore asserted his right to intervene in ecclesiastical affairs outside the southern metropolitan province as early as c.669, when he deposed Chad as Bishop of York and replaced him with Wilfrid. But at this early date, Theodore does not seem to have been granted the pallium nor enjoyed archiepiscopal status. This privilege may have been granted, according to Alan Thacker, in 679, by Pope Agatho in October at Wilfrid's Roman synod (Thacker 2008, 58). However, it is possible that Theodore's receipt of the honour of the pallium took place earlier and should be connected to papal concerns over the monothelete dogma. Theodore was highly regarded in Rome and seen as the most learned expert in these doctrinal complexities. Pope Agatho's letter to Emperor Constantine IV after his 680 Roman council directly alludes to his desire to draw upon Theodore's theological expertise (Riedinger 1990, 132–3; Chadwick 1995, 92). In 678/9, Pope Agatho despatched to England his emissary, John the Archcantor, with a copy of the *acta* of the 649 Lateran Council, to investigate the doctrinal orthodoxy of the English church (HE IV, 18). John was present at the Council of Hatfield which affirmed the orthodoxy proclaimed in Rome in 649. It is in the proceedings of the Council of Hatfield that Theodore is first styled as Archbishop of Canterbury. Although Bede records the Council of Hatfield as taking place in 680, it must surely have been convened in 679 in the run up to Agatho's Roman council at Easter 680 (Cubitt 1995, 252–8). If this earlier date is correct, then the idea that Theodore was first granted the pallium in October 679 is chronologically very difficult. It is unlikely that there would have been sufficient time for Theodore to receive the pallium and convene the Council, particularly since the winter months of November and December were unseasonable times to convene a major council (Cubitt 1995, 25–6).

Theodore's standing in Rome and his role as an expert in the recent doctrinal controversy may have been leading factors in his elevation to the archiepiscopate. His decision to press forward with the creation of new sees would certainly have been strengthened by this direct mark of papal favour. One wonders, therefore, how welcome the complaints of Wilfrid and other Anglo-Saxons in Rome in October 679 against his initiatives would have been. Some compromise was reached in 679: the number of sees was limited to twelve. Moreover, at the Council held the following Easter in Rome to prepare for the Council of Constantinople, Wilfrid was present, and according to Stephen, affirmed the orthodox faith for 'all the northern part of Britain, and of Ireland, and for the islands which were inhabited by the peoples of the English and of the Britons and also the Irish and the Picts' (VW 53; Charles-Edwards 2000, 432). It looks as though, in Rome in 679–80, Theodore's supreme position as archbishop over the church in England and perhaps also in Britain was confirmed. The synod of 679 did not nullify the creation of new Northumbrian sees but rather allowed Wilfrid to select the new bishops. Wilfrid's reported status in Easter 680 seems to signal some recognition of his own enhanced but not archiepiscopal power in northern Britain and Ireland. It may be that some sort of deal was done, a compromise between Theodore's superior powers and recognition of Wilfrid's status in the north and in Ireland and other parts. If Wilfrid was granted far-reaching ecclesiastical authority, this may have been one reason why Ecgfrith so violently rejected the papal ruling. Thomas Charles-Edwards has argued that both Kings Oswiu and Ecgfrith had ambitions to subordinate the north of Ireland, Iona and other parts of Britain to their rule and to the jurisdiction of the English church (Charles-Edwards 2000, 434–5). Having gained the support of Theodore in reducing Wilfrid's power and dividing the Northumbrian diocese to prevent the concentration of so much power in the hand of one bishop, Ecgfrith probably did not wish to have Wilfrid affirmed with such extensive authority. When Aldfrith accepted Wilfrid back in 686, Northumbrian ambitions in Pictland had received a setback at the Battle of Nechtanesmere, and Bishop Trumwine had been forced to leave his diocese. While Wilfrid appears to have been pressing his claims to authority in the Northumbrian church in 686–91, these were disputed. At his final restoration in 706, he appears to have been content with the see of Hexham and control of that community and the other of Ripon, not challenging John of Beverley's position at York.

Wilfrid ended his life in 710 a figure of charisma and authority within his own communities but perhaps not widely influential outside them. His struggles for authority as a bishop and for the privileged status of his own foundations were played out against the background not only of Anglo-Saxon politics and custom but also on an international stage. His links to Frankish circles, and particularly to the bishops and churchmen associated with the foundations of St Columbanus, and his involvements in papal Rome, are vital keys to understanding his career, its triumphs and failures.

Appendix 1: Anglo-Saxon Charters Attested by St Wilfrid

St Wilfrid attests as a witness a number of Southumbrian charters preserved in various archives. The inclusion of incarnational dating in some of these has attracted scholarly attention in the debate over when this practice was introduced, but they are deserving of wider consideration because of their testimony to the saint's activities in the South. Moreover, Kelly's work on early charters, particularly those preserved in the archive of the church of Selsey (founded as a result of Wilfrid's mission), has suggested diplomatic formulae and styles – including the use of incarnational dating – which may be linked to Wilfrid's influence (Kelly 1998, xlv–l). The evidence of charters with Wilfridian connections is therefore a valuable source for the study of his career. Although, as a corpus of material, these charters can be problematic because of forgery and tampering, recent scholarly discussions, notably by Edwards and Kelly, have provided a helpful guide to their reliability (Edwards 1988; Kelly 1998, 2007, 2009).

In what follows, I offer an annotated list of all the charters in which Wilfrid's name appears in the witness list.

S 45: AD 692. Nothhelm, king of the South Saxons, grants 33 hides in Sussex to his sister, Nothgyth. Nothgyth transfers the land to bishop Wilfrid [692×709] with later confirmations

Nothhelm's charter to his sister is largely reliable, although the list of estates may have been tampered with. The transfer to Wilfrid may be authentic, or may have been reworked at a later date. It is dated by the incarnation (Kelly 1998, no. 2, pp. 13–22).

S 47: Æthelberht, king of the South Saxons, to Wilfrid, bishop, grant of ½ a hide at Chichester, Sussex

Kelly (1998, no. 8, pp. 40–1) has convincingly shown that this charter is a forgery.

S 51: AD 676. Osric, king, to Bertana, abbess; grant of land at Bath, Somerset, for a nunnery

Full discussion is given by Kelly who argues that the charter is most likely to be a fabrication based upon an authentic grant of 675/6. She presents arguments favourable to its incarnational dating clause and notes that the witness list has significant contemporary features. But she sounds a note of caution, pointing out that two successive bishops of Winchester attest, and that all the bishops present could have been drawn from the pages of Bede (Kelly 2007, no. 1, pp. 53–62; see also Sims-Williams 1988, repr. 1995; Edwards 1988, 218–23)

S 52: 680 (for 678×693). Oshere, king, to Frithuwald, monk of Bishop Winfrith; grant of land at Ripple, Worcs

Sims-Williams has argued for the authenticity of this charter and suggests emending Winfrith to Wilfrid (Sims-Williams 1988, repr. 1995, 174–83; 1990, 104–5). The authenticity of the charter as a whole is, however, doubtful and Sims-Williams' emendation is not wholly persuasive.

S 53: AD 693×?699. Oshere, king of the Hwicce, to Cuthswith, abbess; grant of land at *Penitanham* and *Dyllwuuida* (?) for the building of a minster

Wilfrid appears on the witness-list with Archbishop Berhtwald and eight other bishops, so that donation may have been made before a meeting of bishops. The charter is undated but can be dated to 693×699 (Sims-Williams 1976, 8–13; 1990, 191, 193–4; Cubitt 1995, 259).

S 72: 680. Privilege of Pope Agatho for Medeshamstede with donations to the same house by King Æthelred

Kelly has demonstrated that this charter is a later forgery (Kelly 2009, no. 2, pp. 160–70).

S 230: 680. Cædwalla, king to Wilfrid, bishop, grant of 70 hides at a number of places in Sussex

Kelly (1998, 99–103) has convincingly shown that this charter is a forgery.

S 232: 673 for?683. Cædwalla, king to Wilfrid, bishop, grant of 55 hides in and around Selsey and 32 hides elsewhere in Sussex

Kelly (1998, no. 1, pp. 3–13) has convincingly shown that this charter is a forgery.

S 235: AD 688. Cædwalla, king of the West Saxons, to Cedde, Cisi and Criswa; grant for the foundation of a minster of land at Farnham, Surrey

An authentic charter, which bears both an incarnational date and an indiction (Edwards 1988, 132–7, 163)

S 1171: AD 685×693, probably 686×688 (March). Œthelred to Æthelburh, abbess for her minster called Barking, grant of 40 hides

An authentic charter which survives in a contemporary copy which appears to have the witness list added a century later (Hart 1966, 122–35; Wormald, 1985, 9, 25).

S 1246: 677 for 687 or 688. Eorcenwald, bishop of the East Saxons, to the nunnery of Barking, grant of privileges and of lands

A difficult charter which shares the same witness list as S 1171 (with the omission of Æthelred) but which is based on genuine material. It is regarded by Wormald as broadly trustworthy. It includes an incarnational date (Hart 1961, 122–7; Yorke, 1985, 5–6; Wormald 1985, 25).

S 1248: AD 693. [? Eorcenwald], bishop to [? St Mary's, Barking] grant of 28 hides at Battersea, 20 at *Watsingaham* (Washingham). The land had been granted to him by Cædwalla, king of Wessex and confirmed by Æthelræd, king of Mercia

Edwards regards this charter as substantially genuine but not without its problems. It represents a grant by Bishop Eorcenwald of London to Barking. The land had been granted to him by Cædwalla and later confirmed by Æthelræd. Edwards has shown how the witness list combines two different sets of attestations, the first belonging to Cædwalla's grant in the 680s and the second to its confirmation by the Mercian king in 693. Wilfrid's attestation belongs to the first witness list from the 680s. The charter includes an incarnational date of 693 (Hart 1961, 135–41; Edwards 1988, 306–8).

Appendix 2: The Chronology
of Stephen's Life of Wilfrid

The occasion of not just one but two lengthy conferences devoted to the life and times of St Wilfrid stimulated new thinking and opened up new questions about the saint and his context. One area for scrutiny was the traditional chronology for the saint's life. The foundation of modern understanding was laid by Charles Plummer in the notes to his edition of Bede's *Historia Ecclesiastica gentis anglorum* first published in 1896 (Plummer 1896, II, 314–29). Plummer's acute penetration and wide erudition makes these pages still an invaluable guide and they have been widely followed, not least by Alan Thacker in his *Dictionary of National Biography* article on Wilfrid, a touchstone in discussions of the saint (Thacker 2004a). Nevertheless, significant developments in early medieval scholarship have overtaken Plummer's account, not least Levison's convincing redating of the death of Wilfrid from 709 to 710 (Stancliffe above). Additionally Paul Fouracre's important paper in this volume sheds new light on the chronology of Wilfrid's travels to Francia, questioning Plummer's calculations. This present paper re-examines the chronology of Wilfrid's career in the light of contemporary sources – Stephen's *Vita*, Bede's *Historia*, diplomatic and other evidence – and puts forward a revised chronology. The close scrutiny of Stephen's *Life* necessary for such a study was very revealing, not only of Wilfrid's career but also of the reliability, practices and skill of his biographer.

Stephen's *Life of Wilfrid* is a work of hagiography and therefore seeks to demonstrate its subject's sanctity and vindicate its hero, exonerating him from the accusations and hostility which Wilfrid attracted during his lifetime. Unlike, for example, both the prose lives of Cuthbert by Bede and the anonymous author, which are largely taken up by miracle stories, the miraculous element in the *Vita Wilfridi* is not pronounced. The *vita* is arranged chronologically, it tells the story of Wilfrid's life from birth to death, finishing with a posthumous miracle, and is divided only into chapters with no book divisions. Although, this is not an uncommon arrangement for a *vita* (the anonymous life of Cuthbert is arranged likewise) it does make Stephen's narrative a biographically-oriented hagiography rather than one, such as Adamnan's *Life of Columba*, arranged by types of miracle (Anderson and Anderson (ed.) 1991). As a work of hagiography, its narrative is not structured by dates – chapters do not generally open by indicating by reference to an external chronology (such as a king list) when the events to be expounded took place. However, close scrutiny reveals a strong underpinning of chronological markers and, indeed, Stephen's sense of chronology is remarkable – very few, if any, chronological errors or displacements can be detected in his *vita*, as will be argued below. This fact has not been fully recognised, partly because Stephen's dating of a key episode in Wilfrid's early career, the assassination of his patron the bishop of Lyons, was judged to have been in error. However, the underlying reliability of Stephen's testimony to this episode has been powerfully restated by Paul Fouracre in this volume (Fouracre above; see also Levison 1913, 164–5).

Given, therefore, that Stephen's account of Wilfrid's stay in Lyons on his first journey to Rome has been a stumbling block for his overall standing, it is important first to consider the question of the dating of Wilfrid's sojourn in Lyons. This episode, like much of the saint's childhood and early career is very loosely dated in Stephen's account. Wilfrid's birth can be reliably pinned down to 634 (for reasons explained below), and Stephen states plainly that Wilfrid left home for the Northumbrian court at the age of 14, thus allowing us to date his entry to Lindisfarne in or after 648. It is Bede who provides greater precision over Wilfrid's journey to Rome because he tells us that Wilfrid came to the court of the Kentish king Eorcenberht during Honorius's tenure of the archdiocese of Canterbury, which is dated 627×631–30 September 653 (Keynes 1986). Wilfrid spent a year in Kent before departing with his fellow Northumbrian, Benedict Biscop, for Rome. However, it is not clear whether Honorius was still alive when the two departed; he died in September 653 and the see was then vacant for almost 18 months, and it is possible that their departure took place in this period since Bede would not have been able to refer to another archbishop as an indicator of the date of their departure. Wilfrid then set out for Rome, stopping in Lyons where Stephen tells us he spent *aliquod spatium* ('certain time', VW 3), while his eager companion, Benedict Biscop sped on to Rome. Wilfrid, having won the favour of the bishop, then also moved on to Rome. Again Stephen is vague about the length of the saint's stay, only recording that he spent 'many months' (*multos menses*) in devotions at the shrines of the saints and was tutored by the archdeacon Boniface who eventually presented him to the Pope (VW 5). After receiving a papal blessing, Wilfrid returned to Lyons where he remained for three years with the bishop, only departing after the latter's death at the hands of Queen Balthild's *duces*.

Plummer dated Wilfrid's second sojourn in Lyons to 654 × 655–657 × 658, calculating Wilfrid's travels on the continent very tightly and effectively giving the minimum period that Wilfrid could have been away. However, there is nothing in the accounts of either Bede or Stephen to require the presence of Wilfrid in England much before 663/4. Stephen (VW 7) tells us that his arrival back in England coincided with the joint rule of King Alhfrith with his father Oswiu, which is usually dated to c. 655–c. 665, and that he gained Alhfrith's favour and received the donation of Ripon from him. Under Alhfrith's patronage, he was ordained priest, and then championed the Roman Easter reckoning at the synod of Whitby. After his victorious leadership, Stephen tells us that he was consecrated bishop at the age of 30. Since, according to the canons, priests could not be consecrated before the age of 30 (but could be consecrated in their 29th year), Wilfrid's priesting must have taken place only slightly earlier. Thus Wilfrid has to be back in England by 663/4 but not necessarily much earlier.

As Professor Fouracre shows very clearly (above), problems over the dating of Wilfrid's residency in Lyons are actually the result of Plummer's narrow temporal window for Wilfrid's first journey to Rome and to the continent. Stephen tells us (VW 6) that Wilfrid was caught up in the events surrounding the Bishop of Lyons's death and charter evidence demonstrates that Aunemundus was alive in August 660. He must have been murdered by 664, the date when his successor, Genesius, attests a charter. Plummer's date must, therefore, be discarded and Stephen's witness to Wilfrid's stay in Lyons given a degree of rehabilitation.

The dating of Wilfrid's first journey to the continent is difficult, therefore, and whether Plummer's close dating is followed or Wilfrid is allowed a rather more leisurely progress, there is still roughly a decade of Wilfrid's life when events are sparse. It is possible that Wilfrid did not leave Kent until 654, spent a year travelling to Rome via Lyons, arriving there 655/6, and returned to Lyons in 656/7 and that his three-year stay in the city was terminated by the death of Aunemundus shortly after August 660. This would bring Wilfrid back to England roughly three years before his consecration as priest in 663/4. A comparison with the early career of his erstwhile travelling companion, Benedict Biscop does little to illuminate this early period, since his whereabouts in the period 653 to 668 (his third journey to Rome when he accompanied Theodore of Tarsus back to Canterbury) are also hard to date. His second visit to Rome took place after the accession of Pope Vitalian in 30 July 657 and before 665/6 when he became a monk at Lérins.

Now let us explore the chronology and temporal markers used in Stephen's *Life of Wilfrid*. As Stancliffe has convincingly demonstrated, Stephen was writing between July 712 and March 714 (Stancliffe above, and see also Thacker above), so within four years at the most of Wilfrid's death in 710. For at least the last few years of Wilfrid's career, Stephen was well-informed. He himself was a close associate of Wilfrid in his later years, travelling to Rome with him in 703/4 and he knew Wilfrid's disciple, Acca, who had also accompanied Wilfrid on this journey. Further, Wilfrid had not long before his death recounted his own life story to Tatberht, later abbot of Ripon (VW 65). Thus Stephen was well-informed by his own memory and by the accounts of those who knew the saint well so that one might expect that his biography would be accurate and chronologically coherent. However, it is now widely recognised that unwritten memories are subject to a good deal of reorganisation and modification, including their temporal frame of reference. Remembered events can easily be transposed to new settings which often provide a more plausible context for the things described than their actual, factual ones (C. Cubitt 2000; G. Cubitt 2007; Lynn Abrams 2010). Stephen's personal involvement in the events he records and his access to personal memories is not a guarantee therefore of the reliability of their chronological framework.

Stephen's chronology can be checked against itself to see if it is internally consistent, and may also be reckoned against externally dated events, such as papal pontificates and the dates of Roman councils. Bede's *Historia ecclesiastica* also provides a good deal of datable material, for example the dates and lengths of Theodore's archiepiscopate and the dates of many kings. But one should note that Bede's own chronology is not always reliable and has been subject to much criticism (see Stancliffe, above). There is additionally a danger of circularity since both Bede and modern historians may be drawing upon information in Stephen's *vita*. A further source which is utilised later in this essay is the handful of charters witnessed by Wilfrid, although their dating is not always straightforward (see appendix 1). It should also be recognised that complete precision in dating Wilfrid's career is not possible because, while, for a hagiographer, Stephen is unusually helpful in locating events, he rarely offers detailed dating; his markers are usually in years and one can not ascertain when in a year an event occurred or, if the year mentioned is that of a pontificate or reign, what the precise dates for these would be. A period of at least two months should also be incorporated into some reckonings to allow for travel to Rome. Reginald Lane Poole calculated, using data from the twelfth century, that a trip from Rome to Canterbury could be accomplished in 29 days by a man riding with great speed and utmost urgency. Sufficient closely dated evidence from the twelfth century survives to suggest that normally such a trip took almost seven weeks (Lane Poole 1934, 263–4). In 1790, William Wordsworth set out to walk from England across the Alps. He departed from Dover on 13 July 1790, and arrived at Lyons on the 4/5th August (Gill 2004). Such reckonings are tricky, however, because Wilfrid's journeys were rarely straightforward. In 703/4, he is said to have made the journey on foot (VW 50); his first journey was interrupted by lengthy stays in Lyons. We know only a little of the other sojourns which Wilfrid made – his trip in 678/9 went via Frisia and he subsequently travelled via the Frankish court of King Dagobert and that of the Lombard King, Perctarit (VW 25–8). Bede tells us that on his last trip to Rome, he paid a visit to the mission of his disciple, Willibrord, in Frisia, and was delayed on his return at Meaux by ill health (HE III, 13). None of Wilfrid's continental peregrinations were therefore simple and direct journeys, all involved stopovers of uncertain duration, and therefore it is impossible to calculate precisely their duration.

Stephen uses two chronologies which can assist us to anchor the events of Wilfrid's life to externally dated historical events. The most common of these is references to Wilfrid's life, often to his age but also to the length of his episcopate. These markers occur throughout the text. Thus we are told that Wilfrid was 14 years old when he left his family for the court of Queen Eanflæd (VW 2), that he was 30 when he was elected bishop (VW 11), that he had been bishop for nearly 40 years when he attended the Council of Austerfield (VW 47) and for over 40 years when at the synod of Rome to which he had appealed against the decisions of Austerfield (VW 54). Finally, in chapter 66, we are told that Wilfrid died in his 76th year when he had been bishop for 46 years. On two occasions, events in Wilfrid's reign are dated to regnal years, his belated restoration following his first appeal to Rome took place in the second year of King Aldfrith's reign (VW 44) and the Council of Nidd took place in the first year of King Osred's reign (VW 60).

Stephen gives other comparatively precise chronological indications, the duration of Wilfrid's sojourns in various places or the length time which had elapsed after his various tribulations. I will list these below:

VW 3: Wilfrid waited for a year in Kent before proceeding with Benedict Biscop to journey to Rome for the first time.

VW 6: Wilfrid stayed in Lyons for three years on his return journey from Rome.

VW 14: Wilfrid retired to Ripon for three years when he discovered that Chad had been consecrated to his see of York.

VW 15: The same period of three years is specified before Archbishop Theodore's reinstatement of Wilfrid.

VW 30: Wilfrid states in his petition to Pope Agatho that he had been controlling the see of York for ten years or more before it was divided against his will. Since he was driven out in 678, ten years earlier would indicate a date of 667–8 which is difficult since he was restored in 669. Possibly, this imprecision is due to the fact that he was consecrated bishop in 664–5 but did not actually govern the see until 669. Alternatively, if the ten years and more are reckoned from the Roman synod of 679 itself, this would give a date of 669.

VW 34: Wilfrid was condemned to nine months' imprisonment on his return to Northumbria with a favourable papal judgment.

VW 43: Theodore announces his desire to make peace with Wilfrid because he foreknows that after 'this year', his death approaches.

VW 44: King Aldfrith summons Wilfrid back to Northumbria in the second year of his reign and restores Hexham and his other properties back to Wilfrid, which the saint holds securely for five years.

VW 46: At the Council of Austerfield, Wilfrid condemns his opponents for rejecting papal decisions for twenty-two years.

VW 53: The Roman synod adjudicating Wilfrid's case sat for four months with seventy sittings.

VW 59: King Eadwulf of Northumbria was driven out after a reign of only two months.

In evaluating this information, one should note that Stephen does not always give such precise indicators of the passage of time; on a number of occasions, he states that events lasted a few weeks or days. However, the dating of these episodes does facilitate the construction of a chronology for the life of Wilfrid, which often can be cross-referenced to other events, such as the reign of a king. The only one of the eleven occasions listed above which raises questions is the reconciliation in London between Theodore and Wilfrid when Theodore states that his death would occur after that year (*Scio enim post hunc annum appropinquantem vitae meae terminu'*: VW 43). The chronology of Wilfrid's career would place this in 686/7 but Theodore did not die until 19 September 690, so the archbishop's premonition might seem a little premature though by no means impossibly early for an old man.[1] It is therefore important to note that the evidence of three charters (S 1171, S 1246 and S 1248) records the presence of Wilfrid at assemblies in the kingdom of the East Saxons in company with Bishop Eorcenwald (whom Theodore had summoned to London with Wilfrid) in the period 686–688, and this adds further support to Stephen's narrative and chronology.

Stephen's statement that Wilfrid died in his seventy-sixth year is likely to be correct given his proximity to Wilfrid in his final years. Stephen does not give any indicator of the year of Wilfrid's death but mentions that he died on a Thursday and that Acca commemorated the saint's death by celebrating every Thursday liturgically as if it were a Sunday (VW 65). Levison argued persuasively for 710 as the year of Wilfrid's death against Bede's statement that he died in 709 since Wilfrid's feast-day was celebrated on the 24 April which fell on a Thursday in 710 and not 709 (Levison 1946, 278–9; Stancliffe above). By this reckoning, Wilfrid must have been born in 634 and become bishop in 664, since Stephen tells us that he was elected in his thirtieth year. Wilfrid's elevation to the episcopate happened after the Synod of Whitby which took place in 664, according to Bede. Stephen records that the Council of Austerfield took place when Wilfrid had been bishop for nearly forty years, that is, before 703–4. Wilfrid journeyed on foot to Rome to appeal against its judgment and was vindicated by a synod of Pope John which lasted for 4 months. At this council, Wilfrid described himself as ruling as bishop for over forty years, giving a date

[1]   See also HE V, 8. I am very grateful to Nick Higham for his helpful discussion of this point.

of 704–5. In the early seventh century, two popes of the name of John ruled successively, Pope John VI (30 October 701–11 January 705) and Pope John VII (1 March 705–18 October 707). Wilfrid had to be back in England before the death of King Aldfrith on 14 December 704 or 705. Scholars mostly agree that Aldfrith died on 14 December 705 (Stancliffe, above). Wilfrid does not seem to have dallied in Rome long after the synod's adjudication but he was delayed in Gaul where he was seriously ill at Meaux. These criteria narrow the period of Wilfrid's stay in Rome to 704 which accords nicely with the pontificate of John VI who died in January 705. A four-month synod could be fitted into the year prior to his death.

This case-study illustrates nicely the relative accuracy and coherence of Stephen's chronology. Although it is not possible to be exact about the dating of particular events, for example, the Council of Austerfield, it is notable that Stephen's own chronology can be meshed harmoniously with dates well attested in other sources such as Pope John VI's pontificate.

Another valuable case-study is the Roman synod of Pope Agatho which exculpated Wilfrid for the first time. Wilfrid was present at the great Easter Synod of Pope Agatho which met in 680 to debate the monothelete controversy in preparation for the 680–1 Council of Constantinople (Easter in 680 fell on the 25th March). Stephen describes how, when Wilfrid was ignominiously deprived of his see by King Ecgfrith and Archbishop Theodore, he predicted the death of King Ælfwine a year later. Ælfwine was killed at the Battle of Trent in 679 so Wilfrid's prediction can be dated to 678. His second journey to Rome was interrupted by a missionary sojourn in Frisia, and visits to Kings Dagobert of Austrasia and the Lombard king Perctarit. This suggests that that the journey was not very speedy, so he may have arrived in Rome in 679. At the Roman synod which adjudicated his case, Wilfrid claims that he had been governing his see for more than ten years before his unjust eviction (VW 30), a date which agrees with his restoration to the see of York in 669 after the arrival of Archbishop Theodore on 27 May of that year.

Wilfrid's political activities intersected with the reigns of a number of kings, Alhfrith, Oswiu, Aldfrith, Eadwulf and Osred of Northumbria, Wulfhere, Æthelræd and Ceolred of Mercia and Coenwalh and Cædwalla of Wessex. These figures appear in Stephen's narrative at key points in Wilfrid's career and it is notable that when these are checked against other chronological data for their reigns (usually the evidence of Bede or the *Chronicle*), they are generally compatible. The same is true for the bishops who also appear in the text, such as Theodore and Berhtwald. For example, we know that Theodore arrived in England in 669. Stephen describes how Theodore restored Wilfrid to his see of York after a period of 3 years in retirement at Ripon. So Wilfrid will have retired to Ripon in 666, suggesting that he spent 2 years in Gaul after his consecration at Compiègne.

Stephen's use of chronological markers and data is therefore remarkably accurate. Stephen may have, of course, checked his own chronology to iron out anomalies but even if this is the case, it is remarkable how well his time frame and dating fit with external criteria, events recorded not only in Bede's *Historia ecclesiastica*, but also with the dates of papal pontificates and reigns of continental kings. This must surely indicate that Stephen was able not only to draw upon recent, accurate and personal memories but also some written chronological data. Some of his information was dated by regnal years so it is possible that he had access to king lists. But given his ability to harmonise events, it is possible that he had annalistic information entered into an Easter table, a hypothesis strengthened by Wilfrid's own championing of the Roman, Dionysiac Easter reckoning. Given Wilfrid's achievement in introducing this paschal computus to England, it is probable that his own foundations were both knowledgeable regarding and committed to the use of these tables. It is likely to have been no coincidence, therefore, that Bede's standing as a master of religious chronology was challenged by a member of Wilfrid's own following. Bede, it is well known, refuted the imputation of heresy made before Wilfrid with some indignation, describing his accusers as *rustici* (Wallis 1999, 405, 415) This rude naming may have been a special insult if, in fact, Wilfrid's following included men very learned in computus and chronology. Secondly, diplomatic evidence suggests that Wilfrid may be associated with the use of incarnational dating in some early charters. He attests a handful of charters which included an incarnational date in their formulation. These include S 235, a grant of King Cædwalla dated to 688 and S 1248, a grant of Eorcenwald, both of which are judged authentic by a number of scholars, and others which are more problematic, such as S 1246, a composite grant (again a donation of Eorcenwald) and S 51. Overall, the diplomatic evidence is difficult but does suggest that incarnational dating was used in the late seventh century, and the presence of Wilfrid in the witness lists of a number of these grants is striking. Recent scholarship has demonstrated that the links between Wilfrid and the diplomatic use of incarnational dating are suggestive, if not conclusive (Kelly 1998, xlvi–xlvii).

A Revised Chronology for the Life of St Wilfrid

634 Birth of Wilfrid into a noble Northumbrian family   VW 1

648 At the age of 14, Wilfrid leaves home for the court of Queen Eanflæd who places him at Lindisfarne in the service of a monk, a retired thegn, there.   VW 2

'post circulum annorum' ['after a succession of years', meaning 'after a few years'], Wilfrid decides to leave Lindisfarne for a pilgrimage to Rome.   VW 3

Before September 653 He is sent by Eanflaed to Kent to King Eorcenberht, during the pontificate of Archbishop Honorius (627×631–30 Sept 653). Wilfrid waits a year there, before setting out with Benedict Biscop perhaps in 654.   VW 3, HE V, 19

Wilfrid travels via Lyons where he stays *aliquod spatium* ['for a certain time'] and is received by Bishop 'Dalfinus', more correctly Aunemundus.   VW 3, 4

?655–6 Wilfrid's visit to Rome. Wilfrid spends *per multos menses* ['many months'] in devotion at the shrines of saints.   VW 5

Wilfrid returns from Rome to Lyons.   VW 5, 6

?660×663 Wilfrid leaves Lyons after the execution of Bishop Aunemundus. Stephen relates that Wilfrid had spent 3 years in Lyons.   VW 6

660×663 Wilfrid returns to England and is recommended to King Alhfrith by King Coenwalh of Wessex. He becomes Alhfrith's religious adviser.[2]   VW 7

Alhfrith grants Wilfrid 10 hides at *Aetstanforda* and then the monastery at Ripon with 30 hides. Bede tells us (*Life of Cuthbert*, 8) that Cuthbert and other Irish/Celtic brethren are driven out.   VW 8

663 Wilfrid is ordained priest by Bishop Agilbert, then visiting Kings Oswiu and Alhfrith (Agilbert had been drive out of Wessex c. 660). If Wilfrid was consecrated at the age of 30 or in his 29th year, as the canons decreed, then this probably took place in 663.   VW 9

664 Synod of Whitby: Wilfrid acts as spokesman for the Roman party including Agilbert and Alhfrith.   VW 10

664 '*post spatium*' ['after a while'] Wilfrid is chosen as bishop at the age of 30. He travels to Gaul for consecration at Compiègne.   VW 11–12

In his absence, Oswiu has Chad consecrated bishop in his place. VW 14

?666 Wilfrid's shipwreck on the South Saxon coast on his return journey to England.   VW 13

---

[2]   Alhfrith became subking after the battle of Winwaed in 655. Coenwalh succeeded Cynegils and was restored to the throne in 648.

?666–669 Wilfrid retires to Ripon as abbot where he remains for 3 years. In this period, he acts as bishop in Mercia for King Wulfhere and in Kent for King Ecgberht, where he ordains many priests including the future bishop, Putta. The see of Canterbury was vacant after the death of Archbishop Deusdedit(d. 14 July 664). Under the patronage of Wulfhere, many monasteries are founded in Mercia and Wilfrid is given Lichfield.

VW 14–15

He returns to Ripon with liturgical teachers, Aedde and Aeona, and with masons. He introduces the Rule of St Benedict. VW 14

Wilfrid acting as bishop in Kent before Theodore's arrival. HE IV, 2

After May 669 Wilfrid is restored to his see by Archbishop Theodore after three years retirement. Wilfrid's restoration of the church at York and the construction and dedication of the church at Ripon both fall within the period 669 to 678. VW 15, 16, 17

670 Death of King Oswiu – Bede reports that he had hoped to go to Rome with Bishop Wilfrid. HE IV.5

Wilfrid's period of harmony with King Ecgfrith and Queen Æthelthryth, when the King was victorious over the Picts. This period ends with Æthelthryth's monastic retirement which took place 672/3 (Thacker, 2004e). VW 19

Wulfhere's attack on Northumbria, probably 670–4 VW 20

Extension of Wilfrid's ecclesiastical rule into Lindsey VW 21

Foundation and construction of Hexham, on an estate given by Æthelthryth and therefore before 672/3, the date of her retirement and departure from Northumbria. VW 22

672 Archbishop Theodore's Council of Hertford – Wilfrid sends proctors. Policy of creating more sees debated. HE IV, 5

673 Ill health of Bishop Bisi of the East Angles and division of his see.

HE IV, 5

Theodore's deposes Bishop Winfrith of Lichfield for disobedience and he retires to Barrow (HE IV, 6). Keynes (1986) gives the dates for this as 672×676 but Stephen's account of his journey to Rome suggests that Winfrith travelled in 678.

675/6 Dagobert II of Austrasia, in exile in Ireland, is restored to Francia through Wilfrid's intervention; Wilfrid receives Dagobert, and equips him for his return to Francia. VW 28

675/6 November 6 – Wilfrid apparently witnesses a donation of King Osric of the Hwicce to Bertana, abbess of Bath. S 51

678 Ecgfrith turns against Wilfrid and he is condemned by Archbishop Theodore who consecrates 3 bishops in new sees carved out of the Northumbrian diocese. VW 24; HE V, 24

Bede dates Wilfrid's expulsion to 678 – and he says that two bishops, Eata and Bosa, were appointed, one for Deira (York) and one for Bernicia (Hexham/Lindisfarne) and additionally Eadhæd was consecrated for Lindsey; all three were consecrated at York by Theodore.   HE IV, 12
Wilfrid predicts the death of King Ælfwine one year later (he was killed in 679).   VW 24

678–9 Wilfrid travels to Rome.

His enemies foment an ambush against him by King Theuderic and Ebroin but their men attack Bishop Winfrith of Lichfield instead.   VW 25
Wilfrid's mission to the Frisians and their leader, Aldgisl. Ebroin and Theuderic attempt to have him captured or killed. Wilfrid over winters in Frisia.   HE V. 19, VW 26–8

679 Wilfrid travels on to King Dagobert II who offers him the see of Strasbourg. He moves on accompanied by Bishop Deodatus.
Wilfrid and Deodatus travel onwards to Italy and are received by King Perctarit.[3]

17 September 679 Convocation of the Council of Hatfield by Theodore
        HE IV, 17

October 679 Lateran Council in Rome rules in Wilfrid's favour. Over fifty bishops and priests meet in the Lateran basilica. In his petition, Wilfrid states that he had governed the see of York for ten years and more when he was driven out. See above for discussion of this dating. Dated by the papal *acta* (Levison 1912, 249–82)   VW 29–32

679 Battle of Trent – Æthelræd of Mercia defeats Ecgfrith and regains Lindsey; death of King Ælfwine. The new bishop Eadhæd is expelled and Theodore places him over Ripon.   HE IV, 12

March 25 680 Wilfrid attends the synod of Pope Agatho. It was presumably during his stay in Rome in 679–80 that Wilfrid obtained a monastic privilege from the pope.   VW 43

680 Wilfrid, having spent *multis diebus* ['many days'] in Rome, returns home via Campania, and crosses into Francia via the Alps. He discovers that Dagobert has been deposed.

680/1 Wilfrid returns to Northumbria and presents the papal documents to King Ecgfrith at a Council. But the Council rules that Wilfrid should be imprisoned for 9 months.   VW 34
Wilfrid's imprisonment first in *Broninis* and then in Dunbar. VW 36–8
Wilfrid is released because of the divine chastisement of the king's wife. Stephen does not indicate for how long the saint had been imprisoned. Sims-Williams (1988/1995, 177) notes that Wilfrid may not have served his full sentence.   VW 39

---

[3] Perctarit is wrongly described as King of Campania. But the chronology works because he was in exile for 9 years (662–71) but ruled Milan 661–688.

681   Three years after Wilfrid's departure (i.e. 678), Theodore consecrates Tunberht to Hexham and Trumwine to the Picts.   HE IV, 12

681   Wilfrid takes refuge with Berhtwald, nephew of King Æthelræd and is given a small monastery. However, he is driven out by Ecgfrith's enmity and flees to Centwine of Wessex whence he is also forced to flee. VW 40
Wilfrid's mission to Sussex: he is received by King Æthelwealh. He spends many months preaching to the South Saxons. Æthelwealh gives his royal vill to be an episcopal see, and then gives 87 hides in Selsey.   VW 41
Wilfrid acted as bishop in Sussex for five years until the death of Ecgfrith which took place in 685. This would place Wilfrid's evangelisation of Sussex in 680/1–685.   HE IV, 13
Wilfrid helps Cædwalla in exile and assisted him in gaining the throne.

Between 3 July 683 (death of Leo II) and 26 July 684 (accession of Benedict)
Wilfrid obtains a ruling, probably the confirmation of Pope Agatho's privilege, from the pope-elect, Benedict II, presumably by sending a legation. This can be dated closely since Benedict in VW 46 is described as *electus*.   VW 43, 46

684   Theodore's Council at *Adtuifyrd*, convened just before the beginning of winter: Cuthbert is elected bishop, initially of Hexham, but because he wishes to be bishop of Lindisfarne, Bishop Eata is transferred back to Hexham.   HE IV, 28

685   Cædwalla gains the West Saxon throne and summons Wilfrid to be his chief councillor.

26 March 685 Cuthbert is consecrated bishop at Easter in York in the presence of 7 bishops, including Theodore, and of Ecgfrith. Cuthbert was probably consecrated to Lindisfarne, and Eata moved to Hexham at this point (Tunberht, the incumbent bishop of Hexham had been deposed).

20 May 685 Death of Ecgfrith at the battle of Nechtanesmere. Acccession of Aldfrith (although this was arguably not immediate). Death of Bishop Eata of Hexham at the beginning of Aldfrith's reign; he is succeeded at Hexham by John of Beverley.

686/7 Theodore, foreseeing the imminence of his own death, summons Wilfrid and Eorcenwald to a meeting in London at which he confesses that he has wronged Wilfrid by depriving him of his property and sending him into exile. He promises to achieve his reconciliation and nominates him his successor at Canterbury but Wilfrid suggests that the succession be decided by a council. Theodore sends letters to King Aldfrith of Northumbria and King Æthelræd of Mercia, and Abbess Ælfflæd. Æthelræd receives Wilfrid and restores his monasteries and properties to him.   VW 43

686 In the 2nd year of his reign, Aldfrith summons Wilfrid back to Northumbria. Restoration of Hexham, then the see of York, and the monastery at Ripon. Stephen says that Wilfrid held Ripon and York for 5 years securely after his exile.

687–8 Cuthbert dies 20 March 687; Wilfrid rules Lindisfarne as bishop for a year and causes much turbulence. This suggests that Wilfrid was in Northumbria until at least around March 688.   HE IV, 29

Wilfrid lives for many years in alternate states of harmony and conflict with Aldfrith. Eventually Wilfrid departs after disagreements over the status of Ripon and Aldfrith's adherence to the rulings of Theodore's middle period. Wilfrid takes refuge with Æthelræd of Mercia.   VW 45

August 687 John of Beverley consecrated Bishop of Hexham.

15 December 686–8–September 701 Wilfrid obtains a ruling, probably confirmation of his monastic privilege, from Pope Sergius.   VW 43, 46

March 686×688? Wilfrid witnesses a grant of Œthelred for Abbess Æthelburh for Barking.   S 1171

687/8 Grant of Bishop Eorcenwald to the nunnery at Barking witnessed by Wilfrid. A difficult charter which is dated to 677 but this should be amended to 687×688.   S 1246

680s Wilfrid witnesses a grant by a bishop, probably Eorcenwald, to St Mary's Barking. The charter is dated to 693 but it incorporates an earlier witness list, with Wilfrid in it, from a grant of Cædwalla from the 680s. S 1248

688 Wilfrid witnesses a grant of King Cædwalla to Cedde, Cisi and Criswa to found a monastery at Farnham (S 235). Wilfrid must therefore have been in Southumbria for at least part of 688.

?690–1 July 692 According to Bede, Wilfrid acted as bishop for the Middle Angles and consecrated Oftfor bishop of the Hwicce at the command of King Æthelræd after the death of Theodore in September 690. Canterbury was vacant until the election of Berhtwald on 1 July 692.   HE IV, 23

July 692×August 693 During his Mercian exile, Wilfrid consecrated Swithberht bishop for the Frisian mission, in the absence of the archbishop elect, Berhtwald of Canterbury who was overseas for his consecration.

HE V, 11

692 or after Wilfrid receives a donation from Nothgyth, sister of King Nothhelm of the South Saxons, of land granted to her by her brother in 692. S 45

693×699 Wilfrid attends a gathering of bishops which witnesses a grant by King Oshere of the Hwicce to Cuthswith for the foundation of a monastery.

S 53

695 Translation of St Æthelthryth at Ely, possibly in the presence of Wilfrid, who attested to the incorruption of her body.   HE IV, 19

702　Council of Austerfield/*Aetswinapathe* is convened by Berhtwald to which Wilfrid is summoned. Wilfrid rebukes the bishops for resisting papal commands for 22 years – since 680, giving a date of 702 for the council. Wilfrid also states that he had been bishop for nearly 40 years – suggesting before 704.　　　　　　　　　　　　　　　　　　　　　VW 46, 47

Wilfrid returns to Æthelræd of Mercia who decides to make enquiries in Rome.　　　　　　　　　　　　　　　　　　　　　　　　　VW 48

Excommunication of Wilfrid's followers.　　　　　　　　　　VW 49

703–4 Wilfrid and his followers travel to Rome on foot, visiting en route Willibrord in Frisia (HE III, 13)　　　　　　　　　　　　　VW 50

Wilfrid is received by Pope John in Rome and attend the papal council in Rome, which lasts for 4 months. In one of the later sessions, Wilfrid states that he has been a bishop for over 40 years which gives a date of 704 or after.　　　　　　　　　　　　　　　　　　　　　　　　VW 50–54

Papal judgment – Wilfrid wishes to remain in Rome to die but is ordered to return home absolved. He returns over the Alps to Gaul.　VW 55

704–5 Wilfrid's seizure at Meaux and his vision of the Virgin and St Michael there.

704–5 Wilfrid visits Willibrord in Frisia on his return journey from Rome.
　　　　　　　　　　　　　　　　　　　　　　　　　　　HE V, 13

Wilfrid returns to England and lands in Kent. Archbishop Berhtwald promises to soften the previous judgments and both travel together to London. Wilfrid visits King Æthelræd who retired in 704.　　VW 57

Wilfrid sends messengers to King Aldfrith who refuses to obey the Roman judgments.

705　Aldfrith is striken with a fatal illness and dies December 705. Before his death, he repented of his obduracy towards Wilfrid. Wilfrid returns to Ripon but is driven out by the new king, Eadwulf. After a reign of 2 months, Eadwulf is himself driven out.

706　Synod of the Nidd in King's Osred's first year. Restoration of Wilfrid: return of Ripon and Hexham.

Death of Bishop Bosa of York; transfer of John of Beverley to York and Wilfrid restored to the see of Hexham　　　　　　　　　HE V, 3

708　Bede addresses his letter to Plegwin, refuting a charge of heresy made in the presence of Wilfrid.

After 709 Wilfrid's dispositions of his property and monasteries in the reign of King Ceolred of Mercia (who reigned after 709)

Thursday April 24rd 710 Death of Wilfrid at Oundle: in his 76th year, after 46 years as bishop.

Bibliography

Abrams, Leslie, 1996 *Anglo-Saxon Glastonbury: Church and Endowment*, Woodbridge: Boydell Press

Abrams, Lynn, 2010 *Oral History Theory*, London: Routledge

Adriaen, M. (ed.), 1971 *Gregorius Magnus homiliae in Hezechilhelem prophetam*, CCSL **142**, Turnholt: Brepols

Adriaen, M. (ed.), 1979 *Gregorius Magnus Moralia in Job*, CCSL **143**, Turnholt: Brepols

Alexander, J. J., 1978 *Insular Manuscripts, 6th to the 9th Century* [A Survey of the Manuscripts Illuminated in the British Isles, I], London: Harvey Miller

Andaloro, M., 2006 *La Pittura medievale a Roma 312–1431, Atlante: percorsi visivi*, Rome: Palombi

Anderson, A. O., & Anderson M. O. (ed. and trans.), 1991 *Adomnán's Life of St Columba*, Oxford: Oxford University Press

Anderson, B., 1991 *Imagined communities: Reflections on the Origins and Spread of Nationalism*, 2nd edn London: Verso

Andrieu, M. (ed.), 1931–61 *Les 'Ordines Romani' du haut Moyen Âge*, 5 vols, Spicilegium sacrum Lovaniense 11, 23, 24, 28, 29, Louvain: 'Spicilegium sacrum Lovaniense' Administration

Angenendt, A., 1982 Die irische Peregrinatio und ihre Auswirkungen auf dem Kontinent vor dem Jahre 800, in H. Löwe (ed.), *Die Iren und Europa im früheren Mittelalter*, Stuttgart: Klett-Cotta, 52–79

Anon, 2001 Notre-Dame-de-Bondeville (Seine-Maritime), Manoir Gresland, *Archéologie Médiévale*, **30–1**, 412–13

Anton, H. H., 1975 *Studien zu den Klosterprivilegien der Päpste im frühen Mittelalter*, Berlin: Walter de Gruyter

Arndt, W., & Krusch, B. (eds.), 1884 *Gregorii Turonensis Opera*, MGH, *scriptores rerum Merovingicarum*, **1**, Hannover: Hahn

Arnold, T. (ed.), 1882–5 *Historia Regum*, in T. Arnold (ed.) *Symeonis Monachi Opera Omnia*, 2 vols, RS 75, vol 2, 3–283

Attenborough, F. L. (ed.), 1922 Laws of Ine, in F. L. Attenborough (ed. & trans.), *The Laws of the Earliest English Kings*, Cambridge: Cambridge University Press, 36–60

Attridge, H. W., and Fassler, M. E. (eds), 2003 *Psalms in Community: Jewish and Christian Textual, Liturgical, and Artistic Traditions*, Leiden: Brill

Audouy, M., 1984 Excavations at the Church of All Saints, Brixworth, Northamptonshire, 1981–2, *Journal of the British Archaeological Association* **137**, 1–44

Augenti, A., 1996 *Il Palatino nel Medioevo: archeologia e topografia (secoli VI–XIII)*, Rome: Bretschneider

Bailey, R. N., 1976 The Anglo-Saxon Church at Hexham, *Archaeologia Aeliana*, 5th ser., **4**, 47–67

Bailey, R. N., 1991 St. Wilfrid, Ripon and Hexham, in C. Karkov & R. Farrell (eds), *Studies in Insular Art and Archaeology*, American Early Medieval Studies **1**, Oxford, Ohio, 3–25

Bailey, R. N., 1992 Sutton Hoo and Seventh-Century Art, in R. Farrell & C. N. de Vegvar (eds), *Sutton Hoo: Fifty Years After*, American Early Medieval Studies, **2**, Oxford,

Ohio, 31–41

Bailey, R. N., 1993 *Saint Wilfrid's Crypts at Ripon and Hexham*, Newcastle upon Tyne: Society of Antiquaries of Newcastle upon Tyne

Bailey, R. N., 1996a *England's Earliest Sculptors*, Toronto: Pontifical Institute of Mediaeval Studies

Bailey, R. N., 1996b Seventh Century Work at Ripon and Hexham, in T. Tatton-Brown & J. Mumby (eds), *The Archaeology of Cathedrals*, Oxford Univ. Comm. for Archaeology Monograph, **42**, Oxford: Oxford University Committee for Archaeology, 9–18

Bailey, R. N., 2009 Anglo-Saxon Art; Some Forms, Orderings and Meanings, in S. Crawford, H. Hamerow, & L. Webster (eds), *Form and Order in the Anglo-Saxon World, AD 600–1100*, Anglo-Saxon Studies in Archaeology and History, **16**, Oxford: School of Archaeology, 18–30

Bailey, R. N., forthcoming Roman or Anglo-Saxon Stone Carvings?, in R. Hall (ed.), *Ripon Cathedral Crossing Excavations*

Bailey, R. N. & Cramp, R. J., 1988 *CASSS 2, Cumberland, Westmorland and Lancashire-North-of-the-Sands*, Oxford: Oxford University Press

Bailey, R. N., & O'Sullivan, D., 1979 Excavations over St. Wilfrid's Crypt at Hexham, 1978, *Archaeologia Aeliana*, 5th ser., **7**, 142–57

Bailey, T., 1976 Accentual and Cursive Cadences in Gregorian Psalmody, *Journal of the American Musicological Soc.*, **29**, 463–71

Bailey, T., 1978 Ambrosian Choral Psalmody: The Formulae, *Studies in Music from the University of Western Ontario* **3**, 72–96

Bailey, T. (ed. and trans.), 1979 *Commemoratio brevis de tonis et psalmis modulandis: Introduction, Critical Edition, Translation*, Ottawa: University of Ottawa Press

Bailey, T., 1980 Ambrosian Psalmody: An Introduction, *Rivista internazionale di musica sacra* **1**, 82–99

Bailey, T., 1993 An Ancient Psalmody without Antiphons in the Ambrosian Ferial Office, *Revista de Musicologia* **16**, 183–90

Baldovin, J., 1987 *The Urban Character of Christian Worship. The Origins, Development and Meaning of Stational Liturgy*, Orientalia Christiana Analecta, **228**, Rome: Pontificale Institutum Studiorum Orientalium

Baring-Gould, S., 1914 *The Lives of the saints,* 3rd edn, Edinburgh: John Grant

Barker, M., 2007 *Temple Themes in Christian Worship*, London & New York: T. & T. Clark International

Barker-Benfield, B. C. (ed.), 2008, *St Augustine's Abbey, Canterbury*, Corpus of British Medieval Library Catalogues **13**, London: British Library

Barral i Altet, X., 1989 Le décor des monuments religieux de Neustrie in H. Atsma (ed.), *La Neustrie: les Pays au Nord de la Loire de 650 à 850: Colloque Historique International*, Beihefte der Francia, **16**, 2 vols, Sigmaringen: Thorbecke, **2**, 209–24

Barral i Altet, X., 1996 Poitiers: Chapelle funéraire dite 'Hypogée des Dunes', in N. Duval et al., *Les premiers monuments chrétiens de la France, **2**, Sud-Ouest et Centre*, Paris: Picard, 302–9

Barrow, J., 2010 The Ideology of the Tenth-Century English Benedictine 'Reform', in P. Skinner (ed.) *Challenging the Boundaries of Medieval History: the Legacy of Timothy Reuter*, Turnhout: Brepols, 141–54

Bassett, S., 1992 Church and Diocese in the West Midlands: the Transition from British to Anglo-Saxon Control, in J. Blair and R. Sharpe (eds), *Pastoral Care before the Parish*, Leicester: Leicester University Press, 13–40.

Bassett, S., 2000 How the West was Won, *Anglo-Saxon Studies in Archaeology and History*, **11**, 108–18

Bauchhenss, G., & Noelke, P., 1981 *Die Iupitersälen in den Germanischen Provinzen*, Cologne: Rheinland-Verlag Gmbh

Bell, D., 2010 Holy Icons: Theology in Colour, http://www.antiochian.org/ 1103744287 (accessed 6/4/2010)

Bernard, P., 2004 A-t-on connu la psalmodie alternée à deux choeurs, en Gaule, avant l'époque carolingienne? 1. Examen critique des sources, *Revue bénédictine* **114**, 291–325

Bernard, P., 2005 A-t-on connu la psalmodie alternée à deux choeurs, en Gaule, avant l'époque carolingienne? 2. Existe-t-il des marqueurs lexicaux de ce type de psalmodie, et sont-ils fiables?, *Revue bénédictine* **115**, 33–60

Berschin, W., 1989a *Opus deliberatum ac perfectum*: why did the Venerable Bede write a Second Prose Life of St Cuthbert?, in G. Bonner, D. Rollason & C. Stancliffe (eds), *St Cuthbert, His Cult and His Community to AD 1200*, Woodbridge: The Boydell Press, pp. 95–101

Berschin, W., 1989b Bonifatius consiliarius: ein römischer Übersetzer in der byzantinischen Epoche des Papsttums, in A. Lehner and W. Berschin (eds), *Lateinische Kultur im VIII Jahrhundert Traube Gedenkschrift*, Erzabtei, St. Ottilien: Eos Verlag, 25–40

Bertolini, O., 1941 *Roma di fronte a Bisanzio e ai Longobardi*, Rome: Istituto di Studi Romani, Storia di Roma, **9**

Bethmann, L., & Waitz, G., 1878 *Pauli historia Langobardorum, MGH, Scriptores rerum Langobardicarum et Italicarum saec*. **6–9, 1,** Hanover: Hahnsche Buchhandlung, 12–187

Biddle, M., & Kjølbe Biddle, B., 2001 Repton and the 'great heathen army', 873–4, in J. Graham-Campbell, R. Hall, J. Jesch & D. N. Parsons (eds), *Vikings and the Danelaw: Select Papers from the Proceedings of the Thirteenth Viking Congress, Nottingham and York, 21–30 August 1997,* Oxford: Oxbow Books, 45–96

Biddle, M., 1994 The Tomb of Christ: Sources, Methods and a New Approach, in K. Painter (ed.), *'Churches Built in Ancient Times': Recent Studies in Early Christian Archaeology*, London: Soc. of Antiquaries of London, 73–147

Biddle, M., 1999 *The Tomb of Christ,* Stroud: Sutton

Bidwell, P., 2010 A Survey of the Anglo-Saxon Crypt at Hexham and its Reused Roman Stonework, *Archaeologia Aeliana*, 5th ser., **39**, 53–145

Billett, J. D., 2011 The Liturgy of the 'Roman' Office in England from the Conversion to the Conquest, in C. Bolgia, R. McKitterick and J. Osborne (eds), *Rome Across Time and Space: Cultural Transmission and the Exchange of Ideas, c. 500–1400,* Cambridge: Cambridge University Press, 84–110

Birch, W. de G., 1885 *Cartularium Saxonicum*, **1**, London: Whiting

Bischoff, B. and Lapidge, M. (eds), 1994 *Biblical Commentaries from the Canterbury School of Theodore and Hadrian*, Cambridge: Cambridge University Press

Bischoff, B., 1952, Das karolingische Kalendar der Palimpsesthandschrift Ambros, M. 12 sup., in B. Fischer & V. Fiala (eds), *Colligere Fragmenta: Festschrift Alban Dold zum 70. Geburtstag am 7. 7. 1952*, Beuron: Beuroner Kunstverlag, 247–60

Bischoff, B., 1990 *Latin Palaeography: Antiquity and the Middle Ages,* trans. D. Ó Cróinín and D. Ganz, Cambridge: Cambridge University Press

Blagg, T., 1981 Some Roman Architectural Traditions in the Early Saxon Churches of Kent, in A. Detsicas (ed.) 1981 *Collectanea Historica: Essays in Memory of Stuart*

Rigold, Maidstone: Kent Archaeol. Soc, 50–3

Blair, J., 1989 Frithuwold's Kingdom and the Origins of Surrey, in S. Bassett (ed.) *The Origins of the Anglo-Saxon Kingdoms*, Leicester: Leicester University Press, 97–107

Blair, J., 2002 A Handlist of Anglo-Saxon Saints, in A. Thacker & R. Sharpe (eds), *Local Saints and Local Churches*, Oxford: Oxford University Press, 495–565

Blair, J., 2005 *The Church in Anglo-Saxon Society*, Oxford: Oxford University Press

Blake, E. O. (ed.), 1962 *Liber Eliensis*, Camden Third Series, **92**, London: Offices of the Royal Historical Society

Bliss, J. (trans.), 1844 *Morals on the Book of Job*, **1**, Oxford: John Henry Parker

Bonner, G., Rollason, D., & Stancliffe, C. (eds), 1989 *St Cuthbert, His Cult and Community to AD 1200*, Woodbridge: Boydell

Borst, A., 1998 *Die karolingische Kalenderreform*, Hannover: Hahne

Bovini, G., 1990 *La Cattedra eburnean del Vescovo Massimiano di Ravenna*, Ravenna: Giorgio La Pira

Brakke, D., 1995 *Athanasius and the Politics of Asceticism*, Oxford: Clarendon Press

Brakke, D., 2006 *Demons and the Making of the Monk: Spiritual Combat in early Christianity*, Cambridge, Massachusetts: Harvard University Press

Brandenburg, H., 2005, *Ancient Churches of Rome from the Fourth to the Seventh Century*, Turnholt: Brepols

Bremmer, R. H., 1990 The Nature of the Evidence for a Frisian Participation in the *Adventus Saxonum*, in A. Bammesburger & A. Wollman (eds), *Britain 400–600: Language and History*, Heidelberg: C. Winter, 353–71

Bresslau, H., 1912–31 *Handbuch der Urkundenlehre für Deutschland und Italien*, 2 vols, 2nd edn, Leipzig: Hans-Walter Klewitz

Bright, W., 1888 *Chapters of Early English Church History*, 2nd edn, Oxford: Clarendon Press

Brooks, N., 1971 The Development of Military Obligations in Eighth- and Ninth-Century England, in P. Clemoes & K. Hughes (eds), *England before the Conquest: Studies in Primary Sources Presented to Dorothy Whitelock*, Cambridge: Cambridge University Press, 69–84

Brooks, N. P., 1984 *The Early History of the Church of Canterbury: Christ Church from 597 to 1066*, Leicester: Leicester University Press

Brown, G. B., 1925 *The Arts in Early England*, **2**, Anglo-Saxon Architecture, London: John Murray

Brown, P., 1981 *The Cult of the Saints*, Chicago: Chicago University Press

Brown, P., 1995 *Authority and the Sacred: Aspects of the Christianisation of the Roman World*, Cambridge: Cambridge University Press

Brown, P., 2003 *The Rise of Western Christendom: Triumph and Diversity, A.D. 200–1000*, 2nd edn, Oxford: Blackwell

Bruns, H. T., 1839 *Canones apostolorum et conciliorum*, Bibliotheca Ecclesiastica, **I**, Berlin: Reimar

Bullough, D. A., 1984 *Albuinus deliciosus Karoli Regis*: Alcuin of York and the shaping of the early Carolingian court, in L. Fenske, W. Rösener & T. Zotz (eds), *Institutionen, Kultur und Gese llschaft. Festschrift für Josef Fleckenstein*, Sigmaringen: Jan Thorbecke Verlag, 73–92

Bullough, D. A., 1991 *Carolingian Renewal: Sources and Heritage,* Manchester: Manchester University Press

Bullough, D. A., 1993 What has Ingeld to do with Lindisfarne?, *Anglo Saxon England* **22**, 93–126

Bullough, D. A., 1997 The Career of Columbanus, in M. Lapidge (ed.) *Columbanus: Studies on the Latin Writings*, Woodbridge: Boydell, 1–28

Bullough, D. A., 2003 'York, Bede's Calendar and a Pre-Bedan English Martyrology', *Analecta Bollandiana* **121**, 329–55

Bullough, D. A., 2004 *Alcuin: Achievement and Reputation*, Education and Society in the Middle Ages and Renaissance **16**, Leiden: Brill

Butler, L., and Morris, R. (eds), 1986 *The Anglo-Saxon Church*, CBA Research Report **60**, London: Council for British Archaeology

Cambridge, E., 1979 C. C. Hodges and the Nave of Hexham Abbey, *Archaeologia Aeliana*, 5th ser., **7**, 158–68

Cambridge, E., 1984 The Early Church in County Durham: a Reassessment, *Journal of the British Archaeological Assoc*, **137**, 65–85

Cambridge, E., 1995 Discussion: pre-Conquest to Thirteenth Century, in E. Cambridge & A. Williams, Hexham Abbey: a Review of Recent Work and its Implications, *Archaeologia Aeliana*, 5th ser., **23**, 51–138, at 72–94

Cambridge, E., 1999 The Architecture of the Augustinian Mission, in R. Gameson (ed.), *St Augustine and the Conversion of England*, Stroud: Sutton Publishing, 202–36

Camden, W., 1637 *Britain, or, A Chorographicall Description of the Most Flourishing Kingdomes, England, Scotland, and Ireland, and the Islands Adjoyning, Translated newly into English by Philemon Holland*, London: Aspley

Cameron, A., & Hall, S. G., 1999 *Eusebius' Life of Constantine*, Clarendon Ancient History Series, Oxford: Clarendon

Campbell, A. (ed. and trans.), 1967 *Aethelwulf: De abbatibus*, Oxford: Clarendon Press

Campbell, A. (ed.), 1950 *Frithegodi Monachi Breviloquium vitae Beati Wilfredi et Wulfstani Cantoris Narratio Metrica de Sancto Swithuno*, Turin: Thesaurus Mundi

Campbell, J., 1979 Bede's Words for Places, in P. H. Sawyer (ed.) *Names, Words and Graves: Early Medieval Settlements: Lectures Delivered at the University of Leeds, May 1978*, Leeds: The University of Leeds, 34–54

Campbell, J., 1986 *Essays in Anglo-Saxon History*, London: Hambledon

Campbell, J., 2004 Bede (673/4–735) in *Oxford Dictionary of National Biography*, Oxford: Oxford University Press: http://www.oxforddnb.com/ article/1922, accessed 9 Feb 2012

Campbell, J., 2010 Questioning Bede, in M. Henig and N. Ramsay (eds), *The Archaeology and History of Christianity in England, 400–1200: Papers in Honour of Martin Biddle and Birthe Kjølbye-Biddle*, BAR Brit Ser **505**, Oxford: Archaeopress, 119–27

Capelle, B., 1934 Le *Kyrie* de la messe et le pape Gélase, *Revue bénédictine* **46**, 126–44

Capper, M. D. T., 2008 Contested Loyalties: Regional and National Identities in the Midland Kingdoms of Anglo-Saxon England, c.700–c.900, Unpublished PhD Dissertation, University of Sheffield

Carte, T., 1747 *A General History of England from the Earliest Times (to A.D. 1654)*, London: Printed for the Author

Chadwick, H., 1995 Theodore, the English Church and the Monothelete Heresy, in M. Lapidge (ed.) *Archbishop Theodore, Commemorative Studies on his Life and Influence*, Cambridge: Cambridge University Press, 88–95

Chadwick N., 1958 *Studies in the Early British Church*, Cambridge: Cambridge University Press

Chaplais, P., 1978 The Letter from Bishop Wealdhere of London to Archbishop Brihtwold of Canterbury: the Earliest Original 'letter close' Extant in the West, in M.

P. Parkes & A. G. Watson (eds), *Medieval Scribes, Manuscripts and Libraries*, Aldershot: Scolar Press, 3–23

Charles-Edwards, T., 1995 The Penitential of Theodore and the *Iudicia Theodori*, in M. Lapidge (ed.), *Archbishop Theodore: Commemorative Studies on his Life and Influence*, Cambridge: Cambridge University Press, 141–74

Charles-Edwards, T. M., 2000 *Early Christian Ireland*, Cambridge: Cambridge University Press

Charles-Edwards, T. M. (trans.), 2006 *The Chronicle of Ireland*, 2 vols Translated Texts for Historians **44**, Liverpool: Liverpool University Press

Chartraire, E., 1911 Les tissus anciens du trésor de la cathédrale de Sens, *Revue de l'Art Chrétien*, **61**, 261–80, 370–86

Chavasse, A., 1958 *Le Sacramentaire gélasien (Vaticanus Reginensis 316)*, Bibliothèque de théologie, 4th ser., **1**. Paris: Desclée

Church, R. W., 1897 *The Oxford Movement: Twelve Years 1833–45*, London: Macmillan

Claire, J., 1962 L'évolution modale dans les répertoires liturgiques occidentaux, *Revue grégorienne* **40**, 231–5

Claire, J., 2006–7 Saint Ambroise et le changement de style de psalmodie: Traces importantes de transformation de la psalmodie sans refrain en psalmodie avec refrain dans le Carême milanais, *Études grégoriennes* **34**, 13–57

Clapham, A. W., 1930 *English Romanesque Architecture before the Conquest*, Oxford: Clarendon Press

Clarke, A., & Hall, R., *Ripon Cathedral Crossing: HARGM: 8682, Archive Report*, York: York Archaeological Trust

Claussen, M. A., 2004 *The Reform of the Frankish Church: Chrodegang of Metz and the 'Regula canonicorum' in the Eighth Century*, Cambridge Studies in Life and Thought, 4th ser., **61**, Cambridge: Cambridge University Press

Claussen, P. C., 2008 *Die Kirchen der Stadt Rom im Mittelalter 105, B. 0–1300*, Stuttgart: Steiner

Coatsworth, E., 2008 *CASSS 8: Western Yorkshire*, Oxford: Oxford University Press

Cohen, D., 2002 Notes, Scales, and Modes in the Earlier Middle Ages, in T. Christensen (ed.), *The Cambridge History of Western Music Theory*, Cambridge: Cambridge University Press, 307–63

Colgrave, B. (ed. & trans.), 1927 *The Life of Bishop Wilfrid by Eddius Stephanus*, Cambridge: Cambridge University Press

Colgrave, B. (ed. & trans.), 1940 *Two Lives of Saint Cuthbert: A Life by an Anonymous Monk of Lindisfarne and Bede's Prose Life*, Cambridge: Cambridge University Press

Colgrave, B., (ed. & trans.) 1956 *Felix's Life of St Guthlac*, Cambridge: Cambridge University Press

Colgrave, B., (ed. & trans.) 1968 *The Earliest Life of Gregory the Great*, Cambridge: Cambridge University Press

Colgrave, B. & Mynors, R. A. B. 1969 *Bede's Ecclesiastical History of the English People*, Oxford: Oxford University Press

Conant, J., 1956 The Original Buildings at the Holy Sepulchre in Jerusalem, *Speculum*, **31**, 1–48

Connolly, S. (trans.), 1995 *Bede: On the Temple*, Liverpool: Liverpool University Press

Constantinescu, R., 1974, Alcuin et les 'libelli precum' de l'époque carolingienne, *Revue d'histoire de la spiritualité* **50**, 17–56

Coplestone-Crow, B., 2009, *Herefordshire Place-Names*, Little Logaston: Logaston Press

Corning, C., 2006 *The Celtic and Roman Traditions: Conflict and Consensus in the Early Medieval Church*, Basingstoke: Palgrave MacMillan,

Courtenay, P., 1998 Saxon and Medieval Leicester: the Making of an Urban Landscape, *Transactions of the Leicester Archaeological and Historical Society* 72, 110–145

Coville, A., 1928 *Recherches sur l'histoire de Lyon du Vme siècle au IXme siècle (400–800)*, Paris: Picard

Craig, D., 1992 *The Distribution of pre-Norman Sculpture in South-West Scotland: Provenance, Ornament and Regional Groups*, Unpublished PhD Thesis, 4 vols, University of Durham

Cramp, R., 1974 Early Northumbrian Sculpture at Hexham, in D. P. Kirby (ed.), *Saint Wilfrid at Hexham*, Newcastle upon Tyne: Oriel Press, 115–40

Cramp, R., 1984 *CASSS,* 1: *Durham and Northumberland*. Oxford: British Academy

Cramp, R., 2005 *Wearmouth and Jarrow Monastic Sites*, 2 vols, Swindon: English Heritage

Crawford, S., Hamerow, H., & Webster, L. (eds), 2009 *Form and Order in the Anglo-Saxon World, AD 600–1100*, Anglo-Saxon Studies in Archaeology and History, **16**, Oxford: School of Archaeology

Crook, J., 1999 Crypts, in M. Lapidge *et al.* (eds), 1999, 10–11

Crook, J., 2000 *The Architectural Setting of the Cult of Saints in the Early Christian West c. 300–c. 1200*, Oxford: Oxford University Press

Cross, F. L., & Livingstone, E. A., 1997 *The Oxford Dictionary of the Christian Church*, 3rd edn, Oxford: Oxford University Press

Cubitt, C., 1989 Wilfrid's 'usurping bishops': Episcopal Elections in Anglo-Saxon England, c. 600–c. 800, *Northern History,* **25**, 18–38

Cubitt, C., 1995 *Anglo-Saxon Church Councils c.650–c.850*, London and New York: Leicester University Press

Cubitt, C., 1996 'Unity and Diversity in the Anglo-Saxon Liturgy', in R. N. Swanson (ed.), *Unity and Diversity in the Church*, Studies in Church History 32, Oxford: Blackwell, 45–57

Cubitt, C., 2000 Monastic Memory and Identity in Early Anglo-Saxon England', in W. O. Frazer and A. Tyrrell (eds), *Social Identity in Early Medieval Britain*, Leicester: Leicester University Press, 253–76

Cubitt, C., 2005 The Clergy in Anglo-Saxon England, *Historical Research* 78, 273–87

Cubitt, C., 2007, 'Bishops and Councils in Late Saxon England: the Intersection of Secular and Ecclesiastical Law', in W. Hartmann (ed.), *Recht und Gericht in Kirche und Welt um 900*, Oldenbourg, Munich, pp. 151–67

Cubitt, C., & Costambeys, M., 2004 Oda (*d. 958*), *Oxford Dictionary of National Biography* Oxford University Press: http://www.oxforddnb.com/ view/article/ 20541, accessed 9 Sept 2010.

Cubitt, C. & Price, R., forthcoming *The Lateran Synod of 649*, Liverpool

Cubitt, G., 2007 *History and Memory*, Manchester: Manchester University Press

Cullin, O., 1991 De la psalmodie sans refrain à la psalmodie responsoriale: Transformation et conservation dans les répertoires liturgiques latins, *Rev de Musicologie* 77, 5–24

Curran, M., 1984 *The Antiphonary of Bangor and the Early Irish Monastic Liturgy*, Dublin: Irish Academic Press

Curtis, L. P., 1968 *Anglo-Saxons and Celts; a Study of anti-Irish Prejudice in Victorian England*, Studies in British history and culture 2, Bridgeport, Conn: Conference on British Studies at the University of Bridgeport

Dailey, E. T. A., 2010 'The *Vita Gregorii* and Ethnogenesis in Anglo-Saxon Britain', *Northern History* **47**, 195–207

Dallas, C., 1973 The Nunnery of St. Kyneburgha, *Durobrivae* **1**, 17

Davidse, J., 1996 On Bede as Christian Historian, in L. A. J. R. Houwen & A. A. MacDonald (eds), *Beda Venerabilis: Historian, Monk and Northumbrian*, Groningen: Egbert Forsten

Davies, W., 1978a *An Early Welsh Microcosm: Studies in the Llandaff Charters*, London: Royal Historical Society

Davies, W., 1978b Middle Anglia and the Middle Angles, *Midland History* **20**, 18–20

Davis, R. (trans.), 1989 *The Book of the Pontiffs (Liber Pontificalis)*, Liverpool: Liverpool University Press

Davis, R., 1992 *Lives of the Eighth-Century Popes (Liber Pontificalis): The Ancient Biographies of Nine Popes from AD 715 to AD 817*, Translated Texts for Historians **13**. Liverpool: Liverpool University Press

Davis, R. (trans.), 2000 *The Book of Pontiffs (Liber Pontificalis). The Ancient Biographies of the First Ninety Roman Bishops to AD 715*, rev. edn, Liverpool: Liverpool University Press

Dawson, D., 1998 Review of Young, F., 1997 Biblical Exegesis and the Formation of Christian Culture, in *Journal of Theological Studies* **49**, 353–8

De Blaauw, S., 1994 *Cultus et Decor. Liturgia et architettura nella Roma tardoantica e medievale. Basilica Salvatoris, Sanctae Mariae, Sancti Petri*, Studi e Testi, Rome: Biblioteca Apostolica Vaticana

De Clerck, P., 1977 *La Prière universelle dans les liturgies latines anciennes: temoignages patristiques et textes liturgiques*, Liturgiewissenschaftliche Quellen und Forschungen **62**, Münster: Aschendorff

Deferrari, J. (ed.), 1963 *The Fathers of the Church: a New Translation, 45, Saint Augustine The Trinity*, Washington DC: Catholic University of America Press

DeGregorio, S. (trans.), 2006 *Bede: On Ezra and Nehemiah*, Liverpool: Liverpool University Press

Dekkers, E., & Fraipont, J. (eds), 1956a *Augustinus, Enarrationes in Psalmos I–L*, Brepols: CCSL **38**

Dekkers, E., & Fraipont, J. (eds), 1956b *Augustinus, Enarrationes in Psalmos LI–C*, Brepols: CCSL **39**

De Rossi, G. B., 1888 *Inscriptiones Christianae Urbis Romae Septimo Saeculo Antiquiores*, Rome: Ex Officina Libraria Philippi Cuggiani

De Vogüé, A., 1972 *La règle de Saint Benoît*, Sources Chrétiennes, **181–6**, Paris: Les éditions du Cerf

De Vogüé, A., 1992 The Master and St Benedict: a Reply to Marilyn Dunn, *English Historical Review*, **107**, 95–103

De Vogüé, A., and Antin, P., 1979 *Grégoire le Grand, dialogues, Tome II (Livres I–III)*, Sources Chrétiennes **260**, Paris: Les éditions du Cerf

Dey, H. W., 2011 *The Aurelian Wall and the Refashioning of Imperial Rome, AD 271–855*, Cambridge: Cambridge University Press

Doppelfeld, O., & Weyres, W., 1980 *Die Ausgrabungen im Dom zu Köln*, Mainz am Rhein: von Zabern

Dornier, A., 1977 The Anglo-Saxon Monastery at Breedon-on-the-Hill, Leicestershire, in A. Dornier (ed.), *Mercian Studies*, Leicester: Leicester University Press, 155–68

Drury, P. (ed.), 1983 *Approaches to the Interpretation of Excavated Buildings*, BAR British Series, **110**, Oxford: Archaeopress

Duchesne, L. (ed.), original publication 1884, reprinted 1981 *Le Liber Pontificalis. Texte, Introduction et Commentaire*, Paris: Bibliothèque des Écoles d'Athènes et de Rome, 3 vols

Dufaÿ, B., & Bourgeois, L., 1998 Rosny-sur-Seine, église Saint-Lubin, in N. Duval et al. (eds), *Les premiers monuments chrétiens de la France, 3, Ouest, Nord, et Est.* Paris: Picard, 227–34

Dumville, D. N. (ed. and trans.), 2002, *Annales Cambriae, A.D. 682–954: Texts A–C in Parallel*, Cambridge: Basic Texts for Brittonic History, 1

Duncan, S. A. J., 1998 Being Different: Schools and Hagiography in Bedan Northumbria, Unpubl PhD thesis, University of Manchester

Duncan, S. A. J., 2000 *Signa de caelo* in the Lives of St Cuthbert: the Impact of Biblical Images and Exegesis on Early Medieval Hagiography, *Heythrop Journal*, **41**, 399–412

Dunn, M., 1990 Mastering Benedict: Monastic Rules and Their Authors in the Early Medieval West, *English Historical Review*, **105**, 567–94

Dunn, M., 1992 The Master and St Benedict: a Rejoinder, *English Historical Review*, **107**, 104–111

Dunn, M., 2000 *The Emergence of Monasticism: From the Desert Fathers to the Early Middle Ages,* Oxford: Blackwell

Durliat, J., 1980 *De la ville antique à la ville byzantine. Le problème de subsistances*, Rome: Collection de l'École française de Rome, **136**

Dyer, J., 1989a Monastic Psalmody of the Middle Ages, *Revue bénédictine*, **99**, 41–74

Dyer, J., 1989b The Singing of Psalms in the Early-Medieval Office, *Speculum* **64**, 535–78

Edwards, H., 1988 *The Charters of the Early West Saxon Kingdom*, BAR, British Series **198**, Oxford: Archaeopress

Ehwald, R. (ed.), 1919 *Aldhelmi Opera Omnia, MGH, Auctores Antiquissimi* **15**, Berlin: Weidmann

Elbern, V. H., 1962 Nouvelles recherches au sujet de la crypte de' l'Abbé Mellebaude, *Bulletin de la Société des Antiquaires de l'Ouest*, 4th ser., **6**, 375–93

Emmerson, R. K., 1981 *Antichrist in the Middle Ages: A Study of Medieval Apocalypticism, Art and Literature*, Manchester: Manchester University Press

Erickson, B. H., 1997 Social Networks and History: a Review Essay, *Historical Methods* **30**, 149–157

Etchingham, C., 1993 The Implications of *Paruchia*, *Ériu*, **44**, 139–62

Etchingham, C., 1999 *Church Organization in Ireland, AD 650–1000*, Maynooth: Laigin publications

Evans, G. R., 1984 *The Language and Logic of the Bible: The Earlier Middle Ages*, Cambridge: Cambridge University Press

Evans, J. G., and Rhys, J., 1893 *The Text of the Book of Llan Dâv*, Oxford

Ewald, P., and Hartmann, L. M. (eds), 1891–99 *Gregorii I Papae Registrum epistolarum*, 2 vols, *MGH Epistolae* **1**, **2**, Berlin: Weidmann

Ewig, E., 1979 Beobachtungen zu des Bischofslisten der merowingischer Konzilien und Bishofs Privilegien, in E. Ewig (ed.), *Spätantikes und Fränkisches Gallien. Gesammelten Schriften (1952–1973)*, **2**, Munich: Beihefte der Francia 3/2, 426–55

Faral, E. (ed.), 1929 *Historia Brittonum*, in E. Faral (ed.), *La Légende arthurienne*, **3**, Paris: Librairie Ancienne Honoré Champion, 4–62

Farmer, D. H. (ed.), 1968 *The Rule of St Benedict: Oxford, Bodleian Library, Hatton 48*, Copenhagen: Rosenkilde & Bagger

Farmer, D. H., 1974 Saint Wilfrid, in D. P. Kirby (ed.) *Saint Wilfrid at Hexham*, Newcastle upon Tyne: Oriel Press, 35–59

Farmer, D. H., and Webb, J. F. (trans.), 1998 *The Age of Bede*, London: Penguin

Faulkner, W., 1966 *Requiem for a Nun*, New York: Random House

Fernie, E., 1983 *The Architecture of the Anglo-Saxons*, London: Batsford

Fernie, E., 1985 Anglo-Saxon Lengths; the 'Northern System', the Perch and the Foot, *Archaeol. J.*, **142**, 246–54

Fernie, E., 1991 Anglo-Saxon Lengths and the Evidence of the Buildings, *Medieval Archaeology*, **35**, 1–5

Ferrari, G., 1957 *Early Roman Monasteries: Notes for the History of the Monasteries and Convents at Rome from the V through to the X Century*, Studi di antichità cristiana **23**, Città del Vaticano: Pontifico Instituto di archeologia cristiana

Ferretti, P., 1938 *Esthétique grégorienne*, Solesmes: Abbaye Saint Pierre de Solesmes

Ferris, I., & Jones, R., 1991 Binchester: a Northern Fort and Vicus, in R. F. J. Jones (ed.), *Britain in the Roman Period, Recent Trends*, **5**, Sheffield: J. R. Collis, 103–9

Ferris, I., & Jones, R., 1995 *Excavations at Binchester Roman Fort, County Durham, 1976–1991: Assessment and Post-excavation Research Design*, Birmingham University Field Archaeology Unit Unpublished Report, **342**

Ferris, I., & Jones, R., 2000 Transforming an Elite: Reinterpreting Late Roman Binchester, in T. Wilmott & P. Wilson (eds), *The Late Roman Transition in the North: Papers from the Roman Archaeology Conference, Durham 1999*, BAR British Series **299**, Oxford: Archaeopress, 1–11

Fillipi, G., 2009 'Un decennio di ricerche e studi nella Basilica Ostiense', in U. Utro (ed.), *San Paolo in Vaticano*, Todi: Tau Editrice, 29–45

Finberg, H. P. R., 1974 *The Formation of England, 550–1042*, London: Hart-Davis

Finsterwalder, P. W., 1929 *Die Canones Theodori und ihrer Überlieferungsformen*, Weimar: H. Böhlaus

Fletcher, E., 1981 *Benedict Biscop*, Jarrow: Jarrow Lecture

Foard, G., *An Archaeological Resource Assessment of Anglo-Saxon Northamptonshire (400 – 1066)*, Available: http://www.le.ac.uk/archaeology/research/projects/eastmidsfw/pdfs/29nhas.pdf Accessed: 1 April 2009

Foley, W. T., & Higham, N. J., 2009 Bede on the Britons, *Early Medieval Europe*, **17(2)**, 154–185

Foley, W. T., 1992 *Images of Sanctity in Eddius Stephanus' 'Life of Saint Wilfrid', An Early English Saint's Life*, Lewiston, NY: The Edwin Mellen Press

Foley, W., & Holder, A. (trans.), 1999 *Bede: A Biblical Miscellany*, Translated Texts for Historians **28**, Liverpool: University Press

Foot, S., & Roffe, D., 2007 Historical Context within Lindsey and Possible Estate Structures, in C. Loveluck (ed.), *Rural Settlement, Lifestyles and Social Change in the Later First Millennium AD at Flixborough, Lincolnshire: Anglo-Saxon Flixborough in its Wider Context*, Excavations at Flixborough **4** Oxford: Oxbow Books, 130–43

Foot, S., 1998 The Role of the Minster in Earlier Anglo-Saxon Society, in B. Thompson (ed.), *Monasteries and Society in Medieval England*, Harlaxton Medieval Studies, **6**, Stamford: Paul Watkins, 35–58

Foot, S., 2006 *Monastic Life in Anglo-Saxon England, c. 600–900* Cambridge: Cambridge University Press

Fouracre, P., 2003 Why were so many Bishops Killed in Merovingian Francia?, in N. Fryde and D. Reitz (eds), *Bischofsmord im Mittelalter*, Veröffentlichungen des Max-Planck-Instituts für Geschichte **191**, Göttingen: Vandenhoeck & Ruprecht

Fouracre, P., 1990 Merovingian History and Merovingian Hagiography, *Past and Present* **127**, 3–38

Fouracre, P., 2008 Forgetting and Remembering Dagobert II: the English Connection, in D. Ganz & P. Fouracre (eds), *Frankland: The Franks and the Worlds of the Early Middle Ages*, Manchester: Manchester University Press, 70–89

Fouracre, P., & Gerberding, R., 1996 *Late Merovingian France: History and Hagiography 640–720*, Manchester: Manchester University Press

Fournier, G., 1996 Manglieu, in N. Duval *et al.* (eds.), *Les premiers monuments chrétiens de la France, 2, Sud-Ouest et Centre*, Paris: Picard, 71–4

Fowler, J. T. (ed.), 1875 *Acts of the Chapter of the Collegiate Church of SS. Peter and Wilfrid, Ripon, A.D. 1452 to A.D. 1506*, Surtees Society **64**, Durham: Andrews

Fowler, J. T. (ed.), 1882 *Memorials of the Church of SS. Peter and Wilfrid, Ripon*, **1**, Surtees Society **74**, Durham: Andrews

Fraipont, J. (ed.), 1965 *Itineraria et Alia Geographica: Bedae Venerabilis, De Locis Sanctis*, CCSL **175**, Turnholt: Brepols, 249–80

Freeman, E. A., 1888 The Ancient British Church, *The [Church] Guardian*, **8** February 1888, 195

Frénaud, G., 1961 'Le culte de Nôtre-Dame dans l'ancienne liturgie latine', in H. Du Manoir (ed.), *Maria: Études sur la Sainte Vierge*, 8 vols, Paris: Beauchesne, **2**, 157–211

Frere, W. H. (ed.), 1901–24 *Antiphonale Sarisburiense*, 3 vols, London: Plainsong and Mediaeval Music Society

Fritze, W. H., 1969 Universalis gentium confessio Formeln, Träger und Wege universalmissionarischen Denkens im 7. Jahrnhundert, *Frühmittelalterliche Studien* **3**, 78–130

Geary, P. J., 1978 *Furta Sacra: Thefts of Relics in the Central Middle Ages* Princeton: Princeton University Press

Geertman, H., 1975 More veterum, *Il Liber Pontificalis e gli edifici ecclesiastici di Roma nella tarda antichità e nell'alto medioevo*, Groningen: H. D. Tjeenk Wiilink

Gelling, M., 1993 Why aren't we Speaking Welsh?, *Anglo-Studies in Archaeology and History*, **6**, 51–6

Gem, R. D. H., 1983 Towards an Iconography of Anglo-Saxon Architecture, *Journal of the Warburg and Courtauld Institutes*, **46**, 1–17

Gerberding, R., 1987 *The Rise of the Carolingians and the Liber Historiae Francorum*, Oxford: Oxford University Press

Gerschow, J., 2005 Liudger und die angelsächsischte Kirche, in G. Iseberg & B. Rommé (eds), *805: Liudger wird Bischof. Spuren eines Heiligen zwischen York, Rom und Münster*, Mainz: Philipp von Zabern, 141–8

Gilbert, E., 1974 Saint Wilfrid's Church at Hexham, in D. P. Kirby (ed.), *Saint Wilfrid at Hexham*, Newcastle upon Tyne: Oriel Press Ltd, 81–113

Gill, S., 2004 'Wordsworth, William (1770–1850)', *Oxford Dictionary of National Biography*, Oxford, Oxford University Press. Available: http://www.oxforddnb.com/view/article/ Accessed 23 Feb 2012

Girard, R., 1961 La crypte et l'église de Saint-Laurent de Grenoble, *Cahiers d'Histoire*, **6**, 243–63

Gneuss, H., 2001 *Handlist of Ango-Saxon Manuscripts. A List of Manuscripts and Manuscript Fragments Written or Owned in England up to 1100*, Medieval and Renaissance Texts and Studies **241**, Tempe, Arizona: Arizona Center for Medieval and Renaissance Studies

Godman, P. (ed. and trans.), 1982 *Alcuin: The Bishops, Kings, and Saints of York*, Oxford Medieval Texts, Oxford: Clarendon Press

Goehring, J. E., 1986 New Frontiers in Pachomian Studies, in B. A. Pearson & J. E. Goehring (eds), *The Roots of Egyptian Christianity*, Philadelphia: Fortress, 237–57

Goffart, W., 1988 *The Narrators of Barbarian History (A.D. 550–800): Jordanes, Gregory of Tours, Bede, and Paul the Deacon*, Princeton, New Jersey: Princeton University Press

Goffart, W., 1990 The *Historia Ecclesiastica*: Bede's Agenda and Ours, *Haskins Society Journal*, **2**, 29–45

Goffart, W., 2005 'L'Historie écclésiastique et l'engagement politique de Bède', in S. Lebecq, M. Perrin & O. Szerwiniack (eds), *Bède le Vénérable entre tradition et postérité*, Lille: Université Charles de Gaulle, 149–58

Gordon, A., 1726 *Itinerarium Septentrionale*, London: printed for the author

Grabar, A., 1972 *Martyrium*, Paris: Collège de France

Gray, T. (trans.), 1990 *The Homilies of Saint Gregory the Great on the Book of the Prophet Ezekiel*, Etna CA: Center for Traditionalist Orthodox Studies

Gregg, R. C. (trans.), 1989 *Athanasius, The Life of Anthony and the Letter to Marcellinus*, New York: Paulist Press

Gretsch, M., 1974 Æthelwold's Translation of the Regula Sancti Benedicti and its Latin Exemplar, *Anglo-Saxon England*, **3**, 125–51

Gretsch, M., 1999 *The Intellectual Foundations of the English Benedictine Reform*, Cambridge: Cambridge University Press

Gretsch, M., 2005 The Roman Psalter, its Old English Glosses and the English Benedictine Reform, in H. Gittos and M. B. Bedingfield (eds), *The Liturgy of the Late Anglo-Saxon Church*, Henry Bradshaw Soc. Subsidia **5**, Woodbridge: Boydell, 13–28

Grocock, C. W., & Wood, I., forthcoming *Abbots of Wearmouth and Jarrow*, Oxford Medieval Texts, Oxford: Oxford University Press

Haddan, A. W., & Stubbs, W., 1869–78 *Councils and Ecclesiastical Documents Relating to Great Britain and Ireland*, 3 vols, Oxford: Clarendon Press

Haines, J., 2008 A Musical Fragment from Anglo-Saxon England, *Early Music* **36**, 219–29

Haldon, J., 1997 *Byzantium in the Seventh Century*, rev. edn, Cambridge: Cambridge University Press

Hall, R., & Paterson, E., 1999 The Ripon Jewel, in J. Hawkes & S. Mills (eds), *Northumbria's Golden Age*, Stroud: Sutton, 268–80

Hall, R., 1993 Observations in Ripon Cathedral Crypt 1989, *Yorkshire Archaeol. J.*, **65**, 39–53

Hall, R., 1995 Antiquaries and Archaeology in and Around Ripon Minster, in L. R. Hoey (ed.), *Yorkshire Monasticism. Archaeology, Art and Architecture from the 7th to the 16th Centuries*, British Archaeology Conference Transactions, **16**, 12–30

Hall, R., 1997 Revelation (over Ripon Cathedral Crypt) Chapter 2, *Archaeology in York*, **22** (3), 26–35

Hallinger, K., 1957 Papst Gregor der Grosse und der heiliger Benedikt, in B. Steidle (ed.) *Commentationes in Regulam Sancti Benedicti*, Studia Anselmiana **42**, Rome: Herder, 231–319

Hanslik, R., 1960 *Benedicti Regula*, CSEL **75**, Vienna: Hoelder

Hanssens, J-M., 1948–50 *Amalarii episcopi Opera liturgica omnia*, 3 vols, Studi e Testi **138–40**, Vatican City: Biblioteca apostolica Vaticana

Harrison, K., 1976 *The Framework of Anglo-Saxon History to A.D. 900*, Cambridge:

Cambridge University Press

Harrison, K., 1984 A Letter from Rome to the Irish Clergy, AD 640, *Peritia*, **3**, 222–9.

Hart, C. R., 1966 *The Early Charters of Eastern England*, Leicester: Leicester University Press

Hart, V., & Hicks, P., 2009 *Palladio's Rome*, New Haven and London: Yale University Press

Hartel, W. de, & Kamptner, M., 1999 *Sancti Pontii Meropii Paulini Nolani opera (pars I), epistulae*, CSEL **29**, 2nd ed., Vienna: Österreichischen Akademie der Wissenschaften

Hawkes, J., 1996 The Rothbury Cross: an Iconographic Bricolage, *Gesta*, **35**, 73–90

Hawkes, J., 1999a Northumbrian Sculpture: Questions of Context, in J. Hawkes & S. Mills (eds), *Northumbria's Golden Age*, Stroud: Sutton Publishers, 204–15

Hawkes, J., 1999b Statements in Stone: Anglo-Saxon Sculpture, Whitby and the Christianisation of the North, in C. Karkov (ed.), *Anglo-Saxon Archaeology: Basic Readings*, New York: Garland Publishers, 403–21

Hawkes, J., 2002a *The Sandbach Crosses: Sign and Significance in Anglo-Saxon Sculpture*, Dublin: Four Courts Press

Hawkes, J., 2002b The Church Triumphant: the Masham Column and the Art of the Church in Ninth-Century Anglo-Saxon England, *Hortus Artium Medievalium*, **8**, 337–48

Hawkes, J., 2003a The Plant-Life of Early Anglo-Saxon Art, in C. Biggam (ed.) *From Earth to Art*, Amsterdam: Rodopi, 263–86

Hawkes, J., 2003b *Iuxta Morem Romanorum*: Stone and Sculpture in the Style of Rome, in G. H. Brown & C. Karkov (eds), *Anglo-Saxon Styles*, Albany NY: SUNY, 69–100

Hawkes, J., 2005 Figuring Salvation: an Excursus into the Iconography of the Iona Crosses, in S. Foster & M. Cross (eds), *Able Minds and Practised Hands: Scotland's Early Medieval Sculpture in the 21st Century*, Society of Medieval Archaeology monograph series **23**, London: Maney Publishers, 259–75

Hawkes, J., 2006 The Anglo-Saxon Legacy, in E. Hartley, J. Hawkes & M. Henig (eds), *Constantine the Great: York's Roman Emperor*, London: Ashgate Press, 104–14

Hawkes, J., 2007a Gregory the Great and Angelic Mediation: the Anglo-Saxon Crosses of the Derbyshire Peaks, in A. Minnis & J. Roberts (eds), *Text, Image and Interpretation: Studies in Anglo-Saxon Literature in Honour of Éamonn Ó Carragáin*, Turnholt: Brepols, 432–48

Hawkes, J., 2007b Viewed through a Glass Darkly: the Questionable Movements of Art in Anglo-Saxon England, in P. Horden (ed.), *Freedom of Movement in the Middle Ages*, Harlaxton Medieval Studies, **15**, Donington: Shaun Tyas, 19–36

Hawkes, J., 2009 The Church Triumphant: the Figural Columns of Early Ninth Century Anglo-Saxon England, *Anglo-Saxon Studies in Archaeology and History*, **16**, 29–42

Hawkes, J., 2011 Design and Decoration: Re-Visualising Rome in Anglo-Saxon Sculpture, in C. Bolgia, R. McKitterick & J. Osborne (eds), *Rome across Time and Space. Cultural Transmission and the Exchange of Ideas, c. 500–1400*, Cambridge: Cambridge University Press, 201–21

Hayes, P., 1988 Roman to Saxon in the South Lincolnshire Fens, *Antiquity* **62**, 321–6

Hayward, P. A., 1999, Demystifying the Role of Sanctity in Western Christendom, in J. Howard-Johnston and P. A. Hayward (eds), *The Cult of Saints in Late Antiquity and the Early Middle Ages*, Oxford: Oxford University Press, 115–42

Heinzelmann, M., 2001 *Gregory of Tours: History and Society in the Sixth Century*, Cambridge: Cambridge University Press

Heitz, C., 1977 Cryptes préromanes du VIIIe au XIe siècle, *Université de Paris X – Nanterre, Centre de recherches sur l'Antiquité tardive et le Haut Moyen-Age*, **11**, 31–45

Hen, Y., 2001 *The Royal Patronage of Liturgy in Frankish Gaul to the Death of Charles the Bald (877)*, Henry Bradshaw Soc. Subsidia Ser. **3**, London: Boydell & Brewer

Hen, Y., 2002 Rome, Anglo-Saxon England and the Formation of the Frankish Liturgy, *Revue Bénédictine* **112**, 301–22

Hen, Y., 2007 Missionaries and Liturgy, in F. J. Felten, J. Jarnut and L. E. von Padberg (eds), *Bonifatius – Leben und Nachwirken: Die Gestaltung des christlichen Europa im Frühmittelalter*, Mainz: Gesellschaft für mittelrheinische Kirchengeschichte, 341–52

Henderson, G., 1999 *Vision and Image in Early Christian England*, Cambridge: Cambridge University Press

Henderson, I., 1986 The 'David Cycle' in Pictish Art, in J. Higgitt (ed.), *Early Medieval Sculpture in Britain and Ireland*, BAR British Series **152**, 87–123, Oxford: Archaeopress

Henderson, W. G. (ed.), 1874 *Missale ad usum insignis ecclesiae Eboracensis*, 2 vols, Surtees Society **59, 60**, Durham: Andrews

Herrin, J., 1987 *The Formation of Christendom,* Oxford: Basil Blackwell

Higham, N. J., 1997 *The Convert Kings – Power and Religious Affiliation in Early Anglo-Saxon England*, Manchester: Manchester University Press

Higham, N. J., 1999 Bishop Wilfrid in Southern England: a Review of his Political Objectives, *Studien zur Sachsenforschung* **13**, 207–17

Higham, N. J., 2001 Britons in Northern England in the Early Middle Ages: Through a Thick Glass Darkly, *Northern History*, **38.1**, 5–25

Higham, N. J., 2005 Guthlac's *Vita*, Mercia and East Anglia in the First Half of the Eighth Century, in D. Hill and M. Worthington (eds), *Aethelbald and Offa*, BAR, British Series **383**, Oxford: Archaeopress, 85–90

Higham, N. J., 2006 *(Re-)Reading Bede: The Ecclesiastical History in Context.* Abingdon: Routledge

Higham, N. J. (ed.), 2007 *Britons in Anglo-Saxon England*, Woodbridge: Boydell.

Higham, N. J., forthcoming, Bede's Agenda in Book IV of the *Ecclesiastical History of the English People*: A Tricky Matter of Advising the King, *Journal of Ecclesiastical History*

Hiley, D. (ed.), 1995 *Oxford Bodleian Library MS. Lat. liturg. b. 5* [facsimile], Publications of Mediaeval Manuscripts **20**, Ottawa: Institute of Mediaeval Music

Hill, P., 1997 *Whithorn and St Ninian: the Excavation of a Monastic Town, 1984–91*, Stroud: Sutton Publishers

Hillaby, J., 1998 St Oswald, the Revival of Monasticism, and the Veneration of the Saints in the Late Anglo-Saxon and Norman Diocese of Worcester, *Transactions of the Worcestershire Archaeological Society* **16**, 79–132

Hinds, A. B. (ed.), 1896 *Northumberland County History*, vol. 3: *Hexhamshire, Pt 1.* Newcastle upon Tyne: Andrew Reid & Co

Hodges, C. C., 1888 Ecclesia Hagustaldensis: *The Abbey of St Andrew, Hexham.* London: privately printed

Hodges, C. C., & Gibson, J., 1919 *Hexham and its Abbey.* Hexham: Gibson & Son

Hodgkin, R. H., 1935 *A History of the Anglo-Saxons*, Oxford: Clarendon Press

Hodgkin, T., 1906 *The History of England from the Earliest Times to the Norman Conquest,* Political history of England **1**, London: Longmans Green and Company

Hohler, C., 1956 The Durham Services in Honour of St. Cuthbert, in C. F. Battiscombe (ed.), *The Relics of Saint Cuthbert*, Oxford: Dean and Chapter of Durham Cathedral, 155–91

Holder, A. G., 1994 *Bede: On the Tabernacle*, Liverpool: Liverpool University Press

Horsley, J., 1732 *Britannia Romana*, London: Osborn & Longman

Hourlier, J., 1973 Notes sur l'antiphonie, in W. Arlt, E. Lichtenhahn and H. Oesch (eds), *Gattungen der Musik in Einzeldarstellungen: Gedenkschrift Leo Schrade*, Bern and Munich: Francke, 116–43

Hubert, J., 1927 L'Abbatiale Notre-Dame de Déols, *Bulletin Monumental*, **86**, 5–66

Hubert, J., Porcher, J. & Volbach, W., 1969 *Europe in the Dark Ages*, London: Thames & Hudson

Huelsen, C., 2000 *Le Chiese di Roma nel Medio Evo. Cataloghi ed Appunti*, original publication Florence: Olschki 1926, reprint Rome: Edizioni Quasar

Huggins, P., Rodwell, K., & Rodwall, W., 1983 Anglo-Saxon and Scandinavian Building Measurements, in P. Drury (ed.), *Approaches to the Interpretation of Excavated Buildings*, BAR British Series, **110**, Oxford: Archaeopress, 21–65

Hughes, A. (ed.), 2000 *Lambeth Palace Sion College ms. L1: The Noted Breviary of York* [facsimile], Publications of Mediaeval Musical Manuscripts **25**, Ottawa: Institute of Mediaeval Music

Huglo, M., 2001 Gallican Chant, in S. Sadie and J. Tyrrell (eds), *The New Grove Dictionary of Music and Musicians*, 2nd edn, **9**, New York: MacMillan, 458–72

Hunt, W., 1900 Wilfrid, in S. L. Stephen & S. S. Lee (eds), *Dictionary of National Biography* **61**, London: Smith, Elder and Company, 238–42

Hunter Blair, P., 1970 *The World of Bede*, London: Secker and Warburg

Hurst, D. (ed.), 1955 *Bedae Venerabilis Opera, Pars III Opera Homiletica*, CCSL **122**, Turnholt: Brepols

Hurst, D. (ed.), 1960 *Bedae Venerabilis Opera, pars II: Opera Exegetica, 3: In Lucae Evangelium Expositio; In Marci Evangelium Expositio*, CCSL **120**, Turnholt: Brepols

Hurst, D. (ed.), 1962 *Bedae Venerabilis, Opera exegetica 2. In primam partem Samuhelis libri IIII. In Regum librum XXX quaestiones*, CCSL **119**, Turnholt: Brepols

Hurst, D. (ed.), 1965 *Bedae Venerabilis Opera, pars III: Opera Homiletica*, CCSL **122**, Turnholt: Brepols

Hurst, D. (ed.), 1969 *Bedae Venerabilis, Opera exegetica 2A. De tabernaculo. De templo. In Ezram et Neemiam.* CCSL **119A**, Turnholt: Brepols

Hurst, D., 1999 *Bede the Venerable: Excerpts from the Works of Saint Augustine on the Letters of the Blessed Apostle Paul*, Cistercian Studies Series **183**, Kalamazoo, Michigan: Cistercian Publications

Hurst, D., and Adriaens, M. (eds), 1969 *Hieronymi Commentarii in Matheum Libri IV*, Turnholt: Brepols

Hurst, D. and Fraipont, J. (eds), 1955 *Beda Venerabilis, Opera homiletica. Opera rhythmica*, CCSL **122**, Turnholt: Brepols

Hutton, M., & Warmington, E. H., 1914 *Tacitus: Germania*, Cambridge, MA: Harvard University Press

Izzi, L., 2010 Rome and Anglo-Saxon England, Unpublished PhD Thesis, 2 vols, University of York

Jaager, W. (ed.), 1935 *Bedas metrische Vita Sancti Cuthberti*, Palaestra **198**, Leipzig: Mayer & Müller

Jäggi, C., 1998 *San Salvatore in Spoleto: studien zu spätantiken und frühmittelalterlichen architektur Italiens*, Wiesbaden: Reichert

James, E., 1988 *The Franks*, Oxford: Blackwell

James, M. R., 1983 *The Apocryphal New Testament*, Oxford: Oxford University Press

Jannet-Vallat, M., 1995 Vienne, basilique Saint-Pierre, église Saint-Georges, in N. Duval et al. (eds), *Les premiers monuments chrétiens de la France, I, Sud-Est et Corse*, Paris: Picard, 254–66

Jeffery, P., 1985 Review of M. Curran 1984, *Worship* 59, 459–61

Jeffery, P., 2000 Eastern and Western Elements in the Irish Monastic Prayer of the Hours, in M. E. Fassler and R. A. Baltzer (eds), *The Divine Office in the Latin Middle Ages: Methodology and Source Studies, Regional Developments, Hagiography*, Oxford: Oxford University Press, 99–141

Jeffery, P., 2003a Review of McKinnon 2000, *Journal of the American Musicological Soc.* 56, 169–79

Jeffery, P., 2003b Monastic Reading and the Emerging Roman Chant Repertory, in S. Gallagher, J. Haar, J. Nádas and T. Striplin (eds), *Western Plainchant in the First Millennium: Studies in the Medieval Liturgy and its Music*, Aldershot: Ashgate, 45–103

Jeffery, P., 2003c Philo's Impact on Christian Psalmody, in H. W. Attridge and M. E. Fassler (eds), *Psalms in Community: Jewish and Christian Textual, Liturgical and Artistic Traditions*, Leiden: Brill, 147–87

John, E., 1970 The Social and Political Problems of the Early English Church, in J. Thirsk (ed.) *Land, Church, and People: Essays Presented to H. P. R. Finberg*, Reading: Agricultural History Review 18, supplement, 39–63

Jones, C. W. (ed.), 1943 *Bedae opera de temporibus*, The Mediaeval Academy of America 41, Cambridge, MA: The Mediaeval Academy of America

Jones, P. F., 1929 *A Concordance to the Historia Ecclesiastica of Bede*, Cambridge, Mass: The Mediæval Academy of America for the Concordance Society

Jones, W. T., 1932 Recent Discoveries at Ripon Cathedral, *Yorkshire Archaeol. J.*, 31, 74–6

Jong, M. de, 2001, Monastic Prisoners or Opting Out? Political Coercion and Honour in the Carolingian Kingdoms, in M. de Jong, F. Theuws & C. van Rhijn (eds), *Topographies of Power in the Early Middle Ages*, Leiden: Brill, 291–328

Kardong, T. G., 1990 The Monastic Practices of Pachomius and the Pachomians, *Studia Monastica*, 32, 58–78

Kelly, S., 1990, Anglo-Saxon Lay Society and the Written Word, in R. McKitterick (ed.) *The Uses of Literacy in Early Medieval Europe*, Cambridge: Cambridge University Press, 36–62

Kelly, S. E. (ed.), 1995 *Charters of St Augustine's Abbey, Canterbury, and Minster-in-Thanet*, Oxford: Published for The British Academy by Oxford University Press

Kelly, S. E. (ed.), 1998 *Charters of Selsey*, Oxford: Published for The British Academy by Oxford University Press

Kelly, S. E. (ed.), 2007 *Charters of Bath and Wells*, Oxford: Published for The British Academy by Oxford University Press

Kelly, S. E. (ed.), 2009 *Charters of Peterborough Abbey*, Oxford: Published for The British Academy by Oxford University Press

Kendrick, T. D., 1939 *Anglo-Saxon Art to A.D. 900*, London: Methuen & Co. Ltd

Ker, N. R., 1941 The Provenance of the Oldest Manuscript of the Rule of St. Benedict, *The Bodleian Library Record*, 2, 28–29

Ker, N. R., 1969–2002 *Medieval Manuscripts in British Libraries*, completed by A. J. Piper, I. C. Cunningham and A. G. Watson, 5 vols, Oxford: Clarendon Press

Keynes, S., 1985 King Athelstan's Books, in M. Lapidge & H. Gneuss (eds), *Learning and*

Literature in Anglo-Saxon England: Studies Presented to Peter Clemoes on the Occasion of his Sixty-Fifth Birthday, Cambridge: Cambridge University Press, 143–201

Keynes, S. D., 1986 Episcopal Succession in Anglo-Saxon England, in E. B. Fryde (ed.), *Handbook of British Chronology*, 3rd edn, London: S. Porter and N. Roy, 209–24

Keynes, S. D., 1994 *The Councils of Clofesho: Brixworth Lecture 11, 1993*, Vaughan paper **38** Leicester: University of Leicester, Department of Adult Education

Keynes, S., 2005 Between Bede and the *Chronicle*: London, BL, Cotton Vespasian B. vi, fols. 104–9', in K. O'Brien O'Keefe and A. Orchard (eds), *Latin Learning and English Lore, I: Studies in Anglo-Saxon Literature for Michael Lapidge*, Toronto Old English Series **14**, Toronto: University of Toronto Press, I, 47–67

Kidd, B. J. (ed.), 1903 *Selected Letters of William Bright*, London: Wells Gardner, Darton & Company

Kipling, R., 1910 The Conversion of St Wilfrid, in R. Kipling, *Rewards and Fairies*, London: Macmillan, 221–42

Kirby, D. P., 1966 The Saxon Bishops of Leicester, Lindsey (*Syddensis*), and Dorchester, *Leicestershire Archaeological and Historical Society* **41**, 1–8

Kirby, D. P., 1973 'Bede and the Pictish Church', *Innes Review* **24**, 6–25

Kirby, D. P. (ed.), 1974 *St Wilfrid at Hexham*, Newcastle: Oriel Press

Kirby, D. P., 1976 '... per universas Pictorum provincias', in G. Bonner (ed.) *Famulus Christi: Essays in Commemoration of the Thirteenth Centenary of the Birth of the Venerable Bede*, London: SPCK, 286–324

Kirby, D. P., 1983 Bede, Eddius Stephanus and the 'Life of Wilfrid', *English Historical Review* **98**, 101–14

Kirby, D. P., 1991 *The Earliest English Kings*, London: Routledge

Kirby, D. P., 1995 The Genesis of a Cult: Cuthbert of Farne and Ecclesiastical Politics in Northumbria in the Late Seventh and Early Eighth Centuries, *Journal of Ecclesiastical History*, **46**, 383–97

Kitzinger, E., 1936 Anglo-Saxon Vine-Scroll Ornament, *Antiquity* **10**, 61–71

Kjølbye-Biddle, B., 1986 The Seventh-Century Minster at Winchester Interpreted, in C. A. S. Butler and R. K. Morris (eds), *The Anglo-Saxon Church: Papers on History, Architecture and Archaeology in Honour of Dr. H. M. Taylor*, Atlantic Highlands, NJ: Humanities Press International Inc, 196–209

Kölzer, T., 2001 *Die Urkunden der Merowinger, MGH, Diplomata Regum Francorum e stirpe Merovingica*, 2 vols, Hannover: Hahn

Krautheimer, R., 1971a Sancta Maria Rotunda, in R. Krautheimer (ed.) *Studies in Early Christian, Medieval and Renaissance Architecture,* London: University of London Press, 107–14

Krautheimer, R., 1971b Santa Stephano Rotundo in Rome and the Rotunda of the Holy Sepulchre in Jerusalem, in R. Krautheimer (ed.) *Studies in Early Christian, Medieval and Renaissance Architecture,* London: University of London Press, 69–114

Krautheimer, R., 1971c Introduction to an 'Iconography of Medieval Architecture', in R. Krautheimer (ed.) *Studies in Early Christian, Medieval and Renaissance Architecture,* London: University of London Press, 116–30 [originally published in *J. Warburg and Courtauld Inst.*, 5, 1942, 1–33]

Krusch, B. (ed.), 1888 *Vita Sanctae Geretrudis, MGH*, scriptores rerum Merovingicarum, 2, Hannover: Hahn, 447–74

Krusch, B. (ed.), 1896 *Passiones vitaeque sanctorum aevi Merovingici et antiquiorum aliquot. MGH Scriptores rerum Merovingicarum 3*, Hanover: Hahn

Krusch, B. (ed.), 1902 Jonas, *Vita Columbani abbatis et discipulorum eius libri duo*, *MGH, Scriptores rerum Merovingicarum* 4, Hanover/Leipzig: Hahn, 1–156

Krusch, B. (ed.) 1920 *Vita Sancti Amandi, MGH, Scriptores rerum Merovingicarum* 5, Hannover/Leipzig: Hahn, 394–485

Laistner, M. L. W., 1939 *Bedae Venerabilis Exposition Actuum Apostolorum et Retractio*, Cambridge, Mass: The Medieval Academy of America

Laistner, M. L. W., 1943 *A Hand-List of Bede Manuscripts*, Ithaca, NY: Cornell University Press

Laistner, M. L. W., 1983 *Expositio Actuum Apostolorum*, CCSL, **121** Turnholt: Brepols

Lang, J., 1988 *Anglo-Saxon Sculpture*, Aylesbury: Shire Publications

Lang, J., 1991 *CASSS 3, York and Eastern Yorkshire*, Oxford: Oxford University Press

Lang, J., 1993 Survival and Revival in Insular Art: Northumbrian Sculptures of the 8th to 10th Centuries, in M. Spearman and J. Higgitt (eds), *The Age of Migrating Ideas*, Edinburgh: National Museum of Scotland, 261–67

Lang, J., 1999 The Apostles in Anglo-Saxon Sculpture in the Age of Alcuin, *Early Medieval Europe*, **8**, 271–82

Lang, J., 2001 *CASSS 6, Northern Yorkshire*, Oxford: Oxford University Press

Lapidge, M., 1975 The Hermeneutic Style in Tenth-Century Anglo-Saxon England, *Anglo-Saxon England* **4**, 67–111

Lapidge, M., 1988 A Frankish Scholar in Tenth-Century England: Frithegod of Canterbury/Fredegaud of Brioude, *Anglo-Saxon England* **17**, 45–65

Lapidge, M., 1989 Bede's Metrical *Vita S. Cuthberti*, in G. Bonner, D. Rollason and C. Stancliffe (eds), *St Cuthbert, his Cult and his Community*, Woodbridge: Boydell Press, 77–93

Lapidge, M., 1996a *Anglo-Latin Literature 600–899*, London and Rio Grande: The Hambledon Press

Lapidge, M., 1996b Byrhtferth and Oswald, in N. P. Brooks & C. R. E. Cubitt (eds), *St Oswald of Worcester: Life and Influence*, Leicester: Leicester University Press, 64–83

Lapidge, M., 2006 *The Anglo-Saxon Library*, Oxford: Oxford University Press

Lapidge, M. (ed.), 2009 *Byrhtferth of Ramsey, The Lives of St Oswald and St Ecgwine*, Oxford: Oxford University Press

Lapidge, M., Blair, J., Keynes, S., and Scragg, D. (eds), 1999 *The Blackwell Encyclopaedia of Anglo-Saxon England*, Oxford: Blackwell Publishing

Lapidge, M., & Herren, M., 1979 *Aldhelm: The Prose Works*, Cambridge: D. S. Brewer

Laporte, J-P, 1988 C. Reliques et documents carolingiens, *Bulletin de la Société Archaeologique et Historique de Chelles*, ns. 8–9, 115–60

Latouche, R. (ed.), 1930–64 Richer, *Histoire de France*, les Classiques de l'histoire de France, 2 vols, Paris: H. Champion

Lawlor, H. J., & Best, R. I. (eds) 1931 *Martyrology of Tallaght*, London: Henry Bradshaw Society **68**

Lawrence, C. H., 1989 *Medieval Monasticism: Forms of Religious Life in Western Europe in the Middle Ages*, 2nd edn, Harlow, Essex: Longman

Lawson, G., 1999 Musical instruments, in M. Lapidge *et al.* (eds), *The Blackwell Encyclopaedia of Anglo-Saxon England*, Oxford: Blackwell Publishing, 328–9

Lawson, G., and Rankin, S., 1999 Music, in M. Lapidge *et al.* (eds), *The Blackwell Encyclopaedia of Anglo-Saxon England*, Oxford: Blackwell Publishing, 327–8

Laynesmith, M., 2000 Stephen of Ripon and the Bible: Allegorical and Typological Interpretations of the Life of St Wilfrid, *Early Medieval Europe*, **9.2**, 163–82

Le Jan, R., 1995 *Famille et Pouvoir dans le monde franc (VIIe–Xe siècle)*, Paris:

Publications de la Sorbonne

Levison, W., 1905 *Vitae sancti Bonifatii archiepiscopi Moguntini, MGH, Scriptores rerum Germanicarum in usum scholarum separatim editi*, 57, Hanover: Hahnsche Buchhandlung

Levison, W., 1912 Die Akten der römischen Synode von 679, *Zeitschrift der Savigny-Stiftung für Rechtsgeschichte*, Kan Abt 33, 249–82

Levison, W. (ed.), 1913 *Vita Bertilae abbatissae Calensis* and *Vita Wilfridi I, Episcopi Eboracensis auctore Stephano*, in B. Krusch & W. Levison (eds), *MGH, Scriptores rerum Merovingicarum* 6, Hanover/Leipzig: Hahn, 95–109, 163–263

Levison, W., 1935 Bede as Historian, in A. Hamilton Thompson (ed.), *Bede, His Life, Times and Writings*, Oxford: Oxford University Press, 111–51

Levison, W., 1946, *England and the Continent in the Eighth Century. The Ford Lectures Delivered in the University of Oxford in the Hilary Term 1943*, Oxford: Clarendon Press

Levy, K., 1998 *Gregorian Chant and the Carolingians*, Princeton: Princeton University Press

Liddon, H. P., 1894 *Life of Edward Bouverie Pusey*, 4th edn, London: Longmans, Green

Liebermann, F., 1889 *Die Heiligen Englands* Hannover: Hahn

Liebermann, F. (ed.), 1903–1916 *Die Gesetze der Angelsachsen*, 3 vols, Halle: Niemeyer

Lifshitz, F., 2006 *The Name of the Saint: The Martyrology of St Jerome and Access to the Sacred in Francia, 627–827*, Notre Dame: University of Notre Dame Press

Lightfoot, J. B., 1890 *Leaders in the Northern Church: Sermons Preached in the Diocese of Durham*, London: Macmillan

Lindsay, W. M. (ed.), 1911 *Isidori Hispalensis episcopi Etymologiarum sive originum libri XX*, 2 vols, Oxford: Clarendon Press

Llewellyn, P., 1971 *Rome in the Dark Ages*, London: Constable

Lombardi, F., 1996 *Roma, le chiese scomparse. La memoria storica della città*, Rome: Palombi

Longhurst, M., 1931 The Easby Cross, *Archaeologia*, 71, 43–7

Love, R. C. 2004 *Goscelin of Saint-Bertin. The Hagiography of the Female Saints of Ely*, Oxford Medieval Texts, Oxford: Oxford University Press

Lowe, E. A., 1929 *Regula S. Benedicti: Specima Selecta e Codice Antiquissimo Oxoniensis Elegit Atque Adnotatione Instruxit*, Oxford: Clarendon Press

Lowe, E. A., 1934–72, *Codices Latini Antiquores*, 11 vols, Oxford: Clarendon Press

Lowe, E. A., 1960, *English Uncial*, Oxford: Clarendon Press

Mabillon, J. (ed.), 1677 *Vita Wilfridi*, Acta Sanctorum Ordinis S. Benedicti, saec 4, pt 1, Paris: Société des Bollandistes, 676–722

Mackie, G. 2003 *Early Christian Chapels in the West: Decoration, Function and Patronage*, Toronto: University of Toronto Press

Mac Lean, D., 1997 King Oswald's Wooden Cross at Heavenfield in Context, in C. Karkov, M. Ryan & R. T. Farrell (eds), *The Insular Tradition*, New York: Garland Press, 79–98

Macalister, R. A. S., 1945–49 *Corpus Inscriptionum Insularum Celticarum*, 2 vols, Dublin: Irish Manuscripts Commission; 1st vol. repr. 1996, Dublin: Blackrock Co.

Magni, M., 1979 Cryptes du haut Moyen Age en Italie: problèmes de typologie du IXe jusqu'au début du XIe siecle, *Cahiers Archéologiques*, 28, 41–85

Maguire, H., 1996 *The Icons of their Bodies: Saints and their Images in Byzantium*, Princeton: Princeton University Press

Maillé, Marquise de, 1971, *Les cryptes de Jouarre*, Paris: Picard

Mann, J., 1994 Allegorical Buildings in Medieval Literature, *Medium Aevum*, **63**, 191–209

Markus, R. A., 1996 *Signs and Meanings. World and Text in Ancient Christianity*, Liverpool: Liverpool University Press

Markus, R. A., 1997 *Gregory the Great and his World*, Cambridge: Cambridge University Press

Martène, E., 1736–8 *De antiquis ecclesiae ritibus*, 2nd edn, 4 vols, Antwerp: Typis Joannis Baptistae de la Bry

Martin, L. T. and Hurst, D. (trans.), 1991 *Bede the Venerable: Homilies on the Gospels*, 2 vols, Cistercian Studies **110, 111**, Kalamazoo, Michigan: Cistercian Publications

Martínez Pizzaro, J., 2008 The King Says No: on the Logic of Type-Scenes in Late Antique and Early Medieval Narrative, in J. Davies & M. McCormick (eds), *The Long-Morning of Medieval Europe: New Directions in Early Medieval Studies*, Aldershot: Ashgate, 181–92

Martiniani-Reber, M., 1986 *Lyon, musée historique des tissus. Soieries sassanides, coptes et byzantines Ve–XIe siècles*, Paris: Editions de la réunion des musées nationaux

Matter, E. A., 1990 *The Voice of My Beloved. The Song of Songs in Western Medieval Christianity*, Philadelphia: University of Pennsylvania Press

Mayr-Harting, H., 1972 *The Coming of Christianity to Anglo-Saxon England*, London: B. T. Batsford; 3rd edn, 1991, University Park, PA: Pennsylvania State University Press

Mayr-Harting, H., 1976, *The Venerable Bede, The Rule of St. Benedict, and Social Class*, Jarrow: Jarrow Lecture

McClendon, C. B., 2005 *The Origins of Medieval Architecture: Building in Europe, A.D. 600–900*, New Haven: Yale University Press

McClure, J., 1984 Bede and the Life of Ceolfrid, *Peritia*, **3**, 71–84

McKinnon, J., 1995 Lector Chant versus Schola Chant: A Question of Historical Plausibility, in J. Szendrei and D. Hiley (eds), *Laborare fratres in unum: Festschrift László Dobszay zum 60. Geburtstag*, Hildesheim: Weidmann, 201–11

McKinnon, J., 2000 *The Advent Project: The Later-Seventh-Century Creation of the Roman Mass Proper*, Berkeley, Los Angeles and London: University of California Press

McKitterick, R., 1977 *The Frankish Church and the Carolingian Reforms, 789–895*, Royal Hist. Soc. Stud. in Hist. **2**, London: Royal Historical Society

McKitterick, R., 1981 The Scriptoria of Merovingian Gaul: a Survey of the Evidence, in H. B. Clarke & M. Brennan (eds), *Columbanus and Merovingian Monasticism*, BAR International Series **113**, Oxford: Archaeopress, 173–207

McKitterick, R., 2008 *Charlemagne: The Formation of a European Identity*, Cambridge: Cambridge University Press

McNeill J. T., and Gamer H. M., 1938 *Medieval Handbooks of Penance, A Translation of the Principal* libri poenitentiales *and Selections from Related Documents,* New York: Columbia University Press

Meehan, D. (ed.), 1958 *Adamnan's De Locis Sanctis*, Scriptores Latini Hiberniae, **3**, Dublin: Institute for Advanced Studies

Mellows, W. T. (ed.), 1949 *The Chronicle of Hugh Candidus*, London: Oxford University Press

Mews, C. J,. 2011 Gregory the Great, the Rule of Benedict and Roman Liturgy: the Evolution of a Legend, *Journal of Medieval History* 37, 125–44

Meyer, A. R., 2003 *Medieval Allegory and the Building of the New Jerusalem,*

Cambridge: Brewer

Meyvaert, P., 1963 Towards a History of the Textual Transmission of the *Regula S. Benedicti*, *Scriptorium*, **17**, 83–110

Michaud, J., 1999 Culte des reliques et épigraphie: l'exemple des dédicaces et des consécrations d'autels, in E. Bozóky & A-M. Helvétius (eds), *Les reliques: objets, cultes, symboles: actes du colloque international de l'Université du Littoral-Côte d'Opâle (Boulogne-sur-Mer), 4–6 Septembre 1997*, Turnholt: Brepols, 199–212

Micklethwaite, J. T., 1882 On the Crypts at Ripon and Hexham, *Archaeol. J.*, **39**, 347–54

Micklethwaite, J. T., 1896 Something about Saxon Church Building, *Archaeol. J.*, **53**, 293–351

Migne, J-P. (ed.), 1845 *Eusebii Hieronym, Opera Omnia*. Paris: PL **22**

Migne, J-P. (ed.), 1862 *Bedae Venerabilis, Opera Exegetica*. Paris: PL **91**

Migne, J-P. (ed.), 1863a *Sancti Ambrosii, Opera Omnia*, Paris: PL **16**

Migne, J-P. (ed.), 1863b *Sancti Augustini, Opera Omnia*, Paris: PL **39**

Migne, J-P. (ed.), 1865 *Sancti Augustini, Opera Omnia*, Paris: PL **38**

Migne, J-P. (ed.), 1874 *Joannis Cassiani, Opera Omnia*, Paris: PL **49**

Migne, J-P. (ed.), 1882 *Sancti Ambrosii, Opera Omnia*, Paris: PL **14**

Miller, A., 1976 *Death of a Salesman*, Penguin Plays, Harmondsworth: Penguin Books

Mitchell, J., 2001 The High Cross and Monastic Strategies in Eighth-Century Northumbria, in P. Binski & W. Noel (eds), *New Offerings, Ancient Treasures: Studies in Medieval Art for George Henderson*, Stroud: Sutton Publishers, 88–114

Mitchell, J., forthcoming Anglo-Saxon Vine-Scroll: Incidence, Sources and Meaning, in L. Cleaver & D. Park (eds), *The Staffordshire Hoard and Anglo-Saxon Art: Material, Contexts and Interpretations*

Mordek, H., 1975 *Kirchenrecht und Reform im Frankenreich: die Collectio Vetus Gallica, die älteste systematische Kanonessammlung des fränkischen Gallien, Studien und Edition*, Berlin: W. de Gruyter

Morin, G., Capelle, B., & Fraipont J. (eds), 1958 *Hieronymus, Tractatus sive homiliae in psalmos. In Marci evangelium. Aliaque varia argumenta*, Brepols: CCSL **78**

Morris, C., 2005 *The Sepulchre of Christ and the Medieval West*, Oxford: Oxford University Press

Mostert, M., 1999 *754: Bonifatius bij Dokkum vermoord*, Hilversum: Verloren

Mountain, W. J., & Glorie F. (eds), 1968 *Augustinus, De trinitate libri XV Libri I–XII*, Brepols: CCSL **50**

Muir, B. J., and Turner, A. J. (eds and trans), 1998 *Vita sancti Wilfridi auctore Edmero: The Life of Saint Wilfrid by Edmer*, Exeter: University of Exeter Press

Nees, L., 2002 *Early Medieval Art*, Oxford: Oxford University Press

Nelson, J. L., 1978 Queens as Jezebels: Brunhild and Balthild in Merovingian History, in D. Baker (ed.) *Medieval Women: Essays Dedicated and Presented to Professor Rosalind M. T. Hill*, Ecclesiastical History Society, *Studies in Church History*, subsidia **1**, Oxford: B. Blackwell, 31–77

Newman, J. H., 1844 *Lives of the English Saints*, London: James Toovey

Nicolai, V. F., Bisconti, F. & Mazzoleni, D., 1999 *The Christian Catacombs of Rome. History, Decoration, Inscriptions*, Regensburg: Verlag Schnell & Steiner GmbH

Norberg, D., 1982 *S. Gregorii Magni Registrum Epistolarum*, 2 vols, CCSL **140, 140A**, Turnholt: Brepols

Nordhagen, P. J., 1965 The Mosaics of John VII (705–707 A.D.): the Mosaic Fragments and their Technique, *Acta ad Archaeologiam et Artium Historiam Pertinentia*, **2**, 121–66

Nordhagen, P. J., 1968 *The Frescoes of John VII (A.D. 705–707) in Sta Maria Antiqua in Rome*, Acta ad Archaeologiam et Artum Historiam Pertinentia, **3**, Rome: Bretschneider

Nordhagen, P. J., 1969 Carved Marble Pilaster in the Vatican Grottoes. Some Remarks on the Sculptural Techniques of the Early Middle Ages, *Acta ad Archaeologiam et Artium Historiam Pertinentia*, **4**, 113–20

Nordhagen, P. J., 1978 S. Maria Antiqua: the Frescoes of the Seventh Century, *Acta ad Archaeologiam et Artium Historiam Pertinentia*, **8**, 89–142

Norris, R. A., 2003 *The Song of Songs Interpreted by Early Christian and Medieval Commentators*, Michigan and Cambridge: Eerdmans

Nowacki, E., 1990 The Performance of Office Antiphons in Twelfth-Century Rome, in *Cantus Planus: Papers Read at the Third Meeting, Tihany, Hungary, 19–24 September 1988*, Budapest: Hungarian Academy of Sciences Institute for Musicology, 79–91

Nowacki, E., 1995 Antiphonal Psalmody in Christian Antiquity and the Early Middle Ages, in G. M. Boone (ed.), *Essays on Medieval Music in Honor of David G. Hughes*, Isham Library Papers 4, Cambridge, MA: Harvard University Department of Music, 287–315

Ó Carragáin, É, 1994 *The City of Rome and the World of Bede*, Jarrow: Jarrow Lecture

Ó Carragáin, É, 1999 The Term *Porticus* and *Imitatio Romae* in Early Anglo-Saxon England, in H. Conrad O'Brian, A. M. D'Arcy & J. Scattergood (eds), *Text and Gloss: Studies in Insular Learning and Literature Presented to Joseph Donovan Pheifer*, Dublin: Four Courts Press, 13–34

Ó Carragáin, É, 2005 *Ritual and the Rood: Liturgical Images and the Old English Poems of the* Dream of the Rood *Tradition*, London & Toronto: The British Library & University of Toronto Press

Ó Cróinín, D., 1982 A Seventh-Century Irish Computus from the Circle of Cummianus, *Proceedings of the Royal Irish Academy*, **82 C.**, 405–30

Ó Cróinín, D., 1985 'New Heresy for Old': Pelagianism in Ireland and the Papal Letter of 640, *Speculum*, **60**, 505–16

Ogilvy, J. D. A., 1967 *Books Known to the English, 597–1066*, Cambridge, Massachussetts: Medieval Academy of America

O'Loughlin, T., 2007 *Adomnan and the Holy Places. The Perception of an Insular Monk on the Location of the Biblical Drama*, London: T. and T. Clark

O'Reilly, J., 1995 Introduction, in S. Connolly (trans.), *Bede: on the Temple*. Liverpool: Liverpool University Press, xvii–lv

Ó Riain, P., 1993 *Anglo-Saxon Ireland: The Evidence of the Martyrology of Tallaght*, H. M. Chadwick Memorial Lectures, 3, Cambridge: Department of Anglo-Saxon, Norse, and Celtic

Ó Riain, P., 2002 A Northumbrian Phase in the Formation of the Hieronymian Martyrology. The Evidence of the Martyrology of Tallaght, *Analecta Bollandiana* **120**, 311–63

Ó Riain, P., 2006 *Feastdays of the Saints. A History of Irish Martyrologies*, Brussels: Société des Bollandists, Subsidia Hagiographica, **28**

Osborne, J., 1985 The Roman Catacombs in the Middle Ages, *Papers of the British School at Rome*, **53**, 278–328

Osborne, J., Brandt, J. Rasmus & Morganti, G. (eds), 2004 *Santa Maria Antiqua al Foro*

Romano cento anni dopo, Rome: Campisano

Osborne, J., & Claridge, A., 1996 *The Paper Museum of Cassiano dal Pozzo*. Series A: *Antiquities and Architecture*, Part **2**: *Early Christian and Medieval Antiquities*, 2 vols, London: Harvey Miller

Oury, G., 1965 Psalmum dicere cum Alleluia, *Ephemerides liturgicae*, **79**, 97–108

Padel, O. J., 1985 *Cornish Place-Name Elements*, Nottingham: English Place-Name Society

Padel, O. J., 1988 *A Popular Dictionary of Cornish Place-Names*, Penzance: A. Hodge

Padel, O. J., 2007 Place-Names and the Saxon Conquest of Devon and Cornwall, in N. J. Higham (ed.) *Britons in Anglo-Saxon England*, Woodbridge: Boydell & Brewer, 215–30

Padel, O. J., 2009 *Slavery in Saxon Cornwall: The Bodmin Manumissions*, Cambridge: Kathleen Hughes Memorial Lectures, **7**

Page, R. I., 1965 Anglo-Saxon Episcopal Lists, Parts 1 and 2, *Nottingham Mediaeval Studies*, **9**, 71–95

Page, R. I., 1966 Anglo-Saxon Episcopal Lists, Part 3, *Nottingham Mediaeval Studies*, **10**, 2–24

Palmer, J. T., 2009 *Anglo-Saxons in a Frankish World, 690–900*, Turnholt: Brepols

Palol, P. de, 1968 *Arte hispánico de la época visigoda*, Barcelona: Ediciones Polígrafa

Paperbroch, D. (ed.), 1701 *Vita Deodati*, Acta Sanctorum, June **3**, Antwerp, 872–4

Parker, M., 1853 *Correspondence of Matthew Parker*, J. Bruce & T. T. Perowne (eds), Cambridge: Cambridge University Press for the Parker Society

Parkes, M. B., 1991 *Scribes, Scripts and Readers. Studies in the Communication, Presentation and Dissemination of Medieval Texts*, London: The Hambledon Press

Parsons, D. (ed.), 1975 *Tenth-Century Studies: Essays in Commemoration of the Millennium of the Council of Winchester and 'Regularis Concordia'*, London: Phillimore

Parsons, D., 2001 The Mercian Church, Archaeology and Topography, in M. P. Brown & C. A. Farr (eds), *Mercia; An Anglo-Saxon Kingdom in Europe*, London: Leicester University Press, 51–68

Peers, C. R., 1931 Recent Discoveries in the Minsters of Ripon and York, *Antiq. J.*, **11**, 113–22

Peers, C., & Ralegh Radford, C. A., 1943 The Saxon Monastery at Whitby, *Archaeologia*, **89**, 64–5

Pelteret, D., 1998 Saint Wilfrid: Tribal Bishop, Civic Lord or Germanic Lord?, in J. Hill and M. Swan (eds), *The Community, the Family and the Saint: Patterns of Power in Early Medieval Europe, Selected Proceedings of the International Medieval Congress, University of Leeds 4–7 July 1994, 10–13 July 1995*, Brepols: Turnholt, 159–80

Périn, P., & Feffer L-C (eds), 1985 *La Neustrie: Les pays au nord du Loire de Dagobert à Charles le Chauvre (viie–ixe siècles)*, Rouen: Musées et Monuments départmental de Seine-Maritime

Petschenig M. (ed.), 1886 *Iohannes Cassianus: Collationes*, CSEL **13** Vienna: Verlag der Österreichischen Akademie der Wissenschaften

Petschenig M. (ed.), 1888 *Iohannes Cassianus: De institutis coenobiorum et de octo principalium vitiorum remediis, De incarnatione Domini contra Nestorium*, CSEL **17** Vienna: Verlag der Österreichischen Akademie der Wissenschaften

Phillips, D., & Heywood, B., 1995 *Excavations at York Minster*, **1**, London: RCHM

Piazzoni, A. M., 1992 Arresto, condanna, esilio e morte di Martino I, in *Martino I Papa e il suo tempo*, Spoleto: Centro Italiano di Studi sull'Alto Medioevo, 187–210

Picard, J-Ch., 1988 *Le Souvenir des évêques: sépultures, listes épiscopales et cultes des évêques en Italie du nord des origins au Xe siècles*, Rome : École Française de Romes

Picard, J-M., 1991 Church and Politics in the Seventh Century: the Irish Exile of Dagobert II, in J-M. Picard (ed.), *Ireland and Northern France AD600–850*, Dublin: Four Courts Press, 27–52

Pirault, L., 2009 La basilique des Champs Saint-Martin à Rezé (Loire-Atlantique) in D. Paris-Poulin, S. Nardi Combescure and D. Istria (eds), *Les premiers temps chrétiens dans le territoire de la France actuelle hagiographie, épigraphie et archéologie: nouvelles approches et perspectives de recherche*, Rennes: Presses Universitaires de Rennes, 181–94

Plummer, C. (ed.) 1896 *Venerabilis Baedae Opera Historica*, 2 vols, Oxford: Clarendon Press

Pontal, O., 1989 *Histoire des conciles mérovingiens*, Paris : Éditions de Cerf

Poole, R. L., 1919 St Wilfrid and the See of Ripon, *English Historical Review*, **34**, 1–24

Poole, R. L., 1934 *Studies in Chronology and History*, Oxford: Oxford University Press

Preest, D., 2002 (trans.), *The Deeds of the Bishops of England (Gesta Pontificum Anglorum)*, Woodbridge: Boydell

Prinz, F., 1965 *Frühes Mönchtum im Frankenreich*, Kempten: Oechselhäuser

Quentin, Dom. A., 1908 *Les Martyrologes historiques du moyen-âge*, Paris: Société des Bollandistes

Radford, C. A. R., 1961 The Bishop's Throne in Norwich Cathedral, *Archaeol. J.*, **116**, 115–32

Raine, J. (ed.), 1864 Prior Richard's History of the Church of Hexham, in J. Raine (ed.), *The Priory of Hexham, its Chronicles, Endowments and Annals*, Surtees Society, **44**, 63–106

Raine, J., (ed.) 1865 *The Priory of Hexham, vol. II, Preface by J. Walbran*, Surtees Society, **56**, i–c

Raine, J. (ed.), 1879 *The Historians of the Church of York and its Archbishops, I*, London: Longman

Rankin, S., 1985 The Liturgical Background of the Old English Advent Lyrics, in M. Lapidge and H. Gneuss (eds), *Learning and Literature in Anglo-Saxon England: Studies Presented to Peter Clemoes on the Occasion of his Sixty-Fifth Birthday*, Cambridge: Cambridge University Press, 317–40

Rankin, S., 2002 Review of McKinnon 2000, *Plainsong and Medieval Music* **11**, 73–98

Rankin, S., 2011 Music books, in R. Gameson (ed.), *The Cambridge History of the Book in Britain*, I: *c. 400–1100*, Cambridge: Cambridge University Press, 482–506

Rankin, S., forthcoming, Alcuin's *De laude Dei* and Other Early Sources of Office Chants. A Paper Given at the 2001 York Quodlibet Conference ('Alcuin of York'), now to appear in a volume in honour of Thomas Forrest Kelly to be published by Harvard University Press

Rauer, C., 2006 Pope Sergius's Privilege for Malmesbury, *Leeds Studies in English*, **37**, 261–81

Reekmans, L., 1970 Le développement topographique de la région du Vatican à la fin de l'antiquité et au début du moyen âge (300–850), in *Mélanges d' archéologie et d'histoire de l'art offerts au Professeur Jacques Lavalleye*, Université de Louvain, Recueil de travaux d'histoire et de philologie, 4th ser., **45**, 197–235

Reynaud, J-F, 1995 Lyon, Basilique Saint-Just, in N. Duval et al. (eds), *Les premiers monuments chrétiens de la France, I., Sud-Est et Corse*. Paris: Picard, 271–7

Richards, J., 1979 *The Popes and the Papacy in the Early Middle Ages, 476–753*, London:

371

Routledge and Kegan Paul

Ridyard, S., 1988 *The Royal Saints of Anglo-Saxon England: a Study of West Saxon and East Anglian Cults,* Cambridge: Cambridge University Press

Riedinger, R., 1990 *Concilium Universale Constantinopolintanum Tertium, Acta Conciliorum Oecumenicorum,* 2nd series, **1**, Berlin: Walter de Gruyter and co

Roberts, A., Donaldson J., Schaff, P., & Wace H., 1994 *Nicene and Post-Nicene Fathers,* Massachusetts: Hendrickson

Roberts, J., 2005 *Guide to Scripts Used in English Writings up to 1500,* London: British Library

Rodwell, W., Hawkes, J., Cramp, R. & Howe, E., 2008 The Lichfield Angel: a Spectacular Anglo-Saxon Painted Sculpture, *Antiq. J.,* **88,** 1–60

Roffe, D., 1986 The Seventh-Century Monastery at Stow Green, Lincolnshire, *Lincolnshire History and Archaeology* **21,** 31–4

Rogerson, A., 2003 Six Middle Anglo-Saxon Sites in West Norfolk, in T. Pestell and K. Ulmschneider (eds), *Markets in Early Medieval Europe. Trading and 'Productive' Sites, 650–850,* Macclesfield: Windgather, 110–21

Rollason, D. W., 1978 Lists of Saints' Resting-Places in Anglo-Saxon England, *Anglo-Saxon England* **7,** 61–93

Rollason, D. W., 1982 *The Mildrith Legend: A Study in Early Medieval Hagiography in England,* Studies in the Early History of Britain, Leicester: Leicester University Press

Rollason, D. W. (ed. and trans.), 2000 *Libellus de exordio atque procursu istius, hoc est Dunelmensis ecclesiae,* Oxford: Clarendon Press

Rollason, D. W., 2004 Osred I (696×8–716), *Oxford Dictionary of National Biography,* online edn, Oxford University Press, Sept 2004 Available: http://www.oxforddnb.com/view/article/20903 Accessed 31 August 2010

Roper, M., 1974a The Donation of Hexham, in D. Kirby (ed.), *Saint Wilfrid at Hexham,* Newcastle upon Tyne: Oriel Press, 169–71

Roper, M. 1974b Wilfrid's Landholdings in Northumbria, in D. P. Kirby (ed.) *Saint Wilfrid at Hexham,* Newcastle upon Tyne: Oriel Press, 61–79

Rosenwein, B., 1999 *Negotiating Space. Power, Restraint, and Privileges of Immunity in Early Medieval Europe,* Ithaca: Cornell University Press

Rosser, S., 1997 Æthelthryth: A Conventional Saint?, *Bulletin of the John Rylands University Library of Manchester* **79 (3),** 15–24

Rouche, M., 1989 Remarques sur la géographie historique de la Neustrie (650–850), in H. Atsma (ed.), *La Neustrie: les Pays au Nord de la Loire de 650 à 850: Colloque Historique International,* Beihefte der Francia, **16,** 2 vols, Sigmaringen: Thorbecke, **1,** 1–23

Rousseau, P., 1999 *Pachomius. The Making of a Community in Fourth-Century Egypt,* Berkeley: University of California Press

Rousseau, P., 2002 *The Early Christian Centuries,* Harlow: Longman

Rubenstein, J., 1999 Liturgy against History: The Competing Visions of Lanfranc and Eadmer of Canterbury, *Speculum* **74,** 279–309

Sapin, C., 1986 *La Bourgogne préromane, construction, décor, et fonction des édifices religieux,* Paris: Picard

Saxl, F., 1943 The Ruthwell Cross, *Journal of the Warburg and Courtauld Institutes* **6,** 1–19

Saxl, F. & Wittkower, R., 1948 *British Art and the Mediterranean,* London: Oxford University Press

Schäferdiek, K., 1994 Fragen der frühen angelsächsischen Festlandmission,

Frühmittelalterliche Studien, 28, 172–95

Schapiro, M., 1944 The Religious Meaning of the Ruthwell Cross, *Art Bulletin* 26, 232–45

Scheil, A. P., 2004 *The Footsteps of Israel, Understanding Jews in Anglo-Saxon England*, Ann Arbor, MI: University of Michigan Press

Schlunk, H. and Hauschild, T., 1978 *Hispania Antiqua: Die Denkmäler der frühchristlichen und west gotischen Zeit*, Mainz: von Zabern

Schoebe, G., 1962 The Chapters of Archbishop Oda (942/6) and the Canons of the Legatine Councils of 786, *Bulletin of the Institute of Historical Research* 35, 75–83

Schweitzer, F. M., 1994 Medieval Perceptions of Jews and Judaism, in M. Perry and F. M. Schweitzer (eds), *Jewish-Christian Encounters Over the Centuries, Symbiosis, Prejudice, Holocaust, Dialogue*, American University Studies Series 9: History, 136, New York: Peter Lang, 131–168

Scott, J., 1981 *The Early History of Glastonbury: An Edition, Translation and Study of William of Malmesbury's De Antiquitate Glastonie Ecclesiae*, Woodbridge: Boydell

Scott, J., 2000 *Social Network Analysis: a Handbook*, 2nd edn, London: Sage

Scragg, D. S. (ed.), 2008 *Edgar King of the English, 959–975: New Inter-pretations*, Woodbridge: Boydell Press

Sennhauser, H. R., 1979 Spätantike und frühmittelalterliche Kirchen Churrätiens, in J. Werner & E. Ewig (eds), *Von der Spätantike zum frühen Mittelalter*, Vorträge und Forschungen 25, Sigmaringen: Thorbecke, 193–218

Shanzer, D. R., 2010 The Tale of Frodebert's Tail, in E. Dickey & A. Chahoud (eds), *Colloquial and Literary Latin*, Cambridge: Cambridge University Press, 376–405

Sharpe, R., 1984 Some Problems Concerning the Organization of the Church in Early Medieval Ireland, *Peritia*, 3, 230–70.

Sims-Williams, P., 1975 Continental Influences at Bath Monastery in the Seventh Century, *Anglo-Saxon England*, 4, 1–10

Sims-Williams, P., 1988 St Wilfrid and Two Charters dated 676 and 680, *Journal of Ecclesiastical History* 39, 163–83, reprinted in Sims-Williams 1995, V

Sims-Williams, P., 1990 *Religion and Literature in Western England, 600–800* Cambridge Studies in Anglo-Saxon England, 3, Cambridge: Cambridge University Press

Sims-Williams, P., 1995 St Wilfrid and Two Charters dated AD 676, in P. Sims-Williams (ed.), *Britain and Early Christian Europe, Studies in Early Medieval History and Culture*, Aldershot: Variorum, unpaginated

Sirat, J., 1983 Stèles et sarcophages du haut moyen âge, *Histoire et Archéologie*, 76, 73–80

Smalley, B., 1964 *The Study of the Bible in the Middle Ages*, Notre Dame: University of Notre Dame Press

Smith, M., 1998 Ideology and Theology: The Irish and the Britons in the Ecclesiastical History in the light of Bede's theology of the Jews, Unpubl. MA Thesis, Centre for Medieval Studies, University of York

Smyth, A., 1975–9 *Scandinavian York and Dublin: The History and Archaeology of Two Related Viking Kingdoms*, 2 vols, Dublin: Templekieran Press

Smyth, M., 2003 *La Liturgie oubliée. La prière eucharistique en Gaule antique et dans l'Occident non romain*, Paris: Éditions du Cerf

Snape, M. E., 2003 A Horizontal-Wheeled Watermill of the Anglo-Saxon Period at Corbridge, Northumberland, and its River Environment, *Archaeologia Aeliana*, 5th ser., 32, 37–72

Southern, R. W., 1963 *St Anselm and his Biographer: A Study of Monastic Life and Thought 1059–c.1130*, Cambridge: Cambridge University Press.

Spearman, M. & Higgitt, J. (eds), 1993 *The Age of Migrating Ideas*, Edinburgh: National Museum of Scotland

Stäblein, B., 1955 Gallikanische Liturgie, in F. Blume (ed.), *Die Musik in Geschichte und Gegenwart* **4**, Kassel and Basel: Bärenreiter, 1299–1325

Stafford, P., 1985 *The East Midlands in the Early Middle Ages*, London: Leicester University Press

Stafford, P., 2001 Political Women in Mercia, Eighth to Early Tenth Centuries, in M. P. Brown and C. A. Farr (eds), *Mercia, an Anglo-Saxon Kingdom in Europe*, London: Leicester University Press, 35–49

Stancliffe, C., 2003 *Bede, Wilfrid, and the Irish*, Jarrow: Jarrow Lecture 2003

Stancliffe, C., 2007 *Bede and the Britons*, Whithorn: Whithorn Lecture 2005

Stancliffe, C., forthcoming Disputed Episcopacy: Bede, Acca and the Question of the Relationship between Stephen's *Life of St Wilfrid* and the Early Prose Lives of St Cuthbert

Stancliffe, C. and Cambridge, E. (eds), 1995 *Oswald. Nortumbrian King to European Saint*, Stamford: Paul Watkins, reprinted 1996

Stenton, F. M., 1943 *Anglo-Saxon England*, 1st edn, Oxford History of England **2**, Oxford: Clarendon Press

Stenton, F. M., 1970 (first published 1933) Medeshamstede and its Colonies, in D. M. Stenton (ed.), *Preparatory to Anglo-Saxon England: Being the Collected Papers of Frank Merry Stenton*, Oxford: Clarendon, 179–92

Stevenson, J. (ed.), 1858 *The Church Historians of England III*, London: Seeleys, later reprinted as Stevenson, J. (trans.), 1987 *Symeon of Durham: A History of the Kings of England*, Felinfach: Llanerch

Stevenson, J. B., 1996 Hiberno-Latin Hymns: Learning and Literature, in P. Ní Chathán and M. Richter (eds), *Irland und Europa im früheren Mittelater: Bildung und Literatur*, Stuttgart: Klett-Cotta, 99–135

Stevenson, W. H. (ed. and trans.), 1904 (repr. 1959), Asser, *De Rebus Gestis Ælfredi*, in W. H. Stevenson (ed.), *Asser's Life of King Alfred*, Oxford: Clarendon Press

Stokes, W. (ed.), 1905 *The Martyrology of Oengus the Culdee: Félire Óengusso Céli Dé*, Henry Bradshaw Society, **29**, London

Stukeley, W., 1776 *Itinerarium Curiosum*, London: Printed for Messrs Baker & Leigh

Taft, R., 1993 *The Liturgy of the Hours in East and West: The Origins of the Divine Office and Its Meaning for Today*, 2nd rev. edn, Collegeville, MN: Liturgical Press

Taft, R., 2003 Christian Liturgical Psalmody: Origins, Development, Decomposition, Collapse, in H. W. Attridge and M. E. Fassler (eds), *Psalms in Community: Jewish and Christian Textual, Liturgical and Artistic Traditions*, Leiden: Brill, 7–32

Talbot, C. H., 1954 *The Anglo-Saxon Missionaries in Germany*, New York: Sheed & Ward

Tangl, M., 1916 *Die Briefe des Heiligen Bonifatius und Lullus*, MGH, Epistolae Selectae, Berlin: Weidemann (reprinted Munich, 1989)

Taylor, H. M., 1968 Corridor Crypts on the Continent and in England, *North Staffs. J. Field Studies*, **9**, 17–52

Taylor, H. M., & Taylor, J., 1961 The Seventh-Century Church at Hexham: a New Appreciation, *Archaeol Aeliana*, 4th ser., **39**, 103–34

Taylor, H. M., & Taylor, J., 1965–78 *Anglo-Saxon Architecture*, 3 vols, Cambridge: Cambridge University Press

Thacker, A., 1982 Chester and Gloucester, *Northern History* **18**, 199–211

Thacker, A., 1983 Bede's Ideal of Reform, in P. Wormald, D. Bullough & R. Collins (eds), *Ideal and Reality in Frankish and Anglo-Saxon Society*, Oxford: Blackwells, 130–53

Thacker, A., 1985 Kings, Saints and Monasteries in pre-Viking Mercia, *Midland History* **10**, 1–25

Thacker, A., 1987 The Social and Continental Background to early Anglo-Saxon Hagiography, Oxford: unpublished D.Phil. thesis

Thacker, A., 1989 Lindisfarne and the Origins of the Cult of St Cuthbert, in G. Bonner, D. Rollason and C. Stancliffe (eds), *St Cuthbert, his Cult and his Community to AD 1200*, Woodbridge: The Boydell Press, 103–22

Thacker, A. T., 1996a Bede and the Irish, in L. A. J. Houwen and A. MacDonald (eds), *Beda Venerabilis: Historian, Monk and Northumbrian*, Groningen: E. Forsten, 31–59

Thacker, A., 1996b Saint-Making and Relic Collecting by Oswald and His Communities, in N. P. Brooks & C. R. E. Cubitt (eds), *St Oswald of Worcester: Life and Influence* Leicester: Leicester University Press, 244–68

Thacker, A., 1998 Memorializing Gregory the Great: the Origin and Transmission of a Papal Cult, *Early Medieval Europe*, **7.1**, 79–84

Thacker, A., 2002 The Making of a Saint, in A. Thacker and R. Sharpe (eds), *Local Saints and Local Churches*, Oxford: Oxford University Press, 45–73

Thacker, A., 2004a Wilfrid [St Wilfrid] (*c*.634–709/10), *Oxford Dictionary of National Biography*, **58**, 944–50 or online edn, Oxford University Press. Available: http://www.oxforddnb.com/view/article/29409 Accessed: 31 Aug 2010

Thacker, A. 2004b Werburh (*d.* 700×07), *Oxford Dictionary of National Biography*, online edn, Oxford University Press. Available: http://www. oxforddnb.com/view/article/29062 Accessed 31 Aug 2010

Thacker, A., 2004c Stephen of Ripon, *Oxford Dictionary of National Biography*, Oxford: University Press. Available: http://www.oxforddnb.com/ view/article/ 8445 Accessed 23 Feb 2012

Thacker, A., 2004d Bosa, *Oxford Dictionary of National Biography*, Oxford, Oxford University Press. Available: http://www.oxforddnb.com/view/article/ 2926 Accessed 23 Feb 2012

Thacker, A., 2004e Æthelthryth [St Æthelthryth, Etheldreda, Audrey]', *Oxford Dictionary of National Biography*, Oxford: Oxford University Press. Available at http://www.oxforddnb.com/view/article/18906. Acessed 22 March 2012

Thacker, A. T., 2007a Rome of the Martyrs: Saints, Cults and Relics, Fourth to Seventh Centuries, in É. Ó Carragáin and C. Neuman de Vegvar (eds), Roma Felix – *Formation and Reflections of Medieval Rome*, Aldershot: Ashgate, 13–49

Thacker, A. T., 2007b Martyr Cult within the Walls: Saints and Relics in the Roman *tituli* of the Fourth to Seventh Centuries, in A. Minnis and J. Roberts (eds), *Text, Image, Interpretation. Studies in Anglo-Saxon Literature and its Insular Context in Honour of É. Ó Carragáin*, Turnholt: Brepols, 31–70

Thacker, A., 2008 Gallic or Greek? Archbishops in England from Theodore to Ecgberht, in P. Fouracre and D. Ganz (eds), *Frankland: The Franks and the World of the Early Middle Ages*, Manchester: Manchester University Press, 44–69

Thomas, C., 1964 Settlement-History in Early Cornwall, I. The Antiquity of the Hundreds, *Cornish Archaeology*, **3**, 70–9

Thomas, C., 1992 *Whithorn's Christian Beginnings*, Whithorn: Whithorn Lecture

Thorpe, L. (trans.), 1974 *Gregory of Tours: The History of the Franks*, London: Penguin Books

Thümmler, H., 1958 Carolingian Period, in M. Pallottina (ed.), *Encyclopedia of World Art*, **3**, New York: McGraw-Hill, 97–104

Trousdale, A., Forthcoming Delegation and Local Authority in the Legislation of King Edmund, 939–46, in G. Owen-Crocker (ed.), *Kingship and Power in Anglo-Saxon England*, Woodbridge: Boydell & Brewer

Turner, A. J. & Muir, B. J. (eds), 2006 *Eadmer of Canterbury, Lives and Miracles of Saints Oda, Dunstan, and Oswald*, Oxford: Oxford University Press

Turner, T. H., 1845 Observations on the Crypt of Hexham Church, Northumberland, *Archaeol. J.*, **2**, 239–42

Tweddle, D., Biddle, M., & Kjølbye-Biddle, B., 1995 *CASSS, 4: South-East England*, Oxford: Oxford University Press

Tyler, D. J., 2007 Early Mercia and the Britons, in N. J. Higham (ed.), *Britons in Anglo-Saxon England*, Woodbridge: The Boydell Press, 91–101

Ussher, J., 1631 *A Discourse on the Religion Anciently Professed by the Irish and Brittish*, London: R[obert] Y[oung] for the Partners of the Irish Stocke

Van Dam, R. (trans.), 1988 *Gregory of Tours, Glory of the Martyrs*, Translated Texts for Historians, Latin Series, **3**, Liverpool: Liverpool University Press

van Egmond, W., 1999 The Audiences of Early Medieval Hagiographical Texts: Some Questions Revisited, in M. Mostert (ed.), *New Approaches to Medieval Communication*, Turnholt: Brepols, 41–67

van Egmond, W., 2004 Radbod van de Friezen, een aristocraat in de periferie, *Millennium: Tijdschrift voor middeleeuwse studies*, **19**, 24–44

Van Rhijn, C., 2009 *Paenitentiale Pseudo-Theodori*, CCSL **156B**, Turnhout: Brepols

Vieillard-Troïekouroff, M., 1976 *Les monuments religieux de la Gaule d'après les Oeuvres de Grégoire de Tours*, Paris: Champion

Vodola, E., 1986 *Excommunication in the Middle Ages*, Berkeley, Los Angeles: University of California Press

Vogel, C., 1952 *La discipline penitentielle en Gaule des origines à la fin du VIIe Siècle*, Paris: Letouzey & Ané

Vogel, C., 1960 Les échanges liturgiques entre Rome et les pays francs jusqu'à l'époque de Charlemagne, in *Le Chiese nei regni dell'Europa occidentale e i loro rapporti con Roma sino all'800*, Spoleto: Settimane di Studio del Centro Italiano di Studi sull'Alto Medioevo, 7, 185–295

Wagner, P., 1921 *Einführung in die gregorianischen melodien: ein Handbuch der Choralwissenschaft*, **3**, *Gregorianische Formenlehre: eine choralische Stilkunde*, Leipzig: Breitkopf & Härtel

Waitz, G. (ed.), 1878 *Pauli Historia Langobardorum*, MGH, *Scriptores Rerum Germanicarum in usum scholarum separatim editi*, Hannover: Hahn

Walbran, J., 1846 On a Crypt in Ripon Cathedral, Commonly called St Wilfrid's Needle, *Trans. British Academy Winchester Congress 1845*, 339–54

Walbran, J., 1848 Observations on the Saxon Crypt under the Cathedral Church at Ripon, Commonly called St Wilfrid's Needle, *Royal Archaeol. Inst., York Meeting 1846*, 1–11

Walker, G. S. M., 1957 *Sancti Columbani Opera*, Scriptores Latini Hiberniae **2**, Dublin: Institute Advanced Studies

Wallace-Hadrill, J. M. (ed. and trans.), 1960a *The Fourth Book of the Chronicle of Fredegar with its Continuations*, London: Nelson

Wallace-Hadrill, J. M., 1960b Rome and the Early English Church: Some Questions of Transmission, in *La Chiese nei regni dell'Europa occidentale e i loro rapporti con Roma sino all'800*, 2 vols, Settimane di studio del Centro italiano di studi sull'alto medioevo 7, Spoleto: Presso la sede cel Centro, **2**, 519–48

Wallace-Hadrill, J. M., 1976 Bede and Plummer, in G. Bonner (ed.), *Famulus Christi: Essays in Commemoration of the Thirteenth Centenary of the Birth of the Venerable Bede*, London: SPCK, 366–85

Wallace-Hadrill, J. M., 1983 *The Frankish Church*, Oxford: Clarendon Press

Wallace-Hadrill, J. M., 1988 *Bede's* Ecclesiastical History of the English People: A Historical Commentary, Oxford: Oxford University Press

Wallis, F., 1999 *Bede: The Reckoning of Time*, Translated Texts for Historians 29, Liverpool: Liverpool University Press

Walsh, J. R., & Beadley, T., 1991 *A History of the Irish Church 400–700 AD*, Blackrock: Columba Press

Walsh, M., & Ó Crónín, D., 1988 *Cummian's Letter* De Controversia Paschali *together with a related Irish Computistical Tract* De Ratione Conputandi, Studies and Texts **86**, Toronto: Pontifical Institute of Mediaeval Studies

Walsh, P. G. (trans.), 1966 *Letters of St. Paulinus of Nola*, 2 vols, New York: Newman Press

Ward, B., 1990 *The Venerable Bede*, Outstanding Christian Thinkers Ser., London: Geoffrey Chapman

Ward-Perkins, B., 1986 *From Classical Antiquity to the Middle Ages. Urban Public Building in Northern and Central Italy AD 300–850*, Oxford: Oxford University Press

Warren, F. E. (ed.), 1893–5 *The Antiphonary of Bangor: An Early Irish Manuscript in the Ambrosian Library at Milan*, 2 vols, Henry Bradshaw Society **4, 10**, London: Harrison

Wasserschleben, [F. W.] H. (ed.), 1885 *Collectio Canonum Hibernensis*, in [F. W.] H. Wasserschleben (ed.), *Die irische Kanonensammlung*, 2nd edn, Leipzig

Watson, W. J., 1926 *The History of the Celtic Place-Names of Scotland*, Edinburgh: William Blackwood & Sons

Weber, R. (ed.), 1953 *Le Psautier romain et les autres anciens psautiers latins*, Collectanea biblica Latina 10, Rome: Abbaye Saint-Jérome

Webster, L., & Backhouse, J. (eds), 1991 *Making of England: Anglo-Saxon Art and Culture, AD 600–900*, London: British Museum Publications

Wells, B. W., 1891 Eddi's Life of Wilfrid, *English Historical Review*, **6**, 535–50

Werner, J., & Ewig E. (eds), 1979 *Von der Spätantike zum frühen Mittelalter*, Vorträge und Forschungen 25, Sigmaringen: Thorbecke

Whitelock, D., 1972 The pre-Viking-Age Church in East Anglia, *Anglo-Saxon England* **1**, 1–22

Whitelock, D., 1976 Bede and his Teachers and Friends, in G. Bonner (ed.), *Famulus Christi. Essays in Commemoration of the Thirteenth Centenary of the Birth of the Venerable Bede*, London: SPCK, 19–39

Whitelock, D. (ed.), 1979 *English Historical Documents*, vol. 1, London: Eyre & Spottiswoode Ltd

Whitelock, D., Brett, M., & Brooke, C. N. L. (eds), 1981 *Councils & Synods With Other Documents Relating to the English Church I, A.D. 871–1204*, 2 vols, Oxford: Clarendon Press

Whitelock, D., Douglas, D. C., & Tucker, S. I. (eds), 1961 *The Anglo-Saxon Chronicle*, New Brunswick: Rutgers University Press

Whitham, J. (ed. and trans.), 1893 *The Offices of St. Wilfrid According to the Use of the*

Church of Ripon, Ripon: Harrison

Wilkinson, J., 2002 *Jerusalem Pilgrims Before the Crusades*, Oxford: Aris and Phillips

Wilkinson, M. J., 2007 *Frederick William Faber: A Great Servant of God*, Leominster: Gracewing

Willems, R. (ed.), 1954 *Augustinus, In Iohannis evangelium tractatus CXXIV*, CCSL **36**, Turnholt: Brepols

Williams, P., 2001 The Meaning of *organum*: Some Case Studies, *Plainsong and Medieval Music* **10**, 103–20

Willis, G. G., 1968 *Further Essays in Early Roman Liturgy*, Alcuin Club Collections **50**, London: SPCK

Wilmart, A., 1934 Un témoin Anglo-Saxon du calendrier métrique d'York, *Revue Bénédictine* **46**, 41–69

Wilson, D., 1984 *Anglo-Saxon Art from the Seventh Century to the Norman Conquest*, London: Thames and Hudson

Wilson, D. M., 1986 England and the Continent in the Eighth Century: an Archaeological Viewpoint, in *Angli e Sassoni al di qua e al di là del mare*, Settimane di studio del centro italiano di studi sull'alto Medioevo, **32**, 219–47

Wilson, F. R., 1862 Hexham Abbey Church, *Trans. Architect. Archaeol. Soc. Durham and Northumberland*, **1**, 19–27

Wilson, H. A., 1918 *The Calendar of St Willibrord*, London: Henry Bradshaw Society, reprinted 1998, Woodbridge: Boydell

Winkelmann, F., 2001 *Der monenergetisch-monotheletische Streit*, Frankfurt am Main: Peter Lang

Winterbottom, M., with Thompson, R. M. (eds), 2007 *William of Malmesbury: Gesta Pontificum Anglorum (The History of the English Bishops)*, 2 vols, Oxford: Oxford University Press

Wood, I. N., 1981 A Prelude to Columbanus: the Monastic Achievement in the Burgundian Territories, in H. B. Clarke & M. Brennan (eds), *Columbanus and Merovingian Monasticism*, BAR International Series **113**, Oxford: Archaeopress, 3–32

Wood, I., 1982 The *Vita Columbani* and Merovingian Hagiography, *Peritia* **1**, 63–80

Wood, I., 1986 The Audience of Architecture in post-Roman Gaul, in L. A. S. Butler and R. K. Morris (eds), *The Anglo-Saxon Church: Papers on History, Architecture and Archaeology in Honour of Dr H. M. Taylor*, London: CBA Research Report, **60**, 74–9

Wood, I. N., 1990 Ripon, Francia and the Franks Casket in the Early Middle Ages, *Northern History* **26**, 1–19

Wood, I., 1994 *The Merovingian Kingdoms 450–751* Harlow: Longman

Wood, I., 1995a *The Most Holy Abbot Ceolfrid*, Jarrow: Jarrow Lecture

Wood, I. N., 1995b Northumbrians and Franks in the Age of Wilfrid, *Northern History* **31**, 10–21

Wood, I., 2001 *The Missionary Life: Saints and the Evangelization of Europe, 400–1050*, Harlow: Longman

Wood, I. N., 2006 Bede's Jarrow, in C. Lees & G. Overing (eds), *A Place to Believe In: Locating Medieval Landscapes*, University Park, Penn: Penn State Press, 67–84

Wood, I., 2008 Monasteries and the Geography of Power in the Age of Bede, *Northern History* **45**, 11–25

Wood, I. N., 2011 The Continental Connections of Anglo-Saxon Courts from Æthelberht to Offa, in *Le relazioni internazionali nell'alto medioevo*, LVIII Settimana di Studio,

Spoleto: Fondazione Centro Italiano di Studi sull'Alto Medioevo, 443–80

Wood, S., 2006 *The Proprietary Church in the Medieval West*, Oxford: Oxford University Press

Woolf, A., 2007 *From Pictland to Alba, 786–1070*, The New Edinburgh History of Scotland, vol. 2, Edinburgh: Edinburgh University Press

Wormald, P., 1976 Bede and Benedict Biscop, in G. Bonner (ed.), *Famulus Christi: Essays in Commemoration of the Thirteenth Centenary of the Birth of the Venerable Bede* London: SPCK, 141–69; reprinted 2006 in S. Baxter (ed.), *The Times of Bede: Studies in Early English Christian Society and its Historian*, Oxford: Blackwell Publishing, 3–29

Wormald, P. 1978 Bede, *Beowulf* and the Conversion of the Anglo-Saxon Aristocracy, in R. T. Farrell (ed.), *Bede and Anglo-Saxon England: Papers in Honour of the 1300th Anniversary of the Birth of Bede, Given at Cornell University in 1973 and 1974*, BAR British Series **46**, Oxford: Archaeopress, 32–95; reprinted 2006 in S. Baxter (ed.), *The Times of Bede: Studies in Early English Christian Society and its Historian*, Oxford: Blackwell Publishing, 135–66

Wormald, P., 1985 *Bede and the Conversion of England: the Charter Evidence*, Jarrow: Jarrow Lecture 1984, reprinted 2006

Wormald, P., 1999 *The Making of English Law: King Alfred to the Twelfth Century*, vol. 1, Oxford: Blackwell

Wright, D. H., 1967 *The Vespasian Psalter: B. M. Cotton Vespasian A. i*, EEMF, **15**, Copenhagen: Rosenkilde and Bagger

Yorke, B. A. E., 1985 The Kingdom of the East Saxons, *Anglo-Saxon England* **14**, 1–36

Yorke, B. A. E., 2004 Cædwalla (*c*.659–689), *Oxford Dictionary of National Biography*, online edn, Oxford University Press. Available: http://www.oxforddnb.com/view/article/4323 Accessed 31 Aug 2010

Yorke, B., 2009 *Rex Doctissimus: Bede and King Aldfrith of Northumbria*, Jarrow: Jarrow Lecture

Young, F., 1997 *Biblical Exegesis and the Formation of Christian Culture*, Cambridge: Cambridge University Press

Zadora-Rio, E., 2005 L'historiographie des paroisses rurales a l'épreuve de l'archéologie, in C. Delaplace (ed.), *Aux origines de la paroisse rurale en Gaule méridionale (IVe–IXe siècles):* actes du colloque international, 21–23 Mars 2003, salle Tolosa (Toulouse), Paris: Errance, 15–23

Zycha, J. (ed.), 1891/92 *Augustinus, De utilitate credendi, De duabus animabus, Contra Fortunatum Manichaeum, Contra Adimantum, Contra epistulam fundamenti, Contra Faustum Manichaeum, Contra Felicem Manichaeum, De natura boni, Epistula Secundini, Contra Secundinum Manichaeum*, CSEL **25**, Vindobonae: Holder-Pichler-Tempsky

INDEX

9.1. Silver sheet from Hexham
(Copyright: The Trustees of the British Museum).

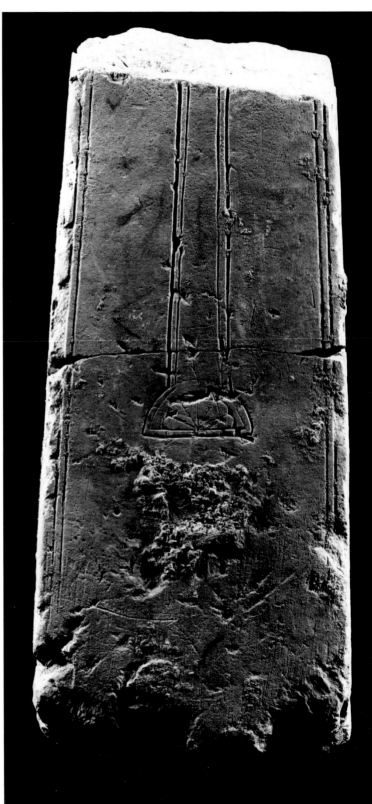

9.2. York: fragment of stèle (Copyright: Corpus of Anglo-Saxon Stone Sculpture: photographer T. Middlemass).

9.3. The Hexham frithstol
(Copyright: Corpus of Anglo-Saxon Stone Sculpture: photographer T. Middlemass).

9.4. Impost from Hexham
(Copyright: Corpus of Anglo-Saxon Stone Sculpture: photographer T. Middlemass).

9.5. Impost from Hexham
(Copyright: Corpus of Anglo-Saxon Stone Sculpture: photographer T. Middlemass).

9.6. Hexham frieze fragment
(Copyright: Corpus of Anglo-Saxon Stone Sculpture: photographer T. Middlemass).

9.7. Ripon capital
(Copyright: Corpus of Anglo-Saxon Stone Sculpture: photographers K. Jukes and D. Craig).

9.8 (opposite) Illustration of St Wilfrid by C. E. Brook,
for Rudyard Kipling's *Rewards and Fairies*, 1910 (publisher's collection).

"A miracle ! A miracle !" he cried

10.2 (above). David Dictating the Psalms, Masham Column, late 8th / early 9th century (Photo: Author).

10.1 (left). Consular Diptych of Aereobindus, 506 A.D. (Photo: Musée National du Moyen Âge – Thermes et Hôtel de Cluny, Paris).

10.3 (opposite, left). A: Easby Cross, late 8th / early 9th century (Copyright: V&A Images / Victoria and Albert Museum, London).

B (opposite right, above): Detail: Apostles (Copyright: V&A Images / Victoria and Albert Museum, London).

C (opposite right, above): Detail: Christ Enthroned in Majesty (Copyright: V&A Images / Victoria and Albert Museum, London).

12.1. Hexham Crypt: Vault of the north side-chamber looking west.
Note the mouldings at the top of the east ribs and the in-curving top of the south rib to the west.

12.2. Feathered tooling on re-assembled collapsed section of wall retaining side of road ramp leading to the south end of the Roman bridge at Corbridge. 0.5m scale.

12.3. Tooling of blocks in west wall of the main chamber in the Hexham crypt. Compare with the tooling shown on Plate 12.2, particularly on the block forming the top of the door on the right-hand side.

12.4–5 (opposite). Two views of the crypt at Ripon Cathedral using a fish-eye lens on the camera to obtain all-round views. The crypt is now the only part of the church dating back to the work commissioned by Wilfrid as abbot in the 660s/670s. Copyright Simon Hill for York Archaeological Trust.

Richard Andrew Hall